i-Net+ Guide to Internet Technologies

Jean Andrews, Ph.D

with Ann Marie Francis

i-Net +™

A CompTIA Certification Program

**COURSE
TECHNOLOGY**

THOMSON LEARNING

Australia • Canada • Denmark • Japan • Mexico • New Zealand • Philippines • Puerto Rico • Singapore • South Africa • Spain • United Kingdom • United States

i-Net+ Guide to Internet Technologies is published by Course Technology.

Senior Product Manager	Lisa Egan
Managing Editor	Stephen Solomon
Production Editor	Elena Montillo
Developmental Editor	Rebecca Holmes
Associate Product Manager	Laura Hildebrand, Elizabeth Wessen
Editorial Assistant	Elizabeth Wessen, Janet Aras
Manuscript Quality Assurance	John Bosco
Manuscript Quality Assurance Engineer	Nicole Ashton
Manufacturing Coordinator	Denise Sandler
Director of Product Marketing	Susan Ogar
Marketing Manager	Toby Shelton
Text Designer	GEX, Inc.
Cover Designer	Abby Scholz

Trademarks

i-Net+, CompTIA, and MeasureUp are all registered trademarks.

Disclaimer

Course Technology reserves the right to revise this publication and make changes from time to time in its content without notice.

The Web addresses in this book are subject to change from time to time as necessary without notice.

For more information, contact Course Technology, 25 Thomson Place, Boston, MA 02210; or find us on the World Wide Web at *www.course.com*.

For permission to use material from this text or product, contact us by
- Web: www.thomsonrights.com
- Phone: 1-800-730-2214
- Fax: 1-800-730-2215

ISBN 0-619-01586-1

Printed in Canada

1 2 3 4 5 6 7 8 9 WC   04 03 02 01 00

BRIEF

Contents

TABLE OF
Contents

CHAPTER NINE
WebTV and Other Internet Appliances   353

CHAPTER TEN
Servers and What They Do   379

CHAPTER ELEVEN
Internet Infrastructure   419

CHAPTER FOURTEEN
Doing Business on the Web   577

Introduction

i-Net+ Guide to Internet Technologies invites you into a lively and insightful grand tour of the many different technologies that make the Internet work. In doing so, this book also prepares you to pass CompTIA's i-Net+ exam. This book will enable you to feel confident when talking with business people as well as technical people about the many features and technologies of the Internet. It will also help you make wise decisions concerning how your business career is linked to the Internet. If you are planning a technical career, consider this book the foundation of your education about the Internet.

This book provides thorough support and preparation for CompTIA's i-Net+ Certification examination. This new, vendor-neutral certification focuses on the technology behind the Internet. Obtaining certification increases your ability to gain employment and improve your salary. To get more information on i-Net+ Certification and its sponsoring organization, the Computing Technology Industry Association, see their World Wide Web site at *www.CompTIA.org*.

FEATURES

To ensure a successful learning experience, this book includes the following pedagogical features:

- **Learning Objectives:** Every chapter opens with a list of learning objectives that sets the stage for you to absorb the lessons of the text.

- **Appealing Art Program:** The text is full of diagrams, drawings, and other visuals to make the many technologies of the Internet easy to follow and understand.

- **Step-by-Step Procedures:** The book has step-by-step instructions that you can easily follow for hands-on experience on all aspects of working with the Internet, including creating web pages, animating graphics, and transferring files.

- **Tips:** Tip icons highlight additional helpful information related to the subject being discussed.

- **Real-Life Examples:** Throughout each chapter, real examples of companies and technologies are given so you can explore how the world is using the Internet.

- **Case Studies:** A thorough, practical example is included in each chapter so you can see how the concepts being covered relate to the real world; the case studies portray actual companies that have used Internet technologies and creative thinking to solve specific problems.

- **End-of-Chapter Material:** The end of each chapter includes the following features to reinforce the material covered in the chapter:

  - **Summary:** A bulleted list is provided which gives a complete but brief summary of the chapter.

  - **Review Questions:** To test knowledge of the chapter, the review questions cover the most important concepts of the chapter.

  - **Key Terms List:** A list of all new terms and their definitions.

  - **Hands-on Projects:** Hands-on projects to help you apply the knowledge gained in the chapter.

  - **Case Study Project:** This hands-on project starts in Chapter Three and continues throughout the book. Using the on-going case study project, you will build a comprehensive web site that includes many of the technologies discussed in each chapter.

- **On the CD-ROM: CoursePrep® Software i-Net+ Test Preparation Software**: 50 test-preparation questions, powered by MeasureUp©, mimic the testing environment so you can practice for exam day.

SUPPLEMENTS

For instructors using this book in a classroom environment, the following teaching materials are available on a single CD-ROM:

Electronic Instructor's Manual: The Instructor's Manual that accompanies this textbook includes a list of objectives for each chapter, detailed chapter lecture notes, suggestions for classroom activities, discussion topics, and additional projects and solutions.

Course Test Manager 1.2: Accompanying this book is a powerful assessment tool known as the Course Test Manager. Designed by Course Technology, this cutting-edge Windows-based testing software helps instructors design and administer tests and pretests. In addition to being able to generate tests that can be printed and administered, this full-featured program also has an online testing component that allows students to take tests at the computer and have their exams automatically graded. The test bank that accompanies this book contains over 100 questions per chapter.

PowerPoint Presentations: This book comes with Microsoft PowerPoint slides for each chapter. These are included as a teaching aid for classroom presentation, to make available to students on the network for chapter review, or to be printed for classroom distribution.

ACKNOWLEDGMENTS

This book has been fun to write, largely because of the tremendous support of the good folks at Course Technology. Lisa Egan, Stephen Solomon, Elena Montillo, Kristen Duerr, John Bosco, and Nicole Ashton: you're a sharp group of people committed to excellence in every way, and it's been a pleasure working with you! Thank you, Tony Woodall, Layton Chauvin, and Don Locke for your outstanding research material. And Layton, your case studies were splendid. Thank you, Becky Holmes, the Developmental Editor, for your diligence and also for your light-hearted humor at just the right times. Thank you, Ann Marie Francis, an incredible writing assistant. Ann Marie, you are a fantastic writer, but more than that, you've become a very close friend. Thank you, Jennifer Dark, my daughter and assistant who is also my friend. The reviewers, listed below, were always diligent and ready to go the extra mile to make this book a success. Thank you so much!

Ric Calhoun, Gordon College

Paul Campano, Union County College

Vicki Cox, Laramie County Community College

Janos Fustos, Metropolitan State College of Denver

Doug Hulsey, Limestone College

Ylber Ramadani, George Brown College

DEDICATION

The teamwork that went into this book is heart-warming and makes me feel so proud to be a part of such an incredible group of people. It's been a pleasure working with you. This book is dedicated to the Glory of God.

PHOTO CREDITS

Figure Number	Credit
3-5	Copyright © 2000 Corel Corporation
3-6	Copyright © 2000 Corel Corporation
3-7	Bob Atkins
3-8	Bob Atkins
3-10	Copyright © 2000 Corel Corporation
3-11	Copyright © 2000 Corel Corporation
3-19	Copyright © 2000 Corel Corporation

Read This Before You Begin

TO THE USER

Before using this book, you should be a computer user and a casual user of the Internet, but no programming or networking knowledge is assumed. After completing the book, you will have an understanding of Internet technologies, which will serve you to:

- Converse effectively with others concerning Internet technologies

- Begin in-depth studies of these technologies to prepare for technical jobs related to the Internet

- Assist people who have Internet-related jobs

- Manage processes using the Internet

- Build web sites of moderate complexity

- Manage client PCs connected to the Internet

Data Disks

To complete the projects in Chapter 3 of this book you need the Data Disk files. Data Disk files are source files that have been created by Course Technology specifically for this book. Course Technology provides the Data Disk files to your instructor in the Instructor's Resource Kit. The files are also available from the Course Technology web site at *www.course.com*.

In most cases, your instructor will copy the Data Disk files to a computer that everyone in the class can access, such as a lab computer or network file server. You can then copy the files to a floppy disk, and label that disk "Data Disk." If you are unsure of what to do, check with your instructor, who can give you more specific instructions.

Using Your Own Computer

You can use your own computer to complete the tutorials, Hands-on Projects, and Cases in this book. To use your own computer, you will need the following:

- **Microsoft Windows 95, Windows 98, Windows NT Workstation, or Windows 2000 Professional.** Your computer must also be configured so that you can connect to the Internet. You will need to be connected to the Internet when you work the chapter exercises.

- **Microsoft Internet Explorer 4 or 5 or Netscape Navigator**. You can download a copy of Internet Explorer 4 or 5 from the Internet Explorer home page at no cost. Connect to *http://www.microsoft.com/windows/ie/*, and then click the Download link from the menu near the top of the web page.

- **Data Disk**. You can get the Data Disk files from your instructor. You will not be able to complete the tutorials and projects in this book using your own computer unless you have the Data Disk files. See the Data Disk section for information on setting up your Data Disk files. The Data Disk files can also be obtained electronically from the Course Technology web site by connecting to *http://www.course.com*, and then searching for this book title.

To the Instructor

To complete the exercises in this book, your students must use a set of user files, which are referred to throughout the book as Data Disk files. These files are included in the Instructor's Resource Kit. They may also be obtained electronically through the Course Technology web site at *http://www.course.com*. Follow the instructions in the Help file to copy the user files to your server or standalone computer. You can view the Help file using a text editor such as WordPad or Notepad.

Once the files are copied, you can make Data Disks for the users yourself, or you can tell users where to find the files so they can make their own Data Disks.

Course Technology Data Disk Files

You are granted a license to copy the Data Disk files to any computer or computer network used by individuals who have purchased this book.

1

USING THE INTERNET

In this chapter, you will learn:

- How to use a web browser to surf the Web
- How to find information on the Internet using search engines and search sites
- About ways a web site attracts and retains customers
- How to send and receive e-mail
- How to access a newsgroup
- About Internet Service Providers, what they do, and how to select one

The Internet has changed the way we communicate. The rise in popularity of the World Wide Web and e-mail have created opportunities and practices that were unimaginable just a few short years ago. The Internet and its services have changed forever the way we communicate with one another, the way we distribute and locate information, and the way we do business. Keeping in touch with family, friends, and business associates around the world is almost effortless. Mass quantities of information are at our fingertips. Businesses see web sites as tools that are as important as ads in the Yellow Pages were a decade ago. More than that, the Web has become a major point of sales and business transactions for many businesses, a trend which is expected to grow explosively in the foreseeable future. Because using the Internet has become essential in most careers today, you don't want to be left behind in gaining the necessary skills and knowledge.

Just knowing how to send an e-mail message or using Yahoo! to find a business's web site is not enough. As more and more businesses use the Web to advertise, serve their customers, and transact business, employees, business owners, and customers need to understand how the Internet works, and how to position themselves successfully within this technology. Now is a great time to learn about the Internet because the opportunities and applications for this knowledge are endless. This book and i-Net+ Certification will serve as your gateway to an exciting future in whatever Internet-related activity or career you choose.

This book takes you from being a casual Internet user to understanding how the Internet works. It describes what each significant piece of software and hardware does, and how all these pieces fit together. It provides a power-packed, yet understandable introduction to all the Internet technologies.

This first chapter is a broad-stroke introduction to the Internet. If you are an experienced Internet user, you can quickly breeze through the chapter. If you are relatively new to the Internet, this chapter shows you the tools that you have at your fingertips to surf the Web, send e-mail, and use chat rooms. It also gives you enough information to make a wise decision when selecting an **Internet Service Provider**—a company that provides access to the Internet for an individual or a business. As you read this chapter, focus on the tools you'll need to use the Internet. Chapter 2 takes you to the next step—understanding how these tools work.

THE INTERNET AND SYSTEMS THAT USE IT

The Internet is a network. More accurately, the **Internet**, which began in the 1960's, is many networks connected together, all of which use the same method of communication. These interconnected networks are called an internetwork, hence the term Internet. The beginnings of the Internet occurred in 1969 when the Advanced Research Projects Agency (ARPA), charged with developing an internetwork that could withstand nuclear attacks on the United States, connected together two university networks over a Wide Area Network called the **ARPANET (ARPA Network)**. This first attempt at a decentralized network using common methods of communication grew over a few short years to cover the globe and to become the Internet of today.

The Internet works because all computers and other devices connected to it are using the same protocols. A **protocol** is a language or a set of rules for communication, and by understanding the protocols used by the Internet you'll understand how communication happens on the Internet.

You can consider the Internet a transportation system for data, much in the way the U.S. Postal Service is a transportation system for letters and package, as seen in Figure 1-1. Many different organizations use and share this transportation system; for example, a mail-order company distributes catalogs through the mail, receives orders and fills these orders, using the U.S. Postal Service. The mail order company shares the postal service transportation system with many other individuals and organizations. The postal service delivers the mail without concern for what's inside those many envelopes, and the organizations that use the postal service don't care exactly how the letters get from one place to another. In Figure 1-1, as far as the person placing an order to the catalog center is concerned, the postal system is simply a "cloud" whose internal workings are of little concern to its user.

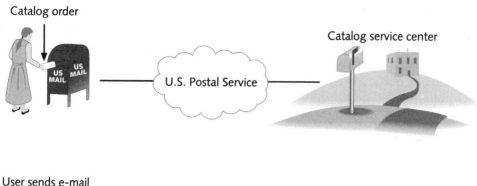

Catalog order

Catalog service center

U.S. Postal Service

User sends e-mail
to a friend

E-mail recipient

The Internet

Figure 1-1   The Internet and U.S. Postal Service are both transportation systems used by other systems to move data from place to place

Similarly, in Figure 1-1, the Internet is used to transmit an e-mail message from one location to another. The Internet really doesn't care what kind of data is being transmitted, and e-mail is only one type of system that uses the Internet to transmit data. Also, the e-mail user is not concerned with how the data gets from its Internet entry point to its exit point (recipient of the e-mail). The Internet is depicted in the figure as a cloud.

Much of this book is devoted to studying the several systems and services that use the Internet. Each of these is designed for a specific purpose, and they are listed in Table 1-1. The first three systems listed are the most popular, and they are introduced in this chapter. The internal workings of the Internet, including the hardware and software that make it work, and how data finds its way from one location to another, are introduced in Chapter 2 and are fleshed out in Chapters 8 and 11.

Table 1-1   Services that use the Internet

Internet Service	Description
World Wide Web	A system for quickly and easily finding and displaying many types of data
E-mail	A one-to-one messaging system
Chat rooms	A system designed for real-time communication
FTP	A system for moving a file from one location to another
Telnet	A system designed to allow a user to issue commands to a computer from a remote location
News groups	A system designed to communicate information to multiple users, all of whom must subscribe to the service. Internet Service Providers often subscribe to newsgroups as a service to their customers.
Gopher	An older utility system designed to locate information on the Internet. This utility has been largely replaced by the World Wide Web.
WAIS (Wide Area Information Server)	An older, mostly outdated system designed to search for and retrieve information on the Internet

The World Wide Web

One of the systems that uses the Internet is the **World Wide Web** (WWW or W3 or "the Web"), which was developed around 1990. The World Wide Web is a collection of interlinked information that is stored on computers all around the world. The information is stored and presented in a way that lets you move around among millions of interconnected documents. Surfing the Web is just like traveling across a giant spider web; you can go from place to place, following these different interconnections.

Most of the information on the World Wide Web is stored in files that are formatted using **Hypertext Markup Language (HTML)**. Essentially, HTML is a set of codes that are included in the text describing how the text should be displayed or printed.

Web communication and standards of HTML are controlled and monitored by the **World Wide Web Consortium (W3C)**, an organization made up of private, educational, and governmental organizations from around the world.

For an overview of the many organizations that are responsible for the various standards that control the Internet, see Appendix B.

The World Wide Web delivers information over the Internet in the form of a **page** or **web page**, which is a file (in HTML format) that can contain text and also can point to other files. These files can contain graphics, and even audio and video clips. The Web uses the **client/server** concept as demonstrated in Figure 1-2. The **client** is a computer that makes a request for data from another computer, called a **server**. The server receives the request, and responds by sending data to the client. The software on the client side that displays a web page is called a **web browser** and the software that processes requests on the server side is called a **web server**. In addition to sending requests to a web server, a web browser can interpret the HTML code in order to display a web page correctly.

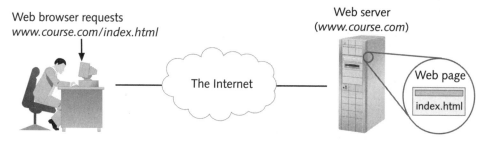

Web browser requests
www.course.com/index.html

Web server
(*www.course.com*)

The Internet

Web page

index.html

Figure 1-2   A web browser (client software) requests a web page from a web server (server software); the web server returns the requested file to the client

When a web browser makes a request for information on the World Wide Web, its request includes the name of a server (*www.course.com* in Figure 1-2) and the name of a specific web page or file on the server that the user wants to see (*index.html* in the figure). This is similar to a buyer sending a catalog order to the catalog service center by U.S. mail, and identifying the catalog order center by its name, address, city, state and zip code. The entity that responds to this request, the web server, searches for the requested page and sends the page back to the browser. A group of web pages on a web server that are managed as a complete unit and work together to present similar information, is called a **web site.** Moving from site to site for information is called "surfing the web." The exact details of how all this works are covered in Chapter 3.

The first publicly available web browser that could display graphics was **Mosaic**, released in 1993 by the National Center for Supercomputing Applications (NCSA) at the University of Illinois. Today, the two most popular web browsers are **Internet Explorer**, distributed by Microsoft, Inc. (65% of users) and **Netscape Navigator**, distributed by Netscape, Inc. (23% of users). The next section describes some interesting things you can do with each of these browsers.

Using Web Browsers

A web browser is a software application on a user's PC that is used to request web pages from a web server on the Internet. The browser requests a web page by sending a URL over the Internet to the server. A URL (uniform resource locator) is an address for a web page file or other resource on the Internet. Figure 1-3 shows some of the parts of a URL. Other parts will be discussed in later chapters.

Figure 1-3   A URL contains the protocol used, the host name of the web server and the path and filename of the requested file

The first part of the URL is **http** (stands for **hypertext transfer protocol**). This part of the URL specifies the rules the web server should use when transmitting the page back to the browser. Recall that rules of communication are called protocols and, although the browser can use several different protocols, http is the one used for web pages. A **hypertext document** is a document that contains text that links to other text, either within the same document file or in another document file.

The second part of the URL is the name of the server being addressed (*www.course.com*) and is called the **host name**. A host name identifies a server within a network. The server name is *www* (a web server) and *course.com* is the name of the Course Technology network, sometimes called the domain name. The web page requested is located in the folder, **myfolder**, on the www server, and the file within that folder is named *myfile.html*.

When people think of URLs, they usually think of only the host name, as in *www.course.com*. This is the URL that requests a default web page. A **default web page** is a page in the main directory of a site that introduces the site and that provides links to other pages in the site. Notice that this URL doesn't specify a certain folder or file. The default web page is the page that is sent to a browser if no other page is specified. The default web page is named index.html, default.htm, welcome.html, or a similar name. It is sometimes known as a web site's home page. The file extension html or htm indicates that the file contains HTML code.

Most browsers are very forgiving about accepting URL shortcuts. For example, all these URLs give the same results: *http://www.course.com*, *www.course.com*, and *course.com*.

In the next section, you'll learn how to use the two most popular browsers, Internet Explorer and Netscape Navigator.

Microsoft Internet Explorer   Microsoft Internet Explorer was first introduced in October 1995, and is free for downloading from the Microsoft web site *www.microsoft.com/windows/ie*. The examples in this section use Version 5.0 (sometimes labeled IE 5), although some people still use earlier versions of the software because of the overhead associated with the later versions. **Overhead** is the amount of system resources required by the software to function, such as space on the hard drive, and computing power. A complete installation of Internet Explorer 5.0 requires 98 MB of hard drive storage.

The basic tools for navigation using Internet Explorer are shown in Figure 1-4. You can request a page by entering the page's address in the Address box labeled in the figure. The example is the Surfing Lobster site at *www.surfinglobster.com*. Use the Back and Forward buttons to move back and forth among the pages you have just downloaded. Internet Explorer is holding these pages in a temporary Internet folder called a cache, and can display them without having to go back to the web server to download again. Use the Stop button to stop downloading the last request and the Refresh button to go back to the server for a fresh copy of the last page requested. Sometimes if a page downloads very slowly, you can press Stop followed by Refresh to speed up the download.

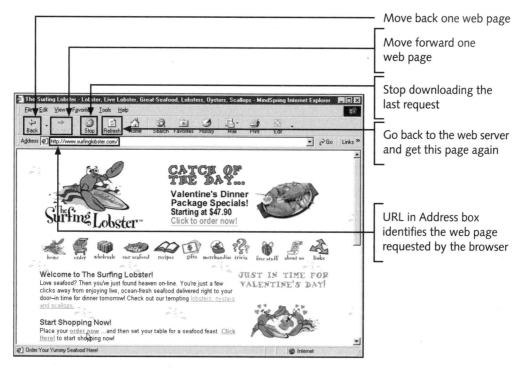

Figure 1-4   Navigating tools using Internet Explorer 5

Netscape Navigator   Netscape Communications, Inc. offers a suite of programs called Netscape Communicator. Netscape Navigator, a web browser, is one of those programs. The entire suite can be downloaded for free. See the Netscape web site, *www.netscape.com*. Navigator 4.7, shown in Figure 1-5, has many of the same features as Internet Explorer 5. For example, you can enter a URL in the Location box (sometimes called the Netsite box), which includes an AutoComplete feature; and reload in Netscape is the same as Refresh in Internet Explorer. Click Shop in the tool bar to access the Netscape online shopping mall. Netscape also has its own search engine, which you can access by clicking the Search button in the tool bar.

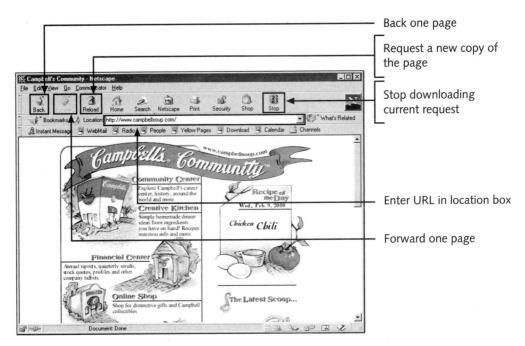

Figure 1-5   Netscape Navigator has similar features as those of Internet Explorer

Next, you'll learn how to use the AutoComplete features, how to save a URL, how to save web pages and other files for off-line viewing, how to limit the web content a user can access, and about browser search features for Internet Explorer and Netscape Navigator.

AutoComplete Feature   Internet Explorer and Netscape Navigator keep track of the URLs you enter in the Address or Location box. Internet Explorer also lacks data you enter in data entry forms on web pages. If you have entered information into an Address box or text box in the past, the browser provides you with a drop down list of previous entries from which you can choose, or the browser will complete the entry for you. To use the drop down list, select an entry and press Enter. For the automatically completed entry, just press Enter and you don't have to complete typing the entry yourself. You can turn this feature on and off. The AutoComplete feature might not be desirable if several users share the PC, because it can remember URLs and user information, including usernames and passwords.

You can control many of Internet Explorer's options, including the AutoComplete feature, from the Internet Properties dialog box. Figure 1-6 shows the Internet Properties dialog box. To customize AutoComplete, follow these directions:

1. Click the **Start** button on the taskbar to display the Start menu, then point to **Settings** to display the Settings menu.

2. Click **Control Panel** on the Settings menu.

3. Double-click the **Internet Options** icon. The Internet Options dialog box opens. This dialog box controls many different Internet settings.

4. Click the **Content** tab. The Content folder opens.

5. Click the **AutoComplete** button under the section labeled Personal Information. The AutoComplete Settings dialog box opens. In this dialog box you can customize the AutoComplete feature by checking different checkboxes that determine when AutoComplete should work.

6. Click **OK** to close the AutoComplete dialog box, then click **OK** to close the Internet Properties dialog box.

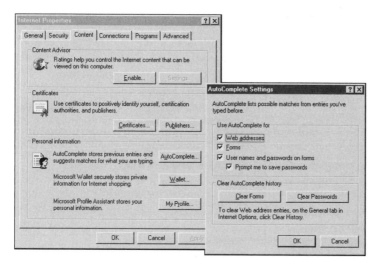

Figure 1-6   Control the AutoComplete feature of Internet Explorer from the Internet Properties window

Saving Web Pages for Later Viewing   You can save a web page so that you can view it later. Netscape Navigator calls this operation "bookmarking" a page. Internet Explorer adds the page to a list of your "Favorites." Follow these directions to bookmark a web page using Netscape Navigator:

1. Make sure Netscape Navigator is showing the web page that you want to bookmark. The URL should be visible in the Location box.

2. Click the **Bookmarks** button on the Location toolbar. The Bookmarks drop down list opens.

3. Click **Add Bookmark** to add the currently displayed URL to the Bookmarks list.

To use the bookmark, click the Bookmarks button on the Navigator toolbar, then click the name of the site you bookmarked from the list in the Bookmark window. Navigator requests the web page.

Netscape Navigator offers a convenient way to organize and edit your bookmarks. You can create descriptions of bookmarks, edit the list, and create desktop shortcuts. Follow these directions to rearrange your bookmark list.

1. Click the **Bookmarks** button on the Location toolbar, then click **Edit Bookmarks** in the drop down list. The Bookmarks window opens.

2. Select the bookmark you want to rearrange, and right click the bookmark. A drop down menu opens.

3. Click **Cut** or **Copy** from the drop down menu.

4. Right click in the new position in the list where you want the bookmark to go, then click **Paste** in the drop down menu.

5. To close the Bookmarks window, click **File** on the menu bar, then click **Close**.

Figure 1-7 shows the process of rearranging a list of bookmarks.

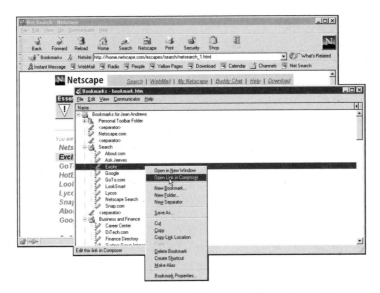

Figure 1-7   Netscape Navigator lets you edit and organize your bookmarks using the Bookmarks window

To add a URL to your list of Favorites in Internet Explorer, follow these directions:

1. Make sure Internet Explorer is showing the web page that you want to add to your list of Favorites. The URL should be visible in the Address box.

2. Click **Favorites** on the menu bar, then click **Add to Favorites**. The Add Favorite dialog box opens. See Figure 1-8. Click **OK** to add the URL.

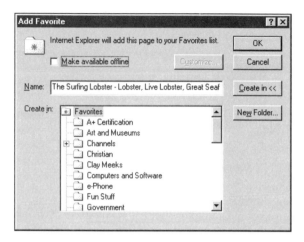

Figure 1-8   Add a favorite web site to the list of favorites

Note that your Add Favorite dialog box might not look like the one in Figure 1-8 because it might not be showing the list of folders into which you can save web pages. To see this list, click the Create in << button.

When you want to request the web page, click Favorites on the menu bar, then click the name of the page you want to see. Note that you can also use the Add Favorite dialog box to organize your Favorites into folders.

Making Web Pages Available for Off-line Viewing   Looking again at Figure 1-8, note the Make available offline option in the Add Favorite dialog box. When you check this option, your web browser saves the web page in a cache so that you can view the page when you are not connected to the Internet. Internet Explorer offers many options for saving pages. For example, you can save some or all of a web site's pages, including graphics and multimedia files. You can select how often saved pages are updated from the original web site; this is called synchronization. You can synchronize web pages on a predetermined schedule, or you can choose to synchronize only when you select this option from the Tools menu. Follow these directions to make a web page available offline in Internet Explorer:

1. Make sure Internet Explorer is showing the Web page that you want to make available offline.

2. Click **Favorites** on the menu bar, then click **Add to Favorites**. The Add Favorite dialog box opens.

3. Click the checkbox **Make available offline**. The Customize button changes from gray to black, to signify that it is now available.

4. Click **Customize**. The Offline Favorite Wizard dialog box opens.

5. Click **Next**. The Offline Favorite Wizard leads you through a series of dialog boxes that lets you set your options for offline viewing. Figure 1-9 shows you the first dialog box in the series. Click **Next** two more times to get to the last dialog box. The last dialog box in the series lets you set a password to control access to this

site offline. Click **Finish** on this last dialog box. The Offline Favorite Wizard closes
and you return to the Add Favorite dialog box.

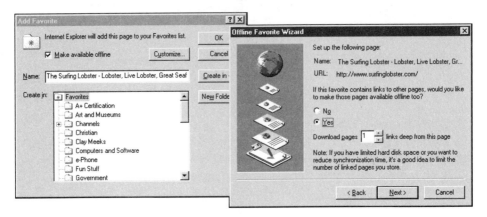

Figure 1-9   Using the Offline Favorite Wizard, you can save some or all of the web pages
on a site for off-line viewing

6. Click **OK** on the Add Favorite dialog box. Internet Explorer copies the pages to
your PC. See Figure 1-10 for an example.

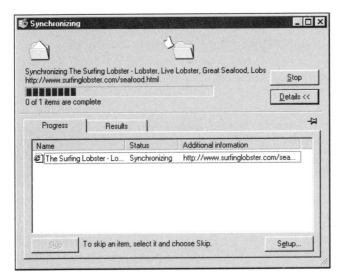

Figure 1-10   Internet Explorer is synchronizing (copying) web pages with pages saved on
a PC for later off-line viewing

When you want to view the web pages offline in Internet Explorer, click File on the menu
bar, then click Work Offline. Then, from the Favorites menu, click the web page you want
to view. Notice that when you are working offline, the only pages available for viewing are

those that you saved to your PC. Other Favorites are grayed–out and not available until you disable Work Offline. To do that, return to the File menu and click Work Offline again.

You can also save web pages for offline viewing in Netscape Navigator. From the File menu, click Save As, and the Save As dialog box opens. From the Save As dialog box, you can save all files referenced by the web page or you can save only the HTML files, which are the text files. Later, when you want to view the saved files, click File from the menu bar, then click Open Page and select the file from the Open Page dialog box. See Figure 1-11. You can browse your hard drive for the file by clicking Choose File. Then click Open to open the file.

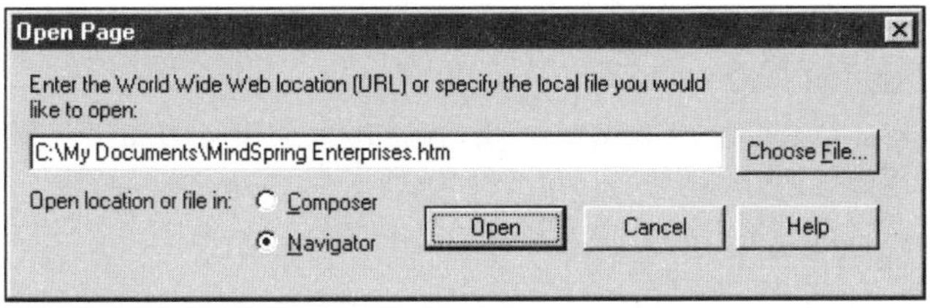

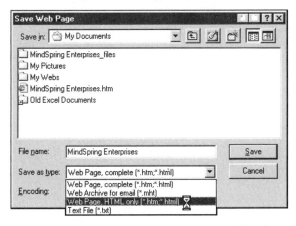

Figure 1-11   Using Navigator, select a file stored on your PC to view offline

Saving Files on the Web to Your PC   Sometimes you want to save a web page to a folder on your hard drive other than the browser cache folder. Perhaps you are learning to use HTML and want to use the source HTML on a web page as an example to follow. The previous paragraph described how to save a web page to a folder on your hard drive of your own choosing using Netscape Navigator (click File, Save As and select the folder). To control where the file is stored on your hard drive using Internet Explorer, follow these directions:

1. Click **File** from the menu bar, then click **Save As**. The Save Web Page dialog box opens. See Figure 1-12.

Figure 1-12   From the Save Web Page window, save web pages to view later when working offline

2. From the Save as type drop down list showing in the figure, click **Web Page, HTML only**, to select what you want to save. This choice saves the text of the web page only, without any of the graphics and multimedia files that are linked to that page. If you choose **Web page, complete** from the drop down list, the web page is saved along with all the graphics and multimedia files that are needed to fully display every item on the page.

3. Click **Save** to save the file.

Follow these directions when you want to view the page:

1. Click **File** on the menu bar, then click **Work Offline**.

2. Click **File** on the menu bar, then click **Open**. The Open dialog box opens.

3. From the Open dialog box, click **Browse** to find the web page on your hard drive. The filename appears in the Open dialog box. Click **OK** to display the page in the browser window.

You can also open the web page file and view the HTML directly by using a text editor or word processor.

Web pages also contain links to other text or to other files. These files can contain different types of data such as text, graphics, or audio. For example, as shown in Figure 1-13, the pointing hand on the web page is a graphic. No graphics can be stored directly into an HTML document because HTML is only text; the document contains a link to a graphic file that contains the pointing hand. Using Internet Explorer, right click on the hand and the drop down menu displays, as seen in Figure 1-13. Select Save Picture As and you can save the graphic file to your hard drive. See Figure 1-14. (If you are using Netscape Navigator, the option in the drop down menu is Save Image As.) As you save the file, you can see that it is named navfwd.gif. (A GIF file is a common type of graphics file that will be discussed in more detail in later chapters.) Later, you can use the pointing hand in one of your own web pages.

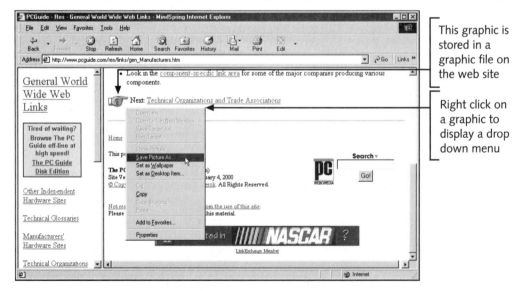

This graphic is stored in a graphic file on the web site

Right click on a graphic to display a drop down menu

Figure 1-13   A graphic on a web page can be saved to a file on your hard drive

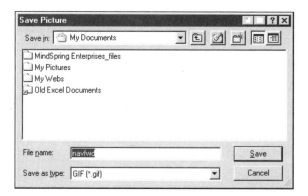

Figure 1-14   A file that is part of a web page can be saved to your hard drive to view or use later

However, some images, photographs, and graphics found on web sites might not be available to you to use on your own web site because of copyright restraints. Logos cannot be used without prior written permission, and other graphics and photos may also be owned by the person or company that created them. When in doubt about your right to use an image, ask for written permission. There are many web sites that offer free images for you to download. Use a search engine such as *www.infoseek.com* or *www.yahoo.com* to find them.

Limiting the Content Available to a Browser   Internet Explorer 5 supports the World Wide Web Consortium's specifications for content selection, called the **Platform for Internet Content Selection** (**PICS**). These specifications allow parents and other responsible individuals (like employers and administrators) to limit the content available to a browser. PICS is a voluntary rating system in which web developers assign their site a rating based on language, nudity, sex and violence. Be aware that not all sites conform to these specifications. Many sites are not rated, and, since web developers assign their own ratings, the results may be somewhat subjective. The settings you choose in Internet Explorer determine which sites the browser displays. If you choose to filter out sites with a certain level of violent content, for example, Internet Explorer checks all incoming pages for the appropriate rating tag, and filters out any sites that contain a rating tag higher than the level you have specified. It also filters out any site that contains no rating, unless you specify that you want to allow unrated pages.

Follow these directions to enable the Internet Explorer Content Advisor:

1. Click the **Start** button on the task bar to display the Start menu, then point to **Settings** to display the Settings menu.

2. Click **Control Panel** on the settings menu.

3. From the Control Panel window, double-click the **Internet Options** icon. The Internet Properties window opens. See Figure 1-15.

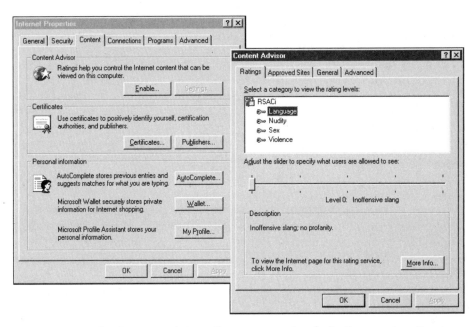

Figure 1-15 The Content Advisor allows a supervisor to limit access to offensive web sites

4. Click the **Content** tab, then click **Enable** in the Content Advisor section of the dialog box, and the Content Advisor window opens, as seen in the figure.

5. For each category (Language, Nudity, Sex and Violence), select one of five levels of filtering and click **OK**. If a supervisor password has not already been set up for this computer, you are prompted to create one. Remember the password because you'll need it to change any of these selections or to disable the feature.

From the Approved Sites tab in the Content Advisor window, you can override the restrictions by entering the URL of any site to which you want to allow access, no matter how the restrictions are set. From the General tab you can specify whether you want to allow Internet Explorer to access unrated sites.

Installing Web Browsers Recall that Netscape Navigator and Internet Explorer are free from the manufacturers. Navigator can be downloaded from *www.netscape.com* and Internet Explorer can be downloaded from *www.microsoft.com/windows/ie*.

As with other software downloaded from the Internet, you can save the compressed file to a folder on your hard drive. After the download is complete, close all open applications and, from Windows Explorer, double click the filename. The file uncompresses and the installation process begins. You are asked to restart your computer before configuration changes go into effect.

If you are downloading Internet Explorer and an older version of the browser is on the PC, it is not erased and you can revert back to it. You can use the Add/Remove Programs dialog in the Control Panel to do this.

About Web Pages

This section takes a closer look at web pages, how they're organized and what special features they can have. Next, it covers how to find information on a web site, and then, how to find information using search engines that search the entire Web.

A Closer Look at Web Pages   Recall that a web page is created using a special language, called the hypertext markup language (HTML). HTML is a form of the **Standard Generalized Markup Language (SGML)**, a standard developed in 1986 in order to retain formatting and linking information in a document as it is moved from one computer or software application to another.

A hypertext document is a document that contains a hyperlink, or special text that is used to point to another location in the same document or another document file. A **tag**, as it applies to SGML and HTML, is a special code written in a document that is interpreted by the software reading the document as a hyperlink, or as a code that describes how certain parts of the text are to be formatted, such as boldface, underlining and indentations.

For example, in a hypertext document such as a web page, this phrase "This is a <B> wonderful </B> day!" is interpreted by the browser as "This is a **wonderful** day!" The tags <B> and </B> mark where boldface begins and ends. Web developers generally use special authoring programs that are designed to insert HTML tags into a document automatically. These programs are called hypertext editors and are used by web page developers so they don't have to type the tags directly into the document. For example, the developer types, "This is a **wonderful** day!" and the hypertext editor substitutes "This is a <B> wonderful </B> day!"

A web browser can display the HTML version of the document before it is interpreted by the browser. For example, using Internet Explorer, click View on the menu bar, then click Source. A text editor displays the page just as it was received by the browser, without interpreting any of the tags. This is a good way to become familiar with HTML. The text editor that Internet Explorer uses is the Windows default text editor, which, in most cases, is Notepad.

Netscape Navigator offers a more sophisticated approach that allows you to see the graphical layout of a web page as well as the HTML code behind the page. Follow these directions to use Netscape Composer, the tool that allows you to view, create and edit web pages:

    1. On the Navigator menu bar, click **Communicator** and then click **Composer**. The Composer window opens.

2. From the Composer window, click **File** on the menu bar, then click **Open Page** and enter the URL of the web page you want to view. See Figure 1-16. Click **Open** in the Open Page dialog box.

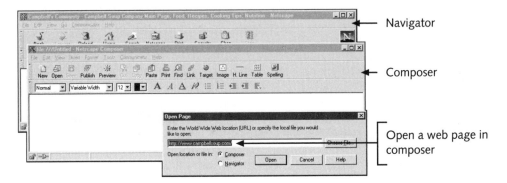

Figure 1-16   Using Netscape Composer, you can view the graphical layout and HTML of a web page

3. The web page is retrieved and displayed with the graphical elements used to create the page outlined with dotted lines. To view the HTML code used to create the page, from the Composer menu bar, click **View** and click **Page Source**. See Figure 1-17.

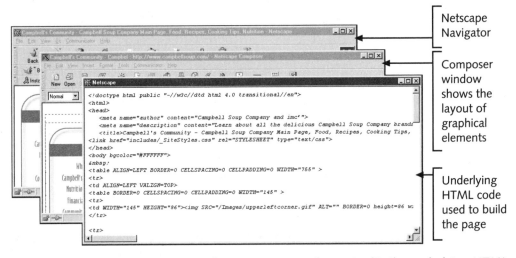

Figure 1-17   Netscape Composer allows you to view, but not edit, the underlying HTML code of a web page

Web Pages Built with Frames   **Frames** allow a web site designer to display different (but usually related) information in two or more separate areas of the screen. More than one web page can be displayed on the same screen, each in its own frame. For example, Figure 1-18

shows the screen divided into two frames; each frame contains a web page, which is stored in its own file. Therefore, it took two HTML files to build this screen. The frame on the left side of the screen has its own scroll bars as does the frame on the right. Most browsers today support frames, but older browsers do not.

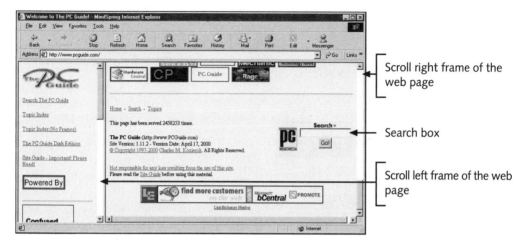

Figure 1-18   A web page using two frames and a search box

Hyperlinks   A **hyperlink**, also called a **hot link** or simply a **link** as mentioned earlier, is a link to another part of the same document or to a different document or file. Hyperlinks appear on a web page as either text or graphics. Text hyperlinks are displayed by the browser in a different color or are underlined. You can tell that something is a hyperlink because your cursor changes to a hand symbol when you move the cursor over the link on the screen. You can execute the hyperlink by clicking on the text or the graphic; the browser jumps immediately to the linked page or section of a page. A hyperlink is written in the HTML document using tags, and is discussed in more detail in future chapters.

Finding Information on the Web

There are many tools and methods available to find information on the Web. In this section you will learn about some of these, including using a browser's search features, searching a single web site for information, and using powerful search engines to find information from any web site anywhere on the Internet.

Searching an Individual Web Site   The web page shown in Figure 1-18 includes a search box. This search box actually links to another web site, *www.pcwebopedia.com*, but many times a search utility searches only on the current site. There are several ways to search a site, which are summarized below.

- **Static index.** A static index is a predetermined list from which you can select an item. The list is created from information from which the developers have decided you might want to search. Figure 1-19 shows an example of a static index search in the form of a drop down list.

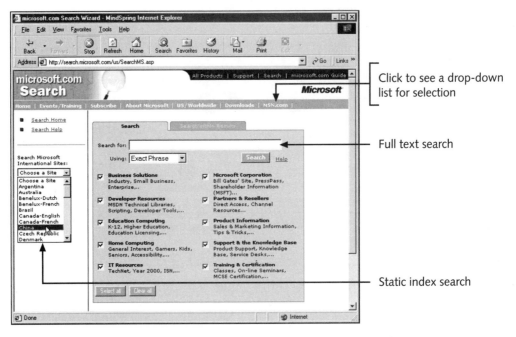

Figure 1-19   Examples of several ways to search a site

- **Site map**. A site map allows you to view a list of all pages on the site, see how the pages are organized and select a page for viewing. Site maps are sometimes written in a column on the left side of the home page, at the top of the home page, or on a separate page that can be accessed from the home page, as shown in Figure 1-20.

- **Keyword index**. A keyword index searches a site based on a list of predefined key words that identify different parts of the web site. For example, an online catalog might offer a keyword search to help you locate different items for sale. You can enter "shoes" or "shirts" in the keyword search box to navigate to those specific items. However, if a word isn't predefined as a keyword, the keyword search won't find it. For example, if you enter "sandals" in a keyword search, and "sandals" wasn't set up by the web designers as a keyword, the search won't take you to the shoe page, even if it offers sandals for sale.

- **Full text index**. A full text index searches the entire text of a site. It does not depend on certain words being predefined as keywords. You enter a word or phrase and the search engine searches all parts of the site for every occurrence of that word or phrase. A full text search would find the page that contains the word sandals in the example given above, because it looks at every word on the page, not just at the predefined keywords. In the example shown in Figure 1-19, you have the option of narrowing down the search to a selected group of pages.

Figure 1-20   A site map lets you quickly find any page on the web site

Search Engines   A **search engine** is a software application that searches for words in documents or in a database. Some search engines search only a single web site, helping you locate information on that site. An example of this type of search engine is AltaVista Search Engine by AltaVista, Inc. (*www.altavista.com*) used as the search engine on the *w3.org* web site owned by the World Wide Web Consortium and on the *amazon.com* web site. The AltaVista Search Engine software can run on Windows NT, UNIX, and Linux platforms. The software version that can support up to 3,000 documents on a single web site costs around $1500. Verity, Inc. (*www.verity.com*) and ZyLab International, Inc. (*www. zylab.com*) also make commercial search engine software, and freeware search engines are also available.

A web site developer first installs the search software on the web site computer, and then uses the software to build an index, which is a database of information on the site. This process is called "indexing the site." The index, once created, works similarly to an index of a book. It contains a list of significant words (called keywords) that the search engine located in the documents and files on the site. When someone performs a keyword search of the site, the search engine software looks in the index for the given keyword and reads the URL of the site of that keyword and then uses the URL to return the page containing the keyword to the user.

Search Engine Web Sites   A search engine can also be used on web sites devoted to the purpose of helping users find information anywhere on the Web. Alta Vista has a web site for that purpose (*www.altavista.com*) as does Lycos, Inc.(*www.lycos.com*), Yahoo! (*www.yahoo.com*), Excite (*www.excite.com*), HotBot (*www.hotbot.com*), and Infoseek (*www.infoseek.com*). All these sites keep databases containing keywords and the URLs where these keywords are located. When you use one of these sites to find information on the Web, you enter a keyword and click a button. The search engine software running on the site's web server searches through the database (index) on the site and returns any matches. The search engine is not searching the entire Web at this point, but only searching the database on the search web site. See Figure 1-21.

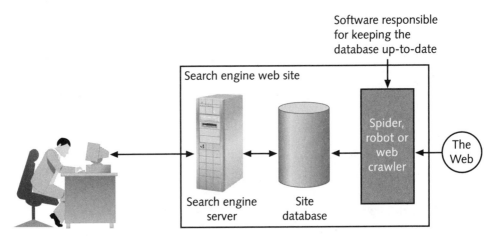

Figure 1-21   When you use a search engine web site to locate something on the Web, the search engine server searches the site's database, not the entire Web

These databases must be kept up-to-date in order to be effective. Information can get into a search engine's database in one of two ways. One way is for someone to enter a specific web site's URL and its keywords into the search engine's database. The other method is for the search engine to go in search of keywords on sites and build the database based on its search results. When a search engine builds a database out of keywords that have been entered by a person, that kind of database is known as a **subject directory**. Yahoo! is an example of a site that maintains a subject directory.

Search engine web sites like Alta Vista use special software called web crawlers, spiders, or web robots to search the entire Web and look for new information to record in the database.

When a spider, web crawler, or a web robot searches for information, the process is called gathering, spidering, and wandering. One example of a search site that uses this method is Infoseek. Its spider is called Sidewinder. The Alta Vista site has a database that is updated daily, and its spider is named Scooter. HotBot uses a spider named Slurp, and Excite has a spider named WebCrawler.

With over one billion documents on the Web, these spiders have plenty to do, moving from site to site looking for keywords to report back to home base. A web developer can aid the process by knowing where to put keywords in the document. Spiders look in the document title and near the top of a web page in the heading area where general information about the page is contained. Some spiders search the first 100 words on a web page, so developers are careful to put important information first. Developers also put keywords within tags called **meta tags**. A meta tag included on the page specifically for a spider or web robot to find and use is called a **meta robot tag**.

Looking back at the web site, *www.surfinglobster.com*, in Figure 1-4, you can see these meta tags by viewing the HTML source text. Using Internet Explorer, first access the web site, then click View on the menu bar, and then click Source. A text editor displays the contents of the web page and shows the HTML. See Figure 1-22. The meta tag META NAME="Keywords" includes all the keywords that the site wants a robot to find and include in search engine databases.

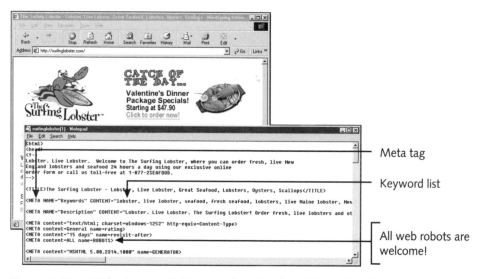

Figure 1-22   Web sites can list keywords to be found by web robots crawling the Web looking for information for database search engines

Once a web robot has visited a site, it revisits the site on a routine basis, looking for changes, so that the search engine database remains current. For more information about search engines, see *www.searchenginewatch.com*, a web site supported by Internet.com, Inc.

Using a Browser's Search Features   Internet Explorer and Netscape Navigator offer convenient ways to access search engine web sites. Using Internet Explorer, follow these directions to instruct the browser to search multiple search engine web sites:

1. Click the **Search** button in the toolbar. The Internet Explorer search options appear in a pane on the left side of the browser window.

2. Enter a search string and click **Search.** A search string is a string of characters for which you want to search. It can be a word or a phrase. The browser accesses several search engine web sites looking for a match, then displays a list of the web sites that it finds.

3. Click on a web site to display its contents.

If you want to use only a single search engine web site as the default for Internet Explorer, at the top of the search pane, click Customize and select Use one search service for all searches and select the search engine from the list of those available. If you want to return to using the Internet Explorer feature of searching multiple search engine web sites, select Use the Search Assistant for smart searching.

When you click the Search button in Netscape Navigator, it calls up the Netscape site, where you can use any of several search engines. See Figure 1-23.

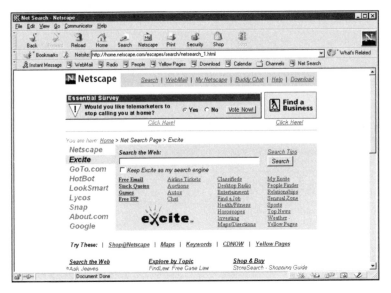

Figure 1-23 Netscape Navigator search button takes you to the Netscape site where you can access several search engines

What Makes a Web Site Great

You've just seen several features of web pages, and how information is found on the Web. Later in this book you'll learn how to create your own web site, and will use all these features just discussed, and more. As both a user and a creator of web sites, you'll be interested in knowing what makes one web site more successful than another. This section addresses several criteria to consider when evaluating web sites.

Evaluating Good Design   Here are some guidelines to use when evaluating the overall design of a web site.

- The very best web sites are *shortcuts*. They are easy to use, creating the feeling for the user that the site is doing its very best to make the entire experience for the user a shortcut to information and doing business.

- The web site should create the feeling of *community*. The site should make the user feel important, respected, served, and a valued member of a community. Many sites accomplish this by offering the user the opportunity to express his or her opinion, with the expectation that someone is listening and the opinion offered just might be published on the site. One of the reasons *amazon.com* is so successful is because it creates a sense of community among book readers by asking for reviews and publishing those reviews.

- Web sites should have a user-friendly home page that should load quickly, get the user's attention, and clearly present what is found on the site. Important information is presented first on the home page; the site doesn't use too many graphics and keeps the download time to a minimum.

- The main menu should display options for the user that clearly state what each option offers. The site should try to make information easy for a user to find.

- Text is kept to a minimum, and written in short, clear paragraphs. A good site uses easy-to-read fonts such as Arial (**this is written in Arial**) and Times Roman (this is written in Times Roman).

- The background is not too busy, but some graphics break up the monotony of the page.

- The best sites use a consistent theme throughout. They use colors, styles, and fonts that complement one another and thought is given to the general layout and planning of each page.

- Finally, a good web site is one that is easy to *find*. A web designer accomplishes this task by putting keywords in meta tags and entering important keywords at the beginning of the site.

Web Sites that Help You Evaluate and Design Web Sites   Some web sites that can help you evaluate other sites and design your own site are:

- *www.builder.com* by CNET
- *www.developer.com* by EarthWeb
- *www.wpdfd.com* by Joe Gillespie
- *www.colin.mackenzie.org* by Colin Mackenzie
- *www.webmonkey.com* by Lycos Network
- *www.shorewalker.com* by Shorewalker.com

- *www.webreference.com* by Internet.com

- *www.webdeveloper.com* by Internet.com

- *www.msdn.microsoft.com* by Microsoft

- *www.projectcool.com* by Project Cool, Inc.

Sometimes it helps to see what *not* to do. Check out *www.webpagesthatsuck.com* (that's: Web Pages That Suck by Flanders Enterprises).

Sending and Receiving E-mail

E-mail was one of the first applications to use the Internet and is now one of the most popular. E-mail is a method for sending a text message or a file to an individual or group of individuals via the Internet. Internet e-mail addresses have three parts: the user name, the @ symbol, and the name of the mail server that receives and then delivers the message. For example, the e-mail address *jsmith@mindspring.com* says that jsmith is the name of the user account on the mail server named mindspring.com.

E-mail consists of four components: the sending client, sending server, receiving server and receiving client. Figure 1-24 shows the process.

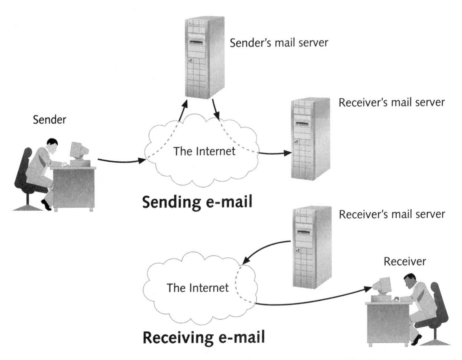

Figure 1-24   Sending and receiving e-mail requires four applications: client and server software to send the message and client and server software to receive the message

The person sending the message has e-mail client software on his PC that communicates with an e-mail server. This e-mail server is most likely located within his company, or, for an individual, at his or her Internet Service Provider, which is his or her entry point onto the Internet. The e-mail server receives the mail from the sender and sends it over the Internet to the mail server identified in the last part of the receiver's e-mail address. The receiving mail server holds the e-mail message in the user account on the server. This user account is identified by the first part of the receiver's e-mail address.

When a receiver checks for mail, e-mail client software communicates with its mail server and requests that all mail under the given user account be downloaded to the client PC. The receiver can then read the e-mail message, as presented by the e-mail client software. You will see the details of how e-mail works in Chapter 4.

There are many popular e-mail client applications. Some of the most popular are Eudora Light and Eudora Pro, available from Qualcomm, Inc. Other client software are Microsoft Outlook Express, which comes with Internet Explorer, and Netscape Messenger, which comes with Netscape Navigator as a part of Netscape Communicator. The example below uses Outlook Express.

Features of E-mail Client Software

In Figure 1-25, Outlook Express displays one open e-mail message. From, To, Subject, and Date are displayed at the top of the message. Folders are used to organize messages and are listed on the left side of the window. An Address Book containing a list of e-mail addresses is listed in the lower left corner of the window. This client software is typical in the way window panes are organized and used.

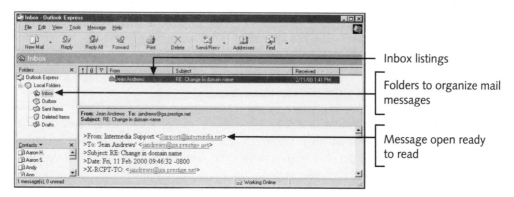

Figure 1-25   Outlook Express, an e-mail client software, comes free with Internet Explorer

Chat Rooms

Chat rooms are a fun way to communicate on the Internet. Conversation is real time among those logged into the chat room because the chat room software displays each message on the screen as soon as it's received. There are thousands of chat rooms running on the Internet, dedicated to thousands of subjects.

Chat Rooms use an application called **Internet Relay Chat (IRC)**, originally written by Jarkko Oikarinen, that, just as with e-mail and the World Wide Web, also uses the client/server method. IRC uses a group of IRC servers in a chat network. See Figure 1-26. Each client makes a connection to the chat room through one of these servers. Once the client is logged onto a server, the server works in cooperation with the other servers on the chat network to manage the conversations in the various chat rooms. Some chat networks are DALnet, EFnet, Undernet, IRCnet, and NewNet. Each of these networks supports a large number of chat rooms called **channels**. EFnet, for example has over 12,000 channels, some for public use and some for private.

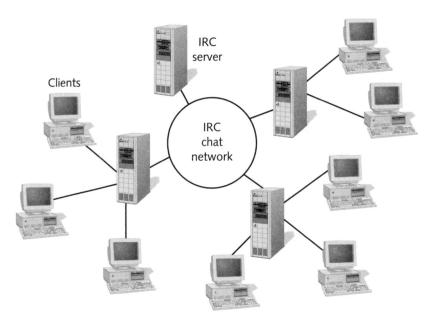

Figure 1-26   An IRC chat network uses a group of servers to manage a chat room; each client must connect to an IRC server

Chat room client software is free and can be downloaded from a number of sites (see *www.coolfreebies.com/chat.html*). Often an Internet Service Provider will include chat room software and access to chat networks in their total package for Internet access. If your ISP does not support chat rooms, you can access them through some web sites such as Yahoo! Chat. For extensive information about chat rooms, see *www.irchelp.org*.

Newsgroups

A **newsgroup** is a service on the Internet or a private network that allows a group of people to post articles and respond to those articles, so that information can be shared among the members of the group. A newsgroup can be private or public. A private newsgroup has limited membership, such as workers within a company, or members of an organization. It may have a subscription fee, such as the newsgroups of ClariNet, a commercial newsgroup organization whose main contributor is United Press International. An ISP can subscribe to ClariNet for a fee, and then can control access to this newsgroup.

Another example of a newsgroup service is Usenet, which consists of thousands of free newsgroups that circulate over the Internet. Usenet is the most popular newsgroup service.

All newsgroups have names. A newsgroup is named using words separated by periods, except for the word news, which is followed by a colon. Each word further defines a category within a category. An example of a newsgroup name is *news:rec.sport.skating.ice.recreational*, which is a UseNet newsgroup devoted to the discussion of recreational ice skating.

Using Newsgroups

Before you can subscribe to a newsgroup, you must have access to a news server, which has access to a newsgroup system like Usenet. For example, your ISP might subscribe to UseNet and provide the newsgroup service to their subscribers. In order to use the service, you need newsgroup client software on your PC (most web browsers have the ability to access newsgroups) and the name of the ISP's news server, so that you can connect to it.

The easiest way to access a newsgroup is to enter a URL in the address box of your web browser, such as: *news:rec.sport.skating.ice.recreational*. The browser loads the newsgroup software and passes to it the name of the newsgroup, rec.sport.skating.ice.recreational. If you are using Internet Explorer, it launches Outlook Express, which is both an e-mail client and a newsgroup client. See Figure 1-27 for a view of this newsgroup discussion using Outlook Express.

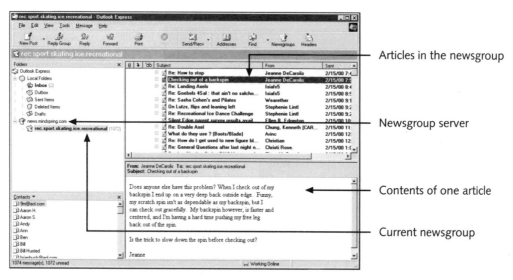

Figure 1-27   Outlook Express is a newsgroup client software as well as an e-mail client

To read an article, click on the article and read it in the box on the lower right. To respond to the article, double-click on the article. An e-mail window opens so that you can write your response. You can choose to send your response only to the author of the article or post to the entire newsgroup.

To browse through a list of newsgroups and select one, follow these directions using Outlook Express:

1. Click **Tools** on the menu bar, then click **Newsgroups**. The Newsgroup Subscriptions dialog box opens. See Figure 1-28.

2. If you can, narrow your selection down by entering a newsgroup high-level name or a description. Or, scroll down the list to find a newsgroup that looks interesting.

3. Click a newsgroup name and then click **Subscribe**.

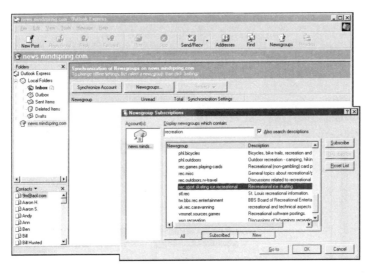

Figure 1-28   A news server lists thousands of newgroups to which you can subscribe

If you are using Netscape Messenger, right-click on the News folder on the left side of the Messenger window and click Subscribe to Newsgroups on the drop down menu. Communicator retrieves the list of newsgroups on the ISP news server and displays them. Select the one you want and click Subscribe.

You've now been introduced to four services that depend on the Internet for communication: the World Wide Web, e-mail, chat rooms, and newsgroups. Next, we take a brief look at the Internet itself, first its infrastructure, and then the different ways that an individual or small company can connect to the Internet.

REAL PEOPLE, REAL PROBLEMS, REAL SOLUTIONS
IF YOU BUILD IT, WILL THEY COME?

Foss & Bourke's traditional business is selling seafood products wholesale to restaurants and markets in the New York area. The Surfing Lobster (*www.surfinglobster.com*) was this well-established company's venture into the world of retail electronic commerce. When they made the decision to sell their products in a retail environment using a web site as their storefront, they employed a development firm that could build the site for them.

Months passed by with very few on-line orders. The owners of the site were baffled. The goal was to expand their business, and it wasn't working. The site that was built for them functioned well enough—it was designed with every component built around a corporate theme. Their product was top quality and competitively priced. Why weren't the orders coming in?

Web search engine and directory placement was the missing ingredient. The site was not placed in web search engines when it was launched. The development firm had not properly coded the site's pages to cooperate with search engines and spiders. People that were using the Internet to find fresh seafood couldn't find the Surfing Lobster!

Did people ever come? Yes! Foss & Bourke found a different Internet services firm to manage their site. The new company had the experience needed in search engine and directory placement. Pages were re-coded and keywords were created that a visitor most likely would use. Competitors' sites were reviewed and compared. With the new firm's efforts, traffic to the site increased dramatically. They also had the expertise to rebuild the Surfing Lobster site and make its design shopper-friendly, just in time for the holiday selling season.

INTRODUCTION TO THE INTERNET INFRASTRUCTURE

The purpose of this section is to give you a very high level view of the Internet's infrastructure. To understand this infrastructure, it is helpful to know a little about how and why the infrastructure came to be.

A Brief History of the Internet

The Internet has been in existence since the late 1960's. Until the late 1980's it was a loosely organized group of interconnected networks that were used predominantly by major academic institutions in the United States for research and development. In 1986, the National Science Foundation formed its network called NSFnet to connect five of these major academic institutions, which were spread from the east coast to the west coast: New Jersey, California, Pennsylvania, New York, and Illinois. Because NSFnet connected smaller networks to each other, it was called a **backbone** network. In 1987, NSF hired a contractor company, Merit, Inc., to increase the speed of this NSFnet backbone network to accommodate the astronomical growth rate of the Internet. At the end of 1989 there were an estimated 130,000 hosts and 650 networks.

It was also becoming apparent that the Internet was being shared by academic and commercial communities. In 1990, IBM, MCI and Merit formed a nonprofit organization called Advanced Network and Services (ANS) to manage the NSFnet backbone. This development was one of the first proof-of-concepts to prove that the primary users of the Internet were fast moving from the academic to the commercial.

In 1995, the National Science Foundation acknowledged that the Internet needed to be managed primarily by commercial companies when it initiated the move to define the infrastructure for the Internet we have today. Three things were done:

- A new backbone, primarily dedicated to the academic community and called vBNS, was created and managed by MCI. NSFnet, its predecessor, was shut down.

- Four **Network Access Points** (**NAPs**) were created, which would tie the several existing commercial backbones to each other and to the vBNS backbone. NAPs are described in the next section.

- Merit was awarded the responsibility for arbitrating the routing of all these backbones at the NAPs. It was agreed that this responsibility would not be awarded to a company that also owned a backbone.

Network Access Points (NAPs)

Figure 1-29 shows the location of the four original NAPs. The NAPs in San Jose and Washington DC are called MAE West and MAE East. A MAE (Metropolitan Area Exchange) is an interconnection point within a metropolitan area. The other two NAPs are in Chicago and New Jersey, although the New Jersey NAP is most often called the New York NAP. These four NAPs were originally managed by Metropolitan Fiber Systems (MFS), Ameritech Advanced Data Systems (AADS), Sprint, and Pacific Bell.

Although the four original NAPs continue to be major Internet connection points or Internet exchange points, there are more than these four today. The original four are called public Internet exchange points, and others, built by privately owned companies, are called private Internet exchange points. Some of these private Internet exchange points are owned by Commercial Internet Exchange (CIX), an organization established in 1991 by several commercial enterprises, to provide exchange points for commercial traffic. Another organization, the Federal Internet Exchange (FIX), is responsible for connection points for the networks of federal agencies. Also, there can be less significant exchange points that serve only two backbone operators where the two backbones simply connect to move traffic from one backbone to the other backbone. Today there are many backbones owned and managed by different companies. Figure 1-30, for example, shows the AT&T backbones, some of which are still under construction.

Figure 1-29   Originally, there were four major Internet connection points where backbones can connect called NAPs

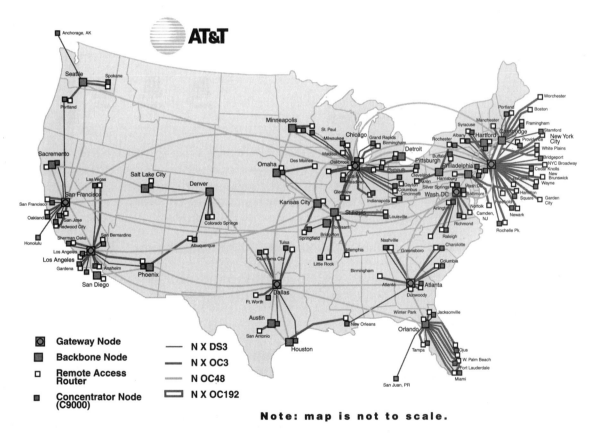

Figure 1-30   AT&T Internet Backbone Network

Large companies that have access to high-speed equipment can connect directly to one of these backbones, but smaller companies and individuals use a provider company to make the connection to a backbone. These Internet Service Providers are the subject of the next section.

INTERNET SERVICE PROVIDERS

An Internet Service Provider (ISP), sometimes called a service provider or access provider, is a business that provides connectivity to the Internet. ISPs can be a small business that provides connectivity in only one city, or a large company with access points in many cities and countries. Besides connectivity to the Internet, most ISPs provide a variety of other services. This section discusses what services an ISP provides, how an ISP connects an individual or small company to the Internet, and gives some guidelines to use when selecting an ISP.

Services Offered by an ISP

The primary purpose of an ISP is to provide access to the Internet. To connect to the Internet, a PC needs a physical connection from the PC to the ISP, software to communicate over the Internet, and an address, so that others on the Internet can identify the PC. An ISP can supply all three of these components, plus a variety of other services.

In order to connect to an ISP, a PC must be using an operating system that supports the communication protocol of the Internet, TCP/IP (discussed in the next chapter). Windows 95, Windows 98, Windows 2000, Windows NT, and the Macintosh operating system all support TCP/IP. Individuals usually connect to the Internet using a dial-up analog telephone line, a faster DSL telephone line, or a cable modem. Application software such as Internet Explorer and Netscape Navigator, that access the World Wide Web and e-mail, can all be downloaded for free from the Internet, but many ISPs include this software on a CD that is given to the user as part of the setup process.

The last thing needed to connect to the Internet is an Internet address so that the PC can be identified on the Internet. These addresses are called Internet Protocol addresses (IP addresses) and are assigned by the ISP when the PC connects to the ISP. The details of how an IP address is assigned to a PC, and how it is used on the Internet are in the next chapter.

Ways to Connect to an ISP

Regular phone lines are the most common way for an individual to connect to an ISP. In addition, there are two high-speed competing methods available—both were introduced to the marketplace at about the same time, cost about the same, and attain about the same speeds. These two methods are DSL lines and cable modems. Most users base their connection decisions on local cable company and phone company services, prices, and availability. Satellite connection is also an option, but it has several drawbacks, and other technologies such as ISDN and T1 lines are too expensive for most individuals. Table 1-2 summarizes the different technologies, which are discussed next.

Table 1-2   Data transmission technologies for personal and small business use

Technology	Access Method	Attainable Speeds	Current Users in U.S.	Comments
Regular phone line	Dial-up	56 Kbps	20 million	POTS – "Plain old telephone service"
DSL	Direct connect	1.5 Mbps downstream and 384 Kbps upstream	1 million	Requires a leased line from phone company
Cable modem	Direct connect	Varies up to 5 Mbps	500,000	Available through cable companies
Satellite	Direct connect	400 Kbps	NA	Only works downstream. Upstream transmission requires a dial-up.
ISDN	Dial-up	128 Kbps	3.2 million	Requires a leased line from phone company

In the table, notice that some services are direct connects and some are dial-up. The difference is in how the connection is made between the two end points. For dial-up, a connection only exists after a phone number has been dialed and a connection has been established. The connection remains intact only as long as both parties are communicating. A direct connect is always connected, similar to the way cable TV works; your television always has access to the cable company and no dial-up is required.

Regular Telephone Lines

Regular telephone lines, the most common way to connect to an ISP, require either an internal or external modem. A modem converts the PC's digital data (data made up of 0s and 1s) to analog data (a continuous and infinite number of variations of frequencies) that can be communicated over phone lines. This conversion is digital to analog going from the PC to the modem and analog to digital going from the modem to the PC. See Figure 1-31.

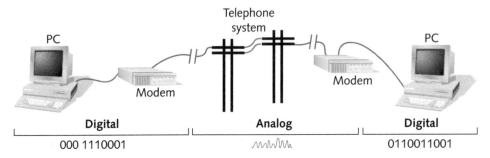

Figure 1-31   Communication is digital from PC to modem and analog from modem to modem

Figure 1-31 shows the telephone system carrying analog data from modem to modem, when in reality, this is seldom true. The data is only analog from a customer's telephone or modem to the telephone company's central office (CO) where it is converted to digital until it reaches the central office of the recipient. If the recipient is an ISP that is using regular telephone lines to connect to its customers, then the data is converted to analog for the final leg of its journey from the ISP's central office to the ISP modem. The fastest possible transmissions over phone lines is 56 Kbps (56,000 bits per second), although speeds this fast are rarely attained, even when both the user and the ISP are using 56K modems. Technology has allowed telephone line communication to attain its maximum speed, opening the way for more advanced methods of communication.

Digital Subscriber Lines (DSL)

The telephone industry has developed several similar technologies that allow data to travel over regular phone lines and remain in a digital state from end to end. These technologies are collectively called **Digital Subscriber Lines (DSL)**. **ISDN (Integrated Services Digital Network)** is an early example of a DSL technology, although ISDN is too expensive to be a realistic solution for individuals.

One type of DSL that is within the price range of individuals is ADSL (asymmetric digital subscriber line). It's called asymmetric because the download speed (from ISP to user) is much faster than the upload speed (from user to ISP). This asymmetrical speed is not usually a problem because most Internet activity involves short transmissions from the user to the ISP (for example, requesting a web page by transmitting a URL), and longer transmissions from the ISP to the user (the web server responds by sending the files needed to build the web page.) Most often when you hear people speaking of DSL lines coming in to their homes to connect to the Internet, the lines are really ADSL. Not all phone lines qualify for DSL and DSL is not available in all areas. A DSL line is leased from the phone company, which provides a converter box on site. From the box, the line connects to an Ethernet NIC (network interface card) in the PC. DSL is direct-connect (always up) as opposed to regular dial-up phone lines. The cost of a DSL line varies greatly; a typical price is $59/month, which includes the services of an ISP.

1

Cable Modem

Cable modem, a popular technology that is also direct-connect, uses cable lines that already exist in millions of households in the U.S. Just as with cable TV, cable modems are always connected.

Cable television lines are analog. Remember that standard telephone lines are also analog. Therefore, just as a standard modem converts your PC's digital signals to analog before sending data to the telephone line, a cable modem converts your PC's digital signals to analog before sending data out on the cable television line. Both types of modem also convert incoming data (from the television cable or the telephone line) from analog to digital. A cable modem connects to an Ethernet NIC in your PC.

Most cable companies provide both upstream and downstream service, although a few provide only downstream service. In this case the connection downstream (data flowing from the ISP to your PC) is a direct connect by cable, but the service upstream is by regular dial-up phone lines. This means that you can receive data over the cable, but to transmit, you must use a regular dial-up. Be sure you understand what you're getting before you lease.

Most cable modem services are also ISPs. Two popular cable modem providers are @Home and MediaOne. See their web sites for more information at *www.home.com* and *www.mediaone.com*. The cost for cable modem service, including ISP cost, is in the range of $35 - $60 per month.

Satellite Connections

Another way to attain high-speed data transmission is by satellites. You lease the service from a provider and mount a satellite dish on your premises. One service provider is DirecPC Satellite Service by Hughes (see the web site *www.direcpc.com*). Using a satellite connection for downstream transmission of data is not a good option, unless you need high speed transmission and live in a remote location that doesn't offer other alternatives. The installation can be complicated and requires a dial-up connection for data to travel upstream.

How an Internet Service Provider Works

Once you connect to an ISP by cable modem, DSL or phone line, the ISP connects you to the Internet. The ISP's equipment can be very simple or complex, depending on the ISP's size. Figure 1-32 shows an example of how a small ISP might connect to the Internet. Because a small ISP is not likely to have the high-speed equipment necessary to connect directly to a backbone, they most likely will subscribe to a regional ISP who will make the backbone connection.

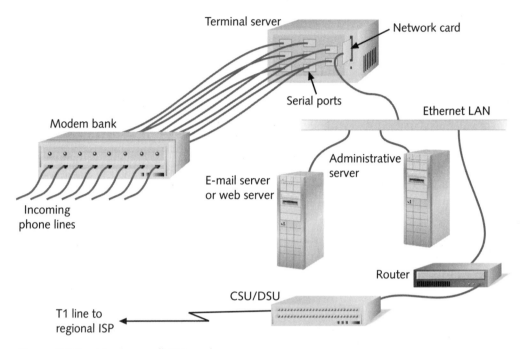

Figure 1-32   How a small ISP works

In the figure, the small ISP uses a T1 line to connect to the regional ISP. A T1 line is a digital dedicated circuit leased from the telephone company that carries the equivalent of 24 phone circuits and can transmit data at 1.5 million bps. Prices for T1 lines vary and are somewhere around $1,000 per month.

The individual phone lines coming in from customers connect to a modem bank. A modem bank is a box that contains several modem cards similar to a modem card that is installed in a regular PC. It takes one modem card to manage one phone line. The modem converts the analog signal from the phone line to digital before it moves the signal on to the terminal server. There is one serial cable connecting the modem bank to the terminal server for each modem card in the modem bank.

A terminal server has a serial port for each of these serial cables coming from the modem bank. It's the job of the terminal server to consolidate all these lines into a single line that connects the terminal server to the local network by way of a single network card in the terminal server. The network cable leaving the terminal server connects to the ISP's LAN. LAN stands for Local Area Network, a group of computers and other devices that is confined to a small area, such as one building.

The LAN might have several computers connected to it. For example, if the ISP provides e-mail and web site services to its customers, there might be a server connected to the LAN that manages both these services. In addition, there most likely will be another computer, called the administrative server in the figure, that manages customer accounts, including managing the process when the customer logs onto the ISP.

There is a router in the figure that is responsible for connecting the LAN at the ISP to the network of the regional ISP. A **router** is a device that connects two or more networks and can intelligently make decisions about the best way to route data over these networks. The two networks here are the ISP's LAN and the regional ISP's network.

Before data gets onto a T1 line, it must be cleaned and formatted by a device called a **CSU/DSU**, which is really two devices in one. The **CSU (Channel Service Unit)** acts as a safe electrical buffer between the LAN and a public network accessed by the T1 line. A **DSU (Digital Service Unit)** makes sure that the data is formatted correctly before it's allowed on the T1 line.

Now let's look at the regional ISP. Figure 1-33 shows how a regional ISP might work. The one in this figure supports several small ISPs and medium size companies that all connect to it using T1 lines, and it also has its own group of individual customers that connect using regular dial-up lines or DSLs. The regional ISP connects to a backbone using a T3 line. A T3 line transmits digital data at 44.7 Mbps and is fast enough to connect to a backbone. The T3 line would enter a data communications center and connect to a backbone by way of a router that belongs to the backbone operator (for example, AT&T or UUNET, which is owned by MCI WorldCom).

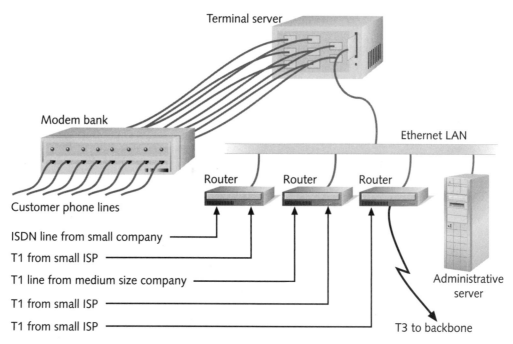

Figure 1-33 How a Regional ISP can work

How to Select an ISP

The type of communication you want should influence your selection of an ISP. For example, there may be only one cable modem provider in your area who is also an ISP. Using another ISP is not an option if you want cable modem. But ISPs provide several services other than connectivity. Some of these services are summarized here. When you're considering an ISP, here are the things to look for, besides types of connectivity (cable modem, DSL, or phone lines).

What You Can Expect from an ISP

An ISP is expected to offer access to the World Wide Web, e-mail services, and possibly FTP services. Some offer chat room and newsgroup services, as well as some space for a personal web site. As you learned earlier in the chapter, each of these services requires a server program running that communicates with the client software on the PC. The ISP provides a computer that has these servers running on it. Depending on the size of the ISP, these servers may share a computer or have a dedicated computer. A computer that is running a program that is a server (such as a web server) is itself called a server. Now you have two definitions for a server: a server can be software that interacts with client software or a server can be a computer that is running server software.

Look for an ISP that offers several e-mail addresses included in a single subscription plan, subscribes to a newsgroup service, and gives you a small amount of space for your personal web site (5 to 10 MB is about right).

Point of Presence

A small ISP might only have local phone numbers to dial for access, but some larger ISPs have local phone numbers in many major cities and other countries. A **POP (Point Of Presence)** is a phone number you can call to access your ISP. If you travel a lot, and need to get on the Internet from other cities, you'll want a local number to dial from several cities, rather than having to make a long-distance call to access your ISP. Some ISPs offer a toll-free number at extra cost.

Even if you're using DSL or cable modem from your home, you'll also want a regular dial-up number you can use in case the cable modem or DSL line is down or you're connecting while on the road.

Performance, Price, and Service

It goes without saying that performance, price, and service are three important factors to consider when selecting an ISP. An ISP should have a technical support desk available in the evenings, on weekends and on holidays. Phone lines should almost never be busy and connections should stay up consistently. The price of unlimited Internet access using a regular phone line, with at least one e-mail address, newsgroup service, and a small amount of personal web space should not exceed $25/month.

Another important service is the ability to access your e-mail from a web site in the event you need to check your mail from someone else's PC. Also look for the ability to forward your e-mail to another e-mail address and leave vacation messages while you're not checking your mail. A vacation message is a message that is automatically delivered to anyone who sends you e-mail.

Some ISPs are free. Broadband Digital Group, Inc. offers FreeDSL for those that have a DSL line (see *www.freedsl.com*). Other free ISPs are Juno Online Services, Inc. (see *www.juno.com*) and Alta Vista (see *www.altavista.com*).

REAL PEOPLE, REAL PROBLEMS, REAL SOLUTIONS
TRAVELING E-MAIL

In early 1999, Frank Delany solved a communication problem in his company when he discovered he could use a web-based e-mail client when he was traveling on business.

The small architectural firm that Frank owns used a local Internet Service Provider (ISP) that handled their Internet connectivity, including e-mail. When he or any of his staff were in the office, their e-mail ran smoothly. Over the past five years or so, Delany and Associates have used e-mail more and more as a communication tool. The company's clients are spread throughout the country. Using e-mail is a cost-effective, efficient means of delivering documents and has actually improved his company's customer service—except when on the road. Getting his messages was always complicated and sometimes impossible when he was anywhere but in the office. Frank had been carrying a laptop computer on business trips primarily to access e-mail, and usually ended up *not* receiving his messages because of connection set-up problems.

When Frank discovered that Yahoo! (*www.yahoo.com*) offered free e-mail accounts accessible through a web browser, he got an idea. At most of the hotels he stayed in, there were business centers with computers that had web access. In airports, he could use either an Internet kiosk or computers in airline business areas. (An Internet kiosk is similar to a phone booth, except that the connection is designed for business travelers to access the Internet.) If he could quickly access the Web for a few minutes, he could get his e-mail without all of the difficulty he usually had. He could easily forward messages from his base e-mail account to another address before he left on a trip. Why keep carrying the laptop and be frustrated? It was the perfect solution for his situation.

Today, when Frank Delany or any of his staff travel on business, they do so without carrying a laptop. All of his staff members have an e-mail account with Yahoo! that they use when on the road. In his company's case, it solved many problems. There isn't the expense of several laptop computers for his staff. The challenge of setting up and getting to the ISP remotely was solved. Even the hassle of carrying a laptop along on trips was eliminated!

CHAPTER SUMMARY

- ❏ The Internet is a group of networks that encircle the entire globe.

- ❏ Applications that use the Internet include the World Wide Web, chat rooms, e-mail, FTP, Telnet, Newsgroups, Gopher, and WAIS. These applications are also known as Internet Services.

- ❏ The World Wide Web is an accumulation of information stored on computers around the world in the form of web pages.

- ❏ A web page is a text document that can contain links to other pages, web sites, or multimedia files.

- ❏ The client/server concept works like this: client software on one computer requests information from server software that is on another computer. Most applications that use the Internet use the client/server concept.

- ❏ A web browser is client software that uses the World Wide Web. Its counterpart server software is called a web server.

- ❏ Examples of web browsers are Mosaic, Internet Explorer and Netscape Navigator.

- ❏ A web browser requests information on the World Wide Web by issuing a URL, which points to a computer and a web page on that computer.

- ❏ Web pages are written as hypertext documents using the HTML language, and are transmitted on the Internet using the HTTP protocol.

- ❏ A cache is a place to store data so that it can be used again.

- ❏ The Windows Control Panel Internet Options allows a user to change settings that affect web browsers.

- ❏ A search engine is software used to search a web site, group of sites, or the entire World Wide Web.

- ❏ Web pages can be divided into frames; each frame is stored in a separate page file.

- ❏ Methods for searching a web site include static index, site map, keyword index, and full text index.

- ❏ A web search site such as Infoseek gets its information by spiders or robots that search web sites.

- ❏ Yahoo! is an example of a subject directory where people request that their sites be registered.

- ❏ A well-designed web site is easy to use, well organized, and uses text, color and graphics effectively.

- ❏ E-mail uses the client/server concept to send text messages from one person to another.

❏ Chat rooms use the IRC application and allow several people to hold a real-time conversation.

❏ In 1993, four NAPs were identified (MAE East, MAE West, New York NAP and Chicago NAP), which were the connecting points for private and public backbones to the Internet.

❏ Most individuals and small companies use an Internet Service Provider to connect to the Internet by way of regular phone lines, DSL lines or cable modems.

❏ Large companies and regional ISPs use T1 and T3 lines to connect to the Internet.

❏ An ISP most often provides e-mail, World Wide Web, chat room, Newsgroups, and FTP services.

❏ Large ISPs have a point of presence (POP) in many major cities and around the world.

KEY TERMS

Advanced Research Projects Agency Network (ARPANET) — The first interconnected network used for free exchange of information between universities, the Department of Defense, and research organizations; a precursor to the Internet.

backbone — A network that connects other networks.

cable modem — A technology that uses cable TV lines for data transmission requiring a modem at each end. From the modem, a network cable connects to a NIC in the user's PC.

cache — Areas of memory or secondary storage where data is kept so that it can be used a second time.

channel — One chat room on a chat network. A channel can be either a private or public chat room.

client — A software program or computer that requests information from another software program on another computer.

client/server — A computer concept where one computer (the client) requests information from another computer (the server).

Channel Service Device (CSU) — A device that acts as a safe electrical buffer between a LAN and a public network such as that accessed by a T1 line.

CSU/DSU — A combination of two devices that serves as the entry point to a T1 or other public network channel. *See* CSU and DSU.

default web page — A web page that is designated as the page to send if no specific page is requested. This page is usually the introductory page of a web site. Also called a home page.

Digital Service Unit or Data Service Unit (DSU) — A device that connects a data terminal equipment (DTE) to a digital communication line such as a T1 line, that insures that the data is formatted correctly.

Digital Subscriber Line (DSL) — A telephone line that carries digital data from end to end that can be leased from the phone company for individual use. DSL lines are rated at 5 Mbps, about 50 times faster than regular phone lines.

frame — As applies to web sites two or more web pages designed to be displayed in a web browser at the same time, either side by side or stacked top to bottom. Each frame can have its own scroll bars.

full text index — A method of locating items on a web site. A full text index searches the entire contents of a web site for the specific word or phrase the you enter in a full text search box. The word or phrase need not have been designated as a keyword.

host name — A name that identifies a computer, printer, or other device on a network.

hot link — *See* hyperlink.

hyperlink — A tag in a hypertext document that links the location of the tag to another point in the same or to a different document. Also called hot link or link.

hypertext — Text in a document that is written with hyperlinks, which are connections between specially marked texts and other locations in the same document or other documents. The hypertext document can be read in a non-linear fashion as the reader moves from one location in the document to other locations by way of the hyperlinks.

Hypertext Markup Language (HTML) — A markup language used for hypertext documents on the World Wide Web. The language uses tags to format the document, create hyperlinks, and mark locations for graphics.

Hypertext Transfer Protocol (HTTP) — The protocol used by the World Wide Web.

Integrated Services Digital Network (ISDN) — A digital telephone line that can carry data at about 5 times the speed of regular phone lines. Two channels (phone numbers) share a single pair of wires.

Internet — A group of computer networks around the world that are connected to each other to create one very large network.

Internet Explorer — Made by Microsoft, the most popular web browser.

Internet Relay Chat (IRC) — The applications software used by chat rooms on the Internet.

Internet Service Provider (ISP) — A business that provides individuals and companies with access to the Internet.

keyword index — A method of locating items on a web site based on an internal list of preselected terms, known as keywords. Usually presented in the form of a field where you can enter a term you wish to search for. Compare to full text index.

link — *See* hyperlink.

meta robot tag — A meta tag that contains a list of keywords left there for web robots to find so that the web page can be located by a search engine.

meta tag — A type of tag in a web page that contains information about the page such as the title of the page and the editor that was used to create the page.

Mosaic — The first web browser sold to the general public that supported graphics.

Netscape Navigator — A web browser that is part of the Netscape Communicator suite of software.

Network Access Point (NAP) — One of four original locations in the United States that serve as major connection points for backbone networks in the U.S. The NAPs were created by the National Science Foundation in 1993.

newsgroup — An Internet service that provides a group of people with a place to post articles and allows people to respond to the articles. Newsgroups are organized around specific areas of interest.

overhead — The storage space, computing power and other resources needed by software or hardware that do not directly add to the intrinsic value of the software or hardware.

page — *See* web page.

Platform for Internet Content Selection (PICS) — An independent organization that provides a voluntary rating system for web pages.

Point of Presence (POP) — A phone number that a user can dial to connect to an Internet Service Provider.

protocol — The rules for communication used by a computer program when communicating with another program.

router — A device that connects networks and makes decisions as to the best routes to use when forwarding messages.

search engine — Software that can be used to search a site, group of sites or the World Wide Web for information. Search engines that search the entire Web use software called spiders or robots to locate information which is stored in a database on the search site for later retrieval.

server — (1) A software program that interacts with client software in a client/server environment. (2) A computer that runs server software and responds to requests for information from client computers.

site map — On a web page, a list of all the pages on a site, showing how the pages are organized. You can select the page you want to view from the list.

spider — *See* web crawler.

Standard Generalized Markup Language (SGML) — A standard for formatting a document so that formatting is retained from application to application, and platform to platform.

static index — On a web page, an index in the form of a predetermined list of terms that allows you to select what you want to see. Usually appears in the form of a drop-down list.

subject directory — A method for locating information on the World Wide Web by which keywords are manually registered into a database for later retrieval.

tag — A code in an HTML document that is used for formatting, inserting graphics, and creating hyperlinks. Most often, a tag has a beginning point and an ending point and each point is enclosed in angle brackets. For example, to bold text, use <B> to begin boldface and </B> to end boldface.

Uniform Resource Locator (URL) — An address for a resource on the Internet. A URL can contain the protocol used by the resource, the name of the computer, and the path and name of a file on the computer.

UseNet — A newsgroup service that consists of thousands of free newsgroups; the most popular newsgroup service.

web browser — A client software program that requests information from another program (the web server) on the World Wide Web.

web crawler — Software that searches the web looking for keywords to record in a search engine database. Also called web robot, spider.

web page — As it pertains to the World Wide Web, a file containing hypertext that is transmitted from a web server to a web browser. The web browser can then display the page to the user. Also called page.

web robot — *See* web crawler.

web server — Computer software that retrieves information in the form of web pages, and delivers those web pages to web browsers upon request. Also, the computer that is running the web server software.

web site — A group of web page files and multimedia files that work together to provide information on the World Wide Web.

World Wide Web (WWW) — One of several applications that use the Internet. This application is a massive accumulation of information stored on computers around the globe in web pages or hypertext documents, graphics, sound, and other multimedia files.

World Wide Web Consortium (W3C) — An organization that controls the standards of HTML and web communications.

REVIEW QUESTIONS

1. Name one example of an application that is dependent on the Internet to work.

2. What is the purpose of Telnet?

3. Name one Internet application that has largely been replaced by the World Wide Web.

4. What software is used as the client software for the World Wide Web?

5. What are the two most popular web browsers today?

6. In the following URL, what is the name of the computer? What is the name of the protocol? What is the name of the web page requested?
   http://www.microsoft.com/index.html.

7. List the steps to mark a favorite URL using Internet Explorer.

8. List the steps to bookmark URL using Netscape Navigator.

9. How do you turn off AutoComplete when using Netscape Navigator?

10. Once you install Internet Explorer 5, how can you revert back to an earlier version of the software installed previously on your PC?

11. How would an HTML document indicate that a word is to be italicized?

12. What is a frame as it applies to web pages?

13. When finding information on a web site, what is the difference between a static index and a site map?

14. Name one example of a web search site that uses a subject directory.

15. Name three web spiders and the sites that use them.

16. What are two strategies to help assure that information on your web site will be found by a web spider?

17. Name three e-mail client applications.

18. Name two chat networks.

19. What was the NSFnet? When was it started and when was it shut down?

20. What is the name of the NAP on the west coast?

21. What device connects two networks?

22. Which is faster, ISDN or cable modem?

23. Which type of technology that is used to connect to an ISP has a different download and upload speed?

24. What port or card does a DSL line use to connect to a PC?

25. If you live in Atlanta and you travel to Chicago and your ISP has a POP in Chicago, what does the ISP give you so that you can connect to the Internet in Chicago?

HANDS-ON PROJECTS

Hands-on
Project

Compare ISPs

Using the web sites of three ISPs that offer service in your area, compare their services by filling in the following chart. Include at least two ISPs that are free.

Internet Service Provider	POPs in other cities	E-mail accounts	Personal Web space	Cost

Beginning with Chapter 3, projects in this book direct you to build your own personal web site that you will progressively build throughout the book. In preparation for these on-going projects, if you don't already have an ISP account or educational institution account that includes space for your web site, sign up for one of these free services that provides personal web space.

Search the Internet for Great Looking Sites

Search the Internet for some great looking sites. Print out the home web page and other significant pages. Write in the margins what looks good to you and why. Also mark what ideas you intend to use when you build your own personal web site.

Install Internet Explorer and Windows Media Player

If the latest version of Internet Explorer and Windows Media Player are not installed on your PC, install them now. Play a radio program while surfing the web.

Research the Internet about Web Robots

Using two or more search engines, print material from web sites that describe in detail how a web robot works.

Research Companies That Build Web Sites

Using a search engine, find three sites that specialize in developing web sites for other companies. List the features that each site offers.

Fast Connection to the Internet

Research the availability and features of DSL and cable modem to your home. How much does the service cost? What is the setup cost? What are the other ISP services that are automatically included in the connectivity cost?

2

HOW THE INTERNET WORKS

In this chapter, you will learn:

♦ About the different components of the OSI model, and how they work together

♦ About the various rules of communication that are used to send data over the Internet

♦ How one computer finds another, and sends data over the Internet

The last chapter introduced two very different ways to look at the Internet. First, you saw the applications that use the Internet: web browsers, e-mail software, newsgroups, and chat rooms. The U.S. Postal Service analogy used in the first chapter let you see that these systems are analogous to a mail order catalog service that places and fills orders. Next you saw a bird's eye view of the infrastructure of the Internet, including backbones and major national connection points for these backbones. Using the U.S. Postal Service analogy, the Internet infrastructure is like looking at the postal service's major national routes used by its large trucks and airplanes.

This chapter continues the process of studying communication on the Internet: how information gets from one location to another, how one computer finds another computer, and about the rules of communication needed so that computers can understand one another. Again, in the U.S. Postal Service analogy the flow of information and the rules of communication is like studying how a letter at one post office finds its way to another post office and ultimately to an individual mailbox.

THE OSI MODEL AND THE INTERNET

When you mail a letter and expect it to reach its destination, you are most likely not aware of the many different systems involved to ensure a successful delivery. Figure 2-1 shows a simple view of those systems. A sender drops a letter in the mail and therefore virtually (not directly) communicates with the receiver.

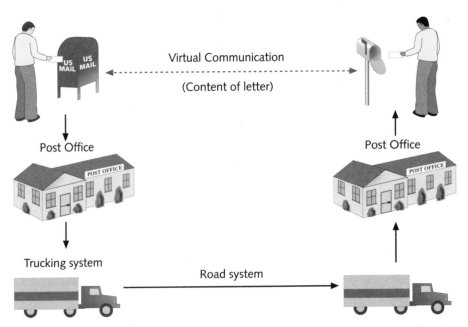

Figure 2-1   Communication is virtual between sender and receiver, but direct between adjacent system in the postal service

A postal carrier picks up the letter, and takes it to the local post office which routes the mail according to zip code. The post office uses a trucking system which uses the public road system to move the letter to the remote post office and finally to the individual mail box.

Think of the Postal Service as a series (or as layers) of related systems. A system that is adjacent to another system must know how to communicate with that other system. One layer is aware of, and must communicate with, the layer above and below it, but need not be aware of a layer remote from it. For example, the trucking system must know and abide by the rules of protocol of the public road system, and will fail if it doesn't follow those protocols. The local post office personnel don't need to know the road system rules for large trucks, and may not even be aware they exist. One way of saying this is that there is direct communication between each layer, but there is no direct communication to non-adjacent layers.

On any network, including the Internet, you will see many similarities with these analogies. The tasks of communicating with another computer can be broken down into separate systems. There are protocols of communication for each of several layers in the system. Each layer must communicate with the layer above it and below it by an established protocol. Virtual communication also takes place as one layer communicates to its counterpart layer on the remote side (for example, when a web browser communicates with a web server).

Just as with the post office, the payload or data is meaningless (not read) by the Internet. And some protocols guarantee delivery (such as registered mail with confirmation back to the sender) and some only promise "best effort delivery."

Understanding the OSI Model

In the 1970s, when manufacturers were beginning to build networking software and hardware to connect computers to one another, each manufacturer developed its own standards of communication within its proprietary network design. In the early 1980s, manufacturers began to standardize networking so that networks from different manufacturers could communicate. Two organizations that were leaders in this standardization effort were the International Organization for Standardization (ISO) and the Institute of Electrical and Electronics Engineers (IEEE).

In an effort to identify and standardize all the levels of communication needed in networking, ISO developed a networking model called the Open Systems Interconnect (OSI) reference model, which is illustrated in Figure 2-2. This model includes all the logical levels of communication needed for one user or application to communicate with another over a network. To accomplish this complete communication, seven layers, or levels, were identified. Just as with the Postal Service analogy of Figure 2-1, communication between adjacent layers is considered direct, but communication between matching layers is considered logical or virtual.

When you study the OSI model, remember that not all networks have a separate layer that matches each of the seven layers. In fact, no network in use today perfectly follows the model, but the model does serve the networking industry as a reference point for discussing different levels or layers in a network. For example, a combination of hardware and software on a network card operates in the Physical layer and the Data Link layer in the model. In Figure 2-2, you can see that these layers are responsible for 1) disassembling data into segments to be assigned to separate packets; 2) later reassembling packets into contiguous data; and 3) passing packets to and receiving packets from the network media or cabling.

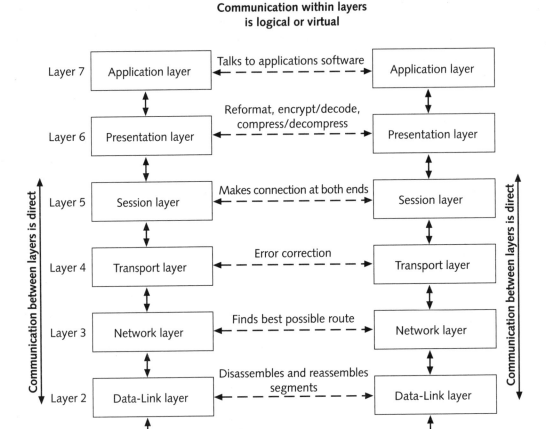

Figure 2-2   The OSI reference model identifies seven layers of network communication within software and firmware

The following section provides an overview of the role each layer plays in a network, starting at the top.

Application Layer

The **Application layer** of the OSI model is responsible for interfacing with application software such as web browsers or web servers. For example, when you enter a URL into a browser address box, the browser communicates the URL to the Application layer of the network software. The communication over the network is transparent to the application from that point forward. The web page is retrieved over the Internet and presented to the browser by the OSI Application layer. For Windows 9x, the Application layer is inherent in the operating system.

Presentation Layer

The **Presentation layer** receives requests for files from the Application layer, and presents the requests to the Session layer (described below). The Presentation layer reformats, compresses, or encrypts data as necessary. These operations are needed in order for the Application layer and the Session layer to communicate, and so that the data can be sent faster and can be secured. An example of the Presentation layer at work is when you use your bank's web site to do your banking, and use an encryption method for security. This encryption software is operating at the Presentation layer.

Session Layer

The **Session layer** is responsible for establishing and maintaining a session between two networked stations or hosts. A session over a network works somewhat like a telephone call over phone lines. The caller makes a call and someone answers on the other end. After both parties know that communication is established, conversation goes in both directions until either the caller or receiver ends the phone call.

The Session layer performs similar duties. Two network hosts attempt to establish a session on a network. Both hosts acknowledge the session, and the session is usually assigned an identifying number. Either host can disconnect a session when communication in both directions is completed. A session between two hosts on a network is called a **socket**. When a session is established, a socket is opened. A disconnected session is called a closed socket.

An example of the Session Layer in operation is when you dial up your ISP and enter your user ID and password. Both ends (your PC and the computer at the ISP) establish a communication session. If your PC senses that the session is broken, it attempts to reestablish the session. Long sessions are not heavily used on the Interent because most connections are temporary, that is, broken as soon as data is successfully transmitted and received. When data is ready to be transmitted again between the same two hosts, the hosts make a new session. Sometimes, however, a session stays intact for several transmissions back and forth.

Transport Layer

The **Transport layer** is responsible for error checking, and requests retransmission of data if it detects errors. The Transport layer guarantees successful delivery of data. On the Internet, the Transport layer is controlled by TCP (Transmission Control Protocol) and, to a lesser degree, by UDP (User Datagram Protocol). These protocols are discussed in more detail later in this chapter.

Network Layer

The **Network layer** is responsible for dividing a block of data into segments that are small enough to travel over a network. These segments of data are called **data packets** or **datagrams** and contain data, along with special identifying information in headers and trailers at the beginning and end of the packet called frames. The headers and trailers identify the packet, its source and destination addresses, and the type of software the data belongs to.

The Network layer is also responsible for finding the best possible route by which to send these data packets over a group of networks. This process is called routing. The Network layer also reassembles the packets once they reach their destination. On the Internet, the Network layer is called IP (Internet Protocol).

Data Link Layer

The **Data Link layer** is responsible for receiving packets of data from the Network layer and presenting them to the Physical layer for transport. If the packets are too large for the Physical layer, the Data Link layer splits them up into even smaller packets than did the Network layer. On the receiving end, the Data Link layer reconstructs the packets into their original size.

Physical Layer

The OSI **Physical layer** is responsible for passing data packets onto the cabling media. At this level, data is nothing but indistinguishable bits. Remember that data is packaged into packets before it is transmitted. This packaging of data has already occurred before it reaches this layer. The Physical layer does not distinguish the frame header or trailer from the payload, or data, within the frame. The Physical layer sees all of it as just bits that need to be passed on.

An example of a device that manages both the Data Link layer and the Physical layer is an Ethernet network interface card installed in a PC. The card receives data packets from the Network layer, and, if the packets are too large for Ethernet traffic, it divides them into smaller packets and then passes them on to the Ethernet cabling.

Network Devices and the OSI Model

When one computer on a network wants to send or receive data from another computer on a network, each computer is called a host, or end point, in the communication exchange. Each host must manage all the layers of communication from the Application layer down to the Physical layer.

However, many devices are involved in the communication between the two end points. One such device is a router, shown in Figure 2-3. Recall that a router is a device that connects two or more networks. If the two hosts are on different networks, there can be one or more routers between them, aiding in the communication. A router is like a traffic cop at an intersection directing traffic in our Postal Service analogy of Figure 2-1. If a U.S. Postal Service truck comes to the intersection, the traffic cop interacts with the truck driver without concern for

2

the cargo he's carrying. A router works at only the lower three layers of the OSI model. Any data traveling through is like cargo in a truck to a traffic cop—it is of little concern.

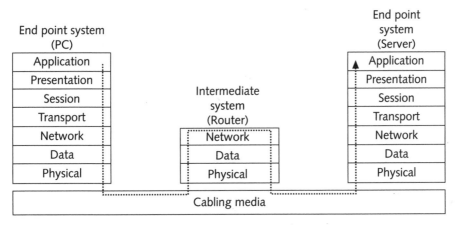

Figure 2-3   The two end-point systems traverse all seven of the OSI layers, but intermediate devices such as a router may only interact with some of the layers

In the example illustrated in Figure 2-3, data begins at the Application layer at one end point and is passed down through the layers of this host, through the cabling media to the router. At the router, it passes up through the lower layers to the Network layer where the router determines the best path for the data to travel to its destination. The Network layer then sends the data down to its lower layers, onto the cabling media and to its destination. At its destination, the data enters at the lowest layer and is passed up through the layers to the Application layer of the destination host.

A process or device that participates in managing data (or some other activity) without being concerned about all the details of the activity is said to be **stateless**, as opposed to a **stateful** process or device that is concerned about every detail or state of the data or activity. A router is a stateless device, because it's not concerned with the content of the data, but a host is a stateful device because it is concerned with every aspect of the data, the content as well as its delivery.

When you connect to the Internet via an Internet Service Provider (for example, from your home computer) your computer becomes one host on the ISP's network. Even though you probably don't have a LAN in your house, your computer is still a networked device once you connect to the ISP, and all the examples that refer to networks also apply to your situation.

The OSI Model Applied to the Internet

You can also use the OSI model to think about how data is transmitted over the Internet. However, the model doesn't translate exactly. The tasks are grouped into four (rather than seven) layers. Three of these four layers are collectively called the **TCP/IP (Transmission Control Protocol/Internet Protocol)** suite of protocols or TCP/IP stack. The TCP/IP protocol suite governs communication over the Internet and traverses the Application layer through the Network layer of the OSI model.

Figure 2-4 shows the four major groupings of the OSI model as applied to the Internet with the top three groups labeled as the TCP/IP suite. Within these layers, several of the more significant protocols are listed and introduced here, but you should know that TCP/IP covers more protocols than just these. This section introduces the TCP/IP "big picture" and the rest of the chapter discusses TCP/IP in more detail.

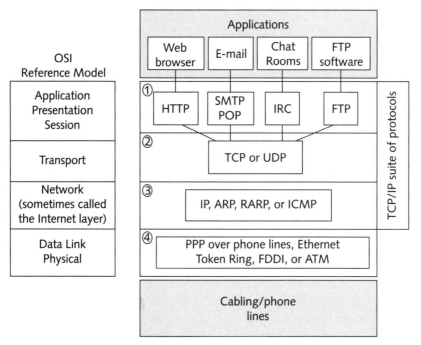

Figure 2-4   An overview of networking software showing the relationships among components

The Application, Presentation, and Session Layers

The Application, Presentation, and Session layers are best treated as a single group instead of three unique layers. In Chapter 1, you saw a few of the applications that use the Internet: web browsers, e-mail, chat rooms, and FTP software. The language or protocol each of these applications uses is listed at the Application, Presentation, and Session layers. The web browser communicates using HTTP; e-mail uses SMTP and POP, chat room software uses IRC, and FTP software uses FTP protocol to communicate at this layer. When one of these applications wants to send data to another counterpart application on another host, it passes the request to an **Application Program Interface (API)** which acts like a messenger service between the application and the appropriate protocol. This high-level application protocol manages the Application, Presentation, and Session layers and communicates with the protocols at the Transport layer.

The Transport Layer

The Transport layer includes two protocols, TCP (Transmission Control Protocol) and UDP (User Datagram Protocol). **TCP** is a protocol that establishes a connection from host to host before it begins transmitting data. Because it first establishes this connection, it is called a **connection-oriented protocol**. **UDP** is a protocol that sends data without caring about whether or not the data is received. It does not establish a connection first; thus it is called a **connectionless protocol**. UDP is, therefore, considered to be a "best effort" transport service, but TCP guarantees delivery. When a TCP packet reaches its destination, an acknowledgement is sent back to the source. If the source TCP does not receive the acknowledgement, it will resend the data or pass an error message back to the higher level protocol. TCP and UDP each serve a different purpose for Internet communication, as you will see later in the chapter.

The Session layer is somewhat of a hybrid layer, as sessions can be managed by one of the high-level application protocols, but a limited type of session is created and managed by TCP at the Transport layer. For this reason, sometimes in other diagrams you'll see the Session layer assigned to the high-level application protocols and sometimes assigned to TCP. Note in Figure 2-4 that the Session layer falls slightly inside the TCP and UDP area.

The Network Layer

TCP and UDP communicate with the Network layer, which is sometimes called the Internet layer. This layer of the TCP/IP protocol suite is responsible for routing. **IP (Internet Protocol)** is the governing protocol at this layer, responsible for breaking up and reassembling data into packets and routing them to their destination. Some of the other supporting protocols include **ARP (Address Resolution Protocol)**, responsible for locating a host on a local network, **RARP (Reverse Address Resolution Protocol)**, responsible for discovering the Internet address of a host on a local network, and **ICMP (Internet Control Message Protocol)**, responsible for communicating problems with transmission to devices that need to know about these problems. These protocols communicate with the Data Link layer protocols.

The Data Link and Physical Layers

When discussing communication over the Internet, the Data Link and Physical layers are generally treated as a single unit, because both of these layers are most often covered by the firmware on a single network interface card. **Firmware** is software that is permanently stored on a microchip. The protocol used depends on the type of physical network that the data is traveling on. For example, for an Ethernet LAN, the protocol is Ethernet, but for a regular phone line, the protocol is PPP.

PPP (Point-to-Point Protocol) is used over phone lines, and allows a PC to connect to a network using a modem. The Point-to-Point Protocol is the most popular protocol for managing network transmission from one modem to another. Ethernet is the most popular network technology used for LANs. Token Ring is also used for LANs. FDDI and ATM are used mostly for fiber-optic high-speed networking. All these technologies are discussed in Chapter 11 except PPP, which is covered in Chapter 8.

The next section begins the process of explaining how protocols work together and communicate with one another by showing how a device or host is identified or addressed at each of these layers. After you understand addressing on the Internet, you can turn your attention to how one device or host uses these addresses to find another device or host on the Internet.

ADDRESSING ON THE INTERNET

Every device on the Internet has a unique address. Part of learning about the Internet is learning how a device (such as a computer or a router) or a program (such as a web server) is identified on the Internet. In our Postal Service analogy, it's like understanding the zip code system, the street address system, and other methods the Postal Service uses to locate individuals and businesses. On the Internet, there are four methods used to identify devices and programs. Each is listed below and then explained. Figure 2-5 shows how each of these addresses relate to the OSI model and which protocols use the different addresses.

- A physical address, also known as a MAC address, is permanently embedded in a network interface card and identifies a device on a LAN.

- An IP address identifies a computer, printer, or other device on the Internet.

- A domain name is an easy-to-remember word or phrase for an IP address.

- A port address is a number that identifies a program running on a computer.

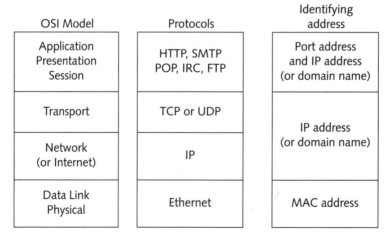

Figure 2-5 How devices on the Internet are identified at different layers of the OSI model

Physical Addresses

A computer, router, network printer or other device on a network connects to the network by way of a network interface card (NIC). When a NIC is manufactured, each NIC is assigned an address at the factory that will never change for that card. It's called the **physical address**, **hardware address**, **adapter address** (the NIC is called an adapter) or **MAC (Media Access Control) address**, and is unique for that card. No two MAC addresses are the same because of the IEEE industry standards created in 1980. The MAC address is built from the vendor's assigned IDs, the model, and the manufacture date.

 When IEEE or other standards organizations announce the creation or improvement of a standard, they do so by issuing a **Request for Comment (RFC)**, which states the proposed standard and requests the industry to comment concerning the proposal. The RFC that created the standard for MAC addresses was RFC 802 named after the year and month the project began. If you'd like to read the standard, see the web site *www.rfc-editor.org*. Search on RFC 802.

MAC addresses are used at the Data Link layer for computers on the same network to communicate. If a host does not know the MAC address of another host on the same network, it uses the higher layer protocols to discover the MAC address.

Computers on different networks cannot use the MAC address for communication, because the Data Link layer protocols only control the traffic on their own networks. In order for a host to communicate with a host on another LAN across the Internet, it must know the address of the host that is used by the TCP/IP protocols. These addresses are called IP addresses; see Figure 2-6.

It is interesting to know a computer's MAC address and its IP address. If your PC is connected to the Internet or any TCP/IP network, follow these directions to display the IP address and the NIC's MAC address in Windows 9x:

1. Click **Start** on the taskbar to display the Start menu, then click **Run**. In the Run dialog box, type **winipcfg** and press **Enter**. The IP Configuration windows opens; see Figure 2-7.

2. Click the NIC from the drop down list of network devices. The Adapter Address displayed is the MAC address. An example of a MAC address is 00-20-78-EF-0C-5A.

3. Click the **OK** button.

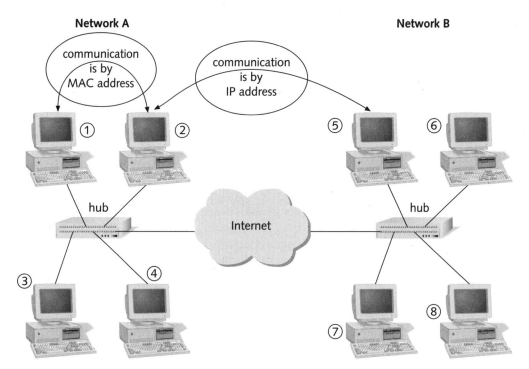

Figure 2-6   Computers on the same LAN use MAC addresses to communicate, but computers on different LANs use IP addresses to communicate over the Internet

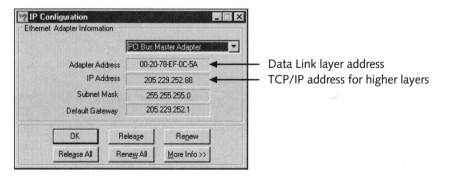

Figure 2-7   Use the Windows 9x WinIPcfg utility to display a PC's IP address and MAC address

As you study how addressing works on the Internet, remember these two important things about MAC addresses: (1) MAC addresses are the most absolute of addresses—a MAC address on a host does not change as long as the NIC doesn't change. (2) All hosts on the same network must communicate by their MAC addresses, which are managed by the Data Link layer protocol that controls the network.

2

IP Addresses

All the protocols of the TCP/IP suite of protocols identify a device on the Internet by its IP (Internet Protocol) address. Each computer, printer, router or other kind of device is assigned one or more IP addresses.

An IP address is 32 bits long, made up of four 8-bit numbers separated by periods. The largest possible 8-bit number is 11111111, which is equal to 255 in decimal, so the largest possible IP address in decimal is 255.255.255.255. Each of the four numbers separated by periods is called an **octet** (for 8 bits), and can be any number from 0 to 255, making for a total of 4.3 billion potential IP addresses (256 2 256 2 256 2 256). However, because of the allocation scheme used to assign these addresses, not all of them are available for use.

The first part of an IP address identifies the network and the last part identifies the host. It's important to understand how the bits of an IP address are used in order to understand how routing happens on the Internet—how the IP protocol is used to locate an IP address anywhere on the globe. When data is routed on the Internet, the network portion of the IP address is used to locate the right network. Once the data has arrived at the local network, the host portion of the IP address is used to identify one computer on the network that is to receive the data. And finally, the IP address of the host must be used to identify its MAC address so that the data can travel on the host's LAN to that host. The next section explains this in detail.

Who assigns IP addresses and tracks these assignments? The work is done under the authority of the U.S. Government and involves several public and private organizations. Later in this chapter is a section that describes how it all works.

Classes of IP Addresses

When a business, college, or some other organization applies for IP addresses, a range of addresses appropriate to the number of hosts on the organization's networks is assigned. IP addresses that can be used by companies and individuals are divided into three classes—Class A, Class B, and Class C—based on the number of possible IP addresses in each network within each class. IP addresses are assigned to these classes according to the scheme outlined in Table 2-1. You can determine the class and size and/or type of company to which the address is licensed by looking at the address. More importantly, you can also determine what portion of an IP address is dedicated to identifying the network and what portion is used to identify the host on that network.

Table 2-1   Classes of IP addresses

Class	Network Octets (blanks in the IP address are used for octets identifying hosts.)	Total Number of Possible Networks or Licenses	Host Octets (blanks in the IP address are used for octets identifying networks)	Total Number of Possible IP Addresses in Each Network
A	0.___.___.___ to 126.___.___.___	127	___.0.0.1 to ___.255.255.254	16 million
B	128.0.___.___ to 191.255.___.___	16,000	___.___.0.1 to ___.___.255.254	65,000
C	192.0.0.___ to 223.255.255.___	2,000,000	___.___.___.1 to ___.___.___.254	254

A Class A address uses the first octet (leftmost) for the network address and the remaining octets for host addresses. A Class A license assigns a single number that is used in the first octet of the address, which is the network address. The remaining three octets of the IP address can be used for host addresses that uniquely identify each host on this network. The first octet of a Class A license is a number between 0 and 126. For example, if a company is assigned 87 as its Class A network address, then 87 is used as the first octet for every host on this one network. Examples of IP addresses for hosts on this network are 87.0.0.1, 87.0.0.2, and 87.0.0.3 (the last octet does not use 0 or 255 as a value, so 87.0.0.0 would not be valid). Therefore, one Class A license can have approximately 256 2 256 2 254 node addresses, or about 16 million IP addresses. Only very large corporations with heavy communication needs can get a Class A license!

A Class B address uses the first two octets for the network portion and the last two for the host portion. A Class B license assigns a number for each of the first two left-most octets, leaving the third and fourth octets for host addresses. The number of possible values for two octets is about 256 2 256 (some IP addresses are reserved, so these numbers are approximations), or about 65,000 host addresses in a single Class B license. The first octet of a Class B license is a number between 128 and 191, which gives about 63 different values for a Class B first octet. The second number can be between 0 and 255, so there are approximately 63 2 256, or about 16,000, Class B networks. For example, suppose a company is assigned 135.18 as the network address for its Class B license. The first two octets for all hosts on this network are 135.18, and the company uses the last two octets for host addresses. Examples of IP addresses on this company's Class B network are 135.18.0.1, 135.18.0.2, 135.18.0.3, and so forth.

A Class C license assigns three octets as the network address. With only one octet used for the host addresses, there can be only 254 host addresses on a Class C network. The first number of a Class C license is between 192 and 223. For example, if a company is assigned a Class C license for its network with a network address of 200.80.15, some IP addresses on this Class C network would be 200.80.15.1, 200.80.15.2, and 200.80.15.3.

Class D and Class E IP addresses are not available for general use. Class D addresses begin with the octet 224 through 239 and are used for **multicasting**, which is when one host sends messages to multiple hosts such as when broadcasting a video conference over the Internet. Class E addresses begin with 240 through 254 and are reserved for research.

 A multicasted video conference uses the UDP protocol because it is a connectionless protocol. Because it is connectionless, it is faster than TCP because it doesn't stop to make a connection, and doesn't add as much overhead information in front of the data. UDP is not as reliable as TCP, but with video conferencing, losing a few data packets here and there is not critical.

Public, Private, and Reserved IP Addresses

When a small company is assigned a Class C license, it obtains 254 IP addresses for its use. If it only has a few nodes (say, less than 25 on a network), many IP addresses go unused, which is one of the reasons that there is a shortage of IP addresses. But suppose that the company grows and now has 300 workstations on the network and is running out of IP addresses. There are a couple of ways to solve this problem. One way is to take into account that not all of these 300 workstations need to have access to the Internet, even though they may be on the network. So, while each workstation may need an IP address to be part of the TCP/IP network, those not connected to the Internet don't need addresses that are unique and available to the Internet; therefore, they can use private IP addresses.

The IP addresses available to the Internet are called **public IP addresses**. If the company is using TCP/IP, the company can make up its own private IP addresses to use on its private network. A large private network that uses TCP/IP is sometimes known as an **intranet**. **Private IP addresses** are IP addresses that are used on private intranets that are isolated from the Internet. Because these nodes are isolated from the Internet, no conflicts arise. The RFC 1918 recommends that the following IP addresses be used for private networks:

- 10.0.0.0 through 10.255.255.255
- 172.16.0.0 through 172.31.255.255
- 192.168.0.0 through 192.168.255.255

When assigning these isolated IP addresses, also keep in mind that a few IP addresses are reserved for special use by TCP/IP and should not be used. They are listed in Table 2-2.

Table 2-2 Reserved IP addresses

IP Address	How It Is Used
255.255.255.255	Broadcast messages
0.0.0.0	A currently unassigned IP address
127.0.0.1	Indicates your own workstation; yourself

All IP addresses on a network must be unique for that network. A network administrator may assign an IP address to a standalone computer (for example, if someone is testing networking software on a PC that is not connected to the network). As long as the network is a private network, the administrator can assign any IP address he or she desires. On an isolated private network (that is, one that is not connected to the Internet), the administrator is free to make up his or her own private IP addresses, although a good administrator avoids using the reserved addresses.

Dynamically Assigned IP Addresses

Another solution for the company that has 300 computers on its network but only 254 IP addresses is to dynamically assign IP addresses. Instead of IP addresses being permanently assigned to workstations (called **static IP addresses**), when a workstation comes online to the network, a server assigns an IP address to it to be used for the current session only (called a **dynamic IP address**). When the session is terminated, the IP address is returned to the list of available addresses. Because not all workstations are online at all times, fewer IP addresses than the total number of workstations can satisfy the needs of the network.

The server that manages these dynamically assigned IP addresses is called a **Dynamic Host Configuration Protocol (DHCP)** server. In this arrangement, workstations are called DHCP clients. DHCP software resides on both the client and the server to manage the dynamic assignments of IP addresses. DHCP software is built into Windows 9x, Windows NT, and Windows 2000. Many Internet service providers (ISPs) use dynamic IP addressing for their dial-up users.

Plans for New IP Addresses

Because of an impending shortage of IP addresses, a new scheme of IP addresses is currently being developed called the **IP version 6 (IPv6)** standard. Current IP addresses using 32 bits have 8 bits in each octet. With the new system, each address segment can have 32 bits, for a total of 128 bits for the entire address. Also, IPv6 will have the added advantage over current IP addressing in that it can automatically assign an IP address to a network device.

Ports

Ports are numbers used to address software or services running on a computer. A host computer may have several services running on it. For example, a computer at an ISP might be running a web server, an e-mail server and a chat room server, all at the same time. How does a web browser on a client PC say, "I want to speak to the web server," and an e-mail client say, "I want to speak with the e-mail server."? The answer is by using a port or a number that has been assigned to the desired service. Each service running on the host is called a **process** and each process is assigned a port. The port is written at the end of the IP address like this: 169.49.209.19:80, separated from the IP address with a colon. A network administrator can assign any number to a process, but there are established port numbers for common services listed in Table 2-3. Unless the administrator has a good reason to do otherwise, he or she uses these common assignments, so the web browser communicates with 169.49.209.19:80 and the e-mail client communicates with 169.49.209.19:25. The combination of IP address and port number is called a **socket**.

Table 2-3 Some common TCP/IP port assignments for well-known services

Port	Service	Description
20	FTP	File transfer data
21	FTP	File transfer control information
23	Telnet	Telnet used by UNIX computers
25	SMTP	Simple mail transfer protocol, client sends e-mail
35	Printer	Private printer service
53	DNS	Domain Name Service (discussed later in chapter)
80	HTTP	World Wide Web protocol
110	POP3	Post Office Protocol version 3, the client receives e-mail
161	SNMP	Simple Network Management Protocol, the TCP/IP protocol that monitors and helps manage network traffic

Domain Names

Sometimes hosts are given alphabetic, or word-based names, in addition to their numeric IP addresses. These alphabetic names are called **domain names**, and they are assigned because IP addresses are numbers, and are therefore difficult to remember, and because companies might want to change their IP addresses without also changing the Internet name by which the outside world knows them. Domain names are an alternate way of addressing a host on the Internet, but all domain names must eventually be mapped onto a host's IP address before contact with the host can take place.

Think of a domain name as a pseudonym or an alias; the real name of the host computer is its IP address. The last segment of a domain name tells you something about the host. Domain names in the United States end in the suffixes listed in Table 2-4. There are other endings as well, including codes for countries, such as .uk for the United Kingdom. Examples of domain names are *course.com*, *pbs.org*, and *leeuniversity.edu*. With the growth of the Internet, there has been a shortage of available domain names; because of this shortage, additional suffixes are being created.

Table 2-4 The highest level domain of a domain name is identified by its suffix

Domain Suffix	Description
.com	Commercial institution
.edu	Educational institution
.gov	Government institution
.mil	U. S. military
.net	Internet provider or network
.org	Nonprofit organization
.int	Organizations established by international treaties between governments

A domain name can further be divided into sub-domains, such as *support.microsoft.com* and *mail.buystory.com*. The first word in the domain name is used to identify a sub-category within the domain *microsoft.com* and *buystory.com*, and is called a **canonical name** or CNAME. A domain name points to an IP address, and a domain name with a prefix can point to another IP address or to a particular folder on the computer that has the IP address for the high-level domain name. See Figure 2-8.

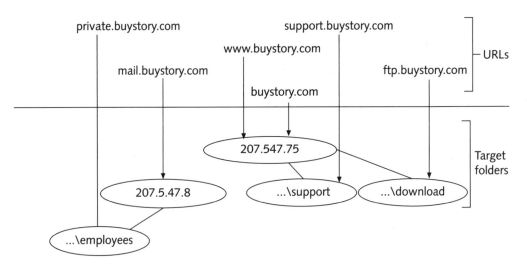

Figure 2-8   Domain names with or without prefixes (CNAMES) can point to IP addresses and folders depending on the mapping strategy used

Assigning and Tracking Domain Names and IP Addresses

The processes of assigning and tracking domain names and IP addresses have always been under the authority of the U.S. Government, although the processes have been administered by several public and private organizations. The system is currently being reorganized to give more authority and responsibility to the private sector.

Originally, IP addresses and domain names were assigned by Network Solutions, Inc. (*www.networksolutions.com*) at the **Internet Network Information Center (InterNIC)** in Menlo Park, California, under the authority of the National Science Foundation. The organization responsible for overseeing this operation is the **Internet Assigned Numbers Authority (IANA)**. See *www.iana.org* for more information about IANA.

Beginning in the spring of 1999, the responsibility for assigning and tracking domain names and IP addresses is being transitioned from IANA to a non-profit, private sector organization regulated by the U.S. Department of Commerce called **Internet Corporation for Assigned Names and Numbers (ICANN)**. ICANN administers a Shared Registration System (SRS) that allows many corporations other than Network Solutions, Inc. to register domain names and IP addresses. However, Network Solutions, Inc. is still responsible for maintaining the master registry of all domain names and IP addresses. A company that can register these names and numbers must be approved by ICANN and is called a **registrar**. For a list of all registrars see the ICANN web site at *www.icann.org/registrars*.

When an individual or organization registers a name or number with one of these registrars, the registrar becomes the sponsor for this name or number. Any changes to it including the contact person or network must be made by this same sponsor. ISPs and web hosting companies who are not official ICANN registrars sometimes offer the service of registering domain names to their customers. In these cases, they are resellers for an approved registrar.

Domain Name Resolution

Domain names and IP addresses are not necessarily permanently related. A host computer can have a certain domain name and can be connected to one network and assigned a certain IP address, and then be moved to another network and assigned a different IP address. The domain name can stay with the host while it connects to either network. It is up to a name resolution service to track the relationship between a domain name and the current IP address of the host computer.

There are two name resolution services that track relationships between domain names and IP addresses: **Domain Name System**, also called **Domain Name Service**, (**DNS**) and Microsoft's **Windows Internet Naming Service (WINS)**. DNS is the more popular of the two because it works on all platforms. At the heart of DNS is a distributed database, which must initially be created manually.

WINS also uses a distributed database, but WINS is only available for Windows networks resolving Windows 9x, Windows NT, and Windows 2000 host names. WINS has an advantage over DNS in that WINS can manage name resolution when IP addresses are dynamically assigned. Windows networks sometimes use a combination of DNS and WINS services.

How DNS Works

DNS uses a hierarchical structure of computers that keep a record of domain names and the location of the host computer that has been assigned each domain name. There are three logical components to DNS: computers searching for the IP address for a domain name, called **resolvers**, servers that contain the information relating domain names to IP addresses, called **name servers**, and the databases of information, called **name space**. The process of discovering an IP address for a given domain name is called **address resolution**.

Name servers are organized from the top down. Network Solutions maintains servers called **root servers** that act as the highest level of authority when locating domain name information. At this time, there are 13 root servers strategically placed all over the world. Under the root servers are top-level, or first-level domain name servers, called Top Level Domains (TLDs), and under them are second-level servers, and so forth.

Each name server holds a piece of the name space (part of the total data needed to resolve names) in entries for each domain name that it knows about. This entry is called a **resource record** or **DNS record**. The contents of these resource records are discussed in Chapter 10.

A network that supports DNS has two or more name servers, called the primary and secondary name servers. The secondary server gets its information from the primary server, and is sometimes called the slave name server. Both servers are considered the authoritative servers for the domain names assigned to their networks. The group of networks for which the name server is responsible is collectively called the name server's **zone**. An **authoritative name server** is the server that has the most current information about a domain name. Figure 2-9 shows a diagram of how these servers are related.

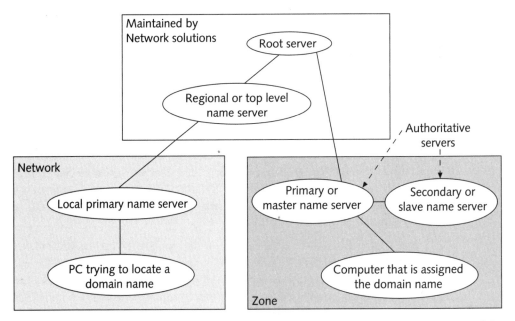

Figure 2-9   The primary and secondary name servers in the host computer's network has the final say regarding where a domain name is to be found

For example, Intermedia.net is an Internet hosting service in California. Many businesses and individuals use the computers there for their own web sites, so the Intermedia.net primary and secondary name servers are the authoritative name servers for all these domain names. When a business registers its domain name with a domain name registrar, rather than giving the IP address that the business's web site has, the business tells the registrar the IP addresses of these two primary and secondary domain name servers at *Intermedia.net.* This information goes into the root name servers at Network Solutions. When others query these root servers for the location of the business' domain names, the root server directs the query to the primary name server at Intermedia.net. This server responds with the IP address that it knows has been assigned to the business's domain name.

For example, *www.buystory.com* is the web site of a business that uses Intermedia.net as its hosting service. When a user at a PC in Maine points her browser to this web site, the PC needs an IP address for that domain name before it can request a web page. It uses the DNS client software to make the request to DNS server software on the local primary name server. (This DNS client and server software is operating at the Applications layer in the OSI model.)

If this is the first time anyone has requested the domain name, the information is not in the name server's database, so it queries its top-level name server. If the top-level name server doesn't know, it queries its root server. If the root server doesn't know, it queries the authoritative name server, which does know! The information is passed all the way back to the PC that initially began the process. Every server along the way saves or caches the data to its name space. This cached entry is assigned a **time to live** (**TTL**), which is the time the data is considered to be good before it needs to be verified.

For example, the owners of *www.buystory.com* might decide to use a different web hosting service and move the domain name to a new network. The owners make the change using their registrar's web site. The primary and secondary name servers at Intermedia.net and the new web hosting company also know the change. The name server on the network in Maine then has incorrect information until it refreshes or updates its name space.

A network administrator uses software settings to control how often a name server refreshes its information. If the time to live is set for several days, which might happen when an administrator is trying to conserve resources, the user on the Maine network might have a frustrating time wondering why the web site is "down."

How to Create and Update a Domain Name

An individual or business purchases a domain name from a registrar of domain names. The initial cost of a domain name is about $70, with a yearly fee after that. The following discussion gives an overview of the process of registering a domain name, using the Network Solutions web site as an example.

To register a domain name at Network Solutions, go to the Network Solutions web site at *www.networksolutions.com*. The web site guides you through the process of registering a domain name. Some of the things you'll have to do include:

- Finding out whether the domain name that you want is available. Network Solutions lets you search the database of domain names.

- Entering the name, address, telephone number and e-mail address for the person who will be responsible for this domain name. Be sure to use an e-mail address that is relatively permanent because Network Solutions will use it to verify that an authorized person is making future changes to the account.

- Entering the information for the primary and secondary domain name servers of the organization that will host the site. For a web hosting service, look for this information on the web hosting service's home page or customer support page.

- Paying for the name with a credit card.

Figure 2-10 shows a domain name being registered on the Network Solutions web site.

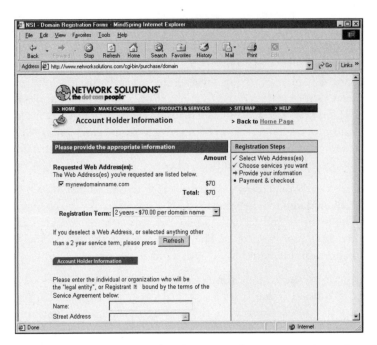

Figure 2-10   Use Network Solutions web site to purchase domain name

Virtual Servers and Virtual Hosting

A discussion of IP addresses and domain names would not be complete without mentioning virtual servers and virtual hosting. When customers share the space and processing power of a server for their web sites, FTP sites, mail sites, and other processes, they can use a **virtual server**. Each customer has a unique IP address. All the IP addresses point to one shared computer, but point to different folders on the computer. A virtual server runs its own processes or programs separately from other programs that are running for other virtual servers on the same computer.

Virtual hosting is a similar technique whereby a company can offer personal web space on a computer by assigning a folder to the web site, but does not necessarily assign the folder its own IP address or give it the right to run its own processes. Having your own IP address and running your own processes generally add to the cost of web hosting. Web hosting will be discussed in more detail in Chapter 10.

2

REAL PEOPLE, REAL PROBLEMS, REAL SOLUTIONS
USE .COM, .NET, OR .ORG?

As an established company in the telecommunications industry, Cathey, Hutton and Associates, Inc. is often referred to as "CHA." The management consulting firm based in Dallas, Texas has been undergoing continuous growth over the last twelve years.

When the company decided to develop and launch a corporate web site, next came the task of choosing a domain name. The principals of the company knew that if they could use the initials "CHA" in their domain name, it would be effortless for their clients to identify. It was a short domain name, and could be easily remembered.

When Cathey, Hutton & Associates set out to register a new domain name, they found that another company had already registered both "cha.com" and "cha.net" leaving the "cha.org" address as their last choice. It was decided to register the ".org" address and use it for their new web site and company e-mail.

Only after the launch of the company's web site did the principals of CHA realize how the domain name they had registered would affect their Internet presence. They learned that using the ".org" top-level domain that most commonly represented non-profit entities was not the best choice for a commercial enterprise.

The company encountered a host of challenges as a result of selecting "cha.org" as their domain name. "Why a dot-org domain name?" became a frequently asked question. "Isn't CHA a *for-profit* business?" was another. Some web search engines rejected their listing because of the misrepresentation. When prospective customers tried "cha.com," they found the Colorado Health & Hospital Association web site and were baffled.

Cathey, Hutton and Associates needed to make a change to their domain name. However, this meant more than just a new registration! The company had five field offices in the United States. They had clients located in almost every state. Communication among offices and clients became increasingly dependent upon the Internet. The company had been using "cha.org" for over two years. Business cards, stationary, and brochures all used the domain name. Existing clients had recorded existing e-mail addresses. What seemed like a simple domain name change was actually a large investment!

Their solution was to systematically rule out domain names more specific to field offices or corporate divisions. They began adding domain names like "cha-marketing.com" and changing printed materials to coincide. The company made changes office by office, until almost everyone was using a specific ".com" address. The change took over a year to complete! The result kept the identity of CHA in the forefront, and added the commercial enterprise connotation to their image.

Changing domain names can be costly. How the customer perceives the domain name can be even more costly! The use of a domain name can go beyond that of a web site URL; it can often be used to portray a company, especially in today's dot-com world.

ROUTING ON THE INTERNET

Now that you have an understanding of how computers are identified on the Internet, the next step is to see how one computer finds another computer on the Internet when it knows an IP address. The next section looks at how networks that make up the Internet are inter-networked together, and how they communicate with one another.

How Data Travels Across Interconnected Networks

Figure 2-11 shows a simplified view of how networks work together to send data over the Internet. A user in California traverses many networks to gain access to a server in New York. Each network operates independently of all other networks, but can also receive a packet from another network and send it on to a third network, while it also manages its own routine, internal traffic.

Networks are connected by routers, which belong to more than one network. In Figure 2-11, Network B contains four routers: Routers 1, 2, 3, and 4. But Routers 3 and 4 also belong to Network C. Network C contains Router 8, which also belongs to the same network as the server in New York that the user wants to access.

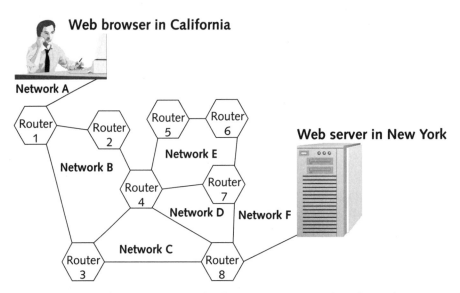

Figure 2-11   The Internet is a web of interconnecting, yet independent, networks

How many paths are there on the Internet by which the user in California can access the server in New York? One path is through Router 1, then 3, then 8, and finally to the server. Data going from the server to the user may travel a different path than data traveling from the user to the server. In fact, if there is a lot of data divided into several packets, each packet may take a different route, and the packets may not arrive at the user's PC in the same order in

2

which they were sent. It's up to the lower layers in the OSI model to sort it all out and reassemble the data before it's presented to the Application layer, and then presented to the browser.

In Figure 2-11, a router that belongs to a network has an IP address on that network. However, if a router belongs to more than one network, it will have one network card for each network it belongs to, and each NIC will be bound to a unique IP address. Router 4 in the diagram belongs to four networks (B, C, D, and E), and would, therefore, have four network cards and four IP addresses, one for each network.

How TCP/IP Routing Works

Suppose a host computer wants to send data to another host. If the first host knows that the remote host is on its same network and it also knows the MAC address of the remote host, it simply sends the data straight through to the Data Link layer. This layer segments the data into packets suitable for the network and sends the data to the Physical layer and onto the cabling media to the remote host.

If the first host knows that the remote host is on a different network on the Internet, it sends the data to the gateway to the Internet. A gateway has two meanings: a device that connects networks, and a device that translates protocols between two networks with different protocols. A common gateway device is a router, which not only can connect two or more networks, but also can decide the best route to send data over several networks.

When a packet arrives at a router, the router decides if the packet belongs to a host within its own network or needs to be routed to a different network. At this point, the router is only looking at the destination IP address of the packet. However, if the packet belongs to its own network, its Data Link layer will transmit the packet by the MAC address, not the IP address. Think of the MAC address as the local address, and the IP address as the Internet address.

How does the sending host know that the remote host belongs to its network or to another network? By comparing the destination IP address to its own IP address. If the network portions of both IP addresses are the same, then it will assume the remote host is on its own network and use the MAC address for communication. If the network portion of the IP addresses are different, then it passes the data off to the gateway for delivery to the remote network.

When a host wants to send data to another host on its own LAN, it may or may not know the MAC address of the destination host but will "learn" the MAC address the first time a packet is sent to it. The host first looks in its cache of addresses for the destination IP address and its matching MAC address. If it doesn't find the entry, then it sends out a broadcast message to every host on its network asking, "Whoever has the IP address xxx.xxx.xxx.xxx, send me your MAC address." The host with the given IP address responds, the cache of addresses is updated, and the packet is sent. A **broadcast** is a message sent to every node on a network. When a host broadcasts a message to discover a MAC address it uses two protocols: ARP (Address Resolution Protocol) at the Network layer and UDP (User Datagram Protocol) at the Transport layer.

When a workstation is first configured to use TCP/IP, one step in the configuration is to associate a MAC address to an IP address. This process is called binding the MAC address to the IP address. When an IP address is bound to the MAC address, TCP/IP data that is addressed to this IP address now has a physical computer or MAC address to send the data to. (The term **binding** refers to associating any OSI layer in the network to a layer just above it or just below it. When the two layers are bound, communication continues between them until they are unbound or released.) Looking back at Figure 2-7, you can see that the IP address in the figure has been assigned to the displayed adapter. In other words, the IP address is bound to this NIC.

Figure 2-12 shows an example of two TCP/IP networks connected by a router. The router (Computer C) belongs to both networks and has an IP address for each network. Think of it as the intersection point of the two networks.

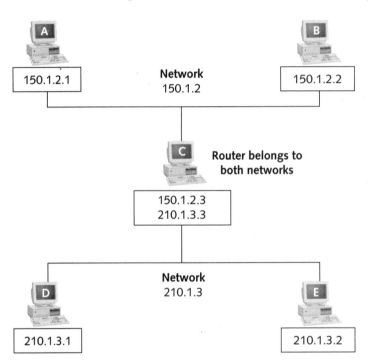

Figure 2-12   Two networks using TCP/IP connected by a router

Suppose both these networks are Ethernet, and Host A wants to send data to Host B, which is on the same network. Host A knows the IP address of Host B. It would also need to know the Ethernet address (MAC address) of Host B in order to send the packet. This is what happens:

1. Host A knows the Host B IP address and turns the job of discovering the MAC address over to ARP (Address Resolution Protocol), which looks up the IP address of Host B in its routing tables on the Host A PC.

2. If ARP does not find the IP address of Host B in its tables, it sends out a broadcast message to the entire network (Hosts B and C in this case) containing a request for the MAC address of Host B.

3. Host B recognizes its IP address and responds with its MAC address.

4. Host A receives the address and updates its routing tables.

5. Host A sends its packet to Host B.

Now suppose that Host A is ready to send a packet to Host E, which is on the other network. Here's what happens:

1. Host A looks at the IP address of Host E and recognizes that Host E does not belong to its network (how it does this will be covered soon).

2. Because Host A is trying to communicate with a different network, it sends the packet to the router of its network, in this case, Host C. Host A knows the MAC address of its router, so it knows where to send the packet. (Host A did not attempt to broadcast for a response from Host E because it recognized that Host E would not hear the broadcast message, since it is on a different network.)

3. Host C receives the packet and looks at the destination IP address. Host C recognizes that the destination IP address is on its second network, so it sends the packet to Host E, just as Host A sent the packet to Host C in the first example. In other words, Host C first looks in its router table. If it doesn't find the IP address of Host E, it sends out a broadcast message to Host E's network, and Host E responds with its MAC address.

Default Gateways

Recall that a gateway can give a network access to other networks. Sometimes a large network has more than one router, as seen in Figure 2-13. The network in the upper left of the figure is 250.1.2 and has two routers (D and E), each belonging to other networks. Host E is designated as the **default gateway**, meaning that hosts on the 250.1.2 network send packets addressed to other networks to this gateway first. The other router, Host D, is called the **alternate gateway** and is used if communication to the default gateway fails.

Suppose Host A on network 250.1.2 wants to send a packet to Host K on Network 210.1.3 in the figure. Host A first sends its packet to the default gateway. If that fails, Host A tries the alternative gateway. Sometimes the default gateway knows that a packet should be routed through an alternate gateway. If so, it sends an ICMP redirect packet back to Host A telling Host A to use the alternate gateway when addressing Host K. The next time Host A attempts to send a packet to Host K, it will read from its routing table to use the alternate gateway.

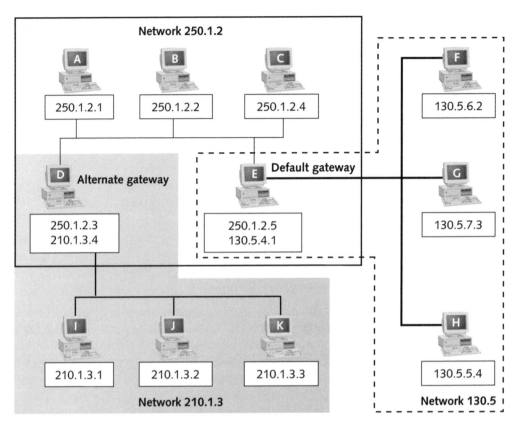

Figure 2-13   A network can have more than one router; one router of the network will be the default gateway

Network Masks

Comparing the network addresses in Figure 2-13 to those of Table 2-1, you can see that networks 250.1.2 and 210.1.3 are Class C networks, and network 130.5 is a Class B network. Also remember that Host A had to determine that Host K was not on its network, but was on a foreign network. How did it know that? By comparing Host K's IP address to the network mask. A **network mask** determines what part of an IP address identifies the network, rather than the host. Host A's network address is 250.1.2. Host A compared these values to the first three octets of Host K's IP address. Because they were not the same, Host A knew that Host K was on another network.

Also notice in Figure 2-13 that the three network addresses are 250.1.2, 210.1.3, and 130.5. By looking at the first octet of each network, you can see that the first two networks are Class C networks (first octets are 250 and 210) and the third network is a Class B network (first octet is 130). This tells you that the first two networks use three octets for the network address and the third network uses only two octets for the network address.

Subnetworks

Remember, from earlier in the chapter, that an IP address contains two parts, a network address and a host address. When a large company applies for a single class license, it is assigned a single network address from which it can create many IP addresses unique to each host in its one network. Also, the company can divide this one network into several **subnetworks** (also called **subnets**) and assign IP addresses to each subnet.

The primary purpose of dividing a network into two or more subnets is to better manage traffic on the network. Recall that a hub indiscriminately broadcasts any data that comes to it to every node on the network, thus generating lots of unnecessary traffic on the network. For a very large network, this can seriously affect network performance. Also, if a host does not know the MAC address of another host on the network, it broadcasts a message to all nodes on the network. By segmenting a large network into individual subnets, the overall effect of all this broadcasting on a network is reduced.

Traffic can better be controlled using subnets because local traffic can be contained within its own subnet, and routers can be effectively used to route traffic from subnet to subnet. TCP/IP can manage this by using not only network addresses, but subnet addresses as well. A few bits at the beginning of the host portion of the IP address are borrowed from the host and used to identify the subnet, and the **subnet mask** tells how many of these bits are used for that purpose.

A subnet mask looks like an IP address, because it has four numbers separated by periods, but it is not an IP address. It's a number that is used to define which portion of an IP address identifies the network (including the subnet) and which portion identifies the host.

An example of a subnet mask is 255.255.240.0. When converted to bits, it looks like this:

     11111111.11111111.11110000.00000000

All subnet masks, when converted to bits, will have all ones on the left and all zeroes on the right. The ones define the network portion (including the subnet) of the mask, and the zeroes define the host portion. The subnet mask above tells us that four bits of the host portion of the IP addresses on this subnet are used for identifying the network. These four bits identify a subnet within the major network. The major network is identified by the first 2 octets of the IP addresses.

A host uses its subnet mask to decide if a destination host is in its subnet. It determines how many bits in a destination IP address belong to the network address by the number of ones in its subnet mask. Once it knows what portion of the destination IP address is the network address, it compares that portion of the address to its own address to decide if the destination address is inside its own subnet. If it is, it attempts to communicate with it directly. If the IP address is outside its subnet, it communicates through the router.

Let's look at one example using these values:

Sending IP address:	130.5.206.189
Destination IP address:	130.5.194.5
Subnet mask:	255.255.240.0

The sending host converts these three addresses to bits, which look like this:

Sending IP address:	10000010.00000101.11001110.10111101
Destination IP address:	10000010.00000101.11000010.00000101
Subnet mask:	11111111.11111111.11110000.00000000

From the subnet mask, the host knows that the first 20 bits of the IP addresses are the network address so it only uses those bits to make the comparison between its IP address and the destination IP address:

Sending IP address, network portion:	10000010.00000101.1100
Destination IP address, network portion:	10000010.00000101.1100

The network portions of the two IP addresses are the same, so the sending host attempts to communicate directly with the destination host rather than sending the data on to its router.

When you configure a computer for TCP/IP, using static IP addressing, you must enter the subnet mask so that the PC can determine if an IP address it wants to communicate with is inside or outside its subnet. For dynamic IP addressing, the subnet mask is not entered because it may vary from session to session. The IP address and the subnet mask for the workstation is assigned each time the workstation logs onto the network. TCP/IP configuration is covered in Chapter 8.

TYING IT ALL TOGETHER

We're now ready to tie all the different protocols together to show how data can travel over the Internet. Let's use an example of a web browser sending a request to a web server. As you read, follow along using Figures 2-14a through 2-14l as your guide. To keep things simple, assume that the web browser knows the IP address of the web server. This would be the case if the user entered the IP address in the browser's address box, rather than the domain name. (If the user had entered a domain name instead, the browser would first need to resolve the domain name before these steps begin because the request requires an IP address.)

In Figure 2-14a, the web browser wants to make a request to a web server, and processes the request using an API call. The API process packages the data using HTTP format, which will include an HTTP header, and addresses it to an IP address and port 80, which is the default port for a web server.

Figure 2-14a   Step-by-step process for a web browser to query a web server

In Figure 2-14b, the HTTP protocol delivers the package to TCP, giving the destination IP address and port. TCP guarantees delivery, and attempts to make a connection to the destination IP address and port. If the connection is made, it prepares the data by attaching a TCP header in front of the data. The header contains:

- Source port

- Destination port

- Sequence number (position of this data segment within a group of segments)

- Acknowledgement number (a message that will be returned to the sender to acknowledge receipt of the data)

- Header length

- Codes that will later help to assure that the data was not corrupted during transmission

Figure 2-14b

In Figure 2-14c, TCP turns to the IP protocol for delivery on the Internet. IP divides the data segment into packets of no more than 65,535 bytes. Each packet contains the TCP header information and the data. IP adds its own header information in front of the TCP header. The IP header contains:

- The version of IP that originated the packet, in the rare event the packet encounters a network that is not using a compatible version of IP. Most networks use IP version 4 (IPv4).

- Length of the IP header, and total length of the packet

- Information that allows IP on the receiving end to reassemble the packets in the correct order

- Time to live (the number of routers the packet can cross, also called the **hop count**). If this number is exceeded, the packet is discarded—a feature that prevents IP packets from bouncing back and forth over the Internet forever.

- The type of protocol that the IP packet is carrying (either TCP or UDP)

- Source IP address and destination IP address

- Information about routing and codes that helps determine whether the IP header was corrupted

Data packets, sometimes called datagrams, are sent out to the Network layer as shown in Figure 2-14d. Each data packet has an IP header, a TCP header, and an HTTP header.

Figure 2-14c

Figure 2-14d

Look at Figure 2-14e. Each time a packet encounters a router, its TTL is reduced by one. If the router must send the packet over a network that cannot handle large packets, the router divides the packet into smaller packets. Ethernet can only handle packets that are under 1500 bytes. Using an Ethernet network might happen in the last hop, when the packet arrives at the destination's local network. The router protocol in the figure is OSPF (open shortest path first), although there are other routing protocols.

Figure 2-14e

In Figure 2-14f, if the packet's TTL is reduced to one, the next router the packet encounters will eliminate the packet. The router sends an ICMP message back to the source IP address, informing the host of the problem.

Figure 2-14f

When the host receives the ICMP message, it resends the packet as shown in Figure 2-14g.

Figure 2-14g

In Figure 2-14h, when a packet arrives at a router that recognizes that the destination IP address is on its network, it sends the packet to the destination host using the MAC address, not the IP address.

Figure 2-14h

Look at Figure 2-14i. Once the packet reaches the Data Link layer of the routing device, if this layer does not have the MAC address in its routing tables, it broadcasts a message to the entire network using ARP protocol at the Network layer and UDP protocol at the Transport layer. The host with the given IP address responds with its MAC address. The router then sends the packet to that host by way of the network card that connects to the LAN to which the host belongs. If the network card discovers that the packet is too big for its network, it divides the packet into smaller packets. This is at the Data Link layer, and an example would be an Ethernet network. The Ethernet NIC would break an IP packet into smaller Ethernet packets before allowing them onto the Ethernet LAN.

In Figure 2-14j, IP at the host is responsible for reassembling the packets into their original order, before passing off the data to TCP. If the Data Link layer on the router had broken up an IP packet into smaller Ethernet packets, the NIC on the destination host would have reassembled the data packets from Ethernet size to IP size before passing them off to IP.

Figure 2-14i

Figure 2-14j

By looking at the protocol entry in the IP header, IP knows to deliver the packet to TCP rather than UDP at the host as shown in Figure 2-14k.

Figure 2-14k

In Figure 2-14l, TCP knows which port to deliver the packet to because of the port information in the TCP header. In our example, Port 80 is a web server which will receive and process the HTTP data.

Figure 2-14l

In this example, the router made routing decisions based on IP addresses. It's important to know that a router works at the Network layer to make these decisions even though once the router decided that the packet belonged to its local network, it relied on its Data Link layer to send the packet to the destination host based on the MAC address.

2

CHAPTER SUMMARY

- The OSI model was developed by the International Organization for Standardization (ISO) to help the industry identify and standardize the different levels of communication on a network.

- There are seven layers in the OSI model: Application, Presentation, Session, Transport, Network, Data Link and Physical. Each layer communicates with the layer above it and below it.

- The Application and Presentation layers interact with applications using the Internet.

- The Session layer establishes a connection that stays intact as long as the hosts want to communicate.

- Most connections on the Internet are temporary, only staying intact long enough for a single transmission.

- The Transport layer on the Internet is managed by either the TCP or UDP protocols.

- The Network layer can divide a segment of data into packets, and is responsible for finding the best possible route across a group of networks such as the Internet. Hosts are identified by IP addresses at this layer.

- The Data Link layer disassembles packets of data into smaller packets as needed to transport over a network, and later reassembles the data at the other end. Nodes on a LAN are identified by MAC addresses at this layer.

- TCP/IP is a suite of protocols that manages communication on the Internet.

- IP works at the Network layer of the OSI model (sometimes called the Internet layer), and uses several less significant protocols such as ARP, ICMP and RARP.

- Four ways to address a device or process on the Internet are IP addresses, port numbers, domain names and MAC addresses.

- IP addresses are managed by InterNIC and can be divided into five classes, A, B, C, D and E.

- Class A, B, and C IP addresses are used by individuals and businesses. Class D is used for multicasting and Class E is used for research.

- An IP address can be permanently assigned to a device (static IP addressing) or a different IP address can be assigned each time the device logs onto the network (dynamic IP addressing).

❒ A process is a program that is running on a computer, and is identified by a port number. The IP address and the port together are called a socket.

❒ Each NIC has a unique MAC address that is assigned to it at the factory, and uniquely identifies a host on a local network.

❒ When a host is configured to use TCP/IP, an IP address is bound to the MAC address.

❒ Domain names are an easy way to remember an IP address, but can also be assigned to different folders on a host so that a host can have many domain names assigned to it.

❒ Registrars approved by ICANN are responsible for leasing and managing domain names.

❒ DNS is a system that helps locate an IP address assigned to a domain name. It consists of a root server managed by Network Solutions, high level name servers (TLDs) in regions of the country, and local name servers responsible for the domain names in their zone.

❒ Virtual servers and virtual hosting are two methods whereby one computer can host many IP addresses and domain names.

❒ A router or host uses a subnet mask to determine if a host with whom it wants to communicate belongs to its network.

KEY TERMS

adapter address — *See* MAC address.

address resolution — The process of discovering an IP address for a domain name.

Address Resolution Protocol (ARP) — A protocol used by TCP/IP that dynamically or automatically translates IP addresses into physical network addresses (MAC addresses).

alternate gateway — An alternate router that is used if the default gateway is down. *See* gateway.

Application layer — The OSI layer responsible for interfacing with the application using the network.

Application Program Interface (API) — A method used by an application program to call another program to perform a utility task.

authoritative name server — The primary or secondary name server over a zone, containing the most authoritative information about domain names in that zone.

binding — Associating an OSI layer to a layer above it or below it, for example, when an IP address (Network layer) is associated with a MAC address (Data Link layer).

broadcast — A message sent from a single host to multiple hosts.

canonical name — As applies to domain names, a name added to the beginning of a domain name that serves as a subcategory of the domain, such as *support.microsoft.com*, where support is the canonical name.

connection-oriented protocol — In networking, a protocol that confirms that a good connection has been made, before transmitting data to the other end. An example of a connection protocol is TCP.

2

connectionless protocol — A protocol such as UDP that does not require a connection before sending a packet. A connectionless protocol provides no guarantee that a packet will arrive at its destination. An example of a UDP transmission is a broadcast to all nodes on a network.

Data Link layer — The OSI layer that disassembles packets and reassembles data into packets, preparing the packets to be passed onto the physical media.

default gateway — The main gateway or unit that sends or receives packets addressed to other networks.

DNS record — *See* resource record.

DNS (Domain Name Service or Domain Name System) — A distributed pool of information (called the name space) that keeps track of assigned domain names and their corresponding IP addresses, and the system that allows a host to locate information in the pool.

domain name — A unique, text-based name that identifies an IP address. Typically, domain names in the United States end in .edu, .gov, .com, .org, or .net. Domain names can also include a country code, such as .uk for the United Kingdom.

Dynamic Host Configuration Protocol (DHCP) — The protocol of a server that manages dynamically assigned IP addresses. DHCP is supported by Windows 9x, Windows NT, and Windows 2000.

dynamic IP addressing — An assigned IP address that is used for the current session only. When the session is terminated, the IP address is returned to the list of available addresses.

firmware — A combination of hardware and software that works together as a unit. Network cards have firmware that controls how the card sends data onto the network cables.

frame — *See* packet.

gateway — Any device that connects two networks of differing protocols, or a device that provides a network access to other networks.

hardware address — *See* MAC address.

hop count — The number of routers a packet passes through as it goes from source to destination. If the hop count exceeds the TTL, the packet is discarded.

Internet Control Message Protocol (ICMP) — Part of the IP layer that is used to transmit error messages and other control messages to hosts and routers.

Internet Network Information Center (InterNIC) — The central group that assigns and keeps track of all Internet IP addresses on the organizational level.

Internet Protocol address (IP address) — A 32-bit address consisting of four numbers separated by periods, used to uniquely identify a device on a network that uses TCP/IP protocols. The first numbers identify the network; the last numbers identify a host. An example of an IP address is 206.96.103.114.

intranet — A private TCP/IP network used by a large company.

IP version 6 (IPv6) — A proposed new version of the Internet Protocol proposed by the Internet Engineering Task Force in 1995. The current version of IP is version 4.

MAC (Media Access Control) — An element of the Data Link layer protocol that provides compatibility with the NIC used by the Physical layer. A network card address is often called a MAC address. *See* MAC address.

MAC address — A 6-byte hex hardware address unique to each NIC card and assigned by manufacturers. The address is often printed on the adapter. An example is 00 00 0C 08 2F 35. Also called adapter address or physical address.

multicasting — A message sent by one host to multiple hosts, such as when a video conference is broadcasted to several hosts on the Internet.

name server — A server that has part of the name space or information needed to resolve a domain name.

name space — The total information that is distributed over many name servers that relate domain names to IP addresses.

Network layer — The OSI layer responsible for routing packets.

network mask — The portion of the IP address that identifies the network; sometimes called a subnet mask. Not all networks use network masks.

node — A device or host on a local network.

octet — An 8-bit number that is part of an IP address. IP addresses are composed of four 8-bit numbers, separated by periods.

packet — Segments of network data that also include header, destination addresses, and trailer information that are sent as a unit using electronic communication. Also called frame.

physical address — *See* MAC address.

Physical layer — The OSI layer responsible for interfacing with the network media (cabling).

Point-to-Point Protocol (PPP) — A protocol that governs the methods for communicating via modems and dial-up telephone lines. The Windows Dial-Up Networking utility uses PPP.

port — A number assigned to a process on a computer so that the process can be found by TCP/IP.

Presentation layer — The OSI layer that compresses and decompresses data and interfaces with the Application layer and the Session layer.

private IP addresses — An IP address that is used on a private TCP/IP network that is isolated from the Internet.

process — An executing instance of a program, together with the program resources. There can be more than one process running for a program at the same time. One process for a program happens each time the program is loaded into memory or executed.

public IP address — An IP address available to the Internet. *See* private IP address.

Request For Comment (RFC) — A document that proposes a change in standards or protocols for the Internet. An RFC can be presented by different organizations, but is done under the general guidance of the Internet Architecture Board (IAB).

resolver — A computer searching for the IP address for a domain name.

resource record — A record on a name server that contains information relating domain names to IP addresses.

Reverse Address Resolution Protocol (RARP) — A protocol used to translate the unique hardware NIC addresses into IP addresses (the reverse of ARP).

root server — A server managed by Network Solutions that contain the highest authoritative information about domain names.

Session layer — The OSI layer that makes and manages an extended connection between two hosts on a network.

socket — A virtual connection from one computer to another, such as that between a client and a server. Higher-level protocols such as HTTP use a socket to pass data between two computers. A socket is assigned a number for the current session, which is used by the high-level protocol. A socket contains the IP address and the port number.

stateful — A device or process that manages data or an activity and is concerned with all aspects of the data or activity.

stateless — A device or process that manages data or some activity without regard to all details of the data or activity.

static IP addressing — IP addresses permanently assigned to a workstation.

subnetwork — Divisions of a large network, consisting of smaller separate networks (to prevent congestion). Each subnetwork (also called a subnet) is assigned a logical network IP name.

subnet mask — Defines which portion of the host address within an IP address is being borrowed to define separate subnets within a network.

TCP/IP (Transmission Control Protocol/Internet Protocol) — The suite of protocols that supports communication on the Internet. TCP is responsible for error checking, and IP is responsible for routing.

Time To Live (TTL) — The time that data is considered to be good, before it must be verified or discarded.

Transport layer — The OSI layer that verifies data and requests a resend when the data is corrupted.

User Datagram Protocol (UDP) — A connectionless protocol that does not require a connection to send a packet and does not guarantee that the packet arrives at its destination. UDP works at the Transport layer.

virtual hosting — A server that provides personal web space on a computer by assigning a folder to the web site, but might not assign the folder its own IP address or give it the right to run its own processes.

virtual server — A server that is used by many customers who share the space and processing power of one server for their web sites, FTP sites, and mail sites. Virtual servers provide customers with unique IP addresses, each of which point to the same computer, but to different folders. A virtual server runs its own processes or programs separately from other programs that are running for other virtual servers on the same computer.

Windows Internet Naming Service (WINS) — A Microsoft resolution service with a distributed database that tracks relationships between domain names and IP addresses. Compare to DNS.

zone — The group of computers on one or more networks that a name server is responsible for, and which contain the most authoritative information about the domain names assigned to these computers.

REVIEW QUESTIONS

1. What organization devised the OSI model? What is the purpose of the model?

2. What is the difference between the Internet and an intranet? How are they alike?

3. Is the IP protocol a stateful or stateless protocol? Why or why not?

4. Which protocol is a "best effort delivery" protocol, IP or TCP?

5. Which protocol is a connection protocol: UDP, TCP or IP?

6. How is the ICMP protocol used on the Internet?

7. Name three ways a host computer can be addressed on a network.

8. On the Internet, the OSI Network layer is sometimes called the _____ layer.

9. What organization is responsible for assigning IP addresses?

10. How many bits are used to write an IP address?

11. What is the class of the IP address, 169.45.66.200?

12. How many IP addresses are there in one Class B license?

13. How is the IP address 255.255.255.255 used?

14. What is the reserved IP address that refers to yourself?

15. How does a port differ from an IP address?

16. When leasing a domain name from a registrar, what IP addresses are required?

17. What are two name resolution services used to track the relationship between domain names and IP addresses?

18. Once a local name server has discovered the IP address of a domain name somewhere on the Internet, if that domain name moves to a new IP address, how does the local name server know about the change?

19. Explain the difference between a virtual server and virtual hosting.

20. What is the process called when an IP address is assigned to a network card installed on a computer? How is the network card identified in this process?

21. When a packet arrives at a router how does the router know that the destination IP address of the packet belongs to one of its networks?

22. How is the TTL entry in an IP packet used?

23. Physically, how can a router belong to more than one network? Logically, how does a router belong to more than one network on the Internet?

24. Explain the difference between a default gateway and an alternate gateway.

25. What is the subnet mask for Class C IP addresses on a network where 1 bit of the host address is used for the subnet address? How many subnets are possible using this arrangement?

HANDS-ON PROJECTS

IP Addresses and Domain Names

1. Your company is establishing a presence in France and has asked you to reserve a domain name in that country. What agency do you use to do that? What is their web site? Print the home page for this agency.

2. What utility program can you use to discover an IP address of a domain name? What is the IP address of *www.microsoft.com*? Point your web browser to the site using the IP address rather than the domain name and print your browser screen. Now add the port address of the web server to the IP address and access the site. Print your browser screen.

3. Sometimes the ownership of a domain name is contested, such as when an unrelated third party leases the name of a celebrity or major corporation as their domain name. Write a brief summary of the rules that ICANN abides by during the judicial process over who gets the domain name. (See *www.icann.org*.)

4. Is *[yourfullname].com* available as a domain name? Go to the Network Solutions web site, enter your name, and print the screen showing if it's available.

Research the Internet

In this chapter, you have been introduced to several organizations that participate in developing standards and protocols for the Internet. One of these organizations is the Internet Architecture Board. Write a brief paper describing who this board is and what the board does. (See their web site *www.iab.org*.)

Using NetStat to Track a TCP Connection

NetStat is a TCP/IP utility that can be used to track a TCP connection. Use it tell Windows 9x to report to you the status of any current TCP connections. Follow these directions to track a TCP connection when accessing the Microsoft web site, reproducing a tracking session shown in Figure 2-15. Print your version of the screen. Netstat and other TCP/IP utilities will be discussed in detail in Chapter 13.

1. Click **Start** on the taskbar to display the Start menu, then point to **Programs** to display the Programs menu.

2. Click **MS-DOS Prompt** on the Programs menu. A window appears, containing the MS-DOS command prompt.

3. Type **NETSTAT** at the MS-DOS command prompt. The results of the command are shown in Figure 2-15, in the first call-out on the figure. These results show that no connections currently exist.

4. Start your web browser, then enter the URL of the Microsoft support site: **support.microsoft.com**.

5. As soon as you enter the Microsoft URL, return to the MS-DOS command window and type **NETSTAT** again while the browser is building the web page. You should see the connection to the Microsoft IP address at port 80.

6. Wait a few moments, then type **NETSTAT** a third time at the MS-DOS prompt. This time you see that no TCP connections exist.

7. Print the screen.

8. At the MS-DOS command prompt type **EXIT** and press **Enter**. The window closes.

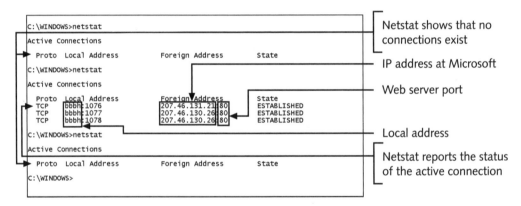

Figure 2-15   By using NETSTAT you can watch TCP establish a connection with another host

Examine Your PC Configuration

If you have a computer connected to the Internet, answer the following questions about your PC configuration:

1. How does your PC connect to the Internet (phone line to ISP, company LAN to ISP, cable modem, etc.)?

2. If you use a phone line to connect to the Internet, what is the phone number you dial to your ISP?

3. Does your PC use a NIC to connect to the Internet? If so, what is the MAC address of the NIC?

4. Does your PC use static or dynamic IP addressing?

5. What is your current IP address and subnet mask?

6. What class IP address are you using?

Learning to Research RFCs

A RFC is the final word on how an Internet technology works. Answer the following questions about RFCs that apply to ports. Use *www.faqs.org* or *www.rfc-editor.org*.

1. What is the earliest RFC that you can find about ports, what they do, and how to use them?

2. List ten or more RFCs that apply to ports, their RFC number, title and purpose.

3. Print the introduction to RFC 1122 and, in a few words, describe its purpose.

4. What service listens at port 37? What is the purpose of this service? (Hint: See RFC 868.)

3

BUILD YOUR OWN WEB SITE

In this chapter, you will learn

♦ How to read and write HTML code to build a moderately complex web site

♦ How to publish a web site

♦ About free resources to help build your web site

♦ About HTML authoring tools, their features and functions

Learning something new is more fun when you learn by doing. This chapter is about doing—building your own personal web site from the ground up. In the first two chapters you gained an understanding of all the components that make up the Internet. That process of learning about Internet technologies will continue throughout the book. Beginning with this chapter, you'll apply what you're learning while you build your own web site. As each new concept is introduced in future chapters, you'll return to your web site to add something new to it—something that applies a new concept, new skill, or new technique. Your web site then becomes not only a point of contact where others on the Internet can meet you, but it also becomes an avenue for you to apply new knowledge and practice new skills.

In order to publish your web site, you need access to some storage space on a web server. The web server that stores your web site files is known as your **web host**. If you are a student at a college or university, you might be assigned space for a web site on your institution's server. If you access the Internet by way of an ISP, check with your ISP to see if your account includes space for a web site. Most ISP accounts include that service, and you can usually find out how to access web site space from the ISP's home page. The web host tells you what URL to use when accessing your web site. For example, the personal web sites hosted by Yahoo! Geocities hosting service all begin with the URL *www.geocities.com*.

Your web host will assign you a user ID, password, and folder for your web files. The web server also determines the file name of the default web page file. Remember from Chapter 1 that the default web page is the web page that the server sends to the browser if the browser asks only for the name of the site (for example, *www.yahoo.com*) and doesn't ask for a specific page on the site (*www.yahoo.com/filexyz.htm*, for example). The web server might require that the default web page have the file name index.htm, index.html, default.htm, or welcome.htm. Look on the customer support pages for the web server or in the documentation that comes with the web site service, for the name of this file and assign that name to your home page.

If you have no way to publish your web site, you can still follow along with the exercises and view your web site using the web browser on your PC in offline mode.

 What's the difference between a web site and a web page? People frequently use these two terms interchangeably. A web page usually implies a single HTML document, whereas a web site implies a web server and any and all interconnected pages that are retrieved with the same default web page or URL. For example, the Microsoft web site, at *www.microsoft.com*, contains many web pages and supporting files about Microsoft products, service, and technology. Your web site might consist of a single web page or it might consist of several pages connected with hyperlinks, and enhanced with sound, graphics, and other multimedia files.

A SIMPLE WEB SITE FROM BEGINNING TO END

In Chapter 1, you learned that a web site is actually a collection of files managed by a web server: HTML files together with text, graphics, and other multimedia files. When someone wants to look at a web site, the web browser contacts the web server, and requests a web page. The web server responds by downloading the requested file to the browser, along with any other files that are needed to build the entire web page.

Creating a web site is a two-step process:

- Create the web page files
- Publish the web site by placing these files on the server

Create a Web Page

In its simplest form, a web page is one file that contains HTML text. You can create this HTML file using any text editor such as Notepad or WordPad. While there are many other tools available to create and publish HTML files, for your first effort, use the tools that are common to every PC: Notepad to create the file, and an FTP utility to publish the file. Later in the chapter, you'll see more sophisticated tools to make your work much easier. To view the HTML file, you can use Internet Explorer or Netscape Navigator.

You should store your web page files in one folder with sub folders on your hard drive. Use Windows 9x Explorer to create a folder. This chapter uses the folder c:\data\webs as an example.

Figure 3-1 shows a simple web page. Follow these steps to create the page with Notepad:

3

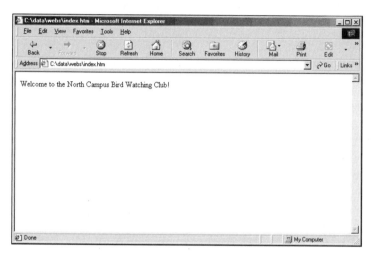

Figure 3-1   First effort at creating a personal web page

1. Click **Start** on the taskbar, then point to **Programs.** The Programs menu opens.

2. Point to **Accessories.** The Accessories menu opens.

3. Click **Notepad.** The Notepad window opens.

4. Type the following text:

   ```
   Welcome to the North Campus Bird Watching Club!
   ```

5. Click **File** on the menu bar, then click **Save.** The Save As window opens.

6. Click the **Save in** drop down list and navigate to and click the folder you created for your web page files (c:\data\webs, in the example).

7. Type **index.htm** in the File name field and click **Save.**

8. To exit from Notepad, click **File** on the menu bar, then click **Exit.**

Follow these directions to view the web page in Internet Explorer:

1. Start Internet Explorer.

2. Click **File** on the menu bar, then click **Work Offline**.

3. In the Address field, type the URL of the file you just created. When you are looking at an unpublished web page—one that is stored on your PC—the URL is the path of the file. In the example given above, the URL is c:\data\webs\index.htm. The web page displays as it will when others view it on the Web.

Why HTML?

The web page you just built was very simple. Let's add one more thing—a new sentence—and you'll see why you need HTML. Follow these directions to open the file you created and add one more line to it:

1. Follow the directions given earlier to start Notepad.

2. Click **File** on the menu bar, then click **Open.** The Open dialog box opens.

3. Click the **Look in** drop down list and navigate to and click the folder that contains your web page file, index.htm.

4. Click the **Files of type** drop down list. A list of file types appears. Use this drop down list to specify that you want to display files with all extensions (including .htm), not just files with the .txt extension. Click **All Files (*.*).**

5. Click the file **index.** Notice that Notepad doesn't display the file extension. Then click **Open.** The file opens.

6. Type the following text on the second line of the file:

   `This month's featured bird is the Bluebird.`

7. Save the file: click **File** on the menu bar, then click **Save.**

8. Exit from Notepad.

9. View the file with your web browser. Review the directions given earlier if you forget how to do this.

Note that the web browser puts the two sentences on the same line. A web browser does not recognize Notepad's command for a line break—it only reads text and HTML. In order to tell the browser to put a line break in the text, you need the HTML code for a line break, which is <BR>. Let's fix it:

1. Using Notepad, open the file index.htm.

2. Type the characters **
** at the end of the first line of text.

3. Save the file and exit from Notepad.

4. Using your web browser, view the file and notice that the browser recognized and used the HTML line break code.

In addition to using a simple text editor to write HTML code, you can also use applications that are designed to create HTML documents. In the previous example, if you had been using a true HTML editor, the editor would have inserted <BR> in place of a line break command at the end of the line. That's one important advantage of using a good HTML editor—it can do a lot of the work for you. At the end of this chapter, you'll learn about several of these editors—some of them free.

In the previous examples, you went back and forth between Notepad and Internet Explorer, using Notepad to edit the file and Internet Explorer to view it. It's easier to switch between these two programs if you use a shortcut:

1. Open Internet Explorer and click **File** on the menu bar. Then click **Work Offline**.

2. In the address field, enter the path to the file index.htm so that the browser is viewing the file.

3. Click **View** on the menu bar, then click **Source**. The browser opens Notepad in a window. From this window you can view and edit the text and the HTML commands. See Figure 3-2 for an example.

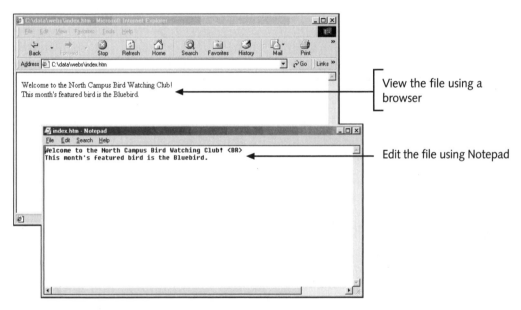

Figure 3-2   Use Notepad to view HTML source code

4. Make a change to the text and save the file. There is no need to close Notepad.

5. Click the browser window to make this the active window.

6. Click **Refresh** or click the address field to highlight the URL, then press **Enter**.

You can make changes in Notepad, save the changes, and immediately view the changes in your browser window. Be sure, however, to save the changes in Notepad before you click the Refresh button if you are using Internet Explorer or the Reload button if you are using Netscape Navigator. It also helps to tile the two windows on your desktop as in Figure 3-2 so you can easily view the contents of both windows at the same time.

Publish the Web Site

When you publish a web site, you copy all the pages and supplemental files needed to build the web site, to the server. To copy files to a server, you need:

- The domain name or IP address of the web server where your web site will reside
- A user ID and password that gives you access to the server and your folder
- The web site file or files, and any supporting graphics files
- A tool to transport files from your PC to the server

The best tool for transporting files from your PC to the server is FTP. If you are working in a computer lab, you might already have FTP installed on your computer. If you are working independently, your ISP or institution might provide you with an FTP utility program, or you might have to get one. This section describes how to download and use FTP, if you don't already have it. Remember that if you are working on a lab computer you may not have permission to download files but you can still read along with the directions to learn about FTP and the download process.

Recall from Chapter 1 that FTP was one of the first services to use the Internet. FTP (which stands for File Transfer Protocol) is an application that can move files from one computer to another. This section shows you how to download an FTP software product and use it. Chapter 4 describes FTP in more detail.

Like other Internet services, FTP uses the client/server model. In order to use FTP, you need the client software on your PC. The host that receives your file must be running the server FTP software. You can download several inexpensive FTP clients from the Internet. The following example uses WS_FTP Pro, which is available from its developer *www.ipswitch.com*.

1. To download FTP client software, use your web browser to go to the web site *www.ipswitch.com* and follow the directions on the site to download WS_FTP Pro. You can evaluate the software for 30 days without cost, so you need not purchase the software now. However, be sure to pay for it if you decide to keep it. When you download the file, it arrives on your PC in a compressed version.

2. Install the compressed FTP software by double-clicking on the filename in Windows Explorer and following the directions on the screen. The installation creates a shortcut on your desktop to FTP Pro.

To connect to the FTP server software, follow the directions below. Note that most Windows-based FTP clients operate in a similar manner. If you have a different client FTP software (CuteFTP, for example) installed on your PC, you'll find that the procedures for connecting to an FTP server and uploading a file are quite similar to those given here. Remember too, that software changes. A newer version of WS-FTP Pro may have been released by the time you read this, so your procedures may differ slightly from those explained here.

1. Start WS_FTP Pro by double-clicking the icon on the desktop.

2. Click **Connect** on the toolbar at the bottom of the window. The FTP Sites window opens.

3. Click **Quick Connect** in the FTP Sites window. The Quick Connect dialog box opens. See Figure 3-3.

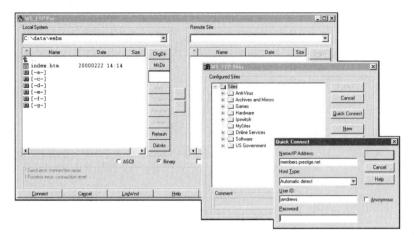

Figure 3-3   Use FTP software to transfer files over the Internet

4. Enter the IP address or domain name of the web server you've chosen for your web site and the User ID and Password that you were assigned or chose when you arranged for the web host service.

5. Don't specify the type of host to which you are connecting. Leave the Host Type drop down menu set to Automatic Detect. Click **OK** to make the connection.

Look at WS_FTP Pro and notice the following information, or look at Figure 3-4:

- Files and folders on the left side of the FTP Pro window are on your PC. This area of the window is labeled Local System. Files and folders on the right are on the remote host; this side is labeled Remote Site. On the Local System side, locate the folder on your hard drive that contains your files, and on the right, locate the folder on the remote computer where you want the files to go. To move up one level in the directory tree, click .. at the top of the list of files. To open a folder, double-click the folder name.

- To move a file, click the filename and drag and drop it on the other side. Or you can click a filename and then click one of the two arrows in between the two windows to move the file from one window to the other.

- Notice that WS_FTP Pro offers radio buttons, or option buttons, at the bottom of the screen where you can select the file format: ASCII, Binary, and Auto. When uploading your web page to the server you should leave the Binary radio button checked. Find the index.htm file you created earlier on your PC and copy it to the web site. For most web hosts, your user ID is all that is needed to get you to the correct folder on the server. So, unless you have reason to do otherwise, put the file in the current folder.

- When you have finished transferring your file, click **Close** on the toolbar at the bottom of the window. The session closes.

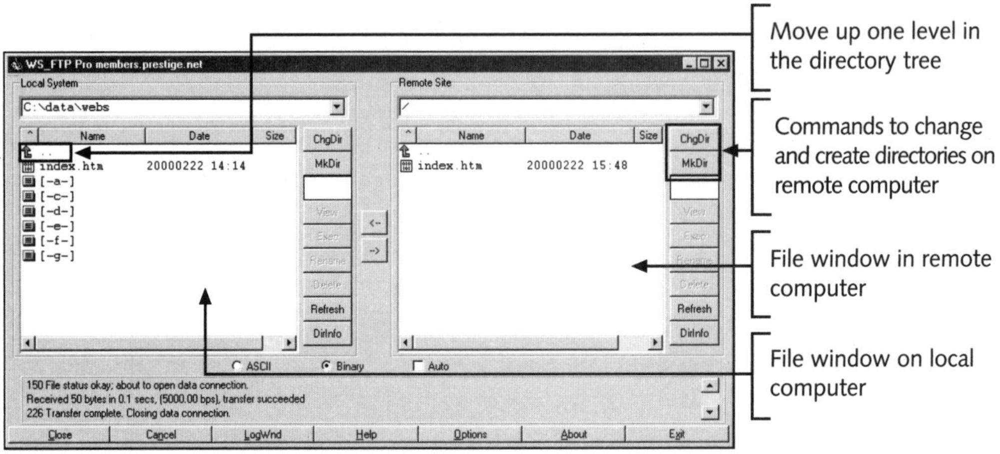

Move up one level in the directory tree

Commands to change and create directories on remote computer

File window in remote computer

File window on local computer

Figure 3-4   The Index.htm file has been copied to the web server using FTP

Once you've transferred your file you can use your web browser to point to the URL of your web site and view it as the world sees it.

The Windows operating system does not distinguish between upper and lower case when naming and recognizing files and folders, but UNIX is case sensitive. Many web servers are UNIX systems. When publishing web pages to a UNIX system, be very careful to use the correct case in all filenames and hyperlinks. To be consistent and avoid potential problems with UNIX systems, always use lower case for all file and folder names, which is the convention used in this book.

LEARNING AND USING HTML

This section introduces several basic HTML commands and presents these commands in the form of examples. You can then use the examples to later create your own web page. When you learn from an example, you get instant results and your success with them will motivate you to try more things on your own.

Appendix C provides a reference of the most common commands, their attributes, and how to use them. You can also look at the web site *www.htmlib.com*. This site provides a comprehensive reference of all HTML commands.

First, let's look at the basic structure of an HTML document and the HTML tools you'll use.

HTML Structure

An HTML document is divided into two parts, the header and the body. The header contains information about the document, such as the editor that created it, and keywords that help a search engine find your page. Information in the header is not displayed on the page by a browser. The body contains the text, links, and graphics that are displayed on the page.

An HTML document contains text and instructions. When a browser displays an HTML document, the text is *displayed* on the browser screen, but instructions are *interpreted* and *executed*. HTML instructions are written in HTML elements called **tags**. Most tags have a beginning point and an ending point in the document. Tags are identified by angle brackets and a **keyword**, which is a word that has a special pre-defined meaning to HTML.

An example of a keyword is **HEAD**. A HEAD tag in HTML defines the document's header. The beginning point of the header is marked by the keyword enclosed in angle brackets like this: <HEAD>. The ending point uses the keyword with a slash like this </HEAD>. An example of a header tag is:

```
<HEAD> header information goes here </HEAD>
```

Most tags use the beginning and ending pairs like the header tag, but some tags are only single entries like the
 (line break) tag used earlier.

All HTML documents should contain a minimum of three tags. These tags:

- Identify the document as type HTML
- Identify the header information
- Identify the body text

The basic structure of an HTML document looks like this:

```
<HTML>
    <HEAD>
        header information goes here
    </HEAD>
    <BODY>
        body of the document goes here
    </BODY>
</HTML>
```

Note that the example in the first part of this chapter omitted the <HTML> and </HTML> tags. Most browsers interpret an HTML document correctly without these identifying tags, but you should always use the tags when you publish web pages to identify the text file as one that contains HTML.

HTML tags are not case sensitive. For example, you can write <HTML> or <Html>. Also, indentations, spaces, and line breaks are ignored. For example, the following example is a valid HTML structure:

```
<HTML><HEAD> header information </HEAD> <BODY>
body of the document goes here </BODY> </HTML>
```

It's also important to know that you can't group the beginning and ending tags so that they overlap other tags. For example, the following structure would cause an error if a browser tried to display it:

```
<HTML><HEAD> <BODY> </HEAD> </BODY> </HTML>
```

You can, however, embed one pair of tags within another pair of tags. This is a valid structure:

```
<BODY> <P> </P> </BODY>
```

In this example, the beginning and ending paragraph tags are embedded within the pair of body tags.

This book always uses upper case for HTML tags to help you identify them, and uses indentations and line breaks to help make the HTML easier to read.

Table 3-1 lists several of the most basic HTML tags and what they do. The next few sections take you through creating web pages using these and other tags. Appendix C contains a much more detailed list of tags and how to use them.

Table 3-1   Some HTML tags

Tag	Description
\<HTML> \</HTML>	Marks the beginning and ending of an HTML document
\<HEAD> \</HEAD>	Marks the header information about the document. Header information is not displayed in the body of the document
\<TITLE> \</TITLE>	Marks the title for the web page that is displayed in the title bar of the browser window
\<BODY> \</BODY>	Body of the document; what's displayed by the browser
\ 	Line break
\<P> \</P>	Beginning and end of a paragraph. These tags create a double space before and after the paragraph and should be used rather than \ \ to accommodate older browsers.
\<H1> \</H1> \<H2> \</H2> .... \<H6> \</H6>	Six levels of headings. H1 uses a large, bold face font. H2 uses a slightly smaller font, and so forth. Use headings tags to format titles and subtitles.
\<B> \</B>	Marks the beginning and end of bold face
\<HR>	Inserts a horizontal line in the document
\<IMG SRC= "filename">	Inserts an inline image file in the document. Include the path to the file relative to the location of the web page.

Learning HTML Step by Step

In the several lessons that follow, you'll learn how to use HTML tags to create great looking web pages. To get the most out of these lessons, follow each step at your computer.

Lesson 1: Headings, Horizontal Lines and Graphics

Graphics, including photographs, clip art, background patterns and artistic fonts, are important elements of web page design. Each graphic is stored in its own graphic file on the web site. When a browser receives a web page from a server, the browser scans the page looking for references to other files and then requests these files from the web server.

When you design a web page, pay attention to the size of any graphics files you use. The larger the file, the longer it takes to download. Long downloads can discourage people from using your site.

Three popular types of graphics files are GIF, JPEG, and PNG:

- **GIF (graphics interchange format)** files, originally developed by CompuServe, have a .gif file extension. They hold clip art that can have a transparent background and need less than 256 colors. GIF files can support animation.

- **JPEG (Joint Photographic Experts Group)** files have a .jpg file extension and are compressed files used to hold photographs. They can have up to 1.6 million colors or be gray scale. JPEG files support animation, but don't allow for transparent backgrounds.

- **PNG (Portable Network Graphics)** files have a .png file extension, and support a transparent background, but do not support animated clip art.

This following section builds the web page shown in Figure 3-5 that uses headings, a horizontal line, and graphics. It builds on the file created at the beginning of this chapter. Follow these steps to create the page:

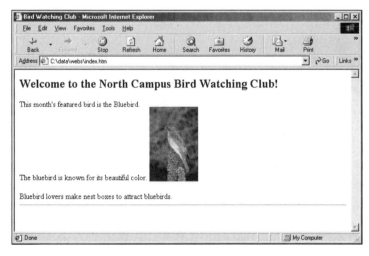

Figure 3-5   This first example of HTML uses a graphics file, a heading, and a horizontal line

1. To create this web page you need a graphic file. The example uses bbird.gif. Copy the bbird.gif file from the Chapter3 folder on your Data Disk into the same folder where the index.htm file that you created earlier in this chapter is stored. (If you have not already created the data disk, see the Introduction to this book for directions.)

2. Start Internet Explorer. Click **File** on the menu bar and then click **Work Offline**.

3. Enter the path and filename in the Address field. For example, enter c:\data\webs\index.htm.

   You are now editing the source file that is located on your PC, not the file that has been uploaded to the web server. Once a file is uploaded to a web server, you can no longer edit it. Instead edit your local copy of the file, and then when you are finished, upload the new copy to the web server, overwriting the file that is already there.

4. Click **View** on the menu bar, then click **Source**. Internet Explorer and Notepad display as in Figure 3-6.

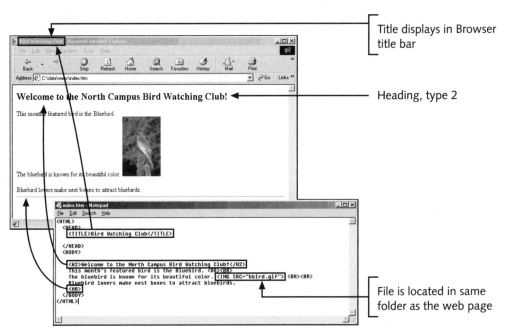

Figure 3-6   The HTML that produced this web page uses a GIF file for the graphics image

5. Enter the following HTML text. Note that this text is also showing in Figure 3-6. Don't enter the line numbers, however. They are only here to help in the explanation that follows this example. Also, even though some of the following lines of

code wrap to the next line, you shouldn't make them wrap when you type in the code yourself. For example, line 6 should be typed all on one line in your file.

```
1.<HTML>
2.   <HEAD>
3.     <TITLE>Bird Watching Club</TITLE>
4.   </HEAD>
5.<BODY>
6.     <H2>Welcome to the North Campus Bird Watching Club!
</H2>
7.   This month's featured bird is the Bluebird. <BR><BR>
8.   The bluebird is known for its beautiful color. <IMG
SRC="BBIRD.GIF">
9.   <BR><BR>
10.  Bluebird lovers make nest boxes to attract
bluebirds.<BR>
11.            <HR>
12.        </BODY>
13.    <HTML>
```

3

6. Click **File** on the Notepad menu bar, then click **Save** to save the file index.htm. Click **Refresh** on the browser toolbar to display the changes.

Here's an explanation of the tags that you used:

- Line 1 specifies that this document is in HTML format.

- Lines 2 through 4 add the header information at the top of the document.

- Line 5 begins the body of the document.

- Line 6 uses the <H2> </H2> tags to format the first line on the web page as a heading, type 2.

- The two line break tags at the end of Line 7 create a double space on the web page. Because some older browsers ignore subsequent <BR> tags, the <P> and </P> tags are often used. Any text within the tags is considered a paragraph unit. Browsers insert a line or two before the paragraph.

- Line 8 contains the reference to the GIF file. The image tag IMG does not contain a path to the file bbird.gif, which means that the file is located in the same folder as the web page file, index.htm.

- Line 11 contains the tag for a horizontal line.

- Line 12 ends the body portion of the document.

- Line 13 ends the HTML portion of the document.

This example uses the <H2></H2> heading tags for the page heading. To see the different size fonts used by the different headings, try substituting <H1></H1> through <H6></H6>.

Lesson 2: Using Hyperlinks to Manage Large Documents

One of the best features of HTML is its ability to let you move around a document via hyperlinks. Instead of having to read a web page linearly (as you would a paper document), you can follow the hyperlinks to skip around on a web page, or to connect to a different web page altogether. Hyperlinks provide a convenient way to navigate around a longer web page.

The web page showing in Figure 3-7 is a long document with a list at the top, under the heading "Bluebird Foundation". Sometimes this kind of list on a web page is referred to as a table of contents. All the items in this list are **hyperlinks**. (Sometimes these hyperlinks are referred to as **links** or **hypertext references**). If you click on any of the links in the table of contents, the browser immediately takes you to that section in the document. These hyperlinks are created with HTML **anchor tags**, which are tags that mark text or a graphic as a link to another point in the same document or to a different document.

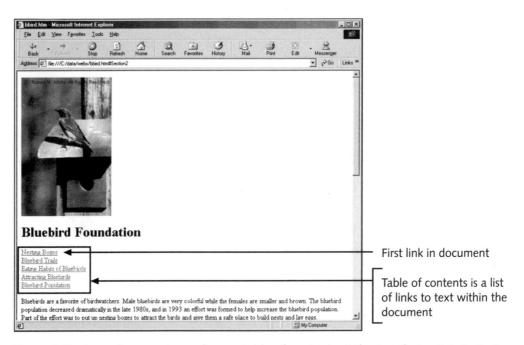

First link in document

Table of contents is a list of links to text within the document

Figure 3-7   Long documents can have a table of contents at the top that points to text within the document

When you want to create a hyperlink from one point in an HTML file to another point in the same HTML file, you need two anchor tags: one that marks the link itself (think of this as the starting point), and one that marks the place to which the link points. This end point is called the **link target**, or the **jump link** (think of this as the destination). For example, in Figure 3-7, the first link "Nesting Boxes" is the first item in the table of contents, and it points to the position later in the document labeled "Nesting Boxes", which is the link target.

As part of creating a hyperlink you must assign the link target with a name. You then use that name when you create the link itself. Think of it this way: the *link* anchor tag says, "take me to the point on this page called xxxx." The *link target* anchor tag says "here is the point on the page that is called xxxx." The HTML for the *link* is shown in Figure 3-8 and the HTML for the *link target* is shown in Figure 3-9.

Here's a brief description of the link and link target tags:

- **\<A HREF="#section-name">link-text\</A>** creates the link; look at Figure 3-8. This tag marks the text or graphic as a link to another section within the same document. In this discussion, **link-text** stands for the text that is the link, in this case the table of contents item, "Nesting Boxes". Section name here stands for the name of the link target. In the example in Figure 3-8, that section is called section1, but you could assign it any name you want. The # symbol indicates that the word following is a section name. The quotation marks are optional, and remind you that this is a term you have created, not an HTML keyword. Remember that you can see this tag in Figure 3-8.

- **\<A NAME="section-name">\</A>** marks a position in a document as the link target, or position that the link points to, and assigns this section a name: section-name. In the example in Figure 3-9, the link target's name is section1. Remember that the quotation marks are optional.

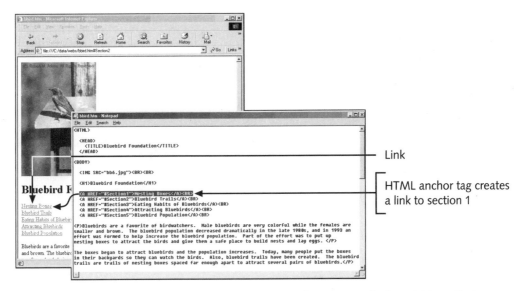

Figure 3-8   A table of contents is created using anchor tags with the HREF attribute

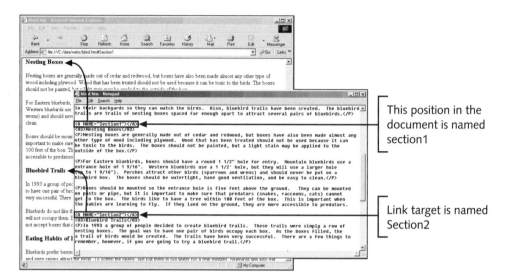

Figure 3-9   The link targets in a long document are created using anchor tags with the NAME attribute

Follow these directions to create this web page:

1. The web page contains the photo of a bird located in a JPEG file called bb6.jpg. To save time typing, most of the text is copied from a text file named bbird.txt. Copy both files (bb6.jpg and bbird.txt) from the Chapter3 folder on your Data Disk into your web page folder.

2. Because this example creates a new HTML file, open Notepad to create the new file.

3. Type the text listed below. Note that this text is also showing at the top of the Notepad screen in Figure 3-8. Remember, don't type the line numbers.

```
1.    <HTML>
2.    <HEAD>
3.    <TITLE>Bluebird Foundation</TITLE>
4.    </HEAD>
5.
6.    <BODY>
7.
8.    <IMG SRC="bb6.jpg"><BR> <BR>
9.
10.   <H1>Bluebird Foundation</H1>
11.
12.   <A HREF="#Section1">Nesting Boxes</A><BR>
13.   <A HREF="#Section2">Bluebird Trails</A><BR>
14.   <A HREF="#Section3">Eating Habits of Bluebirds</A><BR>
15.   <A HREF="#Section4">Attracting Bluebirds</A><BR>
16.   <A HREF="#Section5">Bluebird Populations</A><BR>
```

Here's an explanation of the tags you used:

- Line 8 inserts the file, bb6.jpg, as the first item on the page.
- Line 10 is the title of the article displayed as a heading, type 1, and positioned under the photo.
- Lines 12-16 are the table of contents listed under the title. Each table-of-contents entry is a link to some position within the text. These link targets are named **Section1**, **Section2**, and so forth. Between the pair of anchor tags that make up the link is the text that describes the link. For example, in Line 12, the link text is **Nesting Boxes.** As you can see in Figure 3-7, when the browser displays a link, the link text is underlined and in a different color.

4. Save the file to your web page folder, giving it the name bbird.htm. Don't leave Notepad.

5. Insert the text to finish out the page like this: Move your cursor to the bottom of the Notepad document in preparation to paste some text into the document at that position.

6. Using Windows Explorer, locate the file bbird.txt and double-click on the file-name. This action should open your computer's default text editor, probably Notepad, with the bbird.txt file displayed.

7. Click **Edit** on the menu bar, then click **Select All** to highlight all the text.

8. Click **Edit**, then click **Copy** to copy the selected text to the Clipboard.

9. Click **File** on the menu bar, then click **Exit** to close the copy of Notepad with the bbird.txt file.

10. Return to the Notepad window that is showing the file bbird.htm. Move your cursor to the end of the document. Click **Edit** on the menu bar, then click **Paste** to paste the text from the clipboard into the document.

11. Format the new text for HTML: Add **<P>** and **</P>** tags at the beginning and end of each paragraph to create space between the paragraphs.

12. Format each subheading using type three headings: Insert **<H3>** and **</H3>** tags before and after each heading.

13. At the end of the document, add the **</BODY>** and **</HTML>** tags. Save the file in Notepad.

14. Create the link targets: Position your cursor on the line before the text **Nesting Boxes** (see Figure 3-9) and add the anchor tag: **<A NAME="Section1"></A>**.

15. For each of the other five sections, create anchor tags for **Section2**, **Section3**, and so forth. (You can see the **Section2** anchor in Figure 3-9.)

16. Save the file and click **Refresh** on the browser to display the changes. Or, if you browser isn't already running, load it and enter the folder and filename of this file.

Lesson 3: Using Hyperlinks to Point to Other HTML Files

The previous section demonstrated how hyperlinks can point to different locations within the same HTML file. Hyperlinks can also point to another HTML file, either on the same web site or a different site. In this lesson, you will learn how to use hyperlinks to point to different files on the same web site.

A hyperlink that points to a different file needs only one anchor tag. That tag contains the name of the HTML file that is the destination, or jump link.

The following example uses the index.htm web page showing in Figure 3-5. The procedure makes the word "bluebirds" on the page serve as a hyperlink to the bbird.htm page that you created in Lesson 2. Follow these directions:

1. Open Internet Explorer and set it to work offline.

2. Enter the path and filename of the index.htm file, for example c:\data\webs\index.htm in the browser address field.

3. Click **View** on the menu bar, then click **Source** to view the HTML code in a Notepad window.

4. In place of the word **bluebirds**, insert this: **<A HREF="bbird.htm"> bluebirds</A>**. See Figure 3-10.

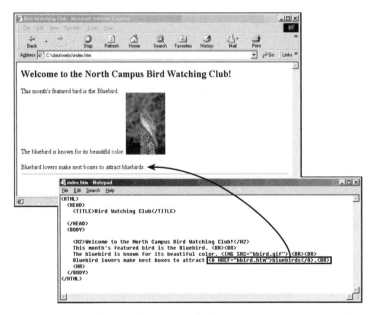

Figure 3-10 The anchor tag with the HREF attribute is used to point the browser to another web page on the same site, creating a hyperlink

5. Save the file and click **Refresh** on the Internet Explorer toolbar to display the changes.

6. Test the hyperlink by clicking on the word **bluebirds** in the browser. The Bluebirds web page displays.

Troubleshooting HTML Errors

If you get errors during the previous exercises, use Table 3-2 as your troubleshooting checklist.

Table 3-2   Errors while developing HTML

Error	What to Check
The link displays as underlined text, but when you click on it, nothing happens	Most likely cause is that the document is linked back to itself (a common error when using one page as a template for other pages). Check the file name in the hyperlink.
The link displays as underlined text, but when you click on it, a message displays telling you that the browser is unable to locate the page or that the page cannot be displayed. This error message is Error Code 404 (file not found).	The browser searched for the link target, but couldn't find it. Check the spelling of the link target name at the link, and at the link target. For links to other files, check the URL including the location of the file and the spelling of the filename. Don't use spaces in the filenames when saving web page document files; this can sometimes confuse older browsers.
HTML code displays in the browser windows	Most likely there is an error in the HTML code so that it doesn't follow HTML syntax (code rules). The browser, therefore, does not recognize the code as HTML, but thinks it's just plain text. Check the syntax carefully against the examples in the book. Look especially for errors in closing quotation marks and closing brackets.
The link works, but all of the text following the link is underlined and has become part of the link	Make sure the closing anchor tag </A> is correctly placed at the end of the appropriate text.
A heading tag or paragraph tag does not work	Check that the tag has both the beginning and ending tags in correct position and correct syntax. Look for tags above this tag that are in error and which therefore have thrown the browser off track before it reaches this tag. Check especially for closing quotation marks.

Lesson 4: Using Hyperlinks to Point to Other Web Sites

In this next lesson, you'll make the bird graphic serve as a hyperlink to the North American Bluebird Society home page at *www.nabluebirdsociety.org*. Creating a hyperlink to another web site is a lot like creating a link to another HTML file on the same web site. Instead of entering the filename in the anchor tag, you simply enter the URL of the site in the anchor tag. This lesson also demonstrates that a graphic can be a hyperlink, just as text can.

Follow these directions:

1. Open your browser and point it to the index.htm file in your web page folder. Click **View** on the menu bar, then click **Source** to view the HTML file in Notepad. See Figure 3-11.

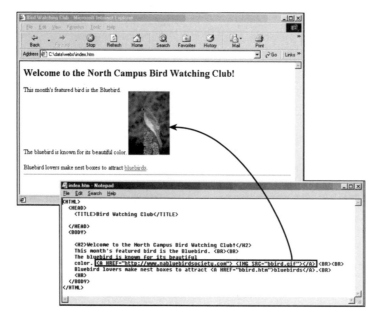

Figure 3-11   The bluebird picture is a hyperlink to the North American Bluebird Society web site

2. Surround the IMG tag for the bluebird graphic with an anchor tag like this:

```
<A HREF="http://www.nabluebirdsociety.org"><IMG SRC="bbird.
gif"></A>
```

3. Save the file in Notepad and click **Refresh** on the browser toolbar to display the changes.

4. Test the hyperlink by clicking on the picture of the bird. The North American Bluebird Society home page displays. Note that if you were working offline, you might see a message from Internet Explorer that tells you the web page is unavailable offline. Click **Connect** in the message window to connect to the web site.

Notice that the picture of the bird now has a box around it, which is the browser's way of saying that this graphic is also a hyperlink. You can turn the border off if you want. To turn

```
 5.   <BODY>

 6.      <TABLE BORDER="1">
 7.         <CAPTION>Bluebird Nest Box Dimensions</CAPTION>
 8.         <TR>
 9.          <TH>Bird</TH>
10.          <TH>Box Floor</TH>
11.          <TH>Box Height</TH>
12.          <TH>Entry Hole</TH>
13.         </TR>

14.         <TR>
15.          <TD>Eastern Bluebird</TD>
16.          <TD>5 x 5</TD>
17.          <TD>9 1/2</TD>
18.          <TD>1 1/2</TD>
19.         </TR>

20.         <TR>
21.          <TD>Western Bluebird</TD>
22.          <TD>5 x 5</TD>
23.          <TD>9 1/2</TD>
24.          <TD>1 9/16</TD>
25.         </TR>

26.         <TR>
27.          <TD>Mountain Bluebird</TD>
28.          <TD>5 x 5 1/4</TD>
29.          <TD>8 1/2</TD>
30.          <TD>1 9/16</TD>
31.         </TR>
32.     </TABLE>

33.   </BODY>
34. </HTML>
```

The table begins at Line 6 and ends at Line 32. The first row is used for headings and begins with line 8 and ends with line 13. The three rows that follow all have four cells each.

2. Save the file in your web site folder. Name the file boxes.htm.

3. Use your web browser to view boxes.htm.

4. Try different values for the BORDER attribute in the <TABLE> tag in Line 6. BORDER="0" is no border at all. Try 0, 3, 5, and 10.

In the above example, a table organizes related information for easy reading. You can also use tables to organize text and graphics on a web page. The table is used as the layout tool with each cell in the table defining one area of the page. A developer might design the page with the table borders showing while developing the page layout, and then hide the table borders after the layout is complete.

Lesson 7: HTML Forms for Data Input

A web page can collect data from the people who view it. Sometimes you want your web page to collect data and transfer it back to the web server, or send it to you or someone else through e-mail. In this section, you will learn how you can create a **form** on a web page, which is an HTML element that allows a web page to collect data and send it back to the web server or an e-mail recipient.

A form can use standard Windows elements like text boxes, checkboxes, radio buttons, drop down lists, and other elements to collect data. Once you enter data into a form, you click a submit button to send the data to a web server or an e-mail address. This section describes how to send the data to an e-mail address. If you want to send the data back to the web server, the web server must have access to a program that can receive and process the data. This powerful feature of the Web is covered in Chapter 6.

Figure 3-13 shows the boxes.htm web page with a form added. Here is a very simple example of the HTML needed to create a form.

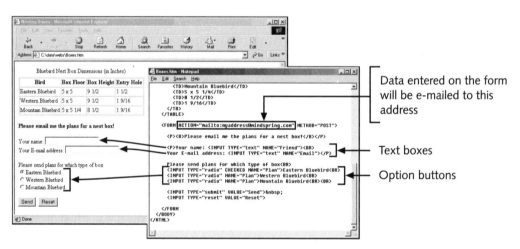

Figure 3-13   The HTML form allows a user to enter data that is sent by e-mail to the site owner

In its simplest form, the HTML form element has these parts:

```
1. <FORM ACTION="mailto:myaddress@mindspring.com"
METHOD="POST">
2.Enter your name: <INPUT TYPE="text" NAME="Friend">
3.<INPUT TYPE="SUBMIT" VALUE="Send">
4.</FORM>
```

Here is a description of the parts of this form:

- The form begins at Line 1 with the <FORM> tag. Form tags must include the ACTION and METHOD attributes. In this example, ACTION tells the browser where to mail the data once it is submitted, and METHOD tells the browser how to mail it.

- Line 2 includes an INPUT tag that is type text. INPUT tags specify the type of element that will appear on the form. A text INPUT tag allows a user to enter data into a text box. Other common INPUT types are CHECKBOX, RADIO, and PASSWORD.

- Also notice the NAME attribute in line 2. The NAME attribute defines the text box to the browser. In other words, the text box is given a name, and in the example above, that name is "Friend." Later, when someone enters data into this text box, the browser will identify the data as having been entered into the text box named "Friend." If someone entered the name "Jennifer" into the text box, for example, the entry in the e-mail message would look like this: Friend=Jennifer.

- Line 3 is a submit button. The VALUE attribute is the text that displays on the button. When someone clicks the submit button labeled Send, the browser e-mails the text associated with Friend to myaddress@mindspring.com.

- Line 4 ends the form.

Follow these directions to create the form showing in Figure 3-13:

1. Open the boxes.htm web page in your web site folder that you created in lesson 6. After the last entry for the table, type in the form tags as shown in Figure 3-13 and listed below. Change the e-mail address in the first line to your own address. Remember, don't type the line numbers, and you don't need to go to a second line as in line 1.

```
1. <FORM ACTION="mailto:myaddress@mindspring.com"
METHOD="POST">

2. <P><B>Please email me the plans for a nest box!</B></P>

3. <P>Your name: <INPUT TYPE="text" NAME="Friend"><BR>
4. Your e-mail address: <INPUT TYPE="text" NAME="Email">
</P>

5. Please send plans for which type of box<BR>
6. <INPUT TYPE="radio" CHECKED NAME="Plan">Eastern Bluebird
<BR>
7. <INPUT TYPE="radio" NAME="Plan">Western Bluebird<BR>
8. <INPUT TYPE="radio" NAME="Plan">Mountain Bluebird<BR>
<BR>

9. <INPUT TYPE="submit" VALUE="Send"> 
```

```
10.<INPUT TYPE="reset" VALUE="Reset">
```

```
11. </FORM>
```

Here's a description of the HTML commands:

- The form begins at Line 1 and ends at Line 11.
- Line 2 uses the bold face tags <B></B>.
- Lines 3 and 4 collect values for Friend and Email into input text boxes.
- Lines 6 through 8 display three option buttons on the form labeled "Eastern Bluebird", "Western Bluebird", and "Mountain Bluebird". The Eastern Bluebird option button is checked, or selected.
- Line 9 uses the non-breaking space code . The purpose of this code is to put a little space between the Send button and the Reset button. You can't get that space by simply entering spaces, because the browser will not display them. Be sure to include the semicolon because some older browsers display the characters " " if the semicolon is omitted.
- Line 10 contains a Reset button. The purpose of a Reset button is to clear all entries on a form so that someone can start over.

2. Save the changes and display the changes in the browser.

3. Enter some data and click **Send**. Check your e-mail inbox for the generated message.

Here is a sample message that you would receive via e-mail:

```
Friend=John+Williamson&Email=JWilliams@peachnet.edu&Plan=Eastern+
Bluebird
```

The first name and value is Friend=John+Williamson. The browser substitutes a + symbol for a space, and each pair of names and values are separated using an &.

Testing Your Site

You should always test your web site before you publish it. You should test the way it looks, and you should also test your hyperlinks. Be sure to test every hyperlink on every page to make certain that each link jumps to the correct location. You should continue to verify your hyperlinks periodically after the site is published. Sometimes web sites change locations, and when they do, your hyperlinks might not point to valid URLs.

In addition to testing hyperlinks, you need to check the appearance of your web page using different web browsers and different versions of a browser. Web browsers interpret HTML in ways that are subtly unique. In addition, individual settings like screen resolution can dramatically affect the way a web page looks. Because you have no idea what type of browser people are using to access your site, it's impossible to test your site using every combination of browsers, screen size, screen resolution, operating system, and browser settings. However, you should make a reasonable effort to test your site with the most common browsers, screen settings, and operating systems.

Before you publish a site, test the site using both Internet Explorer and Netscape Navigator, the two most popular browsers. Test each browser with your screen resolution set to different settings. To change your screen resolution using Windows 9x, follow these steps:

1. Right-click somewhere on your Windows 9x desktop. A drop-down menu opens.

2. Select **Properties**. The Display Properties window opens. See Figure 3-14.

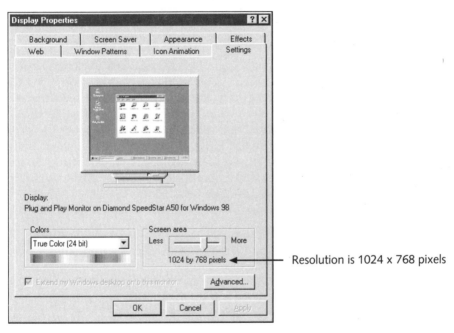

Resolution is 1024 x 768 pixels

Figure 3-14   Test your web pages using different screen resolutions

3. Click the **Settings** tab, if it isn't already showing.

4. Common screen resolutions are 800 by 600 pixels and 1024 by 768 pixels. To change the resolution, move the sliding bar to a new position and click **Apply**. You see a message telling you that Windows is going to resize your desktop. Click **OK**. Your screen temporarily goes blank and then the new resolution takes effect.

5. Windows 9x displays a dialog box giving you the opportunity to return to the original setting. Click **Yes** to keep the new setting.

6. Test your site using both browsers with the new screen resolution.

TAKING HTML FURTHER

Congratulations! You now have a good working knowledge of HTML and several of its more important features. With the tools introduced in this chapter, you can build some very nice multiple-page web sites, complete with graphics, hyperlinks, tables and input forms. You're well on your way to being a successful web page developer.

But you can learn a lot more! You can learn more HTML commands, you can learn about software programs that enhance HTML and you can learn to use HTML editors that make your work easier. This section introduces some of this information.

- *More HTML.* Most of the tags introduced earlier have associated attributes to enhance them, and there are many other tags that weren't covered. In this section, you'll find some resources to help you build your HTML skills.

- *Cascading Style Sheets.* Besides more HTML tags and their attributes, web pages can be enhanced and controlled using an HTML specification called **Cascading Style Sheets** (**CSS**), developed by the World Wide Web Consortium (W3C), that allows a style sheet to be attached to HTML documents. A **style sheet** is a text file with a CSS file extension that contains rules used to control how the browser displays the web page that refers to the style sheet. The style sheet can include information such as what font to use when displaying text marked with a Heading tag, <H1>, what background color to use, or what margins to use for the <P> paragraph tags. A web page refers to the style sheet using the <LINK REL> tag within the <HEAD> and </HEAD> tags of the document.

- *Dynamic HTML and Programs.* HTML and most browsers can run small program segments as part of displaying a web page. These program segments make the HTML dynamic and responsive to the user, the user's browser, and the values the user enters in a form. Some programming languages that you can include in a web page are JavaScript, Jscript, and VBScript (for Internet Explorer only). The program segments are called **scripts** and are executed by the browser. Therefore, a script must be written in a language that the browser can understand.

  Web pages can also run small programs called applets that can be downloaded from a web site. Java is a programming language that is used to write Java applets. Java applets can run on a variety of platforms without having to be altered.

  You can also create program segments that are executed by the web server and which customize the web page before it is sent to the browser, based on information the browser sends to it. Examples of languages used for this purpose are Perl, Java, Visual Basic and C++. You'll see some simple examples of programs executed on the server and by the browser in Chapter 6.

- *HTML Editors.* You can build a web site using just a simple text editor like Notepad, but many tools are available that can help you build a site more quickly. HTML editors are tools that simplify the process by generating HTML code thus saving you time and effort. HTML editors fall into two basic categories: code-based HTML editors and WYSIWYG (What You See Is What You Get) editors. Code-based editors let you edit the HTML code and arrange the tags as you please. WYSIWYG editors are easier to use, because you can work from a visual or graphical view of the web page. The editor generates HTML code behind the scenes as you build the screen.

3

Resources to Help Develop Web-Building Skills

You can use books, web sites and software to help develop your web sites. Check out these sites which have much to offer to both the novice and expert and also offer some free graphics and photos:

- CNET Web Building at *www.builder.com* and *www.cnet.com*

- The Web Developer's Virtual Library at *www.wdvl.com*

- The HTML Reference Library at *www.htmlib.com*

- The Web Diner at *www.webdiner.com*

- Professional Web Design's Table Tutor at *junior.apk.net*

- Strasberg Designs at *www.strasberg.net*

Help files can be another great source of information. HTML editors generally come with a help utility designed to make writing HTML easier. Books are another great source. Try searching the Amazon.com web site on HTML. Check out the rating and reviews of a book before purchasing it.

Using a Simple HTML Code-Based Editor

There are many good code-based HTML editors. This section examines one inexpensive and widely available editor, called CuteHTML, which can be downloaded from the web site *www.globalscape.com* or *www.cutehtml.com*. You can download the product for a free evaluation period. If you decide to buy it, the price is $19.95. Follow these directions to download and use the software:

1. Go to the web site *www.globalscape.com* and follow the directions on the site to download CuteHTML.

2. Double-click on the downloaded file to decompress it and install the software. The installation process creates a shortcut to the software on your desktop.

3. Open the software and then click **File** on the menu bar.

4. Open the folder that contains the web pages created earlier in the chapter. The list of HTML and text files in the folder displays on the left side of the window, and also displays in tabs at the bottom on the window, making for easy access to the files.

5. Double-click on the **bbird.htm** web page on the left side of the screen. The HTML file opens in the editing window. See Figure 3-15. Note how color is used to help you distinguish between HTML code, text, and hyperlinks.

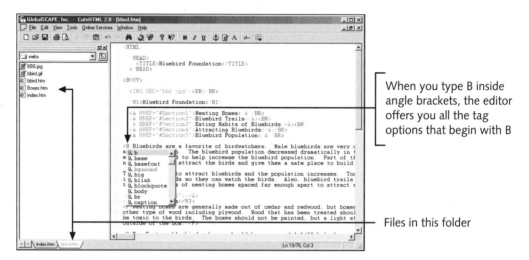

Figure 3-15 The CuteHTML editor gives you choices for tags and their attributes and also color-codes tags and links

6. Try creating a tag. For example, if you want to insert a boldface tag in front of a word, type **<B>**. The editor senses that you are beginning a new tag that starts with a B and automatically displays a list of all tags that start with B. Click the one you want. Then, if that tag has attributes associated with it, the list of attributes for that tag displays for you to make a selection.

7. Just as you did with Notepad, you can save the file and then load the web page in your browser or click **Refresh** if it is already loaded.

Introducing Microsoft FrontPage

You have just seen how a code-based HTML editor can help you write HTML code. This section shows how a GUI HTML editor makes it possible for you to build an entire web site without ever looking at HTML. This example uses one of the most popular GUI HTML editors, Microsoft FrontPage. It gives a quick demonstration of what it's like to build a web site using this type of software.

If you have access to Microsoft FrontPage, you should follow the directions below to create the index.htm page created using Notepad earlier in the chapter.

When you start FrontPage, notice that a blank web page opens, as seen in Figure 3-16. As you work on the page, you can click the **HTML** tab at the bottom of the window to view the code the editor is building behind the scenes for you. If you have Internet Explorer installed, you can click the **Preview** tab to preview the page. On the left side of the window are several different ways to view the web site as you build it.

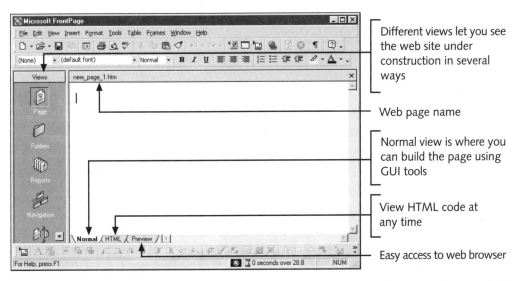

Different views let you see the web site under construction in several ways

Web page name

Normal view is where you can build the page using GUI tools

View HTML code at any time

Easy access to web browser

Figure 3-16   Microsoft FrontPage automatically opens an empty web page when you first execute the software

1. To create a new web page, click **File** on the menu bar, then point to **New** then click **Web**. The New dialog box opens. See Figure 3-17.

Figure 3-17   Specify the location of the web page files

2. Click **One Page Web,** then enter the path on your hard drive where you will store the web pages and click **OK**. FrontPage automatically creates subfolders for the web page and a home page named index.htm. See Figure 3-18.

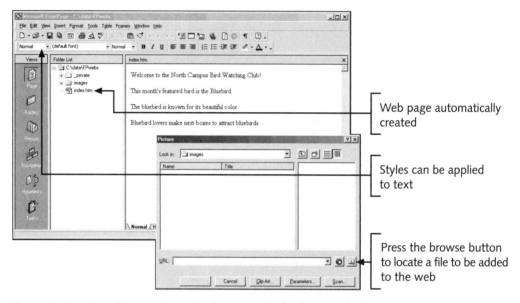

Web page automatically created

Styles can be applied to text

Press the browse button to locate a file to be added to the web

Figure 3-18   FrontPage automatically creates index.htm as the home page for a new web site and subfolders for other files

3. Type the text on the web page as it appears in Figure 3-18.

4. When you are ready to add the bluebird graphic file, position your cursor where you want the graphic to be inserted. Click **Insert** on the menu bar, then point to **Picture** and click **From File**. The Picture dialog box opens. See Figure 3-18. Listed in the box are the images in the images folder that have been inserted into pages that belong to this web site. (Other files in this folder do not display.) Click the **browse** button on the right side of the dialog box to display the Select File dialog box. Click the **bbird.gif** file and click **OK.**

5. To apply a heading tag to the first line of the web page, click anywhere on the line. Click the drop down menu of styles on the far left side of the toolbar, then click on a heading tag.

6. You're now ready to save the page. When you save a file in FrontPage, you need to specify where to save any graphics files embedded in the page. Put the graphics file in the Images folder under the main web page folder. Click **File** on the menu bar, then click **Save** to save the Index.htm file. The Save Embedded File dialog box opens; see Figure 3-19. Click **Change Folder**. The Change Folder dialog box opens. Double-click on the **Images folder** to make it the current folder. Click **OK** to select the folder, and click **OK** again to save the file to the selected folder. The bbird.gif file is copied to the Images folder and the index.htm file is saved.

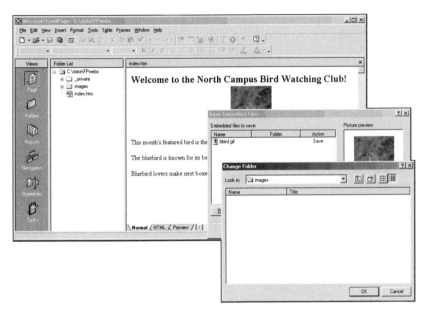

Figure 3-19 Save embedded files in subfolder

7. Next, create a hyperlink to the North American Bluebird Society web site. Right-click on the picture of the bird. A drop-down menu opens. Click **Hyperlink**. See Figure 3-20. The Create Hyperlink dialog box displays; see Figure 3-21.

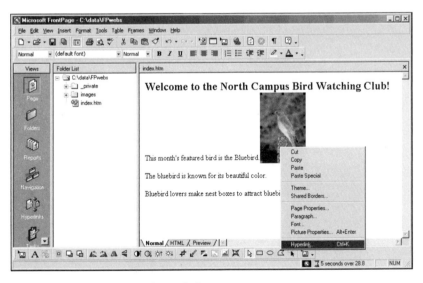

Figure 3-20 Creating a hyperlink

Be sure to include http: in the link

Figure 3-21   Enter the URL of the hyperlink

8. Enter the URL to the North American Bluebird Society web site, including the protocol: **http://www.nabluebirdsociety.org** and click **OK**.

9. Test the hyperlink by selecting the Preview view and then double-clicking on the graphic. Or you can **CTRL click** on the graphic in the Normal view.

10. Save the index.htm page. Then view the HTML created by FrontPage. Click the **HTML** tab at the bottom of the window; see Figure 3-22.

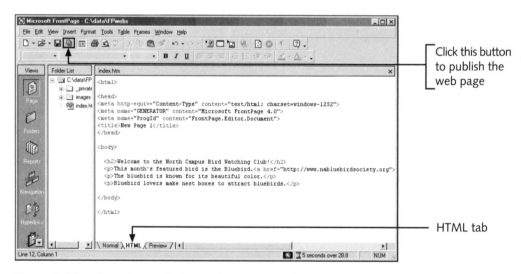

Click this button to publish the web page

HTML tab

Figure 3-22   The HTML tab shows the HTML code

11. Publish the web site using FrontPage. To publish a web site using FrontPage, first save all pages in the site. (In our case, that is just the one page, index.html.) Save the page and then click **Publish** on the toolbar. See Figure 3-22. The Publish Web dialog box opens; see Figure 3-23. Enter the URL for your web site and click **Publish**. Enter the account name and password to the site, if necessary. FrontPage copies all pages to the site, creating subfolders as necessary.

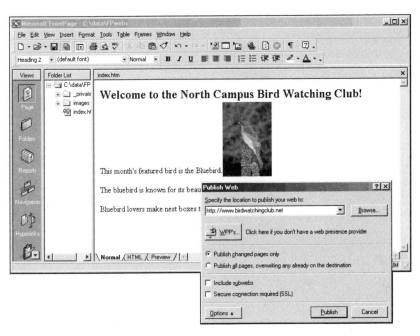

Figure 3-23   Publishing a web site

Survey of HTML Authoring Tools

This section describes several of the more popular HTML editors and gives a little information about each. See their web sites for more information.

Microsoft FrontPage

Microsoft FrontPage was the first to offer the capability to design, create, publish and manage complex web sites to anyone with or without a programming background or an understanding of HTML. FrontPage can create and manage sophisticated web sites, supports frames, and can automatically build a site map with links to each page on the Web from the home page. See *www.microsoft.com* for more information.

Macromedia Dreamweaver

Dreamweaver, by Macromedia, is a favorite WYSIWYG (What-You-See-Is-What-You-Get) HTML editor for professionals. It can be customized using JavaScript, HTML and XHTML. You can edit tags manually in the design view without using the HTML edit window or an external HTML editor. Text data such as tab-delimited files (files that contain data in columns separated by tabs) can be imported directly into an HTML table. The Site Window feature automatically creates a web site map and gives you control over how the map is displayed. You can save the map as a BMP or PNG file and use it on the web site. See *www.macromedia.com* for more information.

Allaire HomeSite

HomeSite by Allaire is an HTML editor that began as a shareware program and has evolved to become one of the most popular code-based HTML editors on the market. Beginners find it easy to master and it's also popular with more advanced users. It has several features: Design View lets you edit in WYSIWYG format. CodeSweeper lets you set rules and filters to cut down on the amount of unwanted additional code generated by some WYSIWYG editors. Tag Inspector makes it easy to modify tags in a document. Support for ASP, DHTML, JavaScript, Perl, SQL and Allaire's Cold Fusion is provided in HomeSite. (Cold Fusion is Allaire's web server.) Many major Web-related software products bundle HomeSite within their software, but it can be purchased as a stand-alone product. For more information see the web site *www.allaire.com*.

NetObjects Fusion

NetObjects Fusion is a good tool for those with little HTML experience, but who want to produce a web site quickly without having to deal with HTML code. However, NetObjects Fusion is not as popular with experienced HTML users. The Site View feature is especially useful in giving an overview of a web site. It's also easy to add a new page to a site where the child page can easily take on the properties of the parent page. (When one page, such as the home page, has a hyperlink to another page, the first page is sometimes called the parent page and the referenced page is called the child page.) One disadvantage of NetObjects Fusion is that it offers no capability to directly edit HTML. See *www.netobjects.com* for more information.

HotMetal Pro

HotMetal Pro by SoftQuad Software, Inc. creates HTML documents that can be viewed in several ways: WYSIWYG, structured view, and a tag view. HotMetal Pro checks the syntax of HTML tags as you create them, offering all possible attributes for the tag. Warning messages are generated when the software senses you're about to put text where it doesn't belong. The software supports style sheets which let you standardize how your text will look on each web page in order to produce a similar look and feel from one page to the next. For more information about HotMetal Pro, see the web site *www.hotmetalpro.com*.

Adobe GoLive

GoLive by Adobe is available for both the Macintosh and Windows systems. The interface is easy to use in its presentation of basic HTML functions, but not as simple when creating style sheets. You can preview your work in any browser. You can use the Inspector window to edit attributes and properties. Icons for all common scripts and objects are on the Palette toolbar. It is easy to alter the shape and course of animation paths and to add frames with the Timeline Editor. For more information, see *www.adobe.com*.

CuteHTML

You saw CuteHTML earlier in the chapter. It's an easy-to-use code-based HTML editor that offers color-coded tags and help when entering tags. When you begin to type a tag, a drop down list of tags opens. When you select a tag, a drop down list of attributes for that tag opens. CuteHTML is inexpensive and can be downloaded from *www.globalscape.com*.

1st Page 2000

1st Page 2000 by Evrsoft, Inc. is a free HTML editor that offers four modes of use: Easy, Normal, Expert, and Hardcore. Beginners are not exposed to complex drop-down menus because the toolbars, buttons, and the interface change depending on which mode you choose. In Normal mode you can use any combination of the toolbars from the Easy, Hardcore, and Expert Mode. The 1st Page 2000 GUI interface is similar to HomeSite but does not have the customization capabilities of HomeSite. The large number of Plug and Play scripts in 1st Page 2000 means you can set up drop-down menus, disappearing text, and create a hit counter without having to know DHTML, JavaScript, or VBScript. You can use a split-screen feature to edit code in one screen and monitor your changes in another. You can set up a Favorites list that contains frequently accessed folders so you can switch among projects and folders freely. You can download a free copy of the software from *www.evrsoft.com*.

THE FUTURE OF HTML

The HTML language has evolved over time and is still changing. The language was originally developed by Tim Berners-Lee, a researcher at the Conseil Europeen pour Recherche Nucleaire (CERN) laboratory in 1989. The current version is HTML 4, which has had varying degrees of input from several standards organizations including the World Wide Web Consortium (W3), the Internet Engineering Task Force (IETF) and the European Computer Manufacturers Association (ECMA). HTML is an application of the **Standard Generalized Markup Language** (**SGML**), which is a standard for several markup languages. (A markup language has special codes that are inserted in a text file to instruct software how to display or print the text. In other words, these codes "mark up" the text.)

A future version of HTML has been named **XHTML** and is an application of an entirely new markup language standard called **XML** (**Extensible Markup Language**) that supports the standards of SGML, while adding flexibility and power. The World Wide Web Consortium is overseeing the development of the specifications that will eventually become XHTML, or more commonly known as XML. Internet Explorer 5 supports XML. See the web site, *www.w3.org* for more information.

REAL PEOPLE, REAL PROBLEMS, REAL SOLUTIONS
IF THE BROWSER FITS

One of the most challenging tasks of a web designer is making sure that a design looks good to every visitor. There is no way to know what type of browser or screen resolution a visitor to any site will be using. Michael McDonough, a Senior Web Designer, knows this first hand.

When Michael first took his graphic design talents to the Web, he used Macromedia Dreamweaver to put together sites. Being new to the web site business, he used Dreamweaver because it acted and worked very much like other Macromedia software with which he was familiar. He could easily create interesting graphics and turn them into great looking web pages.

Indeed, his web sites looked fantastic—as long as they were viewed with Microsoft Internet Explorer and a resolution setting of 800 × 600! Michael's academic coursework did not teach him that not everyone uses Internet Explorer and not everyone has video settings resolved to 800 × 600. The tool he was using to build sites defaulted to produce sites based on a resolution of 800 × 600, and used several scripts that only Internet Explorer would interpret.

Michael's resulting work did not always delight site visitors, or clients. When someone would view a site using a resolution of 640 × 400, he would have to scroll from left to right to read an entire page. Graphic images would sometimes fall off, or wrap on to another line, ruining the presentation. If another visitor had her resolution set to 1024 × 768, the elements wouldn't fill up the page.

If a visitor viewed Michael's work using Netscape Navigator, not all of the scripts and style sheets that were implemented on the site would work correctly. Blank or nonviewable pages, unformatted text, and non-working forms were often the result. In most cases, if a visitor was using the browser provided by America Online, the site could not even be viewed at all!

Michael eventually overcame these problems. He became much more familiar with the advanced use of HTML tags. He learned techniques used by his peers. He tested pages in as many browsers as he could, making adjustments where they were needed. He used browser detection and redirection scripts in certain instances. Michael learned and used professional grade HTML coding software, rather than only WYSIWYG packages like Dreamweaver and Microsoft FrontPage. Today, his talents reach beyond that of design, and also revolve around development.

3

> The predicament in which Michael found himself often happens to people starting out in web design and development. An understanding of what a visitor sees is crucial to being a successful designer or developer. In almost every case, the success of a well-produced web site isn't based on what visitors see through their browsers, it is based on what they *don't* see.

CHAPTER SUMMARY

- A web site requires hard drive storage space on a web server, together with an account and password to the server in order to be published.

- The simplest way to create a web site is to use a text editor like Notepad and use FTP to transfer it from your PC to the server.

- The home page on a web site has a name, such as **index.htm** or **default.html**, which is determined by the web server settings.

- HTML contains instructions called tags that are enclosed in angle brackets. Keywords define the tags. Tags can have attributes that further define the meaning of the tag.

- An HTML document has two parts: the header, which contains information about the document that is not displayed in the browser, and the body, which contains the information to be displayed.

- Some common HTML tags are **<HEAD>**, **
, **<P>, **<B>**, **<HR>**, and **<IMG>**.

- Three types of graphics files supported by the Internet are **JPEG** (for photographs) and **PNG** and **GIF** files (for clip art).

- A hyperlink is a text or graphic in a document that points to another location in the same document or to a different document, either on the same web site or on a different web site.

- Hyperlinks are created using the HTML anchor tags **<A>**. The link is created with the **<A HREF>** anchor tag and the link target is created with the **<A NAME>** anchor tag.

- Files on a web site should be organized so that finding and updating files is easy. Use subfolders under the web site's root folder to hold files.

- An HTML form receives user input that can be e-mailed to a recipient or sent back to the web server for processing.

- A form can use text boxes, check boxes, radio buttons and password boxes. Every form needs a submit button for the user to click to upload the data.

- Before you publish a web site, always test the site on several web browsers and desktop settings.

- Web pages built using HTML can be enhanced with short programs written in Java, JavaScript, VBScript, and C++. These programs can make the HTML dynamic, responding to user input, browser types, and browser settings.

- Programs on the web server written in ASP, Perl, SQL and other languages can customize a web page before it is downloaded to the browser, based on information received from the browser.

- HTML editors are of two types: code based and graphical (also known as WYSIWYG or GUI). An example of a code-based editor is CuteHTML, and an example of a graphical editor is FrontPage.

- HTML is a type of SGML language. The next generation of HTML will most likely be XHTML which is an XML-based language.

Key Terms

anchor tag — An HTML tag that marks text or a graphic that links to another location in the same document or a different document. Anchor tags create hyperlinks. *See* hyperlink.

attributes — A part of an HTML tag that describes how the tag should handle certain tasks.

Cascading Style Sheets (CSS) — A specification for style sheets, developed by the World Wide Web Consortium, which defines how a style sheet controls the formatting of an HTML document. *See* style sheets.

Extensible HyperText Markup Language (XHTML) — Proposed future evolution of HTML. XHTML is an application of XML. *See* Extensible Markup Language.

Extensible Markup Language (XML) — An evolution of SGML that allows developers to create their own tags within a markup language like XHTML.

form — As it applies to HTML, an object in a document that allows the user to input data, which is e-mailed to a recipient identified at the top of the form or is sent back to a program running on the web server.

Graphics Interchange Format (GIF) — A type of compressed graphics file used to hold clip art. The file can contain up to 256 colors. The clip art can have a transparent background and be animated. GIF files have a .gif file extension.

hypertext reference — *See* hyperlink.

Joint Photographic Experts Group (JPEG) file — A type of compressed file commonly used to hold photographs. The file can contain up to 1.6 million colors or be gray scale and does not allow a transparent background.

keyword — A word that has a special pre-defined meaning to the software interpreting a command or instruction.

link — *See* hyperlink.

link target — The point in a document that is assigned a section name and is the destination point for a link or hyperlink identified somewhere else in the document. Also called jumplink.

jump link — *See* link target.

Portable Network Graphics (PNG) — A graphics file used for clip art that supports a transparent background, but does not support animated clip art.

Standard Generalized Markup Language (SGML) — A standard for several markup languages, including HTML.

style sheet — A text file with a .css file extension that contains rules about how a browser should display a web page. A style sheet can include information such as what font to use when displaying text, what background color to use, or what margins to use. A style sheet is attached to an HTML document, and controls the formatting of that document.

tag — The elements of HTML that are interpreted by a web browser as commands to be followed, rather than text to be displayed.

web host — A computer that runs a web server application and stores web site files.

XHTML — *See* Extensible HyperText Markup Language.

XML — *See* Extensible Markup Language.

REVIEW QUESTIONS

1. What are the two major steps to building a web site?
2. What are two examples of file names that are typically used for home pages?
3. Can upper and lower case be used for HTML tags?
4. What is the purpose of the <BR> tag in an HTML document?
5. What tag in an HTML document says the document contains HTML tags?
6. How does a web browser handle indentations and blank lines in a document?
7. What is the purpose of the <P> tag?
8. Name three types of graphics files that web browsers can interpret.
9. What is the purpose of the Refresh button on a web browser?
10. What are the two attributes of an anchor tag that are used to build hyperlinks within a document?
11. What can you do to prevent the browser from drawing a box around a graphic that is serving as a hyperlink?
12. What is the HTML tag that marks the beginning of a new row in a table?
13. What is the HTML tag that marks the beginning of a new column within a row?
14. What is the purpose of the ACTION attribute with a FORM tag?
15. What is the purpose of the Reset button on a form?
16. How is a JavaScript program used within an HTML document?
17. Where might a Perl program be involved with HTML?
18. What are the two types of HTML editors?

19. What is one advantage that a code-based editor like CuteHTML has over Notepad when creating a web page?

20. Name one example of a GUI HTML editor.

HANDS-ON PROJECTS

Practicing HTML

Download the CuteHTML editor from *www.globalscape.com*. Use it to do the following:

1. In the bbird.htm web page built in the chapter, add a hyperlink to the bottom of the page saying "Return to top".

2. In the boxes.htm web page built in the chapter, add a text box that asks "State you live in."

Investigating Hyperlinks

Many ISPs provide the service of registering a domain name for you. The first step is to determine if the domain name is available. Find out how they accomplish that first step:

1. Find a web site other than Network Solutions where you can check to see if a domain name is available.

2. From the web browser, view the HTML source code.

3. Find the link for the search box.

Using a Table as a Web Page Layout Tool

Create a web page with a border on the left side of page to be used as a Site Map to other pages on the site. Make a rough drawing of your site first, as a plan; see Figure 3-24. On the right side of the page, include a page title, a photo or image, and text. Use a table to create this two-column layout. Put the links in Column 1 of the table and the page content in Column 2. This technique is often used by web page developers instead of using two frames, because a table is more likely to be consistently interpreted by browsers than are frames.

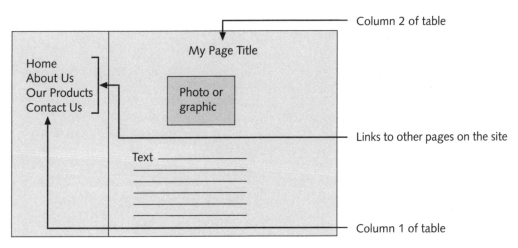

Figure 3-24 A web page is often built using a table as a layout tool

---

CASE PROJECTS

Build Your Personal Web Site

Create and publish your personal web site. It should have the following features and functions:

❑ Use a heading tag on the home page to highlight the title of the page.

❑ Include at least one piece of clip art on your home page (not a photograph).

❑ Create a second page that contains a photograph. You can use your own photos that you take with a digital camera, you can use a scanner to scan an existing photo, or you can have your film developer provide you with digital versions of your photos on CD. If none of these methods is available to you, can you download some free photos from the Internet. For example, see *www.freegraphics.com* or *www.ditto.com*. A newsgroup is also an excellent source of photographs. For example, see *news:alt.binaries.pictures*.

❑ Create a third page that includes a table and a form. Direct the results of the form to your e-mail address.

❑ Test the web site and all its hyperlinks and, if you have the opportunity, publish your site.

Using Web Site Garage

Netscape Navigator offers a web site that can check your site for: problems with performance, compatibility with different browsers, download times, misspelled words, sites that are linked to yours, and so forth. After you have published your personal web site, have Web Site Garage diagnose your site. See websitegarage.netscape.com. Print the results of the tests.

4

E-MAIL, FTP, TELNET, AND NEWSGROUPS

In this chapter, you will learn

♦ How e-mail server and client software work

♦ About software used to manage e-mail bulk-mailing

♦ About MIME file types and how to manage them

♦ How FTP, Telnet, and newsgroups work

In the last chapter you built a web site. It was a good way to learn more about the World Wide Web. This chapter looks at other Internet applications besides the World Wide Web, including e-mail, FTP, Telnet, and newsgroups. Chapter 1 introduced these services briefly, but this chapter digs deeper, discussing how these applications work on both the server and the client, the different protocols they use, and the server-side software available for these services. This chapter also addresses the many different file types that can travel over the Internet, including video, sound, and other multimedia file types; how these file types are identified by web and e-mail software; and how to use the files once they have reached their destination.

E-MAIL

E-mail is a client/server application that is used to send text messages to individuals and groups of individuals. When you send an e-mail message, it travels from your computer to your e-mail server. Your e-mail server sends the message to the recipient's e-mail server. The recipient's e-mail server sends it to the recipient's PC, but not until the recipient asks that it be sent by logging in and downloading e-mail. The different parts of the process are controlled by different protocols.

Figure 4-1 shows the journey made by an e-mail message, and the protocols that control the different parts of the journey. The sender's PC and e-mail server both use **SMTP** (**simple mail transfer protocol**) to send an e-mail message to its destination. Once the message arrives at the destination e-mail server, it remains there until delivery is requested by the recipient. The recipient's e-mail server uses one of two protocols to deliver the message—either **POP** (**Post Office Protocol**) or **IMAP4** (**Internet Message Access Protocol**, version 4). The current version of POP is version 3, often abbreviated as POP3.

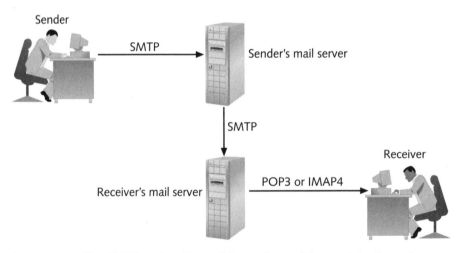

Figure 4-1   The SMTP protocol is used to send e-mail to a recipient's mail server and POP3 or IMAP4 protocol is used to download e-mail to the client

 Recall that Internet protocols are described and defined in a Request for Comments (RFC) sent out to the Internet development community. SMTP is defined in RFC821 and RFC822. When e-mail experts speak of error messages created during e-mail transactions, they sometimes call these messages **822 messages**.

E-Mail Clients and E-mail Servers: How They Interact

E-mail client software communicates with an e-mail server when it sends and receives e-mail. This section describes how a sender's e-mail client software finds the e-mail server and the various ways you can control the process.

Figure 4-1 shows a user with one e-mail server. In fact, it's possible to have two e-mail servers, one for sending e-mail and the other for receiving e-mail. Figure 4-2 shows this arrangement.

4

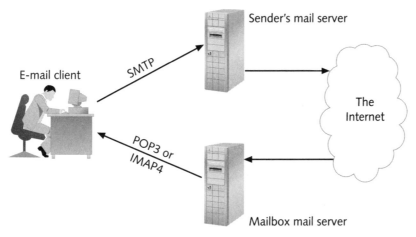

Sender's mail server

E-mail client

SMTP

The Internet

POP3 or IMAP4

Mailbox mail server

Figure 4-2   An e-mail client can use one server to send e-mail and another to receive e-mail

The e-mail server that takes care of sending e-mail messages (using the SMTP protocol) is often referred to as the SMTP server. The e-mail server from which you collect messages that were sent to you is often referred to as the POP server, because it uses the POP protocol.

How does your e-mail client software know the addresses of your e-mail servers? When you configure your e-mail client software for the first time you need to enter this information. If you are connecting to e-mail via an Internet Service Provider, the ISP can tell you these addresses.

TIP   When upgrading e-mail software, look for a feature to import your address book from the old software so you don't have to reenter the e-mail addresses of your friends and associates.

Depending on what e-mail client software you use (for example Eudora, or Outlook Express), these two addresses are entered in a dialog box. Look for menus or icons labeled Options, Preferences, Configuration, Setup, or similar names. After you have entered the addresses, the software saves this and other configuration information in an initialization file, the Windows 9x Registry, or some other location. Remember that the Windows Registry is a database that stores information such as what hardware is attached, which system options are selected, and what application programs should be run when the OS starts. It can also store configuration information needed by Windows applications.

Your e-mail client software might save configuration information in an initialization file. An **initialization file** is an ASCII text file with an .ini file extension. Initialization files are sometimes referred to as INI files. Programs that use initialization files read the files each time they are loaded. The file contains setup parameters, user preferences, and software settings and is stored in the Windows folder or in the application's folder. For example, Eudora, a popular e-mail client software, holds its server settings, along with other settings, in an initialization file named Eudora.ini, which is located in the Eudora folder on the hard drive. Figure 4-3 shows a segment of the file. In this example, the two lines that refer to the two servers are listed below:

```
POPAccount=jdoe@pop.mindspring.com
SMTPServer=mail.mindspring.com
```

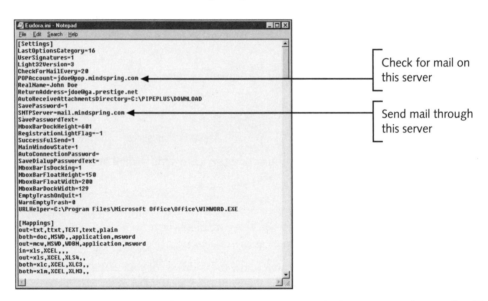

Figure 4-3   The Eudora.ini file contains setup parameters for Eudora. Change this file to point the client to a different e-mail server

The POPAccount line contains the name of the server (pop.mindspring.com) that the client turns to in order to *read* e-mail, and the name of the **POP account** on that server. In the example above, **jdoe** is the name of the account, and **pop.mindspring.com** is the server that manages the account. Therefore, the client software knows to contact the pop.mindspring.com server, and then the server accesses the account for jdoe on that server. It *sends* e-mail out through the host computer named in the SMTPServer line.

If you change ISPs or you have to set up another e-mail account, you may need to change the two server entries. You can do so from within Eudora. In version 3.0, click Tools on the menu bar, then click Options. The Options dialog box opens. Click the Hosts icon on the left to display the POP account server and the SMTP server. See Figure 4-4. Change an entry and click OK to save the changes.

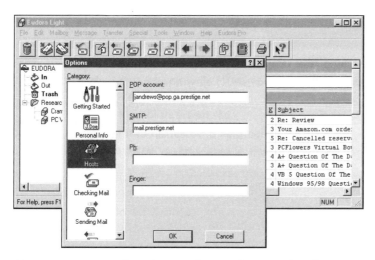

Figure 4-4   Use Eudora Options box to change either the receiving or sending e-mail server

You can also change these two server entries by editing the two lines in the Eudora.ini file. It's useful to know how to modify an INI file when you are troubleshooting potential problems. For example, suppose you are visiting a friend and want to check your e-mail using your friend's Eudora software, but your friend uses a different ISP than you do. You can modify the Eudora.ini file to make it read your mail server's name, then change it back to the original settings when you are done.

In order to make these changes, you need to know your POP account name and the name of your SMTP server. Usually, you can find both these names on your ISP's web site. Here are the steps to edit the Eudora.ini file manually:

1. If Eudora is open, close it. You need to close it because an INI file is only read when the application first loads, and you want Eudora to read your changes when it next loads.

2. Click **Start** on the Taskbar, then point to **Programs**.

3. Click **Windows Explorer** to load Windows Explorer.

4. Click **Tools** on the menu bar, then click **Find**, then click **Files or Folders**. The **Find All Files** dialog opens.

5. In the field labeled **Named**, enter **eudora.ini,** and make sure the local drive is selected in the Look In field, and that the Include Subfolders box is checked.

6. Click the **Find Now** button. The program displays the name and location of the file in a window at the bottom of the dialog box.

7. Double-click on **eudora.ini** to open the file in your default text editor, usually Notepad.

8. Click the line that begins **POPAccount**. The line becomes highlighted to indicate that it is selected. Click **Edit** on the menu bar, then click **Copy**. The line is copied to the Notepad clipboard.

9. Move your cursor down one line and to the beginning of the line. Click **Edit** on the toolbar, then click **Paste** and press **Enter**. The line you copied in step 8 is pasted into the file. Now you have two lines in a row that are identical.

10. Insert a **semicolon** in front of one of the two identical lines. When you put a semicolon at the beginning of the line in an INI file, the line becomes a comment and is ignored by the program when it reads the INI file. It's an easy way to "park" a line of information that you want to use later. Your two lines now look like this:

```
POPAccount=rubyred@pop.fruitful.com
;POPAccount=rubyred@pop.fruitful.com
```

11. Edit the POPAccount line that is not "commented out," so that it points to your e-mail account. Make it look like the POPAccount line listed in Figure 4-3 and shown in the example below:

```
POPAccount=jdoe@pop.mindspring.com
```

12. Save the **eudora.ini** file. Click **File** on the toolbar, then click **Save**.

13. Load Eudora and retrieve your e-mail.

TIP If your friend has set Eudora to reuse previously entered passwords, you will see an error message when Eudora attempts to download your e-mail. This is because Eudora is sending your friend's password to your e-mail account. If this happens, close Eudora and then reopen it. This time it won't have a previous password, and will ask you to enter one. Enter your own e-mail password and Eudora downloads your mail.

After you have read your mail, you should reset the Eudora.ini file back to your friend's POP account. Use Notepad to open the Eudora.ini file and delete the semicolon in front of your friend's POPAccount line. Then delete your entire POPAccount line. Save the file.

It isn't as easy to send e-mail from someone else's account as it is to collect your own e-mail. You might think you could change your friend's INI file and insert the name of your own SMTP server in place of your friend's SMTP server. However, most e-mail servers check the IP address of the sending PC to make sure it's one that is assigned to that ISP. If it's not a valid IP address you get an error like the one shown in Figure 4-5 that says "550 Access denied."

TIP The number 550 in the error message in Figure 4-5 came from the RFC specifications for e-mail protocols. Numbers in the 500 range have to do with server errors. See Appendix D for a list of these error numbers and their meanings.

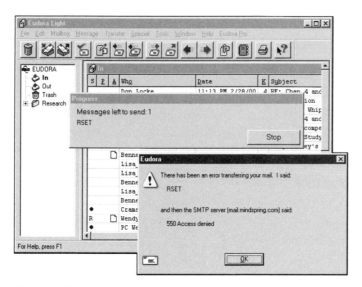

Figure 4-5   Before the e-mail server at the ISP accepts e-mail from a client, it verifies the
IP address. An "access denied" error results if a foreign IP address is sensed

You have two options for sending e-mail from your friend's PC but still retaining your own
e-mail return address:

- One way is to connect to the Internet using your own ISP. You can use this
  method if your friend is using a modem and phone line to connect to the Internet
  and if your ISP has a point-of-presence (POP) in your friend's area. Remember that
  a point-of-presence is a local phone number that you can call to access your ISP. If
  you dial in through your own ISP, your ISP assigns you one of its IP addresses and
  you won't receive the error message 550 that results from an invalid IP address.
  When you're finished, be very careful to make sure to restore any settings in Eudora's
  dialog boxes that you may have changed in order to connect to your own ISP. You
  can read more about how to manage dial up connections in Chapter 8.

- Another way to send e-mail from your friend's PC using your own return address is
  to simply change the Return Address line in the Eudora INI file or in the Eudora
  Options window. Most SMTP servers will send mail using foreign return addresses
  (return addresses using a different mail domain name than the SMTP server).
  Follow the directions given earlier for changing the INI file. When you have finished, be sure to reset the INI file with your friend's return address in the Return
  Address line.

There are two meanings for the acronym POP. Point of Presence refers to a method available for users to access an ISP via a local phone number. Large ISPs have POPs in many
cities. Post Office Protocol refers to the protocol used by e-mail servers and clients that controls how the server sends a message to the client.

The E-mail Protocols and How They Work

The three e-mail protocols are SMTP, POP, and IMAP. This section discusses each of these protocols and gives you enough information to understand how they work and how the dialogue between the server and client transpires. One goal is to prepare you for the times when you see e-mail errors, so that you'll have a general idea of the source of the error and what you must do to resolve it. Another goal is to help you understand how a client and server interact when they create a session, exchange data, and close the session; some of this is general communication knowledge. You can then apply your knowledge to other sorts of servers as well as e-mail servers.

SMTP

SMTP (simple mail transfer protocol) is the protocol used to send e-mail over the Internet. An SMTP transaction begins when an e-mail client program sends an e-mail message to a recipient. The SMTP server responds by receiving the message and sending it on to a recipient server. The recipient server can be either the final destination server of the message's recipient, or it can be an intermediate server that forwards the message on its way to the ultimate recipient server.

The sender SMTP server attempts to make a TCP connection with the recipient server. The SMTP dialogue between servers begins when the recipient responds. The **dialogue** is a series of commands from the sender to the receiver, and a series of replies from the receiver to the sender. While the dialogue is carried out electronically, it is recorded on the server from which you can access a copy if necessary. For example, if you are an Internet support technician working for an ISP and you suspect a problem with the SMTP server, one thing you can do to discover the source of the problem is to have the server display the dialogue. You would then use the dialogue to discover where in the process an error occurred.

It's useful to look at a dialogue (like the one shown in Table 4-1) to see how the two servers communicate with one another. As you look at Table 4-1, keep these things in mind:

- Commands from the sender are four-character words followed by information (called arguments or parameters) that is needed by the receiver to follow the command.

- Replies from the receiver are three-digit numbers with text following. The text is not needed by the sending server, but is useful to humans when they are reading the dialogue.

Table 4-1 lists one example of an SMTP dialogue between servers. In this example, the sending server is named MYISP.NET. It has been sent a message by a user and is ready to send it on to the destination. The receiving server in this example (named OURGLOBE.NET) is an intermediate server. It knows how to get the message to the final-destination server, and agrees to relay it.

Table 4-1   Sample SMTP dialogue between e-mail servers

Server	Command or Reply	Description
Receiving server:		Receiving server is listening on port 25
Sending server:	Uses TCP to connect to the receiving server at port 25	This communication is done using TCP, not SMTP
SMTP Begins:		
1. Receiving server:	220 OURGLOBE.NET	I can open a channel. My name is OURGLOBE.NET
2. Sending server:	HELO MYISP.NET	Hello. We now have a channel. My name is MYISP.NET
3. Receiving server:	250 OURGLOBE.NET	Channel confirmed. I'm OURGLOBE.NET
4. Sending server:	MAIL FROM: tomsmith@myisp.net	I want to send mail from this user
5. Receiving server:	250 ok	Confirmed
6. Sending server:	RCPT TO: jdoe@goodnet.com	The mail goes to this user
7. Receiving server:	251 User not local; will forward to jdoe@goodnet.com	He is not here, but I can forward it on. I'll take the message.
8. Sending server:	DATA	I will send data.
9. Receiving server:	354 send the mail data, end with.	Send the data now ending it with a single period in the last transmission.
10. Sending server:	(e-mail message inserted here)	Series of transmissions here until the entire message is sent.
11. Sending server:	.	Last transmission is only a period.
12. Receiving server:	250 ok	Data transmission is confirmed.
13. Sending server:	QUIT	That's all. I'm closing the channel.
SMTP Ends		
Receiving server:		Waits for next connection

Chapter 2 introduced the term "state." In this example it's easy to understand what a state is. After the command in Line 8 of Table 4-1 and the reply in Line 9, both servers are in the data-sending state. In other words, both servers understand that whatever is sent or received during this current state will be interpreted as data, and not commands. It is clear to both parties what will end the state: the sending server will send a transmission that only contains a period. As soon as the receiving server receives the period, the data-sending state has ended and a new state begins.

While the servers are in the data-sending state, what happens if the sending server sends a command instead of data? The receiving server does not recognize the command, but attempts to process it as data. By establishing states between two communicating parties, the parties are able to carry on business in an organized and predictable fashion.

This table also shows how the error message in Figure 4-5 came to be. A channel between the client software and the server software was first established using SMTP protocol. The client issued the MAIL command. The receiving server looked at the IP address and denied the action. The denial would have been the error code 550. The client gave up and sent the reset command (RSET) to the server saying, "The current mail transaction is aborted." The server responded again with the "550 Access denied" error message.

For a complete list of the reply codes used by the recipient server, see Appendix D. For an in-depth understanding of SMTP, read RFC 821 and RFC 822. See the web site *www.rfc-editor.org* and search for the two RFCs.

POP

The POP protocol is used when a client downloads its e-mail messages from a server. First, the client sends the user ID and password to the server. The server verifies that the user has an e-mail account with the server. Then a session is established between the client and the server. Next, transactions occur as the client requests the mail, and then the session is closed. There are four states during this process:

- Connection is established during the Connecting state
- A session is established during the Authentication state
- Mail is delivered during the Transaction state
- The session is closed during the Update state

Just as with SMTP, the client initiates the process by issuing commands with arguments. The server replies by sending back keywords followed by descriptive text. These replies can contain descriptive text that is intended to be helpful to humans reading the dialogue, but sometimes a reply has text immediately following the keyword that is meaningful to the client software. There are two keywords sent from the server to the client: +OK and -ERR. The first keyword means all is well and the second means there's a problem.

A sample process is shown in Table 4-2. As you read through the example, can you determine the difference between a connection and a session?

In this example dialogue, an error occurred when the client attempted to retrieve a message (RETR in line 14) that it had already told the server to delete. The server replied with an error (-ERR in line 15). Also note that in Line 4, once the session was established, the server locked out all other users from creating a session until this session was over. That's done so that one session can't delete a message that another session still expects to exist. You can see an example of this type of situation by trying to log in to your e-mail server from two PCs at the same time.

Table 4-2 Sample POP dialogue between an e-mail client and server

Client or Server	Command or Reply	Description
Server:		E-mail server is listening on port 110
Client:	Uses TCP to connect to the server (MAIL.GOODNET.COM) at port 110	This communication is done using TCP, not POP.
POP Begins:		
1. Client:	USER JDOE	I want to access this mailbox
2. Server:	+OK	Confirmed. I have that mailbox.
3. Client:	PASS secret	Here is the password.
4. Server:	+OK	The password is verified and the session is established. The server locks the mailbox for exclusive use.
5. Client:	LIST	List all messages in the mailbox.
6. Server:	+OK 2 340	There are 2 messages. The total number of bytes for all messages is 340.
7. Server:	1 100	Message 1 is 100 bytes
8. Server:	2 240	Message 2 is 240 bytes
9. Client:	RETR 2	Give me message 2
10. Server:	+OK message follows	OK, here it comes.
11. Server:	(message sent here)	240 bytes are transmitted.
12. Client:	DELE 2	Delete message 2
13. Server:	+OK message 2 deleted	Confirmed
14. Client:	RETR 2	Give me message 2
15. Server:	-ERR there is no message 2	No can do. You've already told me to delete it.
16. Client:	QUIT	That's all. I'm closing the session.
POP Ends:		
Server:		Server continues to listen at port 110

IMAP

The POP protocol has served us well for years, but it has some limitations that have caused the industry to look toward another protocol for clients to use for reading e-mail. **IMAP (Internet Messaging Access Protocol)** is expected to ultimately replace POP, because it offers more functionality:

- Messages can be archived in folders on the server
- Mailboxes can be shared, so that multiple users can access the same mail
- Users can easily access multiple mail servers

- A user can choose to only read the header information about an attached file without opening the file

- Attached files need not be downloaded with every message.

This last item is useful when the client is connected to the Internet with a slow connection, such as with a phone line, and doesn't want to wait while large attached files download.

The IMAP protocol contains commands that perform the same functions as those in the POP protocol, and the dialogue between the client and server reads like that of POP. But the IMAP protocol set contains many more commands with added functionality. More than 20 RFCs have been written about IMAP since the latest IMAP version 4 was introduced in 1994. For more information, go to the web site *www.rfc-editor.org* and search the database for IMAP.

E-mail Server Software

An Internet Service Provider or large business using the Internet is responsible for providing an e-mail server for its subscribers or employees. E-mail servers are most likely installed on either a UNIX, Linux, Windows NT, or Windows 2000 server. If a computer is powerful enough, it can support more than one type of server software running on it. For example, a computer might run both a web server and an e-mail server. A sampling of e-mail server products is shown below in order from largest to smallest.

Microsoft Exchange Server

This product is a heavy-duty e-mail server designed for large enterprise applications. Exchange Server supports MAPI, POP3, IMAP4 and NNTP protocols. NNTP (Network News Transfer Protocol) is the protocol used by newsgroups.

MAPI (**Messaging Application Programming Interface**) is a specification that allows an application to interact with an e-mail client to send and receive e-mail. For example, a company might have a database that contains a list of customers. From time to time the company might want to send e-mail messages to certain preferred customers offering them special deals based on their high purchasing volume. A Visual Basic application can be written to search the customer database to look for customers who qualify for these special offers. When the application finds a qualifying customer, it uses a MAPI interface to pass an e-mail message to the customer to Outlook Express. Outlook Express receives the e-mail message into its Outbox and then sends the message. The entire process can be automated without any user intervention.

Microsoft Exchange Server supports hot backups (the ability to back up your data while the server is still working) and dynamic rerouting (if an established link is broken, the servers attempt to find a new route). If a new Exchange Server comes on line somewhere in the enterprise, all other Exchange Servers will automatically detect the new server without manual intervention. In addition, the software can track a message anywhere on the Internet in order to troubleshoot transmission problems or track the source of spam (unsolicited messages) or other offensive messages. Servers can work as a cluster of servers; if one server goes down, another server in the cluster picks up the failed server's work. The software has many security features that we will discuss in Chapter 12. For more information, see *www.microsoft.com* or *www.email-software.com*.

NTMail

NTMail by Gordano, Inc. is designed for medium to large companies and Internet Service Providers to run on Windows NT. It supports Auto Responders (a message is automatically sent back to a sender when the message is first received), mail forwarding and list accounts (the same message is sent to multiple addresses).

NTMail can verify that client software with a foreign IP address is not attempting to initiate a message. The purpose of this feature is to allow an ISP to control who can use the SMTP server to send e-mail messages. If only an IP address that is assigned by the ISP can use the service, then the ISP is assured that only subscribers to the ISP are initiating a message.

NTMail limits the maximum sessions from a remote host in order to prevent a **denial of service attack** (a malicious flooding of messages designed to overwhelm and ultimately disable a site). NTMail supports SMTP, POP3, IMAP4, and HTTP. Using the HTTP protocol, NTMail can support a web site providing access so that e-mail users can read their mail. For more information, see *www.ntmail.co.uk*.

ITHouse Mail Server

This product is designed to run on Window 9x or Windows NT, and is written as a compact product for a small to medium-size company. It requires little computing power and will even run on an older 486 PC. ITHouse should be used on a LAN to support in-house e-mail services for employees. As it continually manages the in-house e-mail from employee to employee, it can occasionally log into the ISP to download and upload e-mail from the Internet. ITHouse supports SMTP and POP3 protocols. For more information, see *www.ithouse.com*.

Mailing List Software

There is a growing need for software to manage mailing lists, and there are many software products on the market designed to meet that need. Discussion groups, electronic newsletters, and e-mail advertising campaigns all use this type of software. The software, called a **list server,** manages the mailing lists and the messages sent to that list. Using commands to the list server, an individual can subscribe, unsubscribe, or review the list of subscribers. Some mailing list software supports power users that have special privileges; only they can subscribe or unsubscribe someone from the list.

When you are first added to a mailing list, sometimes the list server sends you an e-mail message explaining how to participate in the discussion group. Be sure to save that message as a future reference. The mailing list has a name, such as OurDiscussionGroup. Messages sent to ourdiscussiongroup@domainname.com, for example, go to everyone on the list. Mailing list software designed for advertising campaigns can individualize a message to address a particular interest or need of the recipient. Some mailing list software products are:

- LISTSERV by Lsoft, Inc. (*www.lsoft.com*)

- Lyris by Lyris Technologies, Inc. (*www.lyris.com*)

- Listproc by the Corporation for Research and Educational Networking (*www.cren.net*)

- NTList by Gordano, Inc. (*www.ntmail.co.uk*)

MIME

E-mail is a useful tool for sending files to other users. You can attach a file to an e-mail message, and the file travels along with the message just as your suitcase travels with you in the trunk of your car. While the content of an e-mail message is in text format, the attached file can be in any format, for example, text, graphics, a word processing document, a sound file, an executable file and so forth. These attached files are most often identified and encoded using a standard called **MIME** (**Multipurpose Internet Mail Extensions**).

The World Wide Web and e-mail both use MIME because both these Internet applications were originally built on the assumption that all the data they would transfer would be text. MIME makes non-text data appear as text, so that these applications can transfer these files. The World Wide Web needs MIME because few web pages are built today with just text. Non-text files such as Java programs, graphics, sound, video clips and other multimedia type files must be transmitted from web server to web browser in order to build a web page. In the discussion that follows, you'll see how developers of e-mail software first attempted to solve the problem of attaching non-text files to e-mail messages using other standards than MIME. Then you'll learn how MIME is used by both e-mail and web software to manage these same non-text files.

Background Information about Attached Files

When the SMTP e-mail protocol was first specified, no provision was made to send any data in messages that was not pure ASCII text. The original ASCII (American Standard Code for Information Interchange) text character set had only 128 characters in it. Each character was assigned a number from 0 to 127, which converted to the binary numbers 0 to 0111 1111. Therefore, only seven of the eight bits that make up a byte were needed to write this character set. Files that follow this format are called **ASCII files**. RFC 821, which defines the

SMTP protocol reads, "The mail data may contain any of the 128 ASCII character codes." Looking back at Table 4-1, when the DATA command was issued and accepted by the receiving server, under this specification, all data that followed could only use 7 bits to a byte and would be interpreted at the other end as belonging to this ASCII character set.

However, many types of data don't follow this coding method. Graphics files and program files (executable files with a .exe file extension) use binary data that can have long series of bits in the data, and word processing documents have embedded codes for formatting that use more than 7 bits. Files that use all 8 bits of the byte and are not readable as text are known as **binary files**. A method was needed to transfer these files using e-mail. One of the first solutions to this problem was **uuencode** (pronounced "you-you encode") and **uudecode** (pronounced "you-you decode"), developed for the UNIX operating system. With these coding and decoding programs, uuencode converts a binary file into a file that uses the seven-bit coding method that SMTP accepts to transport the file. Once the file reaches another UNIX computer, the program on the receiving end, uudecode, takes the coded 7-bit data and decodes it back to the original binary file. Many e-mail software client and server programs still accept files using the uuencode and uudecode methods. Uuencode files have a .UU or .UUE file extension.

Another early method was **BinHex**, a program used by an Apple Macintosh computer to convert a binary file to the 7-bit ASCII text format so that it can be transferred over the Internet. Another BinHex converter program must exist on the recipient's computer to convert the file back to binary before it can be used by the Macintosh computer. BinHex files have a .HQX file extension.

The Internet community developed the current MIME method of transmitting non-ASCII files over the Internet through a series of RFCs over a period of several years. The major RFC for the MIME protocol, RFC 1521, was published in 1993, replacing RFC 1341 produced just a few months earlier. RFC 1521 (see *www.rfc-editor.org*) defines MIME, the coding schemes it uses, and how server and client software communicate information to each other about the files using the MIME specifications.

How MIME Works

MIME is a standard that governs the way a server can send a non-ASCII text file to a client. It tells the client what type of file to expect and what software to use to interpret the file. Information about the MIME file is communicated in a header that precedes the body of a text e-mail message or a web page. The header information indicates what MIME file types are being used, what the encoding method is for the file, and what type of file to expect.

Figure 4-6 shows how the MIME standard encodes and decodes a file for transmission over the Internet using a graphics file Myimage.gif as an example. The steps in the figure are explained below.

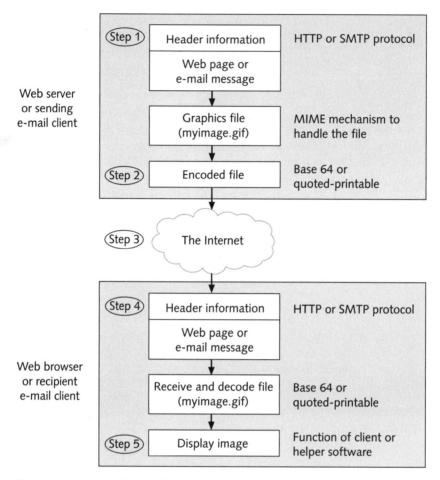

Figure 4-6   How the MIME standard works

Step 1 - Declare the MIME type in header information. The web server or e-mail client creating the web page or e-mail message uses HTTP or SMTP to create a header to the web page or e-mail message declaring that the page or message contains a MIME file type. The header for a web page includes these two (or similar) lines:

```
MIME-Version: 1.0
Accept = image/gif
```

The first line gives the version of MIME, and the second line tells the browser to expect MIME type **image/gif**. MIME types are grouped into several types and subtypes. The type is **image** and the subtype is **gif**. Don't confuse these two header lines with header information that is included in the HTML document itself that you saw in Chapter 3. The header information in this chapter precedes the HTML document, and is part of the HTTP protocol dialogue that occurs before the document itself is transmitted.

An e-mail client creates header information that looks similar to this:

```
MIME-Version: 1.0

Content-Type: application/msword; name="December 1999
newsletter.doc"

Content-Transfer-Encoding: base64

Content-Disposition: attachment;
filename="December2000Newsletter.doc"
```

The MIME type and subtype is **application/msword** and the encoding method is **base64**. There are two primary ways that e-mail data is encoded to conform to the 7-bit ASCII text encoding method: base64 and quoted-printable. **Base64** is used for binary files and other files that contain coded data, and **quoted-printable** is used for text files. Quoted-printable converts the data to a 7-bit coding scheme and base64 uses a 6-bit coding scheme. The base64 scheme takes its name from the 64-code sets it uses. The codes are 0 to 63, which is 000000 to 111111 in binary, thus generating 6 bits for each data item.

Step 2 - Encode the file. The file is encoded in preparation for transmission over the Internet. Although the original MIME specifications only provided for 7-bit coding schemes (base64 and quoted-printable), MIME has been improved so that 8-bit coding can be used (see RFC 1426). Also, support for BinHex files in their BinHex encoded method was added with RFC 1741. Support for Unicode was added by RFC 1641. (**Unicode** is the ultimate replacement for ASCII. It's a 16-bit character set that includes characters for most of the world's writing systems, including the Asian character set.)

Step 3 - Send the files over the Internet. When the transmission begins, HTTP or SMTP sends the header information and then follows it up with the web page or e-mail message.

Step 4 - Client receives the data. The receiving client reads the header information and knows to expect MIME files in the transmission. The client requests and receives the MIME files after it has received the e-mail or web page.

Step 5 - Interpret the MIME file. Depending on the file type, the client interprets and displays the file, or requests that a **helper application** or **external viewer** load and display the file for the user. Web browsers can display GIF files without any help. But, if an e-mail client receives a Word document, it turns the file over to Microsoft Word to load and display to the user. The client is responsible for (1) processing the file itself, (2) calling a helper application to do the job, or (3) if it doesn't know how to process the file itself and doesn't have a helper application identified to do it, displaying a dialog box asking the user to select an application to load and display the file. Examples of helper applications are Lview Pro for graphics files and WinZIP to decompress compressed files.

Suppose, for example, you receive an e-mail message with an attached file that has the ZIP file extension. Your e-mail client software recognizes that the file type is application/zip because that was the information in the message header. You see the file name displayed at the bottom of the e-mail message and double-click on the file to open it. If your system has compression software installed such as PKZip or WinZIP, this software has registered with the system that it will process compressed files that have a ZIP file extension. The client then knows to execute the compression software.

You can view the source data exactly as it was received by the e-mail client using Outlook Express or Microsoft Outlook. Follow these directions in Outlook Express.

1. Open the e-mail with an attached MIME file.

2. Click **File** on the menu bar, then click **Properties**. The Properties dialog box opens.

3. In the Properties dialog box, click the **Details** tab. The message header displays. To see the entire message source, click the **Message Source** button.

Figure 4-7 shows an example of one message source that has a JPG file attached to the message. In the figure you can see the beginning of the encoded JPG file.

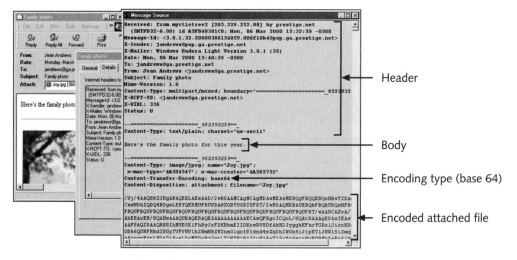

Figure 4-7   Using Outlook Express, you can view the source data exactly as it was sent to the e-mail client complete with header information and encoded attached file

MIME File Types

Several MIME file types were defined initially, and provision was made in the specifications to define new MIME types for the Internet community. If someone wants to do that, he or she can submit the documentation to IANA (Internet Assigned Numbers Authority, see *www.iana.org*), the organization that governs the process and documents the file types for the Internet community. The procedures to register new file types, subtypes, character sets, and conversion specifications are found in RFC 2048 (see *www.rfc-editor.org*). When you register a subtype, you must define the file extensions that will be used for the subtype. For example, a

TIFF file subtype uses the TIF or TIFF file extension. However, the client software first uses the MIME header information to identify the file type rather than the file extension. If the header information does not adequately identify the type, then it uses the file extension to define the file.

You can also use a MIME file subtype that has not been defined to IANA. Suppose, for example, you are developing a web site that will be used by directors of high school marching bands to help them build, compare, and evaluate their musical programs. You decide to build a different MIME type for each musical section (brass, strings, percussion, and so forth) to help identify the best audio application to render the sound when played by the browser. After you have identified the MIME types and the audio application that renders each type, the next step is to register the file type with your web server, which informs browsers about the type. A web server software application will have a menu option to define a new MIME type. To know exactly how to find the menu option, consult the software documentation or online help.

Private MIME types are supposed to begin with X- such as an Audio/X-brass MIME file that has a BRS file extension. Audio is a valid type, but there is no known X-brass subtype, and a file with a BRS file extension will now be known to a client that receives the file as type X-brass. When the browser receives the MIME instructions to receive an X-brass file, at first it will not know what application to use to open the file. You'll have to provide the application to the browser's user who must download it to his or her PC and then use it to open the X-brass file.

The current categories of file types are:

- **Text** - Text files that can be written using a variety of character sets and formatting rules

- **Multipart** - Used to combine two or more body parts into a single message—the parts don't have to be the same type

- **Application** - This file type is a general catch-all for those files that don't fit in one of the other types. Executable files, word processing documents, and unknown file types are transferred using this type

- **Message** - A mail message that has another mail message embedded in it

- **Image** - Graphics files

- **Audio** - Audio or voice data

- **Video** - Video or moving picture data which can include audio data

- **Model** - Virtual reality and other 3-D data

Table 4-3 lists some of the better-known MIME file types and subtypes together with the helper applications that display or use them.

Table 4-3   MIME file types

MIME File Types and Subtypes	File Extensions	Description
Application/mac-binhex40	hqx	Macintosh BinHex 4.0 format
Application/msword	doc, w6w	Microsoft Word document file
Application/octet-stream	bin, exe	Unknown file type that is binary data; client needs to know what application to use to open it.
Application/postscript	ai, eps, ps	PostScript file
Application/rtf	rtf	Microsoft rich text format
Application/zip	zip	Compressed file. Use PKZip or some other compression software to open it.
Image/jpeg	jpe, jpeg, jpg	JPEG file. Use Lview Pro to open it or some other photo editor.
Image/tiff	tif, tiff	TIFF file. Use a graphics editor or photo editor such as Lview Pro
Message/news		A newsgroup file. Use a newsreader program to open it.
Message/rfc822		A standard e-mail message file
Multipart/mixed		The original e-mail client could not make sense of the file extension or its contents but sent it on anyway
Video/quicktime	mov, qt	Quicktime movie file

FTP

Web servers (using the HTTP protocol), and e-mail software (using the SMTP protocol) must both encode data so that it appears like text when it travels over the Internet. However, the **FTP** protocol offers an alternative. FTP can transfer binary files over the Internet without the encoding and decoding overhead, making it a popular protocol for moving files over the Internet. In Chapter 3 you learned to use FTP client software to transfer web pages and graphics files to a web site. In this section, you'll learn more about using FTP, how FTP works, and what happens on the server side of FTP.

FTP is both the name of the protocol and the name of the application that uses the protocol. FTP is the standby, tried-and-true utility to use when you need to get a file from one computer to another on the Internet.

An **FTP site** is a computer that is running an FTP server application. The server application provides directories and folders that contain files for distribution to clients. The site can also receive files transmitted from clients. The FTP server is responsible for managing the user IDs and passwords of those who can access the site, logging in users, and receiving files and transmitting files when requests are made by client FTP software. The server also manages the directories on the computer that the FTP users can access. FTP servers normally listen at Port 21 for client activity, and most web servers have an FTP server running in order to receive changes to web page files from web page developers.

Software manufactures such as Microsoft often provide an FTP site so that users can download the latest software upgrade or patch (a correction for an error in a previous software release). For large organizations, several FTP sites might be maintained in different parts of the world in order to speed up download time over the globe. These are called mirror sites.

Most FTP sites require that a user log in with a valid user ID and password. Some FTP sites are called anonymous FTP sites because they don't require a valid user ID or password. Sites that only allow downloads, but no uploading, are often anonymous FTP sites, meaning that you can log in without a valid ID and password. However, to upload files to a site, you must always log in with a valid user ID and password.

FTP client software can be an application dedicated to FTP such as CuteFTP. A web browser can be used as an FTP client, or an operating system might have an FTP client included in it. If you use FTP a lot, you will want to take the time to download and learn to use a dedicated FTP client such as CuteFTP or FTP Pro because they are easier and quicker to use than other methods. Figure 4-8 shows an example of CuteFTP.

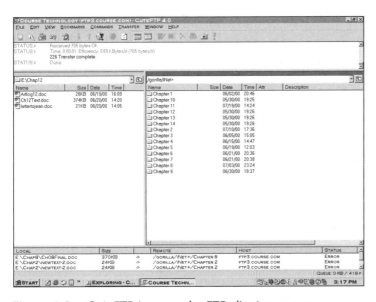

Figure 4-8   CuteFTP is a popular FTP client program

In a dedicated FTP client application such as CuteFTP, files on the client computer show on the left side of the FTP client software window and files on the server computer show on the right side of the window. Downloading and uploading files is as easy as dragging files from right to left or left to right.

If you don't have an FTP client application you can use a web browser or the command-line FTP client included with Windows 9x. Both these methods can serve you well in an emergency when no other tool is available. The following section describes how FTP works. The section then goes on to describe how to use a web browser as an FTP client, and how to use the Windows 9x command-line FTP client.

How FTP Works

An FTP server identifies a user on an FTP site by his or her user ID. When you first log in to an FTP site with a user ID and password, the permissions that have been granted to you determine what the FTP server allows you to do. A user with the correct permissions can copy, delete, and rename files, make directories, remove directories, and view details about files and directories on the remote computer.

FTP client and server software create a session (working at the Session layer of the OSI model) between them after you are logged in. The FTP client has access to the file system on the server, as illustrated in Figure 4-9. An FTP dialog between two computers looks very much like that of an SMTP dialogue. The local computer (the client) issues character-like commands and the remote computer's (the server's) replies are numbers that are interpreted by the local computer.

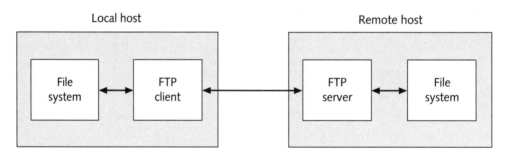

Figure 4-9   FTP client and server software have access to their individual file systems—files can be transferred in either direction

FTP using a Web Browser

Have you ever attempted to download software from a web site and clicked on a hyperlink that says "Click here to download now" or a similar message? If you carefully note the URL after you click to download the software, you will see that the protocol changes from http:// to ftp:// in the web browser address box. The hyperlink directs you to an FTP site; the protocol for that site is not HTTP, but FTP. Your browser is now acting as an FTP client rather than a web client. (Note that you could have accessed the FTP site directly, by entering ftp:// at the beginning of the URL followed by the site domain name or IP address.)

For example, if you are using Internet Explorer you can access the Microsoft anonymous FTP site. Enter **ftp://ftp.microsoft.com** in the URL address box of your browser; see

Figure 4-10. When the browser recognizes that you are accessing an FTP site rather than a web site, the tools on the browser screen change so that the browser looks and acts like Windows Explorer, making it easier to manage files.

Figure 4-10   Web browser's view of an FTP site

For example, suppose you would like to download the Windows 95 clouds wallpaper file and install the clouds wallpaper on your Windows desktop. The URL of the correct site is:

**ftp://ftp.microsoft.com/products/windows/windows95/cdromextras/funstuff/
clouds.exe**

Follow these steps to download the file:

1. Enter **ftp://ftp.microsoft.com** in the URL address box of your browser.

2. Click the drop-down menu on the **Views** button on the far right of the toolbar. Click **as web page** on the menu. Click the drop-down menu again and click **Details**.

3. To open a folder, double-click the folder. A new browser window opens, showing the folder contents. Open the folders in this order: **products, windows, windows 95, cdromextras**, and **funstuff** to see the clouds.exe file.

4. Right-click the file name and select **Copy to Folder**. The Browse for Folder dialog box opens. This dialog box lets you choose which folder on your PC should receive the downloaded file. Select a folder on your PC. It is a good practice to have a folder on your hard drive named Downloads for this purpose.

5. You don't need to log out of this site, because you never logged in. You can close your browser, or enter a new URL to move to a different web page.

Once the file is downloaded, you can execute the file by double-clicking the filename in Windows Explorer.

You cannot upload files to an anonymous site like the Microsoft site, because you must be logged into a site with a user ID and password in order to upload. Your user ID must have permission to upload; this is called write permission or write privileges. If you try to upload a file to a site where you don't have permission to do so, an error occurs like the one shown in Figure 4-11. In the figure, note that the error is identified as error 550 - Access denied.

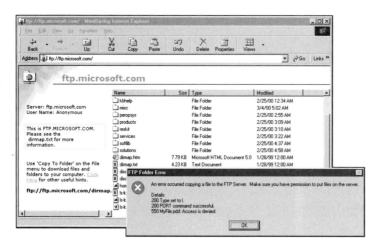

Figure 4-11   An error occurs when you attempt to upload a file to an FTP site where you don't have write permission

If you have a user ID and password with write privileges on an FTP site, follow these directions to use Windows Explorer to upload a file. If you don't have these privileges you can still read this section and look at the figures to see examples of what is happening.

1. Start up Windows Explorer, and find the file that you want to upload. Click the file once to select it.

2. Click **Edit** on the menu bar, and click **Copy** to copy the file to the Clipboard.

3. Close Windows Explorer and open Internet Explorer.

4. Enter the URL of the FTP site to access the FTP site.

5. Click **File** on the menu bar, then click **Login As**. The Login As dialog box displays, as shown in Figure 4-12. Enter your user name and password and click **Login**.

6. Double-click folder names on the site to locate the folder that should receive the file.

7. Click **Edit** on the menu bar, then click **Paste**. The file is copied to the site.

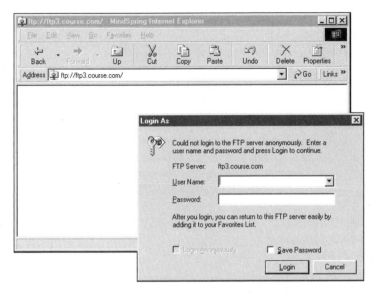

Figure 4-12   Logging into an FTP site with a web browser

Another way to log in to an FTP site is to include the user name and password in the URL like this:

ftp://username:password@hostname:port/pathtothefile/filename

For example, to log in to the ftp site of mydomain.com, you would use this URL:

ftp://myname:mypassword@mydomain.com/myfolder

It isn't necessary to use the port unless the FTP process is listening to some other port than the default port. It is also not necessary to include the folder and file.

FTP from a Command Prompt

Most operating systems including Windows 9x, Windows NT, and Windows 2000 offer FTP client software that runs from a command prompt. Operating FTP from a command prompt is a quick-and-dirty way to transfer files when the computer does not have more user-friendly FTP software installed, or you are testing a series of FTP commands in preparation for writing them into a batch file for later execution. A **batch file** is a file with a .BAT file extension that contains a list of DOS-like commands that can be executed as a group.

To use the Windows 9x FTP software, click Start on the Taskbar. Click Run and type FTP in the Run dialog box. An FTP window opens; see Figure 4-13. The commands in Figure 4-13 are explained in Table 4-4.

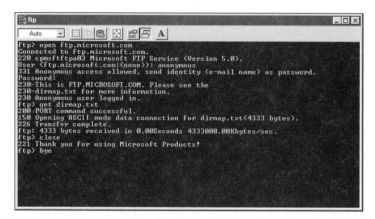

Figure 4-13   An FTP session using the Windows 98 FTP utility

Table 4-4   A sample FTP session from a Windows 98 command window

Client or Server	Command or Reply	Description
Client:	FTP	Type in the Run dialog box to execute the command-based FTP utility. The ftp> command prompt displays in a command window.
Client:	OPEN ftp.microsoft.com	Open a session with a remote computer running an FTP server
Server:	220	Connection confirmed
Client:	User: anonymous	The local computer provides a prompt to enter a user ID for the computer being accessed. Because this is an anonymous FTP site, enter "anonymous."
Server:	331 Send password	The remote computer requests that the user's e-mail address be entered as a password in order to identify the user.
Client:	Password:myemailaddress	The host computer provides a prompt to the user for the password. User enters e-mail address as password.
Server:	230	Confirmed with some directions to user
Client:	Get dirmap.txt	Copy the file Dirmap.txt (or whatever file you want) from the remote computer to your computer.
Server:	200 150 226	Port command successful Opening an ASCII mode data connection for file transfer Transfer complete, returning to command state
Client:	Close	Close the connection to this site
Server:	221	Server says goodbye
Client:	Bye	Close the FTP window

All of these transactions occur during a control state, where commands are issued by the local computer and replies come from the remote computer. During the control state, the protocol that passes commands and their replies is not the FTP protocol, but the Telnet protocol. When the local computer requests a file, the state changes to a data state, at which time data can pass in either direction and the FTP protocol takes over.

These and other Windows 9x commands that can be used during an FTP session are shown in the following table. Note that these commands are only valid if the user is logged onto a site and has the correct permissions.

4

Table 4-5   FTP command line commands

Command	Meaning
ASCII	Sets the file transfer type to ASCII (the default type)
BINARY	Sets the file transfer type to binary (use for all file types except pure ASCII text files)
BYE	Close the FTP program
CD	Change directory
CLOSE	Close the connection to the remote computer
DELETE	Delete file (requires write permission)
DIR	Lists files in the current directory
FTP	Execute an FTP program
GET	Copy a file from the remote computer to the local computer
MKDIR	Make directory (requires write permission)
OPEN	Connect to the remote computer
PUT	Copy a file from the local computer to the remote computer (requires write permission)
RENAME	Renames file on remote computer (requires write permission)
RMDIR	Remove directory (requires write permission)
TRACE	Displays the route each packet takes when running an FTP command

The transfer mode or type used when transferring a file can be critical in ensuring that the file arrives at its destination intact. Use ASCII transfer type when transferring text files, but use binary transfer type for all other types of files. An FTP utility might use ASCII or binary as the default transfer mode or might be able to sense what type of file is being transferred and select the appropriate mode for you. This feature is called Auto mode. You should know how to verify what mode is being used and know how to change the mode as needed. For example, in Figure 4-13, the message "Opening ASCII mode data connection for…" indicates that the mode is ASCII, which is the correct mode for this text file. For a complete listing of FTP commands and replies, see RFC 959 at *www.rfc-editor.org*.

Another protocol similar to FTP is **Trivial FTP** (**TFTP**). It has fewer commands than FTP and can only be used to send and receive files. It can be used for multicasting where a file is sent to more than one client at the same time using the UDP Transport layer protocol. For more information about TFTP, see RFC 1350 at *www.rfc-editor.org*.

TELNET

A Telnet window on a PC is a command window to a remote computer where any command can be executed, just as though the user were sitting at the computer console. Telnet is a popular tool for system administrators. For example, an administrator can use it to control a UNIX computer from a remote location, such as an office down the hall from the UNIX machine or from home. It is even possible to reboot a UNIX computer from a Telnet session if the account that the person used to log into the Telnet session has permission to do so. Telnet was originally used only on UNIX systems, but is now used on Windows NT and Windows 2000 systems.

Telnet is a protocol used to pass commands and replies between the client and the UNIX computer. All UNIX systems support some form of Telnet. Sometimes a UNIX computer cannot run a server program such as an FTP server or an e-mail server, but you can always count on a Telnet session to work if the operating system is running in a healthy state. In fact, a good reason to use a Telnet session is when a system administrator is troubleshooting a problem with an e-mail server or the FTP server is not running properly.

There are several ways to initiate a Telnet session. For example, if you want to create a Telnet session on the computer, mydomain.com at the default Telnet port 23, you can:

- Use the Windows 9x graphical version of Telnet. To run this program, click Start on the taskbar, then click Run. In the Run dialog box type **Telnet mydomain.com 23**.

- You can also open a web browser and enter **Telnet mydomain.com 23** in the URL address box. The web browser senses that you want a Telnet session and opens the Telnet window. It then passes the host and port information to the Telnet utility to open the session.

- Another way you can initiate a Telnet session on the course.com computer using a Telnet utility is to enter this URL in a web browser: **telnet://mydomain.com:23**. On a Windows 9x PC, this action can open a HyperTerminal window, which can serve as a Telnet client. HyperTerminal is a Windows 9x communications utility that can be used in several situations, including as a Telnet client.

- Some web sites are designed to create a link to a Telnet connection. Click on the link and a Telnet utility such as HyperTerminal pops up and accesses a UNIX server. You must then enter a user ID to begin the Telnet session. The next example uses this method.

Many libraries have their online card catalogs available through a Telnet session that is accessed via the World Wide Web. When you log into a library card catalog via a Telnet session, you can search the card catalog, just as if you were sitting at a terminal in the library. For example, follow these directions to access the card catalog of the Free Library of Philadelphia:

1. Using a web browser, access the Free Library of Philadelphia's web site at *www.library.phila.gov*.

2. Click the link to the Catalog. The resulting web page says that if you have access to a Telnet utility, you can use the online catalog and that the user ID is FLPNET.

3. Click the link to Information Gateway. The Windows 9x HyperTerminal window opens, showing the login screen for the UNIX server, which is shown in Figure 4-14. Enter the user ID **FLPNET**. Directions on how to use the catalog display.

4. When you finish, type **Quit** to close the session.

4

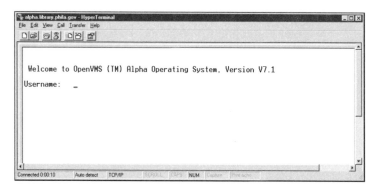

Figure 4-14   HyperTerminal can be used as a Windows 9x Telnet utility

The next example uses Telnet to read e-mail messages and then delete the messages from the server. The commands issued in the session are the same commands that an e-mail client would use to perform the same chores. Follow these directions to log in to your e-mail server and read your mail using Telnet. These directions use a graphical version of Telnet that comes with Windows 9x.

1. Click **Start** on the toolbar, then click **Run**. Type **Telnet** in the Run dialog box. The Telnet window opens.

2. Click **Connect** on the menu bar and then click **Remote System** to open the Connect dialog box, which is shown in Figure 4-15.

3. Enter the name of your POP server. (Remember that POP servers were discussed earlier in this chapter.) The example here uses pop.ga.prestige.net.

4. Enter 110 as the port. (Recall that a POP3 e-mail server uses port 110. If we had wanted to issue UNIX commands in a Telnet session, we would have entered port 23, the default Telnet port.)

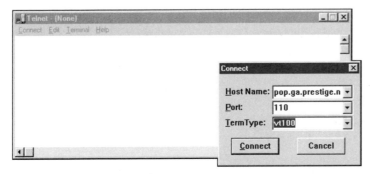

Figure 4-15 Use the Windows 98 Telnet utility to log into a UNIX computer

5. Leave the terminal type at the default value, VT100. Originally, UNIX computers were accessed using mainframe terminals and VT100 was a popular terminal type. When you select VT100, the UNIX computer sends characters formatted for this terminal, which the Telnet client software interprets and displays accordingly. Click **Connect** to connect to the remote computer. Figure 4-16 shows the opening reply of the POP server.

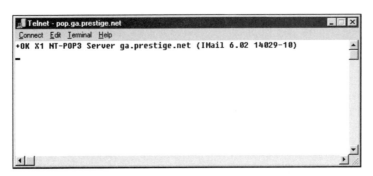

Figure 4-16 After connecting to the e-mail server using Telnet, the server responds with an +OK reply

6. Log in to the e-mail server with your e-mail account and password, using the **POP** commands **USER** and **PASS**. See Figure 4-17 for an example of the screen.

7. Type **LIST** to list the messages and their sizes.

8. Use the **RETR x** (where x is the number of the message you want to see) command to display the contents of a message. Notice that in this raw method of displaying e-mail messages, the header information is clearly visible.

9. After reading a message, use the **DELE x** (where x is the number of the message you want to delete) command to delete it from the server.

10. When finished, use the **QUIT** command to end the session.

11. Close the Telnet window.

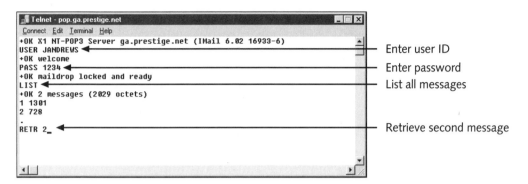

Figure 4-17   Using Telnet, you can read e-mail on an e-mail server using POP commands

NEWSGROUPS

Recall from Chapter 1 that a **newsgroup** is a service on the Internet or private network where a group of people can post articles and responses to those articles, so that information can be shared among the members of the group. Most ISPs subscribe to a newsgroup network and provide a newsgroup server to their customers. The most popular newsgroup network is UseNet; an example of a UseNet newsgroup is news:rec.sport.skating.ice.recreational, which is a newsgroup devoted to the discussion of recreational ice skating.

A newsgroup uses the client/server model. A news server runs on a computer at the ISP. Newsgroup client capabilities are built in to most web browsers. Both Internet Explorer and Netscape Navigator support newsgroups.

You can access a newsgroup by entering the URL of the group in a browser address box. For example, if you enter **news:alt.binaries.pictures.animals** you access a newsgroup devoted to animal photography. When you access a newsgroup, your browser opens your e-mail client software (for example, Outlook Express) so you can view and respond to newsgroup messages. Figure 4-18 shows an example of the newsgroup capabilities of Outlook Express. Click on a news article to view the message. In this example, there is a photograph of cats showing in the window.

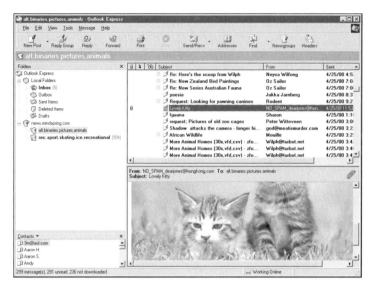

Figure 4-18   Outlook Express is used as a newsgroup client—click on an article to view it

A newsgroup uses the **NNTP** (**Network News Transfer Protocol**) protocol. This protocol works much like SMTP, whereby commands are issued from the client or requesting server as character-based words with arguments following, and replies come from the news server in the form of numeric codes with descriptive text following.

The NNTP protocol has commands that allow a news server to request only those articles it does not already have. An earlier newsgroup protocol, UUCP (UNIX to UNIX copy), sent all of the articles from one server to any other server that requested news from it. This method of indiscriminately sending messages to every host is called **flooding** and results in unnecessary traffic on the Internet.

Figure 4-19 shows an example of how news servers relate to one another and to clients. There are no centralized news servers; each news server carries the same authority as any other server. If a server is configured to get its news from another news server, the server receiving the news is called the slave server. A client connects to a newsgroup by way of an individual server and has access to the news on this one server.

An article in a newsgroup is identified by a Message ID. The NNTP protocol is designed so that a server will not receive duplicate articles (two articles with the same Message ID) and so that two news servers can pass articles in either direction between them. There is also the provision that if a new article has the same message as another article (same body, but different Message ID), the new article will be deleted. This action is done by a robot, a program that automatically runs on the Internet. This robot is called a **cancelbot** and it prevents the Internet and news servers from getting bogged down with redundant information.

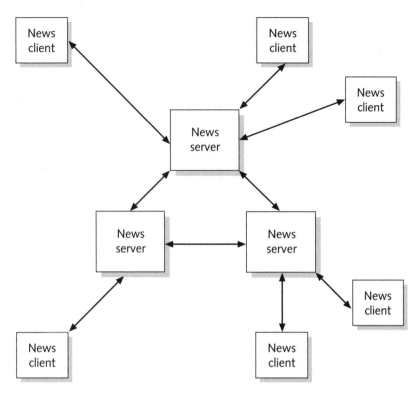

4

Figure 4-19   A news server or client can request news or send news to others using the NNTP protocol. A server can connect to multiple servers or clients, but a client can connect to only a single server

Looking at Figure 4-19, if a client connects to a news server to get news, the dialogue is similar to that in Table 4-6. The same dialogue can also happen between any two servers in the news network. One server gets its news by making the request from another server in the news network. If a server requests a list of articles from another server, it scans the list and requests articles that it does not already have, thus eliminating unnecessary traffic on the Internet.

Table 4-6   Sample dialogue between a newsgroup client and server or between two servers

Client or Server	Command or Reply	Description
Server:		Listening on port 119
Client:	Requests session with news.myserver.com port 119	TCP request for connection to server at port 119
Server:	200 news.myserver.com ready	Connection confirmed
Client:	LIST	What are your current newsgroups?

Table 4-6   Sample dialogue between a newsgroup client and server or between two servers (continued)

Client or Server	Command or Reply	Description
Server:	215	My list follows
Server:	rec.sport.skating.ice.recreational 10 490 500 rec.sport.skating.ice.figure 5 200 205 (others follow)	For this newsgroup, there are 10 articles, number 490-500 For this newsgroup, there are 5 articles, number 200-205
Client:	GROUP rec.sport.skating.ice.figure	I'm interested in this group
Server:	211 5 200 205 rec.sport.skating.ice.figure	Here's what I have about that group
Client:	HEAD 200	Send me the header information for article 200
Server:	221 200 (header follows)	Here is the header for article 200
Client:	ARTICLE 200	Send me the entire article, header and body
Server:	220 200 (article follows)	Here it is
Client:	QUIT	That's all. I'm done.
Server:	205	Goodbye

GOPHERS

A **Gopher** system is a distribution service for text files on the Internet that runs on a UNIX computer using the **Gopher protocol**. Gophers have been largely replaced by the World Wide Web, but occasionally you still see a gopher service running, especially at universities, so you need to be aware of what they are and how they work.

A gopher service runs on a UNIX computer and is responsible for tracking the documents available on the server in the form of a hierarchical site menu called **gopher space**. When you access the service, you can browse the Gopher space by searching through these top-down lists. Locate in the list the article or document you want and the Gopher service finds the article on the server and displays it. Using a web browser, you can enter a Gopher URL like this: **gopher://gopher.tc.umn.edu/**

The resulting Gopher site displays. Figure 4-20 shows the Gopher site at the University of Minnesota. Most web browsers, including Netscape Navigator and Internet Explorer can handle the Gopher protocol.

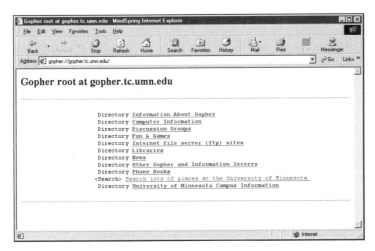

Figure 4-20 A Gopher space is a collection of documents managed by a Gopher service

REAL PEOPLE, REAL PROBLEMS, REAL SOLUTIONS
TOUCHY FTP!

"These HTML files are a mess!" This was a common thought that ran through Tony Burn's mind whenever he would download a web page file from his company's web server. Tony was a graphic designer and used the straightforward Macintosh system to produce eye-catching images for print media. Now the firm that Tony worked for, a large advertising agency, had asked him to learn to edit web pages for the company's site. Along with Tony, they employed the help of a developer who was familiar with their site. The developer's job was to modify the page architecture so that Tony could update the content.

Once the developer placed the modified pages on the web server, Tony used FETCH, a Macintosh FTP utility, to download the files. When they arrived, they were garbled, unformatted and full of unusual characters. Tony would then use BBEdit on his Macintosh, an ASCII text editor similar to Notepad, to go through the code and make it understandable, at least in BBEdit.

After two weeks of painstaking work straightening out the code of each page he downloaded, Tony decided to talk to the developer about the problems he was having. After some testing and discussion, they discovered that Tony was downloading HTML files to his Macintosh via FTP in binary format. The server that was handling the company's web site ran on a UNIX platform, which can be very sensitive to file format.

After the problem was found, file editing was no longer so time consuming! Tony began downloading the HTML files in ASCII format, which kept the properties of the pages intact, allowing him to import the files into BBEdit with no problem. Tony could now focus on design rather than garbled code.

> However, not long after this experience, Tony learned that if he transferred an image file in ASCII format, when it should have been binary, the file arrived on a UNIX computer in a condition unusable by the web server. That's when Tony Burns learned to be very careful when using FETCH to make certain the transfer type was set correctly!

CHAPTER SUMMARY

❐ E-mail uses the SMTP protocol to send text messages over the Internet, and uses the POP or IMAP protocol when an e-mail client requests messages stored on its e-mail server.

❐ Software settings and user preferences are sometimes stored in an initialization file with an INI file extension, or in the Windows Registry.

❐ Both INI files and the Windows Registry can be manually edited, although it is usually better to make changes using the tools available within the software that use these settings.

❐ An e-mail client can use one server to send e-mail (SMTP server) and another to receive e-mail (POP or IMAP server).

❐ SMTP is typical of many client/server protocols in the TCP/IP suite of protocols in that character-based commands are issued from the client, and the server replies with numeric codes.

❐ SMTP dialogs can be viewed by support personnel when troubleshooting problems with e-mail servers.

❐ When a client and server user the POP protocol, the server replies to each command with a positive (+OK) response or a negative (-ERR) response.

❐ IMAP offers the ability to archive old messages in folders on the server, shared mailboxes, multiple mail servers for users, and the ability to only read header information about an attached file without having to download the file. Note that these are enhancements not offered by POP.

❐ Some examples of e-mail servers are Microsoft Exchange Server, NTMail and ITHouse Mail Server.

❐ Mailing list software is called a list server. Examples of list servers are LISTSERV, Lyris, Listproc and NTList.

❐ MIME is a protocol used to transport files attached to e-mail messages and web pages across the Internet.

❐ Uuencode and uudecode on UNIX systems and BinHex on Macintosh computers were two early methods for sending attached files with e-mail messages. The two methods converted the files to a 7-bit format similar to ASCII text that is acceptable to the SMTP protocol.

4

- ❑ An HTTP header to a web page or an SMTP header to an e-mail message contain information about the MIME file type associated with the web page or message.

- ❑ MIME normally uses Base64 or quoted-printable encoding to convert files to a format that SMTP can handle.

- ❑ When an attached file reaches an e-mail client, the client either displays the file or calls on a helper application or external viewer to display the file to the user.

- ❑ MIME file types are identified by a type category followed by a slash and then a subcategory such as Image/gif or Image/jpg.

- ❑ The MIME file types are text, multipart, application, message, image, audio, video, and model. There are many subtypes. Each subtype has one or more file extensions associated with it.

- ❑ Anyone can request that a new MIME file type be recognized by the Internet community by submitting the proper documentation to IANA, the organization responsible for registering MIME file types.

- ❑ An anonymous FTP site does not require a login and is commonly used as a place to get software updates and patches.

- ❑ FTP sites can be accessed by client software such as web browsers, operating system command utilities, or GUI software dedicated to FTP, such as FTP Pro.

- ❑ Telnet is used by UNIX administrators as a method of controlling a UNIX computer remotely.

- ❑ Another use of Telnet is for remote access to a UNIX system by the public, via the World Wide Web; for example, in the case of a library that makes its card catalog available from its web site.

- ❑ UseNet and ClariNet are two examples of newsgroup systems that allow their subscribers to use the Internet to post, read, and respond to articles about a designated subject in a subject-related community of users.

- ❑ Each newsgroup article is assigned a unique Message ID to identify the article. The NNTP protocol used by newsgroup software allows a client or server to receive an article only one time and cull out duplicate articles.

- ❑ A Gopher is a service running on a UNIX computer that manages and provides access to a list of documents stored in a top-down tree called the Gopher space. Gophers have been mostly replaced by the World Wide Web.

KEY TERMS

822 messages — Error messages that occur during e-mail transactions. 822 messages are named after RFC 822, which is the RFC that defines them.

anonymous FTP site — An FTP site that does not require a user to log in with a valid ID or password. Anonymous FTP sites are used to download files, but not used to receive uploaded files.

ASCII files — Text files stored in ASCII format. ASCII stands for the American Standard Code for Information Interchange. ASCII characters are 7-bit characters; each character is assigned a number from 0 to 255. Compare to binary files.

base64 — An encoding method used by MIME to convert a binary file to a 7-bit ASCII text file format so that it can be attached to an e-mail message.

batch file — A file with a .BAT file extension that contains a list of DOS-like commands to be executed as a group.

binary files — Files that use all 8 bits in a byte and are usually not readable by humans. Binary files include graphics files, executable files, sound files; any type of file that is not in ASCII format. Compare to ASCII files.

BinHex — A program used by an Apple Macintosh computer to convert a binary file to a 7-bit ASCII text file format so that it can be attached to an e-mail message. Another BinHex program on the receiving computer must convert the file back to binary.

cancelbot — An Internet robot used by news servers to cull out articles that have the same body content as other articles in order to avoid unnecessary traffic on the Internet and avoid wasting server resources.

denial of service attack — A malicious flooding of messages to an Internet site designed to overwhelm and ultimately disable the site.

dialogue — A series of transmissions between two computers that accomplishes a task such as sending an e-mail message.

external viewer — *See* helper application.

flooding — The indiscriminate sending of messages to every host connected to a computer, which can be a waste of network resources.

FTP (File Transfer Protocol) — The protocol used to transfer files over the Internet such that the file does not need to be converted to ASCII format before transferring.

FTP Site — A computer that is running an FTP server application.

Gopher — A distribution system for text documents stored on UNIX computers. A Gopher is the service responsible for tracking the documents and presenting them to users who access the system.

Gopher protocol — The protocol used by a Gopher service. *See* Gopher.

Gopher space — The top-down hierarchical structure of all the documents on a UNIX computer that is managed by a Gopher server.

helper application — An application used by e-mail client software to interpret and display an attached file to the user. Also called external viewer.

IMAP (Internet Message Access Protocol) — An e-mail protocol that has more functionality than its predecessor, POP. IMAP can archive messages in folders on the e-mail server and can allow the user to choose to not download attachments to files.

IMAP4 (Internet Message Access Protocol, version 4) — Version 4 of the IMAP protocol. *See* IMAP.

initialization file (INI file) — A text file that contains information about application setup and user preferences, which is read by an application when the application first loads.

list server — Software to maintain and manage a list of e-mail addresses and messages to multiple addresses on the list.

MAPI — A specification that allows an application to interact with an e-mail client to send and receive e-mail.

MIME (Multipurpose Internet Mail Extensions) — A protocol that allows non-text files to be attached to e-mail messages or downloaded to a web browser along with a web page. MIME identifies a file as belonging to a category and a subcategory such as Image/gif. Files are encoded using a method that the SMTP protocol can handle when it processes the e-mail message.

newsgroup — An Internet or private network service that provides a forum for group members to post articles and respond to them.

NNTP (Network News Transfer Protocol) — The protocol used by newsgroup server and client software.

POP (Post Office Protocol) — The protocol used by an e-mail server and client when the client requests to download e-mail messages. POP is being slowly outdated by the IMAP protocol. *See* IMAP.

POP account — The name of an e-mail account on an e-mail server where a user receives messages.

POP3 (Post Office Protocol, version 3**)** — Version 3 of the POP protocol. *See* POP.

quoted-printable — An encoding method used by MIME to convert a text-based file to a 7-bit format so that it can be attached to an e-mail message.

SMTP (simple mail transfer protocol) — The protocol used by e-mail clients and servers to send e-mail messages over the Internet. *See* POP and IMAP.

Telnet — A program that allows a computer to be controlled from a remote computer. Telnet applications use the Telnet protocol.

Trivial FTP — A file transfer protocol, similar to FTP, with fewer commands, usually used for multicasting.

Unicode — A 16-bit character set that is expected to ultimately replace ASCII. Unicode includes most of the world's writing systems including the Asian character set.

UseNet — A popular and free system of newsgroups on the Internet containing thousands of newsgroups.

Uudecode — The program that converts a uuencoded file back into the original binary file that it was before it was attached to an e-mail message. *See* uuencode.

Uuencode — An encoding program on a UNIX computer that converts a binary file to a format that can be attached to an e-mail message using the SMTP protocol. Uuencode files have a .UU or .UUE file extension. *See* uudecode.

REVIEW QUESTIONS

1. When is the POP protocol used?

2. Name two features that the IMAP protocol offers that the POP protocol does not offer.

3. When configuring e-mail client software, a POP account is used to (receive/send) e-mail and a SMTP server is used to (receive/send) e-mail.

4. When an SMTP server is sending e-mail to another SMTP server, before the SMTP dialogue can begin, what must both servers do?

5. What are the two general replies that a POP server uses to respond to an e-mail client?

6. What is the purpose of a list server? Name one example of commercial list server software.

7. Why must a binary file be converted to some other format before it can be attached to an e-mail message?

8. What operating system uses the programs uuencode and uudecode?

9. What file extension does a BinHex file have?

10. What two encoding methods does MIME normally use?

11. A MIME type is identified by two words separated by a(n) _____.

12. When a client cannot interpret a MIME file, it calls for a(n) _____.

13. What organization is responsible for registering new MIME file types for the general knowledge of the Internet community?

14. What RFC documents the procedure a developer must follow to register a new MIME file type?

15. List eight major categories of MIME file types.

16. Can a web browser understand and use the FTP protocol?

17. What is the FTP command to copy a file from the local computer to the remote computer?

18. What is the FTP command to copy a file from the remote computer to the local computer?

19. What is an FTP site called that does not require a user to log in before accessing files on the site?

20. What is the default port for Telnet?

21. Can a web browser understand and use the Telnet protocol?

22. Name two newsgroup systems that use the Internet to distribute news.

23. What protocol does newsgroup software use?

24. What is the purpose of a cancelbot?

25. What current Internet service has all but replaced Gopher services?

HANDS-ON PROJECTS

RFC Research

1. What RFC gives the protocol and specifications a news server must use to access the UseNet network? Print the first two pages of the RFC.

2. What RFC describes the Gopher protocol? Print the first two pages of the RFC.

3. List 5 RFCs that describe the IMAP protocol. Print the first two pages of one of these RFCs.

Research Internet Server Software

Use the web site *www.serverwatch.com* and other sites linked to this site to research the following information:

1. List two examples of e-mail server software other than those mentioned in the chapter. List three to six features of each software package, and include the web site of the software manufacturer.

2. Find an FTP server product that can run on a Windows 9x or Windows NT Workstation PC requiring few system resources, and can be used by a small business to distribute software upgrades and patches.

3. Give three examples of news servers that can access UseNet listing the features of each. Include the price and the manufacturer's web site.

File Compression Software

Before you attach large files to e-mail messages, it is a good practice to compress the files using compression software such as PKZip or WinZip. Follow these directions to download and use the software.

1. Find a web site where you can download either PKZip or WinZip. Print the web page describing the software.

2. Download and install the software.

3. Use the software to compress a large file. A TIFF file is a good example of a graphics file that needs to be compressed, but any large file will do. Find a file that is at least 300K bytes. The compressed version of the file should have a .ZIP file extension.

4. E-mail the file to a friend or to yourself.

5. Print the e-mail message showing the attached ZIP file. Using Outlook Express, Microsoft Outlook or some other e-mail client that can display the header information, print the header showing the MIME file type in the header.

6. Uncompress the file. What was the size of the file in bytes before and after compression?

Using Newsgroups

If your ISP supports newsgroups, research these newsgroups to find one that is focused on understanding and using the Internet. What relevant newsgroups do you find? Subscribe to one of these newsgroups for a few days. Print one article from the newsgroup.

CASE PROJECTS

Add an E-Mail Link to Your Web Site

Add an e-mail link to your personal web site; when a user clicks on the link, an e-mail client window should pop up to send you an e-mail message. Publish the web page. Print it showing the new link.

To do this, create a hyperlink like this:

```
<A HREF="mailto:youraddress@yourdomain.com">I want to hear
from you!</a>
```

The text "I want to hear from you!" serves as a hyperlink to an e-mail message addressed to you. Substitute your e-mail address for youraddress@yourdomain.com.

5

SIGHTS AND SOUNDS OF THE INTERNET

In this chapter, you will learn

♦ How to enhance a web site with graphics and sound

♦ How you can add streaming audio or video to a web site

♦ About the different multimedia file types and the software needed to support them

♦ How video conferencing on the Internet works

Multimedia is one of the things that makes the Web so interesting! This chapter will be fun as you learn about the many ways that sights and sounds are delivered over the Internet. You'll learn how they can be incorporated into web sites, how audio and video files are created, compressed, transported, and interpreted, and about the many types of software available to work with multimedia files. Video conferencing is a popular newcomer to the Internet, and using the Internet to make video conference calls to locations around the world is now a reality. Because technology is developing at an accelerated pace, this chapter will introduce you to many of these new technologies, as well as older technologies, so you can follow the developments as they happen with a knowledgeable ear and eye. Also, in this chapter you will learn how to add audio, video, and enhanced graphics to web sites, and about the technology needed to support a client that accesses multimedia web sites.

ENHANCING WEB SITES WITH GRAPHICS AND SOUND

Graphics, video and sound are all included on a web site using one of two basic approaches: streaming or non-streaming data. **Non-streaming data** is data that is downloaded as a file from the server to the browser. When the file arrives at the client, the browser interprets the file and displays or plays it to the user or, if the browser does not support the file type, turns to other software for help. With **streaming data** (either audio or video), the browser (with or without the help of other software) receives the data in a continuous stream. The audio or video data is played to the user as it is received. For example, you can watch the latest news clips as streaming video from the CNN website at *www.cnn.com*. See Figure 5-1. Streaming data is discussed later in the chapter.

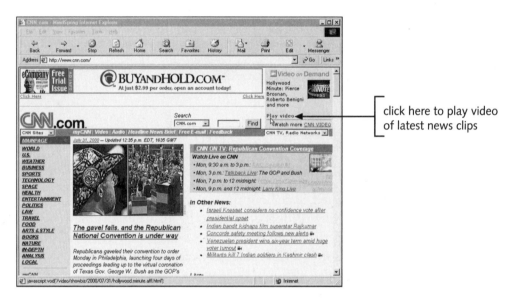

click here to play video of latest news clips

Figure 5-1   Streaming video and audio can be viewed from the CNN web site at *www.cnn.com*

Recall from Chapter 4 that e-mail client software determines a file's type by examining the MIME type declared in the e-mail header information. In the same way, when the browser receives an audio, graphics, or video file, it determines the file type by the MIME file type declared in the HTTP header information.

If the browser does not know how to interpret the file, it must use either a plug-in or a helper application to display the file to the user. Helper applications (sometimes called external viewers), that are used by e-mail applications to display files, were introduced in Chapter 4. A helper application opens the file in a separate window and does not involve the e-mail or browser software.

Plug-ins

A **plug-in**, sometimes called a **browser extension**, is different from a helper application, in that the plug-in enhances the browser, enabling the browser to perform the task. The telltale difference between a plug-in and a helper application is whether or not the software can work independently of a browser (helper application) or whether it requires the browser in order to work (plug-in).

Most plug-ins are developed by third party vendors who create plug-ins and make them available via the World Wide Web. You can find plug-ins that perform all kinds of tasks. Netscape offers links to plug-ins from their web site at *www.netscape.com*. Figure 5-2 shows the Netscape Plug-in Finder, which lists 177 plug-ins. More are being developed every day. Here are some interesting ones:

- Internet Postage at *www.stamps.com* is used to print postage using your computer and printer. Once you sign up for the service, you can use the software to print postage.

- RealAudio at *www.realaudio.com* provides streaming content over the Web. The plug-in allows users to listen to audio over the Internet, and supports .rpm files.

- AnimaFlex by RubberFlex Software can play animations on the Web. The animations that it plays are full screen and are created from small files, usually less than 30K.

- Prizm Plug-in by TMSSequoia allows users to view and change .tif, .gif, .bmp, and .jpg files. The images can be rotated, gray scaled, magnified, and annotated.

- Shockwave by Macromedia is one of the more popular plug-ins. It is used to view and listen to multimedia including graphics and audio.

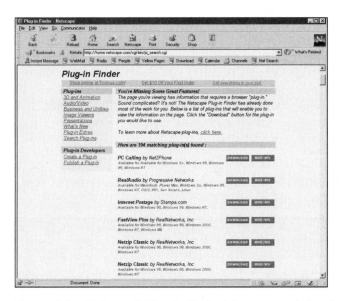

Figure 5-2   Netscape's Plug-in Finder lets you search for plug-ins by platform, file extension, and/or MIME type

These plug-ins can usually be downloaded free of charge through the Netscape site. The manufacturers of the software offer downloads at their sites as well (for example, *www.shockwave.com* and *www.microsoft.com*). Sites like *www.download.com* offer lists of plug-ins that you can search through and download.

Some plug-ins work transparently; that is, you don't even know that the plug-in is helping your browser. Other plug-ins offer you some control over their behavior. For example, the RealAudio plug-in provides a control window that looks like a little CD player, with start and stop buttons, and volume controls. The web page designer decides where and when the plug-in's control window appears.

Most of the time, you do not download a particular plug-in until you have a specific need for it. If a site has files that use plug-ins, it will usually offer you the option of downloading the necessary plug-in. For example, CNN (*www.cnn.com*) uses plug-ins, such as QuickTime for Windows, that allow you to view a video. When you click the video, a program on the web page looks for the plug-in on your hard drive. If you already have the plug-in, the plug-in loads automatically and begins to run. If it is not there, you have the option of downloading the plug-in, as shown in Figure 5-3.

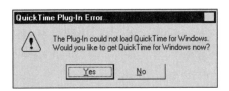

Figure 5-3   When you go to a web site that requires a plug-in that is not installed on your machine, you have the option of downloading the plug-in

If you click the No button, the system does not download the file so you can't view the item that needs the plug-in. If you click the Yes button to download a plug-in, the browser connects to a web site from which you can download the plug-in. In the case of QuickTime, for example, the browser takes you to the QuickTime web site (www.apple.com/quicktime/download). You can follow the directions here to download QuickTime. Other plug-in sites have directions similar to these for downloading QuickTime.

1. Some software vendors, like Apple (the maker of QuickTime), ask for your name and e-mail address and which operating system you are using. Other vendors take you straight to step 4 and do not require that you enter any information.

2. Enter the information requested and click the **Download** button. The File Download dialog box opens, as shown in Figure 5-4.

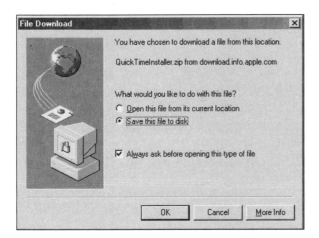

Figure 5-4   Save the plug-in to your hard drive

3. Click the **Save the file to disk** option button and click **OK**. The Save As dialog box opens, shown in Figure 5-5.

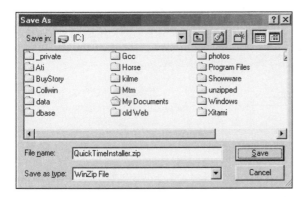

Figure 5-5   When you download a file, remember where you saved the file so you can find it later

4. Choose the directory to which you want to save the file and click **Save.** The file starts downloading to your machine. Once it has finished, the Download Complete dialog box opens, as shown in Figure 5-6.

5

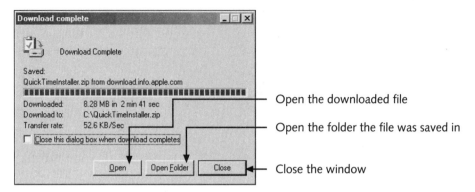

Open the downloaded file

Open the folder the file was saved in

Close the window

Figure 5-6   The download process is complete

> 5. Once the file has been downloaded, it must be installed. Click **Open** and follow the instructions on the screen.

If you are running Netscape Navigator and want to see which plug-ins you currently have installed, you can click About Plug-ins on the Help menu. A list of the plug-ins that are currently installed appears. The list includes which MIME type the plug-in supports, which file types it supports, and whether or not it is enabled. Figure 5-7 shows a sample list of plug-ins as displayed by Netscape.

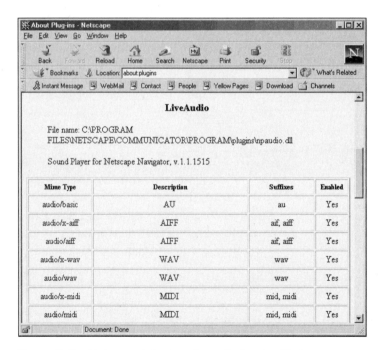

Figure 5-7   Netscape lets you view all plug-ins that are on your computer and what type of files the plug-ins are used with

In the next sections, you will learn how to add audio and video to a web site, and about the different plug-ins that can be used to handle these files. First you'll learn about downloading and playing audio as non-streaming data, and then you'll learn about streaming audio.

Storing Sound in Files

Some popular file types used to store sound are AU, AIFF, MIDI, WAV and MP3 files, although there are several other proprietary type sound files discussed later in the chapter.

- **MIDI (musical instrument digital interface)** sound files are supported by the MPC3 (Multimedia Personal Computer, version 3) standards, which were developed in the early 1990s in an attempt to establish some guidelines for a mushrooming multimedia market. These mostly-outdated standards have had tremendous impact on multimedia technology.

- Sound files called **wave files,** with a .WAV file extension, were developed by Microsoft.

- **AU** files are sound files developed for use on UNIX computers.

- **AIFF** sound files were developed for Apple and Macintosh systems.

- **MP3** is a relatively new type of high-quality sound file that uses MPEG (Moving Picture Experts Group) Version 3 technology, which stores both video and audio in a file using a lossy compression method. **Lossy compression** compresses the data by dropping unnecessary or redundant data.

Audio data, as well as other types of multimedia data, needs to be compressed because when analog data is converted to digital data, the amount of digital data can be quite massive. Sounds are converted to digital data using a microphone and a sound card. You can see a picture of a sound card in Figure 5-8. A sound card receives the analog flow of sound from the microphone and **digitizes** it (converts it to bits: 1s and 0s). This process of approximating an infinite flow of sound such as that received by a microphone into many digital samples is called **sampling**. A sample is taken at a predetermined time interval and then converted to digital data using a predetermined accuracy. The accuracy is stated in bits. An accuracy of 8 bits per sample is not as accurate as 16 bits per sample. This accuracy is commonly referred to as 8-bit or 16-bit sound.

The more samples taken over a period of time, and the more accurate the samples, the more accurate the approximations and ultimate representation of the reproduced sound, but the larger the data file holding those samples. An analogy would be the amount of data collected to measure the height of a mountain at different intervals up the mountain. If you take the measurements every 10 feet and make them accurate to the nearest inch, you will have a much better representation of the mountain than if you take the measurements every 500 feet and make them accurate to the nearest foot, but you will also have much more data. In order to hold many, accurate samples in a data file, the data is often compressed and later decompressed before it is output by the sound card to speakers.

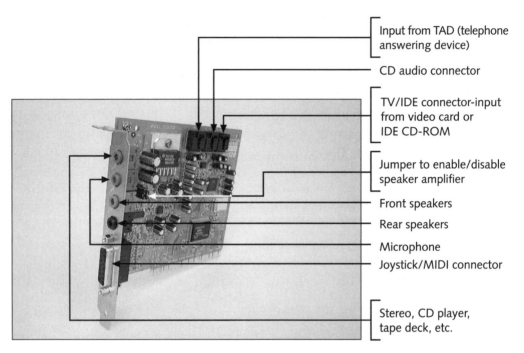

Input from TAD (telephone answering device)

CD audio connector

TV/IDE connector-input from video card or IDE CD-ROM

Jumper to enable/disable speaker amplifier

Front speakers

Rear speakers

Microphone

Joystick/MIDI connector

Stereo, CD player, tape deck, etc.

Figure 5-8 A sound card inputs sound from a microphone and digitizes it so that it can be stored in a sound file

This process of compressing and later decompressing data is called **CODEC** (**compressor/ decompressor**). A CODEC routine that does not drop any data is called lossless compression, as compared to lossy compression. The term CODEC is sometimes used to refer to hardware that converts audio or video signals from analog to digital or from digital to analog. When the term is used this way, it stands for **coder/decoder**.

When you want to include low-quality speech or music sound files on a web site, use either WAV or AU files. For the best quality sound, use MP3 files. There are many sophisticated software applications that allow you to create, edit and add special effects to the different types of sound files. However, if you have a microphone connected to a sound card on your PC, you can use Windows 98 to create a simple WAV sound file:

1. Click **Start** on the Taskbar, and point to **Programs**. Point to **Accessories**, then point to **Entertainment** (or for Windows 95, click **Multimedia**) then click **Sound Recorder**. The Sound window opens. It is illustrated in Figure 5-9.

2. Click the **Record** button (the red dot on the right side of the dialog box) to record, then speak into your PC's microphone. For best results, keep the recording short so the file does not become too large.

3. Click the **Stop** button (the square) when finished.

4. Click **File** on the menu bar, then click **Save As** to save the sound file for later use. By default, Windows saves the file as a .WAV file.

Figure 5-9   Recording sound using Windows 9x

WAV files are easy to create and use, and Internet Explorer and Netscape Navigator support them. The downside is that they can be rather large, so only use them for short introductory sounds.

Adding Sound to a Web Site

Recall from Chapter 3 that to add a graphics file to a web site you store the graphics file on the web site and point to it from a web page using the HTML <IMG> tag. When the web page is downloaded to the browser, the browser scans the page looking for files that are referenced and then requests those files from the server. The server then downloads the file to the browser, which displays it on the page at the location of the <IMG> tag. A sound file can be treated in a similar way using the <BGSOUND>, <EMBED> and <HREF> tags. Remember that you can find a complete list of HTML commands in Appendix C.

Browsers don't generally know how to play sound files without the help of a plug-in or browser extension. Internet Explorer uses Windows Media Player and Netscape Navigator uses LiveAudio which both support AU, AIFF, WAV and MIDI sound files. In addition, Netscape uses Beatnik Player to play **RMF (Rich Music Format)** audio files, which is a proprietary audio file format by Beatnik (see *www.beatnik.com*). Each of these plug-ins provides a window to control volume and to start and stop the sound. The control window can be embedded in the web page as an element on the page much like a graphic. It can also be displayed on the desktop in a separate window, or hidden altogether.

Adding Background Sound to a Web Page

You use a different procedure to add background sound to a web page, depending on whether you are writing for Internet Explorer or Netscape Navigator. Netscape Navigator uses the <EMBED> tag to play a sound file. Some versions of Internet Explorer use only the <BGSOUND> tag and other versions use both <BGSOUND> and <EMBED>.

Background Sounds in Internet Explorer   When you create a web page that will be viewed with Internet Explorer, use the <BGSOUND> tag to create a background sound that plays when your web page is first opened. The plug-in sound window is hidden from view.

Figure 5-10 shows an example of the HTML code for this command. Here's an example of the command:

```
<BGSOUND SRC="chimes.wav" LOOP=1 VOLUME=0>
```

The LOOP attribute determines the number of times the sound file plays (one time in this example) and the VOLUME attribute sets the volume using a value from −10,000 to 0, where 0 is the loudest setting. Place the <BGSOUND> tag inside the <HEAD> tags. Use Internet Explorer and try the example shown in Figure 5-10. Look for the Windows 9x chimes.wav file and other .WAV files in the \Windows\Media folder. Either place the WAV file in the same folder as the web page or, as is customary with web sites, place all sound files in a folder under the web site's root directory named \Sounds. If the files are not in the same folder as the web page, you have to specify where the files are located.

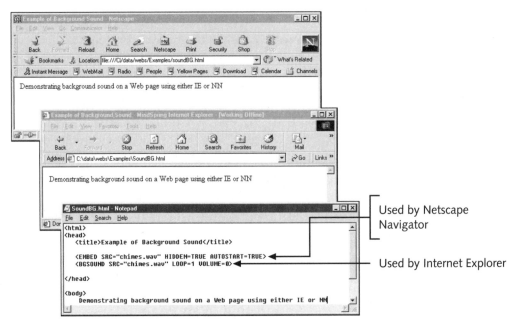

Figure 5-10   Use different methods to add background sound to web pages using Internet Explorer and Netscape Navigator

Background Sounds in Netscape Navigator   The <EMBED> tag was first introduced by Netscape Navigator and later adopted by Internet Explorer, but with a slightly different use. The <EMBED> tag is used to embed any file within a web page. The file can be of any type, including sound and other multimedia file types. You can reference the URL of the plug-in that the browser needs to view or play the file, so that the browser can download the plug-in if it doesn't already have it.

Use the <EMBED> tag to include background sound in a page that will be viewed with Netscape Navigator. (Note that Internet Explorer does not recognize the <EMBED> tag unless it is located within the <BODY> tags; thus, in Internet Explorer, the command doesn't work for background sound). To play the chimes.wav file when the web page is first loaded using Netscape Navigator, use the <EMBED> command within the <HEAD> tags. You can see an example in Figure 5-10:

```
<EMBED SRC="chimes.wav" HIDDEN=TRUE AUTOSTART=TRUE>
```

The AUTOSTART attribute is set to true which causes the sound to play as soon as the page is loaded. The HIDDEN attribute is set to true which causes the sound plug-in to be hidden.

Here's an interesting example of how Navigator can use the <EMBED> tag:

```
<EMBED SRC="chimes.wav" HIDDEN=TRUE AUTOSTART=FALSE>
<A HREF="http://www.yahoo.com"
onmouseover="document.embeds[0].play(false)">Yahoo!</A>
```

In this example, the chimes.wav file is defined in the <EMBED> tag, but not immediately played when the web page is loaded (AUTOSTART=FALSE). Instead, the <A HREF> tag refers to the <EMBED> tag in such a way that, when the user's mouse moves over the hyperlink (onmouseover event) to the *www.yahoo.com* web site, the chimes sound (embeds[0].play). The HTML code and the resulting web page is shown in Figure 5-11. Note that the attribute to the PLAY command is (false). If you change it to (true) then the chimes continue to play without stopping even after the mouse is no longer over the hyperlink.

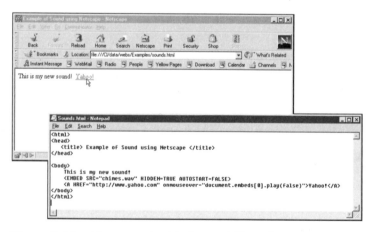

Figure 5-11 Use an embedded sound file to highlight a hyperlink

Sound Files as Hyperlinks

In the previous examples, you saw how to use the <EMBED> and <BGSOUND> tags to put sound files on a web page. You can also place hyperlinks to sound files on your web pages. Simply refer to the sound file name when using the <A HREF> tag:

```
<a href="example.au">Looney Tunes Theme Tune</a>
```

Figures 5-12 and 5-13 show the results of this command in both Netscape Navigator and Internet Explorer. The sound plug-ins for each browser display in a separate window when a sound file is referenced using the <HREF> tag. When you click on the hyperlink in the web page, the plug-in pops up and the sound file plays.

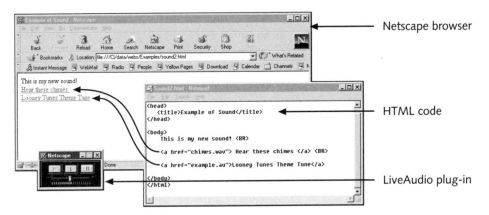

Netscape browser

HTML code

LiveAudio plug-in

Figure 5-12   Netscape Navigator uses LiveAudio to play sound files

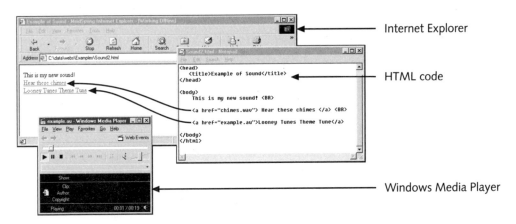

Internet Explorer

HTML code

Windows Media Player

Figure 5-13   Internet Explorer uses Windows Media Player to play sound files

Streaming Audio

In the previous examples, a sound file was downloaded to the browser and then played using a plug-in. This section looks at streaming audio, whereby the sound data is continuously fed from the server to the browser and played as it is received. Neither Internet Explorer nor Netscape Navigator provide built-in support for streaming audio. Both these browsers require that you download a plug-in that can interpret the streaming audio data.

Streaming audio can be stored on a file on the web server, or it can be live streaming data, such as when a live concert or radio is played over the Internet from a web site. For example, to locate the web site of a radio station playing live on the Internet, see *www.broadcast.com*. Click on a link to go to the radio station web site. There you'll find instructions for listening. The site will most likely support one or both of the two most popular plug-ins for streaming audio, either Windows Media Player or RealPlayer G2.

RealPlayer G2 by RealNetworks supports both audio and video streaming data. You can download a free version of the plug-in from *www.real.com*. Windows Media Player by Microsoft also supports both video and audio streaming data and can be downloaded from *www.microsoft.com* at no cost. In order to see and hear streaming data (video and audio), you must have a plug-in installed on your computer since the browsers do not have built-in support for streaming data.

Offering Streaming Data on Your Web Site

If you want to provide streaming audio from your web site, you require a special server to broadcast the data and software to prepare the data. RealNetworks (*www.realnetworks.com*) is one example of a company that provides streaming data servers for web sites. They offer a product called RealServer Basic, which you can download from their web site. RealServer Basic is a 25-stream server, which means that the server has 25 simultaneous sessions of live or on-demand streaming. For larger web sites, or if you wish to run multiple copies of the server, RealNetworks offers RealServer Plus, a 60-stream server, that can be purchased from RealNetworks web site.

Streaming data uses the UDP protocol rather than TCP to transmit the data from the server to the client. Because UDP is not a guaranteed protocol, sometimes quality is not high because packets can be lost. To get around the reduction in quality caused by lost packets, RealNetworks uses an interleave technology, whereby the data is delivered in a staggered fashion so that a few lost packets don't result in an overall decrease in quality. Another difficulty is that UDP packets are sometimes not allowed through an intranet's firewall; those who are connected to the Internet through a firewall are not able to receive streaming data. A firewall is software designed to prevent unauthorized use of an intranet, and is discussed in more detail in Chapter 12.

In addition to UDP, streaming audio and video software use the **RTP (Real Time Transport Protocol)**, which uses **RTSP (Real Time Streaming Protocol)**. You can use **RSVP (Resource Reservation Setup Protocol)** to avoid lost packets by making a bandwidth reservation. RSVP is used with **multicasting**, when one source is sending data to multiple recipients. In effect, a connection is established that is not dropped as long as the data is streaming.

RSVP allows you to reserve bandwidth between your PC and the source. For example, if you know that a certain video is going to be multicast next Wednesday, you may want to reserve a spot so that you can view the video. You first send in an RSVP request (if your browser doesn't offer an RSVP program, you need a separate program to do this). The request goes to the Internet gateway, which will determine if your bandwidth can be met without interfering with others who have already RSVP'd. If it can be, the RSVP request is sent to the next gateway, and the process continues until all the gateways along the route have reserved your bandwidth. If one gateway cannot reserve the bandwidth, all reservations are cancelled.

RSVP has some problems. One problem is that all the network equipment between the source and destination must recognize and support RSVP. If you send an RSVP request through a router which does not recognize the request, it will be denied. In addition, the system provides no way of monitoring or controlling who can send RSVP requests. This could easily result in the system being abused by users who always make these kinds of reservations.

Sometimes streaming data is first buffered on the client in order to get a head start on the data presentation. A buffer of, for example, 15 seconds of data, means that the player can more easily adjust for lulls in data transmission so that it can smooth out the rough spots of presentation.

Metafiles

Any web page that uses streaming data must contain a specific link to a file called a metafile. A **metafile** is a file that contains information about other files. In this situation, it contains the location and filename of the audio or video data. Look at the following example:

> Name of the metafile: **filename1.ram**
> Contents of the metafile: **pnm://server.name.ext/filename2.rm**

Metafiles list the protocol first (**pnm** in the example above). Then the server name is listed, and the filename is listed last. The metafile does not contain the audio or video data, but rather points to a file that does contain the data. The streaming data process, shown in Figure 5-14, works like this:

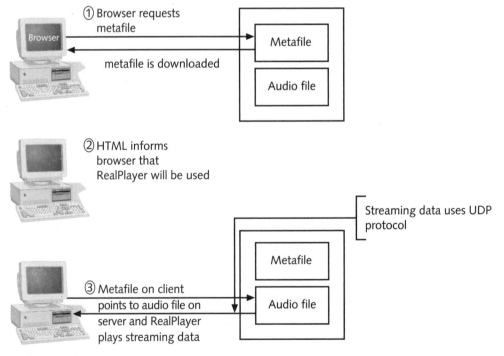

Figure 5-14   Streaming audio technology uses a metafile to point to an audio file on server

- The web page requests the metafile, which is downloaded to the client.

- The <EMBED> or <OBJECT> tag informs the browser of the type of plug-in that is required

- If the browser does not have the plug-in, it points to the URL of the plug-in software (for example, *www.realnetworks.com*) and downloads the plug-in.

- The plug-in is loaded and creates a link to the data on the server as identified by the metafile.

- The streaming data from the server to the client is processed by the plug-in.

With RealPlayer, the audio data is stored on the server in a file with an .RM file extension and the metafile has a .RAM file extension. The metafile is a text file that contains a single URL to the .RM file.

Graphics on Web Pages

Graphics can add interest and generate enthusiasm for your web site, and can promote interaction as shown in Figure 5-15. The single bird on the left is constantly revolving and can be controlled with your mouse. The large graphic on the page contains several hyperlinks. When a graphic is used in this manner, it is called an **image map** or **clickable map**. As you saw in Chapter 3, you can easily include graphics files on web pages. Animation can be included as well, by using animated graphics files, movies and sophisticated plug-ins. This section examines the different graphics file types and explains how to put them on web pages.

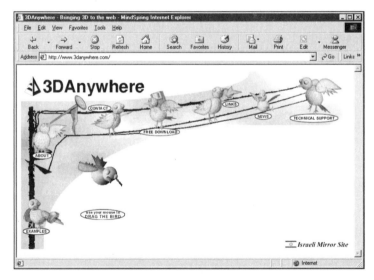

Figure 5-15   Graphics add interest to a site and can promote interaction

Graphic File Types

Graphics files can be categorized as either bit-mapped images or vector images. A **bit-mapped image**, sometimes called a **raster image**, is composed of many small colored or gray dots that, when viewed as a whole, look like an image. **Vector images**, sometimes called **object images**, are created by mathematical equations that communicate to the software how to draw lines and shapes to create the image. Bit-mapped files are easier to import from one software application to another than vector images, because bit-mapped files are easy to display—the software does little more than display a lot of dots. However, the images in bit-mapped files don't enlarge as well as those of vector images. When a bit-mapped image is enlarged, the number of dots don't increase—just the size of each dot increases—so the resolution of the image does not change with the size of the image. See Figure 5-16 a and b for an example of an enlarged bit-mapped image. With vector images, the software completely redraws the image according to the new measurements, so the resulting quality is better.

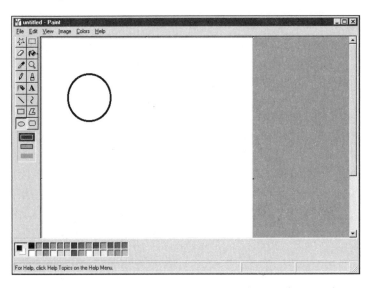

Figure 5-16a   A bit-mapped image is made up of many dots

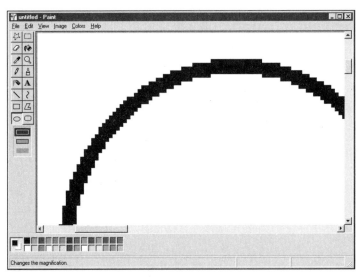

Figure 5-16b   Quality is lost when a bit-mapped image is enlarged

Listed below are several graphic file types that are used on the Web, and information about them.

GIF and GIF89 Files   GIF (Graphical Interchange Format) files are probably the most popular graphics files on the Web. Because they are bit-mapped files, most browsers and other software can easily read them. The **GIF89** version of GIF files supports animation, one transparent background color, and interlacing.

A **transparent background** is a background that is designed to display as the same color as the background of the web page. Often a graphic has a background that is not part of the picture. If the background is transparent, it is not noticed, because it is displayed as the background of the web page. If it is not transparent, the user can see the background of the graphic. Figure 5-17 shows examples of figures with transparent, and non-transparent backgrounds.

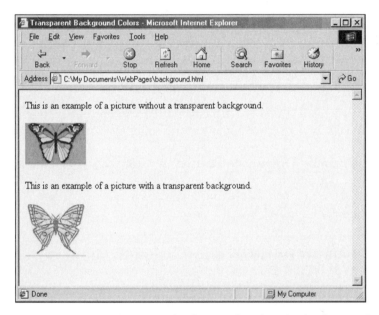

Figure 5-17   A transparent background makes the background of the graphic the same as the background of the web page

Graphics that are **interlaced** are downloaded to a web page in layers so that the first layer draws the graphic from top to bottom with a hazy appearance. Each successive layer makes the graphic appear sharper and clearer. Downloading graphics in this way is more acceptable to many users because they can see how the entire graphic will look without having to wait too long. Graphics that are not interlaced are completely drawn in one pass, from top to bottom, and the user must wait until all the graphic is downloaded to see the entire image.

JPEG Files   JPEG (Joint Photographic Experts Group) files, first introduced in Chapter 3, have a JPG file extension and are most often used to store photographs. JPEG files are more compressed than GIF files because they use a lossy compression method. JPEG files do not support animation, but do support a type of interlacing that makes the photograph appear to fade in slowly on the page. This type of file is called **progressive JPEG**.

PNG Files   PNG (**Portable Network Graphics**) files are a relatively new type of graphic files that use lossless compression, support interlacing and one transparent background color, but do not support animation.

BMP Files   BMP (**Bit-mapped**) files are produced by paint programs such as Microsoft Paint. They are an older type of graphics file that doesn't support high resolution, animation, interlacing or compression. Because they are not compressed and most browsers don't support BMP files, they are not used much on the Web. BMP files are popular on PCs because they are so easy to create and most computers have software to support them.

TIFF Files   TIFF (**Tagged Image File Format**) files are popular for desktop publishing applications. They are often used for photographs and screen captures as well as other graphics. They are bit-mapped images that can use either lossless or lossy compression and offer strong support for color. TIFF files can be rather large and are not supported by most browsers without a plug-in, so they are not as popular on the Web as other file types.

PDF Files   PDF (**Portable Document Format**) is a proprietary file type from Adobe Systems. PDF files are designed to retain the original formatting and yet be easy for anyone to view and print. They are a popular way to deliver software documentation electronically, especially for software that is available via download. You can see an example of a PDF file in Figure 5-18.

PDF files can be created from many different types of electronic documents including word processing files, scanned images, and even web sites. After you create the file, you can use Adobe software to convert the file to the PDF format. PDF files are images of the formatted document and therefore don't allow the user to edit the file. Think of a PDF file as a picture of a formatted document rather than the document itself. PDF files must be viewed by Adobe Acrobat Reader, which is distributed for free. Acrobat Reader is downloaded to the client PC and used as a helper application to read a PDF file. For more information, see the Adobe web site at *www.adobe.com*.

RTF Files   RTF (**Rich Text Format**) files are created by most word processors so that the file can be sent to a user with a different word processor. The files are written using only ASCII codes. The document's formatting is lost when the file is distributed to others, but the ability to edit the file is retained. Compare RTF files to PDF files: a PDF file retains the original formatting of a document file when the file is distributed to others, but, in the process, the ability to edit the file is lost; an RTF file loses the original formatting of a document file when the file is distributed to others, but retains the ability to be edited.

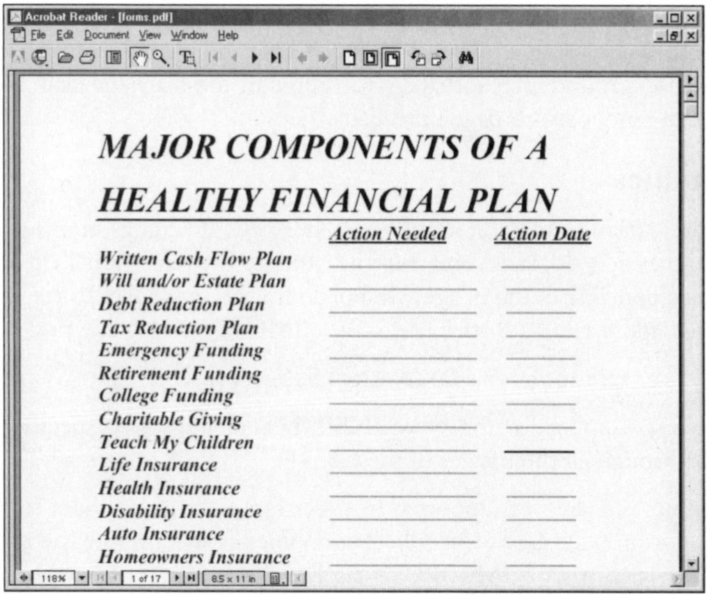

Figure 5-18   PDF files viewed by Acrobat Reader cannot be edited but retain their original formatting

PostScript and EPS Files   **PostScript** is a proprietary technology developed by Adobe Systems (*www.adobe.com*) to allow a software application, such as a word processor or a page layout program, to send commands to a printer that tell the printer how to print a document. PostScript is a **page description language** (**PDL**), which is a language that does more than allow the software to pass the document to the printer; it gives the software the ability to describe to the printer exactly how it wants the printed document to look. PostScript requires a printer that can interpret the commands. PostScript printers cost more than comparable printers that don't understand the PostScript language. The commands sent to the printer are stored in a file with a .PS file extension. An **Encapsulated PostScript** (**EPS**) file contains the PostScript commands as well as a preview image of what the final printed output will look like. PostScript files are only useful on the Web to distribute documents to be printed on a PostScript printer.

> **TIP**   A search engine web site dedicated to helping you locate graphics and photographs on the web in many file formats is *www.ditto.com*.

Web Page Backgrounds

Background texture can add interest to a page and improve its look and feel. To add a background graphic to a web page, use the BACKGROUND attribute of the <BODY> tag like this:

```
<BODY BACKGROUND="texture.gif">
```

This command displays the contents of the texture.gif file to look as though it were the paper on which your web page was printed. Both GIF and JPG files can be used for backgrounds. Beware of background images that are too dense or too busy; they can distract from your message and can render a web page unreadable.

Animated Graphics

Recall from Chapter 3 that GIF files can store animated images. An animated image is made up of several images, and each is displayed one after the other to give the overall effect of animation. A single GIF file contains all the images wrapped into this single file. To use an animated image on a web page, add the LOOP attribute to the <IMG SRC> tag like this:

```
<IMG SRC="animated.gif" LOOP=INFINITE>
```

You can substitute any number for the word INFINITE in the tag to specify how many times the file loops through all the images in the file.

Some types of graphics files are not supported by older browsers. If you want to create your image tags so that, if a browser cannot handle the graphics, it will replace the graphic with text, use the ALT attribute to the <IMG SRC> tag like this:

```
<IMG SRC="Mygraphic.gif" ALT="Your browser does not support
this file type.">
```

You can also control the size of the graphic on your page with the HEIGHT and WIDTH attributes. For example:

```
<IMG SRC="Mygraphic.gif" WIDTH="550" HEIGHT="100">
```

The values for width and height are given in pixels. A **pixel** is the smallest unit of space on a monitor screen that can be addressed by software. The resolution of a monitor screen is measured in pixels (for example, 1024 by 768 pixels).

Figure 5-19 shows three frames of an animated graphic. In the figure, notice that the feather moves to the right in each frame. When the frames are played back-to-back, it looks like the feather is moving to the right. In order to show the feather waving (moving to the right and then back again), frames one and two are shown twice in the animation, so that the animation consists of five frames shown in this order: 1, 2, 3, 2, 1. When the animation is continuously repeated, the feather appears to be waving.

The animation shown in Figure 5-19 was created from a single graphic using Janc's Paint Shop Pro. Paint Shop Pro is a graphics and animation software package that lets you modify graphics and use those graphics to create animation. The company offers a 30-day trial version of the software that can be downloaded from the product web page (*www.jasc.com/psp.html*).

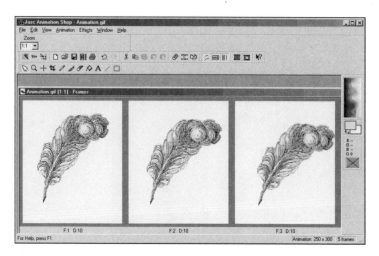

Figure 5-19   An animated file is several images combined together to create the effect that the image is moving

Creating Images   The first step to creating an animation is to modify a graphic so that you have images for each frame of the animation. In the example, the feather has five frames, but only three images are used. Two of the images are used twice. You can create your own animation by downloading the trial version of Paint Ship Pro and installing it on your computer. Use Paint Shop Pro to create a .gif file or download a copyright-free graphics file from the Internet. Then follow these directions:

1. Start Paint Shop Pro by clicking **Start** on the Taskbar.

2. Point to **Programs**, then point to **Paint Shop Pro 6**, and then click **Paint Shop Pro 6**. The Paint Shop Pro title screen appears.

3. Click **Start**. The first time you run Paint Shop Pro, the File Format Associations window opens. In this window you need to tell Paint Shop Pro what types of graphics files to use. Click the option button labeled **CompuServe Graphics Interchange (*.gif)** and click **OK**.

4. Click **File** on the menu bar, then click **Open**. The Open window appears.

5. Click the **Look In** drop-down list, and navigate to and click on the image you are going to animate.

6. Click **Open**. The image opens, as shown in Figure 5-20.

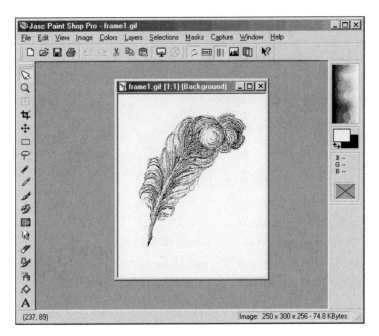

Figure 5-20   Paint Shop Pro can be used to modify images and to create animations

Once the image has been opened in Paint Shop Pro, there are several things you can do to the image. You can modify the image by moving it slightly. Another easy thing to do is to rotate the image slightly. Follow the directions below to rotate the image:

1. Click **Image** on the menu bar, then click **Rotate**. The Rotate window opens. (See Figure 5-21.)

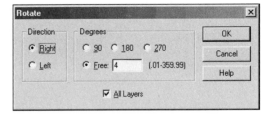

Figure 5-21   Using the Rotate option, you can move the image to the right or left

2. Click either **Right** or **Left** to indicate what direction you want to rotate the image.

3. To rotate the image 90, 180, or 270 degrees, click the appropriate number, or to rotate the image a different number of degrees, enter the number of degrees the image is to be rotated in the Free field. Smaller rotations of 5 to 10 degrees result in smoother animations.

4. Click **OK**. The image rotates.

Although the image does rotate, sometimes the background rotates as well. Figure 5-22 shows an image with the background that was rotated. Notice part of the background is black. This black background can be colored using the tools highlighted in Figure 5-22 and described below.

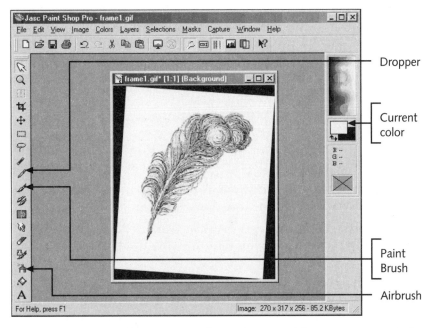

Figure 5-22   Paint Shop Pro provides tools to modify images as needed

The dropper is used to select the current color. The current color is the color that any painting will be done in. To choose a color, select the dropper tool by clicking on it, and then click on any color on the image. The color then appears as the current color (shown on the right hand side of the screen), and if you use the paintbrush or airbrush, the changes takes place in the current color.

The paintbrush is used to paint lines in your image. When the paintbrush is selected, the program paints the current color under the paintbrush as long as you press the left mouse key. If you don't press the mouse button, the paintbrush moves over the image without painting.

Using the airbrush is similar to using the paintbrush, except that the airbrush paints a greater area in one pass. Like the paintbrush, you must hold down the left mouse key to make it paint. Also, since the airbrush paints a wider area, you need to be very careful when you use it. If you get too close to your image with the airbrush, you may paint something you did not intend to paint.

Once the image is complete, it must be saved. Each image should be saved so that it is easy to remember in what order the images need to be placed. To save the image, select File on the menu bar, and click Save As. When the Save As window appears, enter a name for your file and click OK.

Create several images for your animation. Make each image a little different and save each under a different name.

Creating Animation Once you have created the images, you need to join them together to create an animation sequence. Part of the Paint Shop Pro package is animation software. The directions below outline how to use that software to create an animated .gif file.

1. Click **File** on the Paint Shop Pro menu bar, then click **Run Animation Shop**. The Animation Shop title screen appears.

2. Click **Start**. The first time you run Animation Shop, the File Format Associations window opens. In this window you need to tell Animation Shop what types of graphics files to use. Click the option button labeled **CompuServe Graphics Interchange** (***.gif**) and click **OK**.

3. Click **File** on the menu bar and click **Animation Wizard**. The Animation Wizard window appears, asking what the dimensions of the animation are to be.

4. Select **Same Size** and click **Next**. The wizard asks if you want the background to be transparent or opaque.

5. Click on the background type you want and click **Next**. Another window appears asking about positioning of the image.

6. Leave the defaults selected and click **Next**. Another window appears asking if you want the animation to be looped.

7. Enter either the number of loops you want played or select to have the animation played indefinitely. Also enter how long you want each frame to be displayed.

8. Click **Next**. The Animation wizard asks for the frames you want displayed.

9. Click **Add Image**. The Open window appears.

10. Select the frames you want added to the animation by pressing **CTRL** and clicking on the files. To add a second copy of an image (for example, if you want to use an image twice), repeat steps 9 and 10.

11. Once all the images have been selected, click **Open**. The Animation Wizard window displays the files you have selected; see Figure 5-23.

12. If the files are not in the correct order, click on the file that needs to be moved, and click either **Move Up** or **Move Down** to move the file to the correct location.

13. Once the files are in the correct order, click **Next**.

14. Click **Finish** to complete the process. The frames display as they are in Figure 5-19.

15. To view the animation, click **View** from the tool bar, and then click **Animation**.

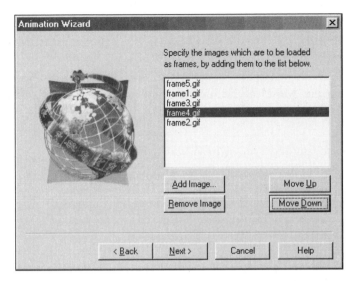

Figure 5-23   Use the Move Up and Move Down buttons to arrange the images in the correct order

16. Save the file so it can be used in future web documents. When you save an animation, the program opens a box labeled Animation Quality Versus Output Size. The slider on the left side of the box lets you choose whether you want a clearer image (resulting in a larger file size), or a lower-quality image (with a smaller file size). Choose your setting and click **Next**.

17. Click **Next** on the last screen, which shows you information about your animation, such as how long it will take to download.

Optimizing Page Download Time

You have just seen how easy it is to add sound and graphics to a web page and it's tempting to go overboard with both. But remember that, as a general rule, if visitors to your web site cannot view a web page within 10 seconds of requesting the page, they are not likely to stay and wait. As a rule of thumb, keep the total size of all files to be downloaded for a single page to about 50K. That way, the page and its sound and graphics should load quickly enough to not discourage your visitors.

MOVIES AND VIDEOS ON THE WEB

The goal of multimedia technology on the Internet is to achieve the same quality as that of television, and, if possible, to make the Web interactive. After several years of research and development, this goal has still not been achieved for many reasons. TV video is transmitted at 30 frames per second. To achieve this same quality of transmission on your computer would require a transfer rate of up to 27 MB of data per second across the Internet—a transmission rate that is currently impossible. Compare that figure to the download rate of a PC connected to the Internet by a regular phone line, which can expect no more than about 53 K per second. It's obvious that your PC cannot approach the quality of TV transmission.

Rather, users must look at the goal of movies and videos over the Internet to be that of easy access rather than high quality. Most Internet users are satisfied with the choppy effect of short newscasts and video conferencing and don't expect to use the Internet to view a movie live from a web site.

Here are the basic steps for putting a movie or video on the Web:

- Create the video using a camcorder or more sophisticated video equipment
- Download the video to your PC
- Edit the video, adding special effects, captions, and so forth
- Compress the video data
- Place the video file on your web site and build the web pages to view it using browser plug-ins

Just as with sound, movies and video can be delivered to a client as either non-streaming (download the file and then play it) or streaming data (play the file as it is downloaded). In this section, you'll learn how both technologies work.

Video File Types

There are three types of video files used on the Web: AVI, QuickTime, and MPEG. **AVI** (**Audio Video Interleaved**) is a Windows video format that is not as popular as MPEG or QuickTime because the files are large and there are sometimes problems synchronizing video with audio. MPEG files, mentioned earlier as a type of audio file, have the advantage of high quality output, and they can support video up to 30 frames per second (the same as TV quality). **QuickTime**, developed by Apple, is the most popular video format. QuickTime movies have a .MOV file extension and the files are smaller than both MPEG and AVI files.

Adding Movies and Videos to Web Pages

Until recently, a movie or video file was referenced on a web page using a hyperlink like <A HREF= "mymovie.avi">. When the user clicked on the hyperlink, a helper application would load and play the movie file. Netscape provides LiveVideo, a plug-in that can play a video file after it is downloaded. LiveVideo supports AVI files on a Windows system.

Movies and videos can now be included on a web page as streaming data using one of three approaches:

- The <EMBED> tag introduced by Netscape can reference a data file and its plug-in. <EMBED> is now supported by Internet Explorer.

- The <OBJECT> tag introduced by Internet Explorer can reference a Microsoft programming object called an ActiveX control that can embed a binary file such as a video file in a web page. The <OBJECT> tag was later enhanced to support more than just ActiveX controls and is being standardized by the World Wide Web Consortium (W3C) and is likely to become the standard way to embed objects in web pages.

- The <APPLET> tag can be used to indicate that a Java applet is included in the web page. Java applets are small programs that can be used to add multimedia such as interactive animations to a web page.

Two popular browser plug-ins that play movies and videos are QuickTime and Microsoft's ActiveMovie.

QuickTime

QuickTime provides the framework for synchronizing video, sound, and text in a web-based presentation. It supports several video compression techniques, and there are several software tools on the market to create and edit QuickTime files, such as Adobe Premiere. The 3D version of QuickTime is called **QuickTime Virtual Reality** (**QTVR**).

QuickTime supports non-streaming data, stored streaming data and live streaming data. Stored streaming data is stored in large data files on the web server. When the streaming begins, the client might accumulate some of the data in a buffer before it begins playing in order to have some leeway to adjust for rough transmissions. Live streaming data, such as radio or live video conferencing, is being created as it is sent downstream.

QuickTime supports many standard video, audio and graphics formats such as WAV, MIDI, Flash, and AVI files. For more information, see *www.apple.com/quicktime*.

Microsoft's ActiveMovie

Microsoft's ActiveMovie supports all the MPEG video formats including MPG, MPEG, MPV, MP2 and MPA, AVI, MOV, WAV, and AIFF file formats. The ActiveMovie plug-in can be referenced in a web page using the <OBJECT>, <EMBED>, or <IMG DYNSRC> tags. This last tag, <IMG DYNSRC> was initially introduced by Internet Explorer to only play AVI files, although other file formats have now been added. For more information, see *www.microsoft.com*.

Add Video to Your Web Site

If your organization has a message that can best be communicated by video, consider adding streaming video to your web site. The steps to do that are outlined in Figure 5-24. The first step is to film the movie using a video camera or camcorder. When you are filming a movie for distribution over the Web, if possible, record activities that have limited motion such as a panel discussion, rather than lots of motion such as a sports event. Lots of motion results in so much change from one video frame to the next that the compression ratio is low and files are too large for easy distribution. Also, to reduce motion from frame to frame, be sure to use a tripod for your camera or camcorder.

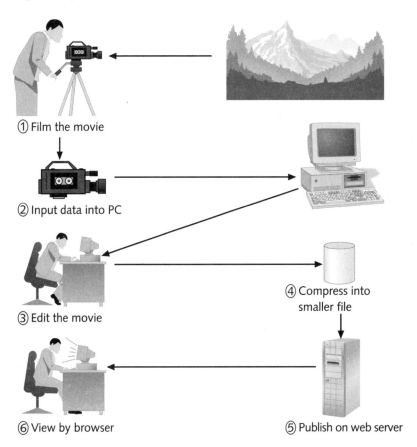

Figure 5-24 Steps to putting video on a web site

There are two basic types of video camcorders: analog and digital. An analog camcorder saves data to traditional videotape that can be played by a VCR. A digital camcorder saves data as bits on a digital storage media. The data can then be downloaded to a VCR tape in a VCR recorder.

Once the movie is filmed, the data must be downloaded to a computer. Data downloaded from an analog camcorder or a VCR requires a video capture card installed in the computer to receive the analog video and audio data and convert it to bits that can be stored in the computer. This process is called digitizing the data. The video capture card has a video-in port that receives the video data, digitizes it, and writes it to video files on a hard drive. The file for even a very short video clip will be very large, so you'll need a lot of empty space on your hard drive. If you have recorded the movie using a digital camcorder, the camcorder will have a cable that can attach to the PC for downloading data to the PC. Because the data is already digitized, no video capture card is required. The data cable from the camcorder connects to the PC through one of the standard ports on the PC. The data is stored directly into a video file. For example, the Digital Cybercam by JVC shown in Figure 5-25 can download data to a PC by way of an Infrared connection, serial port, or IEEE 1394 (FireWire) port.

Figure 5-25　A digital camcorder such as the Digital Cybercam by JVC can be used to download data directly to a PC

The next step is to edit the video file on the PC. A video capture card or a digital camcorder will likely come bundled with software to manage and edit video files. You can use that software or another application such as Adobe Premiere to edit the movie. You can add captions, title frames, or special effects, and cut portions of the video that are uninteresting. After the movie is edited, the next step is to use compression software such as Media Cleaner Pro by Terran Interactive (*www.terran.com*) or Cinepak by Compression Technologies, Inc. (*www.cinepak.com*) to compress the video file into a file small enough for downloading from the Web.

The last step to putting video on your web site is to publish the video file. If you simply plan to download the file for viewing by the browser (non-streaming data), then create a hyperlink to the video file on your web page. However, if you plan to use streaming video so that your users can view the video without having to download the entire file first, then you must install streaming video software on your web server to manage the streaming video process. For example, RealProducer Plus by RealNetworks (*www.realnetworks.com*) can convert compressed video files into a format suitable for streaming video, called RealVideo format. The streaming video is then read and interpreted by a browser using the RealPlayer plug-in.

Some web sites provide live streaming video such as those that support video conferencing or allow users all over the world to watch a live panel discussion. Live data is filmed by a digital camcorder and continuously downloaded to a computer using a port on the computer. Or an analog camcorder is used that downloads data to a video capture card that can support inputting live data. The data is input into software such as RealProducer Pro that converts the data to RealVideo format and makes it available to the live web broadcast. A browser receives a live broadcast using a plug-in such as RealPlayer.

One interesting web site, Web Cam Central (*www.camcentral.com*), tracks other web sites that have web cams and provides some of its own. A web cam is a camera and a web page that provides a live or pre-recorded video broadcast. For example, one of the web cams highlighted by Web Cam Central is Panda Central where you can watch live the activities of baby pandas at the San Diego Zoo. See Figure 5-26.

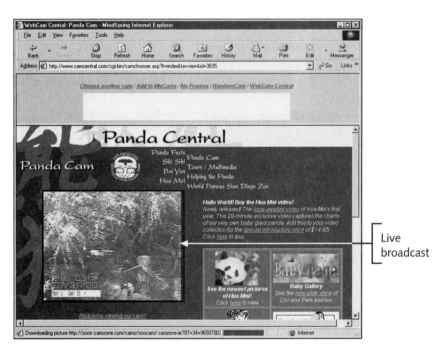

Figure 5-26   Panda Central shows a live web broadcast of pandas at the San Diego Zoo

PROPRIETARY MULTIMEDIA FILE FORMATS

Until recently, a web developer who wanted to include interactive animation on a web site would write the code using HTML or scripting. One language that was once popular for this job was **VRML (Virtual Reality Modeling Language)**. A developer could use VRML to create a sequence of images that collectively created animation, and these images could be manipulated by the user's mouse. VRML has largely been replaced by Java applets and proprietary products.

Macromedia has recently made tremendous headway in the proprietary multimedia market with Flash and Shockwave. **Flash** and **Shockwave** software produce vector-based, interactive, animated files that can be displayed by a browser using free Flash and Shockwave plug-ins. Flash and Shockwave both use streaming media so a Macromedia server is required on the web site. Flash uses vector graphics to produce animated graphics with sound, whereas Shockwave is used mostly in audio and video productions. Macromedia estimates that 80% of web surfers have either the Flash or Shockwave plug-in installed on their browsers to view these popular file formats. Figure 5-27 shows an example of a web site (*www.furniture.com*) that uses Flash to let you move furniture around a room. The site *www.shockwave.com* has several demonstrations of both Flash and Shockwave. Initially there were distinct differences between the two products, but with recent version releases, the differences have become less noticeable.

Figure 5-27   This web site uses Macromedia's Flash to provide interactive animation

Both Shockwave and Flash file formats are stored in files with the SWF (ShockWave Flash) file extension. The files are built using Macromedia software (see *www.macromedia.com*) and then included in web pages using either the <EMBED> tag for Navigator or the <OBJECT> tag for Internet Explorer.

The following example shows the <OBJECT> tag. The ClassID attribute identifies specific Flash commands that are used in the Flash software. Notice that the command also specifies the URL where a user can download the plug-in. The name of the defined object is Motor.

```
<object classid="clsid:D27CDB6E-AE6D-11cf-96B8-444553540000"
       codebase="http://active.macromedia.com/flash2/cabs/
       swflash.cab#version=2,0,0,0" width="8" height="8"
       name="motor">
    <param name="SRC" value="motorwav.swf">
</object>
```

The <EMBED> tag includes the Flash filename, the URL for the plug-in, and the name of the object (Motor). The following example shows an <EMBED> tag to a Flash file:

```
<embed src="motorwav.swf"
pluginspage="http://www.macromedia.com/shockwave/download/"
width="8" height="8" name="motor">
```

VIDEO CONFERENCING OVER THE INTERNET

Video conferencing over the Internet is an exciting technology. The applications are endless, from distance learning, corporate training and marketing, to free long distance video phone calls anywhere on the globe. For example, Akamai, a video conferencing company, provides a full range of video conferencing services (see *www.akamai.com*).

Figure 5-28 shows a sample screen taken from a video conference about e-commerce. In the upper right corner is a video screen of the panel of participants at the conference broadcasted live at the studio. On the left side of the screen is a large area used for a PowerPoint-like presentation where graphics, charts, and text are used to make points and show statistics and concepts.

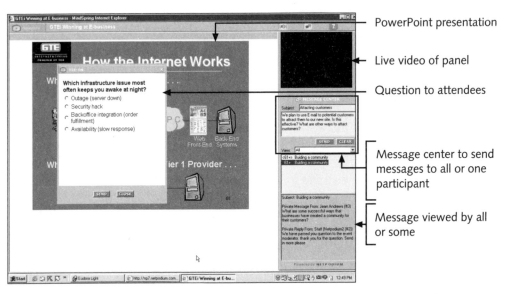

Figure 5-28   A video conference provides video, sound, and interactive graphics

Attendees at the conference can interact in several ways. Periodically, a dialog box opens, asking attendees questions and providing for multiple-choice responses. The results of the poll are displayed in a graphic pie chart, bar chart, and so forth, as shown in Figure 5-29.

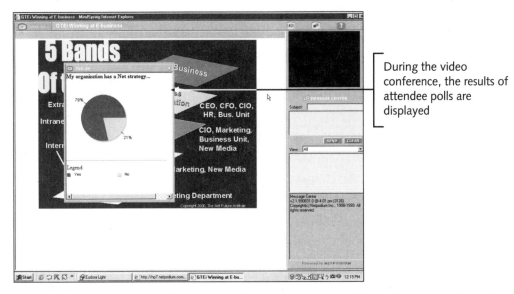

During the video conference, the results of attendee polls are displayed

5

Figure 5-29 For a successful video conference, it is essential that all attendees have the ability to interact

Any conference attendee can pose a question to the panel at any time using the message center on the lower right side of the screen. You can enter a message and then send it to all participants, the panel or to technical support. The ability to communicate with technical support personnel at any point during the conference assures that, if there is a problem with the broadcast, you can get help.

How does this technology work? Prior to the conference, attendees are asked to download the latest version of either RealPlayer or Windows MediaPlayer. Attendees are also asked to set their screen resolutions at a high resolution and download the applets from the Netpodium web site. As a last step to preparing for the conference, attendees are asked to test the entire system using a preflight test routine available on the web site, and shown in Figure 5-30.

The previous example requires sophisticated software and support, but for the average user there are several alternatives that allow you to have your own video conference. One of them is Microsoft's NetMeeting. NetMeeting lets you hold video conference calls if you have a microphone, PC camera, and speakers installed on a Windows 9x, Windows NT, or Windows 2000 system. While viewing and talking with others, you can send text messages, share documents, and draw on an electronic whiteboard that others can see.

There are many software products available for video conferencing. For an extensive list, see *www.thinkofit.com*. Thinkofit is an organization that helps you build video conferencing ability into your web site.

Figure 5-30   Several elements must be in place on the server and client for a successful video conferencing experience

REAL PEOPLE, REAL PROBLEMS, REAL SOLUTIONS
SOUNDS GOOD!

"The site needs sound! A strong, bold racing motor sound! Like the sounds our boats make!" This was one of the first comments the owner of Sonic USA Boats (*www.sonicusaboats.com*) made to my partner and me, owners of Vista 7 West, the web development company hired to build their web site. We were in the process of getting design ideas for the new site, and the word "sound" continued to pop up. Sonic USA of Hollywood, Florida, manufactures first-class, high-performance boats. We knew the site needed to be as eye-catching as the streamlined powerboats were. We also knew that adding sound could really slow down the web site's performance.

The site was to be the first step towards expanding Sonic's operation. The company had been in business for 25 years and was well known in the boating industry. Initially, the three primary goals of the site were to allow prospective buyers an efficient means of receiving a quote, and, to allow the company to sell accessories and to keep up with competitors.

The challenge we faced wasn't in getting the correct sound, or even how to use it effectively. It was adding another large file to a site that was already destined to be graphically rich. We explained to the company's owner that adding the sounds could dramatically decrease page load time, even when used with the most efficient technology. But, he insisted he wanted a motorboat sound.

In almost every case, when our designers go to work on a site, they know that the general rule for total page file size is no more than 50K. Visitors to a site often will leave because of slow page downloads, and once gone, they seldom return. With the tools available today, most web site graphics can be compressed to a usable file size that will keep a site's page in check. When page components like sound files are added, more consideration must be given to the overall design of the page.

In the case of Sonic USA, we convinced the company's owner that the best way to incorporate the use of a motorboat sound was to build an "intro" or "opening" page to the site. This type of page is only for introductory purposes and to make an initial statement for the site. We would use the motorboat sound on the intro page only, making the first page a visitor is presented with, be the one that would catch their attention. It would be designed to set the tone for the company's product and get the visitor to go further into the site.

The designers of Vista 7 West used several technologies to build big, bright graphics, sound, and animation into the site's intro page. A combination of Macromedia Flash, Macromedia Shockwave, JavaScript, and Cascading Style Sheets were implemented to create a page that would load fairly quickly, yet present an image that reflected the company's boats—and have sound!

A secondary static intro page was also designed for the visitor who did not have an updated browser or the correct browser plug-ins to handle the technologies that were implemented. This was done so that visitors would not be discouraged from entering the site if they couldn't experience the sound and animation without the proper plug-ins.

After the site's intro page, very little presentation components were used other than standard graphics and HTML code. JavaScript controls some of the site's navigation, but otherwise it was designed to efficiently deliver what the visitor is looking for.

The Sonic USA web site has all of the components that the owner wanted, and is presented in an effective manner. Adding sounds and animations can deliver an impact, but can also be a deterrent to visitors who will not wait for long page download times. Not all sites can benefit from the use of an intro page. Consider the goals of the site, and then determine what the right choice will be.

CHAPTER SUMMARY

❑ Video, graphical, and audio data can be downloaded from a web site as either non-streaming or streaming data. Non-streaming data is downloaded and then played or displayed.

❑ A browser uses a plug-in or helper application to display or play many multimedia file types.

❑ Common audio file types are AU, AIFF, MIDI, WAV and MP3.

❑ Multimedia digitized data files can be quite large because of the amount of data that is necessary to provide very close approximations of original analog sights and sounds.

❑ Because of the size of multimedia data files, files are often compressed using either a lossy compression or lossless compression method.

❑ You can easily create a WAV sound file using Windows 9x Sound Recorder if your PC has a sound card with a microphone attached.

❑ Sound files can be added to a web page using either the <BGSOUND>, <EMBED>, or <HREF> tags.

❑ Internet Explorer normally uses Windows Media Player, and Netscape Navigator uses LiveAudio or Beatnik Player to play sound files.

❑ The <BGSOUND> tag can be used on a web page to play sound when the page is first loaded by Internet Explorer. For Navigator, use the <EMBED> tag to accomplish the same thing.

❑ Streaming audio and video data require a streaming data server on the web site and a plug-in that supports streaming data on the browser.

❑ Streaming data uses the UDP, RTP, and RTSP protocols. In addition, you can reserve bandwidth for a streaming data session using the RSVP protocol.

❑ Streaming data is often buffered by the browser to get a head start on playing the data so that the browser can smooth out problems with corrupted or missing data packets.

❑ Streaming data uses a metafile that is downloaded to the browser. The browser contains the URL of the audio or video data file.

❑ Graphics can be stored as vector images or bit-mapped images. Vector images are created by software that calculates a series of mathematical equations, and bit-mapped images are created as many dots displayed on the screen.

❑ Common graphic image file types are GIF, GIF89, JPEG, PNG, PDF, TIFF, and BMP files.

❑ PostScript files with PS or EPS file extensions contain printing instructions to a PostScript printer.

❑ Common video file types are AVI, QuickTime, and MPEG.

❑ Movies and videos can be included in web pages using either the <EMBED>, <OBJECT>, or <APPLET> tag.

❑ Two popular browser plug-ins for movies and videos are QuickTime and ActiveMovie.

❑ Macromedia Shockwave and Flash are popular multimedia file formats. They allow a web developer to include interactive animation, video and audio in streaming data from a Macromedia server using Shockwave or Flash plug-ins on the client.

❑ NetMeeting is an example of video conferencing software.

5

KEY TERMS

AIFF file — A sound file that uses the format originally developed for Apple computers.

AU file — A sound file format originally developed for UNIX computers.

AVI (Audio Video Interleaved) — An older Windows video format that is not as well compressed as more recent file formats such as MPEG or QuickTime.

bit-mapped image — An image format that makes up an image from many dots. Also called raster image.

BMP (Bit-mapped) — An older file format that stores an image as many dots of varying colors.

Browser extension — *See* plug-in.

clickable map — *See* image map.

CODEC (compressor/decompressor) — Compressing and later decompressing sound, animation, and video files. MPEG is a common example of a file that goes through the CODEC process. Also stands for coder/decoder when referring to digital-to-analog conversion.

digitize — The process of converting analog data, such as sound, to digital representation of the data in binary (0s and 1s).

Encapsulated PostScript (EPS) — A file format developed by Adobe that includes directions for printing a document to a PostScript printer, and also includes a print preview of the document.

Flash — A popular multimedia file format developed by Macromedia. Flash uses vector-based, streaming data to produce animation, graphics, audio and interactivity.

GIF89 — A version of GIF image that supports animation, transparent background and interlacing.

image map — A graphic on a web page that contains multiple hyperlinks. Also called clickable map.

interlacing — The method of staggering the presentation of data so as to give the overall effect of a smooth transition. Graphics that are interlaced are built on a screen one layer at a time.

lossy compression — A data compression method that drops redundant and near-redundant data, losing some quality in the process, but producing a much smaller data file.

metafile — A file that contains information about other files.

MIDI (Musical Instrument Digital Interface) — A standard for transmitting sound from musical devices, such as electronic keyboards, to computers where it can be digitally stored.

MP3 — A high-quality audio format that uses MPEG, Version 3 technology.

Multicasting — On a network, a type of broadcast message where one source is sending data to multiple recipients.

non-streaming data — Multimedia data that is first downloaded from a web site and then played. Compare to streaming data.

object image — *See* vector image.

Page Description Language (PDL) — A language used to communicate printing instructions to a printer.

PDF (Portable Document Format) — A proprietary file format by Adobe Systems, designed to retain a document's formatting. You can view a PDF file with Adobe Acrobat Reader, a free helper application that can be downloaded from the Adobe web site (**www.adobe.com**).

pixel — The smallest unit of space on a monitor that can be addressed by software. Screen resolutions are normally given in pixels, for example, 1024 by 768 pixels.

plug-in — Software that enhances the ability of a browser to handle certain file types. Also called browser extension.

PNG (Portable Network Graphics) — A graphics format that uses lossless compression, interlacing and transparent background color.

PostScript — A page description language developed by Adobe Systems, used to communicate printing directions to a PostScript printer.

progressive JPEG — A JPEG format that fades a photograph on the screen one layer at a time.

QuickTime — A popular video file format developed by Apple. QuickTime files have a .MOV file extension.

QuickTime Virtual Reality (QTVR) — A version of a QuickTime file format that supports 3D rendering.

raster image — *See* bit-mapped image.

RMF (Rich Music Format) — A proprietary audio file format developed by Beatnik. It requires a Beatnik Player plug-in on the client, which is supported by Netscape Navigator.

RSVP (Resource Reservation Setup Protocol) — A protocol that allows you to reserve bandwidth for upcoming streaming data.

RTF (Rich Text Format) — A file format that converts a word processing document to ASCII code so that another word processor can read and edit the file.

RTP (Real Time Transport Protocol) — A protocol used to transmit real-time data, such as audio, video or simulation data over the Internet. RTP is defined by RFC 1889.

RTSP (Real Time Streaming Protocol) — A protocol that establishes and controls time-synchronized streams of continuous media such as audio and video. RTSP uses the RTP protocol and acts as a network remote control for multimedia servers.

sampling — Part of the process of converting sound or video from analog to digital format, whereby a sound wave or image is measured at uniform time intervals and saved as a series of smaller representative blocks

Shockwave — A popular multimedia file format developed by Macromedia that produces video and audio streaming data.

streaming data — Multimedia data that is played as it is being downloaded. Video conferencing and listening to the radio from a web site are two examples of streaming data.

TIFF (Tagged Image File Format) — A bit-mapped file format used to hold photographs, graphics and screen captures. TIFF files can be rather large and so are not commonly used on web sites.

transparent background — A background that is designed to display as the same color as the background of the web page.

vector image — An image format that composes an image from a series of mathematical equations. Also called object image.

VRML (Virtual Reality Modeling Language) — A language used to create interactive animation on web sites. VRML is not as well-used as it once was, because it's easier for developers to use Flash or Shockwave plug-in software rather than developing their own code.

wave file — A Windows audio file commonly used on web sites for short, low-quality sound

5

REVIEW QUESTIONS

1. What is the fundamental difference between streaming and non-streaming data?
2. How does a plug-in differ from a helper application? Give one example of each.
3. What audio file format was first developed to be used on Apple computers?
4. What audio file format was first developed to be used on UNIX computers?
5. MP3 audio file format is based on what technology?
6. What goal of multimedia technology makes the quantity of data stored so large?
7. What type of multimedia data compression does not lose any data?
8. What HTML tag is used to add sound to a web page whereby the plug-in is always displayed in a separate window?
9. What HTML tag do you use to create a background sound using Netscape Navigator?
10. What HTML tag do you use to create a background sound using Internet Explorer?
11. Name one audio player supported by Internet Explorer.
12. Name two audio players supported by Netscape Navigator.
13. What software produces .RMF files?

14. What are two plug-ins that support streaming audio data?

15. What protocol can be used to reserve bandwidth for upcoming streaming data?

16. Streaming data technology uses a metafile named in an <EMBED> or <OBJECT> tag. What does the metafile contain?

17. What are the two categories of graphic files that are identified by how software displays the data?

18. What software company developed the PDF file format? What helper application is required to view the file?

19. What is one difference between a PostScript PS file and a PostScript EPS file?

20. What is the HTML tag and attribute used to create a background texture on a web page?

21. What company developed QuickTime movie and video format?

22. What is the file extension normally used for QuickTime files?

23. What company developed Flash and Shockwave?

24. What two HTML tags can be used to embed Flash or Shockwave files on a web page?

25. Name a type of graphics file that is vector based.

HANDS-ON PROJECTS

Research PDF Files on the Internet

You work for a hardware manufacturing company that wants to distribute its documentation for products from their web site using the PDF file format. The documentation has been created using Microsoft Word. What software do they need to convert Word documents to the PDF format? How much does the product cost? Print the first page of the URL of the Adobe web site that describes this product.

What are the licensing agreements and terms that you should be aware of in order to provide the users of your site access to the Adobe Acrobat Reader? Print the web page on the Adobe web site that shows these terms and how to provide the reader to your users.

Research Flash and Shockwave

Your employer has asked you to investigate the cost of software needed to develop an interactive multimedia presentation that can be used to train new employees. The presentation should allow for text on the screen along with animated graphics, and allow the trainee to manipulate controls on the screen. Research the *www.macromedia.com* web site to answer these questions.

1. What software is needed to create a Flash file? How much does the software cost?

2. What software is needed to create and edit a Shockwave file? How much does it cost?

3. Which product do you think is the best choice for this job? Explain your answer.

Web Browser Plug-ins

Using Netscape Navigator as your browser, create a web page containing this script within the <BODY> tags. Display the web page to show the plug-ins installed under Navigator. Print the web page.

```
<script language="JAVASCRIPT">
        if (navigator.appName == "Microsoft Internet Explorer")
                document.write ("Plug-ins[] collection not
                supported under IE");
else
        {

                num_plugins = navigator.plugins.length;
                for (count=0; count < num_plugins; count++)
                document.write (navigator.plugins[count].name
                + "<BR>");

        }
</script>
```

5

Research Web Cams

Lynn and Ann Marie Francis are expecting their first child, but they live thousands of miles from both sets of grandparents. Lynn is researching the possibility of a web cam site for their nursery so the grandparents can watch their new grand baby on Lynn's personal web site. Research the hardware and software requirements and the cost for building the web cam site.

Answer these questions:

1. What software can Lynn install on his PC to support live streaming video and audio? (For example, RealProducer Plus at *www.realnetworks.com*.) Print the product web pages showing the price of the product and minimum hardware requirements.

2. What is one example of a digital camcorder that can download live data to the PC? What port is required on the PC? Print the web page showing the specifications for the camcorder and its price.

3. What web server software can Lynn use that will support the streaming video software?

4. What is the total cost of the setup?

CASE PROJECTS

Animated Graphics

Animated gif files are often used to display blinking text or a text box that alternates between two or more messages. Use Paint Shop Pro to create a .gif file that alternates between two or more messages. (The resulting file will contain two images, one for each message.) Add the file to your web site home page making it repeat infinitely.

Add Sound and Test Your Browser

1. If you have a microphone, create a short welcoming message to your web site using Windows 9x Sound Recorder into a WAV file. Play the sound file each time a user accesses your home page.

2. Create a link to your favorite radio station on your home page. When a user moves his or her mouse over the link, sound the chimes or use some other WAV file. Test the link to make sure you can hear your favorite music when you click the link.

Both these tasks use different procedures in Netscape and Internet Explorer. In addition, some versions of Internet Explorer interpret the HTML differently than other versions. Can you make both projects work in both browsers? Make the changes to your web page, then test the page in both Netscape and Internet Explorer. Write a paragraph that describes the HTML you used, whether or not it worked in Netscape and Internet Explorer, and which version of each browser you are using. Compare your results with those of your classmates, especially those who may be using different versions from the browsers that you are using.

Add a Background Texture to Your Web Site

Surf the Web to find a background texture that you like for your web site. Download the texture file to your PC and add it as a background to your web site. (A texture file is generally not copyrighted, so you can do this without violating copyright agreements. However, don't take photographs, logos, or other graphics from web pages for your own site unless you have permission from the web site owner.) Print your home page showing the new background.

6

PROGRAMMING ON THE INTERNET

In this chapter, you will learn

♦ About programs and why they are needed to add functionality to web sites

♦ About server-side and client-side scripting and the differences between the two

♦ About the several programming languages used to build web sites

♦ How to enhance a web site using the Active Server Pages (ASP) methods

♦ How to add a JavaScript program segment to a web site

♦ About cookies and how they are used

♦ About the importance of pre-launch testing and about a testing plan

---

In Chapter 3 you learned how to build a web site using HTML code and HTML GUI editors. In either case, the result is simple HTML, which produces a straight-forward web site whereby each page is a simple rendering of hypertext. Each time users access the site, they always see the same pages with no changes, unless the site developer edits the original pages.

However, sometimes a web site needs to respond to the user or to other outside variables. In order to make a web site responsive to different needs, you need a program. A **program** is a list of instructions that are executed by an operating system or other software. Sometimes the program is written into a text file called a **source file** and then assembled into a coded binary format called **object code** before it is used or executed. The object code is stored into an **executable file**, so named because it is executed by the operating system. On PCs, most executable program files have an .EXE or .COM file extension. Notepad.exe is an example of an executable file. However, a program can also be written as plain text and included in a document. These programs are usually very short and are called **scripts** or **macros**. They are a list of instructions that perform a task, can make decisions based on input, and produce output. A program can be as simple as a single line of instruction such as DISPLAY DATE or can be very complex. The term *script* is generally used to describe a simple program with few decisions and limited input that is stored as text in a document file, and the term *program* refers to a larger group of instructions stored in a program file, although the two terms are sometimes used interchangeably.

WHY PROGRAMMING?

There are two reasons to use programs on the Web: to enable a browser to customize a web page based on user activity or the PC environment, and to enable a web server to customize a web page for a specific browser request. Let's first look at how a program can make a web site responsive to a browser and then we'll look at an example of how a browser can be made responsive. For our web site example, we'll use Amazon.com.

When you want to buy a book on a certain subject from *www.amazon.com*, you enter a subject in a search box on the Amazon.com home page, and then click a button labeled Go! Look at Figure 6-1 for an example of this. When Amazon finds books that match your subject, a new web page appears, with a list of books on that subject. Change the subject, and the same web page displays, but this time with a different list of books. How does a web page display different lists to the user? The process is explained in Figure 6-2.

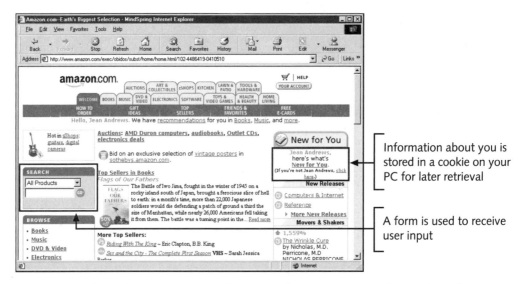

Figure 6-1   This web page receives information from a user into a form. The information is sent back to the server to customize the next web page sent

Once you enter the site's URL, the web browser requests the page, and the web server sends it back to the browser. The home page has a place for the user to enter a subject and click Go!. Recall from Chapter 3 that a web page uses a form to receive input from a user and pass it back to the web server. The subject area and the Go! Button are contained on a form.

When the server receives the form input, it passes the information to a program that is part of the web site. The program receives the subject entered on the home page, searches the database for the books on the given subject, and inserts that list into the web page, which is then downloaded to your browser.

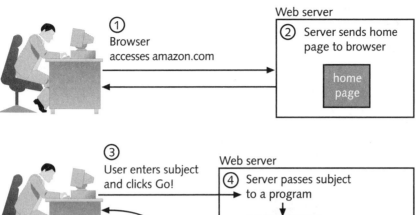

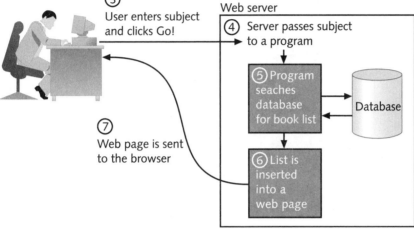

Figure 6-2 A program on the web server is responsible for changing the content of a web page based on information given by the user

These types of web pages, which can change content, are called **dynamic web pages**, as opposed to pages that always display the same information in the same way, which are **static web pages**.

In Figure 6-2, for simplicity's sake, we left out the fact that the home page itself performed some dynamic processing. Once you have purchased something from amazon.com, the home page displays your name on the right side of the screen every time you access the web site. (Note that you won't see this feature the very first time you visit the site.) How does the web site know who you are? Actually, it doesn't until the browser's request reaches the site. When you first visited the site, the site placed a cookie on your PC. When you access the site again, the browser checks for a cookie and, if one is present, the information in that cookie is included in the HTTP header to the web server. Any web page on the server has access to the cookie information. You can read more about cookies later in the chapter.

Programs are also used to make a browser responsive to user input and other external variables. As you have seen from previous chapters, Internet Explorer and Netscape Navigator display web pages slightly differently. In order to accommodate this difference, a web page sometimes contains scripts that are executed by the browser. Figure 6-3 illustrates this concept. When a web page first arrives at the browser, the browser scans the page for scripts and executes these scripts.

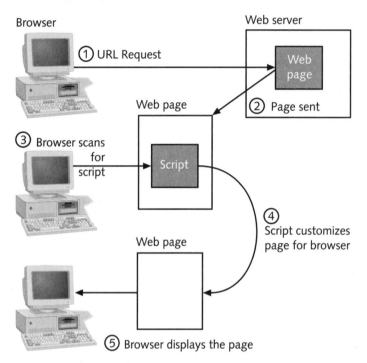

Figure 6-3   A common use of a client-side script is to customize a web page to meet the need of a particular browser

Figure 6-4 illustrates what the script does. The script identifies the browser (either Netscape or Internet Explorer) and then customizes the HTML code for this browser. After the script completes, the browser then interprets the HTML and displays the page. The script substitutes the correct HTML and text in the web page in the place of itself.

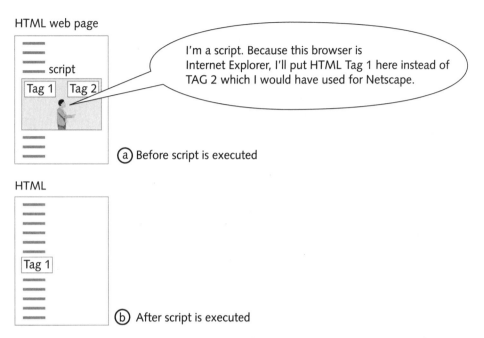

Figure 6-4   A browser executes a script. The script inserts HTML tags and text into the page, and then the browser displays the page

Two Kinds of Programs

Compare Figure 6-2 and Figure 6-3 and note where each of the two programs is executed. In Figure 6-2, the program is executed on the server and is used to search the database for the book list, which is inserted into the web page before it leaves the server. A program executed on the server is called a **server-side script** or server-side program. In Figure 6-3, the script is included in the web page sent to the web browser and is executed by the browser on the PC. The script customizes the HTML code for the browser before the browser displays the page. A script executed on the PC is called a **client-side script** or client-side program.

Figure 6-5 demonstrates that a server-side script is executed on the server and a client-side script is executed by the browser. Notice from this figure that, when a web page reaches the client, there are no server-side scripts in the page because these have already been executed and have substituted their HTML tags and text in the page in place of the script. Client side scripts are generally executed before the browser displays the HTML page, as is the case in Figure 6-5. As you will see later in the chapter, there is also a way that you can design a client-side script that won't execute until the page is displayed by the browser and the user clicks a button on the page, that causes the script to execute.

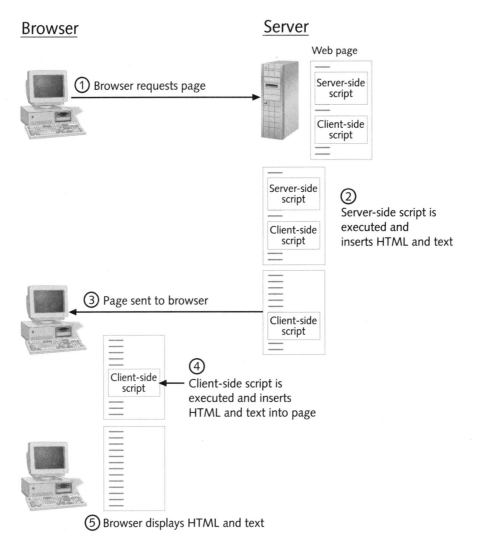

Figure 6-5 Server-side scripts are executed by the server and client-side scripts are executed by the client

Basic Programming Concepts

In order to understand the rest of this chapter, you must know some basic programming concepts. Some of the terms used when discussing programming can be confusing because they are so similar. For example, programming language and programming protocol sound very similar, but they are actually two very different things. A **programming protocol** is a set of rules or standards by which programs interact with the outside world. A **programming language**, on the other hand, is a set of words or codes that are used to write a program.

Two other terms that can be confused are command and argument. A **command** is an order to perform an action, such as to get a file. An **argument** qualifies the action that is stated in the command. To illustrate the difference, look at the following line of HTML:

```
<IMG SRC="SPG193.JPG">
```

In the previous example, IMG is the command. As you already know from Chapter 3, it is a command that tells the system to enter a file in the document. SRC is the argument or attribute that specifies the name of the file. The command cannot work without the argument because the command does not know what file to insert in the document unless the argument tells it.

Some programs rely on objects to perform routine tasks. An **object** is a small program that is designed to perform a specific function. It is like a middle man that manages the interface between the script and some other entity on the server. You first create the object, giving it a name, and then use it to perform tasks. Or, you can use an object that is provided to you by a software application or another developer.

An example of when a web page developer might need an object is when the web page must write text to a text file, but there are no scripting commands or tools to access and write to text files. An object can do the job of the middle man.

Here's an analogy: Imagine that you own a software company and your company has written a new software package. You need someone to write a user guide for this package, but no one in your company knows how to write user guides. So you hire a technical writer who is experienced at that skill. The company then passes the job of writing the user guide to the technical writer. In this analogy, the company (the script) needs a user guide (data written to a text file) so it hires a technical writer (an object) that knows how to do the job. Figure 6-6 illustrates this analogy.

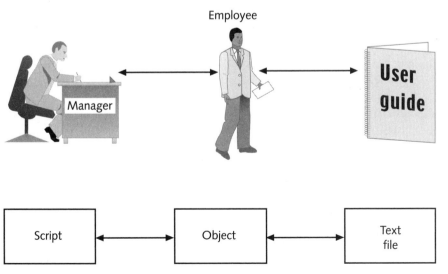

Figure 6-6   An object can be compared to a technical writer who writes a user guide

Programming languages often come with pre-defined objects. A programmer can also use objects that are developed by third-party vendors that can be purchased as add-ons. There are objects to write to text files, print documents on the Windows default printer, retrieve a list of directories on the hard drive, send e-mail messages to an e-mail client and many, many more tasks. A smart programmer learns to never reinvent the wheel in these cases, but instead use preexisting objects to accomplish these tasks. In some cases, where an object does not exist or does not work in the required way, the programmer can write a new object. Once written, it can be used in many different situations by this or other programmers.

Another programming concept is a function. A **function** is a segment of programming code that is executed out of order from the main list of commands on an as-needed basis. Generally, a program is a list of instructions that are executed linearly—starting at the top and going down through the list until all commands are done. A function, on the other hand, is not executed until it is called by another command or outside event. A function itself is a linear list and when it executes, it also does so from the top down. A function has an entry point (where the list begins) and an exit point (where the list ends), and generally, a function does only one thing: it calculates something, displays something, writes something to a file, or some similar event. Figure 6-7 illustrates a function.

Script

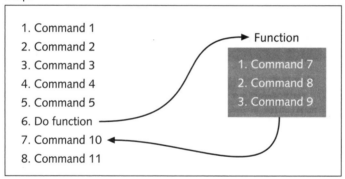

Figure 6-7   A function is not executed until called upon by a command in the main program or by some other event

In the figure, the sixth command called on the function (the action is referred to as a function call). The function performed its three commands and then returned control to the next command after the function call. However, if the command to call the function had not been in the main list, the function would never have executed. You'll see an example of a function later in the chapter. A function occurs when a user clicks a button on a web page, The function doesn't occur until the button is clicked.

The rest of this chapter explains in greater detail how the different programming processes work. There are several tools available on both the server and the client side that are created for different computers (called hardware platforms), different operating systems, different types of data, and different processing needs. You'll learn about the different tools and then you'll learn how to use two of them to enhance a web site, making it responsive to the user.

SURVEY OF PROGRAMMING LANGUAGES USED ON THE INTERNET

As you read in the previous section, a programming language is a set of commands and arguments that have a predetermined meaning to the software that is executing the program. Learning to program involves two distinct skills: learning to use the language (what command does what, and how to qualify the command with one or more arguments) and learning to apply the language to accomplish a task. Many programmers find it easy to learn a new language once they have mastered one language, because they have already learned how to apply a language and because languages often have many similarities.

Languages have evolved over the past 30 years based on changing needs and the competition among manufacturers. Because programming on the Internet has become popular there have already been some evolutions of languages. As you know, the Web is a client-server application with programs that run on the client and on the server. For example, recall that streaming video, discussed in Chapter 5, requires a program running on the server to distribute the video, and a program running on the client to view the video. This section introduces the protocols and languages used on the server. Later in this chapter, you will learn about programs on the client.

Server-Side Programming Protocols

Server-side scripts are interpreted and executed by the web server. Remember that a web server is just a software application designed to manage web sites, and there are many brands of web servers written for many different operating systems. Examples of web servers are Apache, NCSA, Plexus, Open Market, Netscape Commerce Server, and Internet Information Server. Developers cannot always know which brand of web server will be interpreting and executing their scripts and, in many cases, these scripts will be used by several servers on different platforms. Therefore, standards are needed that specify how a server recognizes a script, and how the server and the script interact. These standards are defined in the programming protocols mentioned earlier in the chapter.

CGI Scripts and Programs

The programming protocols for server-side programming have evolved over just a few short years. The first and still very popular way for a program or script to interact with a web server is **CGI (Common Gateway Interface)**, which was originally developed for use on UNIX computers. Figure 6-8 shows how the CGI protocol works. Normally, a URL points to a web page file on a web server. When you are using CGI, however, the URL points to a program file on the web server. The file is an executable binary file that is loaded and executed by the web server when a browser requests that URL. The program then builds a web page that can be sent to the browser.

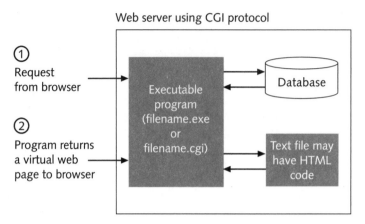

Figure 6-8   A CGI program or script constructs a web page from resources on the server

The program produces output that looks like a web page and can be interpreted by the browser. This kind of web page can be called a virtual web page, because an actual web page that looks just like the one sent to the browser may or may not exist on the server. The program uses the CGI protocol to perform any or all of the following tasks:

- Receive information from the browser about the data it is requesting

- Retrieve information from a database

- Determine information about the environment (such as the date or time)

- Locate text files on the server.

When a browser sends a URL to a web server, how does the web server know whether to pass the requested file to the browser as a web page or execute the requested file as a program? This decision is made based on the parameter settings of the web server software or by following the rules dictated by the software. For example, a popular web server software for UNIX computers is Apache server. By default, this software treats any file stored in the directory named cgi-bin as a CGI program to execute, rather than a web page to download. Another method for identifying a file as a program is to assign it a .CGI file extension, a method used by Apache as well as WebSTAR, a Macintosh web server. This method has the advantage that the program can be stored in any directory.

Though the CGI protocol was first developed for use on UNIX computers, it is now used on Windows and Macintosh systems.

ISAPI (Internet Server Application Programming Interface)

Another protocol is **ISAPI (Internet Server Application Programming Interface)**, which was originally developed by Microsoft for use on Windows NT servers that were using Microsoft web server software, Internet Information Server (IIS). However, the technology has now been ported (computer jargon for "moved" or "transferred") to other platforms.

The ISAPI protocol makes use of Microsoft's dynamic linked library concept, a faster technology than the executable-file concept used by CGI. A dynamic linked library (DLL) is an object or a program that is executed by another program to perform a specific task. A program calls a DLL into action using an application program interface (API) call. An example of a DLL is the print DLL used by Microsoft applications such as Microsoft Word. When Word needs to print a document, it loads and executes the Windows print DLL, turns the job of printing over to it, and moves on to other tasks. Once a DLL is loaded into memory, it can remain in memory until needed again.

ISAPI is a good tool for monitoring interest in a web site. Before the request for a web page is passed to the server, a program using ISAPI examines the request to validate it and logs information about the request into a file for tracking purposes. These files are called **log files** and are used to track errors, interest in the site, user preferences, and so forth.

ISAPI is more difficult for developers to use than CGI because the programs they build must relate to the web server as a DLL rather than as a stand-alone program. A DLL is more restricted by design and is written specifically for the web server that uses it.

Active Server Pages (ASP)

ASP (Active Server Pages) technology by Microsoft is another step in the development of easier and more powerful ways to handle server-side programming. ASP allows you to write a web page with one or more scripts on the page. The server executes the ASP script that uses the ISAPI method to call DLLs to do some of the work of customizing the web page based on information sent from the browser and information about the server environment (such as date and time). After the script has finished customizing the page, the web server sends it to the browser.

Figure 6-9 shows how ASP technology works. The browser requests the web page, which contains the ASP script. The web server recognizes the web page contains an ASP script because the file extension of the web page is .asp. The web server executes the script which has access to system resources on the web site, such as a database, for example. After the script completes, the web page is sent to the browser.

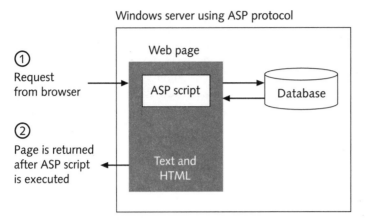

Figure 6-9   Using Windows ASP, an ASP script within the web page has access to resources on the web site

In comparing Figure 6-8 and Figure 6-9, you can see the fundamental difference between a CGI script and an ASP script: with a CGI script, a browser points a URL to a program file, but with an ASP script, the browser points a URL to a web page that contains a script.

Server-Side Includes (SSI)

Server-side Includes (**SSI**) is a simple form of server-side scripting that allows you to use variable values which can be included in the HTML code before it is sent to the browser. For example, you may wish to have your web site display the current day and time. Because the day and time are not constant, you can use SSI to have the site display the variable value.

SSI lets you include a line in the HTML file that indicates that a variable value needs to be entered before the file is sent to the browser. A web server that supports SSI scans a web page before it is sent to a browser and looks for commands to substitute values into the web page. An example of a command is:

```
<!echo var="LAST_MODIFIED"-->
```

When the server sees that command, it gets the last-modified date and inserts it into the web page in the exact place where the command was. It then sends the page to the browser.

There are several variables that the operating system can track and make accessible to a server program; one of these is LAST-MODIFIED. In order for the command to work, though, the system administrator must make the variable usable when the system is set up. If you are creating a web site, it is a good idea to ask which variables can be used and to verify that the variables are set up correctly so that the information can be accessed when the web page is accessed.

Server-Side Programming Languages

There is a variety of programming languages that can use either the CGI or ISAPI specifications. ASP can only be used by two scripting languages, VBScript and JavaScript, and SSI is limited to a few HTML tags. For a language to use CGI, it must be able to receive input and produce output using the CGI specifications. For a language to use ISAPI, it must be able to interact as a DLL to the web server using ISAPI calls. The more popular languages used by CGI and ISAPI are discussed next.

Perl

Perl (**Practical Extraction and Report Language**) was originally written for shell scripts for the UNIX operating system. An operating system's command interpreter is called a **shell** and a **shell script** is a list of commands stored in a file that should be executed by the shell. Recall from Chapter 4 that in DOS or Windows a batch file contains DOS–like commands that should be executed by the command interpreter. A batch file is an example of a shell script. In UNIX, system administrators often use Perl to perform routine utility tasks such as updating or backing up files. Perl was one of the first languages to use the CGI protocol to customize web pages on a server. An advantage of using Perl for CGI programs is that many UNIX administrators and developers already know Perl.

C and C++

C is a popular programming language developed in 1972 by Bell Laboratories and later standardized by the American National Standards Institute (ANSI). The language is compiled, meaning that the file containing the original list of commands (called the source code) is input into another program (called the compiler) to generate a binary encrypted file that becomes the executable file. This file customarily has an .EXE file extension. To run a C program, you execute the .EXE file, but you can't see or modify the original program unless you have the file that contains the source code.

C was originally designed to run on UNIX computers, but there are now C compilers available for most operating systems. The C programming language is a powerful language that allows a programmer to get to and use information that is not available with other, less sophisticated languages like Visual Basic or Perl.

C++ is an updated evolution of C that uses an object-oriented approach to programming. Remember that in programming, an object is anything that is addressed by the program as an entity with properties, attributes, and rules that the program must follow in order to use the object. Some objects are predefined, and others are defined by the programmer. For example, a C++ program can use an object that accesses a database. All the rules and power needed to access the database are conveniently built into the object. The C++ program doesn't need to know exactly how to access the database; it only needs to know how to interact with the object. It's easier to use an object than to reinvent the wheel each time you want to accomplish a specific task; if an object exists that can do that job, then use the object!

C++ is available on most operating system platforms including UNIX, Windows, and Macintosh. The C++ language has many objects that come with the software and other objects that come with the operating system. A developer can also add new objects that come from third-party software vendors, or the developer can write his or her own objects.

Java

Java is another object-oriented language that was developed by Sun Microsystems. It is a highly portable language, meaning that it was designed so that a Java program written under one operating system would also run on others. Small Java programs can be downloaded from a web server and executed by a web browser if the browser is capable of interpreting Java code. These small Java programs are called **Java applets**. Internet Explorer and Netscape Navigator can both handle Java applets, which are often used to add multimedia effects to a web page. Therefore, Java is used as both a server-side language and a client-side language.

Sun also has developed something called **Java Server Pages** (**JSP**), which are similar to Active Server Pages. Java Server Pages can be used to include Java programming in HTML on a web page. These short segments of Java commands inserted inside the HTML web page are called **Java servlets**. The Java servlets are inserted inside HTML the same way that ASP scripts are inserted (refer back to Figure 6-9), and the web page file has a .jsp extension.

A web server must be JSP enabled, which means it must be able to recognize the JSP programming segments inside the HTML and pass these commands to a program designed to interpret Java called a Java compiler. The web server then runs the Java commands to generate a completed HTML web page that is downloaded to the browser. When a Java command inside a JSP web page needs to access resources on the web site such as a database, it will use a Java module designed for that purpose called a **JavaBean**. A JavaBean is a short Java object designed to work as a reusable component in many different situations.

Java servlets by Sun Microsystems and ASP scripts by Microsoft are competing technologies used by the Web. Another competing technology is that of speech recognition on web sites. Microsoft offers **Speech Application Programming Interface** (**SAPI**) and Sun offers **Java Speech API** (**JSAPI**). In addition, Sun has developed a markup language that uses JSAPI called the **Java Speech Markup Language** (**JSML**). All these technologies have the same goal: to enable a web site to recognize and respond to the human voice and to convert text on the web site to speech. The technologies are not yet ready for mass applications, but when they are, one use for them will be for handheld devices that access web sites. A user will be able to speak into the device to use a web site and hear the spoken response from the site.

Visual Basic

Visual Basic (**VB**) by Microsoft, is a very popular language because it is relatively easy to learn and, because it is written by Microsoft, it interacts well with Windows operating systems. Just like C and C++, Visual Basic is a compiled language, meaning that the program is an executable binary file. Visual Basic can use DLLs effectively and is an object-oriented language. Figure 6-10 shows a Visual Basic developer's window. As the developer builds application windows (called forms) and reports to manage and access a database, the developer can call upon several groups of objects to help. The Object Browser window is displayed in the figure. In order to use the object, the developer must know how to write the programming code to interact with the object.

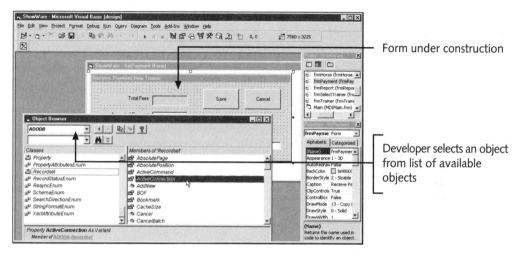

Form under construction

Developer selects an object from list of available objects

6

Figure 6-10   Visual Basic is an object-oriented language. A developer can use the Object Browser window to select an object to include in the application

JavaScript, JScript and VBScript

JavaScript, JScript and VBScript are all scripting languages, meaning that their commands are designed to be included in a web page and executed either by the web server or web browser. A scripting language is not compiled, so the commands, or source code, are readily available in the web page as text and can easily be edited.

VBScript is a subset of Visual Basic for Applications, which is a subset of Visual Basic. Visual Basic for Applications was designed for creating macros for Microsoft products like MS Word or MS Excel. VBScript is designed for writing scripts that can be inserted into web pages. These scripts are executed by either the server or client. VBScript is limited as a scripting language on the client because only Internet Explorer interprets VBScript, although Netscape Navigator can interpret VBScript if the right add-on software is present. VBScript has the advantage over other programming languages because there are many Visual Basic programmers who already know Visual Basic, so learning VBScript is almost effortless.

JavaScript, developed by Netscape for use with Netscape Navigator, resembles Java, but is not a subset of Java in the way that VBScript is a subset of Visual Basic. JavaScript is interpreted by most browsers and is, therefore, the scripting language of choice if you want to serve the most Internet users. JavaScript is also easy to learn. Later in the chapter you will learn to write a short script in a web page using JavaScript.

To compete with JavaScript, Microsoft developed a similar scripting language called **Jscript**, but there are slight inconsistencies between the scripting languages and the way Netscape Navigator and Internet Explorer interpret each. For this reason, it's very important to test a web site using both browsers. Because of JavaScript's popularity and power, an effort has been made by ECMA (European Computer Manufacturers Association), to standardize the language encompassing joint submissions from Microsoft and Netscape. The new hybrid version of the scripting language is called **ECMAScript**. Ideally in the future, ECMAScript will become the accepted standard scripting language used by the entire industry, and all browsers will interpret it the same way, thus making web development much easier.

Learning to Use Scripts

Looking back at Figure 6-5, you see that both client and server scripts can be embedded in a web page. In fact, a web page can have several client and server scripts. For example, in Figure 6-11, the server-side script is executed before the download and the two client-side scripts are executed before the page is displayed. You can also set up the web page in such a way that a client-side script is executed when the user clicks a button on the page.

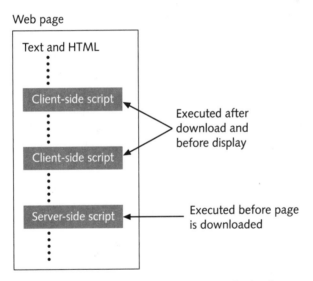

Figure 6-11   A web page can have multiple client- and server-side scripts

All you need to execute a client-side script is a browser; therefore a beginner can easily practice client-side scripting. Simply type the script into the web page and then have the browser view the page. It interprets the script and then displays the page. You'll do this later in this chapter.

Learning to use server-side scripts is a little more difficult because it requires a web server to interpret the script. For an SSI or ASP script, you must type the script into the web page, publish the web page to the server, and then use your browser to access the page. The server retrieves the page, interprets and executes the script, and then passes the results to the browser. If you can publish your web pages to a server that interprets either SSI or ASP, then you can practice these skills. One of the Hands-on Projects at the end of this chapter uses SSI to include a server-side script on your personal web site. You must be using a web server that supports SSI for the script to work. Most servers do support SSI.

In the remaining part of this chapter, you will learn to write some client-side scripts that you can execute with your browser. You will also see some examples of ASP scripts that you will not be able to execute yourself unless you publish the web pages to a web server that supports ASP.

When you want to insert scripts in a web page, you must include tags to mark the beginning and end of the script. Figure 6-12 shows examples of how script tags are entered in HTML code.

6

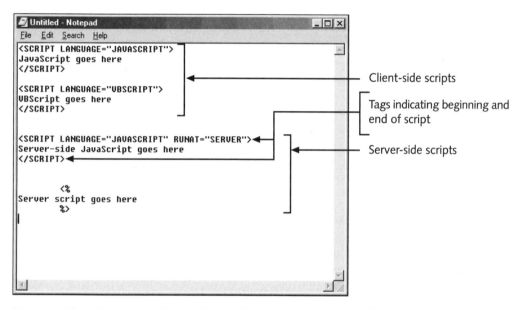

Figure 6-12   Tags are used to indicate where a script begins and ends

Figure 6-12 shows two client-side scripts and two server-side scripts. All work the same way. They have a tag to tell the system that a script follows, and then they have a tag at the end of the script to indicate that the code for the script is completed. If the <%....%> tags are used, the language is assumed to be VBScript.

The server that sees this page will execute the last two scripts and ignore the first two because of the rules that pertain to scripting tags. A server interprets the <SCRIPT> tag without the RUNAT attribute to be a client-side script, and therefore ignores it. Add the attribute RUNAT="SERVER" and the server will execute the script if the server supports ASP. The server assumes the <% ... %> tags are ASP scripts written in the VBScript scripting languages and if the server supports ASP, it will always execute them.

The following sections examine client-side scripting and server-side scripting in more detail. You can follow along by entering the examples from the client-side scripting section, and then running the scripts to see how they work. But, unless you have access to a web server, you will not be able to run the scripts designed for a server.

Client-Side Scripting

In this section, you'll learn to use JavaScript to write a few simple scripts that can be executed by a browser.

Include the Date in a Web Page

In this first JavaScript example listed below and shown in Figure 6-13, the script retrieves and displays the system date. Use Notepad to type the following (don't include the line numbers). Save the file with the name date.htm and then view the file in your browser. Review the steps outlined in Chapter 3 if you need help doing this.

```
1.  <html>
2.  <head>
3.       <title> JavaScript Example </title>
4.  </head>
5.  <body>
6.       Hello, today is
7.       <script LANGUAGE="JAVASCRIPT">
8.            document.write(new Date());
9.       </script>
10. </body>
11. </html>
```

The JavaScript **document.write** command, on line 8, tells the script to write text into the HTML document at the location where the script is inserted. The phrase **new Date( )** retrieves the system date. Each line in a JavaScript ends with a semicolon. In Figure 6-13 you can see the results of the script executed by Netscape Navigator and Internet Explorer that display the system date slightly differently. Look at Figure 6-13 to see an example of this script.

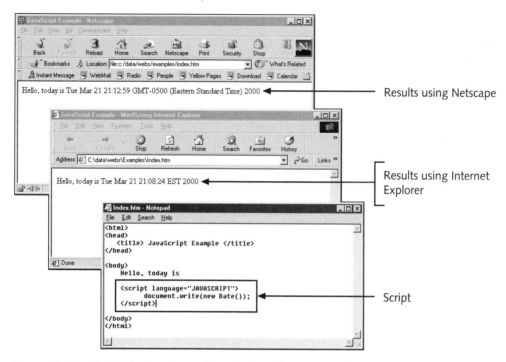

Figure 6-13   A simple JavaScript that displays the system date

Add a Button to a Web Page

The next example introduces some HTML commands that add a button to the web page. When a user clicks the button, a message displays in a box. JavaScript commands are used to create the box and its message.

The program uses the **onCLICK** command, which calls a specific function when the button is clicked. Recall that a function is a segment of scripting that is not executed until an event calls it. In this case, the event is when the user clicks the button on the web page. The function is indicated by the tag **function** and then the name of the function. You can have several functions in one document.

Follow along by entering the code below into Notepad (without the line numbers), saving the file with the name button.htm, and displaying it in your browser.

```
1.   <html>
2.   <head>
3.        <title> JavaScript Example </title>
4.   </head>
5.   <body>
6.        Hello, today is
7.        <script language="JAVASCRIPT">
8.            document.write(new Date());
```

```
9.         </script>
10.        <form>
11.            <input type="BUTTON" VALUE="Click Here"
               onCLICK="MyGreeting()">
12.        </form>
13. </body>
14.        <script language="JAVASCRIPT">
15.        function MyGreeting(){
16.        alert ("I'm learning JavaScript");
17.            }
18.        </script>
19. </html>
```

This example looks more complicated than it is. Here is a breakdown of what the commands are doing. You first saw the <INPUT> tag in Chapter 3 when it was used to create a button to submit data on a form via an e-mail message. Here you use the same <INPUT> tag to create a button that simply says "Click Here." When the user clicks the button, the function executes. You can follow along with each bullet point by looking at the example.

- An input button is added to the HTML by inserting a form, which was discussed in Chapter 3. The form begins on line 10. The input tag is put inside the form tags because it is used to specify an input control for a form. The form tag does not use an **ACTION** method as those in Chapter 3 did because there is no data input into the form for processing.

- The input type is **BUTTON** (line 11). There are several different input types, such as a field, password, check box, and button. Each type of input can reside inside a form.

- The input tag that defines the button is given the value **Click Here**. This is how you specify what is displayed on the button. The code uses the **onCLICK** command to name a function that is performed when the button is clicked. When the user clicks the button, the system calls the function. Remember, a function is a segment of programming instructions that is executed as a single unit from somewhere else in the program. In this case the function is called **MyGreeting()**, and if you look later in the HTML code at line 15, you will find where the function MyGreeting() is defined.

- The function displays a message in an alert box, shown on line 16. An **alert box** in JavaScript is a small box that opens on the desktop and displays a message to the user. It is normally used to get the user's attention to an error or a special condition of which they should be aware.

- Note that the MyGreeting() function has parentheses at the end of the name. A function name always ends with open and close parentheses. Sometime values are included inside the parentheses. The value is then passed to the function for processing.

- Note in line 15 the use of braces { } which mark the beginning and ending of the code that defines the function. In JavaScript, braces are used to mark a segment of code that is to be treated as a unit.

- The part of the script that defines the function is placed below the <BODY> tags of the document because it is really executed outside the body as a called function. The script and the function inside it would never be executed unless the user clicks the button. This is the nature of a function—it's only executed when called upon to do so by some special condition being met, such as the clicking of a button or when an error occurs.

Figure 6-14 shows how both Netscape and Internet Explorer display the code. This method of defining a function that is executed when a button is clicked is a common method used for validating data that the user has entered in an HTML form before the data is sent to the server.

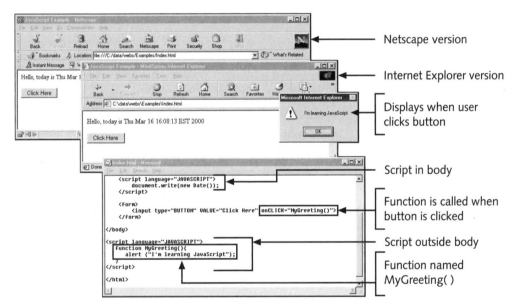

Figure 6-14   A function inside a JavaScript is executed when the user clicks a button

Create a Script that Checks for Errors in User Input

In the following example of client-side scripting, you will see how a script can validate data before the data is sent to the server for processing. It's important to validate data so that bad data is not accepted when a user clicks the Send button. It's the responsibility of developers to prevent bad data from entering a database, and to inform the user of the action being taken. In most cases, the appropriate action is to give the user an opportunity to correct the bad data without having to reenter any data on the form that is already correct.

This web page displays a message to the user and invites the user to enter his or her name and e-mail address and click the Send button to send the data to the server. The client-side script verifies that the e-mail address contains the "@" symbol. Figure 6-15 shows the form for entering the data and the error message that results if the e-mail address doesn't contain the "@" symbol.

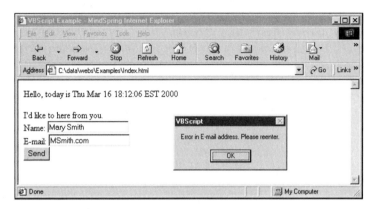

Figure 6-15 An error message displays if the user does not enter an @ symbol in the e-mail address field

When the user enters data in the form, the server receives and processes the data, perhaps entering the information into a database or text file for later use. The name of the web page file that receives the data is UpdateList.asp, which contains an ASP script to process the data. The script below verifies that an e-mail address contains the @ symbol. Again, follow along by typing the script into a file, saving the file with the name errorcheck.htm, and viewing the results. (Remember, don't type the line numbers!)

Also, remember, because the data entered is processed by UpdateList.asp, the data will not be processed unless that file is available.

```
1.  <html>
2.  <head>
3.      <title> VBScript Example </title>
4.  </head>
5.
6.  <body>
7.      Hello, today is
8.
9.      <script language="JAVASCRIPT">
10.         document.write(new Date());
11.     </script>
12.
13.     <form method=GET action="UpdateList.asp">
14.         I'd like to hear from you. <br>
15.         Name: <input type=text name=YourName> <br>
16.         E-mail: <input type=text name=YourEmail> <br>
17.         <input type="BUTTON" VALUE="Send"
                onCLICK="MyCheck(this.form)">
```

```
18.        </form>
19.
20. </body>
21.
22. <script language="VBSCRIPT">
23.        sub MyCheck(MyForm)
24.                if (instr(MyForm.YourEmail.value,"@")=0) then
25.                        msgbox ("Error in e-mail address.
                           Please reenter.")
26.                        else
27.                MyForm.submit()
28.                end if
29.        end sub
30. </script>
31.
32. </html>
```

The first script on the web page is written in JavaScript, but the script to validate the e-mail address is written in VBScript. It is okay to mix scripting languages within a page, and sometimes it is even suggested. Perhaps you have already written a script in VBScript and you are working on another web page that needs the same script. Even though the new web page will have scripts written primarily in JavaScript, why should you spend time rewriting a script you have already written? Instead you can just add the script that was written in VBScript.

The Form Tag   Look first at Line 13, which shows how the FORM tag has been changed from the previous examples. The **METHOD** is **GET** and the **ACTION** calls the web page named UpdateList.asp. A web page that has an .ASP file extension contains Active Server Pages scripting. Because the form method is GET, the contents entered on this form (name and e-mail address) are sent to the UpdateList.asp page as part of the URL. Later in this chapter you'll learn how the data is included in the URL.

The Text Box and Send Button   Lines 15 through 16 display the text boxes for user input, and Line 17 creates the Send button. Line 17 defines these things:

- It makes the input type as **BUTTON**, creating a command button on the page

- The text written on the button is **Send**

- When the user clicks the button, a function is executed named **MyCheck**. When the MyCheck function executes, it will have the contents of the form available to examine. This is because the entry inside the parenthesis following the function name, **"MyCheck(this.form)"** says to execute the function **MyCheck** and send the contents of **this.form** to the function. The function is then free to use all the data that was entered on the form. It will look at the e-mail address but not examine the name.

Defining the Function   The VBScript begins at Line 22 and ends at Line 30 and contains only the single function which begins with **SUB** and ends with **END SUB**. **SUB** and **END SUB** refer to "Begin subroutine" and "End Subroutine" because a function is sometimes called a subroutine.

Line 23 defines the name of the function, **MyCheck**, and says that this function has access to information that it will call **MyForm**. As we saw from Line 17, that information is the data that was entered on **this.form**. The function looks at the e-mail address and makes a decision. Will it display an error message or will it send the data on up to the server to be received by the UpdateList.asp web page? The decision is based on the contents of the e-mail address. Does it contain an @ symbol?

In common English, Lines 24 through 28 read like this:

> If the e-mail address entered into the form does not contain an @ symbol

> Then display an error message

> Else submit the form's data to the web page named earlier at the beginning of the form.

If the e-mail address does not contain the @ symbol, then an error message displays. If the e-mail address does contain the @ symbol then Line 27 is executed, which submits the form contents to the web server and on to the web page UpdateList.asp.

How the Script is Processed   If the user made a mistake, as shown in Figure 6-15, and did not include the @ symbol in the address, he or she can enter the address again and click Send again. When the address is entered correctly, the script sends the data in the form to UpdateList.asp as part of the URL. The URL looks like this:

http://domain.com/UpdateList.asp?YourName=Mary+Smith&YourEmail= msmith@aol.com

Domain.com is the name of the web site from which this web page was retrieved. The URL contains the name of each data item on the form (**YourName, YourEmail**) and the data that was entered into these data items (**Mary Smith, msmith@aol.com**) The plus sign is used instead of a space in the URL and data item entries are separated with the & symbol. Later in this chapter you'll learn what happens on the server side when the UpdateList.asp web page receives the contents of the form.

Accommodating Older Browsers

Some older browsers were not built to interpret scripts. If they encounter the <SCRIPT> tags in an HTML document, they don't know what to do with these tags and simply pass over them. The browser continues on to the next line after the <SCRIPT> tag and tries to interpret that line as HTML. The result can be a browser error, or the browser simply displays the script commands as text on the screen, which results in confusing and meaningless text presented to the user. In order to prevent this from happening, get in the habit of tagging all commands within a script as HTML comments, which older browser ignore if they are erroneously trying to interpret the script as HTML. Newer browsers understand the script tags, and they know to interpret the text between the script tags as commands and not HTML or text. Recall from Chapter 3 that a comment in HTML is marked using the <!-- and -- > tags. When you add these comment tags to the two scripts in the web page shown in Figure 6-15, the result is shown below. Note Lines 10, 12, 25 and 33:

```
1.  <html>
2.  <head>
3.       <title> VBScript Example </title>
4.  </head>
5.
6.  <body>
7.       Hello, today is
8.
9.       <script language="JAVASCRIPT">
10.      <!--
11.              document.write(new Date());
12.      -->
13.      </script>
14.
15.      <form method=GET action="UpdateList.asp">
16.              I'd like to hear from you. <br>
17.              Name: <input type=text name=YourName> <br>
18.              E-mail: <input type=text name=YourEmail> <br>
19.              <input type="BUTTON" VALUE="Send"
                 onCLICK="MyCheck(this.form)">
20.      </form>
21.
22.  </body>
23.
24.  <script language="VBSCRIPT">
25.  <!--
26.      Sub MyCheck(MyForm)
27.              if (instr(MyForm.YourEmail.value,"@")=0) then
28.                      msgbox ("Error in e-mail address.
                         Please reenter.")
29.              else
30.              MyForm.submit()
31.              end if
32.      end sub
33.  -->
34.  </script>
35.
36.  </html>
```

6

Server-side Scripting

Now that you have a brief introduction to scripting on the client side, it's time to look at scripts that are executed by the server before the web page is downloaded to the browser. A server script receives information passed to it from the browser and from files and databases available to it on the server. Recall that when a web server that supports ASP first receives a browser's request, it can scan a web page for an embedded script and execute the script which alters the page before it is downloaded.

One important job that can be performed by server side scripts is maintaining a conversation between a web browser and a web server. A web server keeps no records of previous requests from a web browser or replies to those requests. Recall from earlier chapters that the HTTP protocol used by the World Wide Web is a stateless protocol as compared to other protocols like FTP and SMTP that are stateful protocols. Looking back at Table 4–1 in Chapter 4 at the SMTP dialogue between e-mail servers, you can see that each server is aware of the continuing conversation in the established session. When one server makes a new request or reply, the other server is able to pick up in the conversation where it left off in the previous request or reply. However, with HTTP, when a client is making a series of requests to a web server, since the protocol is stateless, the server treats each request as though it were the first request ever made by this client and has no record of previous communication with it.

Because each request and reply from a web server is independent of other requests or replies, whenever a browser sends a request, it must include all information needed by the server in the request. When the server receives the request, it executes any scripts inside the requested page or, in the case of the CGI method, it executes the requested program. The scripts or program can update a file or database on the server with information from the browser. For example, if a web site processes orders from customers, the program or script updates a database or file with the order information. It then creates or revises a web page that is sent back to the browser that says that the order has been received. Or, it might ask for more information, such as shipping method or credit card information for the order.

In the example of server-side scripting that follows, ASP is the scripting protocol and VBScript is the scripting language on a Windows NT server. Remember that unless you have access to a web server, you will probably not be able to run these examples. The examples require a web server that supports ASP.

Using ASP (Active Server Pages)

Active Server Pages (ASP) is a technology that is included with Microsoft ISS 4.0 and their Personal Web Server 4.0. ASP is designed to allow the web server to interpret scripts and handle them before the scripts are sent to the client PC. ASP works as an object-oriented protocol. Recall from earlier in the chapter that an object is like a middle man that manages the interface between the script and some other entity on the server.

ASP has a big advantage for programmers because it has a lot of predefined objects, which ASP calls ActiveX Data Objects (ADO). These ADOs come with ASP and have been designed to perform features that developers often desire. Therefore, when a developer is using ASP, he can often just locate an ADO to do the job rather than creating the object from scratch. For example, one of the most common things to do with a dynamic web site is to collect information and store the information in a database. ASP has more than one ADO which generates ASP applications that transfer information between the user and a database.

Another advantage of ASP is that it can use JavaScript or VBScript, although by default ASP scripts are written in VBScript. VBScript is quickly becoming the most popular scripting language, so the fact that ASP uses VBScript is helping to make it popular with developers.

Figure 6-16 shows four objects used by ASP pages together with the major functions of these objects.

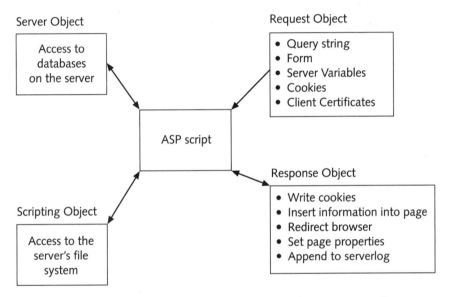

Figure 6-16   An ASP script has access to objects that interact with resources external to the script

- The request object contains information from the browser that made the request.

- The response object enables the script to provide output to the browser.

- The scripting object, among several other things, provides access to the file system on the server. A file system is the drives, directories, and files on the server's secondary storage devices.

- The server object provides access to databases on the server and is discussed in Chapter 7.

Figure 6-17 shows how each object relates to the client and to resources on the web server, including databases and files. Other ASP objects will be introduced in the next chapter.

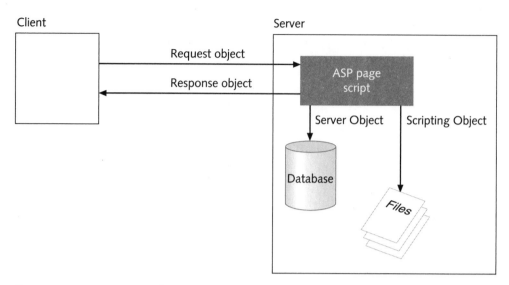

Figure 6-17 Using ASP, the Request and Response objects are used to receive and send data to the client, and other objects have access to resources on the web site

Request Objects

An object is accessed in an ASP script by using the name of the object followed by a part of the object called a property. A property further defines an object and an object has several properties, each used for a different purpose. For example, the request object can be used to get the data that the browser sent to the script in the URL that called the script. To use the request object to enter data into the **YourName** data item, use the script entry **request.querystring ("YourName")**, where **request** is the name of the object, **querystring** is a property of the object, and **YourName** is the name of the data item.

The request object has five properties that the script can draw from for information:

- *Query string.* The browser creates a **query string** that is included in the URL to the server. The content of the query string is the values the user entered into a form on a previous web page. To use this method, the **FORM NAME** tag of this web page must contain **METHOD=GET**.

- *Data from a form.* The browser embeds the values entered into a form into the HTTP header information. This method is more secure, because a user cannot see the values displayed in the address box of the browser in the URL, and because values inside the HTTP header are encrypted. To use this method, the **FORM NAME** tag must contain **METHOD=POST**.

- *Cookies.* The browser sends any values contained in a cookie on the PC, along with the request. The cookie content is embedded in the HTTP header. The request object can be used to read this cookie.

- *Client certificates.* If the PC is using client certificates as a security precaution, the browser sends certificate information to the server inside the HTTP header. Certificates are discussed in Chapter 12.

- *Server variables.* After the request has reached the server, the server can get information about its own environment such as date and time at the server.

Response Objects

The response object includes several properties that are beyond the scope of our discussion, but the most common ones include the ability to:

- Write cookies on the client PC and set the properties of these cookies

- Insert information into the web page

- Redirect the browser to another URL

- Set properties of the web page such as the length of time the page can be cached on the client browser

- Append information to a log file on the server

A log file can be used to determine who has accessed the site, and record any errors that occurred on the site, which can be useful information when you troubleshoot problems with the site.

This next example uses the request object to pass information to the script and the response object to send a message back to the browser. Looking back at the web page shown in Figure 6-15, notice that a person's name and e-mail address was entered into the previous web page. After the e-mail address was validated by a client-side script, the script sent a URL to the web server using the GET method. An example of a URL sent to the server from this web page looks like this:

http://buystory.com/UpdateList.asp?YourName=Mary+Smith&YourEmail= msmith@aol.com

This URL results in the web page Updatelist.asp, that is shown below and in Figure 6-18.

```
1.   <html>
2.   <head>
3.      <title> Server Side Script Example </title>
4.   </head>
5.
6.   <body>
7.      <%
8.      NewName = request.querystring("YourName")
9.      NewEmail = request.querystring("YourEmail")
10.     response.write "Thank you for your request, "
11.     response.write NewName
12.     response.write ". You will hear from us shortly."
```

```
13.     %>
14.     <form>
15.             <input type=BUTTON VALUE="Continue"
                onCLICK="history.go(-2)">
16.     </form>
17. </body>
18. </html>
```

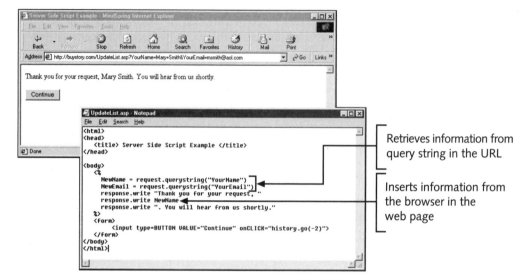

Figure 6-18   The ASP script receives information from the browser in the URL and modifies the web page

Here's a breakdown of the script.

- The script begins in Line 7 and ends in Line 13 with <% and %>. The script uses the request object with the **querystring** property to retrieve data sent to the page via the URL. When you want to use an object in ASP, you write the name of the object, a period, and the name of the property within the object that you want to access or use.

- Line 8 retrieves the value that is named **YourName** into a VBScript variable named **NewName**. This variable becomes a temporary holding place for the data so that you can use the data within the web page. If you want to use the person's name anywhere on the web page, refer to it as **NewName**. In Lines 10 through 12, the response object's write property is used to insert information into the page.

- Line 11 inserts the person's name into the page.

- Lines 14 through 16 are HTML lines to create a button on the page labeled **Continue**. There is a technique demonstrated here that has nothing to do with ASP, but is included to help build your HTML skills. The HTML button created in Line 15 has an **onCLICK** event, which uses HTML code to access the history of web pages accessed by the browser. Later, when the page is downloaded to the browser and the user clicks the continue button, the browser will move backward two pages which, in effect, is what would happen if the user had clicked the Back button on the browser twice.

In this example, the ASP script writes the name of the user on the web page along with a thank you message. When the user reads the message and clicks the Continue button, the browser moves back two pages in its history log.

Writing the Data to a Flat File

In the previous example, the request and response objects were used to receive the data and inform the user that the data had been received. If that was all that happened, the data would be lost because we did not put it anywhere once it was received. In this example, you will add the script commands to write the data to a file so that it can be used at a later date. To do this, you'll use the scripting object, which allows you to interact with files on the server. A simple text-based data file that is not a part of a database is called a flat file. A flat file is a simple and inexpensive way to save data.

The web page containing the script shown below is only responsible for saving the data to the file. Once the data is stored in the data file, someone must be responsible for using FTP to download the flat file to a PC, read the data in the file, and process it.

Remember, since this is a server-side script, it will not work on your machine unless you have a web server that supports ASP. Also in Line 15, replace the path given (D:\FTP\DATAFILES\MYFILE.TXT) with the path and filename you will use on your web server.

```
1.   <html>
2.   <head>
3.      <title> Server Side Script Example </title>
4.   </head>
5.
6.   <body>
7.      <%
8.         NewName = request.querystring("YourName")
9.         NewEmail = request.querystring("YourEmail")
10.        response.write "Thank you for your request,"
11.        response.write NewName
12.        response.write ". You will hear from us shortly."
13.        Const ForWriting = 2
14.        Set FSys = CreateObject("Scripting.FileSystem
           Object")
15.        Set TStream = FSys.OpenTextFile("D:\FTP\DATAFILES\
           MYFILE.TXT", ForWriting)
```

```
16.        TStream.WriteLine (NewName)
17.        TStream.WriteLine (NewEmail)
18.    %>
19.    <form>
20.            <input type=BUTTON VALUE="Continue"
               onCLICK="history.go(-2)">
21.    </form>
22. </body>
23. </html>
```

Our purpose is not to explain every line of this ASP script, but to simply demonstrate how an object can be used to access and write to a flat file on a server. In order to understand all the script, you would need to know how to write complex VBScript scripts, which is beyond the scope of this book. However, here are the high points of using the scripting object to write data to a flat file.

In Line 14 of the script, a scripting object is created that gives access to the server's file system so you can use the files and directories on the server. In Line 15, an object is created which opens an existing file on the server named MYFILE.TXT. In Lines 16 and 17, two new lines of data are written to this text file containing the name and the e-mail address of the user.

The scripting object created in Line 14 is type **FileSystemObject**. This type of object is used to allow a script to interface with files on the server. There are many methods that can be used with this object to create and delete directories and files and update them. The only method used in this example is to open an existing text file, which gains access to that file and its contents. You do that by creating another object that further qualifies or defines the **FileSystemObject**. A text stream object further defines a file system object and is used to read and write data to text files. The object is created in Line 15, named **TStream**, and is used to open the file MYFILE.TXT. The **TStream** object is then used to write two lines to the file.

All About Cookies

Cookies are information sent from a web server to a browser. The information is then stored in a text file on the user's computer to be retrieved by a web server at a later time. Cookies are used to:

- Personalize a web site with the user's name or other information
- Remember what a person has purchased or placed in a shopping cart to purchase later (A **shopping cart** is software used by a server to hold information about items selected for purchase.)
- Track web site activity to see who has visited the site and which pages on the site they access
- Target marketing effort based on your interests

Cookies can contain any information that you enter into a form on a web page and some environmental information about your computer. To know what information a web server can get from your computer, see *www.doubleclick.net*.

A cookie is a shortcut method of tracking information about the user without having to prompt the user each time the information is needed. Without cookies, shopping on the Internet could be much more time consuming, because you might be required to enter all information about your order on every page of the site processing your order. Without cookies, the server would not "remember" anything as you moved from one page to the next page, selecting items to place in your shopping cart, and then making the final purchase. Without cookies, when you got to the final page to place your order, you would need to reenter everything about each item ordered and your billing information. With cookies, the information gathered along the way is available at the last purchase point.

Under Windows 9x, Internet Explorer stores cookies in the Windows\Cookies folder using the filename format **userid@domain.com**. Under Windows NT, Internet Explorer stores cookies in the \WinNT\Profiles\username\Cookies folder. Netscape Navigator stores cookies in a text file, \Program Files\Netscape\Users\yourname\cookies.txt. A cookie can contain encrypted information that only the server that created it can understand. If a cookie is marked as a secure cookie, then it will only be transmitted to the server when a session is secured. Chapter 12 covers how to secure an HTTP session.

Some people are concerned about privacy and don't want cookies stored on a computer. This can be a valid concern when the computer is not your own personal computer, but one at work, in a public library, or other public location. For that reason, browsers provide the option to disable all cookies or prompt the user before writing a cookie. Because cookies are just text files, you generally cannot catch a virus from a cookie. People disable cookies so that companies cannot track their Internet habits. You can read about how to control cookies later in this chapter.

Figure 6-19 shows the process of setting and retrieving a cookie. A cookie is created when the HTTP header contains the command **Set-Cookie**. Information about the cookie is included in the header and a name/value pair contains the data. An example of a name/value pair is **USERID=Mary Smith**. Later, when the cookie is retrieved, the value **Mary Smith** is assigned to the name **USERID**. A cookie can contain multiple name/value pairs.

Later, when the user again requests web pages from the web site that created the cookie, the browser recognizes that it is holding a cookie for this web site and sends the cookie information in the HTTP header when requesting the page. The effect created is a stateful HTTP session in which the browser and server can maintain a dialog using cookies to keep track of where they are in the conversation.

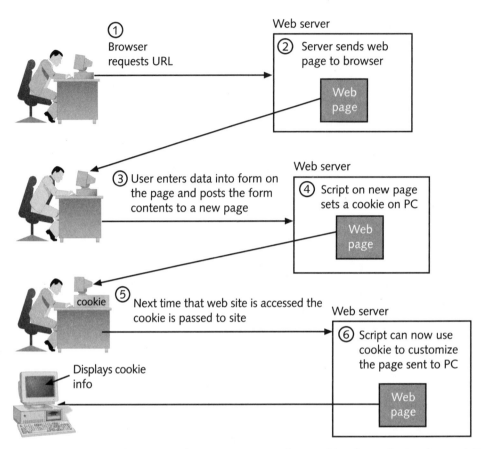

Figure 6-19   A cookie is stored on a users PC to be used by the web site the next time the user accesses the site

Using Cookies

Notice in Figure 6-16 that when using ASP scripting, cookies are listed under both the request and response objects, which means that you can use both these objects with cookies. An ASP script can read a cookie using the request object and write a cookie using the response object. For example, to write the user's name into a cookie on the user's computer, from an ASP script on the server, use this command:

```
Response.cookies("USERID") = NewName
```

To read the user's name from a cookie using the request object, use this command:

```
NewName = Request.cookies("USERID")
```

A cookie has an expiration time that you can set with the response object. To set the cookie expiration property so that the cookie expires on a given date, use this command:

```
Response.cookies("USERID").expires = #1/1/2005#
```

Recall that information about cookies is included in the HTTP header information when it is sent from browser to server or from server to browser. The HTTP header is written first and the web page follows.

Controlling Cookies on a Client

In some situations, people might consider cookies a violation of privacy or security and want to disable the ability of a web server to place a cookie on their computer, or at least to know when a cookie is being put there.

If you are using Netscape Navigator, you can control your cookie settings on your PC. Follow these directions:

1. Click **Edit** on the menu bar, then click **Preferences**. The Preferences dialog box opens.

2. Click **Advanced** in the list of categories. The Advanced settings appear, as shown in Figure 6-20. From this window, you can choose to disable cookies, accept only cookies that get sent back to the server that created them, and warn you before you accept a cookie. The default setting is Accept all cookies. Normally, you would leave it at this setting

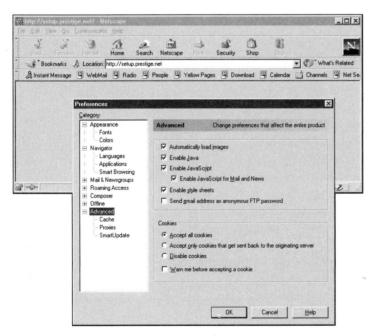

Figure 6-20   Netscape settings to control cookies

If you are using Internet Explorer and you want to change your cookie settings, follow these directions:

1. Click **Start** on the Taskbar, and point to **Settings**, then click **Control Panel**. The Control Panel opens.

2. Double-click the **Internet Options** icon. The Internet Properties window opens.

3. Click the **Security** tab and then click **Custom Level** button at the bottom of the window. The Security Settings window opens, as shown in Figure 6-21.

4. Scroll down to the Cookies section. There you can choose to enable or disable the ability of the browser to write cookies to your computer, or to prompt you before it creates a cookie. When prompted, you can choose to not allow the cookie to be written. Click the option button of the setting you want in each section.

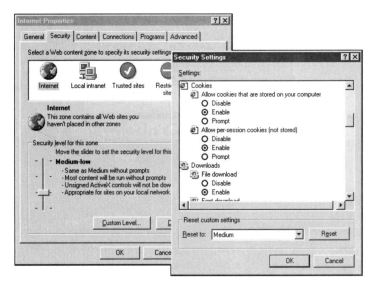

Figure 6-21   Use Internet Options of Control Panel to control how Internet Explorer handles cookies

    For detailed specifications about cookies, see RFC 2109 at *www.rfc-editor.org* and for more information about cookies, see *www.cookiecentral.com*.

PRE-LAUNCH TESTING

Remember from Chapter 3 that before publishing a web page, you tested the page by displaying it using different browsers, screen resolutions, and operating systems. The goal is that when the web site is published, users will find the site as error free as possible and can download the page in a reasonably short time. Scripts that are executed by a browser can be tested using these same methods. However, problems arise when web pages contain server-side scripts. How do you test these pages and their scripts before you publish them to your web site? Server-side scripts cannot be tested by displaying them in a web browser because the browser will not execute them. You must test them using a web server.

There are two approaches to testing server-side scripts: test the site on another server designated as a test server, or test the site in a different directory on the site server itself. When a server is set aside for testing, it is sometimes called the test bed. A test bed is used for large, commercial sites that can afford to keep hardware and software dedicated just to testing.

A less expensive approach is to test using a different directory on the main web server. For example, suppose your web server has the domain name *www.mystore.com* at the IP address 208.30.200.13. The home page for the site is named Index.html and is stored in the root directory of this server or virtual server. Under the root directory are server subdirectories used to hold images and other pages for the site. The directory tree looks like that shown in Figure 6-22.

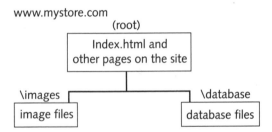

Figure 6-22   Directory structure of a web site

You can create a "mirror" of the site in a directory structure under the root directory for testing changes to the site before you publish the site to the Internet community. Create a directory under the root named Testing, and create the same directories under it that exist under the root. See Figure 6-23 for an example of this. These directories become a virtual test bed and should contain all the files that make up the actual site. Because directory names are named relative to the current folder, if the Index.html page refers to a file in the \Images directory, it looks for a directory immediately under it named Images. If Index.html is on the real site in the root directory, it goes to Images under the root. If Index.html is in the \Testing directory, it goes to \Testing\Images to locate the image file.

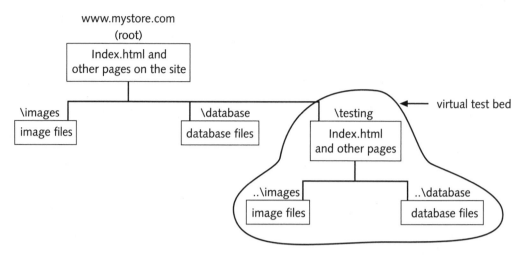

Figure 6-23 Directories under the root directory of a web site can be used to test web pages before they are published to the Internet community

To test changes to your site, using FTP or some other transfer utility, copy the files from your PC to the \testing directory or one of the directories under it. To test these pages, use the URL **www.mystore.com\testing**. After you have tested the site, copy the pages to the root directory to release them to the Internet community.

Some developers prefer to provide some security so that outsiders cannot access the \testing directory or its subdirectories. One simple way to do that is to name the \testing directory a very difficult name such as \X57U23 or something like that. Few web surfers would accidentally stumble upon that URL.

Your site might offer debugging tools for testing ASP scripts. The Microsoft web server, Internet Information Server 4.0, has a built-in Microsoft Script Debugger that helps track errors and passes information about those errors to the developer. Earlier versions of IIS didn't offer this feature.

When testing a site, it's important to have a testing plan rather than to just randomly test whatever functions the web site is intended to do. Write down a detailed list of everything that needs to be tested (all hyperlinks, text boxes, buttons, and so forth) and all conditions under which these things need to be tested (different screen resolutions, operating systems, and so forth). A spreadsheet is a good tool to use for this purpose. Include in the spreadsheet a column to check when the test has been performed successfully. Make up test data that tests all scenarios that the web site should cover. For example, when testing an e-mail address text box, use different types of e-mail addresses and don't forget to include no e-mail address at all in the test data. It has been said that a program or script is no better than the test data that tested it. So be careful to use a complete set of test data.

6

REAL PEOPLE, REAL PROBLEMS, REAL SOLUTIONS
DATA ON THE FLY

Several options crossed Pat Donohue's mind when he was approached with an idea from The Registry Group, a start-up Internet company. The company's idea was to provide a universal gift registry for any given group of individuals using the Web. Pat believed they had a good plan, but also knew they had a limited budget to get the site off the ground. The Registry Group's site, *www.ouregistry.com*, was predicted to generate a large amount of visitor traffic from the start and would need to accommodate a heavy data load.

Pat's firm, Apeweb, LLC (*www.apeweb.com*), was used to working with companies that could afford to build large sites that used strong databases and server products. He knew that the new client needed the right system to get the site to its next funding stage. At that point, the architecture could change and be built with a more robust data support system. To accomplish the initial goal, the only solution was to build a system that would deliver the data resourcefully for a modest cost.

The answer was individual data files, or flat files, for each assembly of people. Pat knew that by building custom scripts, they could accommodate the anticipated visitor traffic. Instead of building a large database to handle the registry groups, he would use a series of scripts that would build small, effective data files on demand. The flexibility of Perl 5, a server-side scripting language, would allow constant creation of new data files that would reside on the server.

After designing the model of the scripts, they were programmed based on the CGI (Common Gateway Interface) model. These scripts would be able to continually build flat data files on demand. When a visitor to the site would create a new group registry, a new data file would be generated and stored on the server. Apeweb programmed a system on Perl scripts that produced individual files that could be accessed and modified. In effect, it was an efficient data file system without a database!

The Registry Group's site continues to grow and attract more traffic still using the flat data file system. *Ouregistry.com* was produced using efficient programming methods that fit budgeting requirements. The next stage of the site is in development by Apeweb—using an SQL database to help manage the site and its growth.

CHAPTER SUMMARY

☐ Scripts are used on either the server (server-side script) or the client (client-side script) to customize a web page. A customized web page is called a dynamic web page, as opposed to a static web page that never changes.

☐ Scripts are short programs that are written as text in a document file.

❑ A common use for a client-side script is to compensate for the slight differences between the way Netscape and Internet Explorer interpret HTML. A script determines which browser is being used and adjusts the HTML accordingly.

❑ Programs and scripts on the server use one of several methods to interface with the web server including CGI (Common Gateway Interface), ISAPI (Internet Server Application Programming Interface), and ASP (Active Server Pages).

❑ CGI originated on the UNIX platform. ISAPI was originally designed to be used by Microsoft web server, Internet Information Server (IIS), using the Windows NT operating system. ASP is used on Windows platforms.

❑ A browser points to a CGI program that generates a virtual web page using various elements on the server. The web page is customized based on information sent to it by the browser.

❑ Scripts using ISAPI relate to web servers as dynamic linked library (DLL) programs that can remain loaded in memory even after the program terminates. Because these DLLs can remain in memory and don't need to be loaded each time they are called, the ISAPI method is generally faster than the CGI method.

❑ Server-side scripts often use log files to track errors and other activity on the web site.

❑ ASP (Active Server Pages) technology by Microsoft provides a method for a web server to look for and execute scripts in web pages before they are downloaded to the client. ASP scripts can be written in VBScript, JavaScript, or JScript.

❑ One of the first languages to use CGI was Perl, which was first used as a UNIX shell scripting language by UNIX system administrators. CGI is now available on most hardware and operating system environments. Other languages often used to write CGI programs are C, C++, Java, and Visual Basic.

❑ Similar to Active Server Pages, Java Server Pages (JSP) is a technology that allows Java programming segments to be written into a web page and executed by the server before the page is downloaded to the browser.

❑ VBScript is a subset of Visual Basic. JScript is Microsoft's look-alike language for Netscape's JavaScript. JavaScript resembles Java but is not a subset of Java. ECMAScript is the up-and-coming standard developed by ECMA (European Computer Manufacturers Association) that encompasses both JavaScript and JScript.

❑ Server and client scripts in HTML are marked using the <SCRIPT> and </SCRIPT> tags. A server script can also be marked using the <% and %> tags.

❑ A web page can contain several scripts for both server and browser written in more than one language.

❑ A function is a program segment that is called from somewhere else in the program to perform a given task.

❑ A client-side script is often used to validate data before it is sent to the server.

❏ In order to not confuse older browsers that don't interpret scripts, enclose all the script commands in HTML comment tags (<!-- and -- >) so the commands will be ignored by these older browsers.

❏ An ASP request object has access to URL query strings, data in the called form, cookies on the client PC, client certificates used to secure a session, and server variables.

❏ The ASP response object can write cookies on the client PC, insert text into the web page, redirect the browser to another URL, set properties of the web page, and append information to a log file on the server.

❏ The ASP scripting object can be used to write data to a text file on the server.

❏ Web browsers offer the ability for users to control if and how cookies are written to their PCs.

❏ A web site that contains server-side scripting should be tested using a web server before the site is published to the Internet community. The site can be tested either using a web server totally dedicated to that purpose, or using a different file location on the same web server used to publish the site.

❏ Test data should be thorough, covering all scenarios expected to be encountered when the site is published.

KEY TERMS

alert box — A message box that can be displayed on the user's screen by a JavaScript to get the user's attention.

argument — In programming, an argument qualifies or modifies the action that is stated in a command.

ASP (Active Server Pages) — A Microsoft technology that allows a web page to contain a server-side script. Some objects that are built into ASP scripting are the request, response, scripting and server objects.

C — A programming language that provides direct access by the programmer to low-level hardware devices such as memory.

C++ — An updated version of C that is object-oriented.

CGI (Common Gateway Interface) — Specifications and protocols used by programs on the server to customize a web page before it is downloaded to the browser. For example, CGI determines how a program can read information in a query string included in the URL to the web site.

client-side script — A script embedded in a web page that is performed by the browser either before the browser displays the page or when the user clicks a button or performs some other action on the page.

command — In programming, an order to perform an action, such as "open a file."

compiling — In programming, the process of changing the source code so that the computer's processor can execute the program.

DLL (dynamic linked library) — A utility program that is called by another program to perform a specific task. For example, a Windows print DLL is called by Microsoft Word to print a document, so that Word does not need to manage the print process. In Windows 9x, DLL files are normally stored in the \Windows\System folder.

dynamic web page — A web page that can be customized by a script or program

ECMAScript (European Computer Manufacturers Association) — A scripting language that encompasses both JavaScript and Jscript, developed with input from both Netscape and Microsoft, designed to ultimately replace both JavaScript and JScript.

executable file — A program file that normally has a .EXE file extension. Using Windows 9x, to execute a program file, from Windows Explorer, double click on the file name.

function — A segment of a program that is assigned a name and sits dormant until called by a command from somewhere else in the program to perform a given task.

ISAPI (Internet Server Application Programming Interface) — A technology developed by Microsoft to be used by the web server Internet Information Server (IIS), so that programs on a web site can be written to interact with the web server as a DLL.

Java — An object-oriented programming language developed by Sun Microsystems. Programs written in Java are designed to easily port to different platforms and operating systems without having to alter the programming code.

Java applet — A small Java program that can be downloaded to a browser and used to perform tasks that the browser cannot do, such as add multimedia effects to a web page.

JavaBean — A short Java program designed to work as a reusable component or object in many different situations.

JavaScript — A scripting language developed by Netscape to be used with Netscape Navigator, but which can now be used by web servers as well as clients.

Java Server Pages (JSP) — A technology developed by Sun Microsystems that uses Java programs called Java servlets in HTML to be executed by the web server before the web page is downloaded.

Java servlet — A short Java program embedded in an HTML document.

Java Speech API (JSAPI) — An interface used by Java programs developed by Sun to recognize voice and convert text to speech.

JScript — Microsoft's version of JavaScript developed to be used with Internet Explorer.

log file — A text file that is used to record activity and events encountered or done by an application.

macro — A script stored in a Word or Excel document for later execution. *See* script.

object — In programming, anything that is addressed by the program as an entity with properties, attributes and rules that the program must follow in order to use the object.

object code — In programming, source code that has been compiled into instructions that can be executed by the CPU.

Perl (Practical Extraction and Report Language) — A programming language originally used to write UNIX shell scripts, but now commonly used to write CGI scripts.

program — A list of instructions to be executed by the operating system or some other software. A program is normally stored on a computer in a program file with a .EXE, .COM, or .SYS file extension.

programming language — A set of commands, and arguments to those commands that have a predetermined meaning to the software executing the program. Examples of programming languages are C++, Visual Basic, and Java.

programming protocol — A set of rules or standards by which programs interact with other programs or resources.

query string — A text-based expression that is included in a URL to a web server to pass information to the web page or CGI program that is requested.

script — A list of programming commands stored in a text file to be executed by the operating system or other software. An example of a script is a Perl script stored in a file.

server-side script — A script that is performed by the server before a web page is downloaded to the browser. The script can be stored alone in a CGI file or embedded in a web page.

shell — An operating system's command interpreter. For Windows 9x, DOS, and Windows NT, the command interpreter is COMMAND.COM.

shell script — A list of operating system commands to be executed by the OS shell. In Windows 9x, a shell script is called a batch file. An example of a shell script or batch file is AUTOEXEC.BAT.

shopping cart — Software used by a commercial web site to hold information about the selections a user has made before the purchase is completed.

source file — In programming, a list of commands that have been entered by a programmer in a specific programming language. These commands cannot be executed until after they have been changed, or compiled, so that the computer's processor can understand them.

Speech Application Programming Interface (SAPI) — An application interface developed by Microsoft for voice recognition and converting text to speech.

SSI (Server Side Includes) — A simple form of server-side scripting that allows you to use variable values which can be included in the HTML code before it is sent to the browser.

static web page — A web page that never changes unless the developer edits the page contents.

VBScript — A subset of Visual Basic designed to be used as a web page scripting language.

Visual Basic (VB) — A popular, object-oriented Microsoft programming language that is easy to learn and interacts well with Windows.

REVIEW QUESTIONS

1. What are two file extensions that a program file can normally have?

2. What is the difference between a dynamic web page and a static web page?

3. What software executes a client-side script? What software executes a server-side script?

4. What are the two protocols used by programs and scripts on a server to customize a web page before downloading to the browser?

5. On what operating system platform was the CGI model first developed?

6. Who developed the ISAPI model?

7. What is the difference between a DLL and a regular program as applied to how the program or DLL is stored in memory?

8. What HTML tags mark the beginning and ending of a script?

9. Active Server Pages scripts by default are written using what scripting language?

10. A server script records an encountered error in what kind of file?

11. What language was first used to write CGI scripts?

12. Small programs that are downloaded to a browser for handling special multimedia effects are normally written using what language? Why is this language the language of choice?

13. VBScript is a subset of what popular programming language?

14. JScript was written by Microsoft to compete with what language?

15. When a JavaScript programmer wants to get the user's attention, he or she will use what programming feature?

16. When a programmer wants to write a short segment of coding to be used as needed from other places in the program, he or she will use a _____.

17. What are four objects provided by ASP technology?

18. If a server-side script needs to access data in a URL query string, the form on the web page calling the URL must use which method in the form tag?

19. Where in a browser request to a web server is the information retrieved from a cookie stored?

20. Name one example of the ASP scripting object.

21. What type of ASP object is used to write data to a text file on the server?

22. What type of web site would use shopping cart software?

23. What HTTP header command is used to write a cookie on the client PC?

24. What are the steps to access the screen to control cookies under Internet Explorer?

25. What tool does Internet Information Server 4.0 offer to help web developers test their ASP scripts?

HANDS-ON PROJECTS

Examine Client-Side Scripts

Access the home page of the *www.amazon.com* web site and view the source code. Search the source code for a client-side script. What is the purpose of this script? How does the script know which browser is being used? Print the script. (*Hint*: Search for the word "script" in the source code)

Research Java on the Internet

Using a search engine, search the Internet for information about Java. Answer these questions:

1. From where does the name "Java" come?
2. When was Java developed?
3. In a brief paragraph describe what Java is best used for.
4. What is the name of Sun's web browser that is designed to handle Java applets?
5. How much does the Java programming language cost?
6. List three books and their publishers that teach Java.
7. What is the most authoritative web site you can find about Java?
8. List three other web sites that are good sources of information about Java.

Research Shopping Cart Software

You work for a small company that is just beginning to plan a web site to sell products. You have been asked to investigate what shopping cart software is available, what are the features of the software, and how much it costs. Research the Internet looking for two shopping cart solutions. For each solution, list these things:

1. What is the name of the software, its manufacturer, the web site to purchase it, and the price?
2. What features does the software offer?
3. How is the data stored in the background? On the server or client? Flat file or database?
4. Does the software use cookies?
5. What kind of web server and operating system does the software require?
6. What kind of technical support does the software manufacturer offer? What kind of documentation comes with the software?
7. What programming skills would be required in house in order to use the software?

CASE PROJECTS

Add a Script to Your Personal Web Site

If your web server supports SSI, add an SSI script to your personal web page that displays the date the web page was last modified. Test the change by publishing the page and displaying it with your browser.

Validate an E-Mail Address on Your Web Site

In Chapter 4 of your on-going project to build your personal web site, you added a feature so that a user could send you e-mail. In this project, add a form to your web site to enable you to receive the e-mail address of a user so that you can contact him or her. Include these features:

❏ Provide a form that includes a text box for the user's name, e-mail address, and mailing address.

❏ Using a client-side script, validate that the e-mail address includes the @ symbol.

❏ When the user clicks the Send button, mail the information gathered in the form to your e-mail address.

❏ If you have access to a web server that provides ASP technology, write the data in the form to a text file on the server to be harvested by you at a later date using FTP.

Create a Test Bed for Your Web Site

Create a virtual test bed on the server where you publish your web site. Create a folder named Testing under the root folder. Store all the files and subfolders under this folder that are normally stored in the root. Access the Testing URL so that it displays your home page. Print the browser screen showing the Testing folder as part of the URL.

7

DATABASES AND WEB HOSTING

> **In this chapter, you will learn**
>
> ♦ What databases are and how they are used on PCs and servers
> ♦ About software used to access and drive a database
> ♦ About some of the programming techniques used to access a web site's database
> ♦ About web hosting and how to select a web hosting service

In the last chapter you learned how to store information collected from a web site user in a flat file for later use. Flat files are a simple solution to the problem of how to provide information to the user and how to retrieve information from the user. In fact, many web sites rely heavily on flat files to provide a catalog of inventory for sale and process those sales.

However, it can be difficult to manage a lot of data using a flat file system. Flat file systems can be slow and cumbersome for the user and are prone to errors. A more up-to-date approach is to use a database to store data, but, with this better technology comes a price. The software needed for a database is more expensive and more difficult to set up, maintain, and use. When adding a database to a web site, you should take into consideration what database software and supporting software the site provides, since limitations of the web server can limit your choices. You will look at all these concerns in this chapter, as well as see some sample coding that shows how a web page can access a database and allow a user to interact with it.

INTRODUCTION TO RELATIONAL DATABASES

Years ago there was some competition between two different kinds of database technologies: relational databases and hierarchical databases. For the most part, the relational database concept won out and hierarchical databases are only used for storing small amounts of data.

A **hierarchical database** uses a top-down design. A top-down design arranges the major categories of data at the top, and the less significant categories are underneath each major category. This type of database design looks like an upside down tree whose branches spread out at the bottom. An example of a hierarchical database is the Windows 98 Registry, which holds user preferences and hardware and software parameters and settings for Windows 98.

A **relational database** holds its data in a group of tables, as shown in Figure 7-1. Each table has columns and rows, with headings at the top of each column describing the data in that column. The column headings are called **field names** and each row of data is called a **record**. Within any column of data, each entry in the column is called a **field**. Each row of data can be uniquely identified by the contents of one or more fields. This field or group of fields is called the **primary key**. For example, in Figure 7-1, the Employee Table contains a list of employees and information about each employee. An employee is identified by his or her social security number (SSN) which is the primary key for this table. Two rows that contain the same SSN would not be allowed into this table.

Tables in a relational database are related to one another by the fields they have in common. For example, in Figure 7-1, the Employee Table is related to the Dependent Table by the SSN of the employee. The Dependent Table can have more than one row for a single employee, depending on the number of dependents this employee has.

If you want to see the list of dependents for an employee, you can search the Dependent Table for all rows that contain the SSN for the employee. If you print a report that contains the employee information as well as his or her dependent information, the report contains data from two tables, Employee and Dependent. To search the database for information is called querying the database and the results of the search are called a **query**. When analysts design a database, they determine several things:

- The number of tables and the name for each table

- The number of columns in each table and the name of each column (field name)

- The primary key for each table

- How the tables can relate to one another by using fields they have in common

This overall design of the database is called the **database structure**. The software that accesses the database (that is, retrieves data from, and enters data into, the database) is called the **database management system (DBMS)**, or **relational database management system (RDBMS)**. The person responsible for managing the database is called the database administrator. A **database administrator** controls who can access the database and what changes they can make to it. The administrator monitors the performance of the database management software and generally assumes responsibility for the integrity of the data in the database.

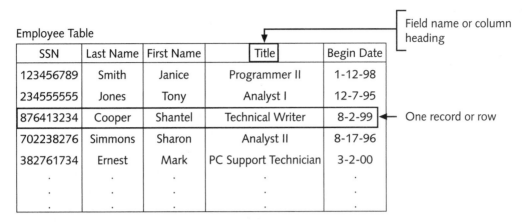

Employee Table

SSN	Last Name	First Name	Title		Begin Date
123456789	Smith	Janice	Programmer II		1-12-98
234555555	Jones	Tony	Analyst I		12-7-95
876413234	Cooper	Shantel	Technical Writer		8-2-99
702238276	Simmons	Sharon	Analyst II		8-17-96
382761734	Ernest	Mark	PC Support Technician		3-2-00

Dependent Table

SSN	Dep No	Last Name	First Name	DOB
123456789	01	Smith	David	8-10-65
123456789	02	Smith	James	12-2-98
234555555	01	Jones	Candy	4-15-72
234555555	02	Jones	Charles	4-15-72

Figure 7-1   A relational database stores data in tables. A table can relate to another table by fields or columns they have in common

The Client/Server Database Model

Originally, database management software applications for personal computers were designed to be used by a single user who would access a database stored on one computer. Soon, however, the need arose for more than one user to access the same data, so the database was stored on a computer on a network that all users could access. Initially, the database management software was still kept on a single user's PC and the centralized computer holding the database was simply a file server with no controlling software. This model is illustrated in Figure 7-2. This file server model made for cumbersome searches. Each time a user wanted to search the database, large chunks of data or even the entire database had to be passed to the user's PC so that the DBMS on the PC could process it. Access time was slow because a lot of system resources were used to pass data back and forth.

Note in Figure 7-2 the symbol of a drum that is used to represent a database. As you saw earlier, the database is really a collection of tables. Each table can be stored in a single file or several tables can be stored in one composite file, which is a large file made up of several components. The file or files are stored on a hard drive. Because a hard drive is physically a stack of platters that hold data, the drum or cylinder symbol is often used to represent data stored on a hard drive in one or more files.

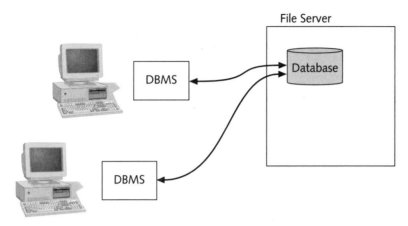

Figure 7-2 Originally, when many users needed to access the same database, the database management software (DBMS) was stored on the users' PCs and the file server only contained the database, but no software to control it

In order to improve performance, the file server model was eventually replaced by another model whereby the database software was divided into two parts: software on the client and software on the server. See Figure 7-3 for an illustration of this concept. On the user's local PC, the client software receives a request from the user and composes a query to the database. It then passes that query to the server software on the file server. The server software processes the query and passes only the data that satisfies the query back to the client. This model of having some of the software on the client and some on the server where the database resides is called the **client/server database model**, and is the model used in most Internet applications today.

However, the Internet model differs from the traditional client/server database model in one significant way: neither the client nor the server portions of the database software are on the PC of the Internet user. When a web browser requests data from a web site, the request goes to a CGI script or program running on the web server, as illustrated in Figure 7-4. The script or program on the server composes a query, and passes it to a database server application. The database server application passes the data back to the script or program, which inserts the data in a web page to be delivered to the browser. The browser, in most cases, is totally unaware of where the data came from. It simply requests a web page along with some parameters, and then receives and displays the page. The client/server database model here is not between the browser and the web server, but between the script or program on the web server and the database application, which may or may not be on the same computer as the web server.

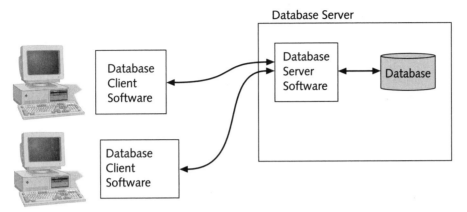

Figure 7-3 With the client/server database model, software on the server controls access to the data resulting in less traffic over the network

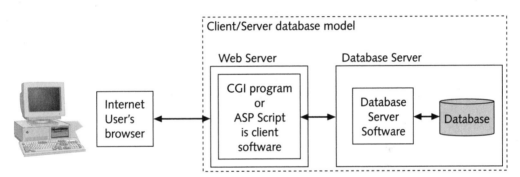

Figure 7-4 When a web browser requests data, the program or script on the web server is the client software in the client/server database model

An important advantage of using the Internet model to access a database like the one illustrated in Figure 7-4 is that the client PC does not need to contain database management software. The browser on the user's PC is detached from the client/server database model because it is only the recipient of the web page that contains the results of the data query. Because database software does not need to be installed and supported on the client PC, many corporations use the Internet model in Figure 7-4 to give their employees access to a database on their Intranet.

Using SQL to Access a Database

As database software began to develop more than twenty years ago, each software manufacturer developed commands and rules to query and update the data. For example, one of the earlier database management applications was dBASE. The dBASE command to access or open a database table was USE, and the command to select a table already opened was SELECT. The command to add a new row to a database table was APPEND. You could remove a row using the DELETE command, change the data in a row using the REPLACE command, and erase all the rows in a table using the ZAP command. Other database applications adopted these and similar command keywords to manage their databases. Over the years, a de facto standard began to emerge that had its roots in dBASE commands, and which was universally accepted as a set of commands and command arguments that could be used to manage a database. This set of commands was called the **Structured Query Language (SQL)**. A **de facto standard** is a standard that does not have an official backing, but which is considered a standard because of widespread use and acceptance by the industry.

Almost every relational database software in use today allows you to use SQL commands to access and update the data. Even though SQL has its roots in dBASE and applications similar to it, the commands are not exactly the same as dBASE commands. For example, to retrieve only the first and last names from the data in the Employee Table of Figure 7-1, use this command:

```
SELECT LASTNAME, FIRSTNAME FROM EMPLOYEE
```

To replace the last name of the employee with the SSN "123456789", use this command:

```
REPLACE LASTNAME WITH "Smithson" WHERE SSN =  "123456789"
```

The major advantage of the universal acceptance of SQL is that programmers can apply SQL skills in many different situations without having to learn a whole new set of commands when they move from one brand of database to another. They only need to learn how to pass an SQL command to the database management software, or database engine. The applications software that provides a user with an interface to the DBMS is called the **database engine**. The computer that runs the DBMS and contains the database is called the **database server**.

Database Management Systems

There are many database management systems on the market today, but this discussion is limited to those that are commonly used on the Internet. Figure 7-5 shows a list of what type of data sources are popular with web sites. Microsoft's SQL Server is the most popular database management system used, followed by Oracle. The third category is ODBC, which is a technology that allows many different kinds of data sources, including Excel and Lotus 123 spreadsheets, to be accessed by a web page script or CGI program.

Other ODBC data sources include database applications like dBASE, FoxPro, and Access. Notice in Figure 7-5 that a flat file, discussed in the last chapter, is also a popular way of storing and accessing data on the Web, followed by several less significant solutions, most of which are commonly used on large mainframe computers.

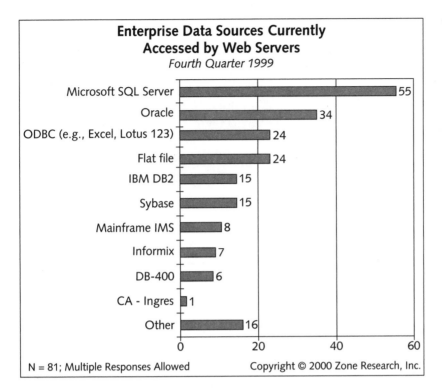

Figure 7-5   Database software used on web sites

Microsoft's SQL Server

SQL Server (pronounced "SEE-qual server") by Microsoft, is a database management system designed for large-scale applications. Because it is made by Microsoft, it has an added advantage in that it interacts well with Windows operating systems (Windows 9x, Windows NT, and Windows 2000) and other Microsoft products such as Office 2000. SQL Server is designed so that it can scale down to be used effectively on a laptop, or can be scaled up to be used as a distributed database run on multiprocessor computers. A **multiprocessor computer** is a computer that contains more than one CPU and is designed for powerful large-scale applications. A **distributed database** is a database that is spread (or distributed) over several computers. Each computer contains a piece of the database, but the database software presents the data to the users so that users see the data as one continuous presentation. In a distributed database, the user is unaware of the fact that part of the data might be stored in Atlanta and the other part in San Francisco. In addition, SQL Server contains sophisticated management software for database administrators and power users.

SQL Server also provides support for data warehousing. A **data warehouse** is a repository for data that has been collected into one or more databases, but which is no longer needed for current processing. Before data warehousing, purged data would simply be backed up to some not-easily-accessible medium like tapes, and never used again. Now, old data can be made accessible from a data warehouse. Warehoused data is useful in many different kinds of situations. For example, it might be used by workers in a company who want to discover trends that can help with marketing, the future direction of the company, and forecasting. Studying data for these reasons is called **data mining**, and data singled out for a particular study is stored in a sub-repository called a **data mart**. Data warehousing is similar to saving the trash so you can rummage through it later! A large company might make a data warehouse or data mart available from a web site on the company's intranet.

Oracle

Oracle, by Oracle Corporation, is a large-scale, highly reliable database management system that traditionally has been used as the industrial-strength database solution for UNIX platforms, although Oracle can also be used on Windows NT and Windows 2000. Oracle is also known for its speed of data access. Oracle, like SQL Server, supports data warehousing, sophisticated management software, and SQL. It also supports the data types needed to hold graphical and audio data, such as photographs, video clips, and images, in a special data field type called a **BLOB (Binary Large Object)**. Oracle can also be scaled down to run on a small PC or laptop. For more information, see *www.oracle.com*.

Using ODBC to Access a Data Source

Oracle and SQL Server are high-end database solutions for multiple users and large quantities of data; however, they are also expensive solutions for small web sites. Less expensive solutions can include FoxPro, Access, Informix, Sybase, and even non-database sources like flat files and Excel and Lotus 123 spreadsheets. All these types of data sources can be accessed directly or can be accessed using technology called ODBC. **ODBC (Open Database Connectivity)** provides a common access method for all these types of data sources and more.

The intent of ODBC is to provide one standardized way to access a data source that developers can use in a variety of applications, operating systems, and data source types. ODBC is a type of API (application programming interface); it provides a way for a program or script to gain access to system resources. ODBC uses SQL as its query language and is one tool that a program or script can use to pass an SQL command to database management software.

ODBC is illustrated in Figure 7-6. Notice in the figure that if the developer chooses not to use ODBC, then the SQL command is passed directly to the database software and the developer must know exactly how to communicate with that software. The advantage of using ODBC over a direct connection is that ODBC provides a standard connection method so that the same methods can be used to connect to many different types of data with standardized results. ODBC provides a set of function calls, a predetermined list of error codes, and a standardized format for the resulting data queries.

ODBC software was designed by the SQL Access Group and has been developed for Windows, UNIX, OS/2 and Macintosh platforms. Both SQL Server and Oracle databases can also be accessed using ODBC methods. Even though Java programs can use ODBC technology, there is a similar and competing technology developed specifically for Java called

JDBC (Java Database Connectivity). JDBC was developed by Sun Microsystems and can only be used with database software that supports it. Informix was one of the first database management system software to provide an interface for JDBC.

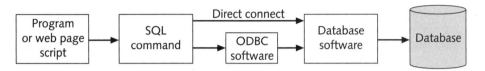

Figure 7-6   ODBC software may be used to pass an SQL command from a program or script to software managing a database

Selecting the Right Database Management System

Selecting the right database product can be critical to the success of your web site. Sometimes the choice is made for you because the database product already is in place within your company. Or, it may be that the web hosting site you are using dictates the choice, or the choice is simply made by others within your organization. However, if you are responsible for selecting a database product, consider these things.

- Product features

- Software, operating system, and hardware requirements

- Technical expertise within your organization

- Overall cost of ownership

Research the database product to know what it can and can't do. For example, if you intend to store and display photographs of your products on your web site, the ability of the database to handle BLOB data types is essential. If you will have many users, some needing different security features than others, verify that the database can handle these different security levels. A database often is designed to be used with a certain operating system. For example, SQL Server works best on a Windows operating system, and Oracle was first designed to be used on UNIX. System administrators and developers in the marketplace will be easier to find and hire if you stick with mainstream database products and their inherent operating systems. Consider the skills already present in your organization and take into account the high cost of training for skills not already present.

You should consider not only the initial cost of purchasing the product, but also consider the total cost of ownership, which can include the cost of hardware, operating system, supporting software, manpower associated with the initial setup and installation, operating and maintenance costs, and support and training costs. Also think ahead to when the database product is out of date and include the cost of upgrades, retraining, and so forth, associated with the update.

SETTING UP A DATABASE ON A WEB SITE

Recall from Chapter 6 that a CGI program and an ASP script can access a database on the server. Look at Figure 6-4 to refresh your memory. The retrieved data can be inserted into a web page before delivery to a browser. Figure 6-4 shows a simplistic view of the process—only showing that it is possible. In this section, you will learn about one method to set up and access a database on a web site: an ASP script that uses ODBC connectivity to access a Visual FoxPro database. Visual FoxPro by Microsoft is a database product that can handle low volume on a web site and is a good inexpensive solution for beginning web sites.

Using ASP Scripts to Access a Database

It is not the intention here to teach all the programming skills required to access a database from a web site, but rather to demonstrate some of the key commands and methods used. You'll see enough, however, to understand the basic flow that a programmer must understand to do his or her job well. In the example that follows, a web hosting service is used, so some of the commands are performed using the web hosting tools made available to the subscriber of the service.

Web hosting is the business of housing, serving, and maintaining files for one or more web sites. When you choose a web host for your web site, the hosting service provides host management software that you can use to set up your database on the web server. You can read more about web hosting later in this chapter.

Step 1: Create the Database

Design the number of tables and column headings in each table needed to hold your data. You'll want to test the database at your PC to make sure it works well and does what it is designed to do.

Step 2: Copy the Database to the Web Site

Recall that FTP is the tool to use to copy all the files that make up the database to the web site server. If you purchase web site space from a web hosting company or ISP, they will most likely have a directory already set up that is designed to hold a database. If not, a good way to keep the database separated from other files on the site is to put the database in a directory named Database directly underneath the root directory. In the example showing in Figure 7-7, the data is stored on the server in a directory named \FTP\crg10\Database, although in the figure you cannot see the directory \FTP in the path.

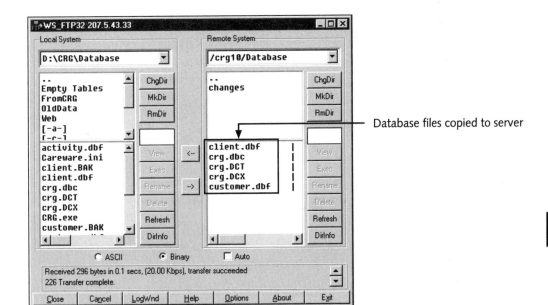

Figure 7-7   Use FTP to copy the database to the web site. This Visual FoxPro database is made up of several files

Step 3: Create an ODBC Connection to the Database

Using the web hosting tools, access the screen to create an ODBC connection. An example screen is shown in Figure 7-8. For this web hosting service, you first locate the directory containing the database, enter a name to be assigned to the data source, and then select the database type from the drop down list of data sources; in this case the type is Microsoft Visual FoxPro Driver.

Step 4: Connect the Web Site to the Data Source

Recall from Chapter 6 that an ASP script communicates with the outside world through objects. In Chapter 6 you saw how the request and response objects were used to receive information from the browser and insert data into web pages that were sent back to the browser. You also saw how the scripting object was used to let the ASP script communicate with a flat file on the server. Recall that in an ASP script, the object type is defined using the name for the type of object at the beginning of the reference, and the action is written next, separated by a period, like this:

```
Response.write "You will hear from us shortly."
```

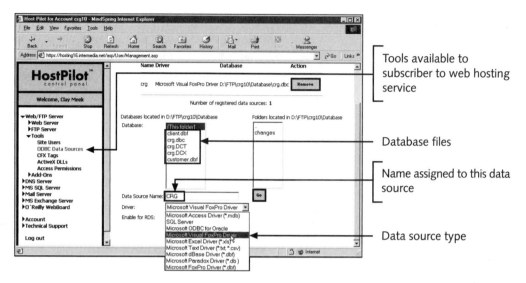

Figure 7-8   To create an ODBC connection to a database, locate the database on the
server, enter a name for the data source and select the data source type

To access a database on the server or on a computer connected to the server, use the application, session, and server objects. Figure 7-9 illustrates how these objects to their jobs. The
application object is used by the ASP script to create an environment or to establish settings
that apply at all times. The application object's commands are executed by the application
object each time the application is loaded into memory, which happens when the web server
starts up. Recall from Chapter 6 that an ASP script has an advantage over a CGI script or
program in that the ASP scripting interpreter, which is part of the web server, need only be
loaded once into memory and, like a DLL, is executed many times from this one load without having to be reloaded each time. Let's say the web server is stopped and restarted at midnight each night as part of the daily maintenance routines. When the reloading happens, the
application object commands are executed and stay in effect until the server is stopped at
midnight the next night. That's the nature of the application object: one time action whenever the server is started.

The session object, on the other hand, is executed each time a new session is established,
which can happen each time a client browser makes a request for a web page containing an
ASP script. During the course of the day, many sessions are opened and closed as browsers hit
the site, and there can be many concurrent sessions as browsers hit the site at the same time.
Use the session object to allow users to maintain a session as they move from one web page
to another. An example of how a session object can be used is when you log onto a secure
server, such as your bank provides, so you can do online banking. These types of sessions have
a timeout period. As long as you are using the session, moving from one page to another
transferring money, viewing your accounts and so forth, the session remains open. When you
log out, close the browser, or simply wait for a period of time, the session closes. You can see

that happen when you log into a banking site, but then don't use the site for a few minutes. When you attempt to use the site again you get a message that says the session has timed out and you must return to the home page and log in again. A session object has a timeout parameter that the web developer can set to determine how long the session remains open without any activity before it will automatically close.

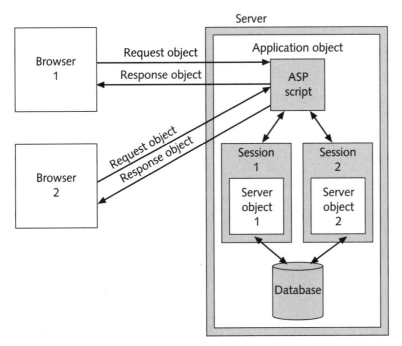

Figure 7-9   An ASP script uses objects to relate to the outside world and to resources on the server

The session object can be used to create a server object, which has the ability to make a connection with a database. This is shown in Figure 7-9. This connection to the database remains intact until the server object is closed or the session object is closed or times out. During the time the server object is active, the ASP script can read and write to the database by referring to this server object using the read and write command set that is defined by the object. The ASP scripting commands to do this are described next.

ASP Scripts to Create the Required Objects

The following script is contained within a special file called Global.asa. If this file exists in the root directory of the web site, whenever the application loads or a web browser hits the site, commands in the script will be executed as they apply.

```
1. <SCRIPT LANGUAGE="VBScript" RUNAT="Server">
2. Sub Application_onStart()
3.     Application("DB_CONNECTION_STRING") = "DSN=CRG;"
```

```
 4. End Sub
 5.
 6. Sub Session_onStart()
 7.     Set Session("DB_CONNECTION") =
        Server.CreateObject("ADODB.Connection")
 8.     Session("DB_CONNECTION").Open Application("DB_
        CONNECTION_STRING")
 9. End Sub
10.
11. Sub Session_onEnd()
12.     Session("DB_CONNECTION").Close
13.     Set Session("DB_CONNECTION") = Nothing
14. End Sub
15. </SCRIPT>
```

First notice that Line 1 defines the scripting language as VBScript, and says that the script is to be executed by the server (not by the client). There are three subroutines in this script. The **Application_onStart** subroutine is executed each time the application loads (at midnight in the previous discussion). The **Session_onStart** subroutine executes each time a browser initially hits the site, and the **Session_onEnd** subroutine executes each time the session is ended.

In Line 3, an application object is created that identifies a database connection. The connection identifies the DSN (data source name) to be **CRG**. Refer back to Figure 7-8 where the web hosting software defined the CRG data source as a Visual FoxPro database stored in a certain directory on the server. The data source was identified as an ODBC connection. Line 3 in this script says to the web server, "This CRG data source, already defined to you, will be used by this application." Later, when the ASP script wants to get access to the data, the server already knows where the data is, what kind of data it is and what kind of connection to use.

In Line 7, whenever a session is created (a browser initially hits the site), a server object is created that is a type ADODB connection within the session. Because of what the server already knows about this connection, the method used to connect to the database will be ODBC, but what is ADODB? **ADODB (ActiveX Data Object Database)** technology is a programming technique developed by Microsoft to be used in Microsoft's programming languages such as VBScript. It allows programmers to query, update, and add data to a database using consistent programming commands and tools from one programming language to another. Think of ADODB as yet one more tool in the group of tools a developer needs to know in order to connect the user to the data. It's the layer between the VBScript and the ODBC connection to the database.

Figure 7-10 illustrates the range of tools available to a developer. Using ADODB commands, the script developer can access the database and read and write to it. Several of the ADODB commands allow the developer to pass SQL commands to the database driver, in this example Microsoft Visual FoxPro. ODBC in this example serves as the pass-through agent, receiving the SQL command from ADODB and passing it on its way.

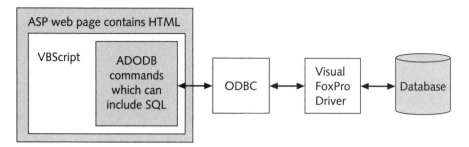

Figure 7-10   In this example, a web developer would need to be familiar with HTML, VBScript, ADODB, and SQL to access the Visual FoxPro database

An interesting observation can be seen in Figure 7-10. Because the developer is using SQL, ADODB, and ODBC to communicate with the database driver, the developer need not understand commands specific to FoxPro databases even though they do exist. Because the web site is developed using these universal tools, later, if it were decided to upgrade the database from FoxPro to some more robust product like SQL Server, it is very likely that the developer would have very little work to do. These same tools and commands that work with the Visual FoxPro driver would also work with the SQL Server driver. This is one big advantage of using these universally accepted tools to interface with a database rather than the tools specific to the database product itself.

Once the connection is created in Line 7, in Line 8 the connection is opened. Now that the connection is open, the scripts in this and other web pages accessed by the browser during this session can use the open connection to read and write to the data.

When the session is closed, Lines 12 and 13 close the connection and remove the connection altogether. You don't want to leave sessions or connections to a database open any longer than necessary because they require system resources to exist.

Step 5: Read and Write to the Database

Recall that SQL is the command set used when a programmer wants to read or write to a database. The SQL command is sent to the database software using software layers. In our example, the SQL command is passed to the ADODB object, which passes it to the ASP server object, which passes it to the ODBC software, which passes it to the Visual FoxPro driver, which interfaces with the database! Looking at the complexity of that last sentence, you can see why web developers that can develop a database-interactive web site require so much skill as well as salary!

An example of a script to compose an SQL command and pass it to the database is show below:

```
1. <SCRIPT LANGUAGE="VBScript" RUNAT="Server">
2.    SQL="Update Customer set Lastname = 'Smithson' where
      SSN = '123456789'"
3.    set rsCustomer = Server.CreateObject("ADODB.record-
      set")
```

```
4.      set rsCustomer = Session("DB_CONNECTION").
        execute(SQL)
5.      rsCustomer.close
6. </SCRIPT>
```

In the script above, you see yet one more object, an ADODB recordset object. A **recordset** is a group of records or rows in a database table that are made available to the program or script for viewing and updating. A recordset is a subset of the database that is currently available. Here's how the script works:

In Line 2, the SQL Update command is composed, but not yet executed. It names the action (**Update**), the table (**Customer**), the new value to be placed in the Lastname column (**Smithson**), and locates the row or record to be updated (where SSN = '123456789'). In Line 3, the recordset is created and named **rsCustomer**. In Line 4 the recordset is acted upon by passing the SQL command to the connection. This action causes the one row to be updated. (Actually, if there were several rows in the table that had this value as the SSN, all these rows would be updated.) In Line 5, the recordset is closed.

What the User Sees

All that you've just seen in the example is happening on the web site. But what does the user see from his or her browser's display screen? Most likely the web pages are set up so that the user first selects the data he or she wants to see, and then clicks a submit button. An ASP script on the requested web page retrieves the data from the database, displays the data, and allows the user to edit it. When the edited data is sent back to the web site, an ASP script on the next web page updates the database with the new data. In all, the user might access several web pages in the process of selecting, viewing, and editing data. The same session applies to all these pages until the user leaves the site or the session times out because of inactivity.

An example of when a user might perform these kinds of tasks is an online banking page that lets a user change his or her personal information, such as mailing address. The user tells the web page that he wants to change his personal information. The script retrieves his current record, with his current name, address and telephone number. The user then edits his address, and clicks on a submit button to send the updated information to the web site, which then updates the database with the new information.

WEB HOSTING

You have just seen how a database can be accessed on a web site, and have examined the tools needed to do the job. Many web sites are maintained in-house where the hardware and software are owned and managed by the company that owns the site. But for small-to-medium size companies, a more cost effective method is to subscribe to a web hosting service that provides the hardware, software, and support for a web site for a monthly subscription fee. When selecting a web hosting site, it's important that you know what services the site offers, and that you select a site that can accommodate your needs. This section is about how to select the right web hosting site for you.

Selecting a Web Hosting Service

Recall from Chapter 2 that a web hosting service can offer you either virtual hosting, where you share the web server with other subscribers, or a virtual server, where you control the web server software yourself. With a virtual server, you can stop and start your instance of the web server software, which can enable you to solve a problem with the web site without involving the technical support staff at the hosting service. When you subscribe to the hosting service, you are assigned a login user ID and password which gives you these rights. You are also assigned an IP address of the site, a directory on the hard drive for your files, and the right to use the software running on the server. You can have your own domain name assigned to the site, and, if the service is provided, create e-mail accounts using your own domain name. Also, look for the ability to use sub-domain or third-level domain names (for example, employees.mydomain.com). Sometimes a web hosting service will also be an ISP and sometimes they don't offer this service. If the hosting service does not offer dial-up numbers to the Internet, then, if you use dial-up, you will also need to subscribe to an ISP for this service.

You will not be able to install your own software on the hosting service's computers, so verify that whatever software your site needs is included in the service. For database-enabled web sites discussed in this chapter, the hosting service must provide the support for the database product you want to use. For example, if you have a SQL Server database that you want to put on your web site, the SQL Server database drivers must be installed and running on the site.

Some of the more important features to look for when shopping for a hosting service are:

- The operating system used (Windows NT, Windows 2000, or UNIX) which determines what software the site supports

- The software and database products the service supports

- Management software available for you to use to manage your site. Some hosting companies require that things like ODBC connections be done only by the service's own technical support and others allow you to do it yourself.

- Technical support staff that are easy to access, friendly, and able to help

- An extensive online knowledge base that you can use. A **knowledge base** is a collection of articles, frequently-asked-questions (FAQs), definitions, and procedures that you can access to find answers to your questions. Figure 7-11 shows an example of a virtual host's knowledge base. Look for articles or white papers with sample coding, easy-to-follow instructions, FAQs, an easy-to-use site map and search utility, and so forth.

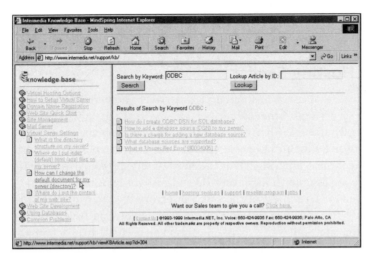

Figure 7-11   A web hosting service should have an extensive knowledge base where you can get answers to your questions about how to use the technology available on the site

- Bandwidth, processor power, and RAM that all affect site performance
- Organized backup and recovery strategy

Even though a local service might offer a slight convenience, don't overlook the possibility of using a service thousands of miles away. Check prices; with over 5,000 web hosting services on the Internet, you should be able to find a fair price. To find a service using web search engines, search on "web hosting" or similar keywords. Also look at *www.internet.com*, which tracks many ISPs that provide web hosting services. Table 7–1 lists the features of three different plans advertised by one hosting service and an explanation of these features.

Table 7-1   Features of three web hosting plans offered by a web hosting service

Plan	A	B	C	Description
Monthly charge	$24.95	$49.95	$79.95	
One-time setup fee	$25	$50	$80	
Initial disk storage	50 MB	100 MB	150 MB	Hard drive space for web pages, database, and other files
Microsoft Windows NT 4.0/ IIS 4.0	x	x	x	Operating system and web server
Online Site Management Control Panel	x	x	x	Tools you will need to manage your site without involving their technical support staff
Unlimited e-mail accounts	x	x	x	
Unlimited FTP access	x	x	x	

Table 7-1   Features of three web hosting plans offered by a web hosting service (continued)

Plan	A	B	C	Description
Unlimited traffic	x	x	x	
CGI support	x	x	x	
Mail server with 50MB initial storage and DeskPilot Web-based Mail Management	x	x	x	This service allows you to set up e-mail accounts using your own domain name (name@yourdomain.com)
FrontPage 98/2000	x	x	x	Recall from Chapter 3 that FrontPage is used to develop web pages
Macromedia DreamWeaver	x	x	x	Recall from Chapter 3 that DreamWeaver is used to develop web pages
Microsoft Access support	x	x	x	Provides support for an Access database
InterDev	x	x	x	A Microsoft product to build sophisticated database-enabled web sites
ASP (Active Server Pages)	x	x	x	Microsoft IIS interprets ASP scripts in web pages
PaymentNet	x	x	x	An authorization service for credit card transactions
Cybercash	x	x	x	Allows secure credit card transactions over the Internet
Access to log file and ability to view WebTrends reports	x	x	x	View information about traffic to your site, errors, transactions, and so forth
Unlimited ODBC source set up	-	x	x	You can have as many ODBC connections as you like
FoxWeb	-	x	x	Windows-based development tool to build interactive web sites to FoxPro and SQL Server databases
Cold Fusion 4.01	-	x	x	High-end development tool for database-enabled web sites (see www.allaire.com)
Secure Certificate Installation	-	x	x	For secure transactions over the Web
Verity Collections search engine	-	x	x	Software to provide full search engine for your site

7

Table 7-1   Features of three web hosting plans offered by a web hosting service (continued)

Plan	A	B	C	Description
StoreFront	-	x	x	Can provide shopping on your web site
Drumbeat	-	x	x	Web page development tool
Perl support	-	x	x	Recall from Chapter 6 that Perl is a scripting language that can be used for CGI scripts.
Microsoft Index Server	-	-	x	Software that can index your site and provide a powerful search utility for the site
Cold Fusion Custom Tag and ActiveX DLL and OCX Registration	-	-	x	Customize Cold Fusion functionality
Intermedia.NET Ciao! chat server	-	-	x	Add live chat sessions to your web site
PLAN ADD-ONS:				
Additional disk space (no setup fee)	x	x	x	$5/month for 25 MB
Additional domain names (no setup fee)	x	x	x	$5/month each
MS SQL Server	-	x	x	$50/month, 10MB database disk space
Additional MS SQL database disk space	-	x	x	$1/month per 5MB
Mailing lists	x	x	x	$10/month per list
Advanced DNS management	x	x	x	$10/month
O'Reilly WebBoard	x	x	x	$20/month

REAL PEOPLE, REAL PROBLEMS, REAL SOLUTIONS
THE SINGLE PAGE

Managing content, pricing and product availability is a daily chore for almost every large on-line retail operation. For Direct Swimming Pool Products (*www.swimmingpools.com*), managing hundreds of HTML pages was getting out of hand. The site had been growing consistently over the past two years, and with the growth came more products and more changes to product data.

The electronic commerce software they had been using to run their on-line store used a flat-file system and a tab-delimited text file to manage product information. (A tab-delimited file uses a tab to separate one value in a row from the next.) The software required that an actual physical HTML page be on the web server in order to display each product. In other words, if Direct Swimming Pool Products (DSPP) had 500 products in their catalogue, 500 HTML pages had to be produced! The continuous chore of keeping track of all of these HTML pages was not only cumbersome but expensive.

The web development firm that DSPP employs to help manage their site decided that an entirely new electronic commerce software package needed to be implemented, one that used a strong database that could handle the company's ever-growing product line. With a true database management system, DSPP could keep control over the products easily with a user interface to the database.

One of the key reasons for using a database for the on-line retailer was the elimination of hundreds of HTML pages. By using a database along with Active Server Page technology, only a few actual pages needed to be developed to display product information in a browser. The new pages would be generated dynamically from the database upon request from a user. With the new software and the database it was no longer necessary to create a new HTML page each time a new product was added to the catalogue!

Expanding on the use of the database, the web development firm built as many pages as possible based on dynamic templates. Any site information that would be frequently updated or modified used a template page that pulled data from the database. Even the home page was designed to pull certain product information that could be changed from the management interfaces.

Instead of the DSPP staff having to manage both a flat-file data system and hundreds of HTML pages, the new system allows the staff to focus on the product data only. Many site functions are now entirely controlled by the SQL database, including reporting and accounting. By using a database, their on-line operation has increased efficiency and effectiveness!

7

CHAPTER SUMMARY

◻ The two types of database architectures are a relational database and a hierarchical database. Most databases today are relational, but smaller databases such as the Windows 9x Registry can use a hierarchical architecture.

◻ A hierarchical database uses a top-down design like an upside-down tree with branches at the bottom.

◻ A relational database is a collection of tables that can be related to one another by columns they have in common. Rows in a table are called records, which are made up of individual fields. Each field has a field name, which is the same as a column heading name.

- One field in a table is denoted as the primary key for the table, which uniquely defines a record in a table. No two records in a table can have the same primary key.

- The design of tables and field names is called the database structure, which is determined by an analyst when the database is first created.

- Requests for information to a database are called queries.

- A database administrator is responsible for the integrity of the data, security to the database, and monitoring the performance of the database software.

- The client/server database model has some of the database management software on the client and some on the server that contains the database.

- On the Internet, the program on the web site serves as the client in the client/server database model and the database server software together with the database may be on the same computer as the web server or may be on another computer.

- SQL is the de facto standard for the command set used to interface with most databases.

- A database management system (DBMS) is the software that interfaces directly with the database. The commands inherent within the DBMS can be used to interact with the database or you can use universal database tools such as ODBC, Microsoft ADODB and SQL.

- The two most popular database products used on the Internet today are SQL Server and Oracle, both of which support BLOB data types, data warehousing, multiprocessors, and distributed databases.

- A universal technology to connect a program to a database source is ODBC, initially developed by the SQL Access Group: it is available under Windows, UNIX, OS/2 and Macintosh operating systems.

- JDBC is similar to ODBC and developed specifically to interface with Java programs.

- When selecting a database product consider the product's functionality, the software and hardware requirements, the overall cost of ownership, and the technical expertise already within your organization.

- An ODBC connection or a direct connection can be used to access a database on a web site. If ODBC is used, your web hosting service must support it.

- An ODBC connection must be created, identified within an ASP script, and then opened from within the script.

- To access a database using ASP scripting, once a connection to the database is made, use ADODB methods to create a recordset object and then pass SQL commands to the recordset and ultimately on to the database.

- When selecting a web hosting service, look for several essential features including the software products it supports, management software that empowers you to manage your own site without involving technical support, an extensive online knowledge base, and enough computing power to give good performance. For good performance, look for adequate bandwidth to the site and CPU processing power and RAM on the Web and database servers.

❑ Also expect a good web hosting service to offer multiple mail boxes that can be set to use your own domain name, unlimited FTP access, and unlimited traffic to the site without additional charges.

KEY TERMS

ADODB (ActiveX Data Object Database) — A Microsoft technology designed to provide a standard set of commands to interface between a program and a database.

BLOB (Binary Large Object) — In a database, a data type used to hold large quantities of data such as that required for photographs, video clips, images and audio.

client/server database model — A method to optimize performance of a database that is being used by multiple users on a network. Some of the database management software resides on the user's PC and some of it resides on the server that is holding the database. The client/server model replaced the earlier file server model.

data mart — A portion of the data in a data warehouse that is identified as useful to a certain target group of data miners.

data mining — Studying data in a data warehouse with the intention of discovering information useful to predict future direction for a company.

data warehouse — A repository of data that has been collected into one or more databases, but is no longer needed for current processing. Data warehouses are used to discover market trends and for forecasting.

database administrator — The person responsible for the overall integrity of the data in a database and the security to the database. The database administrator also monitors the performance of the database software and can adjust parameters to optimize performance.

database engine — The database applications software that provides an interface between the user and the DBMS.

database management system (DBMS) — Software that controls a database, receiving commands from the user or other software and executing those commands on the database. The DBMS is responsible for maintaining the integrity of the database structure. Also called relational database management system (RDBMS).

database server — The computer that contains the database and the DBMS.

database structure — The design of a database including the number of tables in the database, the field names of each column within a table, the primary key of each table and how tables can relate to one another.

de facto standard — A standard that does not have an official backing, but is considered a standard because of widespread use and acceptance by the industry.

distributed database — A database that is stored on more than one computer. Portions of the database can be presented to the user in such a way that the user is unaware that the data is coming from more than one computer.

field — In a relational database, a single entry in a table that occurs at the intersection of one row and one column and the data contained within that entry.

field name — In a relational database, the column heading on a column within a table.

hierarchical database — A database architecture that uses a top-down design with major categories at the top and less significant categories at the bottom. The Windows 98 Registry is an example of a hierarchical database.

JDBC (Java Database Connectivity) — A technology similar to ODBC that provides an interface between a Java program and a database.

knowledge base — A collection of articles, frequently-asked-questions (FAQs), definitions and procedures offered by an organization as part of its customer service.

multiprocessor computer — A computer that contains more than one CPU designed for powerful large-scale applications and network traffic.

ODBC (Open Database Connectivity) — A technology initially developed by the SQL Access Group and later supported by most database and operating system manufacturers that provides a connection between an application and a database on a network

Oracle — A high-end, highly reliable database and DBMS originally designed for a UNIX system, which is popular on the Internet for database-enabled web sites.

primary key — In a relational database, the field or fields that are defined as the entries that make a single row unique within the table. Therefore, no two rows within a table can have the same primary key.

query — A request for data from a database that can be used for an on-screen display or in a printed report. Most database queries are done using SQL. *See* SQL.

record — In a relational database, one row within one table of the database.

recordset — In Microsoft ADODB technology, a group of records in a database currently available to a program to be written to or read from.

relational database — A database architecture that holds data in a group of tables that can be related to one another by columns they have in common. Most databases today use this structure.

relational database management system (RDBMS) — *See* database management system.

SQL Server — A high-end, robust database and database management system made by Microsoft for a Windows system.

Structured Query Language (SQL) — A set of commands and arguments used to manage a database that is universally accepted as the defacto standard by the industry. Most relational databases accept SQL commands.

REVIEW QUESTIONS

1. What are the two types of database architectural designs?
2. The Windows 98 Registry is a small windows database. Which type of database architectural design does the Windows 98 Registry use?
3. What is one row in a table of a relational database called? What is a column heading in the database called?

4. What is the name of the field or fields in a database table that uniquely identifies a record?

5. In a table of employees for a company, what is a likely primary key for this table?

6. What person is responsible for the security, performance, and integrity of a database?

7. In the client/server database model, is there database software on the client machine? On the server machine? What advantage does this model have over the earlier file server model?

8. What is one important advantage that accessing a database from a web browser on a user's PC has over the pure client/server database model?

9. What type of standard is the SQL standard?

10. What is another name for a DBMS?

11. What are the two most popular databases used on the Internet?

12. How does a data mart differ from a data warehouse?

13. Which is a more robust database, SQL Server or Access?

14. Oracle was originally developed for what operating system?

15. What is the purpose of a BLOB data type?

16. Name two databases that support BLOB data types.

17. When connecting to a database from a program or script, what is a common way to make the connection that was developed by the SQL Access Group?

18. JDBC for Java programs competes with what universally accepted technology?

19. In order to create an ODBC connection to a data source, what are two things you need to know?

20. When using ASP, when are the commands in the application object executed?

21. Name seven costs that should be considered when calculating the total cost of ownership for a database management system.

22. What programming technique used by VBScript and other Microsoft programming languages allows a programmer to communicate with a DBMS using an ODBC connection?

23. **Select**, **Update**, and **Replace** are all examples of commands that are part of the _____ language used to communicate with many types of databases.

24. When selecting a database product to be used on a web site, why must the database product be supported by the web hosting service for the site?

25. What is the difference between an ISP and a web hosting service?

HANDS-ON PROJECTS

Your company has decided to create a web site to market its products and you have been assigned the task of recommending a database product and a web hosting service to be used. Use the Internet to research the material you need to answer these questions and to make your recommendations and support your decisions. Do the following projects in order:

BLOB Data Types

The company wants photographs of each product on the site. You discover that the Information Systems group in your company already has Informix and FoxPro expertise so you are considering one of these two databases as your recommendation. Does Informix or FoxPro support BLOB data types? Print the web page to support your answer.

SQL Server vs. Oracle

You are comparing SQL Server and Oracle for your database. Print web pages from three web hosting services that support SQL Server and three web hosting services that support Oracle.

Analyzing Costs

There are 30 users in house that need access to the data. What is the cost of the SQL Server software for these 30 users? Print the web page showing the cost.

Credit Card Transaction Management

You decide that you will recommend Cybercash as the software to manage credit card transactions on your site. Print the web pages of three web hosting services that provide support for Cybercash.

Finding a Web Hosting Service

You are now ready to make your recommendation and have decided to recommend SQL Server with an ODBC connection using ASP scripting and Cybercash. Find three web hosting services that support these choices. Evaluate the knowledge base and site management software for these three services. Among the three, which service, in your opinion, offers the best knowledge base and site management software? Print web pages to support your opinion.

CASE PROJECTS

Find the Best Web Hosting Service for your Web Site

Do some research to find a web hosting package for your web site. Find out the costs, and what features are included in the fee. Then discover what features cost extra, and determine whether they would be useful for your web site. Write up a short report that outlines your results, and tells why this web hosting service is better than the free space offered by your college or your ISP.

8

INTERNET CLIENTS

In this chapter, you will learn

♦ About ways to physically connect to the Internet, including phone lines, ISDN, cable modem, and DSL

♦ About the detailed steps needed to connect to the Internet using a phone line and modem

♦ How to connect a PC to the Internet when the PC is on a LAN

♦ How to install a web browser and manage the browser cache

The Internet is an amazing resource, but in order to make full use of it, your personal computer must have the necessary hardware and software and must be configured correctly. This chapter is about what must first happen at the client PC before that PC can connect to the Internet. As is typical with all Internet technologies, several hardware and software layers must be in place for a successful Internet experience for the user. These components at the client PC include:

- Phone line or cable that connects the PC to the outside world

- Network card or modem to connect the PC to the phone line or cable

- Software to control the network card or modem

- Operating system configured to interact with the software that controls the card or modem

- Applications software to use the Internet, such as web browsers and e-mail clients

In this chapter, you will learn about each of these components, what choices are available when selecting a physical connection to the Internet, how to configure a personal computer to connect to the Internet, and how to load web browser software to use the connection. The emphasis is on understanding how the different protocols and layers of software are installed and configured, and how they work together to accomplish a task.

USING A PHONE LINE TO CONNECT TO THE INTERNET

The most popular way for a home PC to connect to the Internet is to use a regular phone line. In order for a PC to make a successful connection, these things must be in place:

1. A modem to allow communication over phone lines and software to control the modem (this software is called a device driver)

2. Software to allow the modem to interface with a network such as the Internet (for Windows 9x, use the Dial-Up Networking utility)

3. TCP/IP protocol software to communicate over the Internet

4. Phone number, user ID, password, and other information needed to connect to an ISP

5. Applications software to use the Internet (for example, a web browser)

This section explores the first four components in the list and explains in detail how to install a modem and its controlling software, and how to connect to the ISP using the modem. The last part of the chapter addresses installing applications software to use the Internet. In the chapter, step-by-step instructions are given for Windows 98; these instructions are the same as those for Windows 95. Windows NT and Windows 2000 have slightly different step-by-step procedures, but the concepts and general directions are the same.

Mapping the Components to the OSI Model

The components listed above can be mapped to the OSI model to help you understand where each one fits within the different layers of the OSI model (see Figure 8-1). Recall from Chapter 2 that TCP/IP is the protocol suite used to communicate over the Internet and that it works at the Transport and Network layers of the OSI model. These layers communicate with the Data Link and Physical layers, which, on a network, are accomplished by a network interface card installed in the PC. However, when your PC is communicating using phone lines, it has no network card; a modem serves this purpose instead. With a modem, however, two levels of software at the Data link and Physical layers are required: software to control the phone connection and software to control the modem, which together make the modem look and act like a network interface card to TCP/IP.

In contrast to earlier discussions of the OSI model, this discussion begins at the *bottom* of the protocol stack, with the modem. We take this approach because the bottom layers are the foundation and must be in place before the high-level layers will work.

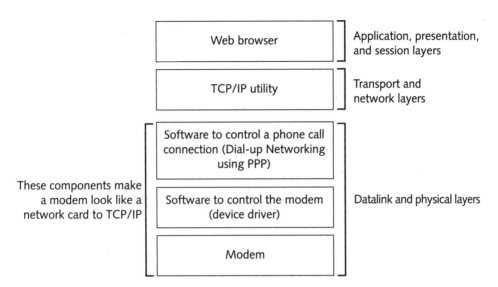

Figure 8-1 When using phone lines to connect to the Internet, these components must be in place

8

Modems: An Introduction

Computers are digital or binary; regular phone lines are analog. In other words, data is stored in a computer as either 0s or 1s, but data travels over phone lines as a continuous flow with infinitely many variations of data. A **modem** is a device that converts analog data suitable for transmission over a phone line, to digital data, suitable for a computer. The word *modem* comes from modulator/demodulator, which means to convert from analog to digital and digital to analog. A modem can be either an external device, as shown in Figure 8-2, or it can be an internal device that is installed in an expansion slot inside a computer, like the one shown in Figure 8-3. A phone line connects to a modem or telephone using either an RJ-11 or an older RJ-12 connector. These connectors are shown in Figure 8-4.

To connect to the Internet using a phone line, you must first install and configure a modem, and then install the software that drives the modem. Software that controls a hardware device such as a modem is called a **device driver**. This software may be included with Windows or you may install it on the PC from a CD or disk that comes with the device. Once the device driver and modem is installed, you should then be able to make a phone call to another computer and establish the connection between computers.

However, if the remote computer is an access computer at your ISP and you want to connect through it to the Internet, more configuration and software is required. Recall that the Internet uses TCP/IP for communication so TCP/IP must be installed on your PC and configured according to the requirements of your ISP. Then your PC must have applications software installed to use the Internet, such as a web browser. In this section, we discuss how to install and configure a modem and connect to an ISP using TCP/IP. Installing browser software comes later in the chapter.

Figure 8-2 SupraSonic external modem

Edge connectors insert into expansion slot on the PC's system board

Figure 8-3 3Com U.S. Robotics 56k Winmodem modem card

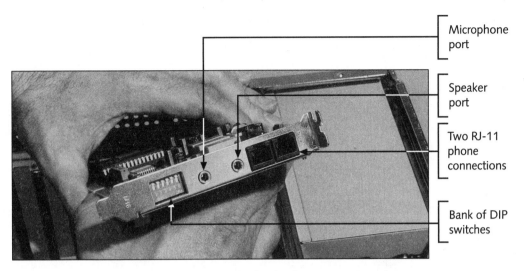

Microphone port

Speaker port

Two RJ-11 phone connections

Bank of DIP switches

8

Figure 8-4 Ports and DIP switches on the back of an internal modem

Install the Modem and Its Drivers

The modem is the middle man between the computer and the telephone system. It is where data is converted to travel between the two systems. Figure 8-5 shows an illustration of two modems at work. A device like a modem that is responsible for managing communication between devices is called a **data communication equipment (DCE)** device and the computer or terminal that is communicating with another device is called the **data terminal equipment (DTE)**.

If the modem is an external device as shown in Figure 8-5, the modem cable connects the modem to a **serial port** on the back of the PC. The port can have either 9 pins or 25 pins and is designed according to the serial port standard called the **RS-232 standard** or, more recently, the **EIA/TIA-232 standard**. Serial ports are used to connect a PC to devices that communicate data serially (one bit follows the next in single file) rather than using a parallel port which transmits data in parallel (8 bits abreast move down the cable at the same time).

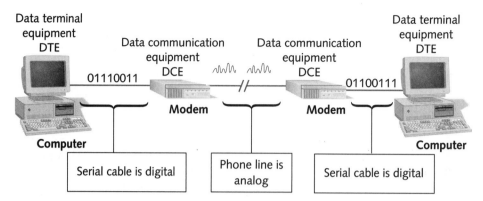

Figure 8-5 A modem converts digital data that a computer uses to and from analog data that can travel over phone lines

If the modem is an internal modem, the modem card is inserted in an expansion slot inside the PC and communicates with the CPU through lines connecting the slot to the CPU, that are embedded on the system board. These embedded lines are collectively called a bus, and modems can use either an **ISA bus** or a **PCI bus.** Figure 8-6 shows how internal and external modems connect to PC system boards. ISA buses transmit data either 8 or 16 bits at a time and the PCI bus uses a 32-bit wide **data path.** The PCI bus is also much faster than the ISA bus, so if you have a choice, use a newer PCI modem card for your PC rather than an older ISA modem card.

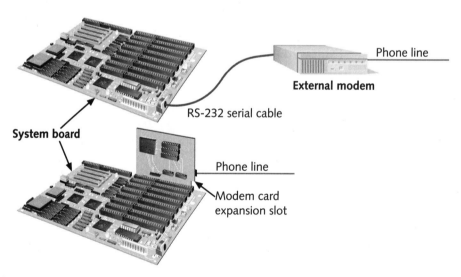

Figure 8-6 An external modem communicates with the processor (CPU) by way of a serial cable, and an internal modem uses either the PCI or ISA bus on the system board

Most input/output devices have two requirements: a device needs a method for communicating with the CPU and it needs a method for the CPU to communicate with it. Both internal and external modems have these same two requirements but they are met in different ways. The external modem connects to the PC by way of a serial port. The serial port controls the communication between the modem and the CPU. For an internal modem, the resources for communication are assigned directly to the modem card and the modem card controls communication between it and the CPU.

External modems require less setup than internal modems. If you have an external modem, once you've plugged the modem cable into the serial port, you are ready to install the device driver. However, if you are using an internal modem, you need to understand how the modem communicates with the CPU, and you must know how to configure the modem for your individual PC.

How Internal Modems Communicate

When a device like an internal modem wants to communicate with the CPU, it uses a line or wire on the system board that connects to the CPU to hail the CPU to get its attention. The line on the system board that the device uses is called an Interrupt Request Number (IRQ) because each line is numbered and is used to interrupt the CPU with a request.

When the CPU wants the attention of a device (to send data to it or request data from it), the CPU uses another group of lines on the system board called address lines. It sends numbers down these address lines to the device called I/O addresses or I/O ports, because the CPU can address an I/O device by using these numbers, much like ports are used by servers. A device knows what I/O addresses have been assigned to it and when these specific numbers are read off the address lines, the device responds to the CPU.

When a modem is first configured, it is set to use a specific IRQ and group of I/O addresses, which are called system resources. On older devices you had to assign these numbers manually by setting hardware switches on the device, but newer devices can be assigned system resources by the installation software when the system first starts up. This newer method of dynamically assigning system resources to hardware devices is called **Plug and Play** and makes installing a new device much easier because you do not have to deal with setting hardware switches on the device. Whenever possible, be sure to buy Plug and Play devices. Windows 9x and Windows 2000 support Plug and Play, but Windows NT does not.

In computer jargon, an old device that uses older technology is called a legacy device. If your modem is a legacy device, then you must assign the IRQ and I/O addresses yourself. You make these assignments by setting jumpers or DIP switches on the modem card. You can see the DIP switches in Figure 8-4 on the back of the card. Figure 8-7 shows an example of jumper switches on a card. The positions of these jumpers and switches tell the system to use a certain IRQ and group of I/O addresses. The documentation that comes with your device should tell you several possible correct positions for your jumpers or switches. Later in this section you can read how to determine which positions to choose. Some devices support both manual technology and Plug and Play. If this is the case, you might have to set the

8

jumpers or DIP switches to tell the system to use Plug and Play and then leave the actual assignments of IRQ and I/O addresses up to Windows Plug and Play.

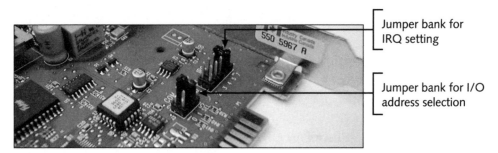

Jumper bank for IRQ setting

Jumper bank for I/O address selection

Figure 8-7   A modem will have jumpers to set IRQ and I/O address values. The default jumper settings should be set to use Plug and Play rather than to dictate these values

Jumpers are short pins sticking up off the card with caps on them, as shown in Figure 8-7. Either remove or insert a cap over two pins to open or close the jumper. If the modem card uses DIP switches, as shown in Figure 8-4, set a DIP switch by flipping one or more of the small switches in the back. Remember that the modem documentation tells you how to set the jumpers and switches, and what settings are recommended.

However, in order to know which IRQ and I/O addresses to assign to a card, you must also know what resources are already being used by your system. For Windows 9x, use Device Manager to display a list of used and available resources. Follow these steps:

1. Click **Start** on the Taskbar, point to **Settings**, and click **Control Panel**.

2. Double-click the **System** icon. The System Properties window opens.

3. Click the **Device Manager** tab, shown in Figure 8-8, and then click **Computer**.

4. Click the **Properties** button. The Computer Properties window opens.

5. Look for IRQ and I/O addresses that are not used. Compare those not currently used with those that the modem card documentation says the modem can be assigned. For example, if the modem says it can use either IRQ 9 or 10 and you see that 9 is already in use, set the modem to use 10.

Sometimes a modem's documentation will specify a COM port rather than an IRQ and I/O address range. A COM port is a predetermined setting for a device's IRQ and I/O address range. COM 1 means IRQ 4 and I/O addresses 03F8 through 3FFF. COM 2 represents IRQ 3 and I/O addresses 02F8 through 2FFF.

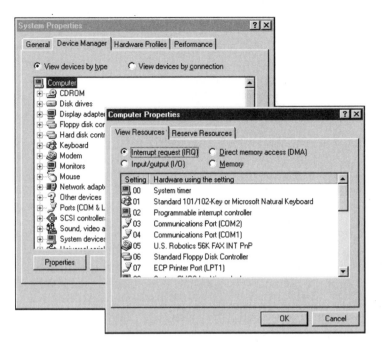

Figure 8-8   Use Windows 9x Device Manager to determine what system resources are available before installing a legacy modem card

Note in Figure 8-8 that COM1 is assigned IRQ 4 and COM 2 is assigned IRQ 3. If you click on the I/O radio button, you will see that COM 1 is assigned I/O addresses 03F8 through 03FF, and COM 2 is assigned I/O addresses 02F8 through 02FF. Any device including the serial ports and a modem card can use COM 1 and COM 2. If your modem is an external modem using the 9-pin serial port, then that port will most likely be using the COM 1 resource assignments showing here in Device Manager.

After you have decided what IRQ and I/O address or COM port you can use, set the DIP switches or jumpers to configure the card to use these resources. Remember that this step is not necessary if you can configure the card to use Plug and Play, which will make the IRQ and I/O address selections for you.

Installing and Configuring an Internal Modem

If the modem is a legacy modem card, then set the DIP switches and jumpers to use IRQ and I/O addresses that are not currently used by other devices installed on the system. If the modem card can be configured as Plug and Play, then use that configuration rather than selecting your own system resources. (Most likely you will activate Plug and Play by setting a

8

jumper or DIP switch, or Plug and Play might be permanently enabled so no action is required on your part.) Here are the basic steps to installing an internal modem:

1. Wearing an anti-static bracelet to prevent damaging any computer parts with static electricity, turn off the PC, unplug it, open the computer case, and install the modem card in an empty expansion slot on the system board.

2. Replace the case cover, plug the power back in, and power up the PC.

If the modem is Plug and Play, Windows 9x automatically detects the new device and steps you through the process of installing the device drivers for the modem. If the modem is a legacy modem card, you must start up the configuration process yourself. Access the Control Panel and double click the **Add New Hardware** icon. Follow the directions to add a modem and install the device driver.

Windows provides device drivers for many modems. In addition, most modems come with their own device drivers on a disk or CD. Whenever possible you should use the device drivers that come with your hardware; these are usually better than those provided by Windows because they are more up-to-date, and they are customized for the specific hardware. During configuration, when Windows asks about the device drivers, click **Have Disk** and provide the drive letter (either floppy or CD/ROM) of the driver files. The installation completes. The last step is to connect a telephone line to the Line-In RJ-11 port on the back of the modem card.

Once the modem is installed, you can verify that it is working by using it to make a phone call. Just ahead is the section that explains how to do this.

Installing and Configuring an External Modem

External modems are much simpler to set up than internal modems. The serial port takes care of communicating with the CPU, and you don't need to set any jumpers or DIP switches, or assign IRQs. Plug the modem cable into the PC's serial port. Connect a telephone line to the Line-in RJ-11 port on the back of the modem. Don't forget to plug the modem's power cord into a wall socket or power strip.

Access the Control Panel and double-click the **Add New Hardware** icon. Follow the directions to add a modem and install the device driver. If your modem came with a device driver on a disk or CD, use that instead of the one provided by Windows. During configuration, when Windows asks about the device drivers, click **Have Disk** and provide the drive letter (either floppy or CD/ROM) of the driver files. The installation completes.

The next section explains how to test your modem to make sure that it is working correctly.

Verifying that Your Modem is Working

Windows 9x provides HyperTerminal, a simple communication utility that you can use to make a phone call with your modem. Some Windows systems provide Phone Dialer, which also makes a phone call using your modem. Follow these directions to test your modem with HyperTerminal:

1. Click **Start** on the Taskbar, then point to **Programs**. Point to **Accessories**, then point to **Communications**, then click **HyperTerminal**.

2. Double-click the **Hypertrm.exe** icon in the HyperTerminal window.

3. When the Connection Description dialog box opens, enter a description of the connection (for example, **test modem**) and click **OK**.

4. Enter a phone number and click **OK**. Click **Dial** to make the call. Even if you dial an out-of-service number, you can still hear the modem making the call. This confirms that your modem is installed and configured to make an outgoing call.

If you don't see HyperTerminal under the Accessories group of Windows, it might not be installed. To install a Windows utility, use the Add/Remove Programs icon in Control Panel.

You can also communicate directly with your modem using the same set of commands that software uses to communicate with modems. Knowing something about these commands can be useful when you are troubleshooting a problem connecting a modem with an ISP. Follow these steps in Windows 9x to send modem commands directly to your modem:

1. Start HyperTerminal, using the directions given above.

2. When the Connection Description dialog box opens, don't enter anything. Click **Cancel**.

3. The HyperTerminal command line window opens, as shown in Figure 8-9.

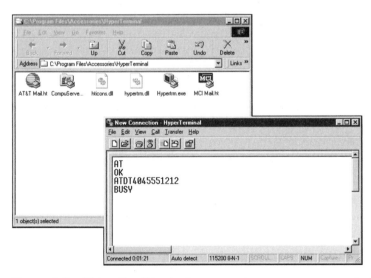

Figure 8-9 Using the AT set of commands, you can communicate directly with a modem, bypassing layers of software. This can be useful when troubleshooting problems connecting to the Internet

4. Enter **AT**, which says to the modem, "I want your ATtention." The modem responds with OK.

5. To dial an out-going call, enter **ATDT** followed by the phone number to call. Almost all modem commands begin with AT. The DT says to "Dial using Tone dialing." In Figure 8-9 the modem attempts the call and responds that the line is BUSY.

When you know a few important AT commands, you can control a modem without having to use applications software. This method can be useful when troubleshooting problems connecting to an ISP because it helps you eliminate the modem as the source of the problem. Table 8-1 lists some important modem commands. Most of these commands are preceded with AT.

Table 8-1   AT commands for modems

Command	Description	Sample Commands
AT	Get the modem's attention	AT (modem should respond with OK)
D	Dial a number	ATDT4045551212 (dial using tone dialing) ATDT9, 4045551212 (get an outside line, use comma to pause)
H	Hang up	ATH
*70	Disable call waiting	ATDT*70,4045551212
Z	Reset the modem	ATZ0 (reset to those settings found when first power on)
&F	Restore factory defaults	AT&F (this method is preferred to ATZ when trying to solve a modem problem)
+++	Tells the modem to return to command mode	+++ (Follow each + with a short pause. Use this when trying to unlock a hung modem. Don't begin the command with AT.)

At this point in the process of connecting to the Internet, your modem should be functioning correctly. You can use HyperTerminal to verify that the modem is installed and working.

Install Dial-Up Networking

Dial-up Networking (DUN) is a process that enables a PC to use a modem and a phone line to connect to a network, just as if that PC had a network card (sometimes called a network adapter or NIC) and network cables. Once connected, the PC behaves just like a node on the network and can take advantage of all the network's resources. The modem behaves just like a network card, providing the physical connection to the network and the firmware at the lowest level of communication in the OSI model. The modems and phone lines in between are transparent to the user, although transmission speeds with direct network connections are much faster than with dial-up connections. This section covers how to use the

Windows 9x Dial-Up Networking utility to create a dial-up networking connection. There is other software available to make this connection in addition to that Dial-up Networking by Windows. Sometimes an ISP provides its own dial-up networking utility.

How Dial-Up Networking Works

Dial-Up Networking uses **PPP (Point-to-Point Protocol)** to send packets of data over phone lines. The process is illustrated in Figure 8-10. PPP works in the Data Link layer in the OSI model. Recall that while the Internet uses TCP/IP packets to transmit data, PPP can transmit other types of data packets used on networks other than just TCP/IP networks. PPP encloses a TCP/IP packet within its own header and trailer information. This header and trailer information is only used while the packet is on the phone line. Once off the line, the PPP header and trailer information is stripped from the packet before it continues over the network. The TCP/IP frame is enclosed in the PPP header and trailer and then presented to the modem for delivery over phone lines to a modem on the receiving end. The modem on the receiving end passes the packet to the PPP utility, which removes the PPP header and trailer information before sending the packet on its way.

8

Figure 8-10   The PPP line protocol supports TCP/IP packets as they travel over a phone line from the client to the ISP

In Figure 8-11, you can see how the PPP, TCP, and IP protocols act like envelopes. Data is put into a TCP envelope, which is put into an IP envelope, which is put into a PPP envelope for travel over the phone lines and network. When the phone line segment of the trip is completed, the PPP envelope is discarded. PPP is sometimes called a bridging protocol or, more commonly, a **line protocol**. An earlier version of a line protocol is **Serial Line Internet Protocol (SLIP)**, which also supports a TCP/IP network, but is seldom used today.

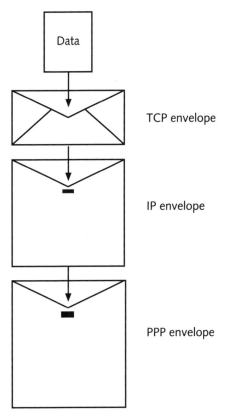

Figure 8-11   The PPP envelope is used only as long as the packet is traveling over the phone lines and then it is discarded

Creating a Dial-Up Connection

This section describes how to create a connection using Dial-Up Networking in Windows 9x. The process creates a Dial-Up Networking icon on your desktop that you can use to make a phone call to connect to a network. After you have created the Dial-Up Networking icon, the next step is to configure the connection represented by the icon to use the protocol of the network to which you want to connect.

For example, if you wanted to connect to your company LAN from home and the LAN uses Novell Netware, you would then configure the Dial-Up Networking connection to use the Netware protocol suite, IPX/SPX. However, to connect to the Internet through an

ISP, you must configure the connection to use the protocol of the Internet, which is TCP/IP. Later in this chapter you will learn how to install TCP/IP and configure a Dial-Up Connection to use it.

Install the Dial-Up Networking Utility The procedure to install Dial-Up Networking and create a connection icon is the same for Windows 98 and Windows 95. If the Windows 9x Dial-Up Networking utility is not installed, then you must install it. Double-click **My Computer** on the Windows desktop. If Dial-Up Networking is installed you see an icon, as shown in Figure 8-12.

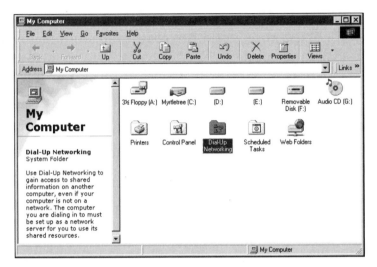

Figure 8-12   Check My Computer to see if Dial-Up Networking is installed

If it is not installed, follow these directions to install Dial-Up Networking:

1. Access the **Control Panel** and double-click **Add/Remove Programs**.

2. Click the **Windows Setup** tab.

3. Click **Communications** and then click the **Details** button. The right-hand window of Figure 8-13 shows the components of the Communications group of Windows 98.

4. Click **Dial-Up Networking** and then click **OK** to install the component. You might be asked for the Windows 98 CD-ROM or disks.

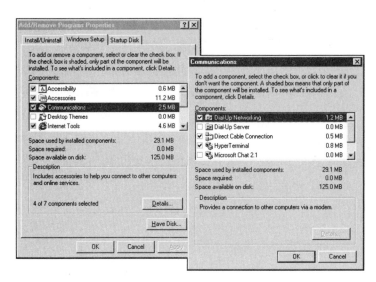

Figure 8-13   Install Dial-Up Networking from the Add/Remove Programs window accessible from the Control Panel

Create the Connection   Follow these directions to create a connection icon:

1. Once Dial-Up Networking is installed, double-click the **Dial-Up Networking** icon in **My Computer** and then double-click the **Make New Connection** icon. The Make New Connection dialog box appears.

2. Enter some text that describes the computer you will be dialing, select your installed modem in the drop-down list, and click **Next**. If you are getting ready to create the connection to your ISP, enter the name of your ISP, but recognize that the connection will not work until you later configure this connection to use TCP/IP.

3. In the next dialog box, type the phone number to dial and click **Next** to continue.

4. Click **Finish** to build the icon. The icon displays in the Dial-Up Networking window. Dial-Up Networking uses default values for the properties of this icon. To view these values, right-click the icon and select **Properties** on the drop-down menu that displays.

5. Click the **Server Types** tab that is shown in Figure 8-14. Verify that PPP is the selected Dial-Up service for the connection and that the TCP/IP checkbox is checked so that a TCP/IP network can use the service. Click **Cancel** to return to the Dial-Up Networking window.

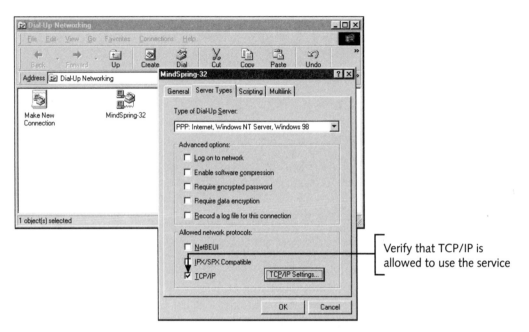

Verify that TCP/IP is allowed to use the service

8

Figure 8-14   Use the Properties box of the Dial-Up icon to verify that PPP is the Dial-Up service and a TCP/IP network can be used by the service

Verify that the Connection is Working   Even though you won't be able to connect to your ISP yet (because you haven't set up TCP/IP), you can still verify that your Dial-Up Networking icon is working. Double-click the icon just created, and click Connect. You should hear the modem dialing. If you like, you can create a shortcut on the desktop to the service. To do that, right-click on the icon and select Create Shortcut on the drop-down menu.

Because you have not yet configured your Dial-Up connection to communicate with your ISP, you will not be able to make a successful connection to the Internet at this point. However, it's important to verify that the modem can at least dial out through the connection. If you can hear the modem dialing a number and you can hear the remote end pick up and attempt to make a connection, most likely the modem and the Dial-Up connection are both working properly. Later, when you are configuring the connection to use TCP/IP, if you have a problem, you can be confident that the problem is with TCP/IP and not the modem or the Dial-Up connection.

This method of approaching an installation one step at a time and verifying successes along the way helps keep troubleshooting as simple as possible. For example, as a last resort to verifying that the Dial-Up connection and modem are working correctly, you can enter the phone number of a friend in the Connect To box and click Connect. You should be able to hear your friend say "Hello" when he or she picks up on the other end. The connection immediately breaks, since the Dial-Up process does not recognize a modem on the other end. This process verifies that your modem and connection are working correctly.

When Windows 9x installs Dial-Up Networking, it also "installs" a Dial-Up Adapter. In terms of function, think of a Dial-Up Adapter as a virtual network card. It is a modem playing the role of a network card for Dial-Up Networking. You can see your new Dial-Up Adapter listed under Network adapters in the Device Manager. You can also see it listed as an installed network component, under the list of installed components in the Network window of Control Panel.

Install and Configure TCP/IP

In the previous section you learned how to install and use a modem to make a phone call and how to use Dial-Up Networking to allow your modem to connect to a network. The next step in connecting to an ISP is to install and configure TCP/IP to communicate with the Internet, which is the subject of this section.

About the TCP/IP Protocols on the PC

Recall that the Internet uses the TCP/IP suite of protocols for communication. In Chapter 2 you saw how an application, such as a web browser, uses an API call to pass requests to TCP/IP, which does all the communicating for the browser. Originally, Windows 3.x and DOS did not provide the TCP/IP utility software suite (sometimes called a **TCP/IP stack**) necessary for this communication on the Internet, but Windows 95 and Windows 98 now include this software.

When upgrading a PC from Windows 3.x to Windows 9x, if Windows 9x finds a TCP/IP stack already installed, it will not overwrite that software with its own version. For that reason, you may find a PC that you are trying to connect to the Internet is still using an old, legacy version of TCP/IP, which can make a successful connection to the Internet difficult. If you are having problems getting TCP/IP to work, then suspect that a PC has a legacy TCP/IP stack installed and search the hard drive for the file called **Winsock.dll**. Normally a DLL file is stored in the \Windows\System directory, but Winsock.dll can be found in other locations, so search the entire drive. If you find the file, delete it, then uninstall the old TCP/IP software, uninstall Windows TCP/IP and reinstall Windows TCP/IP. One example of a TCP/IP stack used by DOS with Windows 3.x is Trumpet Winsock, which provides its own version of Winsock.dll. It installs Winsock.dll in a directory named \TRUMPET and also installs the path to the directory in the Autoexec.bat file executed by Windows each time it loads.

The TCP/IP utility for Windows 9x offers these components:

- The core group of TCP/IP protocols and services includes TCP, IP, UDP, ARP, ICMP and DNS. All these protocols were discussed in Chapter 2. If you don't recall the purpose of each one, review that chapter before continuing.

- Support for API calls to TCP/IP, including Windows Sockets and NetBIOS (discussed later in this chapter)

- Tools for diagnosing problems with TCP/IP, including ARP, FTP, NBSTAT, NET-STAT, PING, Route, Telnet, TRACERT, IPCONFIG, and WINIPCFG. FTP and Telnet were covered in Chapter 3, and these other troubleshooting tools will be covered in Chapter 13.

- Client for DHCP. Recall from Chapter 2 that DHCP is used to assign an IP address dynamically each time a PC uses TCP/IP to connect to a network such as the Internet.

- Client for WINS. Recall that WINS is one way of finding the IP address for a domain name.

- Point-to-Point Protocol (PPP), discussed earlier in the chapter, is a protocol used by a modem to connect to a network.

Figure 8-15 shows the relationship among several of the TCP/IP protocols supported by Windows 9x, Windows NT, and Windows 2000.

8

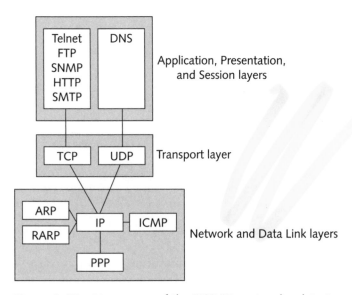

Figure 8-15   How some of the TCP/IP protocols relate to one another

Installation Steps

TCP/IP may already be installed on your PC. Follow these directions to verify that it is installed. If it isn't installed, continue with the directions to install the TCP/IP protocols:

1. Access the **Control Panel** and double-click the **Network** icon.

2. Click the **Configuration** tab. You can see a list of installed network components as shown in Figure 8-16. Look for TCP/IP in the list.

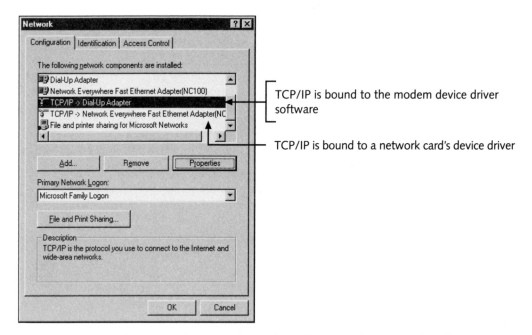

TCP/IP is bound to the modem device driver software

TCP/IP is bound to a network card's device driver

Figure 8-16 Use the Network icon in Control Panel to see what network utilities are installed and to add or remove these utilities

3. If you don't see TCP/IP anywhere on the list, then it is not installed and you should click **Add**. The Select Network Component Type dialog box opens.

4. Double-click **Protocol** in the list. The Select Network Protocol dialog box opens. Click **Microsoft** in the Manufacturer's list. Click **TCP/IP** in the Network Protocols list and click **OK**. See Figure 8-17.

TCP/IP installs and then binds itself to any installed netword card or Dial-Up Adapter so they can communicate over the TCP/IP network. Remember that binding means to associate one layer in the OSI model to a layer either directly above or below it. In this case, the Dial-Up Adapter, using the PPP protocol and the modem device driver as a pair, serves as the next lower layer in the OSI model. Verify that TCP/IP is bound to the Dial-Up Adapter by looking for the connection in the Network window (look at Figure 8-16 again). If TCP/IP is not bound to the Dial-Up Adaptor, then verify that TCP/IP is checked as an "Allowed network protocol" under the Properties window of the Dial-Up Networking icon for the mode.

TIP When you are having a problem connecting to the Internet, one thing you can try is to uninstall and then reinstall TCP/IP. Use the Network icon of Control Panel to do that.

The next step is to configure the TCP/IP-bound Dial-Up Networking connection to use the settings provided by your ISP.

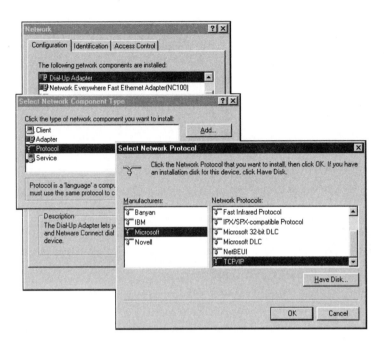

Figure 8-17   Install the TCP/IP protocol

Configure Your TCP/IP Dial-Up Connection for Your ISP

In order for your PC to connect to an ISP and use the Internet, you need the following information:

- Phone number of the ISP

- User ID and password for the ISP

- An IP address (may be assigned by your ISP when you first connect)

- The IP address of the default gateway (may be assigned by your ISP when you first connect)

- A subnet mask (may be assigned by your ISP when you first connect)

- The IP address of a domain name server (may be assigned by your ISP when you first connect)

All the terms mentioned in this list have been introduced and explained in earlier chapters. Here is a review:

- Every computer using the Internet must be assigned a unique IP address.

- A gateway is a computer or other device that allows a computer on one network to communicate with a computer on another network. A default gateway is the gateway a computer uses to access another network if it does not have a better option.

- A subnet mask is a group of four numbers (dotted decimal numbers) that tell TCP/IP whether or not a remote computer is on the same or a different network.

- A domain name server is a computer that can find an IP address for another computer when only the domain name is known.

- A computer might have a permanently assigned IP address (static IP addressing) or be assigned a different IP address each time it logs on to the network (dynamic IP addressing). Most ISPs use dynamic IP addressing.

Verify the Phone Number

Follow these instructions to verify the phone number of the ISP or to enter a new phone number:

1. On the Windows desktop, double-click **My Computer** and then double-click the **Dial-Up Networking** icon.

2. Right-click the **Dial-Up connection** icon for your ISP and click **Properties** on the drop-down menu. The dialog box for this connection opens. Click the **General** tab.

3. Change the phone number if necessary and click **OK** to save your changes. You can also permanently set the ISP's user ID and password from this Properties box.

Select the Type of IP Addressing

Most ISPs use dynamic IP addressing. You can specify the type of addressing from the Dial-Up Networking icon Properties window accessed in the previous step. Click the Server Types tab and click TCP/IP Settings. The TCP/IP Settings dialog box opens, as shown in Figure 8-18. Follow these directions:

1. In the TCP/IP Settings box, click **Server assigned IP address** if your ISP uses dynamic IP addressing. If your ISP uses static IP addressing, click **Specify an IP address** and enter the address given you by your ISP.

2. If your ISP provided you with the IP addresses of a DNS, then click **Specify name server addresses** and enter the IP address of the Primary and Secondary DNS.

3. Most likely you should check the bottom two boxes on this form to **Use IP header compression** and **Use default gateway on remote network**, but follow the directions given you by your ISP.

4. Click **OK** to close the TCP/IP Settings window. Click **OK** again to close the Dial-Up Networking icon.

You should now be able to connect to your ISP, although you will not be able to use the connection until you install applications software such as a web browser.

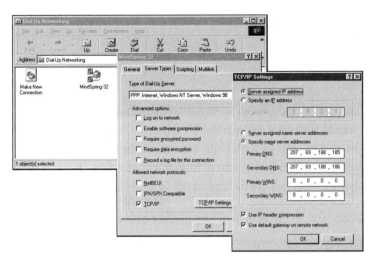

Figure 8-18   When using a modem to connect to the Internet, enter TCP/IP settings with information provided by your ISP

Connect to Your ISP

To connect to your ISP, double-click the Dial-Up Networking shortcut on the desktop and enter your User ID and password. Then click Connect. You should hear your modem and the modem at the ISP negotiating the connection and then all is quiet. If you have a web browser installed, you should be able to use this software now.

When you connect to a network where the server assigns the IP address to the client, the server also assigns the IP address of the default gateway and the subnet mask that the PC must use. The default gateway is the IP address of the server at the ISP that provides access to the Internet, and the subnet mask is needed so that the PC can find this server on the ISP's network.

After you have connected to the ISP, you can see what assignments have been made, using one of the TCP/IP utilities. For example, follow these instructions to use WinIPcfg:

1. Click **Start** on the Taskbar and click **Run.** Enter **WINIPCFG** in the Run dialog box and click **OK.** The IP Configuration window opens, as shown in Figure 8-19.

2. Click the **Dial-Up Adapter** in the drop-down list and note the IP address, subnet mask, and default gateway for the current session. If there is no connection at present, these values are all zero.

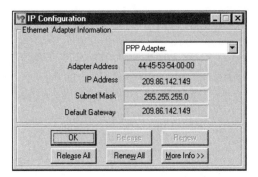

Figure 8-19   Use the TCP/IP utility WINIPCFG to know the IP address, subnet mask, and default gateway currently assigned to your PC

Multipoint Connections

When a PC communicates with another computer using only a single connection, the connection is said to be **point-to-point**, which is the type of connection just described. However, Windows 98 also supports PPP Multilink protocol, which allows you to use two or more physical connections for a single virtual dial-up link called a **multipoint connection**. For example, if you have a PC or notebook computer that has two modems installed and you have access to two phone lines, you can use both the connections together to create a single dial-up with twice the bandwidth! The protocol that enables you to do this is called **PPP Multilink** (**MP**) and is defined by RFC 1717 and RFC 1990. Follow these directions to create a Dial-Up Networking icon that uses MP:

1. Install and verify that both modems are working properly when each is used on a regular point-to-point connection. For best results, the modems should be the same speed.

2. Create a Dial-Up Networking icon for the first modem and test a connection using that dial-up.

3. Right-click the **Dial-Up** icon in the Dial-Up Networking window and click **Properties**. The Dial-Up Networking Properties box opens. Click the **Multilink** tab.

4. Click the checkbox **Use Additional Devices** and click **Add**. Select the second modem from the list of available devices. Then click **OK**.

5. Test the multipoint connection by dialing out, using the directions given earlier in the section.

USING CABLE MODEM, ISDN OR DSL TO CONNECT TO THE INTERNET

Even though phone lines are analog when they leave a customer's home or business, once they reach the telephone company's central office, the phone company converts both voice and data to a digital form to travel over long distances. Then the digital data is converted back to an analog signal just before it reaches the customer's location; this usually happens at the customer's central office.

The problem with slow analog lines can be greatly improved by using phone lines that are digital all the way from one customer to the other. This is often done for large commercial customers. One example of a digital line is a T1 line, which carries the equivalent of 24 phone circuits and can transmit data at 1.5 million bits per second (Mbps). Prices for T1 lines vary and are somewhere around $1200 per month. These lines are sometimes installed as private circuits connecting two locations of the same company.

A T1 line is too expensive for personal or small business users, so several technologies have emerged to compete for the home and small business market for high-speed data transmission. Five technologies, listed in Table 8-2, are currently prominent in the marketplace. Note the access method listed in the table: dial up (create a connection by dialing a number) or direct connect (the connection is "always up").

8

Table 8-2 Data Transmission Technologies for Personal and Small Business Use

Technology	Access Method	Attainable Speeds	Current Users in U.S.	Comments
Regular phone line	Dial-up	53 Kbps	20 million	POTS – "Plain old telephone service"
ISDN	Dial-up	128 Kbps	3.2 million	Requires a leased line from phone company
Cable modem	Direct connect	Varies up to 5 Mbps	500,000	Available through cable companies
DSL	Direct connect	1.5 – 32 Mbps downstream and up to 1 Mbps upstream	1 million	Requires a leased line from phone company. There are several types of DSL lines offering different speeds.
Satellite	Direct connect	400 Kbps	NA	Only works down stream. Upstream transmission requires a dial-up.

Using These Devices with TCP/IP

When using any of these technologies, if you are connecting a single PC to the Internet using an ISP, then the TCP/IP settings are no different from those used by a modem-to-phone line connection. Figure 8-20 shows that, regardless of how the connection is made (cable modem, DSL, etc), TCP/IP manages the connection to the ISP in the same way. As you see in Figure 8-20, cable modem, DSL and a LAN all use a network card in the PC for the physical connection. The network card provides a network port for a network cable. For cable modem service to the Internet, the other end of the network cable connects to a cable modem. For DSL, the other end of the cable connects to a DSL box and, for a LAN, the other end of the network cable connects to a network hub. For each of these types of Internet connections, generally the installation goes like this:

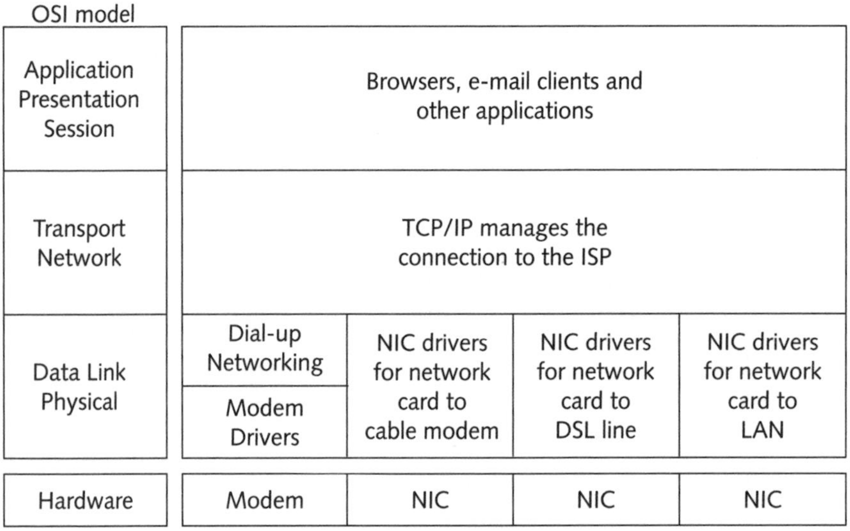

OSI model

Application Presentation Session	Browsers, e-mail clients and other applications			
Transport Network	TCP/IP manages the connection to the ISP			
Data Link Physical	Dial-up Networking / Modem Drivers	NIC drivers for network card to cable modem	NIC drivers for network card to DSL line	NIC drivers for network card to LAN
Hardware	Modem	NIC	NIC	NIC

Figure 8-20   TCP/IP manages a connection to an ISP the same way, regardless of the network media used at the lower layers of the OSI model

1. Install the network card and the drivers to control the card.

2. Use a network cable to connect the PC to a cable modem, DSL box or network hub.

3. Install TCP/IP and bind TCP/IP to the card.

4. Configure TCP/IP to connect to the Internet or LAN.

5. Install the applications software (for example, a browser) to use the connection.

In the following section, you'll learn about the different ways to connect to the Internet using these faster-than-phone line connections and the details of installing these services.

Cable Modem

Regular phone lines require a dial-up connection. In moving to the next generation of data transmission for the home and small business, the choice is a direct connection and speeds measured in Mbps (million bits per second) rather then Kbps (thousand bits per second). A direct connection means that the line is always up; there is no need to establish a connection every time you want to connect to the Internet. **Cable modem**, a popular technology that is direct connect, uses cable lines that already exist in millions of households in the U.S. Just as with cable TV, cable modems are always connected. Simply turn on the PC and you're up. Cable modem uses a technology called **data over cable service interface specification (DOCSIS)**.

With cable modem, you install an Ethernet network interface card in your PC. When the cable company installs the service in your home, they provide an external modem that converts the analog signal coming over the cable to digital before it is sent to the Ethernet NIC in your PC. The modem designed for the DOCSIS interface is likely to be leased to you as part of the cable modem service.

Most cable companies provide upstream service (data flowing from your PC to your ISP) by cable but a few companies do not. In this case the connection downstream (data flowing from the ISP to your PC) is a direct connect by cable, but the service upstream is by regular dial-up phone lines. This means that you can receive data over the cable, but to transmit, you must use a regular dial-up connection. Be sure you understand what you're getting before you lease.

Also, the cable coming to your home is not a single point-to-point connection from your home to the cable company as a phone line system is, but rather is a **point-to-multipoint** connection, whereby the signal from the cable company is sent to multiple destinations. Your connection is one of many in the neighborhood that all tie to a single backbone cable coming into the neighborhood. For this reason, you can see degradation in service if many people are using cable modem in your area and are therefore competing for the same bandwidth.

When you lease cable modem service, you are most likely also agreeing to use the cable modem company as your ISP. Two popular cable modem providers are @Home and MediaOne Express. See their web sites for more information at *www.home.net* and *www.mediaone.com*. The cost for cable modem service including ISP cost is in the range of $35-$60 per month.

As described earlier, the cable TV company provides a cable modem when you first subscribe to the service and some companies also provide a network card and network cable. The cable modem uses a regular TV cable cord to connect to a TV cable wall outlet. Figure 8-21 illustrates

8

what the arrangement looks like. The cable modem also has an electrical connection to provide power to the box. Before you can set up cable modem on your PC, you must first install the network card and its drivers and then connect the PC to the cable modem box by way of a network cable. Your cable modem company will provide you with the TCP/IP settings to use to configure TCP/IP. Some cable modem companies will do the entire installation for you. A service technician will come to your home, install the network card, and configure your PC to use the service.

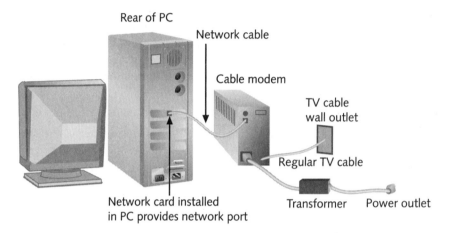

Figure 8-21 Cable modem connects to a PC through a network card installed in the PC

If you don't have on-site service from the cable modem company, you can use the instructions in the next section to install a network card and configure the network card and TCP/IP.

Install the Card and TCP/IP

The first step is to physically turn off the PC and install the network card in an expansion slot. Once you've installed the network card, turn on the PC. When Windows loads, it senses the new device and launches the Add New Hardware Wizard, which steps you though the process of loading the device driver software to control the card. Once the NIC is installed, it is listed in the Network window of the Control Panel as an installed network device. Figure 8-22 shows this window.

Notice in Figure 8-22 that TCP/IP is bound to the network card (last entry in the window). If TCP/IP is installed, it will automatically bind to the card when the card is installed. If you don't see the entry in the Network window as shown in Figure 8-22, then you must install TCP/IP. To do that, access the Control Panel and double-click the Network icon and follow the directions given earlier in the chapter to install TCP/IP. You may be asked for your Windows 98 CD. At the end of the installation, you will be asked to reboot your PC. After you reboot, check the Network window again and look for the entry to confirm that TCP/IP is bound to the network card.

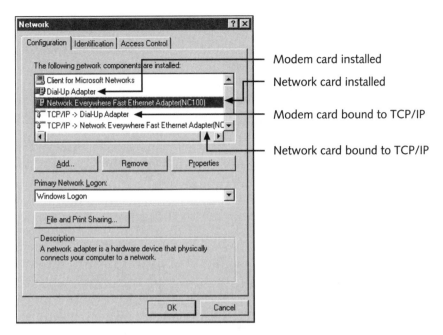

Modem card installed

Network card installed

Modem card bound to TCP/IP

Network card bound to TCP/IP

Figure 8-22   A network card is listed in the Network window as an installed network device when using DSL, cable modem or a LAN to connect to an ISP

If TCP/IP is not bound to the card, follow these direction:

1. Select the card and click the **Properties** button. The network card Properties window opens.

2. Click the **Bindings** tab.

3. Check **TCP/IP** and click **OK**. You should now see TCP/IP bound to the card in the Network window.

Determine the MAC Address of Your Network Card

The next step is to determine the MAC address of your network card and give this information to a help desk technician at the cable modem company. The technician enters the MAC address into an online list of valid addresses that identify your PC as a subscriber to the cable modem service. When the PC first connects to the service, the system recognizes the PC and assigns to it a valid IP address, subnet mask, IP address of the default gateway and IP address of a domain name server. To determine the MAC address of the network card, use WinIPcfg. Follow these directions:

1. Click **Start** on the Taskbar and click **Run.** Enter **WINIPCFG** in the Run dialog box and click **OK**. The IP Configuration window opens

2. Select the network card from the drop down list and read the **Adapter Address** in the window. Give this value to the cable modem help desk.

Configure TCP/IP to Connect to the Cable Modem

Now configure TCP/IP to use the network card to connect to cable modem. To do that, follow these directions:

1. Start the **Control Panel**, then double-click the **Network** icon. (Or you can right-click the Network Neighborhood icon on the desktop and select Properties on the drop-down menu.) The Network window opens.

2. Click the entry in the window where TCP/IP is bound to the network card and click **Properties**. The TCP/IP Properties window opens. See Figure 8-23.

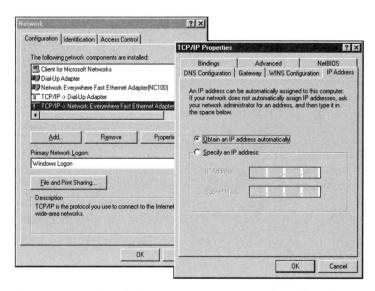

Figure 8-23   Set TCP/IP bound to the network card to obtain an IP address when it first connects to the cable modem

3. Click the **IP Address** tab and click the option button **Obtain an IP address automatically**.

4. Click the **WINS Configuration** tab and select **Use DHCP for WINS Resolution**. See Figure 8-24. Note that your cable modem provider might instruct you to configure this setting differently.

5. Click the **DNS Configuration** tab and select **Disable DNS**. (DNS will be enabled once the PC connects to cable modem and receives the necessary information.) As in the previous step, your cable modem provider might instruct you to configure this setting differently.

6. Click **OK**.

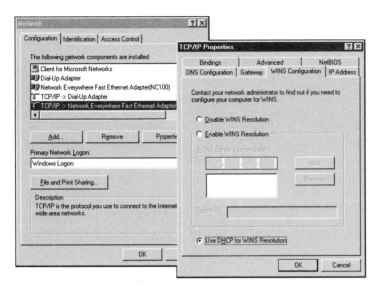

Figure 8-24   WINS configuration settings for a TCP/IP connection

Connect all the Cables

The next step is to connect the cable modem to the network port. To do that, shut down the PC and connect one end of the network cable to the network port on the back of the PC. Connect the other end of the cable to the cable modem. Be sure the cable modem is plugged in and turned on. There is usually a switch on the back of the box. Connect the TV cable from the TV cable outlet to the cable modem. (Refer back to Figure 8-21.) Turn on the PC.

When the PC starts up, you should immediately be connected to the Internet. Test the connection using your web browser or e-mail client. If you are not connected, try the following:

- Use WinIPcfg to access the IP Configuration window. Select the network card. Click **Release All**. Wait a moment and click **Renew**. Check for Internet connectivity again.

- If the above did not work, turn off the PC and the cable modem. Wait a full five minutes until all connections have timed out at the cable modem company. Turn on the cable modem and then turn on the PC. After the PC boots up, again check for connectivity.

- If this doesn't work, call the cable modem help desk. The technician there can release and restore the connection at that end, which should restore service.

Digital Subscriber Line (DSL)

In the race to produce a fast data transmission technology that is affordable for home use and that offers a direct connection rather than a dial up, the telephone industry has developed several similar technologies which are collectively called **Digital Subscriber Line (DSL)**. (ISDN is an early example of DSL.)

One prominent version of DSL is **Asymmetric Digital Subscriber Line** (**ADSL**), which is 50 times faster than ISDN and is direct connect. (Asymmetric refers to the fact that upstream transmission is not necessarily run at the same speed as downstream transmission.) When using the Internet, most transmission is downstream (downloading web pages) so the asymmetric technology is a viable option for home use if the emphasis is on using the Internet. ADSL uses a standard for transmission called **G.Lite** sponsored by ITU. To have a DSL connection, you must lease the line from the phone company, which provides a converter box on site. From the box, the line connects to an Ethernet NIC in your PC just like cable modem.

A DSL line is like a phone line in that it is point-to-point so that you don't need to be concerned that you will be competing with others in your area for bandwidth, as is the case with cable modem. The cost of an ADSL line varies greatly, anywhere from $35 to $85 per month, depending on your location.

A DSL installation is very similar to that of a cable modem installation. You first install the network card and bind it to TCP/IP. Then configure TCP/IP to obtain an IP address automatically. You will need the help of the DSL provider's help desk to set up your PC at their end. They will need to know the MAC address of your network card and will instruct you concerning any TCP/IP settings. Some DSL services include a complete installation. The company will send a service technician to your home to install the network card and configure your PC to use its service.

Integrated Services Digital Network (ISDN)

Integrated Services Digitial Network (ISDN) is a technology developed in the 1980s that uses regular phone lines, and is accessed by a dial-up connection. For home use, an ISDN line is fully digital and consists of two channels, or phone circuits, on a single pair of wires called B channels and a slower channel used for control signals, called a D channel. Each B channel can support speeds up to 64,000 bps. The two lines can be combined so that, effectively, data travels at 128,000 bps, which is about three to five times the speed of regular phone lines.

These ISDN lines with two B channels and one D channel are called **Basic Rate Interface** (**BRI**). Because these ISDN lines are designed for small business and home use, the two lines can support voice communication, fax machines, and computers. Logically, the two circuits are two phone lines that can each have different phone numbers, although most often only one number is assigned to both lines. Besides the BRI, there is a faster ISDN interface called **Primary Rate Interface** (**PRI**), designed for business use, that consists of 23 B channels and 1 D channel. With a PRI, you can combine several of the 23 B channels into a single fatter channel called an H channel for heavy business use.

In order to use an ISDN line at your business or home, you must have the following:

- An ISDN line leased from the phone company

- An ISDN device on your computer or connected to your computer (comparable to a modem for a regular phone line)

- If the ISDN device is installed on your computer, then you must have ISDN software on your PC to manage the connection

If you plan to use an ISDN line to access the Internet, then in order for you to see a performance gain, your service provider must also have an ISDN line. If you plan to use the ISDN line for telecommuting, then your place of business must also have ISDN in order for performance to improve.

The single ISDN device that connects to the ISDN line at your home can be an expansion card inside your PC or can be an external device. If the device is external and is using a serial port on the computer system, then the serial port does not make a distinction between communicating with an ISDN device or with a modem, since all its communication is digital in either case. There are three choices for connecting to ISDN:

- **Internal card**: An internal card is less expensive than the other two choices, but limits the use of the ISDN to when your computer is on. (When the computer is off you can't use the ISDN line for voice or a fax machine.)

- **External device**: An external device requires a connection to your PC. If you connect the device by way of your serial port, you have a bottleneck at the serial port; the device can communicate to your PC only as fast as the serial port speed.

- **External device and network card**: You can use an external device connected to your PC by way of a network card. The price is higher, but this solution offers the most advantages: the PC does not have to be on to use the ISDN line, and the network card is faster than a serial port.

The telephone company's responsibility for the phone system ends at your house. Inside your house, you are responsible for your home phone network. When you use ISDN you need a device that connects these two systems; this device is called an **NT1** (**Network Termination 1**) device. The device is installed outside your home. You also need another device called a **TA (Terminal Adapter)**. This device can be a box sitting beside your PC or a card inside the PC. The two major manufacturers of TAs in the United States are Eicon Technologies and 3Com. See their web sites at *www.eicon.com* and *www.3com.com* for more information. Sometimes a TA device is called an ISDN box or is incorrectly called an ISDN modem. A modem converts digital signals to analog and analog signals to digital. An ISDN circuit is digital all the way; no modems are needed, so it's not correct to call this device a modem.

8

Satellite Service

Another way to attain high-speed data transmission is through the use of satellites. You lease the service from a provider and mount a satellite dish on your premises. One service provider is DirecPC Satellite Service by Hughes (see the web site *www.direcpc.com*). Using a satellite connection for downstream transmission of data is not a good option unless you need high speed transmission and live in a remote location that doesn't offer other alternatives. The installation can be complicated and requires a dial-up connection for data to travel upstream.

CONNECTING A PC ON A LAN TO THE INTERNET

When a PC is connected to a Local Area Network (LAN), the configuration required to connect to the Internet is different than when a single PC is connected directly to an ISP. This section addresses what these differences are, and how to configure a PC when it is connected to a LAN that uses one of several configurations to manage TCP/IP and Internet access.

Many companies today are concerned about security to their LAN when users on the LAN need Internet access. This concern is very valid, because data on a company's LAN can be mission-critical to the company's success, and hackers are becoming more sophisticated and knowledgeable day by day. Keep security in mind as you read about the different ways a LAN administrator can set up a LAN to maintain a balance between supporting the needs of the users and protecting the company's data and resources.

About Software and Protocols Controlling a LAN

Before you can understand how to connect a PC on a LAN to the Internet, you need to understand how each computer on a LAN uses the operating system and protocols to communicate with other computers on the LAN. The operating system used by the network determines how the client computers on the LAN are configured, how one computer or node finds another node on the LAN, how one application communicates with another application over the network, and how the client must be configured to connect to the Internet.

A LAN might have a network operating system that controls every computer on the LAN (called a domain model or domain networking) or each computer might manage itself on the LAN (called a peer-to-peer model or peer-to-peer networking). For peer-to-peer networking, each computer on the LAN controls communication to and from it and is responsible for managing its own resources on the LAN. In the domain model, one computer on the LAN is the domain controller and manages the communication and resources for all computers on the LAN. This computer has a network operating system (NOS) installed on it which controls the network.

The three most popular network operating systems are NetWare by Novell, UNIX, and Windows NT (upgraded to Windows 2000). In a peer-to-peer network, each computer can use any personal computer operating system that supports peer-to-peer networking such as

Windows 98, and for computers on a domain-controlled network, the computers that are not the domain controller can use any of these same operating systems.

In addition to each computer needing an operating system, the entire network needs a single protocol that every computer on the LAN uses for communication. In some cases two protocols are used in order to accommodate various needs of the network. Windows 9x, Windows NT and Windows 2000 all support several protocols for networks. The two most popular are TCP/IP and NetBIOS. Because the protocol for the Internet is TCP/IP, if computers on a LAN access the Internet, then the LAN must be using TCP/IP. You can read more about protocols and network operating systems in Chapter 11.

NetBIOS (Network Basic Input Output System) is a network protocol that provides an application programming interface (API) that allows one application to communicate with another application on the same LAN. NetBIOS is useful when two or three computers are networked together in a small business. Because NetBIOS does not support routing, it does not support Internet communication. If NetBIOS is required because of applications used on the network and if computers also need access to the Internet, the solution is the **NetBIOS over TCP/IP (NetBT)** protocol, a protocol that allows NetBIOS API calls over a TCP/IP network (see Figure 8-25).

8

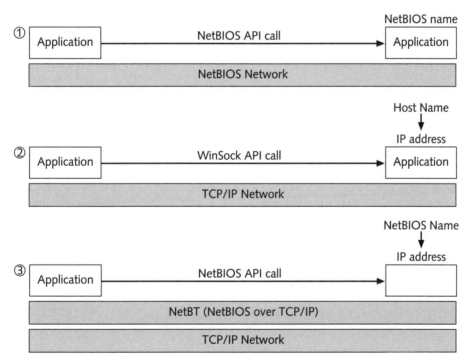

Figure 8-25   Three ways a Windows network can work

NetBIOS networks require that each computer on the network have a NetBIOS name. These names are usually assigned when the operating system is installed. Windows identifies computers on a NetBIOS network by NetBIOS names. In contrast, TCP/IP identifies computers by IP addresses, but TCP/IP also allows a computer to be assigned a character-based host name, which is easier to remember than an IP address. On a TCP/IP network, the host name must be associated with an IP address before one computer can find another on the network. Recall that this process is called name resolution.

Applications using NetBIOS use NetBIOS API calls to communicate with other applications on the network. Applications that are using TCP/IP to communicate over the network use a type of API call to TCP/IP that is known as **Windows Sockets** (**WinSock** for short). WinSock is a part of the TCP/IP utility software installed with TCP/IP.

An application can make a NetBIOS API call to another computer on a network and identify the remote computer by its NetBIOS name even though the network is using TCP/IP (refer to Figure 8-25). When dealing with these hybrid networks, know that the NetBIOS name of the remote computer must be related to an IP address before TCP/IP can make the connection. Later in this chapter you can learn how this is done.

Connecting a LAN to the Internet

In order to understand how a client on a LAN might be configured to access the Internet, you first need to look conceptually at the different approaches. A network is usually set up so that there is only one entry point to the Internet, called the gateway. Remember from Chapter 2 that a gateway is more a concept than a device. It can be a computer or it can be some other device that physically connects a network to another network. This section discusses three different approaches to connecting to the Internet through a gateway.

In Figure 8-26, the PCs on the LAN can't get to the Internet because they are not using TCP/IP, but instead are using another type of network protocol such as NetBIOS or IPX/SPX by NetWare by Novell. This type of network security is called **protocol isolation**. Users can place files on the Windows NT or UNIX server, which has access to the Internet and could even be used as a web server to the Internet. Files downloaded from the Internet to this server might be made available to users on the LAN. In this situation, security is high, but users can't surf the web. There is one exception: If the Windows NT or UNIX server has a web browser installed on it, then a user sitting at this one computer could surf the web.

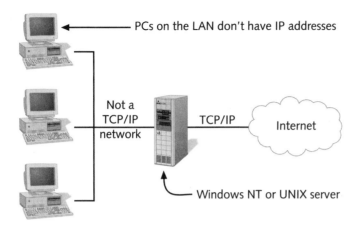

PCs on the LAN don't have IP addresses

Not a
TCP/IP
network

TCP/IP

Internet

Windows NT or UNIX server

Figure 8-26   Using protocol isolation, users cannot see the Internet but can pass files back and forth to it

8

In Figure 8-27, the LAN is using TCP/IP and a router is serving as the gateway to the Internet. Recall that a router is a device that connects two or more networks and manages the traffic between them. PCs are assigned valid public IP addresses that can be used on the Internet and users have full access to the Internet. This configuration gives users the access they might need, but there is little security involved. Data on the network is highly subject to hackers in this configuration.

A network manager could introduce some level of security if the router is a Windows NT or UNIX computer, or is a dedicated router from a vendor that supports software that filters IP packets. When a router is used in this filtering capacity, it is called a firewall. A **firewall** is any device that prevents unwanted traffic between two networks.

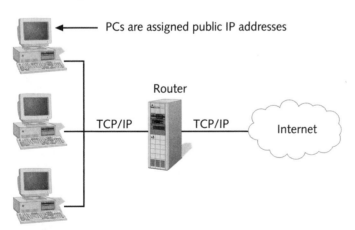

PCs are assigned public IP addresses

Router

TCP/IP

TCP/IP

Internet

Figure 8-27   Using router security, the router serves as the gateway to the Internet

With proxy server security, shown Figure 8-28, the router is replaced by a proxy server that serves as a firewall. A proxy is something or someone who stands in the place of another. A **proxy server** uses a process called **Network Address Translation (NAT)**, and is a computer that makes a connection to other computers on the Internet on behalf of computers on its private network. The other computers on the network are assigned private IP addresses that will not work as valid IP addresses on the Internet. When one of these computers tries to access the Internet, its IP address reaches the proxy server, which substitutes its own IP address before sending the request over the Internet. All activity from this network to the Internet appears to be coming from this one proxy server. When the proxy server receives the response from the Internet it passes it on to the PC on the network that made the request.

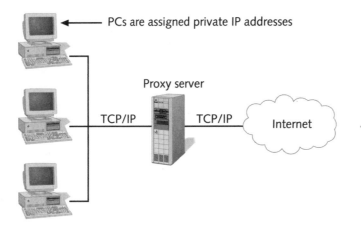

Figure 8-28   Using a proxy server, PCs on the LAN access the Internet with the proxy server filtering traffic

A proxy server can filter out any IP packets it wants to, limit the IP addresses and ports on the Internet with which a PC can communicate, and take other measures to control traffic to and from the network. Much administrative monitoring of Internet traffic is possible with a proxy server. The server can also speed up Internet access by caching data that users request from the Internet often. Windows 98 Second Edition and Windows 2000 offer a proxy service called Internet Connection Sharing (ICS). It is intended to be used on a small LAN to allow several computers to share a single IP address and access to an ISP. You can read more about proxy servers in Chapters 10 and 12.

Connecting the Gateway to the Internet

In all the situations described in the previous section, the computer designated as the gateway has access to the Internet. This access can be by way of any of the methods discussed earlier in the chapter. For example, the gateway can have modem card installed and use a Dial-Up connection to the ISP. (The ISP is not showing in Figures 8-26, 8-27, and 8-28, but is used to connect the gateway to the Internet.) Using a phone line to connect all users on a LAN to the Internet would most likely not be suitable because it is so slow. The gateway could use a cable modem, DSL, ISDN or other type of connection. The choice for the type connection partly depends on the amount of traffic the gateway must support. For a small LAN of less than 15 users with moderate needs for Internet access, cable modem or DSL should provide adequate bandwidth.

Looking at the illustrations in Figures 8-26, 8-27, and 8-28, you can see that two lines are coming from the computer that is acting as the gateway. One line in the drawing connects the computer to the LAN and the other line connects the computer to the ISP and on to the Internet. Physically, this situation calls for two connections on a single computer. The connection to the LAN is always done by a network card, but the connection to the ISP might be a network card, modem, or ISDN card. If the connection to the ISP is by way of a network card, such as would be the case if the connection is using cable modem or DSL, then the computer has two network cards installed. One card is bound to the protocol used by the LAN and the other card is bound to the protocol used by the ISP's network, which will always be TCP/IP. An example of this situation is presented in Chapter 13.

How Computers Find Each Other on a LAN

When an application using NetBIOS or Windows Sockets wants to communicate with another computer on the same TCP/IP LAN, the requesting computer knows the NetBIOS name or host name of the remote computer. But before TCP/IP communication can happen between the two computers, the first computer must discover the IP address of the remote PC. The process of discovering the IP address of a computer when you know the host name or NetBIOS name is called name resolution. For an application using NetBIOS, the computer runs through the following checklist in this order to discover the IP address. (A computer that is using just TCP/IP and not NetBIOS uses DNS to resolve the name, not WINS, and begins at Step 5 below.)

1. The computer checks the NetBIOS name cache. This cache is information retained in memory from name resolutions made since the last reboot.

2. If the computer has the IP address of a WINS server, it queries the server. Recall from Chapter 2 that a WINS server is a Windows NT or Windows 2000 server on the network that maintains a database of NetBIOS names and IP addresses.

3. The computer sends a broadcast message to all computers on the LAN asking for the IP address of the computer with the broadcasted NetBIOS host name.

4. The computer checks a file named LMHosts, which is stored in the \Windows folder on the local computer. This file, called a host table, contains the NetBIOS names and associated IP addresses of computers on the LAN if someone has taken the time to manually make the entries into the file.

5. If the IP address is still not discovered, the computer assumes the network is using DNS instead of WINS, so it checks the file in the \Windows folder named Hosts. The Hosts file is another host table that contains host names and associated IP addresses that is similar to the information kept by DNS servers.

6. If the computer has the IP address of a DNS server, it queries the DNS server.

Both the LMHosts and Hosts files are in the \Windows folder and are called host tables. **LMHosts** serves as a local table of information similar to that maintained by a WINS server for NetBIOS names, and **Hosts** serves as a local table of information similar to that kept by a DNS server.

If you look in the \Windows folder of a Windows 9x computer, you will see a sample of each file named LMHosts.SAM and Hosts.SAM. Open each file with Notepad to examine it. Entries in a host table file that begin with the # symbol are comments and are not read by the name resolution process. There are many commented lines in the sample files. You can add your entries to the bottom of the file without the # symbol. An example of this file is shown in Figure 8-29. Note in this figure that the IP addresses begin with 10. Recall from Chapter 2 that these numbers are reserved for private IP addresses.

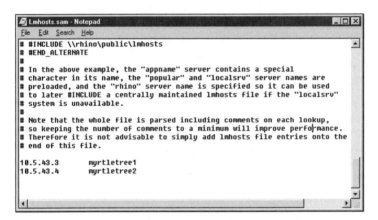

Figure 8-29   LMHosts is used to resolve names when using NetBIOS

Configuring a PC on a LAN to Connect to the Internet

Now that you understand the different ways a client might be configured on a network to get access to the Internet and to discover IP addresses of other computers on the network, you are ready to learn how to use the Windows 9x tools to make these configuration settings. This section looks at the TCP/IP settings needed to connect users on a network to the Internet. Recall that the protocol used by the network must be TCP/IP in order for all users to access the Internet from a network.

To configure TCP/IP correctly for a PC on a network you must know the answers to these questions:

- Does the network use a proxy server? If so, what is the IP address of the server?

- What is the IP address of the default gateway if one is used?

- Is static IP addressing or dynamic IP addressing used? If static IP addresses are used, are the IP addresses public or private?

Follow these directions to tell TCP/IP to use a proxy server to connect to the Internet:

1. Access the Control Panel and double-click the **Internet options** icon. The Internet Properties window opens.

2. Click the **Connections** tab and click **LAN Settings**. The LAN Settings window opens. Check **Use a proxy server**.

3. Enter the IP address or domain name of the proxy server and the port that you want the client to use. For example, if you want the proxy server to be used when using the World Wide Web, enter 80 as the port.

4. If you want a proxy server to be used for other Internet services, click **Advanced**. The Proxy Settings window opens as shown in Figure 8-30. Enter the name of each proxy server and the port to use. Click **OK** to save your changes.

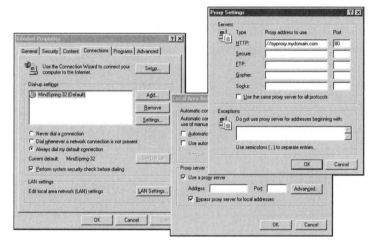

Figure 8-30   Tell TCP/IP to use a proxy server to connect to the Internet

To set a default gateway to the Internet:

1. Access the Control Panel and double-click the **Network** icon. In the Network window, click the **Configuration** tab.

2. Select the TCP/IP binding to the NIC used to access the LAN and click **Properties**. The TCP/IP Properties box for that binding opens. Click the **Gateway** tab. See Figure 8-31.

3. Enter the IP address of the gateway, click **Add** and click **OK** to save your changes.

From this TCP/IP Properties box you can also enable either DNS or WINS and enter the IP addresses of the DNS or WINS servers.

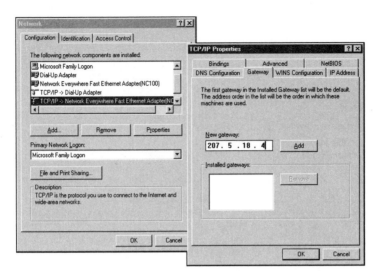

Figure 8-31   Use the TCP/IP Properties window to enter a gateway IP address to the Internet if one is used

To specify dynamic or static IP addressing, follow these directions: From the TCP/IP Properties window, click the **IP Address** tab. For static IP addressing, click **Specify an IP address** and enter the IP address assigned to this workstation and the subnet mask See Figure 8-32 for an example of this screen.

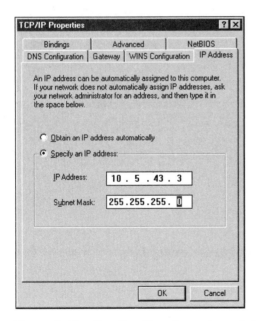

Figure 8-32   Specify either dynamic or static IP addressing on your LAN using the TCP/IP Properties window

Configuring a PC to Share Resources with Others on the LAN

If users on a LAN are working on a common project and need to share applications and files or need to share printers, then all these users must be assigned to the same workgroup on the LAN. In Windows, a workgroup is a group of users on a LAN that share common resources. Windows makes these resources available by way of Network Neighborhood. The Network Neighborhood icon is found on the desktop. Double click it to see the names of all computers on the LAN that are in your workgroup. Using Network Neighborhood, you can copy files from one computer to another, use the applications installed on one computer from another computer, and share printers. Figure 8-33 shows an example of Network Neighborhood.

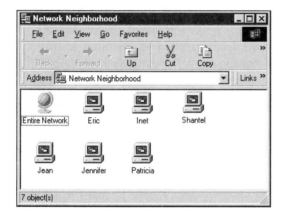

Figure 8-33   Network Neighborhood shows all computers on the LAN in a common workgroup

Workgroups can be effective when several people work on a common project. For example, if you and others in your group are building a web site, sharing resources on the LAN can be an effective method of passing web pages around as they are built. Or one computer on the LAN can be designated as the file server. The user of this computer makes a portion of hard drive space available for the entire web site files. All users have access to this one resource and the web site files are neatly kept in a single location.

To set up a workgroup and assign a computer a name within the workgroup, follow these directions:

1. Access the Control Panel and double-click the **Network** icon.

2. Click the **Identification** tab. See Figure 8-34.

3. Enter the name of the workgroup (Golden in this example). All users in the workgroup must have the same name entered in the window on their PC.

4. Enter the name of the computer (Patricia in this example). Each computer name must be unique within the workgroup.

5. Click **OK** to exit the window. The computer should now be visible in Network Neighborhood as Patricia on all computers in the workgroup.

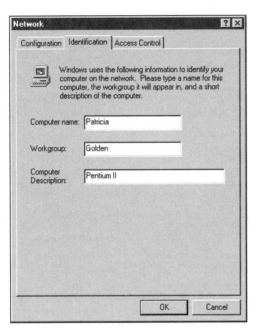

Figure 8-34   Each computer in a workgroup must be assigned a name that other users on the network will see in their Network Neighborhood window

INSTALLING AND MANAGING INTERNET EXPLORER OR NETSCAPE NAVIGATOR

By now you already have experience downloading and installing a web browser, but here is a quick review. Microsoft recommends the following minimum hardware and software needed to support Internet Explorer Version 5:

- 486DX/66 MHz or higher processor
- Windows 95, Windows 98, Windows NT 4.0 with Service Pack 3, or Windows 2000
- 16 MB (megabytes) of RAM for Windows 9x or 32 MB for Windows NT/2000
- From 45 MB to 111 MB of hard drive storage, depending on the options installed
- A mouse and an Internet connection

To download and install Internet Explorer, go to the *www.microsoft.com/ie* site and click Download Now. Follow the directions that will step you through the process. If you don't already have a web browser installed and cannot access the Microsoft web site, you can use their FTP site at *ftp.microsoft.com*. Windows 9x has an FTP utility included with the operating system, so you should be able to use that to get started. See Chapter 4 for directions using Windows FTP.

To download Navigator Netscape, go to the Web site *www.netscape.com* or use the FTP site *ftp.netscape.com/pub/netscape6*. Download the Netscape Setup program and then execute it from your PC.

Browser Caching

An important part of managing web browser software on a user's PC is managing browser caching, which can speed up Internet access. Recall that a cache is a place where the computer holds frequently used data for later use. A cache can sometimes be memory and sometimes be hard drive space, and clients, servers, and several types of Internet hardware use caching to speed up Internet use. Internet Explorer caches web pages to the hard drive and Netscape Navigator caches them to the hard drive and to memory for as long as the browser is loaded. With Internet Explorer, you can control the amount of hard drive used for caching and with Navigator you can control the amount of memory and hard drive space used.

Caching speeds up Internet access because the browser will display a page that is cached from memory or the hard drive, rather than going back to the web site to get the page. The disadvantage of caching is that, if the web site updates the web page, the page displayed by the browser might be out of date. Another disadvantage is that hard drive space is used that might better be allocated for other purposes. Therefore, you might want to reduce the size of the hard drive cache to conserve space or increase it if you have plenty of hard drive space to spare. To clean up a cluttered hard drive, you can clean the cache, which also assures you that all pages displayed will be current because the browser must go to the site for a new copy.

Managing the Web Browser Cache

To change the size of the Internet Explorer cache and clean the cache, follow these directions:

1. In Internet Explorer, click **Tools** on the menu bar, then click **Internet Options**. The Internet Options window opens.

2. Click **Settings** and the Settings window opens, as shown in Figure 8-35. Notice the location of the cache: C:\WINDOWS\Temporary Internet Files.

3. Change the size of the cache and click **OK** when done. This setting determines how large the folder can become.

To clean out the cache, click Delete Files, then, in the dialog box that opens, click OK when asked, "Delete all files in the Temporary Internet Files folder?"

8

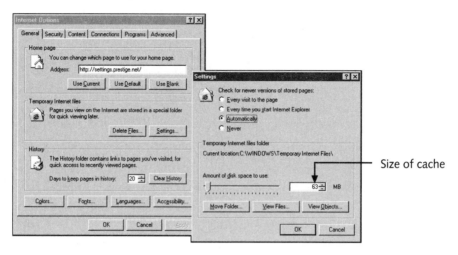

Size of cache

Figure 8-35   Use Internet Options of Internet Explorer 5 to manage the web browser's cache settings

To manage your cache settings in Netscape Navigator, follow these directions:

1. Click **Edit** on the menu bar, then click **Preferences**. The Preferences window opens.

2. From the list of categories on the left side of the window, click on the + symbol to open the **Advanced** list. Then click **Cache** under the Advanced choices. The cache Preferences window opens on the right side of the window, as shown in Figure 8-36.

You can adjust the amount of memory and disk caches given in Kilobytes. Having too large a memory cache hinders the performance of other applications that are open, but setting the cache to zero means that you will be unable to print web pages. If you are not squeezed for hard drive space or memory, set the disk cache at about 8,000 Kbytes and the memory cache at about 1,000 Kbytes.

To change the folder where the disk cache is kept, enter a new folder name in the Disk Cache Folder field. You might want to move the location of the cache if you are trying to free up the space on one logical drive (for example, drive C) and have a second logical drive available to hold the cache (for example, drive D).

To empty the cache, click Clear Memory Cache or Clear Disk Cache. Because the browser takes time to search through the cache, it's a good idea to clear the cache out every now and then to improve performance.

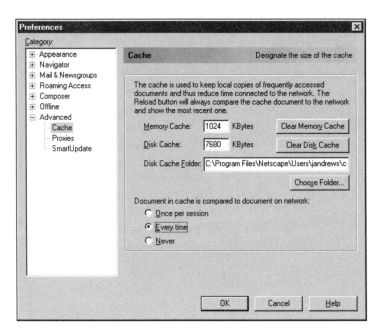

Figure 8-36   Managing the browser cache for Netscape Navigator

At the bottom of the window you can control how often the browser compares the pages in the cache to those on the web site. **Once per session** is recommended, which means that the page in the cache is compared to the web site only the first time you access the site during the current Internet session.

Web pages are also cached on proxy servers and other cache servers. This method of caching, which helps not only one user but can help all users on the LAN, is discussed in Chapter 10.

REAL PEOPLE, REAL PROBLEMS, REAL SOLUTIONS
UPDATE YOUR BROWSER

With a small and steadily growing local network, keeping users' software up to date was always a challenge for Terri Adams. As the network administrator, one of her duties was to make sure that the 75 workstations in the office had current versions of software installed.

Because her company used several Internet and intranet based applications, it was vital to keep browsing software updated. The company used Internet Explorer from Microsoft (*www.microsoft.com*) on every machine that was part of the local network. Terri found that the browser software changed often—more often than any other application in use by the company. She was constantly downloading software patches and upgrades to keep up with the changing technology. (A **software patch** is a fix for a software problem or bug and is downloaded from the software manufacturer's web site and then installed over the existing software.)

A little over a year ago, Terri's job was made a little easier. Microsoft began providing a small piece of software, a "wizard," that could detect which Internet Explorer components were installed on any of the network computers, and then download and install missing items. The wizard could be downloaded over the Internet to a local machine and executed. It would then look at the local browser, operating system, and installed components to determine which new software needed to be downloaded. After the determination process was complete, the wizard stepped through to download the new software and components. When the download was complete, the installation was complete!

Terri soon found that she could keep users' Internet browsing software updated easily. One of the components from Microsoft would even notify Terri if newly published critical updates were available. Before she installed the wizard software, downloading a new browser or updating a current one could be a time-consuming task, because browser software, plug-ins, and components all had to be downloaded independently.

In Terri's organization, the chosen browser is Internet Explorer, but Netscape Navigator has a similar feature to help you keep track of updates, new plug-ins, and fixes. The update wizard is called SmartUpdate and can be accessed from the Netscape web site at *www.netscape.com*. Click on the link to SmartUpdate.

Whether browser software is running in a network environment or at home, the update software that is available can be a helpful timesaver. The technology to *keep up* with technology continues to innovate and improve.

CHAPTER SUMMARY

❑ To connect to the Internet from a PC using a phone line, the following must be in place: the phone line with a dial tone, the modem, the software to drive the modem (device driver), an operating system configured to interface with the device, TCP/IP stack, and applications software to use the Internet.

❑ To connect to the Internet with a phone line by way of an ISP, you need to know the phone number, user ID, password and TCP/IP configuration, which includes static versus dynamic IP addressing, and DNS server IP addresses.

❑ A modem and the modem's device driver operate at the Data Link and Physical layers of the OSI model.

❑ A modem (stands for modulation/demodulation) is a device that converts digital data to and from analog data and serves as the middle man between a PC, which is digital, and a phone line, which is analog.

❏ Device driver software that controls a modem can come from the modem manufacturer or from Windows. It is best to use the manufacturer's software when you have a choice.

❏ A modem is a DCE (data communications equipment) device and a computer is a DTE (data terminal equipment).

❏ Modems can be external or internal devices. External modems use a serial cable connecting to the serial port of a PC. An internal modem uses either an ISA or PCI expansion slot on the system board of the PC.

❏ The speed of a phone line connection is partly determined by the speed of the serial port to the modem, the modem itself and the quality of the phone line.

❏ A modem, like all I/O devices, requires an IRQ and a range of I/O addresses to communicate with the CPU.

❏ Use Windows 9x Device Manager to determine the system resources currently used by devices on your system and look for available resources a new modem can use.

❏ Plug and Play modems are automatically configured by the system without having to manually set jumpers and DIP switches to select the system resources for the modem to use.

❏ A COM port is a predetermined set of IRQ and I/O addresses that can be used by a device such as a modem or serial port.

❏ Windows HyperTerminal is a useful tool to determine that a modem is working properly and to diagnose problems with a modem before or after a system is configured to connect to the Internet.

❏ Software and people can communicate with a modem using a set of commands called the AT command set. These commands can be useful when troubleshooting modem problems.

❏ Dial-Up Networking is a Windows utility that allows a modem connected to a phone line to look and act like a network card to TCP/IP or some other network protocol stack.

❏ PPP (Point-to-Point Protocol) is a line protocol and manages the transmission of data packets over phone lines. PPP supports TCP/IP data packets and is used when a computer connects to the Internet using phone lines.

❏ SLIP is an older line protocol and is not as powerful as PPP.

❏ After installing a modem, the next step to connect to the Internet is to install and configure Dial-Up Networking to use the modem to connect to your ISP.

❏ TCP/IP software was not a part of DOS or Windows 3.x but is included in Windows 9x, Windows NT and Windows 2000. When Windows is installed, if it finds a legacy version of TCP/IP installed, it will not overwrite that software.

❏ The TCP/IP utility for Windows includes the core protocols, support for Windows Sockets (WinSock) and NetBIOS, diagnostic tools, client for DHCP, client for WINS and PPP.

8

❑ If your ISP uses dynamic IP addresses, then you do not need to know the IP address of the client, the default gateway, or subnet mask because these are dynamically assigned each time the PC logs onto the ISP's network.

❑ Use WinIPcfg to verify that an IP address, subnet mask and default gateway have been assigned when using TCP/IP.

❑ Phone lines use a point-to-point connection, but Windows 98 supports a multipoint connection, whereby two or more physical lines can be used to create a single logical connection which increases the resulting bandwidth.

❑ Some faster ways to connect to the Internet from a home or small business are ISDN, cable modem, DSL, and satellite.

❑ ISDN for home use is a digital phone line that is equivalent to two regular phone lines (B channels) and one slower controlling channel (D channel), and is called a BRI (Basic Rate Interface).

❑ ISDN for business use is equivalent to 23 phone lines (B channels) and one D channel and is called a PRI (Primary Rate Interface).

❑ To connect a home PC to ISDN, you can use an ISDN card in the PC, a network card connected to an ISDN device, or a serial port connected to the ISDN device.

❑ Cable modem uses cable lines from a TV cable company that connect to a modem in your home. The modem then connects to a network card in your PC by way of a network cable.

❑ A DSL line is a leased digital phone line that needs a converter box at your home. The box connects to a network card in your PC by way of a network cable.

❑ A Windows network can use NetBIOS or TCP/IP or a combination of both. Nodes on a NetBIOS network are identified by a NetBIOS name. Nodes on a TCP/IP network are identified by a host name and an IP address.

❑ LAN administrators are concerned with LAN security when PCs on the LAN connect to the Internet, and therefore use a network configuration that provides that security. Possible options are protocol isolation, router security, and security provided by proxy servers.

❑ When protocol isolation is used, the PCs on the LAN cannot connect to the Internet but can access files on a server that does interact with the Internet.

❑ With router security, PCs are assigned public IP addresses and can have full access to the Internet. This setup offers little support for LAN security unless the router includes filtering software that controls traffic to and from the Internet.

❑ When a LAN uses a proxy server, PCs on the LAN are assigned private IP addresses and do not connect directly to the Internet. Instead, the interaction with the Internet is all done by the proxy server.

❑ A computer finds another on a network using a DNS server, a WINS server or one of two host tables stored on the computer: LMHosts or Hosts.

❐ For Windows 9x, use the Internet options and Network icons of Control Panel to con-
    figure a PC on a LAN to access the Internet.

❐ Internet Explorer uses a hard drive cache and Netscape Navigator uses memory and
    hard drive caches to speed up Internet access.

KEY TERMS

Asymmetric Digital Subscriber Line (ADSL) — A type of DSL line that is asymmetric, which means that data travels downstream at one speed and upstream at a
different (slower) speed.

Basic Rate Interface (BRI) — An ISDN standard that allows for two B channels and
one D channel on a single ISDN line. A B channel is equivalent to a regular phone line
and a D channel is a slower channel used for control. *See* PRI.

cable modem — A technology that allows data transmissions over cable TV lines. The
data traveling over the cable is analog and is converted to digital by a cable modem
before it is passed to a computer by way of a network cable and NIC installed in the PC.

data communication equipment (DCE) — A device, such as a modem, that is
responsible for the communication between two other devices, such as a PC and a server.

data path — On a system board, a group of embedded wires on which data can travel. A
data path is part of a bus.

data terminal equipment (DTE) — The term used to refer to a computer and a remote
computer or terminal to which the computer or terminal is attached.

device driver — A small program stored on a hard drive that tells the computer how to
communicate with an input/output device such as a printer or modem.

Dial-Up Networking (DUN) — A Windows utility that allows a modem connected to a
phone line to look and act like a network card, so other higher-level utilities and software
can use a phone line to connect to a network.

Digital Subscriber Line (DSL) — A leased digital phone line that uses direct connection
(always up). A DSL line connects to a data converter installed at your site, which connects
to your PC by way of a network cable and network card.

DOCSIS (Data Over Cable Service Interface Specifications) — The communications
standards that are used by cable modem.

EIA/TIA-232 standard — *See* RS-232 standard.

firewall — A device that prevents unwanted traffic from entering or leaving a network.

G.Lite — A communication standard sponsored by ITU used by ADSL.

Hosts — A text file located in the Windows folder that contains NetBIOS names and their
associated IP addresses, that is used for name resolution for a NetBIOS over TCP/IP
network.

Integrated Services Digital Network (ISDN) — A communications standard that can
carry digital data simultaneously over two or more channels on a single pair of wires
(BRI standard) at about five times the speed of a regular phone line connection, or up to
23 channels for heavy business use (PRI standard).

8

ISA bus — A bus or group of wires embedded on a system board that provide a group of expansion slots on the system board that can be used to attach expansion cards, such as a modem card, to the board. An ISA bus can have either an 8-bit or 16-bit data path.

line protocol — A protocol used to send data packets destined for a network over phone lines. PPP and SLIP are examples of line protocols.

LMHosts — A text file located in the Windows folder that contains NetBIOS names and their associated IP addresses, that is used for name resolution for a NetBIOS over TCP/IP network.

modem — From MOdulate/DEModulate. A device that modulates digital data from a computer to an analog format that can be sent over telephone lines, then demodulates it back into digital form.

multipoint connection — A connection between two devices in which more than one physical connection is used to create the appearance of a single connection. Two computers connected to each other using two phone lines and two modems on each computer is an example of a multipoint connection.

NetBIOS (Network Basic Input Output System) — A Windows application programming interface (API) that allows one application to communicate with another application on the same LAN. NetBIOS cannot be used to cross from one network to another because it does not support routing.

NetBT (NetBIOS over TCP/IP) — A protocol that is used when NetBIOS program calls are made over a TCP/IP network.

Network Address Translation (NAT) — A process that converts private IP addresses on a LAN to the proxy server's IP address before the data packet is sent over the Internet.

NT1 (Network Termination 1) — A device used in an ISDN setup that is the point of interchange between the phone company and your internal home or business network. (An NT1 is a box outside your house where your ISDN line connects to the phone company service.)

PCI bus — A bus on a system board that provides four or more expansion slots that can be used to attach expansion cards such as a modem to the board. A PCI bus has a 32-bit data path.

Plug and Play — A technology in which the operating system and BIOS are designed to anotomatically configure new hardware devices to eliminate system resource conflicts (such as IRQ and I/O address conflicts).

point-to-multipoint — A connection between one device and several other devices where data travels from the original device to multiple destinations. An example of point-to-multipoint communication is cable modem.

point-to-point — A dedicated connection between two devices using a single physical connection.

PPP (Point-to-Point Protocol) — A line protocol used by Dial-Up Networking and other software to send data packets over phone lines. PPP works at the Data Link layer of the OSI model and can support TCP/IP and NetBIOS packets.

PPP Multilink (MP) — A Windows utility that allows a PC with more than one modem or other communication device to create a multipoint connection.

Primary Rate Interface (PRI) — An ISDN standard designed for heavy business use that allows for up to 23 B channels and 1 D channel on a single ISDN leased line. *See* BRI.

protocol isolation — A type of network security whereby computers on the network don't use TCP/IP and therefore cannot communicate over the Internet.

proxy server — A firewall device that can filter traffic in and out of a network. The proxy server communicates with computers on the Internet on behalf of computers on the network making the request.

RS-232 standard — The standard that determines the design and function of a serial port or serial cable. Also called the EIA/TIA-232 standard.

Serial Line Internet Protocol (SLIP) — An older, mostly outdated line protocol used to send data packets over phone lines. SLIP does not support encrypted data as does PPP.

serial port — A port on the back of a computer used for transmitting data serially or in single file. Serial ports are used by a mouse, modem, or other device that uses serial communication with a computer. A serial port has either 9 or 25 pins.

SNMP (Simple Network Management Protocol) — A protocol that is included with Windows but must be installed separately that provides system management for TCP/IP networks.

Software patch — A segment of computer code that fixes a bug or provides a new feature. Software patches can be downloaded from a software manufacturer's web site and then installed over existing software.

TA (Terminal Adapter) — An internal or external device that converts an ISDN data stream into a signal that is suitable for a regular analog telephone or a computer. Sometimes called an ISDN card or ISDN box.

TCP/IP stack — A group of TCP/IP utilities and protocols that make up the total TCP/IP group needed to support traffic over a TCP/IP network such as the Internet. TCP/IP software on a PC is sometimes called the TCP/IP stack.

Windows Sockets (WinSock) — A part of the TCP/IP utility software that manages API calls from applications to other computers on a TCP/IP network

REVIEW QUESTIONS

1. Software that controls an input/output device, such as a modem or printer, is called a(n) _____.

2. Data in a computer is _____, but data traveling over a phone line is _____, and a _____ converts the data between the two states.

3. What are the two names for the standard that controls a serial port?

4. What two types of buses on a system board can be used to support a modem card?

5. What are the two types of system resources required by a modem?

6. Which is faster, an ISA bus or a PCI bus?

7. What does the word "modem" mean?

8. When installing a modem, what device will prevent you from damaging the PC from static electricity as you work?

9. A phone jack on the back of a modem or modem card is called a _____ port.

10. What Windows utility can be used to make a phone call using commands from the modem AT command set?

11. What modem command will cause a modem to hang up?

12. What modem command will restore the modem to factory defaults?

13. What Windows utility makes a modem appear to be a network adapter to TCP/IP?

14. What protocol manages data packets over phone lines?

15. Name one protocol that is supported by SLIP.

16. The TCP/IP utility software suite is sometimes called a TCP/IP _____.

17. What are the steps to verify that TCP/IP is bound to a network adapter?

18. If you determine that TCP/IP is not bound to a Dial-Up Networking network adapter, what should you first check?

19. When an ISP uses dynamic IP addressing, what values are assigned to the client each time it connects to the ISP?

20. After you are connected to your ISP, what TCP/IP utility can you use to see the IP address assigned to you by the ISP?

21. What should you do to improve browser performance that has degraded over time?

22. Which is a faster connection for home use, ISDN or cable modem?

23. Which of the following uses asymmetric communication, cable modem, ISDN, regular phone lines, or ADSL?

24. Which service uses an analog data stream, cable modem or ISDN?

25. Which type of communication service might experience a degradation in service if many people in your neighborhood use the service?

26. What is the purpose of the NetBT protocol?

27. TCP/IP supports both WinSock and NetBIOS. Compare the two.

28. If you wanted the most security on your LAN, which would you use, router security or a proxy server? Why?

29. Which type of network security uses public IP addresses? Which type uses private IP addresses?

30. If a company is using a router to connect to the Internet and is running low on IP addresses for its growing number of computers, why might the company switch to using a proxy server to connect to the Internet?

HANDS-ON PROJECTS

Research Cable Modem in Your Area

Research the possibility of installing cable modem at your home. Answer the following:

1. What is the name of the cable modem company in your area? (If you don't have a company in your area, use one in a nearby city to answer the remaining questions.)

2. Print the home page of the company's web site

3. Is the cable service two-way or downstream only?

4. How much are the startup expenses? What is the monthly fee?

5. Does the company also serve as an ISP? If so, what services are included? (web page space, e-mail accounts, and so forth)

6. If the company is an ISP, can you use their cable modem service and not use the ISP service?

Research DSL in Your Area

1. What is the company that offers DSL in your area? (If DSL is not offered in your area, answer the remaining questions for a nearby city.)

2. How much does DSL service cost? What additional features are included with the service?

3. Are you required to use the phone company's ISP service if you select DSL?

4. What equipment are you required to buy or lease to use the service?

5. Compare DSL to cable modem above. Which is the better buy for you? Why?

Investigate Your PC Configuration

1. Does your PC have a Hosts or LMHosts file in the \Windows folder? If so, print the contents of the file.

2. Does your PC use static or dynamic IP addressing to connect to the Internet? List the steps you used to determine the answer to this question. Print the screen showing the answer.

3. Using a PC with a modem, use HyperTerminal to dial a friend's home phone number. Print the HyperTerminal screen showing the results of the call.

Research Modems for Purchase

A friend of yours has a Pentium PC with 32 MB of RAM, and a 2 GB hard drive. The PC does not have a modem installed. She has asked for your help to purchase and install a modem so she can connect to the Internet. Answer these questions to get started on the project:

1. What is the cost of a PCI modem card that is Plug and Play? Print the web page of a shopping site showing the modem and price.

8

2. You want to verify that you can get support from the modem manufacturer if you have problems with the modem. Print a help page from the web site of the modem manufacturer.

3. Print the same pages as above for a second modem using a different manufacturer.

Use a Browser Help Utility

Using your browser's help utility, print instructions for changing the size of the browser cache and cleaning out the cache.

Download and Use NetMonitor

NetMonitor by Kissco, Inc, is a shareware product you can download from the Internet for free to monitor your Internet connection. It reports your connection speed, your IP address, download speeds, routes taken to web sites, and registered owners of these sites. Go to the web site *www.freenetmonitor.com* and download the software. Install it on your PC to monitor your Internet connection. Use it to report on your connection speed to the Internet.

CASE PROJECTS

Test Your Web Site Using the Latest Browsers

As new browser versions become available, it is important for web site developers to be aware of these new versions and test their web sites to verify that the browsers interpret them correctly. Do the following to download the latest versions of Internet Explorer and Netscape Navigator and test your site using these browsers:

1. Access the Microsoft web site, *www.microsoft.com/windows/ie*. What is the latest version of Internet Explorer? What are its advertised features?

2. Download Internet Explorer and print your personal home page viewed by this latest version.

3. Access the Netscape Navigator web site, *home.netscape.com/smartupdate*. What is the latest version of Navigator? What are its advertised features?

4. Using SmartUpdate, download Navigator. Print your personal home page viewed by this latest version.

WebTV and Other Internet Appliances

In this chapter, you will learn

♦ About thin clients and the technological trends in devices used to access the Internet

♦ About Microsoft WebTV and how it can be used by PCs and other devices

♦ How Internet telephony works and the different hardware and software devices that use the technology

♦ About appliances, other than computers, that can connect to the Internet, and about some of the concerns and challenges of these new technologies

---

The Internet is an exciting adventure in new technologies. It's interesting to discover the creative ways these technologies can be applied to improve communication and to access information. We have yet to see just how far existing technology can take us, let alone the new technology that appears on the market every day. Client devices for accessing the Internet (other than personal computers) are such new technology and are changing so fast, that it's difficult to keep up. Definitive trends have not been fully established. This chapter looks at some of the emerging trends and standards. Remember that it remains to be seen how this area of Internet development will proceed in the future as the leaders and standard-bearers are yet to be clearly established. In this chapter you will first learn about WebTV (one of the few established technologies in this area), devices used to make phone calls over the Internet, wireless devices, thin clients, and other Internet appliances.

THIN CLIENTS

When computers were first used as business tools before the invention of the personal computer, large mainframe computers housed both software and data. The data was made accessible to users by a device called a dumb terminal. A **dumb terminal**, in its simplest form, is a monitor and a keyboard connected to a mainframe computer with no processing power of its own. A user at the terminal turns it on and enters a user ID and password to log onto the mainframe computer, which is connected to the terminal by cabling. The dumb terminal can do nothing on its own; it is simply an input/output device. The VT100 is an example of one of the more popular terminal types.

Then, in the 1980s, the personal computer became popular as a computing device. It had its own processing power, and was therefore called a stand-alone system. These two approaches for providing access to data and software (mainframe vs. stand-alone) merged when technology was developed that allowed a personal computer connected to a mainframe to look and act like a dumb terminal. Telnet is an example of a software application used by a PC that enables the PC to play the role of a dumb terminal to a UNIX computer.

The next trend in computing access was the client/server model, in which some of the computing is done on the PC and some computing is done on a server connected to the PC by a network. This model is the most prevalent model used on the Internet. However, there is also a definite trend back in the direction of the dumb terminal/mainframe approach with the development of many thin client devices. A **thin client** is a device that does little or no processing of data, relying on the server to hold the data and the server's software to process the data. The server in this model is sometimes called a **fat server**. In the industry, the client/server model generally means that data processing is shared by both parties, whereas the **thin client/fat server model** means most, if not all, of the data processing is done by the server. An example of a thin client is the Winterm 3200LE (see Figure 9-1) by Wyse, the market leader in Windows-based thin clients. This thin client is capable of using office applications, web browsing and e-mail and costs less than $600.

Thin clients usually come preloaded with a reduced version of an operating system. For example, Compaq offers a thin client using the Stinger operating system from Be Inc. and another Compaq thin client uses Windows CE. Also, Linux is a popular OS for thin clients. Unlike a PC operating system, the OS is only responsible for communicating with the server and is not used to install and load software or manage floppy drives and hard drives, because all these resources reside on the server.

When choosing between personal computers and thin clients in a business environment, which approach is best? It depends on how many are needed and what you want them to do. The advantage of using thin clients is that they generally cost less than personal computers and are easier to support. However, they don't have the computing power or total functionality that a PC does, and therefore require heavy support from powerful servers to carry the burden of providing both software and data to the thin client.

Figure 9-1 The Wyse Winterm 3200LE is an example of a Windows-based thin client

9

The decision between PC and thin client is most often based on how the device will be used. For general office applications, web surfing and e-mail, thin clients connected to a powerful server is probably the best choice. For web site developers, programmers, and those requiring heavy-duty computing power, personal computers are needed. Also, setting up an environment to support thin clients can be expensive because of the cost of a high-end fat server. Therefore, if the office is small (fewer than five workstations), it's probably more cost effective to use PCs networked together as a peer-to-peer network and avoid the high overhead of supporting a few thin clients.

Internet Appliances

The question also arises, just how thin (and inexpensive) can you get? The Wyse Winterm 3200LE shown in Figure 9-1 costs several hundred dollars but can support office applications like Excel and MS Word. But, if web browsing and e-mail is all you need there are many less costly solutions. For home use, there's a growing market for devices that can provide only limited access to the Internet—just web browsing and e-mail only—which cost under a hundred dollars. When the client gets that "thin" they are no longer considered a thin client, because they are really not computers, but are rather called **Internet appliances**.

A computer, by definition, is a device that computes or processes data, and Internet appliances have little or no processing power. An Internet appliance is a device that can access the Internet and use it for limited applications such as e-mail and web surfing. An example of an Internet appliance is i-Opener by Netpliance, Inc., shown in Figure 9-2. I-opener is a box with an LCD panel and keyboard that has an internal modem, a web browser and an e-mail client built in. It also provides a port for add-on devices such as a printer. The embedded client software supports several, but not all, MIME types. (Recall that a MIME type file is a file that can be attached to e-mail messages or included in the files needed to build a web page and must have software installed on the client to interpret the file.) For example, i-opener can read and display JPEG files, but can't handle Shockwave because the plug-in to interpret JPEG is included in the software preinstalled in the device, but no software to interpret Shockwave files is installed, nor can it be. The device is, therefore, limited in functionality, but the cost is under $100, and it is very easy to use.

Figure 9-2   An example of an Internet appliance is i-Opener by Netpliance, Inc.

In general, Internet appliances work very much like the dumb terminals of the 1970s and are sometimes called terminals, although they do have some limited processing power, and therefore are not really "dumb." They have microchips that contain the OS and software to access and use Internet services. Some manufacturers require that you use their ISP, which provides the support the Internet appliances need to work. Their functionality may be limited, but they are the tool of choice in many situations. In the next section, you'll learn about one of the more popular Internet appliance technologies, WebTV by Microsoft.

WebTV

WebTV is a two-fold technology. **WebTV** brings the Internet and interactive shows to your television, and **WebTV for Windows** brings television to your computer. WebTV in a set-up box can turn your television into an Internet appliance. When it is used to view web pages on your television screen, WebTV acts as a browser; consequently, web developers must consider if their web pages are going to be interpreted by WebTV and make the necessary adjustments to the code.

WebTV can also support **interactive television** which enables you to participate as you watch television shows that are designed for user interaction, if you have the right equipment. As the technology of computers and television comes together, interactive television is gaining popularity. Users can play along as they watch their favorite game shows, vote in a survey, or e-mail questions to guests on a talk show as they watch the program.

Watching TV on Your Computer

Windows 98 comes with Microsoft WebTV for Windows, which is different from WebTV. Microsoft WebTV for Windows offers television viewing over the computer, while WebTV offers Internet access using the television. For example, with Microsoft WebTV for Windows, users can watch television on their computer monitors as they work on other projects. Multiple windows on PCs provide the ability to work on an application in one window while you watch the news in the corner of your monitor in another window. You can also participate in interactive TV, for example, to use your computer to compete against other viewers on game shows.

Turning your computer into a television is not hard. As figure 9-3 shows, the computer receives input from a TV cable. A TV cable is hooked to the computer by a WebTV-compatible TV tuner card, which is installed in the computer. The cable provides the television broadcast signals, which are then displayed on the monitor.

To participate in interactive television, the system must have a connection to the Internet. This connection provides the means for data to be transmitted from your computer when you are using interactive television. Note that in Figure 9-3 you can see a TV cable connected to the PC by way of a tuner card, but this connection cannot be used for Internet access. To access the Internet using TV cabling, a cable modem is required that is an external device. Recall that the cable modem connects to the PC by way of a network card.

9

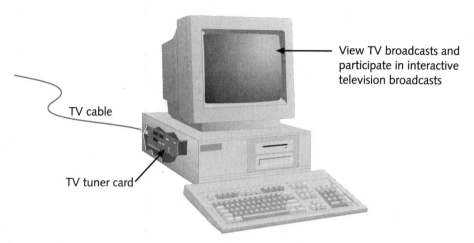

View TV broadcasts and
participate in interactive
television broadcasts

TV cable

TV tuner card

Figure 9-3 You can use Microsoft WebTV for Windows to view TV broadcasts using a
PC that has a TV tuner card installed

The list below outlines the minimum hardware requirements for watching TV on your
computer:

- Intel Pentium compatible 120 MHz processor

- 16 MB RAM

- 1 GB disk space

- Super VGA monitor

- Television tuner card with the drivers to support WebTV for Windows

- Cable or antenna connection

- Internet connection (in order to have interactive ability)

- Mouse with two buttons

Although the above will work, it is recommended that you have the following in addition
to the list above before you try to install and use WebTV for Windows:

- Intel Pentium compatible 200 MHz processor

- 32 MB RAM

- 2 GB disk space

- 28,800 bps (or faster) modem

- Sound card

- Wireless keyboard with pointing device

Windows 98 comes with Microsoft WebTV for Windows, although it is often not installed when Windows 98 is installed and must be installed later. To install WebTV for Windows on your computer follow these steps:

1. Click **Start** on the Taskbar, point to **Settings**, and click **Control Panel**.

2. Double-click the **Add/Remove Programs** icon.

3. Select the **Windows Setup** tab. After Windows finishes searching for components, the **Add/Remove Programs Properties** window opens.

4. Check the box in front of **WebTV for Windows** and click **OK**.

5. Follow the directions on the screen, inserting the Windows disk when necessary. Windows will prompt you to reboot the machine once or twice depending on the hardware configurations.

To run WebTV for Windows, click Start on the Taskbar, point to Programs, point to Accessories, point to Entertainment, and click WebTV for Windows. When you first run WebTV for Windows, the system walks you through configuration. When you configure the program, you connect to the Internet to download the current TV schedule for your area. Entering your zip code ensures that you will get the correct schedule. Figure 9-4 shows the WebTV schedule.

9

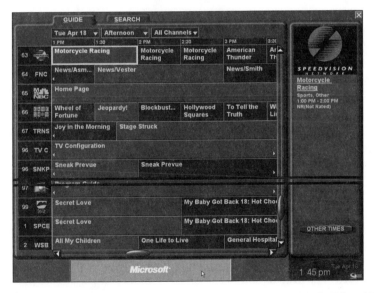

Figure 9-4   Using WebTV for Windows, you can see your local TV schedule and watch a TV show on your PC

The WebTV schedule can be viewed by date and time or by category (sports, kids, comedy). The WebTV schedule allows you to click on the show you want to watch. If the time of the show is not convenient, WebTV for Windows offers the option to view other times that the selected show is scheduled to be broadcasted.

WebTV Through your Television

WebTV allows people to use a regular television to access the Internet and e-mail. An inexpensive Internet appliance using an ordinary television as its display device, WebTV accesses the Internet using a regular phone line and can be used to send and receive e-mail messages and for web browsing. This service is ideal for people who are not comfortable with computers but want to access web sites and use e-mail to stay in contact with friends and family, as well as for those people who are technically proficient and just want one more option for high-tech communication. Using a transceiver, the television becomes the display device. A video cable connects the transceiver to the television, and a phone line is used to connect the transceiver to the Internet and the WebTV Network. A remote control and wireless keyboard are used to navigate the Internet. Figure 9-5 illustrates this option of WebTV.

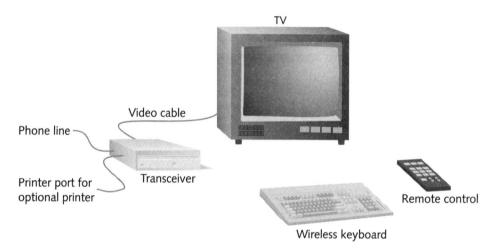

Figure 9-5   Using WebTV technology, you can access the Internet through a regular phone line using a TV as your monitor

As Figure 9-5 shows, the transceiver also has a printer port to allow for printing. There are several printers that will work with WebTV, but all printers require an IEEE1284 cable. An **IEEE1284** cable is a cable that adheres to the strict requirements of the IEEE organization for the 1284 specifications for parallel port communication. Look for IEEE1284 printed somewhere on the cable to assure you the cable uses these higher standards. Ordinary parallel cables will not work with WebTV. Although the system has features similar to a computer (Internet, e-mail, printing), it is not a computer and there are several things it cannot do that a computer can.

One of the drawbacks of WebTV is that it does not have a hard drive and, therefore, has no place to store files. Because of this limitation, many popular software packages that are considered industry standards cannot be used with WebTV. WebTV does not have Adobe Acrobat Reader, a program used to read text files in PDF format, so WebTV users cannot read PDF files. This can present problems if you try to view web documents in PDF format.

Also, WebTV can display only two types of video clips: Video Flash and MPEG. And because it cannot store files, pictures cannot be scanned and saved by WebTV. WebTV has its own browser, so you can't use either Internet Explorer or Netscape Navigator.

One feature of the Internet that is becoming popular is instant online communication; however, this feature is unavailable with WebTV. For example, AOL Instant Messenger offers this feature to Internet users. With AOL Instant Messenger, you can enter the AOL Instant Messenger screen name of friends and family, and if anyone on the list is online when you log on to the Web, Instant Messenger notifies you. At that point, you can send instant messages back and forth that only you and the receiver can read. Because the messenger software must be downloaded and WebTV terminals cannot download software, these programs cannot be used by WebTV users.

To use WebTV and your television to access the Internet, you must have a television, a transceiver (the Internet appliance), subscription to a WebTV service, and a phone line. Currently, there are five companies that make these Internet appliances for WebTV: Philips Magnavox, Sony, Mitsubishi, RCA, and EchoStar. EchoStar only manufactures hardware for people with satellite service. While there are several service packages that you can choose from when you subscribe to WebTV, all offer the ability to access the Internet and send and receive e-mail without having a computer. Many of the services also offer interactive TV so the viewer can participate in TV shows.

Interactive Television

WebTV provides interactive television. The goal of interactive television is to provide interactive web sites that are related to specific television shows. Web pages that are designed for a specific show will draw in viewers of the show, and viewers will continue to browse the web page to find more information about the show they are watching. For example, if you are watching the World Series, interactive television may show statistics for the current batter. You can use the Internet connection to view additional information about the team. Or if your favorite sitcom is on, a trivia question about the show may pop up. You interact by answering the question, which is transmitted through the Internet. Figure 9-6 illustrates how interactive television works on a TV equipped with a WebTV device.

When a television show is broadcast, the picture is created on the screen one line at a time (there are a total of 528 lines for each frame). There is an analog stream of data to build the first line then a quick blank interval while the pointer beam returns to the beginning of the next line. When the last line is created, a **VBI** (**vertical blanking interval**) is sent while the pointer beam returns to the top of the screen for the next frame. The VBI is a blank space between frames that normally does not carry any data. With regular television, the signals are received through the television cable to the transceiver and are simply passed on to the television.

With interactive television, hyperlinks for the Web are embedded in the VBI. The WebTV transceiver scans the VBI for hyperlinks. When the technology detects a hyperlink in the VBI, it accesses the Internet. The data from the Internet is displayed on the television screen. At this point, WebTV is serving as a web browser, receiving interaction from the user and passing it on to the web server by way of the Internet accessed phone line.

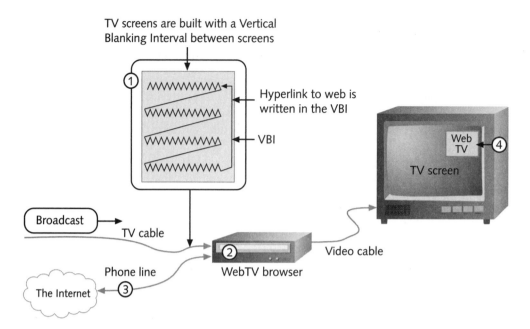

Figure 9-6   With interactive television, a link to a web page is embedded in the television broadcast analog stream; WebTV intercepts the link and retrieves the web page over the Internet, displaying it on the TV screen

The **Advanced Television Enhancement Forum** (**ATVEF**) was created to provide direction and standards for the interactive television industry. The ATVEF has developed a specification standard for the technical content of interactive television to allow the broadcasts to be transmitted by any network to any receiver (analog, digital, cable, and satellite) that is compliant with the specification. Microsoft has been a leader in the development of the group. For more information on ATVEF and WebTV including what you must do to make a web page WebTV-compliant, see *www.webtv.net*.

WebTV HTML Links

As you know, WebTV acts as a browser to interpret HTML and display it as a web page on your television. Because the television is a different technology from the traditional computer monitor, various attributes have been added to HTML tags to work with WebTV. For example, developers can set both the background color (BGCOLOR) and the cursor color (CURSOR) for input fields on forms. Because it is often difficult to see the information on a television screen, developers use the additional colors to make it easier for the viewer. For a complete listing of HTML tags that work with WebTV, go to the web site *developer.webtv.net*.

INTERNET TELEPHONY

Telephony is the technology of telephones, and **Internet telephony** is the technology of using the Internet to make phone calls. It has been estimated that by early 2001, the Internet telephony market will reach $63 billion dollars a year. Early Internet telephony involved one PC with a microphone, speakers, and software connected over the Internet with another PC with the same setup. Today, however, there are several Internet telephony implementations including:

- PC to PC with each PC equipped with microphone, speakers and matching software

- PC to phone using an ITSP (Internet Telephony Service Provider)

- Phone to phone using an ITSP at both ends

An **ITSP** (**Internet Telephony Service Provider**) is similar to an ISP but provides access between the Internet and the public telephone network. For a phone call on the Internet to reach a regular telephone, an ITSP must make the conversion between the two networks and complete the process by dialing the telephone number for the destination phone. If the ITSP is located within the destination number's local area, the phone call does not incur long distance charges even if it is initiated from another continent.

The Internet and the public telephone network are two entirely different types of networks. As you already know, the Internet manages data on the network in data packets, and the data is divided into packets for transmission across the Internet. Each packet might take a different route to reach its destination. It's up to the computer at the receiving end to reassemble the packets into the original order and maintain the continuity. A network that uses this approach is called a **packet-switching network**. In contrast, the public telephone network is a **circuit-switching network**. With this type of network, when one telephone dials another, a physical or virtual circuit is created between the two end points. This circuit remains open and dedicated to this specific call until the call is completed. Continuous data is free to flow in both directions (called full-duplex, as opposed to only one direction at a time, which is half-duplex) until the call is ended. Because of this circuit-switching approach, the public telephone network is called the **Public Switched Telephone Network** (**PSTN**).

An **IP telephony switch** is a device that can make the switch between PSTN and IP. At the heart of an ITSP is an IP telephony switch converting data between the two networks. While the voice data is traveling on the Internet, it is compressed and converted to data packets using the application-level protocol **VoIP** (**Voice over IP**).

Implementations of Internet telephony are continually improving as this exciting new technology is gaining momentum and the technology is advancing. This section addresses several past, present and upcoming implementations.

PC-to-PC Implementation

The earliest attempts at using the Internet for voice communication required that both parties have a computer equipped with software, a sound card, microphone and speakers. This is illustrated in Figure 9-7. Each computer in this configuration is called an **IP Telephony terminal**, and the PSTN is not involved because the communication is between two PCs. Voice data remains digitized and in data packets from source to destination. Early attempts at this implementation were not of the highest quality because the software supported only half-duplex communication and data was not sufficiently compressed, so conversations were choppy and full of static. Internet telephony today yields crisper, clearer voice quality, similar to that of cellular phones. All calls are free and no long distance charges are incurred with this type of implementation because the PSTN is not involved.

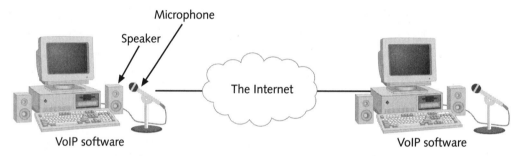

Figure 9-7   Two PCs connected to the Internet equipped with microphones, speakers and telephony software can be used for telephone calls exempt from long distance charges anywhere in the world

Most Internet telephony software supports conferencing with more than two parties on a call. Be aware that if the call must pass through a firewall, you might encounter problems because the firewall might not allow VoIP packets to pass through. Popular Internet telephony software for PC-to-PC conversations, which include the ability for conferencing (and even video conferencing if each PC is equipped with a video camera), are Microsoft Netmeeting (*www.microsoft.com*), CU-SeeMe by White Pine Software (*www.cuseemeworld.com*), and Internet Phone by VocalTec (*www.vocaltec.com*). These and several other telephony software applications also include the ability to use an electronic whiteboard that is shared between parties to make for an effective business meeting over the Internet.

PC-to-Phone Implementation

During a PC-to-phone session, a PC initiates the call using VoIP software such as Internet Phone or Net2Phone from Net2Phone, Inc. (*www.net2phone.com*). Net2Phone comes packaged with Netscape Navigator, Version 6. The software provides a GUI interface that looks like the keypad of a cellular phone. To use the software to make calls to a regular telephone, you must subscribe to an ITSP to make the transition to PSTN, as shown in Figure 9-8. When you subscribe to the service, you are assigned a user ID and password that is required to use the service. Rates other than the base subscription rate may apply.

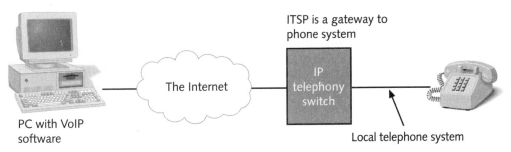

PC with VoIP
software

ITSP is a gateway to
phone system

The Internet

IP
telephony
switch

Local telephone system

Figure 9-8   When calling a regular telephone over the Internet you must subscribe to an
ITSP in the local calling area where you would like to call

Companies are developing that manage the ITSP subscriptions for you, and some of them offer
the service for free. For example, Dialpad.com, Inc. is a company that offers free Internet phone
calls to anywhere in the United States. For more information, see *www.dialpad.com*. When
making phone calls from your PC, a headset like the one shown in Figure 9-9 connected
to your sound card is more convenient and provides better sound quality than a microphone and speakers.

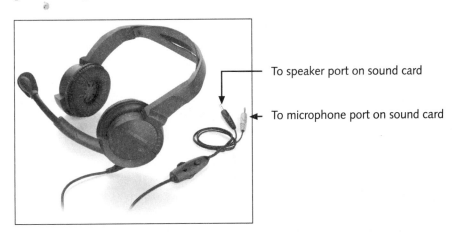

To speaker port on sound card

To microphone port on sound card

Figure 9-9   For voice communication from your PC, a headset can be used instead of a
microphone and speakers; the headset attaches to both the microphone input
and the speaker output of the PC sound card

Phone-to-Phone Implementation

A relatively new Internet telephony implementation is phone-to-phone where you initiate
an Internet call from a phone. This technology requires a special type of "telephone" that is
really not a telephone at all, but an Internet appliance that supports an Internet telephony
software application. The device is called an **IP phone**. Figure 9-10 illustrates how it works.

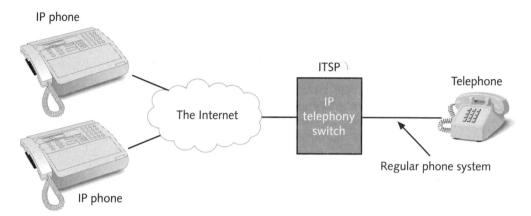

IP phone

ITSP

Telephone

The Internet

IP telephony switch

Regular phone system

IP phone

Figure 9-10   In a phone-to-phone system, an IP phone only needs an Internet connection, but a regular phone requires an ITSP to receive a call over the Internet

An example of an IP phone appliance is the Solphone PCA (Personal Communication Assistant) by Soliton Systems (*www.solitonsys.com*). The phone showing in Figure 9-11 can make both traditional (PSTN) and Internet phone calls. You press a button to switch between the two systems. When it's an IP phone, it can use either a LAN connection, cable modem or DSL to connect to the Internet. Once on the Internet, the phone call can go to either a regular phone or another IP phone or PC.

Figure 9-11   The Solphone PCA is an IP phone that offers voice and fax over the Internet

Another device by Aplio, the Aplio/PRO, lets you turn your regular telephone into an Internet appliance to make an Internet call. This device is shown in Figure 9-12. The device connects between a regular telephone and a LAN connection so that phone calls are routed over the Internet. The device has an embedded application that is based on the Linux operating system, which is also embedded in the device.

Figure 9-12   This Aplio device connects a regular telephone and a LAN to route phone calls over the Internet

9

WIRELESS INTERNET

As people get busier and work increasingly outside the office, the need for flexible Internet and e-mail access increases. Studies also show that the demand for wireless technology will continue to increase. Industry analysts predict that within the next two years:

- There will be more than one billion wireless subscribers worldwide.

- 70 percent of new cellular phones will have some form of Internet access.

- 80 percent of new Personal Digital Assistants (PDAs) will be Web-connected.

- 63 percent of Web transactions will be generated from mobile devices.

- More than 80 percent of new applications deployed to mobile workers and other consumers will be designed for non-PC devices.

This section is about wireless Internet devices, the protocol these devices use, and the technological trends.

Using Wireless Technology to Browse the Internet

Although wireless devices like cellular phones, for example, advertise Internet access, they don't display information like your computer does, and they are not designed to surf the Web. Rather, they are designed to get specific information from the Web, for example, stock quotes, e-mail, and sports scores. The screens on the devices are small, and they don't have the capability to display large graphics and banners or streaming video, but there is still much that you can do with the wireless devices. You can search for a restaurant, buy a CD, read the latest headlines, find an address, or even book a flight. However, you are limited to the pre-determined features and options provided by the device.

Most of the wireless devices are menu-driven, which means that you select where you want to go from a menu rather than by typing in a URL. Once the browser has been launched, you will be charged for the time you are connected. The browser brings up a menu of the most popular sites that are designed for wireless technology. From the menu, you can select a site, for example, CNN. Or you can type in a site's name, but it is a long process if you have only the number keys. For example, on some systems, to type the letter 'C' you would have to press the number 2 four times. And since no standards have been determined, the keys used to enter punctuation may be different for each device on the market. Figure 9-13 shows a cellular phone that has Internet access.

Figure 9-13   Cellular phones use menu-driven commands when they access the Internet

Usually you have no choice about a device's Internet Service Provider because most wireless devices are purchased through plans that bundle the technology with the ISP. For example, if you purchase a phone from Sprint, Sprint would also be the ISP for the device. As with most ISPs, there is a fee involved.

Most web sites are still not designed with wireless technology in mind, but the devices do come with software to convert HTML. However, the conversion process takes time and it is difficult to navigate through a site that is written in traditional HTML, because most HTML sites are not designed to be menu-driven.

Most of the sites that are designed for wireless technology are menu-driven. If you visit the CNN site, for example, you can browse the headlines and use the menu to choose a story you want to read. But again, because the screens are small, you may get only one or two lines of the article at a time.

Wireless Application Protocol

The high demand for wireless access to the Internet, including web pages and e-mail, led to the creation of the **Wireless Application Protocol** (**WAP**). One goal of WAP is to bridge the gap between the needs of traditional Internet access devices (such as a computer) and wireless Internet access devices. WAP is a communication standard designed for mobile Internet access. This standard outlines how information from the Internet is transmitted to mobile users. It includes protocols for designing applications and is supported by over 1200 companies. The WAP forum continues to set standards for the wireless industry. For the latest WAP developments, go to *www.anywhereyougo.com*.

One feature of WAP is the Wireless Markup Language (WML). **WML** is a markup language that is very similar to HTML, but it is derived from SGML and XML. While HTML creates web pages, WML pages are known as WAP pages. In addition, WMLScript, which is similar to JavaScript, is designed to work with WAP Internet devices. There were three major considerations that had to be addressed when WML was created:

- Wireless devices have narrow bandwidths (from 9.6 to 14.4 kbps) and limited network connections.

- Wireless devices have small display areas (three to four lines of text with no more than 20 characters per line) and limited input keys.

- Wireless devices have limited memory.

Because of these limitations, WML has a limited tag set and some of the tags have a different syntax when compared to HTML. WML files are organized differently than HTML documents. WML files are called **decks** and are divided into cards. **Cards** are sections of the deck that fit onto one screen.

When a wireless device requests information from the Internet, it does so through a WAP gateway at its ISP. When the gateway requests a web page, if the web site is WAP compliant, it presents WML and WMLScript data to the gateway. If the web site is not WAP compliant, it presents regular HTML web pages. The wireless device is able to interpret both WML and HTML although HTML interpretation might present poorly formatted information on screen. Figure 9-14 illustrates the entire process according to WAP standards. The process goes like this:

- Wireless devices use a cellular connection to transmit data the same way your telephone line sends data when you have a regular connection. The wireless device transmits its request for data to the gateway at the ISP.

- The gateway then takes the request to the Internet and retrieves the data in either HTML or WML and WMLScript.

- The gateway receives the data from the Internet, and converts it into compressed binary code.

- The binary code is transmitted over the airwaves back to the wireless device.

- The wireless devices have micro-browsers that interpret the code and display the information on the screen.

9

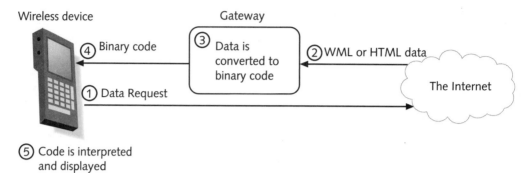

Figure 9-14   How wireless devices use the WAP specifications to access the Internet

Uses of Wireless Devices

There are many wireless Internet-accessible devices on the market today such as phones, pagers, and personal digital assistants. While these devices have their limitations, they also offer some advantages over traditional Internet access via your computer. The main advantage of these devices is their size. Providers are taking advantage of the small size and portability of these devices to offer services that are impractical or unnecessary on a traditional desktop computer with Internet access, but which are quite valuable to a person on the road.

One popular service that is being provided to customers with wireless Internet devices is instant notification, or alerts. If you were invested heavily in a particular stock, for example, wouldn't it be nice to be notified immediately if the value changed? Then you could access your portfolio and decide if you should make any changes. Alerts can be sent to remind you not to miss your 4:00 dentist appointment or to mail your cousin's birthday card. These alerts are sent as text to pagers, cell phones, or PDAs. Figure 9-15 shows a pager that has received a text message.

Figure 9-15   New pagers are being designed to display text messages

Yahoo! (*mobile.yahoo.com*) even offers alerts on auction items, so you can be notified when a particular item goes on sale. To sign-up for alerts, you just go to the site (like Yahoo!) and subscribe to the alert. When you need to be notified, the site automatically sends you a message. To make the site work with your device, however, you need to have a text messaging feature turned on by your ISP, and they may charge extra.

Go2 Systems (*www.go2online.com*) is one of many locator services that are targeting the wireless user. If you are in an unfamiliar city or area of town and you want to find the nearest Waffle House, for example, you can use your wireless Internet-accessible cell phone or PDA to log on to Go2. After entering your current location the service tells you where the nearest Waffle House is and the fastest way to get there. As the services grow, they will also offer additional services like the option to make a reservation at the hotel it just located for you.

For companies that have people on the go, wireless technology offers another benefit: wireless access to the company's intranet over the Web. This access is especially useful to service technicians and salespeople who travel around the country. Many times technicians cannot update records and orders until they return to the office, often several days after the work for the customer has been completed. The customer is not billed until the order is entered in the system. With a PDA, the technician can update the order and bill the customer instantly at any place and any time. So instead of the bill being mailed a week after the work is done, it is mailed the same day, reducing turnaround time and increasing cash flow. Figure 9-16 shows a PDA that can be used for Internet access.

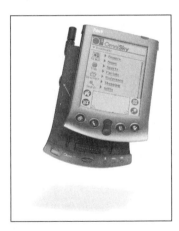

Figure 9-16   Personal Digital Assistants can be used to access either the Internet or an intranet

Fixed Wireless

Although the Internet appears to be everywhere, there are still people who pay a long distance phone charge for access. And there are people who want high speed connections, but do not have local access to a cable modem or DSL. The major long-distance companies are trying to grab that market by offering wireless access to the Internet with your PC. **Fixed**

wireless systems use a wireless router or modem and a data point at your house. The data point may be a small antenna on top of your roof or another similar technology. The technology allows the data to be transmitted through the airwaves rather than traditional wires.

Fixed wireless offers advantages to people whose only other option is dial-up. With fixed wireless, the Internet is always on, extra phone lines are not needed, and data transmission is faster than dial up (up to 100 times faster). Although it has several benefits, fixed wireless Internet is not expected to replace the cable modem or DSL because they are both available to the public now, and fixed wireless is a new technology that is available only in limited areas. As the availability of fixed wireless increases, the number of people with cable modems and DSLs will also increase. Unless those people are unhappy with their current services, there will be no reason for them to switch to fixed wireless.

REAL PEOPLE, REAL PROBLEMS, REAL SOLUTIONS
AS MOBILE AS COMPUTING GETS!

Passing through as many as 10 airports a week, Richard Larson was constantly on the go. Business meetings spread across the country kept the consulting executive rushing from city to city. He carried the least amount of luggage that he could, but he always had his laptop computer stuffed in his oversized briefcase. He used the laptop during or immediately after most meetings, and it was his most common connection with his office. In the evenings at hotel rooms, he would use his laptop to upload and download important files via the Internet. Quite often, the notes he would take during the meetings would be turned in to presentations or reports for the next day's appointment.

The laptop computer that Richard carried with him was compact and state-of-the-art. However, after a year of relentless travel, the computer was becoming a bother to use and carry from meeting to meeting. He was tired of the additional weight in his briefcase, the unpacking and packing, the plugging in and waiting for the computer to boot, and the awkward presence the laptop made. He sometimes felt like a pad and pencil would be a better alternative, but the time it would take him to type the information he had gathered from his notes outweighed that option.

He began to look at a solution: Personal Digital Assistants (PDAs). When he started researching PDAs, he realized that they are mini-computers, and are often referred to as hand-held computers. They include software for keeping schedules, taking notes, and recording addresses and phone numbers. Additional software can be purchased for use with the PDA that allows him to do just about anything he can do on his laptop.

A PDA provides a small, accessible means of meeting most of his requirements. These electronic devices are small and very portable. When folded, most are about the size of a checkbook and they use software that he is familiar with. Many use popular applications designed to work specifically with a PDA, such as Microsoft Office. Almost all of the PDAs he looked at have built-in modems and can connect either to the Internet or to another computer easily and quickly.

Richard purchased a PDA, and began to use it at his meetings. At first, the small screen and keyboard were difficult to use. He found himself taking notes by hand at times, using the PDA when he could. After a few meetings, and with practice, he found that he could enter data just as quickly as he could on his laptop. Over time, he discovered that the PDA was just the tool he needed.

For this active businessman, the PDA offered many benefits. Because of the small amount of battery power needed to run the PDA, he no longer had to worry about weakening batteries during long meetings. The PDA could easily connect to the Internet, handling all of his data communication needs. The physical size of the handheld computer made for a much lighter and less cumbersome load through his hectic travel schedule. Even computing while in flight became a simple task!

On the rare occasions when Richard Larson is in his office, he connects his PDA directly to his desktop computer for file upload and download. A Personal Digital Assistant was the solution to his predicament!

9

CHAPTER SUMMARY

- ❐ Technology, standards, and trends in the Internet appliances market are constantly changing because the industry is young and leaders and standard-bearers have not yet emerged and been identified.

- ❐ Early computing efforts used a dumb terminal to connect to a mainframe computer. Later, the focus changed to stand-alone personal computers, then to a hybrid technology called the client/server model. Recently, the trend has started to change to the thin client/fat server model, which in some ways is reminiscent of the dumb terminal/mainframe model.

- ❐ A thin client is a computer that has little processing power and is primarily used to connect to a powerful server (fat server) that provides the applications software and data, and processes both.

- ❐ When choosing between using PCs or thin clients in a business environment, the most important thing to consider is user needs. If the number of workstations is small, the thin client model may be too expensive a solution.

- ❐ Using an Internet appliance to access the Internet is a relatively new technology and includes wireless, thin clients, WebTV using television, IP phone, and a wide variety of up-and-coming implementations of this technology.

- ❐ One disadvantage of an Internet appliance is that your choice of Internet applications such as e-mail and web browsers are limited on an appliance, and installing new software is, in most cases, impossible. Most Internet appliances do, however, offer the ability to upgrade the existing software installed on the application.

- ❐ A standard operating system for thin clients and Internet appliances has not emerged, but contenders are Windows CE, Linux and Stinger by Be Inc.

❑ WebTV is often used along with interactive television to make it possible for TV watchers to access the Internet and interact with a web site that is synchronized with the TV show they are watching.

❑ WebTV for Windows on a PC can be used to watch television on your PC, including interactive television.

❑ When using WebTV with a television and a transceiver set-top box to access the Internet, applications are limited only to web browsing and e-mail. The type of attached files that WebTV can interpret is also limited and includes JPEG, but does not include PDF file format.

❑ Current manufacturers of WebTV appliances are Philips Magnavox, Sony, Mitsubishi, RCA, and EchoStar.

❑ With interactive television, the vertical blanking interval between frames is used to hold the hyperlink of a web page that is synchronized with the TV show. Requesting the web page and allowing the user to interact with it is a separate function from displaying the TV show on the television screen, even though both applications are sharing the TV screen.

❑ The organization that controls the standards and directions of interactive television is the Advanced Television Enhancement Forum (ATVEF), which has the strong support and endorsement of Microsoft.

❑ Web pages designed to be used with interactive television use specific HTML tags and methods to account for the relatively low resolution of television screens and the limited number of plug-ins that WebTV can support.

❑ Internet telephony is the technology of using the Internet for voice communication. The protocol that defines Internet telephony is the Voice over IP (VoIP) protocol.

❑ Early implementations of Internet telephony included PC-to-PC communication, although phone-to-phone communication is now possible.

❑ A phone that can initiate a phone call over the Internet without first involving the regular telephone system is called an IP phone and must have a direct connection to the Internet.

❑ If a phone call over the Internet is directed to a regular telephone, then the call must be converted from the packet-switched Internet to the circuit-switched public telephone system using an IP telephony switch.

❑ An IP telephony switch is provided by an ITSP in the local area where Internet calls are directed. Users can subscribe to an ITSP, which permits them to place phone calls over the Internet to telephones in the ITSP service area.

❑ Some examples of software that a PC can use to place Internet phone calls are Microsoft Netmeeting, CU-SeeMe, Internet Phone, and Net2Phone.

❑ There are several Internet appliances on the market that can be used to place Internet calls from a regular phone, an IP phone, or a cellular phone.

❑ Wireless Internet appliances use the Wireless Application Protocol (WAP) which specifies how information from the Internet is converted, transmitted and delivered to wireless devices.

❑ When a wireless device requests a web page, if the web site is WAP compliant, it presents the web page in a scaled down and specialized markup language called WML (Wireless Markup Language) and the page is called a WAP page. The WAP page is sent over the airwaves to the wireless device by the WAP gateway.

❑ Fixed wireless is an exciting new alternative for homes or businesses that are too remote to have access to DSL, cable modem, or other high bandwidth Internet technology. Using an antenna on top of your house or office, you can access the Internet with two-way communication that is up to 100 times faster than regular phone lines.

KEY TERMS

Advanced Television Enhancement Forum (ATVEF) — An organization that provides direction and standards for the interactive television industry.

card — As applies to WML, a section of a WML file (a deck) that fits on the screen of a wireless Internet device – *See* deck.

circuit-switching network — A type of network that creates a physical or virtual dedicated circuit between end points. After the connection is established, data flows continuously from point to point. The public telephone network is an example of a circuit-switching network. Compare to data-packet network.

deck — As applies to WML, a file containing text to be displayed on wireless Internet devices. *See* card.

dumb terminal — Used with a mainframe computer, the terminal is little more than a monitor and keyboard that is used to connect to the mainframe as an input/output device. All processing of data is done on the mainframe.

fat server — A powerful server that is used to support the software, processing and data needs of a thin client.

fixed wireless — A technology that uses an antenna or similar receiver/transmitter device for wireless communication, which can be used for Internet access in remote locations.

IEEE1284 — A standard for parallel communication used by parallel ports and cables.

interactive television — A technology to combine a web browser such as WebTV with a television show so that a user can interact with a web site that is synchronized with the TV show.

Internet appliance — A device other than a computer that is used to access the Internet as a client with limited applications.

Internet telephony — The technology of using the Internet to make phone calls.

IP phone — An Internet appliance used to initiate or receive a phone call made over the Internet. It uses a direct connection to the Internet. For example, it connects to a LAN, cable modem or DSL line.

9

IP telephony switch — A device that can make the switch between PSTN and IP.

IP Telephony terminal — A device such as a PC that can be used to initiate or receive voice communication over the Internet.

ITSP (Internet Telephony Service Provider) — An organization similar to an ISP that provides access to the regular telephone system from the Internet. An ITSP is used when you want to make a phone call on the Internet to a regular telephone.

packet-switching network — A network that works by sending data broken down into individual packets from point-to-point. Each packet is capable of taking a different route to the destination and then the data is reassembled at the destination point. The Internet is an example of a packet-switching network. Compare to circuit-switching network.

Public Switched Telephone Network (PSTN) — The traditional public telephone network, which uses a circuit-switching technology.

telephony — Telephone technology.

thin client — A computer that does little processing of data, contains a limited version of an operating system and applications software, and depends on a fat server for its data and most of the software it needs.

thin client/fat server model — A client/server model in which the client computer performs little if any processing because the majority of the processing is done by the server.

VBI (vertical blanking interval) — In a television analog data stream, the interval that does not carry visual data needed to cover the time it takes for the pointer beam to move from the bottom of one frame to the top of the next frame. The VBI carries hyperlink information for interactive television.

VoIP (Voice over IP) — The protocol used to send voice data over the Internet.

WebTV — A system for displaying information from the Internet on a television screen and to support interactive television.

WebTV for Windows — A Windows component that supports television on a PC by way of a TV tuner card.

Wireless Application Protocol (WAP) — A protocol that specifies how information from the Internet is formatted, transmitted and received by wireless Internet appliances.

WML (Wireless Markup Language) — A markup language that is used to build web pages for transmission to wireless devices using the WAP protocol.

REVIEW QUESTIONS

1. Give one example of a thin client.
2. Explain how a thin client and a fat server work together.
3. When would a company benefit from a thin client?
4. Why are thin clients not recommended for everyone?
5. What is an Internet appliance?
6. How are Internet appliances different from a thin client?

7. What are the hardware requirements to run WebTV for Windows on your PC?

8. List the steps for installing WebTV for Windows on your PC.

9. WebTV can be used to access the Internet with your TV. What type of people is this option geared towards?

10. Who makes the Internet appliance (transceiver) used with WebTV?

11. What types of video clips can WebTV display?

12. List any disadvantages to using your WebTV and your television to access the Internet rather than your PC.

13. How is interactive television different from regular television?

14. How does interactive television work?

15. What does ATVEF stand for?

16. What is the purpose of the ATVEF?

17. Where can you get more information on ATVEF?

18. List three Internet telephony implementations.

19. What is an ITSP and what does it do?

20. Explain a packet-switching network.

21. An IP telephony switch switches between _____ and _____.

22. Name some software packages that allow PC-to-PC conversations.

23. Why was WAP created?

24. What is WML and what is its purpose?

25. Explain how a PDA gets data from the Internet.

HANDS-ON PROJECTS

Research Internet Telephony

Your company has headquarters in your local community and has just opened a branch office in London. The company is anticipating extensive phone conversations between headquarters and the branch office and has asked you to research some ways to save money by using the Internet for telephone calls between the two cities instead of standard long-distance phone calls. Prepare a short paper that reports your findings and recommends some options. Include in the report at least one solution for each of the following three options. For each solution, state the cost of initial setup and on-going costs and the advantages and disadvantages of using that solution:

❑ **Option 1** PC-to-phone: Include the initial cost of equipment at both ends and the on-going costs including a subscription to an ITSP in London for calls going from headquarters to London and a subscription to an ITSP in your local area for calls going from London to headquarters.

- **Option 2** PC-to-PC: This option should be considerably less expensive than the other options, but the disadvantages will be greater.

- **Option 3** Phone-to-phone: Include material printed from the web site of at least one company that manufactures an IP-enabled telephone.

Investigate Wireless Communication

You are working for a company that provides in-home health care for the elderly and disabled. The service employs medical professionals to visit clients and perform medical check-ups. The employees are asked to stop by the office each night to submit the paperwork for the day, but the visits often take longer than scheduled and the nurses cannot always make it to the office before it closes. This creates a problem because if the records are not updated in a timely manner, a nurse could be sent to the client without a complete medical history.

The company is interested in some type of wireless communication to allow the records to be updated remotely and has asked you to do the groundwork. Research the available technology. Also, determine the cost of the technology, and the advantages and disadvantages. Prepare a paper outlining your findings.

Research Thin Client

As your company grows, it is becoming more interested in new, less expensive technology to use in the offices. One option that has been mentioned is thin clients. Find three companies that make thin clients. For each company, determine the hardware requirements, operating systems, and applications it will support, and the cost.

Case Project

Research WebTV

Research WebTV development and determine the best background and foreground colors for your web site so that it can easily be viewed by WebTV users. Then make the appropriate changes to your web page.

Research Internet Telephony

Find companies that offer a method to allow visitors to make free long distance calls from your web site. Determine what you would have to do to make your site qualify for free long distance and put the **Call For Free** button on a web page on your site.

10

SERVERS AND WHAT THEY DO

> **In this chapter, you will learn:**
> ♦ About the role servers play on the Internet
> ♦ About the many different types of servers on the Internet and what they do
> ♦ About different features of various servers used on the Internet

As you recall from earlier chapters, most Internet services use the client-server model. Recall also that the term *server* has two meanings. It can refer to the computer that is used to provide data or services for other computers, or it can refer to the software running on that computer that provides a service to other computers (which are called clients).

As hardware, a server is no different from any other computer except it needs to have enough power, speed and storage capacity to handle the traffic and demands of its users. As software, a server can provide a variety of different services. Already in this book you have seen many different types of software servers including web servers, e-mail servers, FTP servers, DNS servers, and newsgroup servers. This chapter not only summarizes the functions of these servers, but adds to the list several other types of servers. The goals of this chapter are to help you understand the roles that many types of servers play on the Internet, to know the features to look for when evaluating a server application, and to understand how they all work together to create the powerful communications experience of the Internet.

OVERVIEW OF SERVERS

There are several different types of servers, and each performs a different function. Figure 10-1 shows some of the more common servers. This figure shows a few ways that servers can relate to clients and to the Internet, but in no way is it intended to show all configurations, because the possible configurations are endless. In previous chapters you have been introduced to several of these servers and there are some new ones in the figure. Listed below are the servers shown in the figure and discussed in this and other chapters.

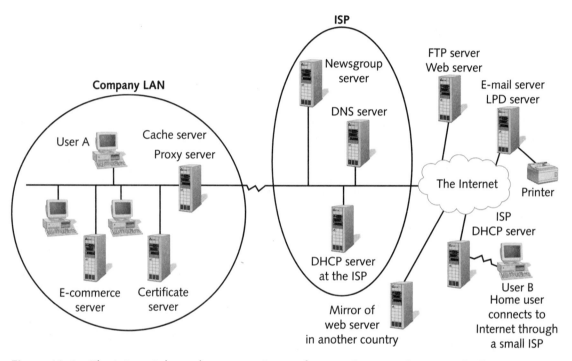

Figure 10-1   The Internet depends on many types of servers to support communication and provide information

- *A cache server* improves performance by caching data, thereby reducing the necessity of requesting data across the Internet.

- *A certificate server* manages certificates, which are binary data that can be used as a digital signature to provide security for electronic transactions and business.

- *A DHCP server* is responsible for assigning an IP address to a client when the client logs on to a TCP/IP network.

- *A directory server* provides information to computers on a network about resources on the network.

- *A DNS server* is responsible for tracking domain names assigned to IP addresses

- *An e-commerce server* manages the processes of buying and selling over the Internet, including credit card transactions.

- *An e-mail server* receives and sends e-mail messages and attached files to clients and other e-mail servers.

- *An FTP server* manages files and directories, allowing users to log on and download or upload files to and from the FTP site.

- *A list server* manages mailing lists to groups of e-mail addresses, distributing e-mail messages to those on the list.

- *A mirrored server* is a server that carries the same data and services as another server in order to be a backup of the other server and to provide easier access to users.

- *A newsgroup server* works in a network of other news servers to send and receive articles posted to newsgroups. Subscribers use newgroups to communicate about a given newsgroup subject.

- *A proxy server* manages the traffic over the Internet for other computers on a company network. The proxy server uses its own IP address for Internet traffic in proxy for other computers on the network.

- *A Telnet server* provides a way for remote users to control a remote computer through a console window on their computer screen.

- *A web server* manages web sites and provides web pages to clients as requested by the client.

- *An LPD server* is connected to an Internet printer, and manages print jobs that are sent to the printer over the Internet.

Notice from the list of servers that you can divide the servers into two basic groups based on their primary functions. The goal of some servers is to help with communication over the Internet (DNS servers, DHCP servers, cache servers, proxy servers, mirrored servers, and directory servers). The primary function of the other group of servers is to provide data or services to users on the Internet (web servers, e-mail servers, list servers, FTP servers, news servers, e-commerce servers, certificate servers, LPD servers, and Telnet servers). The rest of this introductory section talks about the general features of all servers. This chapter covers those servers whose primary function is to provide data and services to users. It then discusses servers that are focused on helping with communication on the Internet.

Server Port Assignments

As you learn about servers, recall from Chapter 2 that each server that is running on a computer is assigned a port number from 0 to 65,535 so that clients can access the server by way of this port. For example, web servers use port 80. All browser clients know that to connect to a web server on a computer, they need to communicate the IP address of the computer and the port number of the server and use the correct protocol that the server is expecting, which, in this case, is HTTP. A list of the standard port numbers for common applications is shown in Table 10-1. Although these are the standard ports, they are not the required ports for each protocol. All the protocols can be assigned to any port, but they are normally assigned to their default port.

Table 10-1 Port assignments for servers

Server	Protocol	Default Port
FTP server	FTP	20 for data and 21 for control information
Telnet server	Telnet	23
E-mail server	SMTP	25
E-mail server	POP3	110
Web server	HTTP	80
News server	NNTP	119

Another point to keep in mind as you study these different servers is that a computer can have more than one server running on it. For example, a web server and an e-mail server can run on the same computer at the same time. They can do this because they use different ports and each is listening for client activity at its own port.

It is not uncommon in a small organization for a computer to run several servers at the same time and for one software application to provide more than one server. For example, the software application SyGate by Sybergen is a proxy server, a cache server and a DHCP server. The SyGate Manager is showing in Figure 10-2. Notice the checkbox labeled Enable Built-in DHCP Server. SyGate is discussed in more detail later in the chapter.

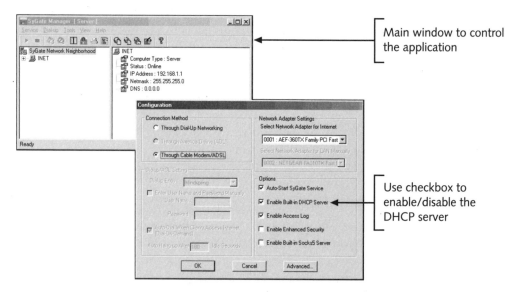

Figure 10-2   More than one server can be included in the same application. A server can be enabled or disabled using application settings

Server User Interfaces: GUI vs. Command Driven

Consider a server as a software application that must be installed and managed by someone who might carry the title of system administrator, network administrator, or, for web servers, webmaster. This administrator must have a way to set options, monitor the performance of the server, and troubleshoot problems as they arise—the user interface is the tool that allows the administrator to do these jobs. In the following discussion, consider the user to be the administrator responsible for managing the software using this interface.

Servers can be either command driven or have a graphical user interface. Servers with a **command-driven interface** require the user to enter commands to achieve a desired result. The commands can consist of words or characters, but they must be entered in the correct format or the server will not accept them. MS-DOS is an example of command driven software; you can see the MS-DOS command line in Figure 10-3. The user must know the correct commands and their syntax to use MS-DOS.

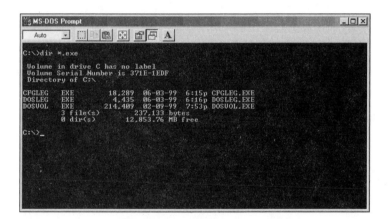

Figure 10-3   MS-DOS is a command-driven system

Servers are often controlled by configuration or initialization files. These are text files that contain options and parameter settings that the software reads when it is first loaded. An administrator can change a setting such as a port number by changing an entry in the text file. The next time the server is loaded it will pick up the new setting.

For example, a web server might have a configuration file named CONFIG.TXT that is stored in a configuration folder under the main folder for the application. An entry in that text file might be PORT = 80. If the administrator wants to change that port to 8080, the administrator must change the text in the configuration file to PORT = 8080. The application must be restarted before the change takes effect. Notepad or any other text editor can be used to edit these files.

One example of a server that is controlled by configuration files is the Apache web server. The set of configuration files is stored in the Conf folder under the main Apache folder as shown in Figure 10-4. The main configuration file is named Httpd.conf. Figure 10-5 shows a sample entry in that file that specifies the port that the server uses and the e-mail address where problems with the server will be reported.

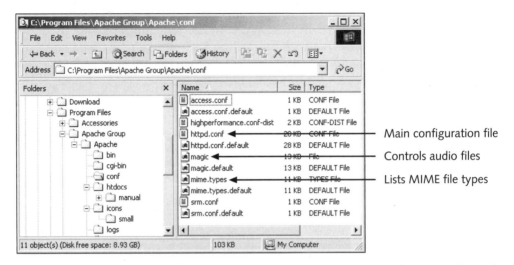

Main configuration file

Controls audio files

Lists MIME file types

Figure 10-4   An administrator can control a server by entries in configuration files. This group of text files controls the Apache web server

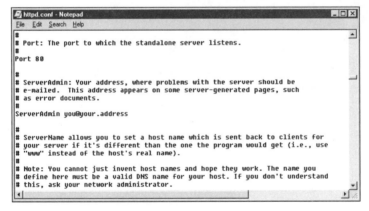

Figure 10-5   Sample entry in a web server configuration file

A **graphical user interface** (**GUI**), on the other hand, has icons that the user can select to perform a function or run a program. One popular program that uses GUI is Windows. Windows uses a GUI to make it easier for a user to access a program or file. Web servers use a GUI to make it easier for the webmaster to work with the server. For example, the SyGate server uses a GUI window showing in Figure 10-2 to configure the server. If a webmaster is comfortable with web servers but is not familiar with a particular web server, he or she can use a GUI to hunt through menus and icons to find the needed settings or options to set.

For example, a web server application might have a menu option that is labeled Options. When the administrator clicks Options and then clicks Port, a dialog box opens that shows the current port to be 80. The administrator changes the value to 8080 and exits the menu. The web server must then be stopped and restarted for the change to take effect. Configuration data can be stored in configuration files that belong to the application, or, for Windows systems, it can be stored in the Window Registry.

Running Servers as Background Services

In general, a server is software that runs in the background on a computer and waits for activity from other programs. The programs being supported are clients that are communicating to the computer by way of TCP/IP. When a program runs in the background, it can process data and execute tasks even though these jobs are not visible on the screen and the program is not accepting input from the keyboard. In Windows, a program running in the background to support other programs is called a service. In UNIX systems, the program is called **daemon**. Some programs run in the background, and other programs run in the foreground. A program that is running in the foreground is one with which you can communicate via the keyboard or mouse.

For example, after the Apache web server has been installed under Windows 2000, you can then install the server as a background service. See Figure 10-6. The service then automatically loads every time Windows 2000 is loaded. Note in Figure 10-6 that you can also manually start and stop Apache using the Start and Stop features in the Apache web server group.

10

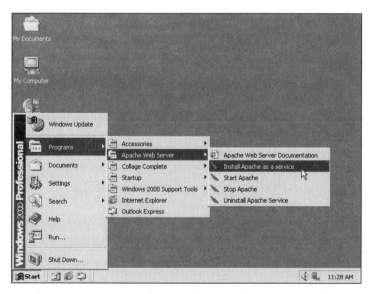

Figure 10-6   A server application can be run on a computer as a service that is automatically started every time the OS loads

A computer can run multiple services at the same time. In Windows 2000, you can view the services that are running on the system using the Component Services window. Follow these directions:

1. Click **Start** on the Taskbar, point to **Settings**, and click **Control Panel**. The Windows 2000 Control Panel opens.

2. In the Control Panel, double-click the **Administrative Tools** icon. The Administrative Tools window opens.

3. Double-click **Component Services** icon. The Component Services window opens, as shown in Figure 10-7.

4. Click **Services (Local)** to view the list of services currently running.

Note in the figure that the Apache service is running and has been loaded automatically at startup. Also note in the figure that two other services are running as clients, DHCP Client and DNS Client. It's interesting to note that this computer is a server to some applications and a client to others, as indicated in Figure 10-7. Notice too, that the window does not indicate which applications are client applications and which are server applications. Administrators are aware of this from their knowledge of the software.

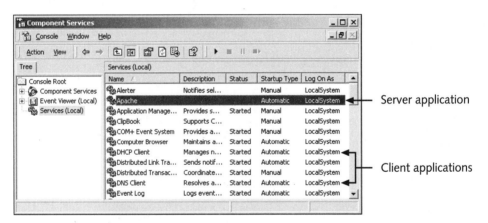

Figure 10-7   Windows 2000 shows the list of currently running services

Tracking Information in Log Files

Servers often track information about their activities in log files. These log files are text files that can then be used by administrators to troubleshoot problems with the software, track activities in order to analyze traffic patterns or user preferences, or look for clues that hackers are using the server. A server should be able to turn off its logging capabilities since this slows down the performance of the system. An administrator will choose to use the feature only in certain situations.

Operating System Platforms

A web server must be installed on the operating system for which it is built. The primary operating systems on the Internet are UNIX, Windows NT, and Windows 2000. The OS also determines many of the features and options available to support the server. For example, if you are selecting a virtual server company and want to use VBScript as your scripting language, you must select a service that has a web server installed on a Windows platform since VBScript is only supported by Windows and not UNIX. If you want to make the best use of Perl scripts, find a service that uses the UNIX platform, and if you want to use ODBC for your database connectivity, you must have a Windows platform.

SERVERS THAT PROVIDE DATA AND SERVICES TO USERS

Looking back at Figure 10-1, you can see that servers that provide data and services to users (for example web and e-mail services) can be located on a company LAN. The LAN might have partial, full, or no access to the Internet, or the server might be located so that it has full access to the Internet. In either case, the server works the same way; it provides its data and services to clients that make requests to it.

The location of the requesting computers is generally not important. In Figure 10-1, user A is on a company LAN and user B is connected from his home to the Internet by way of a simple ISP connection. A web server or news server generally does not know or care how a client got to the point of requesting data or a service. The exception to this is when a server is set up so that it only responds to those clients that have a predefined IP address (that is, one that is already known to the server). ISPs set up their servers this way to prevent anyone but their own subscribers from using the server.

10

The rest of this section discusses individual types of servers in detail. Some information is a recap of previous chapters but is included here for easy reference.

Web Servers

A web server delivers documents that have been formatted as HTML. For this reason, web servers are also called HTML servers. Web servers can exist on a company intranet to only serve corporate clients or they can be made available to the entire Internet. Web servers have been discussed throughout the book, but this chapter goes into more detail about what features a web server might have.

There are a wide variety of web servers available, many of which you can download for free. One of the most common free web servers is Apache, a software package developed by the Apache Group (*www.apache.org*), a nonprofit organization of volunteer software developers.

Apache can run on either a Unix machine or a Windows 98/NT/2000 machine. Although there are countless others, Apache is a good example of a web server for several reasons. It has been on the market for some time, so most of the bugs have been corrected; it is fairly easy to set up and configure; and it is widely used in the industry. Other web servers that are popular include Microsoft's Internet Information Server (IIS) (*www.microsoft.com*) and BorderManager by Novell (*www.novell.com*). Both IIS and BorderManager are common servers found in larger companies.

How a Browser Accesses a Web Server

A web server stores information and programs. It executes these programs and provides information based on client browser requests. It provides HTML pages and other files as they are requested by clients using the HTTP protocol.

From a user's perspective, a web server is a place to go to get information from the World Wide Web. A user enters a URL (Uniform Resource Locator or Universal Resource Locator) into a browser client's address box to make a request to a web server. The URL is an address used to locate resources on the Web. Each URL has several parts:

- It begins with the protocol that must be used to access the information. If the protocol is not specified, the browsers assume HTTP.

- The next item is the name of the server indicating where the resource can be found.

- The URL may also have a path to the resource at the end of the URL. The path tells where the information can be found on the server.

- Sometimes the port is included in the URL. When the port is included, it is listed after the name of the server, but before the path. You only need to include the port if it isn't a standard port, as outlined in Table 10-1.

The domain name in the URL must be converted to an IP address before the URL can be sent over the Internet. A browser sends the domain name to a DNS server that is responsible for returning the corresponding IP address to the browser. The browser then substitutes the IP address for the domain name and makes the request over the Internet to the web server. Routers along the way use the IP address to locate the server. Once the computer with the correct IP address is located, the computer uses the port number to determine which server running on the computer gets the request. When the web server receives the request, it locates the requested web page and its associated files and sends these files to the browser.

The next section introduces some of the features of a web server and how they work from the perspective of the administrator or webmaster who is responsible for managing the server, setting its options, and monitoring its performance.

Virtual Servers and Virtual Hosting

Many companies are anxious to enter the World Wide Web, but once they discover the total cost of owning a web server, maintaining the server, and keeping a connection to the Internet, they get discouraged. The expense may just be too large for a small company, or a larger company may want to "test" the Internet to see if it is right for the company. One option for such a company is to lease part of a web server from a company with an existing server. Virtual servers and virtual hosting were introduced in Chapter 2 as a solution to this problem of wanting to have a web site while making a very low initial investment.

Recall from Chapter 7 that when a company contracts with a virtual server company, there are usually several web features and services that are offered. These usually include one or more domain names and assistance in registering those domain names. Other services include e-mail addresses using your own domain name, directories for the file storage on the web server, help in creating a web site, and access to a host of tools and software applications to manage the site. Virtual servers always include some tools for accessing a database and you are always allowed to use your own domain name, for example, *www.yourname.com*. In addition, you should be able to carry on full e-commerce on your site using secured credit card transactions. And, because you use your own domain name, your customers should not be able to distinguish the difference between your web site in house and your web site at a virtual server company.

One company that offers virtual servers is Intermedia.NET (*www.intermedia.net*). They offer three different plans, each offering increased features and disk space. Intermedia.NET is not an Internet Service Provider, however, so you must also subscribe to an ISP to connect to the Internet. Once connected, you can update your account through the Intermedia web site, and all file transfers are also handled through the web site. You can control your site when you log onto their web site, create and delete e-mail accounts, add domain names and sub-domain names, and activate support tools such as ODBC. For example, in Figure 10-8, as the site administrator leasing a virtual server from Intermedia.NET, you can add, delete, and edit your registered domain names that point to the site. If the web server is down because of an error, you can stop and start the web server without having to involve technical support.

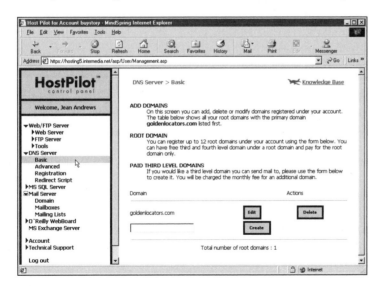

Figure 10-8 Using a virtual server web site, a subscriber can control the domain names pointing to the site

Virtual hosting (sometimes called web hosting) offers less power to the subscriber than does a virtual server. When you use virtual hosting, your domain name usually (but not always) includes the name of the company offering the virtual hosting. For example, if you are an AOL subscriber, you have a limited amount of space on the web server that you can use to create a web site. But the domain name on that site would be something like *www.aol.com/yourname.html*. Most likely you will not be able to do e-commerce on your site and will not have access to powerful database tools. Occasionally, a virtual hosting service allows you to use an Access database on your site, but you may be limited in the tools you can use to interface with it. To use a virtual hosting site, you only need a tool, such as FTP software, to send files to the site.

The newest version of Microsoft's IIS supports virtual servers and virtual hosts. In the past, multiple web sites residing on one web server all had to have unique IP addresses. But IIS is now capable of handling several domain names under a single IP address. IIS uses HTTP 1.1 host headers to accomplish this, but not all browsers support HTTP 1.1. Because the feature is not supported by all browsers, it is best used in an intranet environment until the majority of browsers support HTTP 1.1.

Most virtual hosts handle multiple domain names on the same server by having the URL serve as a path to a file. When you create a web page through your ISP (such as AOL), you are not assigned an IP address. Rather, the URL (for example, *www.aol.com/yourname.html*) includes the server and the filename for your web site.

What is the best way to set up a virtual server? Remember that a single computer can run many different services, including many copies of the same server software. When you set up a computer as a virtual server, arrange for each company that is leasing a virtual server site to run its own instance of Apache. In other words, if there are four virtual servers on a computer, Apache server is loaded four times at startup, once for each company. Each instance of Apache is set to look to a different default directory for its HTML documents. In the configuration file for each instance of Apache, an entry should point to the company that this server is servicing. The entry looks like this:

```
Listen www.smallco.com:80
```

If you are offering virtual hosting services, you can use a single instance of Apache server to service all virtual hosts. However, this arrangement is not desirable if all these hosts have a lot of traffic because they are all competing for the one resource. Another reason this is not a good solution is that if one company has problems with its web site, it can cause the service to lock up, which brings down not only its own web site, but all other web sites as well. When shopping for a virtual server company, be sure to find out if your virtual server lease is running its own private instance of the web server or if you are sharing the instance with other virtual servers.

Protocols Supported

All web servers support HTTP (otherwise they would not be web servers!), and most also support FTP so that developers can send files to the site from remote locations. Sometimes a web server application also includes an e-mail application so that you don't have to purchase additional software. Another option is to buy several server applications, one for each protocol, and install them on the same or different computers.

If you want to use your web server for e-mail, the server must support e-mail protocols. As discussed in Chapter 4, Simple Mail Transfer Protocol (SMTP) is used to send e-mail messages from your computer to the server, and either Post Office Protocol, version 3 (POP3) or Internet Message Access Protocol, version 4 (IMAP4) is used to receive messages from the Internet to the client.

Another important feature to consider is support for secure protocols. Secure protocols are used to encrypt all incoming and outgoing data so that it cannot be read or modified in transit. A secure protocol used by web servers is SSL (secure sockets layer). When you see a URL with *https*: at the beginning instead of *http*, you know that this web server is using SSL protocol for security.

Having a secure protocol is especially important if you are working in an environment where you are sending and receiving sensitive or confidential data. The secure protocols work to make sure that the data cannot be read by anyone other than the intended recipient. Secure protocols are covered in Chapter 12.

Although it is considered by many to be outdated, Gopher is still supported by many web servers. Gopher is a protocol that was developed at the University of Minnesota and was named after the school's mascot, "The Golden Gopher." Gopher is a menu driven, text-based information service, and is used to view text files that can be located anywhere on the network. Gopher has largely been replaced by the World Wide Web.

10

Security

It is important to make sure that whichever web server you use, it provides adequate security. Security involves making sure the right people can get in and making sure the wrong people are kept out. It also involves giving people access to only the information they need and making sure that information is not intercepted while it is in transit. Security is covered in detail in Chapter 12, but this next section looks at a few basic features of web servers that pertain to security.

Access Control   **Access control** allows the web server to limit which files a user can read or write to, based on the user's IP address or user ID. User IDs are used with passwords. However, user IDs and IP addresses can be falsified and passwords can be discovered, so some servers offer advanced methods of access control, such as digital signatures. Digital signatures are used to verify that the person sending or receiving a message is who he says he is.

There are even more advanced methods of access control that include biometrics, or the use of human characteristics for identification. Fingerprints, eye retinas, voice patterns, and face patterns are all a part of biometrics, and they can all be used to ensure that the person accessing the server is legitimate.

Encrypting Protocols Because the Internet is a public network, it is always possible that data will be intercepted while it is being transferred. In order to avoid the risk of an unintended party seeing your data, the data is encrypted, or sent in a format that cannot be read by anyone other than the intended receiver.

The SSL protocol introduced earlier also supports encryption so that if data is intercepted as it is sent across the network, it cannot be read. The data is decoded or decrypted by the SSL protocol when it reaches it proper destination.

Chroot Environments Some computers using the UNIX operating system offer an option to run in chroot mode. **Chroot mode** restricts the portion of the file system that is occupied by the server. If a server is running in chroot mode, the files outside of the server are invisible to the server. And, of course, if they are invisible, they are also inaccessible.

Running in chroot mode offers security because all private files can be kept outside of the server area. That way, the server cannot accidentally access a file that is not intended for public viewing. If your company is concerned that other companies who share your virtual server might have access to your sensitive data, look for this feature on the UNIX computer supporting the servers.

Server Side Scripting

Recall from Chapter 6 that a script is a short program that is executed or carried out by another program. Programming languages that are designed to create scripts are referred to as scripting languages. Some of the more popular scripting languages are Perl and JavaScript. These languages are usually easier to code than other languages (such as C or C++), but they take longer to run because each instruction has to be handled by another program before it can be processed. The type of scripts that a web server supports is more a function of the computer's operating system than the web server software itself. For example, VBScript is supported by Windows and not UNIX, and Perl is most often found on UNIX platforms. But JavaScript is universally supported on most operating system platforms. For more detailed information about scripting, refer to Chapters 6 and 7.

Standard CGI-Based Scripts Common Gateway Interface (CGI) is the specifications that define the way for a web server to pass a web user's input to an application program running on the server, get a response, and pass data back to the user. Remember from Chapter 6 that CGI allows a web developer to write a program that creates a dynamic web page that can interact with a database, and can receive and process input from a user.

An example of CGI at work is when a web page contains a form for the user to complete. The browser receives the data entered into the form by the user and sends the data back to the web server. The web server then passes the information to the application program that is running on the server. Once the data is processed by the application, the application program sends a response to the web server and the server forwards that response to the user. All this interaction between the web server, the resources on the server, and the application follows the CGI specifications.

One advantage of CGI scripts is that they are consistent among operating systems. The advantage of this is that CGI scripts can be used regardless of the OS that is running on either the client or the server computer. It can be used with Windows, Macintosh, UNIX, and other operating systems. Always expect a web server to support CGI if you want it to support web sites that involve interaction with users. The most popular language used for CGI scripts is Perl.

Server-Side Include   Server-Side Include (SSI) is a simple form of scripting that allows you to include variable values in the HTML code before it is sent to the browser. For example, you may wish to have your web site display the current day and time. Because the day and time are not constant, you can use SSI to find and display the date.

SSI scripts include a line in the HTML file that indicates that a variable value needs to be entered before the file is sent to the browser. A web server that supports SSI scans a web page before it is sent to a browser, looking for commands to substitute values into the web page. An example of a command is:

```
<!--echo var="LAST_MODIFIED"-->
```

When the server sees that command, it finds the date the page was last modified, and inserts it into the web page in place of the command. It then sends the page to the browser.

LAST_MODIFIED is only one of several variables that the operating system can track and make accessible to a server program. In order for the command to work, though, the system administrator must make the variable usable when the system is set up. If you are creating a web site, it is a good idea to ask which variables can be used and to verify that the variables are set up correctly so that the information can be accessed when the web page is accessed.

Database Interfaces

Many web servers use CGI to interface with web site databases. Recall from Chapter 7 that there are other methods. A popular interface is ODBC for Windows systems which can interact with ASP scripts embedded in web pages. For UNIX systems, JDBC uses a technology that is similar to ODBC. Before selecting a web server or a virtual hosting service, find out what databases the server supports and what tools are supported to interface with the database. Recall from Chapter 7 that popular databases are Oracle and SQL Server and that the most common set of commands to query and update a database is SQL.

Ability to Monitor Performance

Many web servers allow you to monitor their performance. What this means is that the software oversees the computer system to determine if it can handle the tasks that are being requested of it. Performance monitoring is also useful when a system manager is making changes to the system. As a change is made, a manager can look at real-time data to ensure that the changes are not causing a lapse in performance.

For example, Microsoft's IIS uses Performance Monitor and Event Viewer, a program that comes with Windows NT and Windows 2000, to monitor performance. The program allows the administrator to monitor the activities of the server and the network. As the program monitors the network, it collects data, and that data can be exported so that it can be analyzed in a spreadsheet or database program.

FTP Server

Recall from Chapter 4 that an FTP server makes files and directories available to remote users. Users log on to the server with a user ID and password. The user ID is assigned certain privileges needed to retrieve and delete files on the server, copy files to the server, make directories, and delete directories. For security reasons, the user ID and password are both managed by the server software and not the client. FTP servers usually run on the same computer that is running a web server because web developers often use FTP to put new web pages on the web site. FTP is also used by software manufacturers to provide a place for users to download new releases of their software. For detailed information about FTP, see Chapter 4.

List Server

Chapter 4 discussed e-mail servers and how to send and receive e-mail messages. One thing that most e-mail servers do not do is maintain mailing lists. Rather, a list server usually does this job. While a list server may seem similar to a news server, the most obvious difference between a list server and a news server is that a list server sends posted messages to the list members' e-mail boxes, and a news server collects the posted articles and users have to retrieve the articles manually. Examples of list servers are LISTSERV and Majordomo. Some list servers can be downloaded for free.

One purpose of a list server is to provide a means for people to subscribe and unsubscribe to mailing lists without the administrator of the list having to intervene. When you want to subscribe to a mailing list, you simply send an e-mail message to the list server. The list server then processes the request and you are added to the mailing list. If you later want to be removed from the list, simply send another message asking to "unsubscribe." Sometimes a mailing list is managed by an administrator who has control over who goes on and off the list. These types of mailing lists are often used by organizations or corporations for private discussion groups within the corporation.

Many list servers have a feature which allows users to search archives. Although this may not sound like an important feature, it helps both the subscribers and the postmaster. The subscribers can search by keyword. For example, if you remember reading a message about Humphrey Coliseum at Mississippi State University, you could search for "Humphrey" and the list server would bring up all messages that contain "Humphrey." Then you could review the messages to find the one that you were seeking.

Archives also help the postmaster because they reduce the number of user questions. Instead of posting a message and waiting for a response, a subscriber can quickly find the information in the archives.

Less sophisticated list servers send an individual e-mail message to everyone on the list, but some list servers make better use of resources. If many recipients are on the same domain, which is likely when a mailing list targets those in the same organization, the list server only sends the message to the targeted e-mail server one time with a long list of recipients. This function makes it possible for small computers to handle large lists.

News Server

Part of the TCP/IP suite is the Network News Transfer Protocol (NNTP), a protocol for transmissions within newsgroups. Remember that a newsgroup is a group of users that have a common interest and that share information. Newsgroups are organized by subject hierarchies. The first few letters of the newsgroup represent the major subject category, and the rest of the name indicates the sub-categories. For example, the newsgroup **comp.ibm** is about IBM computers, and **comp.ibm.as400.rpg** is a newsgroup about the RPG programming language as it pertains to the IBM AS/400 computer. Some of the more common major subject categories are listed in the table below.

Table 10-2   Newsgroup subject categories

Abbreviation	Subject Category
news	News
rec	Recreation
soc	Society
sci	Science
comp	Computers
alt	Alternate

Many newsgroups use Usenet, a worldwide network of servers that pass messages among each other, though other newsgroup networks are also available. The messages are similar to e-mail messages, but they contain additional headers and are referred to as news articles. When a news article is posted on one server, it is then passed to the other servers, but it does not take a specific path.

There are thousands of news servers which make up the Usenet network. Each of the servers stores messages and passes the messages along using NNTP. The network is decentralized; all the servers are at an equal level. A news article originates on one server and is passed around until all the servers have it. But NNTP offers no guarantee that a message will make it to all the servers. As a matter of fact, it cannot even guarantee that an article will make it past the originating server.

After posting a message, a user may decide to cancel it. Most newsgroups allow a user to send a command to cancel a message if the user is the same person who wrote the original message.

Sometimes newsgroups have a moderator. When a message is sent to a moderated news group, the message must be approved by the group's moderator before it can be posted. Newsgroups are moderated to prevent unwanted messages. For example, a moderator may refuse a message selling a product. Also, a moderator rejects **flames**, rude messages that are directed as an attack against another user.

Before you subscribe to a newsgroup, you should watch the newsgroup for a few days. This allows you to become familiar with the way the newsgroup works, and prevents you from posting comments or questions that may be unwanted. Newcomers are also asked to learn **netiquette** (short for **net**work et**iquette**), which are the basic rules of courtesy used when sending electronic messages. The basis of netiquette is to use common courtesy when sending e-mails, participating in newsgroups, using chat rooms, or engaging in other Internet services. Another netiquette lesson is to read the group's FAQ (Frequently Asked Questions) which are usually posted with the newsgroup. For more information about newsgroups and how they work, refer to Chapters 1 and 4.

Mail Server

E-mail servers use SMTP protocol to receive e-mail from clients and to send e-mail to other e-mail servers on the Internet. E-mail servers also store e-mail messages and their attachments for accounts they manage. Clients can request that these messages be downloaded to the client PC using the POP3 or IMAP4 protocols. Just as with web servers, an e-mail server can exist on a corporate intranet to serve only the corporation, or it can serve the Internet at large. ISPs generally provide an e-mail server for their customers. E-mail servers were covered in detail in Chapter 4.

Certificate Server

Certificates are used to maintain security when sending and receiving data and messages over the Internet. Both people and companies can get certificates, but the certificates are usually managed by an outside company. When each party of a communication has a certificate, it can be verified that both parties are who they say they are. The details of how certificates work and the circumstances in which they are used are covered in Chapter 12.

The server that issues and maintains certificates is a **certificate server**. If a company has sensitive data that it sends to customers over the Internet, the company may want to issue certificates to its customers to make sure that the data is not intercepted by someone else and the identity of the company is verified. The customer can get a certificate from a certification agency, or the company can set up its own certificate server. The server would allow the company to act as its own certification agency and issue certificates to internal and external users. Looking back at Figure 10-1, the company LAN in the figure has an internal certificate server that could serve internal and external users.

E-commerce Server

The process of buying and selling services and products over the Internet is known as **e-commerce**. Companies that are using the Internet to sell their goods are often using a virtual server, but as e-commerce grows, many companies are beginning to see cost savings by purchasing their own e-commerce server. **E-commerce servers** (sometimes called **e-servers**) are servers that are designed to handle all aspects of e-commerce, including taking orders, processing payments, sending verifications, and printing packing slips.

Currently, Hewlett Packard (*www.hp.com*) and Sun Microsystems (*www.sun.com*) have the largest number of e-commerce servers in use and are the leaders in the e-commerce field. However, with the growth of e-commerce, many other companies are beginning to heavily market their e-commerce servers. The market will remain open for some time while the best features are determined. You can read more about e-commerce in Chapter 14.

LPD Server

LPD (Line Printer Daemon) servers are used to accept and process print jobs that are sent over the Internet. With an LPD server, a user in one location can send a document to a printer that is connected to the Internet at a different location. The LPD server is connected to one or more printers, and each printer is assigned a URL. The print jobs must use LPR (Line Printer Remote), which is a protocol that is used to send print jobs over the Internet. Clients that use LPR are sometimes referred to as LPR clients.

10

The process of sending a print job over the Internet is very similar to sending data over the Internet. Every print job has two parts: a data file and a control file. The data file contains the data that is to be printed, and the control file has instructions on what to do with the data file and how to print the document. When someone using an LPR client requests that a document be printed on a printer somewhere on the Internet, the LPR client sends the data file and the control file to the IP address for the LPD server. The server then forwards the print job to the proper printer.

Telnet Server

A Telnet server provides a way for a user to remotely control a server. This works well for system administrators who want to manage a server from the office down the hall or from home. Telnet was discussed in detail in Chapter 4. Telnet has traditionally been used only to access UNIX computers, but Windows NT and Windows 2000 now offer Telnet servers as part of their administrative tools.

SERVERS THAT ENABLE INTERNET COMMUNICATION

Servers that facilitate communication over the Internet include DNS servers, DHCP servers, cache servers, proxy servers, mirrored servers, and directory servers. This section looks at each of these servers, what they do, and how they fit into the overall communication scheme of the Internet.

DNS Server (Name Server)

A DNS (Domain Name Server) server maintains a database of host computers and their IP addresses so that when a client makes a request by the host name, the DNS server can find the IP address for that host. DNS servers, officially called name servers, were first introduced in Chapter 2. Usually only ISPs and large corporations with extensive intranets have DNS servers.

A DNS client is known as a resolver. A resolver is software that is used to find an IP address for a domain name. Resolvers are part of TCP/IP on the client. When you enter a domain name, your browser notifies the resolver and the resolver finds the IP address that corresponds with the domain name. Name servers and resolvers are the terms used in technical literature, but most people refer to them as DNS server and DNS client, which are the terms used here.

The data that DNS servers use to track domain names and IP addresses is called zone data and is stored in zone data files. These zone data files are sometimes just called records. The process of discovering the IP address for a domain name is called name resolution, or just resolution. It is also possible to find the domain name for a given IP address; the process is called reverse resolution or reverse mapping.

In Chapter 2 you learned the various levels of DNS servers including the root, top level, secondary, primary, master, and slave DNS servers. If you need a review of these terms, look back at Chapter 2. The key to understanding how one of these servers works is to examine the entries in a data file the server uses. Table 10-3 lists some of the records that might appear in one of these files with an explanation of how the records are used.

Table 10-3   An example of a DNS record

Lines in the DNS record	Description
IN SOA mycompany.com postmaster.mycompany.com	This start-of-authority (SOA) record tells other DNS servers the name of this DNS server and the e-mail address of the person to whom error messages can be sent. There can be only one SOA record in a DNS file. The record has several other entries which are not shown.
IN NS ns2.hostcompany.net IN NS ns3.hostcompany.net	These two lines show the two authoritative name servers. There can be more than two servers listed here. The first is the primary server and all others are secondary servers. These entries are called NS (name server) records.
IN HINFO SUN4/110 UNIX	This HINFO (hardware information) record identifies the type of computer and operating system used.
Buystory.com. IN A 207.5.47.75	This line identifies the host, buystory.com, assigning it an IP address. This line is called the A (Address) record.
207.5.47.75 IN PTR buystory.com	This PTR (pointer) record does reverse resolution, mapping IP address to domain name. An A record and a PTR record would never be found in the same data file because the file is designated as a resolution file or a reverse resolution file, but never both.

Table 10-3   An example of a DNS record (continued)

Lines in the DNS record	Description
IN MX 10 buystory.com	This line is called the MX (mail transfer) record and says that all mail coming to the buystory.com domain goes to the buystory.com computer.
www IN CNAME buystory.com ftp IN CNAME buystory.com pop IN CNAME buystory.com mail IN CNAME buystory.com smtp IN CNAME buystory.com	These lines, called CNAME records, show the canonical names for buystory.com called the CNAMEs. These CNAMEs are the valid prefixes for buystory.com (example: mail.buystory.com). Using CNAME records, you can refer to mail.buystory.com as just "mail" in other DNS records.

When a DNS server is first installed, the zone data file must be created and then the DNS server must be told the name of the file and where the file is located. This information about the file might be given to the server in a configuration file or through menu options and parameters.

Directory Server

Directories can serve different functions. When you are working with a network, you might use directories to let you know where files and devices are located, as shown in Figure 10-9. Windows 2000 calls its directory to track resources on a network Active Directory. On the Internet, a DNS server can use a directory for its data file that hold information about IP addresses and domain names. A program that accesses and manages a directory is called a **directory server**.

A **directory** stores information, and the information in a directory is read more often than it is written. Because a directory does not have to be updated constantly, it does not need a high-powered update feature. Rather it needs to be able to handle a high volume of searches and to provide results for queries quickly. Because of these requirements, directories usually have a simple update utility that can update anything in the directory, and they usually concentrate their power in the query functions.

A directory follows an upside-down tree structure with the root at the top and branches underneath the root in a hierarchical structure, as shown in Figure 10-9. Items near the bottom of the directory are subordinate to items above them. When you query the directory, it searches the top layers first and then drills down to items underneath them until the right information is located.

10

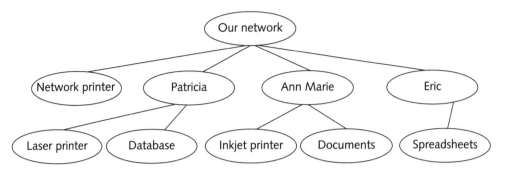

Figure 10-9 Information about resources on a network can be kept in a directory

Directory servers sometimes use a protocol called the **Lightweight Directory Access Protocol (LDAP)** to access directories, as illustrated in Figure 10-10. LDAP was designed to run over TCP and can be used on the Internet or on a corporate intranet. LDAP is a "lighter" version of DAP (Directory Access Protocol), meaning that LDAP has less code than DAP. One reason the code for LDAP is lighter is that the original version of LDAP did not have security features.

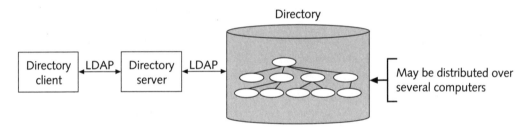

Figure 10-10 LDAP can be used by a program to query a directory

As Figure 10-10 shows, LDAP directory service is based on a client-server model and it works very simply. The data for the LDAP directory resides on one or more servers. When an application or user needs information from a directory, the user's application acts as a client to the directory server and makes the request to the server. The server uses the LDAP protocol to query the directory. The server then provides the answer or a link to where the client can get more information.

One important thing to realize is that even though the LDAP directory can reside on more than one server, all the servers have access to the same directory information. Therefore, if you requested the same query of all the servers, you would get the same result. The only time the information is different is when the LDAP directory data is being updated. When that happens, one server may have the new information, and another server may have older information. But the system is designed to make sure that all servers will have the same information in a short period of time.

Cache Server

As you will recall from Chapter 8, caching is storing frequently used information in a temporary place so that it can be accessed faster. There are different types of web caching including browser-based caching, also discussed in Chapter 8. Browser-based caching is set up at the browser level; Internet Explorer and Netscape Navigator both support caching. Browsers allow the user to indicate how much hard drive space should be allocated to web caching.

Another type of caching happens at the server level. A **cache server** is a server that saves web pages and other files that users have requested so that when the page is requested a subsequent time, it can be retrieved without accessing the Internet. The cache server is placed between the users and the Internet, and it often resides on a router or proxy server.

Web caches are very useful for large companies which use the Internet for daily activities. There are billions of web pages, but only a small fraction of those pages are accessed on a regular basis. A cache helps by storing frequently accessed pages so that when they are requested, they can be accessed from the cache rather than the Internet, which speeds up retrieval time. For example, Yahoo! (*www.yahoo.com*) is one of the most popular sites on the Internet. The Yahoo! logo can be stored in the cache so that it does not have to be downloaded each time the page is accessed. This saves the amount of time that it takes to load a page.

Cache servers can run on systems such as a proxy server or a router, or they can be set up as a dedicated computer system. Wherever they are located, they are designed to speed up the transmission time and they all work in the same way. Figure 10-11 shows a cache server that resides on a router, and illustrates how web caching can be set up at the network level.

10

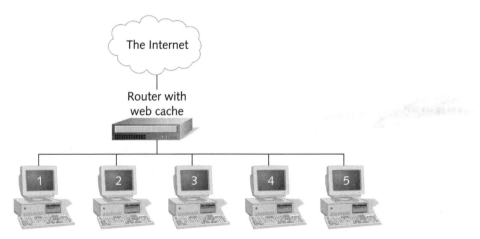

Figure 10-11   Web caching is used to speed data transmission

If computer 2 in Figure 10-11 requests a web page, the router receives the request and checks with the web cache to see if the page is in the cache. If the information is not in the cache, the router directs the request to the Internet. When the request is answered, the information is sent back to router. When the router gets the information, it saves a copy of the page in the cache and sends a copy to computer 2. Later in the day, if computer 5 requests the same information that computer 2 requested earlier, the request goes to the router, the router checks the cache, and because the information is in the cache, the data from the cache is sent back to computer 5.

Because web sites change and objects on those sites also change, the cache must be able to determine if the copy of the object in the cache is "fresh" or current with the objects on the web server. If the web site has been updated, the cache must retrieve a new copy from the web server. There are three basic ways that the cache server ensures that it has the freshest object:

- The cache server can send a "get if modified" request to the web server. Only objects modified since the last request are sent to the cache server.

- The server can use freshness data to determine how fresh an object is. For example, HTTP 1.0 includes a time expiration date in the object's header which can be evaluated to determine if a stored object has expired.

- The server can look at the elapsed time since the object was last modified to judge the life expectancy of each object.

There is also a new trend with web caching which vendors are referring to as active caching. Active caching takes place one of three ways:

- When there is little or no traffic to the server, the cache server can send "get if modified" requests to store fresh objects from sites that are frequently accessed.

- The cache can be set to automatically refresh data at a specified time or at certain intervals.

- The network administrator can configure the cache to evaluate the logs of past requests and anticipate which sites will be requested in the future. Then the cache can refresh those frequently requested sites.

Mirrored Server

If a company has a web site that has a lot of traffic, they often set up a **mirrored server**, which is a second server that contains all the files of the main server. A mirrored server is an exact replica of the main server. It is updated as often as the main server to ensure that both servers contain the same data. The mirrored server serves two purposes: it provides another server for traffic, thereby decreasing download times for consumers, and it serves as a backup if the main server goes down.

On a network with a mirrored server, the main server and the mirrored server are tied together with a simultaneous two-way communication link. Although the two servers are linked, they are usually stored in different locations. That way, if one server was disabled because of fire, flood, or other disaster, the second server would not be affected.

As Figure 10-12 shows, mirroring is a fairly simple process. The steps below outline how mirroring works.

1. The main server creates and sends a message packet that contains the files needed to update the mirrored server. At the same time, the main server starts a timeout sequence.

2. The mirrored server receives the packet and makes sure that there are not any errors.

3. The mirrored server sends a transmit acknowledgement back to the main server.

4. Once the main server receives the acknowledgement, it cancels the timeout sequence and lets the operating system know that the acknowledgement has been received.

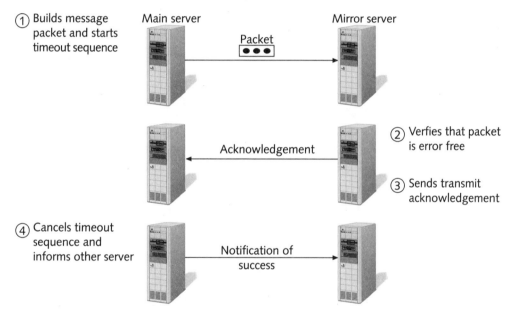

Figure 10-12   The basic mirroring process

Using a Mirrored Server as an Additional Server

Web sites that get a lot of traffic often need more than one server to handle the traffic. And if the traffic comes from different parts of the world, they may want to have servers in different locations to provide the best services for their customers. For example, a company in Japan that has a good bit of Internet traffic from the United States may decide to have a mirrored server in the United States.

Mirroring is often transparent to the user, but there are times when you can see that you are using a mirrored server. For example, the popular web site *www.download.com* provides you with the ability to download a variety of software applications. They use mirrored servers all around the world. You can select the best location from which to download your software to ensure minimal download time. Obviously, if you are in Melbourne, Australia, it's faster to download a file from an Australian server than from one located in the United States. Figure 10-13 shows some of the mirrored servers at *www.download.com*.

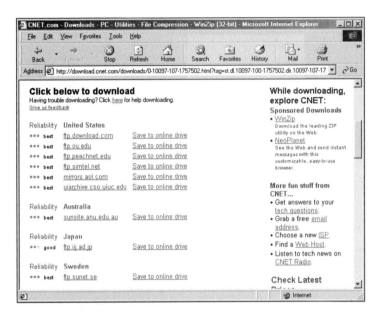

Figure 10-13   In this example, the file to be downloaded can be accessed from many different locations

Using a Mirrored Server as a Backup Server

When a company becomes dependent on its server and stores most or all of its information on that server, the server must be backed up on a regular basis. Although it is possible to back up a system to a portable medium such as disks or tapes, another option is to have another server which is an exact replica of the main server—a mirrored server.

A mirrored server acts as a very effective backup system. If the main server goes down, it is faster and easier to switch operation to a mirrored server than it is to restore information from disks and tapes. When a mirrored server is used as a backup for a server, it is designed so that it constantly copies short segments of files from the main server as they are updated. This makes sure that the mirrored server remains up-to-date with the main server.

Proxy Server

A **proxy server** is a server that acts as an intermediary between another computer and the Internet. In the corporate environment, the main purpose of a proxy server is to provide web access for computers that are located behind a corporate firewall. Corporations that are concerned about security sometimes limit the amount of activity allowed over the Internet, but many employees need to access the Internet to do their job. A solution is to use a proxy server as the go-between.

A **firewall** is more a concept than a device. It is used to limit the traffic between the Internet and a network in order to secure the private network. The proxy server itself can be the firewall when it is configured to filter the traffic allowed to pass through. Or the firewall can be a router that is between the proxy server and the Internet, which also filters traffic.

Some ISPs limit access to a single IP address. In this situation, a network could use a proxy server to provide access to the Internet for its computers. If a proxy server does all Internet activity with its own IP address, the ISP is satisfied and all computers on the private network have Internet access. This solution is becoming a common practice for small networks in homes and small businesses.

In addition to optional firewalls, most proxy servers come with caching systems. The caching systems work like those described in the earlier section; the firewalls provide extra security measures and are discussed in detail in Chapter 12.

10

Figure 10-14 shows how a proxy is set up in relation to a network. When a user on a network with a proxy server requests a web page from the Internet, the request first goes to the proxy server. If the proxy server is also acting as a firewall, the proxy server filters the request to make sure that it does not break any security standards. Next, if the proxy server has a cache, it looks in the cache to see if the request can be handled without accessing the Internet. If it doesn't find the requested web page, it sends the query over the Internet using its own IP address instead of that of the requesting PC. Because the proxy server substitutes its own IP address for that of the requesting PC before accessing the Internet, a proxy server is called a **Network Address Translator** (**NAT**). For more information on NATs, refer to RFC 1631. When the server receives the web page, it passes it on to the PC.

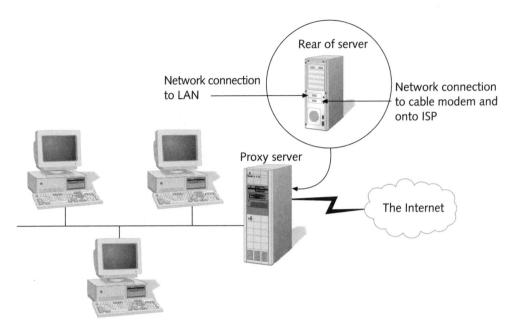

Figure 10-14 A proxy server stands between a private network and the Internet

A Proxy Server Used as a Firewall

When a proxy server is acting as a firewall, it can filter traffic in both directions. It can filter traffic that is coming in to the network from outside computers, and it can filter traffic that is leaving the network. One way to filter incoming traffic is to limit communication from the outside to specific ports on the inside of the private network. Some firewalls maintain a list of ports to which they prevent access.

Firewalls filter outgoing traffic through a variety of methods. One method is to examine the IP address of the destination web site against a list of either allowed addresses or forbidden addresses. For example, SyGate for Home Office, a proxy server by Sybergen Networks (*www.sygate.com*), allows the system administrator to prepare a list of IP addresses that are restricted for users. Or, system administrators can list only those IP addresses that users are allowed to access.

SyGate calls these lists of IP addresses the Black and White Lists. If the Black list is enabled, users cannot access an IP address on the list. If the White list is enabled, users are allowed to access these IP addresses and no others. Also, the Black and White lists can apply to only certain IP addresses on the LAN and not to others. The IP addresses on the Internet apply to web servers, e-mail servers, Telnet servers, or all servers, depending on the ports included on the list. Figure 10-15 shows SyGate's Black and White List Editor, which is used to determine web site access. The Internal IP Address on the left of the Add BWList Item dialog box is the IP address of a single user on the LAN. The External IP Address on the right side of the box is the IP address of the web site, e-mail server, or other server that the user or entire network is being restricted from using.

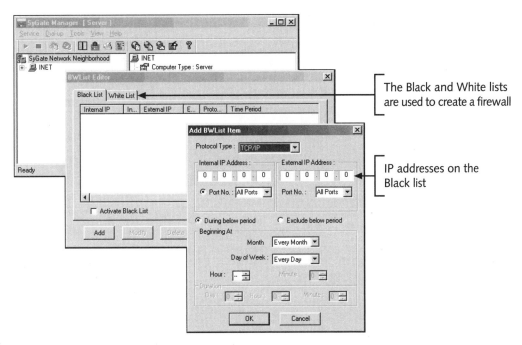

The Black and White lists
are used to create a firewall

IP addresses on the
Black list

10

Figure 10-15 Proxy server software like SyGate can be used to create a firewall for a
private LAN or a personal computer

Configuring a Browser to Use a Proxy Server

When a user accesses a web site through a proxy server, he or she is usually not even aware
that the proxy server exists. All transactions appear to be taking place directly between the
user and the Internet. Even when a user is denied access to a site, he or she often assumes
it is a problem with the web site, not a proxy server that is restricting access. However, the
proxy server is not completely invisible. A user's PC must be configured to use a gateway
to access the Internet as described in Chapter 8. In most situations, this is all that is necessary to use the proxy server. However, it might become necessary to force the browser to
use the proxy server. To configure Internet Explorer to access the Internet using a proxy
server, follow these steps:

1. Click **Tools** from the menu bar, then click **Internet Options**.

2. Click the **Connections** tab.

3. Click the **LAN Settings** button. The Local Area Network Settings dialog
   box opens. See Figure 10-16.

4. Click on the checkbox labeled **Use a proxy server** and enter the address and
   port for the server. To configure a different proxy server for each protocol, click
   on the **Advanced** button.

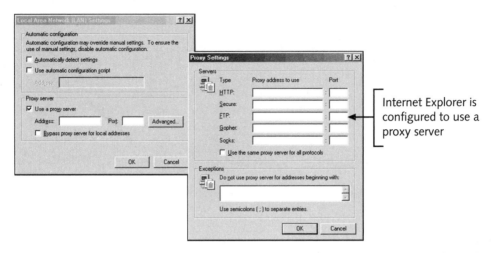

Figure 10-16   Options to configure Internet Explorer to access the Internet through a proxy server

5. In the appropriate fields on the Proxy Settings Screen, enter the addresses to be used for each protocol, and click **OK** to save your changes.

If you are using Netscape and you want to configure it to work with a proxy server, you can follow these directions.

1. Click **Edit** on the menu bar, then click **Preferences**. The Preferences dialog box opens.

2. Click the **+** sign to the left of **Advanced** and then click **Proxies**. The Proxy window opens.

3. Click the option button labeled **Manual Proxy Configuration**, then click the **View** button. The Manual Proxy Configuration dialog box opens, as shown in Figure 10-17.

4. Enter the IP addresses for the proxy servers that you want to use for each of the protocols listed, then click **OK** to save your changes.

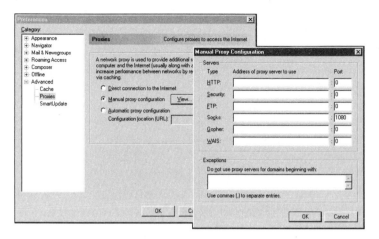

Figure 10-17 Set Netscape Navigator to use a proxy server using the Preferences window

DHCP Server

A **DHCP (Dynamic Host Configuration Protocol) server** is a service that assigns IP addresses to computers on a network when they first access the network. Recall from Chapter 8 that DHCP is used when computers are assigned dynamic IP addresses (that is, the IP address changes each time the computer access the network), rather than static IP addresses (the IP address is permanently assigned to the computer). ISPs use DHCP to assign an IP address to a computer when it first connects to the ISP to access the network. For dial-up connections, a new IP address is assigned to the computer and remains with the computer as long as it's connected. The next time it connects, it gets a new IP address.

When computers are connected to a LAN that is using dynamic IP addresses, a DHCP server must be running on the LAN to assign IP addresses, and each computer on the LAN must be configured to access that server to get an IP address at startup. Recall from Chapter 8, that in addition to an IP address, DHCP servers can also tell the computer:

- The IP address of the DNS server

- The IP address of the default gateway to the Internet

- The subnet mask of the network

You can use the WinIPcfg utility to see your assignments once you have connected to the network or to the ISP. Follow these directions to use WinIPcfg in Windows 9x.

1. Click **Start** on the Taskbar, then click **Run** and type **winipcfg** in the Run dialog box. The IP Configuration window opens, as shown in Figure 10-18.

2. Select the adapter card that you are using to connect to the ISP or network from the drop down list to view the current assignments.

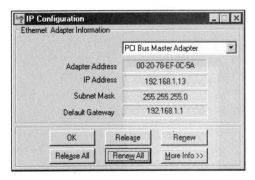

Figure 10-18   Use the IP configuration utility to know what assignments a DHCP server has made to your PC on a network

Notice in Figure 10-18 that the IP address assigned is a private rather than a public IP address. This indicates that the PC is on a private network. If it is to access the Internet, it must do so through a proxy server.

Proxy server applications often provide a DHCP service. The proxy server software should allow the administrator to enable or disable the DHCP server as needed because other software might be running on a network that already provides the service.

REAL PEOPLE, REAL PROBLEMS, REAL SOLUTIONS
TO BE VIRTUAL?

Jay Logan and his small team were assigned the task of deploying their company's web site. Jay's company, a regional home accessory retailer, had been making plans to offer a small selection of products for sale online. His team of five consisted of a manager from each division—operations, sales, marketing, distribution, and accounting. Their plan was almost complete, and ready to be executed. They had assembled their online catalog, set up a system to handle orders through their central distribution warehouse, and hired a web development firm to build the e-commerce site. The only unsettled point to their plan was where to place the completed web site.

There were several options available. Their first choice was to install web server hardware and software on their local network. Another option was to buy the hardware and software and place the system remotely at a web hosting company, or "co-locate." Their third option was to host the site virtually at a web hosting company.

Placing a web server within their local network made sense, but only before they analyzed the cost! It would mean hiring another staff member to handle the server, paying for extra network bandwidth, and then adding the cost of the actual hardware and software. After more analysis, the cost for an internally hosted web server became less and less attractive.

Remotely hosting their site was next on their list. Jay had done extensive research into co-location of web servers and found that, once again, cost was an issue. Even though co-locating their server was more affordable than internally hosting the site, it was still very expensive, especially when the team considered that their new on-line venture would take at least nine months to start generating considerable traffic. The initial setup and monthly cost of a co-located server seemed to be more than what they wanted to spend.

Their last, but as it turned out, best, option was to host the site *virtually* and share the costs of web site hosting with other site owners. The cost of hosting their site on a virtual server was much less than their other options. After some research, the team realized that for the traffic they expected in their first year, most virtual hosting companies offered more than enough bandwidth with their service. They could choose which hosting components would best serve their e-commerce needs such as on-line payment processing, database servers, and mail servers. They didn't need to be concerned with hiring additional staff or paying for hardware and software. All this came at a fraction of the cost of either hosting the site internally or co-locating.

Jay and his team decided to go with the virtual hosting option. They knew that as the site's traffic grew, they could always move to one of the other hosting alternatives.

After the site launched on a virtual host server, their time spent analyzing this part of their plan paid off. The virtual host performed very well, and the site operated as planned! The company's site also turned out to be a successful e-commerce site, and continues to have a growing number of visitors. Even after a year of operation, Jay has found that the virtual hosting company continues to accommodate their site without fail!

10

CHAPTER SUMMARY

- ❑ A server can be either software that provides a service to other software or it can be the computer on which the server software is running.

- ❑ Servers can be classified as those that provide data and services to users on the Internet or those that aid in communication over the Internet.

- ❑ Each server runs as a background process on a computer. It is started and stopped either manually or automatically when the operating system first loads.

- ❑ Each server listens at a port, which is a number assigned to it that client software uses to identify the service it is looking for on the computer.

- ❑ A server is controlled by an administrator who uses configuration files, a command-driven interface, or a GUI interface.

- ❑ Configuration files are text files that are read by the server each time it loads to get the information it needs to customize settings and preferences.

- ❑ Client software and server software can run on the same computer. For example, a computer can run a DHCP client and a web server at the same time.

- ❑ Apache by the Apache Group is a common web server that will run on both a UNIX and Windows platform.

❑ Browsers access web servers using a URL.

❑ Virtual hosting is often used by individuals and small companies to reduce the cost of owning a web site.

❑ Virtual hosting provides less power and functionality than do virtual servers.

❑ Web servers should support several protocols including HTTP, SMTP, POP3, IMAP4, SSL, and Gopher.

❑ When selecting a web server, consider the scripting languages and the database interfaces it supports.

❑ A server should have tools available to measure performance.

❑ Web servers most likely include an FTP server to be used by developers for uploading web pages.

❑ List servers are used to manage large mailing lists.

❑ News servers work by getting news articles from other news servers. Clients can post new articles to their local news server.

❑ Mail servers use SMTP, POP3 or IMAP4 protocols and are used to send and receive e-mail messages.

❑ Certificate servers are used to manage digital signatures. Digital signatures are used to secure transactions on the Internet or a private network.

❑ E-commerce servers support a wide range of commercial transactions including credit card transactions.

❑ Telnet servers are used by remote users to log on to a server. UNIX computers have always used Telnet. More recently, Windows supports Telnet.

❑ A DNS server is sometimes called a name server and is responsible for relating domain names to IP addresses and IP addresses to domain names. There are several layers of DNS servers beginning with root DNS servers at the top of the hierarchy.

❑ A DNS server uses data files that contain DNS records to hold information about domain names and IP addresses. Each DNS record has a name and a designated function.

❑ A directory is a database that holds information about resources on a network. LDAP is a protocol that is often used to access a directory.

❑ A cache server can reside on a router, a proxy server, or a computer dedicated for that purpose. A cache server is used to improve performance by caching information on the web so that traffic over the Internet is reduced.

❑ A mirrored server can be used to back up the primary server and to provide improved performance by strategically locating the mirrored server in a different part of the world. Large, international corporations frequently mirror web servers and FTP servers.

❐ A proxy server provides web access to other computers on a private network, substituting its own IP address for the other computer before sending a request over the Internet. A proxy server sometimes acts as a firewall and is sometimes used to reduce the cost of an ISP service that charges by the number of IP addresses using the service.

❐ A DHCP server provides dynamic IP addresses to other computers on a network.

KEY TERMS

access control — A feature of a server that limits which files or directories a user can read or write to based on his user ID.

cache server — A server that can reside on a router or computer that caches information retrieved from the Internet in case it is requested again, in order to reduce traffic over the Internet and improve performance on the local network.

certificate server — A server that issues and revokes certificates, which are binary data used to identify a user on the Internet in order to secure electronic business transactions.

chroot mode — A function of UNIX that restricts the portion of the file system that a service running on the UNIX platform can access.

command-driven interface — A software interface that requires the user to enter a command to achieve a desired result. MS-DOS is an example of software that uses this type of interface. Compare to GUI.

daemon — In UNIX, a program that runs in the background to support or serve other programs.

DHCP (Dynamic Host Configuration Protocol) server — A service that assigns dynamic IP addresses to computers on a network when they first access the network.

directory — A database that tracks resources on a network.

directory server — A server that accesses and manages a directory.

e-commerce — Buying and selling products and services over the Internet.

e-commerce server — A server designed to handle all aspects of e-commerce, including taking orders, processing payments, sending verifications, and printing packing slips.

firewall — Software or hardware that limits traffic between the Internet and a private network or single computer.

flame — A rude message sent over the Internet.

graphical user interfaces (GUI) — A software interface that provides icons, menus, and windows in order for a user to command the software. Windows is an example of software that uses a GUI. Compare to command-driven interface.

LDAP (Lightweight Directory Access Protocol) — A protocol used by client and server software to access a directory.

LPD (Line Printer Daemon) — A server that is responsible for receiving and processing print jobs that are sent over the Internet.

10

LPR (Line Printer Remote) — The protocol that controls how print jobs are sent to printers over the Internet.

mirrored server — A server that is an exact replica of another server that is used to reduce traffic on the main server. This improves performance for the benefit of the user. Mirrored servers also serve as a backup for the main server in case the main server fails.

netiquette (network etiquette) — Basic rules of courtesy used when sending electronic messages.

Network Address Translator (NAT) — A device that substitutes its own IP address for that of another computer. *See* proxy server.

proxy server — A server that acts as an intermediary between another computer and the Internet. The proxy server substitutes its own IP address for the IP address of the computer on the network making a request, so that all traffic over the Internet appears to be coming from only this one IP address.

service — A program that runs in the background to support or serve other programs.

REVIEW QUESTIONS

1. What is the standard port assignment for a web server?

2. What are two types of interfaces that a server can offer a user or administrator?

3. What is the name for a file that is read by a server when it first loads that contains parameters and settings for the server?

4. A program that runs in the background in Windows 2000 to be used by other programs is called a(n) _____.

5. What are three operating systems that are commonly used to support servers on the Internet?

6. If you want to use ODBC for database connectivity, what is one operating system that you cannot use?

7. Name one brand of web server software.

8. What is one disadvantage of several virtually hosted web sites using the same instance of a running web server?

9. List at least three protocols that you would expect a web server to support.

10. When you see HTTPS: at the beginning of a URL in a web browser address box, what protocol is the browser currently using?

11. Name two scripting languages that might be supported by a web server.

12. What technology does a web server use to pass data that it has received from a browser to a program to process that data?

13. Name two database software applications that are commonly used to support a database on a web site.

14. Name one brand of list server software.

15. What protocol do news servers use?

16. A rude message sent in a news article is called _____.

17. What is the purpose of an SOA record in a DNS data file? How many SOA records are there in a DNS file?

18. Which DNS record identifies the host, assigning it an IP address?

19. Which DNS record applies to e-mail transfers?

20. What protocol does a directory server normally use?

21. What is the main purpose of a cache server?

22. What are two purposes of a mirrored server?

23. Explain the difference between a DNS server and a DHCP server.

24. Explain how a proxy server can also act as a firewall.

25. Under what circumstances is a proxy server *not* a firewall?

HANDS-ON PROJECTS

Research List Servers

10

Your company has asked you to make a recommendation for the purchase of a list server needed by the marketing department. Fill in the following table for four different list server products. Based on your findings, which product do you recommend? Why?

Criteria for the list server:

- Will be used to send about 1,000 messages a day to customers.

- Will be installed on a Windows 2000 platform. GUI interface is preferred.

- Each recipient must be able to see his or her own e-mail address and no other recipient address.

- Must be able to manually edit the e-mail message to any one recipient before it is sent.

	Product 1	Product 2	Product 3	Product 4
Product name				
Manufacturer				
Web site of manufacturer				
Can handle 1,000 messages per day				
Will install on Windows 2000				
Masks list of recipients from each recipient				
Can edit individual messages before they are sent.				
Price of product				

Research Groupware Applications

Sometimes several servers come packaged in a single application called groupware. Research the web site *serverwatch.internet.com*, which lists several groupware products, and list the type of servers that each of these products includes:

1. eRoom
2. TeamWare Office
3. WebBoard
4. Netscape Proxy Server
5. SyGate
6. Trumpet FireSock
7. WinGate Pro

Research Microsoft Proxy Server

Microsoft offers proxy server software called Microsoft Proxy Server. Answer the following questions about this product:

1. What is the URL of the Microsoft web site that gives information about this product?
2. What is the price of Microsoft Proxy Server?
3. What operating system platforms can it run on?
4. What is the latest version number of Microsoft Proxy Server?

Research Web Servers

Use the web site WebServer Compare (*webservercompare.internet.com*) to compare web server products. This site is shown in Figure 10-19. Answer the following questions:

1. Explain each of the nine criteria listed in Figure 10-19 used to compare web server products.
2. Print the home pages of the product manufacturers of five web server products that match all criteria and support all operating systems listed.

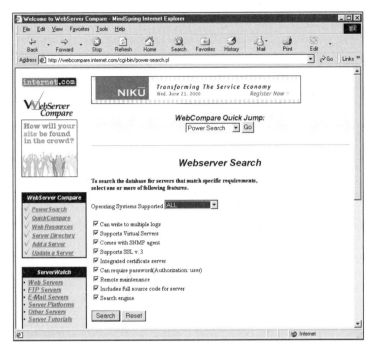

Figure 10-19   WebServer Compare's web site can be used to compare web server products based on nine criteria

Web Servers That Support E-mail

Find a web site on the Internet that supports E-mail. Print the logon web page to the e-mail server. What web server software is being used on this site?

11

INTERNET INFRASTRUCTURE

In this chapter, you will learn

- ◆ How to compare network operating systems
- ◆ About the different local network technologies, including Ethernet, Token Ring, and FDDI
- ◆ About the devices and technologies used to connect networks and manage traffic among networks
- ◆ How to compare the bandwidth technologies used on LANs, WANs and the Internet
- ◆ About the practical aspects of designing and building a small-business LAN connected to the Internet

In earlier chapters, you were introduced to some of the hardware devices and software that allow PCs and servers to communicate with one another. Examples of this kind of technology include regular phone lines and cable modem on the local level, and T1 lines and backbones on the regional and national levels. This chapter goes deeper into what types of networks exist including the hardware, software, and protocols they use, and about the different bandwidth technologies available today on which these networks depend. Most of the material in this chapter focuses on the lower two layers of the OSI model, the Data Link and Physical layers. You will see as you read on that what happens at the local level form the building blocks that make up the Internet. Much of the material in previous chapters will come together in this chapter as a unified whole. At the end of the chapter, you'll see a real-life example of how one small business incorporated some of the technologies of this chapter to build a LAN as well as to access the Internet.

WHAT IS THE INTERNET INFRASTRUCTURE?

The Internet is a collection of networks connected to one another by a maze of connecting devices and high-speed cabling and wireless technologies. These networks form the building blocks that are collectively known as the Internet infrastructure.

When you study the Internet infrastructure, much attention is given to how much data can travel over a given communication system in a given amount of time. This measure of data capacity is called **bandwidth** or data **throughput** and is often measured in bits per second (bps), one thousand bits per second (Kbps) or million bits per second (Mbps). The Internet is dependent on technologies that provide varying degrees of bandwidths, each serving a different purpose and following a different set of standards.

A local area network has a much lesser need for data throughput than does a national backbone. In between these two systems are many regional systems that require varying degrees of medium bandwidths. Figure 11-1 shows an illustration of various types of networks and their bandwidths. You can compare these networks to our road system. Streets in a subdivision (a local network) are designed for small amounts of traffic. Side streets and country roads are designed for low-to-medium degrees of traffic and major highways for medium-to-high traffic. Then there are major freeways (the national backbones) that are designed for the fastest and most amount of traffic. Local networks don't connect directly to backbones, just like a street leaving a subdivision doesn't connect directly to a freeway because the sudden change in bandwidth would stress both systems. You'll see many other similarities to road systems as you read this chapter.

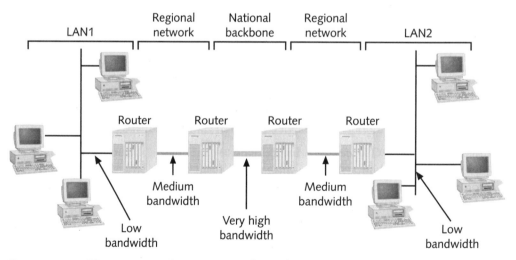

Figure 11-1   The Internet infrastructure is dependent on varying degrees of bandwidth technologies and devices

In the chapter, you'll begin by studying the infrastructure of the local network, beginning with its operating systems and then its physical technologies. Consider local networks one of the basic building blocks of the Internet. Next you'll look at the connecting devices that are designed to connect two or more networks of differing bandwidth and differing technologies. Last, you'll look at the several different technologies for medium-to-high bandwidths that are devoted to connecting networks together across short to long distances.

OPERATING SYSTEMS ON THE NETWORK

A LAN needs software to control how users can access each other and share resources on the LAN. Two approaches to managing network resources are the peer-to-peer model and the client/server model.

In the **peer-to-peer model**, each computer on the LAN has the same authority as other computers. Each computer user decides to share a resource on his or her computer such as a file, a database, or a printer. By sharing these resources, this computer becomes the server to other computers on the LAN. Windows 9x and Windows NT Workstation are examples of operating systems that can support a peer-to-peer network.

For example, several computers using Windows 98 in a small business or home can be connected together using an Ethernet hub to form a small LAN, as shown in Figure 11-2. One or more computers on the LAN might have a network connection such as a phone line, DSL line, or cable modem to connect to the Internet. Or, as in the figure, the cable modem can connect directly to the hub and on to the Internet. In this situation, each PC on the LAN is responsible for managing its access to the Internet through the cable modem.

11

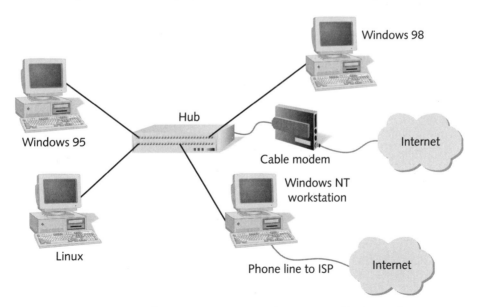

Figure 11-2   On a small peer-to-peer network, some or all PCs can have access to the Internet and no one computer controls the network

In a **client–server model**, sometimes called a **domain model**, one or more computers control how all resources on the LAN are used and who can access these resources. The network is administered from this controlling computer in the network. The system administrator, who is responsible for the network, sets up user accounts and assigns user privileges to network resources. Software, data, and printers can be shared only when the system administrator has allowed that right to a user account.

An operating system that can provide this level of control, monitoring, and support to a network is called a **network operating system** (**NOS**). The most popular network operating systems are Windows NT and Windows 2000 by Microsoft, Novell by Netware, and UNIX. A network operating system is installed on the server computer and other operating systems can be installed on the client computers in the network. It is a common practice for the server to use one OS and the clients to use another. For example, the server might use UNIX and the clients on the LAN use Windows 98 or Windows NT Workstation.

If the organization provides services over an intranet or the Internet, such as a web server or an e-mail server, the computer or computers that provide that service require an operating system to run the service. This operating system is responsible for managing these service programs and the resources they require. If a service such as a web server must accommodate thousands of hits per day, then the OS must be robust enough to handle the volume.

The operating system that controls the LAN need not be the same OS that manages the services to the Internet or intranet. For example, in Figure 11-3, an organization might use one server to control the LAN and another server to provide services over the Internet. The server that controls the LAN is using the network operating system Windows NT Server. When Windows NT Server controls a LAN, it is called the **domain controller**.

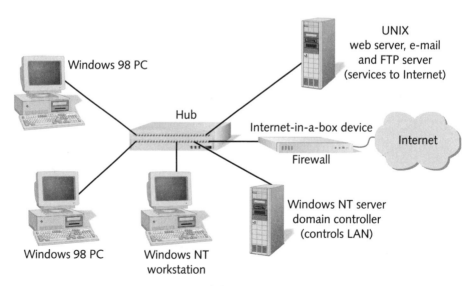

Figure 11-3   One NOS can control the LAN and another NOS can be used for services provided over the Internet

The server that runs the software to provide services to the Internet (a web server, FTP server, and e-mail server) is using UNIX as the NOS. Windows NT Server is great at managing a LAN, and UNIX is a great choice as an OS for a web server, so in this example, each OS is doing the job for which it is best suited. However, using more than one network operating system within an organization comes with a price. Most network and system administrators specialize in a single NOS; when you use more than one NOS, you might have the added overhead of requiring a different system administrator for each server.

Also, notice in Figure 11-3 that a firewall provides access to the Internet. The device in this example is called an Internet-in-a-box and provides the interface between the Internet and the LAN and is discussed later in the chapter. Also, note that the user PCs on this LAN use Windows 98 and Windows NT Workstation. There is no problem with having several different operating systems for user PCs on the same LAN as long as each operating system can access the network using the proper protocols.

Finally, know that the configuration shown in Figure 11-3 is not the only configuration possible to accomplish the goals of supporting both the LAN and the Internet services. For example, the Internet connection could go directly to the UNIX server and it could then serve as the firewall, eliminating the need of an added device. Or, the firewall box could sit between the Internet and the UNIX server and not be directly connected to the LAN. A network architect would make the decisions as to how the network should be configured based on the volume of traffic, security requirements, budget, business needs, and technical expertise within the organization.

11

Operating Systems for the Client

On a LAN, each personal computer must have an operating system that is capable of interfacing with a network interface card and the resources available on the network. The most popular personal computer OS is Windows 9x. Other options are Windows NT and Linux.

Windows 9x

Microsoft has a suite of operating systems designed for varying needs. Windows 9x is the low-end operating system used for personal computers. It is backward compatible with DOS, Windows 3.x, and legacy hardware devices, and is an excellent choice as a personal computer OS. It supports network access and can be used in a peer-to-peer or client/server network. Using Windows 9x, you can give others on the network access to files and folders on your hard drive (or even the entire hard drive) and to a printer that is directly connected to your PC. For this feature, file sharing must be installed, as was covered in Chapter 8.

To use the sharing feature of Windows 9x, you first must make sure your computer is set up for share-level access control. To do this, follow these steps:

1. Click **Start** on the Taskbar, point to **Settings**, and click **Control Panel**.

2. Double-click the **Network** icon. The Network window opens.

3. Select the **Access Control** tab.

4. Make sure **Share-level access control** is selected. If not, select it.

5. Click **OK**.

To make a folder available to others on the network, follow these directions:

1. Find the folder in Windows Explorer, and right-click on the folder. A drop down menu opens.

2. Click **Properties** from the drop down menu and the Properties dialog box opens. See Figure 11-4.

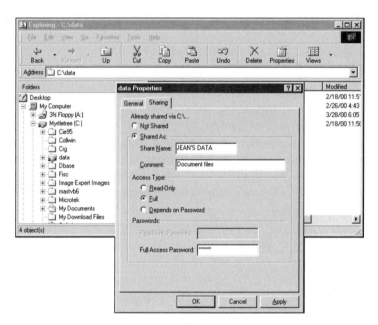

Figure 11-4   Using Windows 98, a user on a network can share a folder with others on the network

3. Click the **Sharing** tab in the dialog box.

4. Click the **Shared As** option button. In the Share Name field, enter a name that others on the network can use to identify the folder.

5. In the Full Access Password field, enter a password others must use to access this resource, then click **Apply**. Others on the network can then see the folder as an icon in their Network Neighborhood window.

This is an example of how a peer-to-peer network works. Each user is responsible for administering and controlling access to the resources at his or her workstation.

In addition to one or more operating systems, a network also requires a network protocol so that all PCs on the network are using the same standards for communication on the network.

The network protocol selected must be supported by every operating system on the network. To see the network protocols that are supported by Windows 9x, follow these directions:

1. Click **Start** on the Taskbar, point to **Settings**, and click **Control Panel**. Double-click on the **Network** icon. The Network window opens.

2. Click the **Add** button. The Select Network Component Type window opens. Select **Protocol** and click the **Add** button. The Select Network Protocol window opens. The window showing in Figure 11-5 displays the four network protocol manufacturers supported by Windows 98. In the figure, Microsoft is selected and on the right side of the window you can see the several different network protocols supported for a Microsoft network.

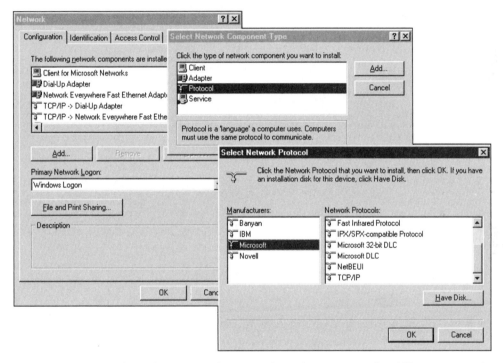

Figure 11-5   Use the Select Network Protocol window to view the different network protocols supported by Windows 98

3. Click **Cancel** three times to exit each of the three windows.

Looking at Figure 11-5, you can see that one protocol that is supported for a Microsoft network is TCP/IP. If the local network is to have access to the Internet, this protocol must be used. Sometimes, however, a network must support more than one network protocol, because each protocol is used for a different purpose. For example, if an application is running over the network from a server to different computers on the LAN and the application requires the NetBIOS protocol, then this protocol must be installed on each computer on the LAN. In order for these same computers to access the Internet, the TCP/IP protocol must also be installed.

Windows NT Workstation

Windows NT offers two operating systems, Windows NT Workstation and Windows NT Server. Windows NT Workstation works well as a stand-alone OS or as an OS on a PC that is part of a peer-to-peer network or client/server network. The OS looks and feels very much like Windows 9x, but at its behind-the-scenes foundation, it is a very different operating system. Figure 11-6 shows the Windows NT desktop.

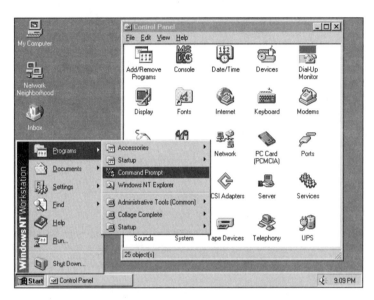

Figure 11-6   The Windows NT desktop is similar to that of Windows 9x

Recall that Windows 9x continues to support older hardware and software. However, Windows NT and Windows 2000 do not support legacy software or hardware. Instead, these operating systems manage hardware and software with a heavy hand, expecting these components to follow the rules of relating to a true 32-bit OS. For example, older 16-bit legacy software could use memory addresses to access RAM directly, but 32-bit software must interact with the OS, which accesses memory for it. If a 16-bit program attempts to access memory directly in a Windows NT environment, the software will produce a general protection fault error and Windows NT will terminate it. All the Windows NT and Windows 2000 operating systems work this way, which is why NT stands for new technology.

When considering whether to use Windows NT or Windows 2000 on a computer, verify that all the hardware and software already installed on the PC is compatible with this new way of doing business. For hardware, check the Hardware Compatibility List (HCL) on the Microsoft web site. If your specific hardware is not listed, you most likely won't be able to successfully install Windows NT on the system. If software was written originally for DOS or Windows 3.x, it may or may not work. Check with the software manufacturer or simply load the software on a Windows NT computer and test it. Most software designed for Windows 9x is 32-bit software and will work under Windows NT.

The underlying difference between 16-bit software and 32-bit software is the mode that the CPU is operating in when the software is executed. A CPU can work in real mode or protected mode. **Real mode** accesses memory and the hard drive directly using a 16-bit data path, and **protected mode** accesses memory and the hard drive indirectly using a 32-bit data path. DOS applications all use 16-bit real mode, but Windows 3.x uses a hybrid real mode and protected mode called a virtual real mode. Windows 9x supports all three, but Windows NT only supports virtual real mode and protected mode.

Linux

There was a time that UNIX was not considered a viable option as a personal computer OS, but that changed when Linux was invented. Linux was written by Linus Torvalds in 1991 with the help of volunteers all over the world. Linux was designed as a scaled-down version of UNIX. It is free, although companies offering Linux charge a price for the documentation, technical support and add-on modules. Linux is small enough to fit and run on a 486 computer, yet has network capabilities similar to a full-fledged commercial version of UNIX. For a time, Linux was considered only a training tool to learn UNIX, because it could be installed on an inexpensive low-end PC and easily used in a training environment or at home. Linux is no longer considered just a training tool, and is rapidly gaining acceptance as an operating system of choice in certain situations.

Linux is an excellent NOS to use in a small company environment with low-volume traffic for intranet services. It is a popular OS for Internet-in-a-box devices. It can be used as the OS for a web server or proxy server for a LAN. (Recall that a proxy server is software that acts as the middle man between the Internet and other PCs on the network.) Apache Server, a popular web server application, is often used on a UNIX or Linux platform. Even though Linux is not generally considered the OS for high-volume traffic that UNIX is known to handle, several high-traffic web sites now run successfully using Apache Server on a Linux platform, and the industry's perception of Linux is changing at a fast pace.

Linux's popularity is also growing. Apple, Computer Associates, Compaq, Corel, Dell, Hewlett-Packard, IBM, Informix, Intel, Lotus, NAI, Netscape, Novell, Oracle, SAP, and Sybase are among the companies that have recently provided support for their products using the Linux OS. The largest drawbacks to using Linux in a corporate environment are not so much the technical strength of the OS, but the support and standards surrounding it, lack of application software written for it, lack of experienced technical people, and lack of a user-friendly interface.

Linux is very different from Windows. In order to evaluate Linux as an operating system, you need to understand the difference between an operating system kernel and operating system shell. The operating system **kernel** is that part of the operating system that interfaces with hardware, including the NIC that accesses the network; see Figure 11-7. The user or applications software cannot command the kernel directly, but must go through a command

11

interface called the **shell**. Applications software also must interface with the OS through the shell and, in most cases, cannot access the hardware directly. (Recall that older DOS applications could do that when the CPU is running in real mode.) The Linux kernel is considered a much more stable operating system kernel than the Windows kernel, which results in fewer Linux crashes than Windows crashes in comparable situations.

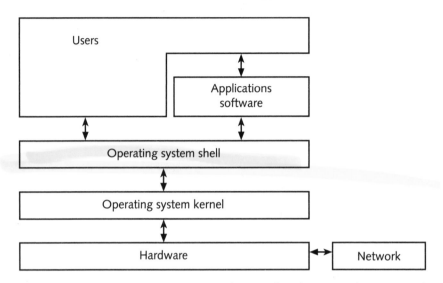

Figure 11-7 An operating system is the interface between the users and applications software and hardware which accesses the network

Most people are accustomed to using the Windows operating system graphical user interface (GUI) that many users take for granted and assume is present in all operating systems. This interface is Windows's GUI operating system shell. However, Windows also offers a command-line shell where users can enter commands as text. You can access the Windows command-line shell and enter commands that look and work like older DOS commands. The shell is often called the DOS box and you can see it in Figure 11-8. To access the DOS box in Windows 9x, click **Start** on the taskbar, point to **Programs**, then click **MS-DOS Prompt**. For Windows 2000, click **Start**, point to **Accessories**, and click **Command Prompt**. For Windows NT, click **Start**, point to **Programs**, and click **Command Prompt**.

In Windows, the GUI shell is the default shell. If you want a command-line shell, you must load a DOS box. In contrast, Linux and UNIX use a command-line shell as the default shell, and a GUI shell is an add-on feature. This difference in approach to a shell is one of the major differences between Linux and Windows. Figure 11-9 shows the default Linux shell interface for users. The command entered is ls -l /. This command requests a list of all files in the / directory, which, in UNIX, is the root directory. The command is similar to the DIR command in DOS.

Figure 11-8   Windows 98 offers a command-line shell where DOS-like commands can be typed in a "DOS box"

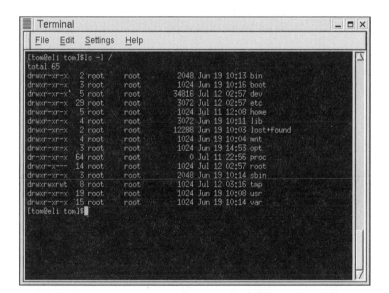

Figure 11-9   Linux uses a command-line shell as its default shell

Notice how the list of files and directories is displayed in Figure 11-9. The first column gives information about the type of file or directory and the read and write privileges assigned to it. The fourth column shows the size of the file or directory, and the next columns show the date and time the file or directory was last updated. The last column is the name of the file or directory. Recall from Chapter 4 that when you access an FTP site that is run by the UNIX operating system, you are likely to see a directory list that looks like this one.

Linux is not as popular an operating system for a personal computer as Windows because of this less-than-friendly shell. GUI shells are available for Linux that make it look and feel more like a Windows environment, but these are not widely used. As these GUI shells become more popular and applications software companies begin writing their applications to run on Linux, the popularity of Linux as a desktop OS will increase. Three administrative packages for Linux include Red Hat's Linux, Caldera's Open Administration System, and SuSE's Yet Another Setup Tool (YAST).

Network Operating Systems

Recall that a network operating system manages network resources. This section looks at the more popular operating systems and focuses on how to select the right one for the job. Selecting the right network operating system is an important decision, one which affects many other technical and business issues, so the decision should be made with care. Some criteria to consider when selecting a NOS are:

- *Reliability* How reliable is the OS? Even a small percentage of file corruption can be unacceptable. When a problem occurs, how quickly can the OS recover without requiring manual intervention or even a reboot?

- *Performance* Can the NOS handle the volume and type of traffic that you expect? Some operating systems handle high volume traffic with file sharing on a LAN better than they handle high volume hits to a web server. Some operating systems might perform best with lower-rate traffic, but might be more stable than another OS that can handle a higher volume of traffic. Know what the OS is good at and use it in that environment.

- *Adaptability* If you look again at the network that is diagrammed in Figure 11-3 you can see a variety of operating systems, equipment, software, and business needs. In the real world, things are seldom straightforward and the latest technology is sometimes mixed with legacy hardware and software. The NOS should be able to handle a mixed bag of software and hardware. For example, what programming languages can the OS support (Java, FORTRAN, COBOL and C++)? Can it handle older 16-bit applications if they are still used within the organization? Can it handle thin clients and PDAs as well as PCs?

- *Ease of Use and Ease of Installation* How easy is it to install? What expertise is required for the installation? What GUI interface features are available? How easy is it to administer? For example, in a small organization, you might hire a consultant to install the NOS and set everything up, but a non-technical end-user must administer the NOS on a daily basis. He or she would need to be able to set up a new user account, reset a forgotten password, change the authority of a user account to use network resources, back up the data to tape, and so forth. How much training and technical expertise must an administrator have to do these daily administrative chores and how much will that training cost? Closely examine the system monitoring tools, GUI based administrative tools, SNMP support, system management products available for the NOS, and all the documentation that goes with the products.

- *Affordability* Don't just consider the initial price of the NOS, but consider the on-going expenses of supporting the entire environment. Consider costs for upgrades, technical support services, hardware maintenance, training end users and technical professionals within the organization, and so forth.

- *Security* What security features does the NOS offer? How well is the data shielded from willful destruction or accidental corruption? Can the NOS protect you from a denial-of-service attack? Can the NOS manage encrypting data and certificates? You can read more about security in Chapter 12.

- *Scalability* Most companies have a growth plan. Take a close look at yours and evaluate how well the NOS can fit into the plan. The cost of hardware stays about the same from year to year, but the quality of that hardware is constantly improving. For example, for the past 12 or 15 years, you have been able to buy a high-quality personal computer for about $2,000. In 1987, that $2,000 would buy you an IBM Model 30 with a 10 MB hard drive, an Intel 8088 CPU running at about 4.7 MHz, 2 MB of RAM with a 13 inch monitor, keyboard, and mouse. This was a great system at that time! Today, that same $2,000 will buy you a 12 GB hard drive, a Pentium CPU running at 800 MHz, 256 MB of RAM, a 17-inch high-resolution monitor, keyboard and mouse—same price; much more power. The point is that you don't want to spend your money this year for a server you won't need until next year. The server power will sit unused for one year while the quality of the server you could have bought next year for the same money would be much improved. For this reason, many organizations will choose to put off that purchase until the hardware is needed. You want the NOS to be scalable to the extent it can work with a server that has one processor today but might have two more processors added to it next year.

The next section introduces several popular network operating systems and some of the advantages and disadvantages of each.

Windows NT Server and Windows NT Enterprise Server

Windows NT Server was introduced as an NOS into the marketplace at the same time Microsoft released Windows NT Workstation. Windows NT Server is designed to create and support a client/server network for a LAN called a domain. In this context, a domain is a network where access to resources on the network is centrally controlled, compared to a peer-to-peer network where each computer on the network controls access to its own resources. One Windows NT Server computer is designated the **primary domain controller** (**PDC**), which stores and controls a database of (1) user accounts, (2) group accounts, and (3) computer accounts. This database is called the directory database or the **security accounts manager** (**SAM**) database.

An administrator can update the directory database on the PDC from any workstation or server on the domain. One or more read-only backup copies of the directory database can be kept on other computers. Each computer with a backup of the directory database is called a **backup domain controller** (**BDC**). See Figure 11-10.

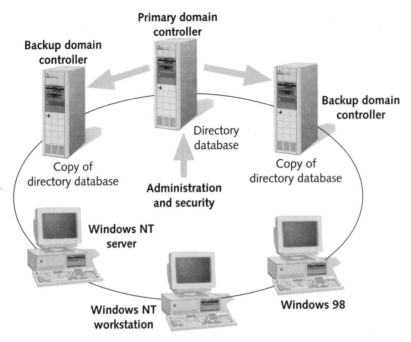

Figure 11-10   A Windows NT domain

Windows NT Enterprise Server was released after Windows NT Server. Windows NT Enterprise Server is designed to handle high-end computers supporting large database systems. With the release of Windows NT Enterprise Server, Microsoft set the precedent that it would release different NOSs for different size systems rather than make a single NOS highly scalable.

Windows 2000

Windows 2000 is a series of operating systems, each designed for a particular size computer and computing needs. Windows 2000 includes four operating systems:

- *Windows 2000 Professional* This OS is designed to ultimately replace both Windows 9x and Windows NT Workstation as a personal computer desktop OS. It is an improved version of Windows NT Workstation, using the same kernel approach to hardware and software, and includes all the popular features of Windows 98. It supports Plug and Play, a Control Panel with an Add/Remove Hardware icon, improved backup utility, FAT32 file system (allows for larger and more efficient logical drives on a hard drive than did DOS or Windows 95), virtual private network support, and security features. Hardware and software must qualify for the OS. For hardware, check the Hardware Compatibility List at *www.microsoft.com/hcl*.

- *Windows 2000 Server* This OS is the improved version of Windows NT Server and is designed as a network operating system for low-end servers. Just as with Windows NT Server, it can be a domain controller for a network and is a powerful file server and printer-sharing server.

- *Windows 2000 Advanced Server* This network operating system has the same features as Windows 2000 Server, but is designed to run on more powerful servers. It supports large numbers of processors and can support up to 64 GB of memory.

- *Windows 2000 Datacenter Server* This network operating system is another step up from Windows 2000 Advanced Server and is designed to support up to 16 processors. It is intended to be used in large enterprise operations centers such as those needed to support data warehousing.

Netware by Novell

Netware by Novell, Inc. (*www.novell.com*) was, for many years, the tried-and-true industry-accepted solution to LAN management. Even with the strong inroads into the NOS market made by Microsoft, Novell Netware is still considered the fastest, most effective NOS for file sharing across a LAN. Netware uses a suite of protocols collectively called **IPX/SPX (Internetwork Packet Exchange/Sequenced Packet Exchange)**, which are supported by Windows 9x, Windows NT, and Windows 2000. The IPX portion of the protocol is the Network layer responsible for routing, and the SPX portion of the protocol manages error checking, making it the Transport layer. IPX/SPX is similar to TCP/IP.

Netware is installed on the server that controls the LAN, and each computer connected to the LAN must run a Netware client to interact with the server and provide a logon screen when the user first accesses the network. Windows operating systems all include this Netware client. There is also a DOS Netware client available so that a DOS computer can log into a Novell Netware LAN.

Because Netware does not use TCP/IP, it is not a viable NOS for servers that provide services over the Internet although other software can be running on the network to provide TCP/IP.

UNIX and Linux

Until recently, UNIX was the only tried-and-true viable option for a network operating system that would provide services over the Internet. TCP/IP was born in a UNIX environment, and, for many, to think "OS for the Internet" is to think "UNIX." UNIX can also support a LAN as a file and database server, managing user accounts and access privileges. UNIX was also the first, and still is the most popular, NOS for mid-size servers to support thin clients. Java was developed in a UNIX environment to support thin clients served by

11

a UNIX computer. The first web servers used UNIX. Today, 48% of web servers on the Internet use UNIX as compared to 33% that use Windows NT. UNIX is the accepted mainstay for the firewall market. Many popular firewall applications (SunScreen, BorderWare, Checkpoint) were originally designed to be used on a UNIX platform.

UNIX is not an easy operating system to learn. Even though it does offer a GUI interface, a system administrator cannot fully perform his or her job without a working knowledge of a somewhat cryptic command-line shell. Installing UNIX and installing hardware devices on a UNIX system require expertise far beyond that of a casual user.

There are several hardware manufacturers that offer their own version of UNIX. IBM's UNIX is called AIX. Sun's UNIX is named Solaris; Compaq has a version of UNIX named Tru64 UNIX, and Hewlett-Packard's UNIX version is called HP-UX.

Linux was mentioned earlier as an operating system for a personal computer, but is fast becoming a viable option as a NOS. Red Hat, Inc. sells an impressive version of Linux that has proven to be competitive as a NOS for Internet services. Latest studies show it performing at about 40% of the speed of Windows NT Server. See *www.redhat.com* for more information about Red Hat Linux. For information about the at-large Linux OS see these web sites: *www.linux.org* for general information about Linux, *www.linux.org/docs/index.html* for Linux documentation, and *www.linuxnewbie.org* for information for new users of Linux.

To use UNIX is to know its reliability. Months in a data center can go by and no one on the technical staff can remember when the UNIX server last had to be rebooted. UNIX is a highly scalable, high performing, powerful, highly reliable NOS that carries with it the overhead of requiring an experienced, well-trained administrative and technical staff.

Now that you have an understanding of the purpose of the operating systems on a local network, you can turn your attention to the hardware that creates the network.

UNDERSTANDING LANS AND HOW THEY WORK

A **LAN (local area network)** is a group of computers and other devices spread over a limited area and connected in such a way that any device can gain access to any other device on the LAN. All workstations, printers, and file servers connected to the LAN are accessible to PCs on the LAN. In today's business environment, access to the Internet is important to many business functions, so the LAN often provides a method for a user's PC to connect to the Internet by way of a gateway. The hardware devices used to connect to and build a LAN, and the software that control them is the subject of this section.

Network architecture is the overall design of the network, including the physical components, network technologies, interfacing software, and their protocols needed to establish reliable communication among nodes on the network. (A **node** is one device on the network such as a workstation, server, or printer.) The three most popular physical network technologies for local networks are Ethernet, Token Ring, and Fiber Distributed Data Interface (FDDI). An older type of network technology is Attached Resource Computer network (ARCnet), which is seldom seen today.

Each type of architecture is designed to solve certain network problems, and each has its own advantages and disadvantages. Network architectures differ from each other in many ways. In this discussion, you'll learn about two basic differentiating characteristics—how computers are logically connected and how traffic is controlled on the network.

Ethernet

Ethernet is the most popular network technology used today. There are three variations of Ethernet, primarily distinguished from one another by speed:

- *10-Mpbs Ethernet* The first Ethernet specification was invented by Xerox Corporation in the 1970s, and later in 1980, was enhanced and became known as Ethernet IEEE 802.3 after the organization that sponsored the specification, the Institute of Electrical and Electronic Engineers. This type of Ethernet operates at 10 Mbps (megabits per second) and uses **unshielded twisted-pair** (**UTP**) cable or **coaxial cable**. Unshielded twisted-pair cable uses a connector that looks like a large phone jack and is called an **RJ-45 connector**, and coaxial cable uses a **BNC connector** that looks like a TV cable connection. There are several grades of cables. Category 5 (Cat-5) UTP cable is the most common.

    There are several variations of this speed of Ethernet. **10Base5 Ethernet** (sometimes called **Thicknet**) uses thick coaxial cable. **10Base2 Ethernet** (sometimes called **Thinnet**) uses a less expensive, smaller coaxial cable. Thicknet and Thinnet can both be used on the same LAN. Figure 11-11 shows several types of cables used with Ethernet.

- *100-Mpbs Ethernet or Fast Ethernet* This improved version of Ethernet (sometimes called **100BaseT**) operates at 100 Mbps and uses **shielded twisted-pair** (**STP**) cable. 100BaseT networks can support slower speeds of 10 Mbps so that devices that run at either 10 Mbps or 100 Mbps can coexist on the same LAN. One variation of 100Mbps Ethernet is called **100BaseFX**, which can support fiber optic cable. Fiber optic cable is also shown in Figure 11-11.

- *1000-Mpbs Ethernet or Gigabit Ethernet* This latest version of Ethernet operates at 1,000 Mbps and uses twisted-pair cable and fiber optic cable. While not yet widely used, Gigabit Ethernet is expected to be used for high-speed LAN backbones and for server-to-server connections.

11

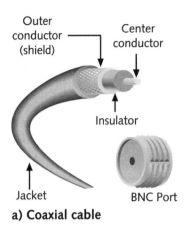

a) Coaxial cable

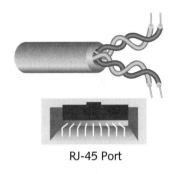

b) Unshielded twisted-pair (UTP)

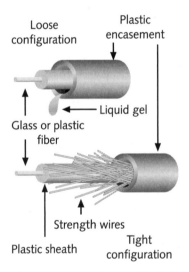

c) Fiber-optic cables with tight and loose sheaths

d) Shielded twisted-pair (STP)

Figure 11-11   Networking cables

Ethernet Topology

Ethernet networks can be configured as either a bus topology or a star topology. **Topology** is the arrangement or shape used to physically connect devices on a network to one another. Figure 11-12 shows an example of a bus and a star topology. A **bus topology** connects each node in a line and does not include a centralized point of connection. Cables just go from one computer, to the next one, and the next. A **star topology** connects all nodes to a centralized hub. PCs on the LAN are like the points of a star around the hub in the middle. A **hub** is a device used to connect nodes on a LAN.

Bus design

Terminator   Terminator

a) Ethernet can be constructed with a bus design.

Star design

b) Ethernet can be constructed with a star design using a hub.

Figure 11-12   Ethernet is a simple and popular network technology

11

The star arrangement is more popular because it is easier to wire and to maintain than the bus arrangement. Also, in a bus arrangement, the failure of one node affects all the other nodes because a failed node cannot pass data to the next node down the line.

In a star topology, a hub works by passing all data that flows to it to every device that is connected to the hub. A hub does not read the destination address at the beginning of a data packet and make decisions about where to send the packet, as routers do. It simply broadcasts the data packet to every device. For this reason, a hub can generate a lot of unnecessary traffic on a LAN. This can result in slow performance when a lot of nodes are connected to a hub. To solve this problem, an Ethernet LAN is often broken into more than one LAN called LAN segments. Each LAN segment is connected to other segments by a bridge, switch, or router. These devices are discussed later in the chapter. When you divide a large LAN into several smaller LANs, the broadcasted traffic over any individual LAN is reduced. A small hub, like the one shown in Figure 11-13 costs less than $300.

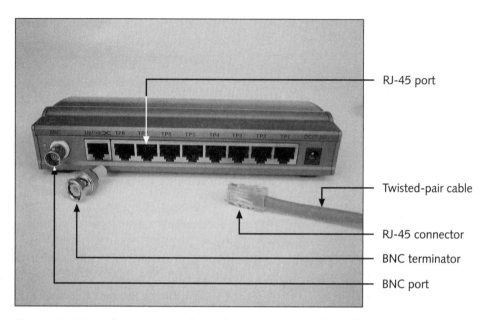

RJ-45 port

Twisted-pair cable

RJ-45 connector

BNC terminator

BNC port

Figure 11-13 A hub is a pass-through device to connect nodes on a network

How Ethernet Controls Data Traffic

An Ethernet network is a passive network, meaning that the networked computers, rather than a dedicated network device, originate the signals that manage the network. (A dedicated network device is a device, such as a hub, used solely to support a network; other devices on the network, such as PCs, have functions other than networking.) Ethernet works much like an old telephone party line, where each computer is like a party line caller. When you wanted to make a call on a party line, you had to pick up the telephone and listen. If there was a dial tone (carrier), then you could make a call. If someone else was talking, you would have to hang up and try again later. If two people attempted to make a call at the same time, both calls would fail. They would each need to hang up and begin again. The first one back on the line would be able to make a call.

Similarly, a computer that wants to send packets over Ethernet first listens on the network for silence. If it hears nothing, it begins to transmit. As it transmits, it is also listening. If it hears something other than its own data being transmitted, it stops transmitting and sends out a signal that there has been a **collision**, which occurs when two computers attempt to send data at the same time. A collision can cause packets that were just sent to be corrupted. Each computer waits for a random amount of time and then tries to transmit again, first listening for silence. This type of network technology is called a **contention-based** system because each computer must contend for an opportunity to transmit on the network.

Computers using Ethernet gain access to the network using the **Carrier Sense Multiple Access with Collision Detection (CSMA/CD)** method. The name of the method describes the three characteristics of the way computers communicate on

Ethernet: (1) a computer must sense that the network is free to handle its transmission before initiating a signal (*carrier sense*), (2) many computers use the same network (*multiple access*), and (3) each computer must detect and manage collisions (*collision detection*).

Network Interface Card (NIC)

A computer connects to a LAN by way of a network interface card (NIC), sometimes called an adapter. Figure 11-14 shows a photo of a NIC. Recall from earlier chapters that every NIC has a uniquely assigned address called a MAC address that identifies the card at the lowest layers of the OSI model. (The NIC's MAC address is associated with an IP address when TCP/IP is bound to the NIC.) Sometimes a NIC provides more than one cable connector in order to accommodate different cabling media, and is therefore called a combo card. The combo card in Figure 11-14 has a port for a BNC connector for a Thinnet connection and an RJ-45 port for twisted pair. Only one of the two ports is used on a LAN.

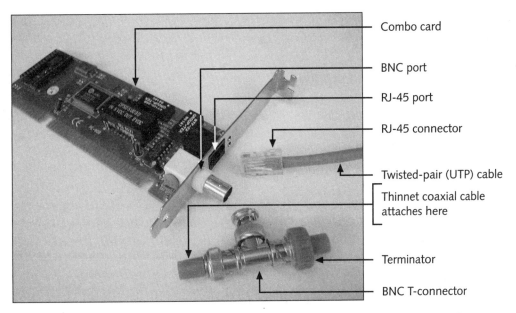

Figure 11-14   This Ethernet combo card can use either a BNC or RJ-45 connection, depending on the cabling system used

Notice in Figure 11-14 the shape of the BNC connector, which is called a T-connector. It can be used to connect PCs together in a bus design as shown in Figure 11-12a. A terminator connected to the right side of the T-connector in Figure 11-14 indicates that this connector will be placed on a PC on one end of the Ethernet bus. In contrast, the twisted-pair cable in Figure 11-14 can be used to connect the PC using this NIC to a hub in an Ethernet star design as in Figure 11-12b.

Repeaters

Because signals transmitted over long distances on a network can weaken, devices are added to amplify signals in large LANs. For example, for a 10BaseT Ethernet cable, if the cable exceeds 100 meters (328 feet), amplification is required. A **repeater** is a device that amplifies signals on a network. There are two kinds of repeaters. An **amplifier repeater** simply amplifies the incoming signal, noise and all. A **signal-regenerating repeater** reads the signal and then creates an exact duplicate of the original signal before sending it on. Ethernet uses a signal-regenerating repeater.

Token Ring

A less popular LAN technology is Token Ring, which was developed by IBM and transmits data at 4 Mbps or 16 Mbps. Logically, Token Ring networks are arranged in a ring topology. However, physically, stations are connected to the network in a star formation. The ring formation describes how a token is passed around a ring from one node to the next until it ends up back at its starting point. The star formation describes how each node is physically connected to a centralized device. The centralized device is called a **controlled-access unit** (**CAU**), a **multistation access unit** (**MSAU** or sometimes just **MAU**), or a **smart multistation access unit** (**SMAU**). Figure 11-15 shows a sample Token Ring configuration with three workstations connected to an MSAU, although the MSAU in the figure can support up to eight workstations. One end of the MSAU has a Ring In (data flows into the MSAU) connection and the other end has a Ring Out (data flows out from the MSAU) connection.

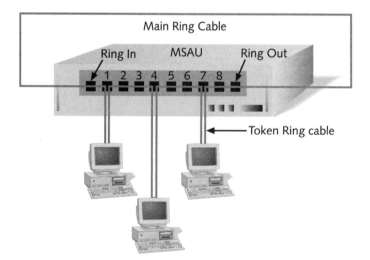

Figure 11-15   A Token Ring network uses a centralized device called a multistation access unit

Each workstation contains a Token Ring LAN card with a 9-pin connector for the Token Ring cable, which connects each workstation to an MSAU. Token Ring cables can be either UTP or STP cables that have two twisted pairs, for a total of four wires in the cable.

The entire Token Ring is made up of not only the main ring, but also the cabling to each PC on the Token Ring. Looking at Figure 11-15, you can see that a Token Ring network is said to be a physical star, but a logical ring. All workstations connect to a centralized MSAU, but you can also follow the ring path around the entire network. The ring path in the figure goes from the Ring In on the MSAU down to each PC and back again, to the Ring Out, which connects back to the Ring In.

The Main Ring Cable in the figure can also connect to another MSAU. Several MSAUs can be strung together in a big ring, each supporting its own group of workstations. Even though there can be several MSAUs in a ring, there is still only a single token traveling the ring.

Communication on a Token Ring

Communication and traffic on a Token Ring network are controlled by a **token**, which is a small data frame with a special format that travels around the ring in only one direction. One station receives the token from the preceding station, called its **nearest active upstream neighbor** (**NAUN**), and passes it on to the next station on the ring, called its **nearest active downstream neighbor** (**NADN**). As one station passes the token to the next station, it can attach data in a frame to the token. The next station receives the token together with the data frame and reads this data frame. If the frame is intended for it, it changes 2 bits in the frame to indicate that the data has been read by the intended station. It then passes the token and the data frame on. When the token and frame are received by the station that sent the frame, it sees that the frame was successfully received and does not send the frame on again. In this case, it releases the token by passing it on to the next PC, without a data frame attached. However, if the amount of data requires more than one frame, instead of releasing the token, the PC sends the next frame with the token. In either case, the token is passed on to the next PC, and data is never on the ring without the token preceding it.

Any PC receiving a token with no data frame attached is free to attach a data frame before passing on the token. The token is busy and not released to another PC until the sending PC has received word that the data was successfully received at its destination. In other words, the only PC that should remove a data frame from behind the token is the PC that attached it in the first place.

FDDI

Fiber Distributed Data Interface (**FDDI**, pronounced "fiddy") is a ring-based network, like Token Ring, but does not require a centralized hub, making it both a logical and physical ring. FDDI provides data transfer at 100 Mbps, which is much faster than Token Ring or regular Ethernet, and a little faster than Fast Ethernet, which also runs at about 100 Mbps. At one time, FDDI used only fiber-optic cabling, but now it can also run on UTP. FDDI is often used as the network technology for a large LAN in a large company or large ISP. FDDI is also used as a backbone network to connect several LANs in a large building.

FDDI uses a token-passing method to control traffic, but FDDI is more powerful and sophisticated than Token Ring. FDDI stations can pass more than one frame of data along the ring

11

without waiting for the first frame to return. Also, once the frames are transmitted, the sending station can pass the FDDI token on to the next station to use, so that more than one station can have frames on the ring at the same time. With Token Ring, a data frame is only found traveling behind the token. With FDDI, data frames travel on the ring without the token. A PC keeps the token until it has sent out its data and then passes the token on. Possessing the token gives a PC the right to send data. A token is released (sent on) when the PC has finished transmitting.

Of the three networks just discussed, Ethernet is by far the most popular; it is the least expensive and simplest to install and maintain.

INTERNETWORKING DEVICES

You have just seen how a LAN is constructed using hubs, repeaters, and cabling. You have also read about the role that desktop and network operating systems play on a LAN. Next, this chapter looks at LANs as the building blocks to a maze or web of networks across a WAN or across a country. Devices that connect a LAN to other LANs include switches, routers, gateways, and bridges. As you study a working definition of each, you'll notice that there is overlap in the way they function and how they are defined. The device can be a physical box (like a router) or it can be a concept such as a gateway, when a PC with appropriate software is strategically located between the LAN and the Internet. Relating each device to the OSI model helps to clarify the distinctions among the various devices.

Bridges and Switches

Hubs can support only a limited number of nodes, and as the number of nodes increases, performance, speed, and reliability can drop for the overall network. One method used to prevent this kind of congestion is **segmentation**, which splits large networks into smaller LANs. Each segment contains two or more computers, and the segments are usually connected by bridges or switches. Figure 11-16 shows a photo of a bridge.

Both bridges and switches use the MAC address to determine where to send packets. They maintain routing tables that list which computers are connected to each hub, and use the information from the routing tables to determine where to send a packet based on its final destination. Because the devices use only MAC addresses to make decisions, they operate at the Data Link level of the OSI model. Figure 11-17 shows how bridges and switches relate to the OSI model.

Figure 11-16   A bridge

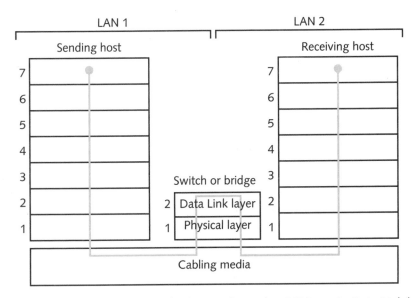

Figure 11-17   A switch or bridge works at the OSI layer 2, Data Link layer, where MAC addresses are used to send a data packet to the right LAN

What is the difference between a bridge and a switch? The main difference is how they work. A bridge broadcasts data to one or more LANs while a switch knows which LAN a packet should be sent to. Let's examine how a bridge works first.

In order to determine which network the packet should be sent to, the bridge creates and maintains a routing table that lists the computers on each LAN. A separate table is kept for each LAN. When a data packet reaches the bridge, the bridge looks at the packet's destination address, then searches the routing table for the originating LAN, looking for the destination address of the data packet. If it finds the address in this routing table, it drops the packet, knowing that the packet will have already reached its destination, because it was broadcast to all nodes on the LAN by the LAN's hub.

If the bridge did not find the destination address in the routing table for that LAN, it broadcasts the packet to all nodes on all LANs it is connected to *except* the LAN that the packet came from. Therefore, a bridge only makes a single decision, "Is this packet destined for a node on its own network?" If the answer is "No," then the bridge simply broadcasts it to all other LANs.

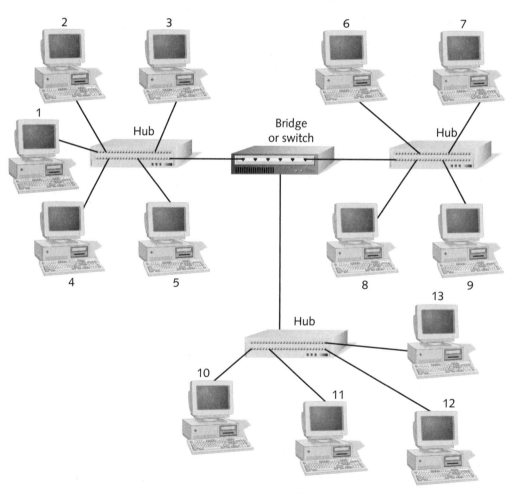

Figure 11-18   A bridge or switch connects two or more LANs and decides to allow or prevent the packet from passing through based on its destination MAC address

Figure 11-18 shows three LANs connected by a bridge. The bridge has created routing tables outlining which computers are connected to each hub (each hub is connected to a separate port on the bridge). There are two different scenarios that may occur. The first is that a computer sends a packet to another computer in the same LAN. Let's say that computer 3 sends a packet to computer 4. Because the packet must pass through the LAN's hub and a hub broadcasts all data packets it receives to all nodes on the LAN, the packet is sent to the bridge. The bridge looks at the routing tables for computer 3's LAN and sees that computer 4 is on that LAN, so the bridge filters out the data packet (drops it).

The second scenario is that a computer may send a packet to another computer on a different LAN. For example, computer 7 sends a packet to computer 10. The packet is sent from 7 to the bridge. The bridge looks at the routing tables for computer 7's LAN, and does not see computer 10. It then broadcasts the data packet to the other two LANs. When the packet reaches each hub, the hub on each of the two LANs broadcasts the packet to all nodes on its LAN.

You can now clearly see why bridging does not work well with large networks (such as the Internet). Broadcasting messages over several large networks would produce much unnecessary traffic on these networks. Bridging is effective at separating high-volume areas on a LAN and works best when it is used to connect LANs that usually do not talk outside of their immediate network.

A switch, on the other hand, does not work by sending broadcast messages. Just like bridges, switches also keep tables of all the MAC addresses of all the devices connected to the switch. They use these tables to determine which path to use when sending packets.

In the example above, if computer 7 sends a packet to computer 10, the switch receives the packet because the hub on computer 7's network is broadcasting. Using the destination address in the header of the packet, the switch would refer to its tables and determine the LAN to which the packet is addressed. The switch then forwards the packet to the proper LAN, rather than broadcasting the packet to all the LANs.

Although the switch can send data to devices in the LANs to which it is connected, anything that needs to be sent outside of the immediate area must be sent through a router.

Routers

A **router**, shown in Figure 11-19 can also serve as a link between connected LANs. It can route data to the correct LAN in a way that is similar to a switch's method.

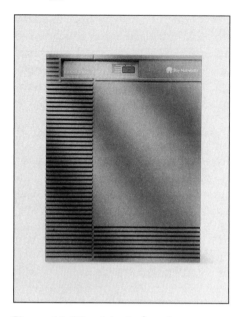

Figure 11-19   A typical router

However, a router can also forward a message to its correct destination over the most efficient available route to destinations far removed from the LANs it's connected to. Switches and bridges use MAC addresses to make decisions, but routers use IP addresses to determine the path to send a packet. The use of the IP address moves the router up the OSI model. It operates at level 3, Network layer, as shown in Figure 11-20.

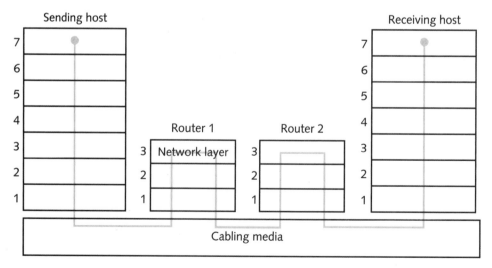

Figure 11-20   Routers work at the OSI layer 3, Network layer, where IP addresses are used to find the best route from source to destination

Like switches, routers use tables to determine the best route for the data to take to reach its destination. The difference is that the tables that the router creates and maintains are not limited to devices physically connected to the router, the tables contain IP addresses rather than MAC addresses, and the tables have all the available routes and their current conditions. This allows the routers to make much more sophisticated decisions when determining the path to send a packet.

When the router receives a packet, it first looks at the packet's destination address. Once it has the address, the router can use the tables and the current conditions of the network to decide which would be the best path for the packet to take. If there is not a good route directly to the destination, the router may forward the packet to another router. When a packet is being sent across a network, it may go through several routers. When a packet is sent from one router to another, this is called a **hop**.

Routers are usually found on complex networks that have multiple LANs, and they work well with Internet environments because they use IP addresses.

When routers communicate with other routers to build routing tables and determine availability of routes, four protocols are used: RIP, OSPF, BGP, or DVMRP. They all operate at the OSI Network layer and are very complex communication protocols.

- **RIP (Router Information Protocol)** is an older protocol used to build routing tables by broadcasting messages to all routers on the network. Entire routing tables are shared among routers using RIP.

- **OSPF (Open Shortest Path First)** was built to improve on the shortcomings of RIP. It uses multicasting instead of broadcasting to exchange routing information among routers. (Recall that broadcasting is indiscriminately sending data to every node on a network compared to multicasting which sends data to specific multiple nodes.) Instead of broadcasting entire routing tables, using OSPF, routers exchange information about these tables so they can build their own tables based on the shared information. Using OSPF, a router can get the information it needs from other routers to calculate the shortest path to send a packet across networks.

- **BGP (Border Gateway Protocol)** is used to manage data packets destined for remote locations of the Internet. It is sometimes called the long-distance protocol.

- **DVMRP (Distance Vector Multicast Routing Protocol)** is used for connectionless data packet delivery to a group of hosts.

Gateways

As discussed in Chapter 2, a gateway can refer to any device that acts as the entry or exit point for a network. In this definition, a router would be an example of a gateway. However, there is another use of the term gateway; a **gateway** allows you to connect networks that use different protocols (i.e., TCP/IP and IPX/SPX). The gateway converts the data as it is sent, so that it can be understood by the protocol of the receiving network.

11

One example of a gateway at work is shown in Figure 11-21. The e-mail system in the example is proprietary; it does not send messages in SMTP (Simple Mail Transfer Protocol). For the e-mail system to work, a gateway must be in place that acts as a translator and converts messages to and from SMTP format. In the example, the following process takes place when an e-mail is sent:

1. An e-mail message is sent from the e-mail client to the proprietary e-mail server.

2. The e-mail server sends the message to the Internet.

3. The gateway to the Internet translates the e-mail into SMTP.

4. The e-mail is then sent over the Internet.

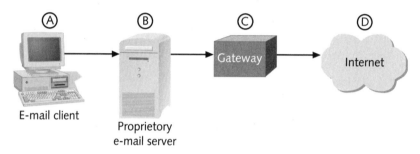

Figure 11-21   The gateway converts data so it can be understood by the receiving network

Gateways are a combination of hardware and software. A gateway may reside on a router, server, microcomputer, or mainframe. Different gateways translate different data. The example above discussed an e-mail gateway, but gateways can also be used to manage access between a LAN and the Internet, between a PC and a mainframe, or between different networks.

Internet-in-a-Box

An **Internet-in-a-box** device is becoming a popular Internet access solution for small businesses. These devices combine a variety of technologies, such as Internet connectivity, web access, e-mail, firewall, and other networking capabilities, into a single easy-to-manage unit.

Generally, a box comes with an internal expansion card to connect to your ISP (via modem, ISDN, DSL, etc.) and a network card to connect to the network hub. It has an embedded OS that manages the software servers that can include proxy, web, e-mail, DHCP, and DNS. It also can include a **cache-in-a-box**, which is both the hardware and software necessary to implement web caching for a network. Once a device is set up, it can be maintained through a web browser and can usually be managed with minimal training. Companies that manufacture Internet-in-a-box include eSoft, Inc. (*www.esoft.com*), Ramp Networks, Inc. (*www.webramp.com*), 3Com Corporation (*www.3com.com*), and Lucent Technologies (*www.lucent.com/ins*).

Team Internet, manufactured by eSoft, Inc., is an example of Internet-in-a-box; see Figure 11-22. It is simply a computer without a monitor or keyboard, but with a CPU, memory, and a hard drive that uses Linux as its operating system. The network administrator accesses the device using a browser from any workstation on the LAN.

Figure 11-22 Team Internet Model 100 Internet-in-a-box supports 2–25 workstations and serves as a router, firewall, e-mail server, and web server

11

In Figure 11-23 you can see the main menu of the Team Internet Model 100 administrative software. To access the menu, the administrator uses a browser to access the URL of the device like this: http://192.168.1.1:8000/. The IP address is that assigned the device and the controlling software running on the device is listening at port 8000. From this menu and its submenus, which are all web pages written in HTML, you can control the Model 100 software and the hardware.

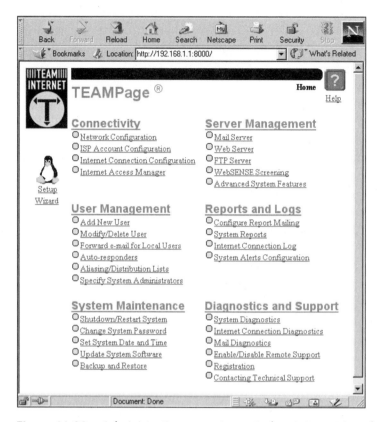

Figure 11-23   Administrative menu to control an Internet-in-a-box

Figure 11-24 shows the Network Configuration screen. On this screen you can change the IP address and subnet mask of the device, enable or disable the RIP protocol, and enable or disable the DHCP server. If the DHCP server is in operation, the administrator must provide a range of IP addresses it can assign to workstations logged into the LAN.

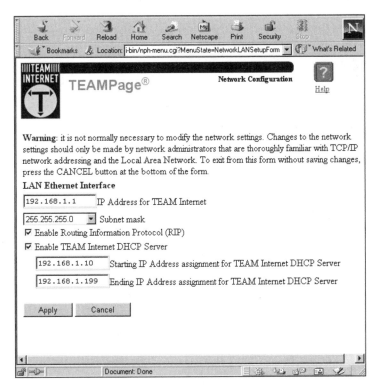

Figure 11-24 Network configuration screen for an Internet-in-a-box

On the Account Information screen shown in Figure 11-25, an administrator can set up a new e-mail account for a user, control the user's access to the Internet, and control the user's access to the LAN from a remote device such as a phone line. This last option is shown in Figure 11-25 as a drop-down menu labeled RAS Access, which stands for Remote Access Service.

Figure 11-25   Setting up a new user to access the Internet and have an e-mail account
using an Internet-in-a-box

If an administrator plans to use the Internet-in-a-box as a firewall, the box must be placed
between the LAN and the Internet connection. Otherwise, it can be set up as a computer
on the LAN. A box that is serving as a firewall must have two IP addresses assigned to it (public and private).

Figure 11-26 shows how an Internet-in-a-box can be used with a LAN. The computers on
the LAN are connected to the hub, which is connected to the Internet-in-a-box. When you
access the Internet from the LAN, your data must go through the Internet-in-a-box device,
which can serve the network as a proxy server.

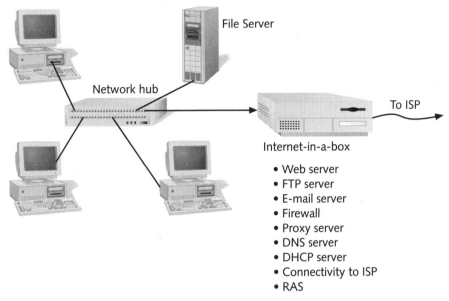

File Server

Network hub

To ISP

Internet-in-a-box

- Web server
- FTP server
- E-mail server
- Firewall
- Proxy server
- DNS server
- DHCP server
- Connectivity to ISP
- RAS

Figure 11-26   An Internet-in-a-box can provide a variety of services and is ideally suited to a small business requiring mild Internet access

11

WAN BANDWIDTH TECHNOLOGIES

Bandwidth refers to the capacity of a communications system to transmit data. The greater the bandwidth, the faster the communication. In digital systems, bandwidth is the measurement of data transmission in bits per second (bps). In analog systems, bandwidth measurement is the difference between the highest and lowest frequency that a device can transmit. Frequencies are measured in cycles per second, or hertz (Hz). Because computers are digital, they use bps to measure bandwidth.

Today's computer connections include several different bandwidth technologies. Chapter 1 covered the most common methods of connecting to an ISP, and the speeds that can be obtained. Technologies covered in Chapter 1 included POTS, DSL, cable modem, and satellite. These services are reasonably priced and are used in homes across the country. Other methods of connecting to the Internet are available that are not as reasonably priced for personal use and are more commonly found in businesses. Table 11-1 is a comprehensive list of all the available technologies. Additional details of the common technologies used today are found after the table.

Table 11-1   Common bandwidth technologies

Technology	Maximum Throughput Speeds	Common Uses
GSM mobile telephone service	9.6 to 14.4 Kbps	Wireless technology used for personal and business mobile telephones
Regular telephone(POTS)	Up to 56 Kbps	Home and small business access to an ISP using a modem
X.25	56 Kbps	Provides communication between mainframes and terminals.
ISDN	64 Kbps to 128 Kbps	Small to medium size business access to an ISP
IDSL	128 Kbps	(ISDN Digital Subscriber Line) Home and small business access to an ISP
DSL Lite or G.Lite	Up to 384 Kbps upstream and up to 6 Mbps downstream	Less expensive version of DSL
ADSL	640 Kbps upstream and up to 6.1 Mbps downstream	(Asymmetric Digital Subscriber Line) Most bandwidth is from ISP to user
SDSL	1.544 Mbps	(Symmetric DSL) Equal bandwidths in both directions
HDSL	Up to 3 Mbps	(High bit-rate DSL) Equal bandwidths in both directions
Cable modem	512 Kbps to 5 Mbps	Home or small business to ISP
VDSL	Up to 55 Mbps over short distances	(Very high data rate DSL) Future technology of DSL under development
Frame Relay	56 Kbps to 45 Mbps	Businesses that need to communicate internationally or across the country
Fractional T1	N times 64 Kbps (where n = number of channels or portions of a T1 leased)	Companies expecting to grow into a T1 line, but not yet ready for a T1
T1	1.544 Mbps	To connect large companies to branch offices or an ISP
Token Ring	4 or 16 Mbps	Used for local network
Ethernet	10 or 100 Mbps	Most popular technology for a local network
T3	45 Mbps	Large companies that require a lot of bandwidth and transmit extensive amounts of data
OC-1	52 Mbps	ISP to regional ISP
FDDI	100 Mbps	Supports network backbones from the 1980s and early 1990s. Also used to con-

Table 11-1   Common bandwidth technologies (continued)

Technology	Maximum Throughput Speeds	Common Uses
ATM	25, 45, 155, or 622 Mbps	Large business WANs and LAN backbones
OC-3	155 Mbps	Internet or large corporation backbone
Gigabit Ethernet	1 Gbps	New under-development technology
OC-24	1.23 Gbps	Internet backbone uses optical fiber
OC-256	13 Gbps	Major Internet backbone uses optical fiber
SONET	51, 155, 622, 1244, or 2480 Mbps	(Synchronous Optical Network) Major backbones

T Lines and E Lines

The first successful system that supported digitized voiced transmission was introduced in the 1960's and was called a T-carrier. A **T-carrier** works with a leased digital communications line provided through a common carrier such as BellSouth or AT&T. Although it was originally intended for voice, the line also works with data. The system has grown to become a popular choice for Internet access for larger companies. The leased lines are permanent connections that use **multiplexing**, a process of dividing a single channel into multiple channels that can be used to carry voice, data, video, or other signals. There are several variations of T-carrier lines; the most popular are T1 and T3 lines. For a T1 line, multiplexing allows the line to carry 24 channels, and each channel is capable of transmitting 64 Kbps. So, a T1 line can transmit a total of 1.544 Mbps. If a T1 is used for voice only, it can support 24 separate phone lines, one for each channel. A T3 line can carry 672 channels, giving it a throughput of 44.736 Mbps. T1 and T3 lines can be used by a business to support both voice and data, with some channels allocated to voice and others to data.

The E-carrier is the European equivalent of the American T-carrier. The E-carrier is a digital transmission format devised by ITU (International Telecommunications Union; for more information, see *www.itu.int*). An E1 line can transmit data at a rate of 2.048 Mbps, and an E3 line can work at speeds of 34.368 Mbps.

Both T-carriers and E-carriers use four wires, two for receiving and two for sending. Originally, copper wires were used (telephone wiring), but digital signals require a clearer connection, so shielded twisted-pair wiring is preferred. The carriers need repeaters that can regenerate the signal every 6,000 feet. Businesses with multiple T1s generally use coaxial, fiber optic, or microwave cabling. With T3, microwave or fiber optic is required.

A **fractional T1 line** is an option for organizations that don't need a full T1 line. The fractional T1 allows businesses to lease some of the channels of a T1 line rather than leasing all 24 channels. This type of arrangement is also good for businesses who expect to grow into a T1 line eventually. Because each T1 channel has a throughput of 64 Kbps, a fractional T1 can be leased in 64 Kbps increments.

X.25 and Frame Relay

Both **X.25** and **frame relay** are packet-switching communication protocols designed for long distance data transmission. As you recall from earlier chapters, packet switching technology divides data into packets and sends each packet separately; it is the technology used by the Internet. Remember too, that each packet may be sent on a different path. This technology works well because it can use the bandwidth more efficiently.

Frame relay is based on X.25, but it is a digital version, whereas X.25 is an analog technology. Because frame relay is digital, it can support higher throughput of up to 1.544Mbps, compared to X.25 which supports up to 56 Kbps. X.25 was popular for about 20 years and was the most common packet switching technology used on WANs. Frame relay, which was standardized in 1984, began replacing the X.25, but new technology is already being created that is replacing frame relay.

Both X.25 and frame relay use **Permanent Virtual Circuits** (**PVC**). PVC is a permanent logical connection between two nodes. PVCs are not dedicated lines, like the T-carriers. Rather, when you lease a PVC, you specify the nodes (two end points) and the amount of bandwidth required, but the carrier reserves the right to send the data along any number of paths between the two stationary end points. You then share the bandwidth with other users that lease the X.25 or frame relay.

The biggest advantage of X.25 and frame relay is that you only have to pay for the amount of bandwidth you require. Frame relay is also less expensive than newer technologies available, and it has worldwide standards already established. But because both X.25 and frame relay use shared lines, throughput decreases as traffic increases.

Circuits for X.25 are not readily available in North America, but frame relay circuits can be found fairly easily. International businesses that communicate oversees may use frame relay to connect offices.

ATM

Asynchronous Transfer Mode (**ATM**) is a very fast network technology that can be used with LANs as well as WANs. It uses fixed-length packets, called **cells**, to transmit data, voice, video, and frame relay traffic. Each cell is 53 bytes, 48 bytes of data plus a 5 byte header. The header contains the information necessary to route the packet. Because all the packets used by ATM are the same size, it is easy to determine the number of packets and the traffic flow, which helps utilize bandwidth.

ATMs also use virtual circuits, meaning that the two end points are stationary, but the paths between these two end points can change. They can use either PVCs or **switched virtual circuits (SVCs)**. SVCs are logical point-to-point connections that depend on the ATM to decide the best path to send the data. The routes are determined before the data is even sent. In contrast, an Ethernet transmits the data before determining the route it will take; the routers and switches are responsible for deciding the paths.

ATMs achieve a throughput of 622 Mbps, which make them popular for large LANs because they are faster then Ethernet at 100 Mbps. An ATM network works best with fiber-optic cable so that it can attain high throughputs, but it will also work with coaxial cable or twisted pair.

TYING IT ALL TOGETHER

This section uses all the different components of a network infrastructure in a real-life example of how a small business built a network with Internet access for all employees using the LAN. The company, the Customer Retention Group, LLC, (*www.crg10.com*) is a small start-up company that provides services to businesses to help the business retain its customers. The service is labor intensive, in part because it includes providing handwritten thank you notes and personal phone calls to clients' customers. The business also wants to allow its employees to telecommute, accessing the database of customers from their homes using a dial-up phone line connection. The company turned to Omega Computer Systems, Inc. (*www.omegacomputers.com*) for a networking solution, and to a local freelance software developer for their database solution.

As you work your way through this example, note the order in which decisions were made. First, the goals of the business and the business needs were defined. These business needs drove every other decision. Second, the software was designed to meet the business goals and needs, and third, the hardware infrastructure was designed to support the software needs. This order is important because too often in the decision making process, technology, rather than business needs drives the process, which is like the proverbial tail wagging the dog.

Business needs and goals as they apply to the company's technology infrastructure were:

- Provide the tools needed for employees to service customers; the tools are primarily a database of activities to perform and methods to report and track those activities

- Provide a way for business clients to update their customer list on the Internet

- Provide a way for employees to telecommute with access to the database

- Provide Internet access to every employee workstation at the primary work location

- Allow for growth

- Keep initial expenses to a minimum

11

The applications software to meet these goals was designed to meet the immediate and future business needs and to be implemented in three phases:

- Build an inexpensive database that would be used initially just on the LAN with a user interface on each PC. The database selected was Microsoft FoxPro with a user interface built with Visual Basic.

- As soon as the customer base merits it, make a portion of the database accessible to the Internet using ASP technology with ODBC access to the FoxPro database. Use a web hosting service for the initial web deployment. (Recall from Chapter 7 that ODBC is a way to connect to a database using ASP server side scripts.)

- As soon as volume on the LAN and the Internet merits it, convert the database to SQL Server.

Based on the business needs, software design, and database design, Omega Computer Systems recommended building an Ethernet LAN with an ISDN line to a local ISP for Internet access using the components outlined below. The components are illustrated in Figure 11-27.

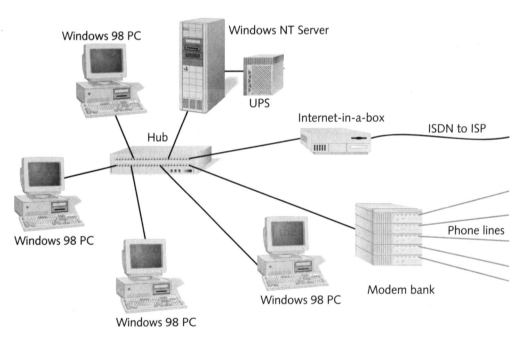

Figure 11-27   A solution for a small business LAN includes an Internet-in-a-box with an ISDN connection to an ISP

- **Server:** Hewlett Packard E60 Pentium III, 500 MHz server with 128 MB of installed RAM and a tape backup system using Windows NT Server as the network operating system

- **Workstations on the LAN:** PCs with 400MHz Celeron processors with 64 MB of installed RAM

- **Internet-in-a-box:** A Team Internet device from eSoft, Inc. with an ISDN connection for Internet services

- **Modem bank for telecommuters:** Shiva LANRover E/Plus modem bank that can support 24 ports, but initially installed with one 4-port modem card

- **UPS:** (A UPS is a device that provides power when the electricity goes off) APC Smart-UPS 700

- **Printers**: Okidata Okipage 18N laser printer and Hewlett Packard Deskjet 830C

The Team Internet device from eSoft, Inc. (*www.esoft.com*) is the Model 100 and is shown in Figure 11-22. It provides Internet services to workstations on the LAN. The device has an RJ-45 port to connect to an Ethernet LAN and an ISDN connection going to an ISP and on to the Internet. It uses the Linux operating system and can be remotely set up and managed using a web browser from any user's PC on the LAN. The device offers these services:

- An e-mail server capable of supporting most e-mail client software. Also uses LDAP to allow you to view all the directories of e-mail accounts.

- WebSense software, which does content filtering to limit web surfing by LAN users

- Built-in firewall which can inspect incoming data packets to determine if they have been requested by an authorized user on the LAN

- Squid software, a proxy server that caches FTP files and web pages to speed up response time. The proxy server makes it possible to use private IP addressing on the LAN

- Third party Virtual Private Networking (PPTP) servers (VPN and PPTP are discussed in Chapter 12)

- Apache web server for Internet/intranet web sites

- FTP server with space for file storage

- DHCP server which can be disabled for static IP addressing on the LAN

- DNS server for all clients on the LAN

- Remote Access Service (RAS) so that a user can dial into the LAN from a computer using a regular phone line.

11

Omega Computers agreed to install the complete solution, get everything configured and running properly, and train the CRG staff in their use. Omega Computers also recommended another vendor to install the network cabling, a service that included the cabling, one hub, and labor. Windows NT Server was selected as the NOS because there was no one technical onsite, and it would be easier to train a non-technical person to administer the LAN using Windows NT Server rather than other solutions. Omega Computers would serve as the technical support to the LAN and NOS when needed.

Two ISDN lines served for both data and voice communication. The local ISP provided access to the Internet, but another service was selected for the web hosting service because the local ISP did not support ASP, ODBC, SQL Server or FoxPro.

Six workstations were initially planned, but the LAN is expected to eventually support up to 30 workstations. It was agreed that when it reached this many workstations, it might be necessary to add a bridge or switch to segment the network in order to improve performance.

Because the company wanted to begin small, the installation was done in stages:

Stage 1: A simple peer-to-peer network was installed using the cabling with hub and four workstations using Windows 98. An ISDN device connected to one workstation gave Internet access to just this one workstation. Occasionally, when another PC needed Internet access, the user would use a modem and regular phone line to dial up the ISP. One PC on the LAN held the FoxPro database and shared it with other PCs on the LAN. Some PCs had printers installed locally. Each PC with a printer shared it with others on the LAN.

Stage 2: New workstations were added as new employees were hired. The Team Internet device was added to manage Internet access, and the ISDN device was no longer needed. The LAN was still administered as a peer-to-peer network and one PC was still used as the database server.

Stage 3: The Windows NT server was installed to hold the database and administer the LAN, and the modem bank was added.

Stage 4: The database was converted from FoxPro to SQL Server. The front-end application to the database for LAN users and the web site scripts were converted to interface with SQL Server instead of FoxPro. Because ODBC was used as the interface tool between the software and the database, the conversion went very quickly.

REAL PEOPLE, REAL PROBLEMS, REAL SOLUTIONS
INCREASING THE PIPE

Leslie German needed more bandwidth. His growing law firm was relying more and more on the Internet to conduct day-to-day business. The firm had grown from a staff of 25 to over 40 in just six months, and every employee was connected through the local network to the Internet.

Leslie managed and administered the law firm's local network. He could see that users were beginning to take advantage of Internet video conferencing, uploading and downloading large amounts of data, and generally pushing the limit of their 128K ISDN connection. With more users expected over the next six months, he knew it was time to look at·other means of connecting to the Internet.

Since the time that Leslie had the ISDN line installed, new options had been introduced for connectivity. Some of them were scalable, some of them not. Most were expensive and would need drastic changes in budgetary planning. He narrowed his options to a fractional T1, frame relay, and SDSL.

Installing a T1 line seemed like a good choice, especially because he could purchase bandwidth in levels of usage. The connection was reliable and could be in use for a long time to come. The disadvantage was cost. Installing a T1 meant a very large expenditure for new routing and switching equipment.

Frame relay, after taking a closer look, didn't make much sense. The law firm had just purchased a new telephone system that did not involve frame relay in any aspect. The feature that is one of the attractive aspects of frame relay is the ability to mesh telecommunications with connectivity. In Leslie's case, it didn't make a difference. Frame relay systems also performed best when there were multiple locations involved—the law firm had no plans for opening offices in other locations. And again, cost was a factor.

The third choice was SDSL. Although it was a newer technology, it made sense. Leslie would not have to make major changes to network hardware, other than the router. Levels of bandwidth could be purchased in levels, much like a T1. The SDSL connection was consistent, constant, and digital. On top of these advantages, the cost was a fraction of a T1 or frame relay.

Leslie made the choice to replace the existing ISDN line with SDSL. A 384K level was purchased initially. The law firm was able to implement the new connection with no change to workstations, and instantly realized the benefits of more bandwidth!

11

CHAPTER SUMMARY

- The two approaches to managing network resources are peer-to-peer and client/server.

- In peer-to-peer networking, all the computers on the LAN have the same authority, and each can act as a server to all the other computers.

- The client/server networking model has one or more computers that manage network resources for all other computers on the network. These servers require a network operating system.

- Windows 9x is a low-level OS primarily used for personal computers.

- Windows NT offers two operating systems: Windows NT Workstation and Windows NT Server.

- Linux is a scaled-down version of UNIX and is small enough to run on a 486 computer, but has network capabilities similar to a full-fledged commercial version of UNIX.

- Windows NT has one computer that is designated the PDC (primary domain controller), which stores a database of user accounts, group accounts, and computer accounts.

- Windows 2000 includes four operating systems: Windows 2000 Professional, Windows 2000 Server, Windows 2000 Advanced Server, and Windows 2000 Datacenter Server.

- Novell Netware is a popular NOS that can provide fast file and database access.

- Novell Netware uses a suite of protocols called IPX/SPX, which generally correspond to the TCP/IP protocols.

- The underlying structure of the network is determined by the network technology. The three most popular physical network technologies are Ethernet, Token Ring, and Fiber Distributed Data Interface (FDDI).

- The most popular network technology used today is Ethernet, which can be configured either as a star or bus.

- Ethernet is a passive network, which means that the networked computers originate the signals that manage the network (rather than a dedicated device).

- A collision occurs when two computers try to transmit data at the same time over the same line.

- A Network Interface Card (NIC) is used to connect a computer to a LAN.

- Repeaters are used to amplify or retransmit a signal when it is being sent over long distances.

- A Token Ring network uses a token to transmit data. Data is added to the token as the token passes around the ring of computers.

- Bridges and switches both use the MAC address to determine where to send packets.

❏ A bridge broadcasts messages to all networks to which it is connected.

❏ Switches use routing tables to determine where a packet should be sent based on its MAC address.

❏ Packet-switching divides data into packets (or segments) and sends each packet independently.

❏ Routers use IP addresses to determine paths to send packets.

❏ Gateways work as a combination of hardware and software to connect two networks of different protocols.

❏ Web caching can be used to store frequently used web pages in a temporary place to decrease download time.

❏ Bandwidth is the transmission speed of data.

❏ T-carriers work with leased digital lines and use multiplexing, a process of dividing a single channel into multiple channels that can be used to carry voice, data, or video.

❏ X.25 and frame relay are both packet switching communication protocols. X.25 is analog and can handle a throughput of 56 Kbps, whereas frame relay, which is digital, can support up to 1.544 Mbps.

❏ ATM (asynchronous transfer mode) sends data in fixed-sized cells (53 bytes).

11

KEY TERMS

100BaseFX — A variation of 100BaseT that supports fiber optic cable.

100BaseT — An Ethernet standard that operates at 100 Mbps and uses STP cabling. Also called Fast Ethernet.

10Base2 — An Ethernet standard that operates at 10 Mbps and uses small coaxial cable up to 200 meters long. Also called Thinnet.

10Base5 — An Ethernet standard that operates at 10 Mbps and uses thick coaxial cable up to 500 meters long. Also called Thicknet.

amplifier repeater — A repeater that does not distinguish between noise and signal. It amplifies both.

ATM (asynchronous transfer mode) — Network technology that uses cells of a fixed length to transmit data.

bandwidth — The transmission speed of data.

(BDC) backup domain controller — A server on a Windows NT network that contains a read-only copy of the domain database.

BGP (Border Gateway Protocol) — A routing protocol used by routers to manage data packets destined for remote locations of the Internet. It is sometimes called the long-distance protocol.

BNC connector — A connector used with coaxial cable. It is often called a T-connector because of the T shape. The long end of the T connects to the NIC and the two short ends can connect to cable or end a bus formation with a terminator.

bus topology — A LAN in which all the devices are connected to a bus, or one communication line. Bus topology does not have a central connection point.

cache-in-a-box — The hardware and software necessary to implement web and FTP caching for a network.

CAU (controlled-access unit) — *See* MSAU.

cells — Used in ATMs, cells are packets of data that are a fixed length of 53 bytes.

client/server model — A network of computers that have one or more computers that control the resources for all computers on the network. Also called domain model.

coaxial cable — Networking cable used with 10-Mbps Ethernet

collision — When two computers send a signal on the same channel at the same time.

contention-based — A network system in which each computer on the system must compete for the opportunity to transmit a signal on the network.

CSMA/CD (Carrier Sense Multiple Access with Collision Detection) — A protocol that Ethernet networks use to monitor the network to determine if the line is free before sending a transmission.

data throughput — The measurement of data capacity, stated in bits per second (bps), thousands of bits per second (Kbps), or millions of bits per second (Mbps).

domain controller — A server on a Windows NT network that contains a database of user accounts and passwords that controls access to the network.

domain — In Windows NT, a logical group of networked computers, such as those on a college campus, that share a centralized directory database of user account information and security for the entire domain.

domain model — *See* client-server model.

DVMRP (Distance Vector Multicast Routing Protocol) — A routing protocol used by routers for connectionless data packet delivery to a group of hosts.

FDDI (fiber distributed data interface) — A ring-based network that does not require a centralized hub and can transfer data at a rate of 100 Mbps.

fractional T1 line — A T1 line that has more than one company leasing the line. Each company is given a specific number of channels, totaling 24.

frame relay — A packet-switching communication protocol that uses digital technology, which can support data transmission speeds of up to 1.544 Mbps.

gateway — (1) Any device that acts as the entry or exit point for a network. (2) A device that allows two networks of different protocols to be connected.

hop — The trip a packet makes between two routers or a router and its final destination.

hub — A device used to join or connect all the nodes of a LAN in a star formation.

Internet-in-a-box — A device that acts as web server, e-mail server, and basic network server to provide Internet access.

IPX/SPX (Internetwork Packet Exchange/Sequenced Packet Exchange) — Protocol used by Novell Netware, which corresponds to the TCP/IP protocols.

kernel — Core portion of an operating system that loads applications and manages files, memory, and other resources.

LAN (local area network) — A network that covers a relatively small geographical area.

MAU (multistation access unit) — *See* MSAU.

MSAU (multistation access unit) — A centralized hub used in token ring networks to connect stations. Also called CAU and MAU.

multiplexing — The process of dividing a single channel into multiple channels that can carry voice, data, video, or other signals.

NADN (nearest active downstream neighbor) — In a token ring environment, the station that receives the token just after the current station.

NAUN (nearest active upstream neighbor) — In a token ring environment, the station that receives the token just prior to the current station.

network architecture — The overall design of a network. It includes hardware, software, and protocols.

node — Any computer, workstation, or device on a network.

NOS (network operating system) — An operating system that resides on the controlling computer in the network. The NOS controls what software, data, and devices a user can access.

OSPF (Open Shortest Path First) — A routing protocol built to improve on the shortcomings of RIP, used by routers that use multicasting instead of broadcasting to exchange routing information among routers.

PDC (primary domain controller) — Used in Windows NT, the server that stores and controls a database of user accounts, group accounts, and computer accounts.

peer-to-peer model — A network of computers that are all equals, or peers. Each computer has the same amount of authority and each can act as a server to the other computers.

protected mode — A mode of CPU operation. When a CPU operates in protected mode, it accesses memory and the hard drive indirectly, using a 32-bit data path.

PVC (permanent virtual circuit) — A permanent logical connection between two nodes or fixed end points that allows data to follow any number of paths when being transmitted.

real mode — A mode of CPU operation. When a CPU operates in real mode, it accesses memory and the hard drive directly, using a 16-bit data path.

repeater — A device that amplifies signals on a network so they can be transmitted further down the line.

RIP (Router Information Protocol) — An older routing protocol used by routers to build routing tables by broadcasting messages to all routers on the network.

RJ-45 connector — An attachment used with UTP (Unshielded Twisted Pair cable) that connects the cable to the NIC.

11

router — A device used on networks to send packets across multiple networks, finding the best available route.

SAM (security accounts manager) — Used in Windows NT, the database of user accounts, group accounts, and computer accounts.

segmentation — When a larger network is divided into smaller segments to increase speed and reliability.

shell — An operating system component responsible for providing an interface for users to enter OS commands.

signal-regenerating repeater — A repeater that is able to distinguish between noise and signal. It reads the signal and retransmits the signal without the accompanying noise.

SMAU (smart multistation access unit) — *See* MSAU.

star topology — A LAN in which all the devices are connected to a central hub.

STP (shielded twisted-pair) — A cable that is made of one or more twisted pairs of wires, which is surrounded by a metal shield.

SVC (switched virtual circuit) — A logical point-to-point connection that depends on switches to decide the best path to send the data. ATM uses SVC.

T-carrier — A system that provides leased digital communications lines through a common carrier such as Bell Atlantic or MCI; typically used for voice and data transmission.

thicknet — *See* 10Base5 Ethernet.

thinnet — *See* 10Base2 Ethernet.

token — A frame that is used on token ring networks to send data from one station to the next.

topology — The arrangement used to connect nodes on a LAN, either in a star or a bus function.

UTP (unshielded twisted-pair) — A cable that is made of one or more twisted pairs of wires, which is not surrounded by a metal shield. Compare to STP.

X.25 — A packet-switching communication protocol which uses analog technology and which can support data transmission speeds of up to 56 Kbps.

REVIEW QUESTIONS

1. Name the three most popular network technologies for local networks.
2. What is the difference between 100BaseT and 100BaseFX?
3. How is a bus topology different from a star toplogy?
4. Does a hub interpret the data that it transmits between computers?
5. How does Ethernet work?
6. When is a repeater needed for a 10BaseT Ethernet cable?
7. Explain how data is transmitted in a Token Ring environment.
8. What does FDDI stand for?

9. Explain the difference between a peer-to-peer model network and client-server model network?

10. What is the primary function of a NOS on a network?

11. List four popular operating systems for personal computers today.

12. What does the NT in Windows NT stand for? Why did it get this name?

13. How would you determine if your hardware is compatible with Windows NT?

14. What is the average price of Linux?

15. When selecting a NOS, what is important to consider?

16. What information does a PDC store?

17. IPX/SPX are used by which NOS?

18. What is the difference between a bridge and switch?

19. Explain packet-switching.

20. What is a hop? What device counts hops?

21. What is the advantage for a company to get a fractional T1 line over a regular T1 line?

22. What are PVC and SVC?

23. What is the cell size for ATM technology?

24. What is the purpose of RAS?

25. Which is faster, T3 or OC-3?

11

HANDS-ON PROJECTS

Internet-in-a-box

The chapter highlighted an Internet-in-a-box device from eSoft, Inc., Team Internet Model 100. Find another example of an Internet-in-a-box from another vendor that offers comparable features to the Model 100. Print web pages describing the box and list the features available. Include how an administrator would access software to control the box.

Research Linux

1. What is the official mascot for Linux? Who chose it and why?

2. Find a web site from which you can download a free version of Linux and print the web page that allows you to download the OS. What organization makes the OS available for downloading?

3. Find a web site that gives you the instructions for installing Linux. Print these instructions.

Research LAN Hardware

Your company is installing a LAN and has asked you to research the purchase of a hub. The hub should work on an Ethernet LAN that will contain 100BaseT devices and slower 10-Mpbs devices all using Cat-5 cable. The hub should support up to 30 devices. Give your employer three options to choose from. Include the web site, vendor, model, model features, and price for each of the three selections. Print the web page for each selection.

Installing a PC on a LAN

Your employer has asked you to install a PC on the company's LAN. The PC does not have a NIC installed, so the first job is to research and purchase a NIC. The LAN is Ethernet using UTP cabling with an RJ-45 connection. Give your employer three options for purchase. Include the least expensive NIC you can find. What features does it lack compared to more expensive versions?

CASE PROJECT

Link to Information about Internet Connectivity Devices

Build a new web page on your personal web site and create a link to it from your home page. Label the linked page "Information about the Internet." On the web page, put links to the following web sites. Include on the page a sentence or two about the link.

- A local provider of cable modem.

- A local provider of DSL

- A manufacturer of a router showing information about the router

- A manufacturer of an Ethernet hub showing information about the hub

- A manufacturer of a network interface card showing information about the card

Print the source code for the home page and the new web page and print the browser screen displaying each page.

12

INTERNET SECURITY

In this chapter, you will learn

♦ About the different ways that computers and networks can be attacked

♦ How to safeguard a network's resources from unauthorized access

♦ How to protect your own privacy when you access the Internet from your home computer

♦ What virtual private networks are and how they ensure a secure connection so that data can be transmitted over the Internet

In the last chapter, you learned about network architectures and how to set up a LAN so that users can have access to different devices and files. In this chapter, you will learn how to protect your network so that the wrong people cannot gain access to private information. This chapter discusses the different ways that people illegally intrude on a network, and what a damaging effect it can have. You will then learn how you can protect both your network's information and your personal information from intruders through methods such as installing firewalls, using intrusion detection software, and implementing authentication systems. The chapter also covers virtual private networks, what they are, and how they provide secure transactions across the Internet.

TYPES OF INTRUSION

Everybody is talking about Internet security. Interest in this topic is at an all-time high, as Internet users and developers alike grapple with the challenges of providing easy access to information while still maintaining a user's privacy. Recently the magazine *PC Week* (*www.pcweek.com*) created a special web site and invited hackers to try to penetrate it. The web site, which is no longer active, ran on Linux and Windows NT servers with all the standard security features: a firewall, an intrusion detection system, and a locked-down server. All the precautions that would be initiated by a security-conscious company were put in place on the web site. The magazine then issued a press release inviting the public to break into the site.

Only seven minutes after the press release hit the wire, the magazine registered the first attempt at hacking the site. Several approaches were made to penetrate the web site, and it took the successful hacker only 20 hours to break into the site and change the home page to read "This site has been hacked. JFS was here." Although most people do not have the knowledge to hack into a site like the one created by *PC Week*, enough people do, and as a consequence, security is of top concern to most network administrators.

Hackers usually attack a site for one of two reasons: to disable the site or to obtain information. Their reasons for wanting to attack a site vary. Some hackers are just intrigued by the challenge. Others are looking for revenge. Still others want to find information to sell. First, let's look at some of the types of intrusion. Later in the chapter you will learn ways to protect yourself from intrusions.

Flooding

A common type of security breech is known as flooding. Flooding attacks usually render the server unable to function. Flooding is a type of Denial of Service attack. **Denial of Service (DoS)** attacks overload the server with false requests so that the server is unable to process actual requests. Or, if the server still can process requests, its performance is too slow to be beneficial. In early 2000, a series of DoS attacks disabled many of the Internet's top web sites including Yahoo!, eBay, CNN.com, Amazon.com, and Buy.com. Several types of flooding attacks are described in the following sections.

SYN Flooding

SYN flooding gets its name because it takes advantage of the synchronization feature of TCP. Recall from earlier chapters that the TCP protocol is responsible for managing the delivery of packets between client and server. When a client attempts to communicate with a server, TCP first attempts to establish communication between the two computers using what is called a "TCP three-way handshake." Once the handshake is completed, the client and server are free to communicate data back and forth. The handshake goes like this, and is illustrated in Figure 12-1:

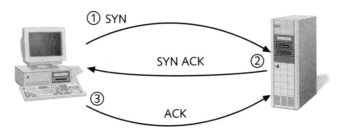

Figure 12-1   In a normal SYN operation, TCP on the client and the server uses a three-step handshake to establish a TCP connection

1. *TCP on the client sends a SYN (synchronize start) packet to TCP on the server.* The packet contains the source (client) IP address and the destination (server) IP address.

2. *TCP on the server responds with a SYN ACK (synchronize acknowledge).* When the server receives the SYN packet, it responds to the source IP address with a SYN ACK packet and creates an entry in a queue for not-yet-completed connections. This queue of half-completed connections can hold from six to 128 connection entries depending on the operating system and its settings. Windows NT normally can hold 6 entries and UNIX normally holds 32 entries. These entries are expected to last only a few milliseconds until the handshake is completed, although an entry in the queue can remain there up to about one minute, again depending on operating system settings. If the server does not hear back from the client, after the one minute expires, the entry is deleted.

3. *TCP on the client completes the handshake by sending an ACK (acknowledge) packet to the destination server.* When the client receives the SYN ACK packet from the server, it completes the handshake with an ACK to the server. When the server receives this packet, the connection is complete and the entry is removed from the pending-connections queue. The two computers are then free to begin transmitting data.

A SYN flood is illustrated in Figure 12-2. When the first computer sends the initial SYN packet to begin the TCP connection process, instead of sending its own IP address as the source IP address in the data packet, it supplies an invalid IP address that cannot be accessed. When the server responds with the SYN ACK packet, it responds to an IP address that seems valid, but is not available. The server keeps trying to send the packet and waits for a response until the pending connection times out and the entry in the pending queue is deleted, which can last up to a minute. In the meantime, the server is being flooded with other false SYN packets—as many as 200 per second. The server cannot keep up with the requests, and the buffer of pending connections fills. When legitimate users try to access the server, they are denied access because of the congestion.

12

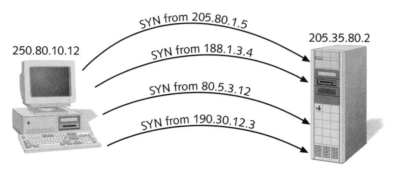

Figure 12-2   In a SYN flood, a server is flooded with TCP handshake requests from many false IP addresses

If the invalid source IP address is consistently the same IP address for all the TCP handshake requests, it might be possible to track the attack back to its source, using tracing tools that are discussed in the next chapter. However, to make the attack more effective, the hacker usually inserts a different source IP address in the SYN packet for each request. Therefore, each packet appears to be coming from a different inaccessible IP address. This way, the attempts to connect appear to be coming from all over the Internet, and are very difficult, if not impossible, to trace to the source. The only way to trace the packets is to go through all segments of the Internet between the source and the target, which is difficult since each segment may have a different owner. And because SYN flood attacks, unlike other flood attacks, require only minimal bandwidth, the SYN flood does not put a strain on any devices between the source computer and the target computer, making the attack unnoticed by each segment of the network.

In addition, hackers sometimes find security weaknesses in servers in different locations on the Internet and use these servers to initiate their attacks. Rather than the attack coming from only one physical source, which might be traceable, the attack comes from several sources from around the world. Figure 12-3 illustrates this point. The owners of these sources are not aware that their servers are being used to initiate a DoS attack because the processes are automated and not visible to system administrators monitoring these servers. Later in the chapter you'll read about how a hacker can find and use these servers with security weaknesses. SYN flooding requires that the hacker understand how TCP connections work and be able to program changes to the headers of TCP/IP packets.

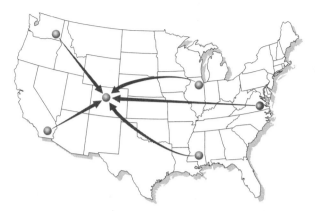

Figure 12-3 Hackers can use unsuspecting servers with weak security to initiate a DoS attack causing the attack to come from many areas of the country

Ping Flooding

Ping (which stands for **Packet InterNet Groper**) is a simple program that allows one computer to send a packet to another computer and then receive a reply. Ping is a simple tool used to discover if another computer is available for communication on a TCP/IP network. The name comes from submarine sonar, which broadcasts a signal, called a ping, that hits surrounding objects and makes a sound revealing the object's size and position. The ping program is a very helpful program for debugging network problems, but it also can be dangerous when hackers decide to implement a ping flood.

Ping flooding (also known as **ICMP flooding**) is when a host is flooded with ping requests. As the host tries to respond to the requests, it gets bogged down and cannot function, causing DoS. This type of flooding is fairly common because it does not require a lot of special knowledge. A variation of ping flooding is the **Ping of death** attack, which occurs when a hacker uses the ping protocol to send a packet that is larger than the standard 64 bytes. Most systems cannot handle packets larger than 64 bytes and will completely shut down when hit with the ping of death.

Figure 12-4 shows an example of the ping command. You can try using it yourself. You must be connected to the Internet to ping another computer on the Internet. Follow these directions:

1. Using Windows, click **Start** on the Taskbar and point to **Programs**, and then click **MS-DOS prompt**. Windows opens the MS-DOS command entry window.

2. At the command prompt, type **ping** followed by a space and the domain name or IP address. For example to ping buystory.com, type **ping buystory.com**. The buystory.com server responds. Information about the communication displays in the MS-DOS command window. This information includes the IP address of the server.

12

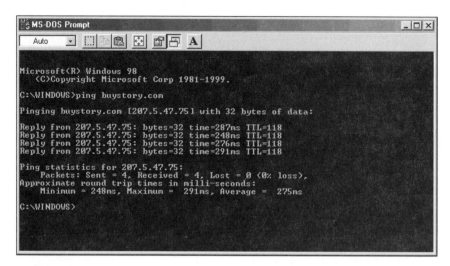

Figure 12-4   Ping can be used to test the connection between two parts of a network

Mail Flooding

Another type of flooding that can result in DoS is **mail flooding**. Mail flooding is when hackers send numerous huge e-mail messages to an e-mail server. As the server receives all the messages, it runs out of disk space, which causes the system to crash.

Spam is a form of mail flooding. **Spam** is unsolicited e-mail messages that are usually trying to sell a product, and are sent in bulk. Spam can quickly fill mailboxes. Many e-mail systems allot only a limited amount of hard drive space for each mailbox. When the mailboxes fill with spam, legitimate messages are rejected.

Spam has become such a nuisance to computer users that many e-mail systems offer spam rejection services. When a user receives spam, he can indicate that he does not wish to receive any more messages from the sender by sending a message to the e-mail system (usually by forwarding the original message to a special mailbox). The e-mail system then automatically sends a message to the return address on the spam message requesting that no more messages be sent. From that point on, all e-mail messages sent with a return address that is the same as the address on the spam message are rejected, and the user never sees the messages.

Free e-mail systems are often targets for mail flooding. One example of mail flooding happened to Australia's free e-mail provider *freemail.com.au*. A hacker sent a large number of junk e-mail messages to users all over the world selling a wide variety of products—everything from hair-loss treatments to Viagra. The hacker used a string of meaningless characters at *freemail.com.au* as the return address on the junk e-mail messages. When people received these annoying messages, they replied with a spam rejection message. The spam-rejection responses to a non-existent address flooded Freemail's system. They received 60 million messages in a 48 hour period. (On a normal day, they receive between 400,000 and 500,000 messages.) The servers were so busy sorting through e-mails addressed to a fictional user at *freemail.com.au*, that legitimate messages could not get through.

Data Theft

Hackers often want to steal information from a network. For example, if a thief knows that the network has a database of customers that includes credit card information, he may want to steal the account information for personal use. Or if an ex-employee has found a job with a competitor, she may want to get data to share with her new employer. No matter what the reason, if data gets into the wrong hands, it can cause a company to lose its business.

How do people break into a network and steal information? They often monitor the network until they find an opening. Once they have an opening or a port that will allow access to the network, they can install programs that allow them future access to the files, and they can scan the network for user IDs and passwords. If they find a working user ID and password, they can sign onto the network and appear as a legitimate user, when they are really stealing information.

Hackers can also try to intercept data as it is transmitted across the network, an attack known as **man in the middle**. The man in the middle attacks can include the interception of e-mails, files, chat dialogs, and other data. In addition to stealing information, the hacker may intercept and change the data and then send it on its way. This causes problems because it may take some time before someone notices the change. For example, many companies today allow customers to order merchandise from their web sites. These companies often have the whole process of receiving an order, preparing a packing slip, and processing the charges done electronically. If a disgruntled employee drastically lowers the price of a product, it may take some time before the company notices the change. In the meantime, the company is losing money each time that product is sold over the Internet.

Computer Infestations

The intrusions discussed so far have the intent of halting resources or stealing data. Another type of intrusion is a virus. A **virus** is a program that can replicate itself by attaching itself to other programs. Viruses usually spread through infected e-mail messages that arrive with a virus in an attachment. The infected program must be executed for the virus to execute. When a virus executes, it may simply replicate itself, or it may also cause harm to a system by immediately performing some damaging action. A virus may be programmed so that it is triggered to perform a negative action at some future point in time, such as on a particular date (for instance, Friday the 13th).

A virus is different from a **worm**, which is a program that spreads copies of itself throughout the network without needing a host program. A **Trojan horse** is a third type of computer infestation that, like a worm, does not need a host program to work—rather, it substitutes itself for a legitimate program.

The most common of the three kinds of infestations is a virus. A virus is called a virus because (1) it has an incubation period (does not do damage immediately), (2) it is contagious (can replicate itself), and (3) it is destructive. Viruses are often programmed to hide in order to avoid detection by anti-virus software.

12

What kind of damage does a virus do? It really depends on the virus. Some viruses do nothing more than make annoying messages pop up when a certain program is opened. Figure 12-5 shows a virus that simply displays garbage on the screen. But other viruses, the viruses that make the headlines, attack hard drives, delete files, and cause systems to crash. Each virus is a little different than all other viruses, which is one reason computers are so susceptible to them.

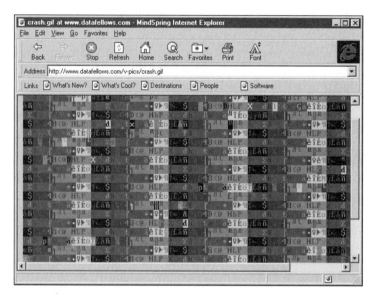

Figure 12-5   The crash virus appears to be destructive, making the screen show only garbage, but does no damage to the hard drive data

A Trojan horse is an infestation that masquerades as a legitimate program. The term Trojan horse comes from Homer's *Iliad*, which took place during the Trojan War. In the story, the Greeks gave the people of Troy a wooden horse as a peace offering, but the horse actually contained Greek warriors, who, once they were in the city, were able to defeat the citizens of Troy.

One interesting example of a Trojan horse is the AOL4FREE program. This program originally was an illegal program that could provide unauthorized access to America Online. After the program's usefulness was blocked by AOL, a new program emerged, also calling itself AOL4FREE that was not an online access program at all, but a destructive Trojan horse. People passed the program around, thinking that it would provide illegal access to AOL; however, if executed, it actually erased files on their hard drives.

A worm is a common way to attack a network, where it creates problems by overloading the network as it replicates itself. Worms are often hidden in Trojan horse programs, and they are damaging just by their presence alone, rather than because they perform a specific damaging act, as a virus does. A worm overloads memory or hard drive space by replicating itself over and over again.

Cookies

Although cookies are not considered by everyone to be a type of intrusion, many people feel that cookies allow companies to intrude on privacy rights. Recall from Chapter 6 that a **cookie** is just data that is stored on the client's system by a web site for later retrieval. Many companies use cookies with their web pages. When a user accesses a web page that uses cookies, the cookie is placed on the user's hard drive. The next time the user accesses the same web site, the browser sends the information in the cookie back to the web server. When you access a web page that remembers your name, the site is using cookies to store your personal information. Web sites use cookies so they can provide a more personal web page to their customers. Cookies are also used to trace customer's browsing habits and for marketing research.

DoubleClick (*www.doubleclick.com*) is one company that uses cookies to track the web-surfing habits of countless Internet users. DoubleClick, an Internet advertising company, puts banners on web pages advertising a wide range of products. The first time you access a web page with a DoubleClick banner, the ad puts a cookie on your hard drive. Once the cookie is on your hard drive, any time you go to a web site with a DoubleClick banner, the cookie sends the URL of the page you are visiting to DoubleClick's server, and your habits are tracked.

Although the information is linked to the computer and not the user, some people are concerned that too much information is being gathered without the user's knowledge. When DoubleClick announced that it planned to create a database with the names of users, their e-mail addresses, and other personal information (including items purchased over the Internet), along with their surfing habits, numerous civil suits were filed against DoubleClick for alleged privacy breaches.

12

PROTECTION STRATEGIES

As you can see from the earlier discussion, it's very important to protect your resources. The strategies you would use vary according to what you are protecting and how intense you want the protection to be. One thing to remember when implementing protection strategies is that all areas of a network need to be protected. If one area is left unprotected, an intruder can find access to your data.

The protection strategy you choose is partly determined by what you want to protect. Some of the entities you can protect are shown in Figure 12-6 and described next.

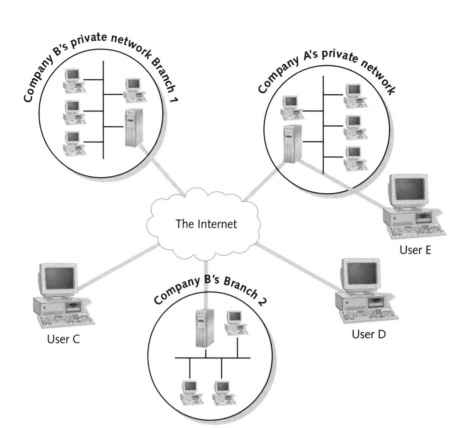

Figure 12-6   Protection strategies depend on what you are protecting

You can protect:

- **A private network or intranet.** This type of network belongs to a single company or organization, and only those who belong to the organization or company use the network. With this type of network, there are no branch offices in other locations. In Figure 12-6, Company A has a private network. If the network uses TCP/IP, then it is called an intranet; otherwise, it is simply called a private network. Protection strategies in this case are mostly limited to authenticating users when they first log on to the network using user IDs and passwords. Authentication occurs at a server that is designated as the secure gateway to the network. When a single user accesses a secure gateway, the term used is **client-to-gateway security**. Employees who use the intranet might need to access resources outside the network such as web sites on the Internet. In this case, because there is an avenue for employees to access the Internet, there might also be an open door for hackers to gain access to the private network through this access method. In addition, an employee such as User E in Figure 12-6 might need to access the network by way of a dial-up connection to a server supporting Remote Access Server (RAS).

- **An extranet.** Corporations might also allow customers and suppliers to have limited access to the corporate intranet to improve business. This access to a private network from outside individuals or companies who use the services of the intranet but might not be validated as full-fledged network users must be protected and secured. This is another type of client-to-gateway security. In Figure 12-6, if Company A allows Company B to access an inventory database on its private network, this connection between the two company networks is called an extranet. An **extranet** is a network between two or more organizations that is a private physical or virtual network.

- **Transactions between individuals and a web site.** Transactions might be performed by individuals accessing your company's web site to purchase a product or exchange information in which the individual does not need to log onto the company's private network. With these kinds of transactions, the transaction itself must be protected (for example, protecting the customer's credit card number). This is an example of a limited application of client-to-gateway security, in which the client does not need to access the network, but the transaction itself needs protecting. For example, in Figure 12-6, if User C makes a purchase from Company A's web site, the transaction must be protected.

- **Transactions between individuals across the Internet.** E-mail sent over the Internet, and FTP services might also need to be secured and authenticated. When two individuals want to send secure e-mail or FTP documents, the term used to describe the security involved is **client-to-client security**. For example, in Figure 12-6, if User C and User D communicate important and personal e-mail messages, client-to-client security is needed.

- **Virtual private network.** A corporate intranet might have a branch in another city that also has a network. When the Internet is used to connect these two corporate networks belonging to the same company, a resulting virtual private network is created and must be protected from outside interference. This structure requires **gateway-to-gateway security**. For example, in Figure 12-6, Company B has two branch offices and wants these two private networks belonging to the same company to have open, but secure communication, so a virtual private network is needed.

12

As you read about the different methods of protecting a network, remember that some methods might be used in all the above situations and some only are practical in a particular circumstance. The goals of a security system are:

- To provide **privacy** to ensure that the intended recipient of data is the only one who reads it

- To provide **authentication** to ensure that a user or computer is who or what they say they are

- To protect **data integrity** to ensure that data is not altered in transit by those intending harm

- To provide **non-repudiation**, which establishes proof that a message was sent or received so that the person sending or receiving the message cannot deny his action

- To be **easy to use** so that customers, employees, and associates are not unduly hampered by the security measures taken

Each of these aspects of a security system are defined and explained in this section.

Authentication

Authentication is the process of ensuring that a person or computer is who or what it says it is before that person or computer is allowed access to a secured network or secured data. There are several methods of authentication, and each method varies in the amount of security it offers. The more sensitive the data or the network, the more advanced authentication method you should implement. Authentication on a network is normally performed by the network operating system that is managing the network. If the user is dialing directly into a RAS server, the server can authenticate the phone number of the caller by using caller ID. RAS servers also support callback, whereby a user dials in and is authenticated by a user ID and password. Then the call is disconnected and the server calls the user back at the number given by the user. This helps to alleviate long distance charges for employees on the road. Callback can also be configured to call back at a specific location, therefore using it for added security.

User IDs and Passwords

The most common authentication method available for a network is user IDs and passwords. A **user ID** is a code that is used to indicate who the user is. Most network operating systems allow each ID to be assigned certain rights that apply to only that ID or group of IDs. These rights allow users to access certain files, programs, databases, and directories. The **password** is a group of characters that the user must enter, in addition to the user ID, that give access to the network. If the user does not know both the user ID and the password, he is denied access to the network.

The network operating system allows the system administrator to define what files or folders the user has access to and what type of access the user has. A user may have read, write, or no access. **Read access** means that the user is allowed to read the file, but he cannot make changes to it. **Write access** allows the user to read the file, make changes, save those changes, and delete the file. **No access**, of course, denies the user any access to the file.

An important part of security is making sure that each user has access to the right files or folders. For example, a new employee in the Information Systems Department needs access to the holiday schedule for that department, but she does not need the right to change the schedule, so she should get only read access to the file. But if the department has a vacation schedule file that each employee needs to update when they plan to take time off from work, the employee does need write access. And, naturally, all employees should have no access to payroll files except those employees directly involved in the payroll process.

The biggest problem with passwords is that many people do not keep their passwords secret. They often choose a password that is easy to remember, such as a birthday or a pet's name. But, if a password is easy to remember, it is also easy to guess. Another problem with passwords is that many people have so many passwords to remember that they write them down. Once a password is written down, it can be found and used by anyone. On the other hand, a forgotten password can be a very frustrating problem for a user and an annoyance for network administrators to correct. A good, effective password is one that has a mixture of letters, numbers, and symbols, and does not have any logical meaning.

Smart Cards

For systems that require more security than that provided by passwords, smart cards may be an option. **Smart cards** are cards that are about the size of a credit card with an embedded microchip in the card. The chip enables the card to hold data or programming that can authenticate a user who is accessing a network. One example of a smart card is SecurID by RSA Security (*www.rsasecurity.com*) shown in Figure 12-7. The number in the upper right corner of the card changes every 60 seconds and is synchronized with authentication software running on the server that gives access to a secured network. If you are an employee who is telecommuting from home and accessing the network using the Internet or a direct phone connection, you can enter the number shown on the SecurID card along with your user ID and password as part of the authentication process. This method of securing a network proves that you have a valid ID and password and are in possession of this card.

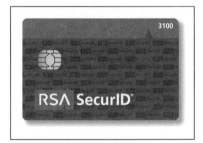

12

Figure 12-7   A smart card such as this SecurID card is used to authenticate a user gaining access to a secured network

Less intelligent smart cards can hold data on a magnetic strip, similar to the way an ATM card holds data. The data on the card usually is a code to run a program. When smart cards are used for authentication, they store the user's profile including which files the user should have access to.

These smart cards are designed to be read by a special machine that has a slot into which you can insert the card. If the card is to be used to verify who you are, you must insert the card when the machine is booted. The machine uses the data on the card to determine which functions you are authorized to perform.

The major disadvantage of this type of smart card is that a reader device must be installed on each computer or other network device where the user must gain access. This type of smart card is more popular in Europe than in the United States. For more information about smart cards, see Smart Card Central Inc. at *www.smartcardcentral.com* and the Smart Card Industry Association at *www.scia.org*.

Digital Certificates

When you receive a letter, the signature on the letter serves as visual verification of the identity of the letter writer. In electronic communication it is impossible to visually verify the identity of the person sending the communication. To help prevent people from falsifying their identities and to make sure that when a message is received it has not been altered, digital certificates were created.

Congress has recently passed a bill which will allow consumers to agree to major business transactions over the Internet. The bill will allow consumers to complete transactions such as purchasing a car, closing a mortgage, or buying life insurance without a pen and paper. Rather, all contracts will be sealed with a digital signature and the contracts will be as legally binding as traditional contracts.

A **digital certificate**, sometimes called a **digital ID**, is a digital signature that verifies the sender's identity. It is a binary file that is stored on your hard drive, usually as part of your Windows Registry information. The file contains identifying information about you. It usually includes the serial number, the expiration date, and the certification authority that issued the certificate. The certificate also contains your special code, which is used when files are sent to you. This code, called a **key**, is explained later in the chapter.

Another feature of digital certificates is to assist in non-repudiation. **Non-repudiation of origin** prevents the person who sent the message from claiming he was not the person who sent it. **Non-repudiation of delivery** is used so that the receiver of the message cannot deny getting the message. With digital certificates, only the intended receiver can read the message because only the intended receiver will have the key to open the message.

The only way to obtain a digital certificate is through a **certification authority** (**CA**), and it is the CAs job to verify that you are who you say you are. The two largest certification authorities are VeriSign (*www.verisign.com*) and Thawte (*www.thawte.com*). Digital certificates are sometimes used to help create a **virtual private network** (**VPN**), whereby hosts on the Internet can communicate to one another with as much privacy as if they were on a private network. For example, if a corporation wants to give certain vendors, customers, or suppliers access to the corporate intranet, the corporation can authenticate the user by requiring that the user have a digital certificate. When the user logs on to the intranet, the certificate is presented to prove the user is who he or she says. Most times, certificates are presented by a browser to the server doing the authentication without the user's intervention. For complete privacy, the data sent across the Internet must be coded so that others cannot read it, which is called encryption. Data encryption is covered later in the chapter.

Sometimes an organization uses a third party such as VeriSign to provide the CA services, or the organization might choose to provide their own CA services. A CA service requires a certificate server such as Microsoft Certificate Service, which is part of Windows NT and Windows 2000. For example, a large corporation might issue each employee a certificate that the employee must use in order to log on to any network within the organization. By using certificates, the need for network administrators to maintain user IDs and passwords for individual networks within the organization is lessened. And employees only need to manage their one certificate rather than having to keep up with many user IDs and passwords. When an employee leaves the company, the certificate is revoked.

Types of Digital Certificates There are five types of digital certificates. Each type of certificate is listed below, along with a definition and an example of when the certificate would be issued.

- A *client SSL certificate* is used to identify the client to the server in an SSL environment. (SSL environments are discussed later in this chapter.) Usually, the client is considered the same as the individual using the computer. If you have accounts with a mortgage company, the company may issue you a client SSL certificate so that you can access your accounts in a secure manner over the Internet. Since the server knows who you are by your certificate, you can access only your records.

- A *server SSL certificate* is used to identify the server to the client in an SSL environment. Businesses that use the Internet as the medium for sales transactions usually have server SSL certificates. These certificates allow customers to verify that the company is legitimate and to use an encrypted SSL session to prevent credit card and other personal information from being stolen. Server SSL certificates are a standard among companies that use the Internet for business transactions.

- An *S/MIME certificate* is used to sign and/or encrypt e-mail. Employees who send e-mails with sensitive information (such as payroll or personnel changes) use the S/MIME certificate to prevent the e-mail from being read by someone else and to sign the e-mail so the receiver is sure of who sent it.

- An *object-signing certificate* is used to sign files such as programs downloaded from the Internet. Companies that provide software to be downloaded from the Internet use object-signing certificates to provide company information to their customers. The customers can use this information to determine if they want to do business with the company.

- A *CA certificate* is used to identify certification authorities, the agencies responsible for issuing digital certificates. Certification authorities use CA certificates to show their customers that they are a trusted authority and that they can legitimately issue digital certificates.

12

What is in a Digital Certificate? Most certificates today conform to the X.509 certificate specification. This specification is recommended by the International Telecommunications Union (ITU), and has been recommended since 1988. The specification outlines what information is included in each certificate. Certificates cannot be read by humans; they must be read by a computer. The example below shows a digital certificate displayed in 64-byte-encoded form.

```
-----BEGIN CERTIFICATE-----
MIICKzCCAZSgAwIBAgIBAzANBgkghkiG9w0BAQQFADA3MQswCQYDVQQGEwJVUzER
MA8GA1UEChMITmV0c2NhcGUxFTATBgNVBAsTDFN1cHJpeWEncyBDQTAeFw05nZEw
MTgwMTM2MjVaFw050TEwMTgwMTM2MjVaMEgxCzAJBgNVBAYTA1VTMREwDwYDVQQK
EwhOZXRzY2FwZTENMAsGA1UECxMEUHViczEXMBUGA1UEAxMOU3VWCM15YSBTaGV0
dHkwgZ8wDQYJKoZIhvcNAQEFBQADgY0AMIGGJAoGBMr6EziPGfjX3URJgEjmKigG
7SdATYazBcABU1Avyd7chRkiQ31FbXFOGD3wNktbf6hRo6EamM5/R1AskzZ8AW7L
iQZBcrXpc0k4du+2Q6xJu2MPm/8WkuMOnTuvzpo+SGXelmHVchEqooCwfdiZywyz
NmmrJgaoMa2MS6pUkfQVAgMBAAGjNjA0MBEGCQCGSAGG+EIBAQQEAwIAgDAfBgQb
HSMEGDAQgBTy8gZZkBhHUfWJM1oxeuZc+zYmyTANBgkqhkiG9w0BAQQFAAOBgBtz
I6/z07Z635DfzX4XbAFpj1Rl/AYwQzTSYx8GfcNAqCqCwaSDKvsuj/vwbf91o3j3
UkdGYpcd2cYRCgKi4MwqdWyLtpuHAH18hHz5uvi00mJYw8W2wUOsYORC/a/Idy84
hW3WwehBUqVK5SY4/zJ4oTjx7dwMNdGwbWfpRqjd1A==
-----END CERTIFICATE-----
```

As you can see, a digital certificate can only be understood by software that is programmed to read it. The certificate is made up of two sections: the data section and the signature section. Below is the same certificate as above, but it is in a format that you can understand.

```
Certificate:
  Data:
    Version: v3 (0x2)
    Serial Number: 3 (0x3)
    Signature Algorithm: PKCS #1 MD5 With RSA Encryption
    Issuer: OU=Ace Certification Authority, O=Ace Industry, C=US
    Validity:
      Not Before: Mon Jul 24 16:12:04 2000
      Not After:  Sun Jul 24 16:12:04 2002
    Subject: CN=Jane Doe, OU=Finance, O=Ace Industry, C=US
    Subject Public Key Info:
      Algorithm: PKCS #1 RSA Encryption
      Public Key:
        Modulus:
          00:ca:fa:79:98:8f:19:f8:d7:de:e4:49:80:48:e6:2a:2s:86:
          ed:27:40:4d:86:b3:05:c0:01:bb:50:15:c9:de:dc:85:19:22:
          43:7d:45:6d:71:4e:17:3d:f0:36:4b:5b:7f:a8:51:a3:a1:00:
          98:ce:7f:47:50:2c:93:36:7c:01:6e:cb:89:06:41:72:b5:e9:
          73:49:38:76:ef:b6:8f:ac:49:bb:63:0f:9b:ff:16:2a:e3:0e:
          9d:3b:af:ce:9a:3e:48:65:de:96:61:d5:0a:11:2a:a2:80:b0:
          7d:d8:99:cb:0c:99:34:c9:ab:25:06:a8:31:ad:8c:4b:aa:54:
          91:f4:15
    Public Exponent: 65537 (0x10001)
```

```
  Extensions:
    Identifier: Certificate Type
      Critical: no
      Certified Usage:
        SSL Client
    Identifier: Authority Key Identifier
      Critical: no
      Key Identifier:
        f2:f2:06:59:90:18:47:51:f5:89:33:5a:31:7a:e6:5c:fb:36:
        26:c9
Signature:
  Algorithm: PKCS #1 MD5 With RSA Encryption
  Signature:
  6d:23:af:f3:d3:b6:7a:df:90:df:cd:7e:18:6c:01:69:8e:54:65:fc:06:
  30:43:34:d1:63:1f:06:7d:c3:40:a8:2a:82:c1:a4:83:2a:fb:2e:8f:fb:
  f0:6d:ff:75:a3:78:f7:52:47:46:62:97:1d:d9:c6:11:0a:02:a2:e0:cc:
  2a:75:6c:8b:b6:9b:87:00:7d:7c:84:76:79:ba:f8:b4:d2:62:58:c3:c5:
  b6:c1:43:ac:63:44:42:fd:af:c8:0f:2f:38:85:6d:d6:59:e8:41:42:a5:
  4a:e5:26:38:ff:32:78:a1:38:f1:ed:dc:0d:31:d1:b0:6d:67:e9:46:a8:
  dd:c4
```

The data section includes the following information:

- The version number of the X.509 that the certificate supports (usually this is version 3)

- The serial number

- The name of the authority that issued the certificate

- The dates and times when the certificate is valid

- The person or company to whom the certificate was issued

- The algorithm used to encode the certificate

- Additional information such as the type of certificate

The signature section of the certificate includes the following:

- The algorithm that was used by the certification authority to create the digital certificate

- The certification authority's digital signature

How Digital Certificates Work The process of getting a digital certificate and using the certificate involves three parties: the person needing the certificate, the authority issuing the certificate, and the company with whom the person wants to use the certificate. Figure 12-8 shows how certificates work. In the example, an individual vendor uses a digital certificate to do business with a corporation over the Internet:

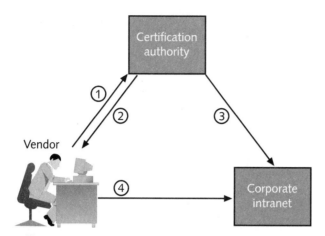

Figure 12-8   Digital certificates can be used to authenticate a user when accessing a corporate intranet

The steps below outline how digital certificates work, as shown in Figure 12-8.

- **Step 1:** An individual who is the point of contact for a vendor doing business with a corporation applies to a certification authority (CA) for a certificate. The process requires that the individual prove his or her identity. Sometimes this is done through an automated process and sometimes it requires a personal interview.

- **Step 2:** The CA validates the identity of the individual and issues a digital certificate. The certificate most often includes a public key (public keys are covered later in the chapter).

- **Step 3:** The CA sends a message to the corporate intranet indicating that a digital certificate has been issued to the vendor. The CA is also responsible for monitoring the certificate and its life cycle and revoking the certificate if that becomes necessary (for example, if the vendor goes out of business or the individual leaves the company).

- **Step 4:** When the individual attempts to log on to the corporate intranet, the individual's browser presents the certificate to the secure gateway. The secure gateway validates that the certificate is one issued by the CA and allows the individual access to the intranet.

For more information about the X.509 specifications, see RFC 2459 at *www.rfc-editor.org*.

How to Protect Your Digital Certificate   Because your digital certificate contains information to identify you, it should be kept secure. If someone gets a copy of your digital certificate, they can pretend to be you when they engage in electronic transactions. Because the information is stored on your hard drive, you should protect your hard drive from unwanted users. The easiest way to protect the information itself is to require a password to access it. Requiring a password prevents anyone who does not know the password from copying, deleting, or changing your digital certificate.

In addition, most software programs that use digital certificates allow you to require a password before the certificate is used. For example, if you are using Outlook Express to send a message and require that a password be entered before the digital certificate is used, when you choose to sign the message with your digital certificate, you must enter a password for the digital certificate before the message can be sent. The steps involved in adding a password to your digital certificate for use with Outlook Express are covered later in this chapter. Some of the programs also let you decide to not require a password before using your digital certificate. If you choose not to require a password, your digital certificate will not be secure. Not having a password has been compared to signing all the checks in your checkbook so you will have one less thing to complete when you write checks.

If you require more protection for your digital certificate than a password, you may want to store your digital certificate away from your computer. Digital certificates can be stored on a PCMCIA card or a smart card. These devices are removable, allowing you to keep the certificate in a separate location from your computer.

Encryption

Because the Internet is a public network, anyone can gain access. Therefore, files that are sent over the Internet can be altered or intercepted. In order to make sure that data cannot be read if it is intercepted while it is being transmitted, it is coded so that it cannot be accessed by anyone but the intended receiver. **Encryption** is the process of coding data to prevent unauthorized parties from being able to change or view it.

The encryption process is fairly simple. The sending computer uses encryption software to encrypt the file. Encryption software converts the file into a form that is unreadable, most often through the use of a mathematical formula. This unreadable data is called **ciphertext**. Part of the formula that is used to encode the data is called a **key.** In its simplest form, encryption requires this same key be used when the data is decoded or decrypted so that it can be read. This method of encryption where only a single key is used, is called **private key encryption** or **symmetric encryption**, and is illustrated in Figure 12-9.

12

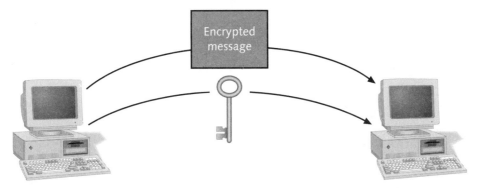

Figure 12-9   A key, which is required to decode an encrypted message, is sent along with the encrypted message, but by a different route

The data and the key are sent to the receiving computer, but they are sent separately and on different paths. When the receiving computer has both the key and the data, it can decrypt (decode) the file and then read the file. The length of the key determines how effective the encryption is. The longer the key, the more secure the data, which makes sense because there are more possible combinations as the key length grows. It has been proven that a key that is 40 bits long can be cracked in about six hours by systematically using every combination of 40 bits until the correct combination is discovered. Therefore, if you want a stronger security method, use longer keys. Keys that are 128 bits are considered long enough for very strong encryption, as there are trillions of possible combinations of zeros and ones, and 128-bit encryption is often an option. Until recently, it was illegal to distribute 128-bit encryption software outside the United States as it was considered a security risk.

Even so, the security is weak when both the key and the message are sent to the recipient, because it is possible that both could be intercepted and the message could be read or altered. In 1976, a solution to this problem was proposed: an encryption method was developed that involved two keys, a public key and a private key. Encryption that uses a public and private key is called **asymmetric encryption** or **public key encryption** and is discussed next.

Public Key Encryption

Public key encryption requires two keys: a public key and a private key. Each user has two keys, and those keys correspond with each other. The public key is available to anyone, and the private key is kept on the user's computer and should be secure. The public key is the key that is used to encrypt the message, and the corresponding private key is the only key that can decrypt the message.

Figure 12-10 shows how public key encryption works. When you want to send an encrypted message to a recipient, you must first request the recipient's public key. The message is then encrypted with the recipient's public key, and sent to the recipient. The recipient uses his private key to decrypt the message before it can be read. If the recipient wants to send an encrypted reply back to the original sender, then the recipient must first request the sender's public key in order to encrypt the message.

The added value and protection of having public keys and private keys over having just a single key is that if the public key is intercepted in transit, it will not matter because an encrypted message cannot be read without the private key, which is never exposed to Internet traffic.

Use public key encryption when you need to send confidential documents by e-mail or FTP. To be effective, both you and all the parties with which you confidentially communicate must subscribe to a public key encryption service such as VeriSign. This group of parties is called a **Public-Key Infrastructure** (**PKI**). For example, employees in an attorney's office and employees of various clients might form a PKI in order to communicate over the Internet in privacy.

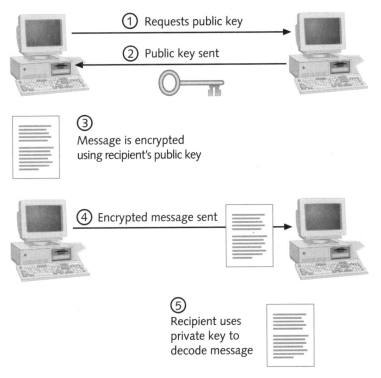

Figure 12-10   Public key encryption uses two keys, the recipients' public key to encrypt the message and his private key to decrypt it

12

Signing up for secure e-mail through VeriSign is not difficult. They even offer a free 60-day trial digital certificate for personal use. In the instructions, VeriSign calls a digital certificate a digital ID. You first fill out the necessary forms on the VeriSign web site, get your digital ID PIN from VeriSign through your e-mail, use the PIN to pick up your digital ID from VeriSign, and install the digital ID onto your PC. The instructions below outline how to get a free 60 day trial digital certificate from the VeriSign web site. Remember, though, that web sites change often, and although these steps were accurate at time of publication, there may be changes.

1. Go to the VeriSign web site (*www.verisign.com*).

2. Click **Secure E-mail** located in the middle of the screen.

3. Click the **Try It!** button to select the option to try a digital ID free for 60 days.

4. Click **Class 1 Digital ID**. VeriSign takes you to a web page that has a form for you to complete. The form asks for your basic information including your name, e-mail address, and billing information (if you choose to purchase the ID instead of using the free 60-day trial).

5. Complete the form.

6. Click the **Accept** button. A message appears asking you to confirm your e-mail address.

7. If the address is correct, press **OK**; otherwise, press **Cancel**. Then another message appears to let you know that the system is creating a new key for you.

8. To set the security level, click **Set Security Level**. A screen appears that allows you to select the appropriate security level; see Figure 12-11. If you select High security, you must enter a password every time your private key is to be used. Medium security should be selected if you want to be notified each time the key is used, and low security automatically grants permission to use your private key. Once you have selected a security level, click **Next** and then click **Finish**.

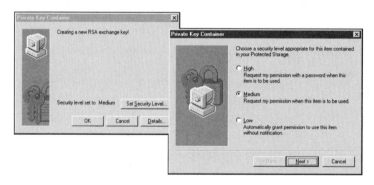

Figure 12-11   VeriSign lets you determine the amount of security needed

9. Click **OK** in the message box. Another message box appears with the message "Signing data with your private exchange key!"

10. Click **OK**. When the data has been sent, the web site changes to indicate that you are on step two of the process.

11. At this point you need to check your e-mail. In your e-mail, you will find a message from VeriSign that has your digital ID PIN.

12. Copy the PIN using the copy and paste feature of your computer.

13. Click the web site link included in the e-mail (*digitalid.verisign.com/enrollment/mspickup.htm*).

14. Use the paste feature of your computer to paste your digital ID PIN into the field on the web page.

15. Click the **Submit** button; see Figure 12-12. After the PIN has been submitted, the digital ID has to be installed on your machine. Figure 12-13 shows the screen for installation.

16. Click the **Install** button, and the system installs your digital ID into your Windows Registry.

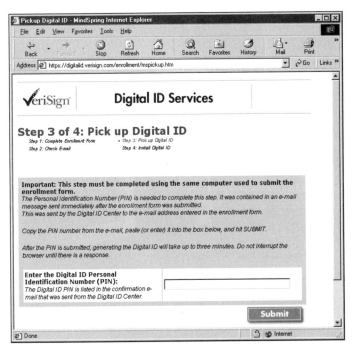

Figure 12-12   To pick up your digital ID, you must know your digital ID PIN

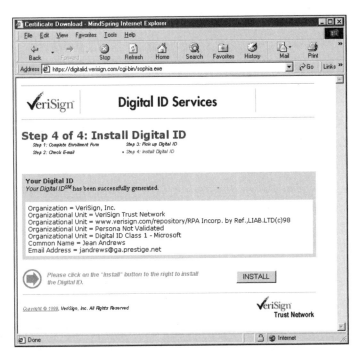

Figure 12-13   Once the digital ID has been created it must be installed

Now that you have your digital ID and it has been installed into your Windows Registry, how do you use it? The first thing you have to do is set up your e-mail client software to use the digital ID to send secure e-mails. In our example, we'll use Outlook Express 4 to go through the steps to use a digital ID. If you are using an e-mail client other than Outlook Express 4, see the VeriSign help desk at *www.verisign.com/client/help/index.html* for instructions specific to your client.

1. Click **Tools** on the menu bar, then click **Accounts**. The Internet Accounts windows opens.

2. Click the **Mail** tab. In the list of accounts, double-click one account in the list. The Mail Account Properties window opens, as shown in Figure 12-14.

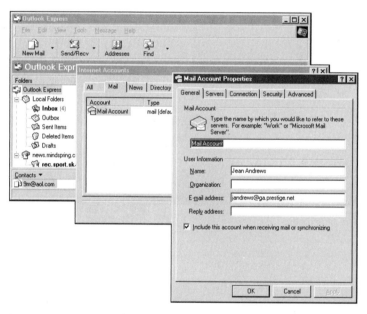

Figure 12-14   Use the Account Properties window of Outlook Express to set up the client software to use a digital certificate

3. Click the **Security** tab and click the checkbox to **Use a digital ID when sending secure messages from**.

4. Click on the **Digital ID** button. The Select Certificate window opens, as shown in Figure 12-15. Select the digital ID you want to use and click **OK**.

5. Click **Close** in the Internet Accounts window.

When you compose a message, you can select encrypt and/or sign on the Tools menu to sign or encrypt a message. If you want to have all messages you send signed, select Tools on the menu bar, then select Options. Click the Security tab, then select to have all outgoing messages encrypted and/or all outgoing messages digitally signed by putting a checkmark next to the appropriate selection.

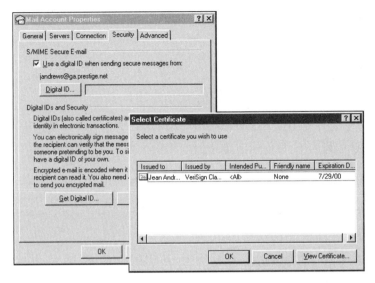

Figure 12-15 A certificate must be selected to correspond with the mail accounts

Figure 12-16 shows a message that was both digitally signed and encrypted. You can see two icons on the right side of the screen: a ribbon and a padlock. These indicate that the message was digitally signed (the ribbon icon) and encrypted (the padlock icon). When the message is sent, the e-mail software uses your private key to digitally sign it. If you requested medium security with private keys, a message appears letting you know that your private key is about to be used, as in Figure 12-17. If you requested high security, you would be required to enter a password before the message could be sent.

12

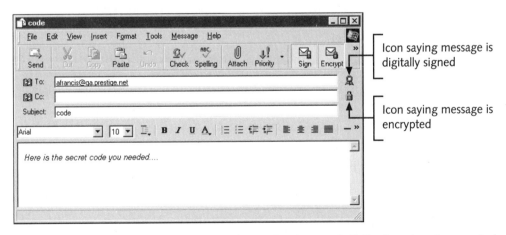

Figure 12-16 Icons on the message indicate that it was digitally signed and encrypted

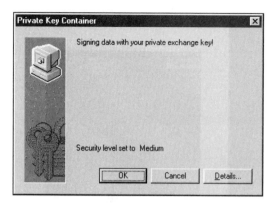

Figure 12-17   With medium security, a message appears to let the user know that the private key is being used

Pretty Good Privacy Encryption

Pretty Good Privacy (PGP) encryption is another encryption protocol. It is used to:

- Encrypt and decrypt messages that are sent over the Internet

- Send digital signatures to ensure the identity of the sender

- Verify that the message was not altered during transmission

Pretty Good Privacy is used by several encryption products. Norton Secret Stuff is a free program which is available from Symantec (*www.symantec.com*) that you can use to encrypt files using PGP encryption. You encrypt your file with Norton Secret Stuff, and then can send the encrypted file over the Internet as an attachment to an e-mail message. The message recipient must decrypt the file with a similar product that uses the PGP encryption method.

Figure 12-18 shows how PGP works. It uses three keys: the receiver's public key, the receiver's private key, and a short key that is generated by the encryption software. Here are the steps:

- When a message is first sent, it is encrypted using a short key, which is a faster encryption process than encrypting with a public key.

- The encrypted message is then combined with the short key, and they are both encrypted using the receiver's public key. They travel together as a package over the Internet.

- When the receiver gets the message, he uses his private key to decrypt both the message and the accompanying short key. At this point, the message is still encrypted with the short key encryption protocol.

- Finally, he uses the short key to completely decrypt the message.

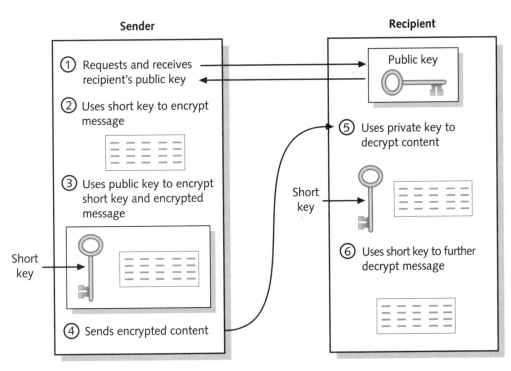

Figure 12-18 With Pretty Good Privacy Encryption, three keys are used: a short key and the recipient's public and private keys

12

Secure Multi-Purpose Internet Mail Extensions

Recall from earlier chapters that **Multi-Purpose Internet Mail Extensions (MIME)** specifications outline how electronic messages and attachments are transmitted. It increased the types of data that could be included in the messages. Internet mail can use MIME to include text other than ASCII, messages that are non-text (multimedia), messages of unlimited length, binary files, and non–ASCII information in message headers.

The secure version of MIME is **Secure Multi-Purpose Internet Mail Extensions (S/MIME)**. S/MIME works in a similar way as public key encryption and is a competing technology. A message is sent with the receiver's public key, and the message can be opened only with the receiver's private key. S/MIME capabilities are included in newer versions of e-mail client software, such as Microsoft Outlook 98.

Firewalls

One of the most important things to do when setting up network security is to install a good firewall. A **firewall** controls information that is sent and received from outside the network. The firewall is a set of programs that can reside on the network's gateway, which is the connection point between the internal network and outside communication. A firewall can be installed on several different types of gateways, including a router, a server, or a separate PC.

The best way to ensure that no one from the outside accesses the network is to restrict all outside users. However, this is obviously unrealistic because it contradicts one of the purposes of a network in today's information-driven economy—to allow communication between people and computers on the network and those using the Internet. Therefore, a firewall is used to ensure all communication received from outside users and computers is legitimate.

A firewall examines all incoming packets to determine if the packets should be forwarded to their final destination. There are a number of ways that the firewall can determine if the packets are legitimate, but the most common way is to look at the source IP address and to compare it to a pre-defined list of accepted sources. If the address is on the list, the packet is forwarded. Otherwise, it is rejected.

Firewalls can be used on personal computers as well as on networks. When a personal computer has an "always on" connection to the Internet, such as a cable modem or DSL, it is a good idea to install a personal firewall. Having a constant connection to the Internet means that people can use software to examine the ports on your PC to determine if one is open. An open port can then be used to penetrate your system. A script or program used to scan for open ports is called a **port scanning script** and is one major tool a hacker uses to penetrate a network or computer. Recall that an open port implies that a connection is established between a program or process running on your PC and a program running on another computer on the Internet. A hacker can use this open port to communicate with the process running on your PC to gain access to resources and data on your computer or network.

If a hacker finds his way in, he can steal any information kept on your computer. Most people keep more information than they realize on the computer, including bank account details, tax returns, credit card numbers, and passwords. Usually somewhere on the computer is personal information about the user, such as address, phone number, and e-mail address. With this information, a thief could easily steal your credit card numbers and run up a huge bill and run down your credit rating.

A personal firewall filters information, blocks open ports, and stops suspicious programs (primarily those programs containing ActiveX controls and JavaScript routines). Zone Labs (*www.zonelabs.com*) offers a firewall that can be downloaded for free if it is to be used for personal use only. As shown in Figure 12-19, the firewall allows the user to set the level of security. The firewall also requests permission from the user prior to allowing any programs access to the Internet. All open ports are blocked, as are any probes from web sites. Other personal firewall software include McAfee Firewall by Network Associates (*www.mcafee.com*) and Personal Firewall 2000 by Norton (*www.symantec.com*).

Web sites like Secure-Me (*www.secure-me.net*) let you test your connection to see how much information an outsider could find out about you. Figure 12-20 shows what information the web site can provide for you.

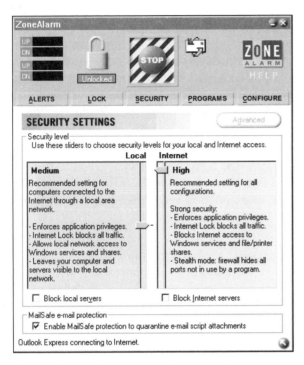

Figure 12-19   ZoneAlarm allows you to determine the amount of security the
firewall provides

12

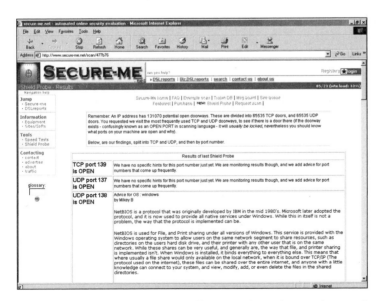

Figure 12-20   Secure-Me.net offers a probe to let you know of any areas potential hackers
may try to use to gain access to your system

Intrusion Detection Software

Just as a burglar alarm for your home alerts you to an intruder, **intrusion detection software** lets you know when someone has tried to break into your network. Because the Internet makes it so easy for people to try to gain access to your resources, it is necessary to have software installed to let you know when an attack has been attempted. Once you have registered attacks, you can make the necessary provisions to guard against them in the future.

Intrusion detection software packages provide alarms, usually in the form of a flashing message to the network administrator, that go off when suspicious activity is spotted. Some of the packages also send e-mail to a specified address or call a pager and leave a code to indicate that there has been suspicious activity on the network. If the activity is caught in time, the location of the perpetrator can be pinpointed, and proper action can be taken.

Good intrusion detection software packages keep logs that can be used as evidence if you wish to press charges against hackers. They also track suspicious activity both inside and outside the network. Inside the network, a disgruntled employee may try to change a user's authority or search for passwords. Outside the network, a hacker may try port scanning scripts to find access to your data. Intrusion detection software also notes **multiple log-in failures**, which happen when a user keeps trying to access the network with an invalid password or user ID. Multiple log-in failures can indicate that an unauthorized user is trying to access network resources. One problem with intrusion detection software is that it might set off an alarm when the activity is harmless. Too many false alarms can cause a user or administrator to ignore a true attack.

Some intrusion detection software packages also offer the ability to view all activity on the network as it occurs. As the network administrator monitors activity, he or she can control what files users have access to and what functions they can perform. One such system is IP-Watcher, by En Garde Systems, Inc. (*www.engarde.com*), which allows you to view activity and stop any activity that is not appropriate.

Electronic Transaction Protocols

As the number of companies that sell merchandise over the Internet grows, so does the concern that the transactions are not secure. New protocols are being developed to help address these concerns and to make sure that all transactions that take place over the Internet are secure. Two of the more popular protocols include secure sockets layer and secure electronic transaction.

Secure Sockets Layer

Secure sockets layer (SSL) is a protocol that was developed by Netscape to provide security between application protocols (such as FTP, HTTP, or Telnet) and TCP/IP. SSL provides data encryption and server authentication, and can provide client authentication for a TCP/IP connection. It is implemented in both Netscape Navigator and Internet Explorer to provide a secure connection when customers are placing orders over the Internet using a browser and a web site. When you see an address that starts with https://, you know that it is a secure connection.

A browser accessing a secure site uses encryption to scramble credit card information without any interference or knowledge of the user. By default, browsers use a method of encryption that uses a 40-bit key, although you can download a version of Netscape Navigator or Internet Explorer that uses a 128-bit key called 128-bit encryption.

SSL uses public and private keys and is similar to the public key method described above, but is a little more complicated. Figure 12-21 shows one of several ways that SSL can work. The sender and the recipient first exchange public keys. (When two people communicate a lot, they already hold each other's public key, so this first step might be unnecessary.) The sender then encodes the message using her private key and the recipient's public key. When the receiver gets the message, she must decrypt the message first with her private key and then with the sender's public key. Using the double set of keys makes sure that the person who is sending the message is who she says she is, because no one else could create a message with her private key. SSL uses digital certificates to achieve this security.

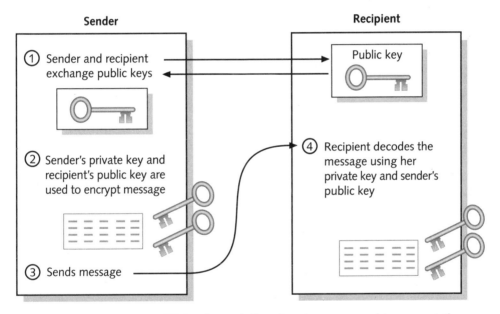

Figure 12-21   Using one SSL implementation, two keys are used to encrypt the message and two keys are used to decrypt it

Secure Electronic Transactions

Secure electronic transaction (SET) is a protocol that is designed to offer a secure medium for credit card transactions. It uses digital signatures to verify that both parties involved in the transaction are who they say they are. SET also protects the information in the transaction (including credit card information) from being stolen or altered during the transaction, which protects all parties including the consumer. SET offers an additional protection to the consumers by providing a mechanism for their credit card number to be transferred directly to the credit card issuer for verification and billing without the merchant being able to see the number.

Let's examine how SET works. When a customer opens a Visa or Master Card account, he is issued a digital certificate that can be used as a credit card for online purchases. The certificate contains a public key and expiration date, and it is signed by the bank to verify that it is valid. Merchants that sell products on the Internet receive certificates from the banks. The certificates include the merchant's public key and the right to use the bank's public key.

When a transaction is made, the customer's browser receives the merchant's public key and the bank's public key, and uses the merchant's certificate to confirm that the merchant is valid. Before the browser sends the order and payment information, information about the purchase is encrypted with the merchant's public key and the payment information is encrypted with the bank's public key, as illustrated in Figure 12-22. This ensures that the merchant cannot read the payment information because the bank's private key is required to open that portion of the message.

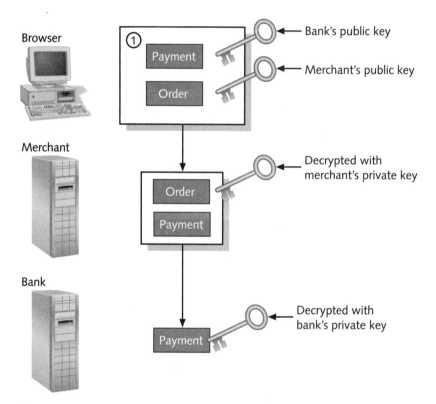

Figure 12-22   Using SET security, a merchant cannot read credit card information because it requires the bank's private key for decryption

Once the merchant gets the information, the customer's digital signature is verified to make sure the customer is valid. There are external companies that do the verification, or the banks may be asked to perform the service. Once the information is verified, the merchant sends the payment portion of the message to the bank. The bank uses its private key to open the message, and verifies the merchant using the digital signature of the merchant. The bank then sends authorization to the merchant, who fills the order.

Protecting Privacy

Just as it is important to protect against people getting into your network and your computer, it is also important to make sure you protect your privacy. Protecting your privacy includes making sure that no one is able to gain access to any of your personal information. When you are on the Internet, it is easy for people to find information about you. The information they find may be only your e-mail address, or it may include financial account information.

As discussed in the previous section, firewalls are one way to make sure that no one is able to access your computer while you are connected to the Internet. But there are other ways to ensure that your privacy stays private. The next section examines some of those methods.

Controlling Cookies

One of the first steps to protecting your privacy is to limit cookies. Both Netscape and Internet Explorer have options to let you reject any cookies. If you have Netscape, you can limit your cookie intake this way: select Edit on the menu bar, select Preferences, then click Advanced. On the screen shown in Figure 12-23 you can set various levels of control through several different check boxes. If you click the checkbox labeled Accept only cookies that get sent back to the originating server, you limit companies like DoubleClick from gathering browsing information about you. Internet Explorer users can control cookies through the Internet Options dialog box. To see this box, select Tools on the menu bar, then click Internet Options, then click the Security tab to select a desired level of security, as shown in Figure 12-24.

12

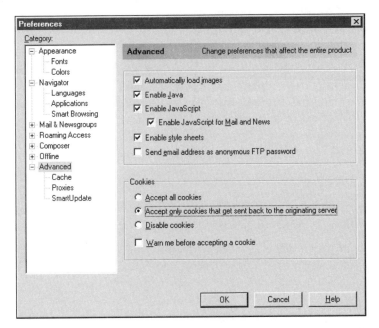

Figure 12-23   Control cookies using Netscape Navigator Preferences window

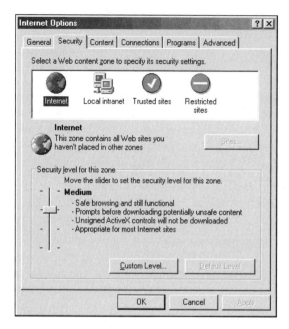

Figure 12-24   Internet Explorer allows you to set the level of security when accessing the Internet

Unfortunately, many web sites, including Yahoo! (*www.yahoo.com*) and Amazon (*www.amazon.com*) rely so heavily on cookies, that it is difficult to get around if you do not allow your browser to accept cookies. And still other sites will not let you in unless you have cookies enabled, which makes it frustrating if you are trying to get information and you keep getting stopped because you will not accept cookies.

One option is to accept the cookies but delete them regularly. Software has been designed just for that purpose. Webroot's (*www.webroot.com*) software, Window Washer, purges all cookies, along with the cache, auto complete data forms, and history each time you shut down your machine. If you have sites that you trust, you can set Window Washer to save cookies from those sites but to delete all other cookies.

Eliminating Spam

Another thing you can do to protect your privacy is to limit how much information you volunteer to people. Many sites request that you complete forms with personal information. Because the information that these sites collect is often added to a database that is sold to advertisers, you should only complete forms for web sites that you trust.

If you do complete a form, it will almost always require an e-mail address. The minute you submit your e-mail address, you are likely to receive unsolicited e-mail messages. Forms usually have a box to check if you do not want to receive future notices from the company, so to avoid some junk e-mail, request that you are not added to any lists. Be careful though, because some forms are worded so that if you do check the box, you are requesting to be added to the mailing list.

Another option is to create a separate e-mail account just for junk mail. You can obtain a free e-mail address at places like *www.hotmail.com* and *www.mailcity.com* and use the account for any mailing lists. Also use this address if you post to a bulletin board, which is a popular place for advertisers to find e-mail addresses.

If you do receive e-mail from an obvious bulk e-mail system (they contain subject lines like "$$$ Make Money Now $$$$" and "FREE FOR THE TAKING!!!!"), do not respond to the message. If you do respond, it only tells the sender that it is an active e-mail address, and you will probably never get off the mailing list.

Protecting Against Viruses

With over 50,000 computer viruses in the world, virus protection is essential to keeping a system secure. The most common protection against viruses is antivirus software. There are several packages available that are designed to protect systems against virus attacks. Two of the more popular software packages are Norton AntiVirus by Symantec (*www.symantec.com*) and McAfee Virus Scan by McAfee (*www.mcafee.com*). Antivirus software should be installed on servers as well as individual PCs. Antivirus software for networks can manage virus protection for all network servers including the mail server, file server, and the SMTP gateway. The Trend Micro (*www.antivirus.com*) software package NeaTSuite is an example of network antivirus software that scans all incoming and outgoing e-mail, Internet activity, and file transfers for viruses and malicious code.

The most common type of virus is one that is hidden in e-mail attachments, and this trend is increasing; however, you can also get a virus from a bulletin board, FTP archive, floppy disk, or a repair service. In order for a virus to execute and do damage (called dropping its payload), the virus must be contained within a program that is executed. Because an e-mail message is only text, the message itself cannot contain a virus, but the virus is hidden in a program in an attached file. Document files can contain macros, which are short programs designed to enhance a document, and most e-mail viruses are hidden within these document macros. The virus cannot damage your system if you don't open the attachment; therefore, never open an attached file unless you trust the person sending it to you. However, hackers can cleverly tempt you to open an attachment. For example, the destructive Mother's Day virus e-mail showing in Figure 12-25 contains a message clearly designed to tempt the reader to open the attached file. This file is not a document at all, but a Visual Basic program that destroys files on the hard drive.

Most antivirus software works by using a **checksum**, a value that is calculated by applying a mathematical formula to data. When the data is transmitted, the checksum is recalculated. If the checksums do not match, the data has been altered, and a virus is potentially the problem. This process of calculating and recording checksums to protect against viruses is called **inoculation**.

12

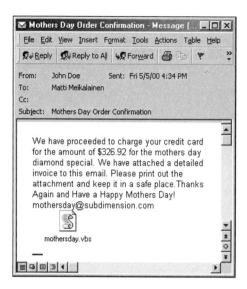

Figure 12-25   The Mother's Day virus sent e-mails indicating that the receiver's credit card had been billed. When the document was opened, it deleted files from the computer's hard drive

The antivirus software applications are designed to alert the user of potential viruses, but the user must do more than install the software. The software must be running at all times, and it should be set up so that it scans the system for viruses every time the computer boots. If the software is not running, it will not be effective.

Another problem with antivirus software is that viruses are designed to elude it. As new viruses are created—and there are between 200 and 300 new viruses discovered each month—antivirus software companies provide updates to the software. The updates offer protection against the newest viruses. But if the updates are not loaded on the machine, the software cannot detect the new viruses, so it is essential to make sure updates are installed on a regular basis.

One of the best ways to protect yourself against viruses is to stay informed. Web sites like *www.datafellows.com* and *www.symantec.com* provide descriptions of the latest viruses as well as any virus threats that are hoaxes; see Figure 12-26. Hoaxes can be almost as damaging as actual viruses because the e-mails that are generated about the false viruses can cause mail flooding.

Be suspicious of e-mails that come from unknown senders, especially if the e-mail has an attachment. Approximately 55% of viruses are acquired through e-mail attachments, so you should open only those attachments that are from someone you know and trust. And if you are not sure of what the attachment is, it is better to ask the sender rather then to risk getting a virus.

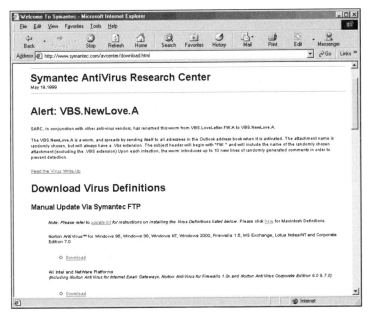

Figure 12-26   Web sites like Symantec post virus alerts and offer downloads to update antivirus software

VIRTUAL PRIVATE NETWORKS

12

A **virtual private network** (**VPN**) uses a public network to provide a secure connection between two parts of a private network or between a remote user and the network. Although by definition the public network does not have to be the Internet, typically the Internet serves as the public network for VPNs. VPNs can be used to connect an individual computer to a LAN (for example, a telecommuter connects to his company's network from his home computer), or they can be used to connect two LANs (such as a branch office connecting to the corporate network).

VPNs are gaining popularity with businesses because they offer networking capabilities at reduced costs. Prior to the VPN concept, if two branches of the same organization, each with its own private network, needed to communicate in privacy, the only solution was to lease a private, dedicated line such as a T1 line or lease a portion of a shared circuit such as Frame Relay. This approach creates a **dedicated private network** (**DPN**) and can be expensive for small corporations, but is a common solution for large banks, the military, and very large corporations. With a VPN, there is no longer a need to lease a private circuit, because the Internet can be used as the public network to connect each branch of the private network. The savings can be considerable, but the primary issue is privacy.

What is needed to set up a VPN? First let's examine how VPNs work, then what hardware and software is necessary for a VPN.

Tunneling

VPNs use a technique called tunneling to allow the two ends of the VPN to communicate. **Tunneling** is a process by which a packet is encapsulated in a secure protocol before it is sent over a public network. In VPNs that deal with the Internet, the packets are encapsulated in one of several competing secure protocols before they are embedded in the IP protocol to travel the Internet. Once the packets are received at the remote private network, the IP protocol header and trailer information is removed from the packet, and the private network protocols are free to transmit the packet.

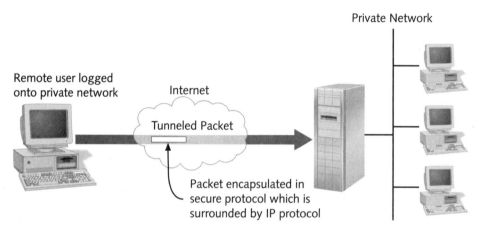

Figure 12-27 With tunneling, packets can travel over the Internet in a virtual private network (VPN)

Figure 12-27 shows an example of tunneling. In the example, the single PC contacts the office network router. The office network determines if the user is valid (usually by checking a password), and if he or she is validated, the VPN software establishes the connection. Data packets transmitted over the Internet have tunneling headers added to packets. When the packet arrives at the office network router, the VPN software removes the tunneling header information from the packet and it is forwarded to its final destination. If the public network is the Internet, as in Figure 12-27, IP protocol is used to transmit the packet between the user and the private network.

The way that a packet is encapsulated and encrypted depends on the protocol. There are four primary protocols that can be used with VPNs to create tunnels: Layer 2 Forwarding (L2F), Point-to-Point Tunneling Protocol (PPTP), Layer 2 Tunneling Protocol (L2TP), and Internet Protocol Security (IPsec). Three of the protocols work at level 2 of the OSI model (Data Link layer), while only one, IPSec, operates at OSI model level 3 (Network layer). In Figure 12-28, there is a fifth protocol, Internet Key Exchange (IKE), that works with IPSec, but at the Application layer of the OSI model.

OSI layers applied to the Internet

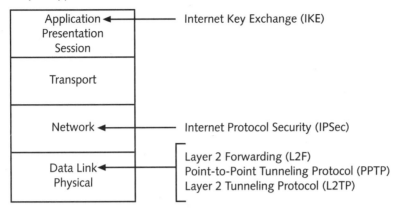

Figure 12-28   The major tunneling protocols used to create virtual private networks

Data Link Layer Protocols

There are three tunneling protocols that operate at the Data Link layer of the OSI model: Layer 2 Forwarding (L2F), Point-to-Point Tunneling Protocol (PPTP), and Layer 2 Tunneling Protocol (L2TP). **PPTP** is the most common tunneling protocol. It is based on **Point-to-Point Protocol** (PPP), a remote-access standard that was created by Microsoft that is used by both the Windows and Macintosh operating systems for dial-up connections. Like PPTP, PPP also works at the Data Link layer of the OSI model. The difference between PPP and PPTP is that PPP is used to manage packets over analog phone lines and PPTP is used to secure private packets over any public network. Another difference between PPP and PPTP is that PPP is dropped as soon as the packet reaches the ISP, because an analog phone line is no longer used and PPP is no longer needed. On the other hand, PPTP is a tunneling protocol that remains with the packet until it reaches its destination at the gateway to the private network.

L2F is a tunneling protocol that was developed by Cisco and which works in a way that is very similar to PPTP. It requires that the ISPs on both ends support the L2F protocol. **L2TP** is a combination of PPTP and L2F that enables ISPs to operate VPNs.

All of the data link layer protocols encode data so that it can be transmitted in private across the Internet. PPTP and L2F use relatively weak authentication and encryption techniques. Because L2TP builds on the features of PPTP and L2F, its authentication and encryption techniques are stronger. L2TP is sometimes used in conjunction with IPsec.

Because PPTP, L2F, and L2TP work at the Data Link layer of the OSI model, they can support protocols other than TCP/IP, such as Novell's IPX or Microsoft's NetBEUI. But, IPsec only works with TCP/IP. IPsec is considered a stronger solution to authentication and encryption than any of the three Data Layer protocols when it is used over the Internet.

12

Internet Protocol Security

Internet Protocol Security (**IPsec**) was developed by the Internet Engineering Task Force to be used as a standard platform for creating secure networks and electronic tunnels. **IPsec** is a suite of protocols that are used for secure private communications over the Internet. Of all the VPN protocols, IPsec is the only one that operates at OSI model level 3 (Network layer). It takes security one step further than the other protocols by verifying and encrypting each packet of data at the Network layer to ensure maximum protection.

IPsec uses three keys: a public key, a private key, and a session key; see the illustration in Figure 12-29. When a message is sent, a function on the sender's machine authenticates the message and can apply an optional digital signature. The data is then encrypted with a public key. The data is sent over the Internet using a secure tunnel. It is then encrypted once again in the tunnel with a session key. At the end of the tunnel, the message is decrypted with a session key, then again using a private key. When the message gets to the receiver's PC, the sender is verified. Once the sender has been verified, the message can be read by the receiver.

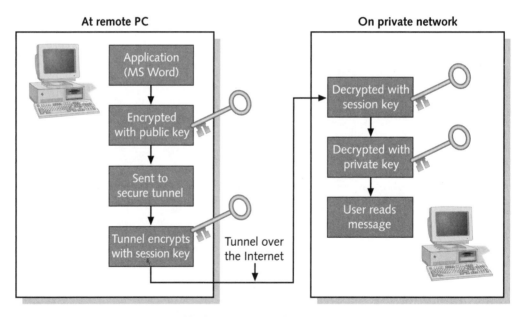

Figure 12-29 IPsec uses a public key, a session key, and a private key to secure data over a VPN

VPN Hardware and Software

A VPN needs three components for optimum performance, though not all parts are necessary if the network doesn't need a high degree of security:

- A security gateway that controls access to the private network

- A certificate authority (either internal or external to the company) to issue and revoke public and private keys and digital certificates

- A security policy server to authenticate users trying to access the network

A **security gateway** is a firewall. It stands between the Internet and the private network, as illustrated in Figure 12-30. It is responsible for encrypting and decrypting packets and tunneling them over the Internet. The security gateway can be a router, a dedicated hardware device, or a server that is also performing other duties than just securing the network. Dedicated hardware devices come in various sizes, and can handle as few or as many users as needed. For example, the VSU-1200 by VPNet (*www.vpnet.com*), shown in Figure 12-31, can accommodate up to 7,500 users at one time. Another example is VPN-1 Gateway by Check Point (*www.checkpoint.com*).

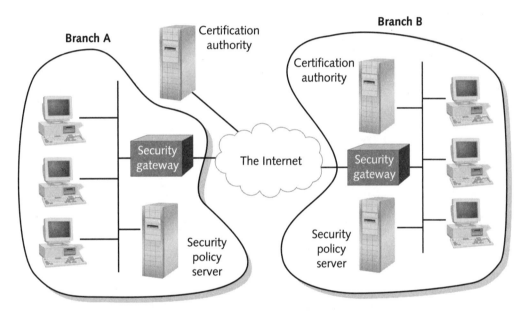

Figure 12-30 To fully function a VPN needs a security gateway, security policy server, and a certification authority for each branch of the private network

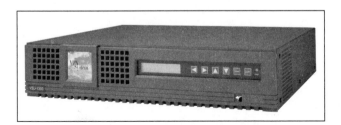

Figure 12-31 The VSU-1200 is one example of a VPN hardware device that serves as the security gateway to the private network

An example of a server acting as the security gateway is Windows 2000 Server using an IPsec third party software or Windows 2000 client. Citrix (*www.citrix.com*) is a popular source for this type of third party security gateway software. For less secure networks, the security gateway can be a PC using Windows 98 and PPTP tunneling.

The **security policy server** is responsible for authenticating those users who have access to the private network. It can be as simple as a Windows NT server that is managing user IDs and passwords, or it can be more sophisticated. For strong authentication, a network might require a digital certificate from every user. If a corporate VPN is also serving as an extranet to vendors, business partners, and preferred customers, the VPN might require each outside individual to obtain a digital certificate from an outside certification authority

The Certification Authority responsible for public and private keys and digital signatures can be external or internal to the network. In Figure 12-30, Branch A uses an external Certification Authority, but Branch B uses an internal CA. In other words, the corporation can manage its own certificates or out-source that responsibility to a third-party vendor such as VeriSign. If people other than employees are allowed access to the private network, then an external CA is needed.

For more information about VPNs, see the web site of the Virtual Private Network Consortium at *www.vpnc.org* and the First VPN's Research Home at *www.firstvpn.com/research/rhome.html*.

REAL PEOPLE, REAL PROBLEMS, REAL SOLUTIONS
WHY A CERTIFICATE?

When Roger Caldwell was nearing the end of a well-executed electronic commerce project for a local retail company, only a few details remained before the site could launch. He had overseen the project from the very beginning. Roger was appointed by the web development firm for which he worked to manage all aspects of the site, so he had overseen the project from the beginning. One of the remaining details was to install a secure certificate on the site's server.

Terry Gunn, the vice president of the retail company for which the site was being built, didn't quite understand why her company needed to spend an additional $125 - $350 for a "secure certificate." The company had already spent thousands of dollars in development and planning for the site. Although the costs were anticipated to build the state-of-the-art e-commerce site, Terry didn't believe she needed to approve the expenditure.

After Roger heard the news that the retailer wasn't going to purchase a certificate, he requested a meeting with Terry. He also asked two people from the retail company who were experienced Internet users to join the meeting. Although the two people, John and Sandra, were not directly connected to the project, he though it would help if he could have a third opinion about the use of security on the Internet.

As soon as the meeting began, Roger explained to the small group what the issue was, and why he thought the site needed a secure certificate installed. His main point was that visitors to the site would be asked for sensitive information if making a purchase. To "secure" their site's server, Roger would use Secure Sockets Layer (SSL) technology to provide a safe way to transmit the sensitive information, such as credit card numbers, e-mail messages, surveys, and other personal data. Without securing the server, visitors to the site who made purchases could potentially be at risk if a party other than the company intercepted any of the transmitted data.

Terry admitted that she had no idea what the secure certificate was. Sandra added to the group's discussion by suggesting another important detail: Confidence in the site! She explained that when she is on the Internet shopping for products, she always checks to see if the site she is visiting uses SSL. This gave her extra confidence in making a purchase from the site because she felt that the owner of the site was interested in protecting her information.

During the meeting, John pulled up a few web shopping sites that he frequented. He demonstrated to the group how a site's certificate could be checked and verified by using controls in the computer's browser. He also pointed out the small bright yellow lock that displayed while on a site that used SSL.

Terry soon agreed that the site did indeed need to have a secure certificate installed. The cost of the certificate was minimal compared to the possibility of a lost customer. Roger also pointed out the two major firms that supplied secure certificates, Thawte (*www.thawte.com*) and Verisign (*www.verisign.com*). He explained the differences in the two companies, and their products. During the meeting, they decided which firm to use.

That afternoon, Roger worked with the hosting company to create the proper encryption codes needed to issue the certificate. Within a few days, the certificate was ready and installed on the web server. Roger's development team made the proper changes within the site's code in order to use the Secure Socket Layer technology. Proper exposure was also installed within the site to make sure that visitors would be aware that the site used a secure certificate.

To date, the company has never had a direct question about the security of the site. By using the certificate appropriately, Roger's firm produced a successful and safe e-commerce site.

12

CHAPTER SUMMARY

❒ Flooding attacks usually result in denial of service, preventing the server from being accessed by legitimate users.

❒ There are several different types of flooding, including SYN flooding, ping flooding, and mail flooding.

❒ When a client communicates with a server, the two computers use a TCP three-way handshake to synchronize the two machines. SYN flooding uses an invalid return address so the synchronization feature of the TCP cannot complete, thereby disabling the system.

❒ When hackers implement a SYN flood, it is difficult to track them down because the flood does not put a strain on any devices other than the one being attacked. Attacks can also be implemented so they appear to be coming from various locations over the Internet.

❒ Ping flooding works by flooding a system with invalid ping requests. Each ping request must be answered, and as the computer tries to answer invalid requests, it cannot respond to valid requests.

❒ Most systems cannot handle ping requests with packets over 64 bytes.

❒ Another form of mail flooding occurs when mailboxes are full of spam, or unsolicited e-mail messages.

❒ E-mail users continue to get unwanted mail, called spam, and ISPs are trying to respond to complaints about spam by offering spam blocking services.

❒ There are many different reasons why a hacker may try to steal data. Common reasons include to gain profit by selling the information, to get revenge on an ex-employer, or to face a challenge.

❒ The attack known as "man in the middle" happens when attackers intercept data that is being transmitted across a network.

❒ Viruses can be designed to do different types of damage, from being nothing more than a nuisance to destroying files.

❒ Trojan horses present themselves as legitimate programs, but once they are executed, they harm the computer system.

❒ A common way to attack a network is to use a worm, which overloads the network resources making the network unusable.

❒ Web sites use cookies to store information about users and to track browsing habits for market research.

❒ Many customers are uncomfortable with the information that web sites can gather using cookies, and are trying to limit the amount of information that can be collected and what can be done with that information.

❏ One of the most important aspects of a network administrator's job is to make sure that the network is protected from unauthorized users and from unauthorized programs.

❏ When you are trying to determine a protection strategy, you have to consider what you are protecting: a private network or intranet, an extranet, transactions between individuals and a web site, transactions between individuals across the Internet, or a virtual private network.

❏ You also have to be aware of what you are trying to accomplish, which is usually one or more of the following: provide privacy, provide authentication, protect data integrity, provide non-repudiation, or just be easy to use.

❏ Because computers make it easy to say you are someone you are not, processes have been created to ensure authentication.

❏ The combination of user IDs and passwords is the most common authentication method today.

❏ A user can have access to files and drives on a network as defined by his user ID.

❏ A good password is a mixture of letters, numbers, and symbols that does not have a logical meaning.

❏ Smart cards provide another method of authentication. Smart cards can hold data about the card holders and then be used to provide access to a single computer or a network.

❏ Digital certificates provide digital signatures that verify that the sender is actually who he says he is.

❏ Digital certificates are issued only by certification authorities, and the biggest certification authority is VeriSign.

❏ One important use of digital certificates is to provide non-repudiation.

❏ There are five types of digital certificates: client SSL certificate, server SSL certificate, S/MIME certificate, object-signing certificate, and CA certificate.

❏ Digital certificates can be divided into two parts, the data section and the signature section.

❏ Because digital certificates act as your signature, they must be protected. Using passwords is the most common way to protect a digital certificate, although some people store the certificate on a device separate from their computer (such as a PCMCIA card or a smart card).

❏ Data that is sent over the Internet is often encrypted using keys to make sure that the data cannot be read by anyone other than the intended party.

❏ Encryption methods vary. The most secure method uses three keys; other methods use one or two keys.

❏ Firewalls can be used on both personal computers and networks, and serve to control information that is sent and received by the computer or network.

12

❑ Firewalls work by examining all incoming packets and determining if the packet needs to be forwarded to its final destination or if it should be rejected.

❑ Intrusion detection software monitors if and when an unauthorized person tries to gain access to your computer or network.

❑ SSL works with both Netscape Navigator and Internet Explorer to provide a secure connection between application protocols.

❑ Credit card transactions over the Internet often use SET to ensure that the transaction is secure and that the credit card information cannot be stolen while it is being transmitted.

❑ A good way to protect your privacy on the Internet is not to volunteer any unnecessary information.

❑ Programs are available which will delete all cookies from your machine on a schedule that you determine.

❑ Antivirus software is only useful if it is updated on a regular basis. It must scan the computer at startup and scan all e-mails and file transfers as they are received.

❑ Antivirus software is available for personal systems and for networks.

❑ One of the best protections against viruses is staying informed about new viruses and about virus hoaxes.

❑ A virtual private network creates a secure connection between two parts of a private network over a public network (typically the Internet).

❑ Virtual private networks use encryption and tunneling to make sure that the connection is secure.

❑ Encryption is the process by which data is coded so that it cannot be read or intercepted by another user.

❑ There are two basic categories of encryption: symmetric encryption (private key) and asymmetric encryption (public key).

❑ Private key encryption uses one key for both the encryption and decryption process.

❑ Public key encryption uses two keys—the public key for encryption and, the private key for decryption.

❑ There are four tunneling protocols currently used for virtual private networks: Layer 2 Forwarding, Point-to-Point Tunneling Protocol, Layer 2 Tunneling Protocol, and Internet Protocol Security.

❑ Three of the tunneling protocols are in level two of the OSI model: Layer 2 Forwarding, Point-to-Point Tunneling Protocol, and Layer 2 Tunneling Protocol.

❑ Internet Protocol Security (IPsec) is the only tunneling protocol that operates at level three of the OSI model. IPsec is also the only tunneling protocol that uses three keys: a public key, a private key, and a session key.

KEY TERMS

authentication — The process of verifying that a person or computer is actually who or what they say they are.

certification authority — An agency that is authorized to distribute digital certificates.

checksum — A number that is calculated for a data file using a mathematical formula. A checksum usually uses the number of bits in the data as part of the formula to produce a unique number.

ciphertext — Encrypted data that is generated by an encryption program.

client-to-client security — The type of protection strategy that is needed when two individuals communicate over the Internet. It includes protection strategies for e-mail exchanges and FTP.

client-to-gateway security — The type of protection from intrusion needed by a private network or intranet. In client-to-gateway security, one user accesses the network via a secure gateway.

cookie — Data that is sent from a web server to the client and is stored on the client's hard drive.

dedicated private network (DPN) — A type of private network where two or more sites communicate over a private, dedicated line such as a T1 line or lease a portion of a shared circuit such as Frame Relay. Compare to virtual private network.

Denial of Service (DoS) — Attacks on servers which are designed to overload the server, therefore preventing it from processing legitimate requests.

digital certificate — An electronic profile that can be used when sending messages to authenticate the sender of the message. A digital certificate includes a key used to decode messages. Also called digital ID.

encryption — The process of coding data to prevent unauthorized parties from viewing or changing the data

extranet — A network between two or more organizations that is a private physical or virtual network

firewall — A set of programs used for security that controls what information is sent and received by a personal computer or a network.

gateway-to-gateway security — The type of protection from intrusion needed by a virtual private network, to ensure reliable and secure communication among private networks that belong to the same organization, but which are located in different places.

ICMP flood — *See* ping flood.

inoculation — The process of calculating two checksums, one before and one after data is transmitted, and comparing those checksums to ensure that a file has not been altered.

Internet Protocol Security (IPsec) — A suite of protocols that are used for private communication over the Internet.

intranet — A type of network that belongs to a single company or organization and only those who belong to the organization or company are allowed to use the network.

intrusion detection software — Software that monitors activity on a network to alert the network administrator of any suspicious activity.

12

key — Part of the formula that is used to encode and decode information. A key must be used when data is encoded, then again to decode the data.

Layer 2 Forwarding (L2F) — A tunneling protocol which connects two computers through the Internet, providing them with a secure connection.

Layer 2 Tunneling Protocol (L2TP) — A tunneling protocol that combines PPTP and L2F to allow Internet Service Providers to operate virtual private networks.

mail flooding — A type of denial of service attack in which an SMTP host is sent a large number of huge e-mails, thus overloading the system.

man in the middle — An attack in which e-mail, files, chat dialogs, and other data are intercepted as they are being transmitted across a network.

Multi-Purpose Internet Mail Extensions (MIME) — Specifications that describe how an electronic message is organized. MIME enables users to include text other than ASCII in e-mail and web pages.

multiple log-in failures — A type of failure caused by a user's repeated attempts to log on to a system with an invalid username and/or password.

no access — As applied to network privileges, no access prevents a user from viewing or changing a specified file or group of files.

non-repudiation — The process of verifying that a transaction occurred, including verifying the people or entities involved with the transaction.

non-repudiation of delivery — Providing proof that a specific message was received by its intended recipient, so that the receiver cannot deny getting the message.

non-repudiation of origin — Providing proof of the origin of a message so that the sender cannot deny sending it.

password — A group of characters that a user must enter, in addition to the user ID, to gain access to a network.

ping — A program that allows one computer to send a packet to another computer and then receive a reply.

ping flood — A type of denial of service attack that happens when a host is flooded with ping requests to the point that the server cannot function; also known as ICMP flooding.

ping of death — A type of denial of service attack that happens when a ping is sent with a packet larger than the standard 64 bytes, causing the system that received the ping request to shut down.

Point-to-Point Tunneling Protocol (PPTP) — Tunneling protocol that is based on PPP, which allows two computers to maintain a secure connection over the Internet.

port scanning script — A script or program that a hacker can use to discover an open port on a computer. A hacker can use an open port to penetrate a computer or network and steal data.

Pretty Good Privacy encryption (PGP) — A popular encryption protocol that uses three keys: a private key, a public key, and a short key that is generated by the encryption software.

private key encryption — An encryption protocol that uses a single key, the private key, for both encryption and decryption. Also called symmetric encryption.

public key encryption — An encryption protocol that uses two keys, a public key for encryption, and a private key for decryption. Also called asymmetric encryption.

Public Key Infrastructure (PKI) — A group of parties who subscribe to a public key encryption service such as VeriSign in order to communicate over the Internet in privacy.

read access — As applied to network privileges, read access allows a user the right to view a file, but not make any changes to it.

Secure Electronic Transaction (SET) — A protocol that offers a secure medium for credit card transactions using digital signatures.

Secure Multi-Purpose Internet Mail Extensions (S/MIME) — A secure version of MIME that works like public key encryption.

Secure Sockets Layers — A protocol that uses both the sender's and receiver's public and private keys to ensure a secure transaction.

security gateway — A device that provides security for a network. See firewall.

security policy server — A server that is responsible for authenticating users who have access to a private network.

smart cards — Cards that can hold data and can be used for authentication when accessing a computer or network.

spam — Unsolicited e-mail messages that are usually trying to sell a product and are sent in bulk to large groups.

SYN flooding — A flooding attack that uses the synchronization feature of TCP to cause a server to shut down.

Trojan horse — A program that appears to perform legitimate functions, but actually is damaging to the system.

tunneling — A process by which a packet is encapsulated in a special secure protocol so that the packet can be sent through the Internet.

user ID — A code that indicates who the user is. The user ID has certain rights associated with it, including rights to files, functions, and programs.

virus — A program that can replicate itself by attaching itself to other programs, and which can cause damage to your computer or network, ranging in severity from mild to disastrous.

virtual private network (VPN) — A network that uses a public network, usually the Internet, to provide a secure connection between two private networks or a node and a private network.

write access — As applied to network privileges, a user with write access to a file can view it, change it, and save changes to that file.

worm — A program that spreads copies of itself throughout the network without needing a host program.

12

REVIEW QUESTIONS

1. List three types of flooding attacks.

2. Explain the TCP three-way handshake.

3. How does the TCP three-way handshake relate to SYN flooding?

4. Does a SYN flood require a lot of bandwidth to be effective?

5. How do you run the ping command?

6. List three reasons a hacker may try to steal data.

7. What is meant by the term "man in the middle"?

8. How is a virus different from a worm?

9. Why is a Trojan horse difficult to detect?

10. What type of digital certificate is used when two individuals send secure documents to each other?

11. How do cookies work?

12. Name three protection strategies to keep your network secure.

13. Explain the difference between an extranet and a virtual private network.

14. What is one example of authentication?

15. What is meant when a user is said to have read access to a file?

16. What constitutes a good password?

17. What constitutes a bad password?

18. How does a smart card work?

19. What information is contained in a digital certificate?

20. Where would you go to obtain a digital certificate?

21. Why is it important to keep your digital certificate secure?

22. Why is it important to keep antivirus software updated?

23. What does a personal firewall do?

24. What are some suspicious activities that intrusion detection software might watch out for?

25. Why would you want to restrict the use of cookies on your machine?

26. Name one thing you can do to help eliminate spam.

27. What type of flooding involves ICMP replies?

28. Name a web site that provides information on the latest virus alerts.

29. What are the different types of encryption?

30. Explain the difference between private key encryption and public key encryption.

31. What is one type of encryption that competes with PGP?

32. What are the different tunneling protocols? What type of network uses tunneling?

33. Which tunneling protocol operates at level three of the OSI model?

HANDS-ON PROJECTS

Personal Privacy Research

Go to the DoubleClick web site (*www.doubleclick.com*). Use the site to investigate what information about your computer can be determined by any web site you access. Print the report.

Digital Certificate Research

Obtain a digital certificate through VeriSign. Install the certificate, and set up your browser to use the certificate when you send messages. Arrange to send an encrypted and digitally signed message to a friend who also has a digital certificate. Then have the friend reply with a message that is also encrypted and signed. Print documents showing that you performed this exercise.

Security Research

Super Supplies, a company specializing in office supplies, has just purchased a direct connection to the Internet so they can implement a new web site. The web site will run from a server, which will function as both the e-mail server and the web server. While the executives are excited about the progress, they are concerned about security because there have been so many news reports of security problems with the Internet. You have been hired as a consultant to determine what security measures should be taken.

The company has requested that you provide a recommendation of hardware and software necessary to provide a secure connection to this server. Also, you have been asked to provide a list of procedures that the company should follow, and when they should be done. Write up your recommendations.

12

VPN Research

The small company that you work for has just started allowing employees to telecommute. Two of the employees got permission to telecommute long distance, and moved out of state. Now that the company is paying for the long distance phone bills, it would like to see what alternatives are available.

Research what would be required to set up a virtual private network. Determine both the hardware and software requirements for the central office and for any remote offices. Write a short report that contains the results of your research.

Encrypting Files using PGP

You have been asked to discover a way that important graphics files can be encrypted so that these files can be sent across the Internet attached to e-mail messages. You have decided to investigate using Pretty Good Privacy (PGP) for Personal Privacy as the solution. Download a free version of the software from *web.mit.edu/network/pgp.html* and use it to encrypt a graphic file. What is required so that the receiver of the file can decrypt it?

Personal Firewalls

Download and install one of the personal firewall products mentioned in the chapter. After the software is running, use your PC to access web sites, send and receive e-mail, and upload and download a file using FTP. What does the firewall software show on the screen and ask you when you do each of these tasks?

13

SOLVING CLIENT PROBLEMS

In this chapter, you will learn

♦ About tools to help solve problems with Windows 98 and applications software

♦ How to manage antivirus software to protect your desktop

♦ How to solve problems with browsers

♦ How to troubleshoot and solve problems when connecting to the Internet

---

You have learned much from previous chapters about how the Internet works and how client software on the PC connects with and interacts with software on servers. This chapter applies this knowledge and teaches you to solve problems that occur when a personal computer is used to connect to and use the Internet.

The most popular operating system for personal computers today is Windows 98, so this chapter focuses on that operating system. It gives you some basic insights into the tools and methods you can use to troubleshoot and solve problems with Windows 98; specifically, problems that affect Internet client software installed on a PC. You will then turn your attention to applications software on the PC with the focus on browsers and other client software and software to protect the security of the PC, including antivirus software. Next, you will learn about the tools available to solve problems using TCP/IP to connect to the Internet. In the last part of the chapter, you will see how all this information ties together as you follow along in a real-life situation of bringing up a small LAN with Internet connectivity.

SOLVING WINDOWS 98 PROBLEMS

Solving problems with Windows 98 and applications software can require a depth of knowledge beyond the scope of this book. Entire books are written about how to support Windows 98. Rather than try to teach you everything about Windows 98, the goal of this chapter is to empower you as a novice troubleshooter, so that you can solve some common problems, and also know the general direction to take to solve complicated ones. Even if you can't solve a very difficult problem yourself, it certainly helps to be able to communicate effectively with a PC technician who can, and this chapter prepares you to do just that.

Microsoft Windows 98 is a suite of programs that work together to manage the hardware and software installed on a PC, interact with the user, and manage a network connection. When you first install Windows 98 from a CD, if you choose to do a typical installation, not all these programs are installed on your hard drive and are therefore not available for your use. In order to configure a PC to connect to the Internet, you must know how to find out what components are installed and how to add these missing components.

In addition, Windows 98, like all software, is not without errors. Occasionally, Microsoft will release an update to Windows 98, called a patch, to fix specific problems. In addition, as new features are written, new releases to Windows 98 are made available for purchase. Currently, Windows 98 is in its second edition, with a new edition expected before this book goes to print. The next section shows you how to determine what components are installed and how to download and install Windows 98 patches.

Managing Applications and Windows 98 Components

The first thing to learn about is how to add and remove an application. The Add/Remove Programs icon under the Control Panel is responsible for listing and managing the installation and removal of applications software, including browsers, e-mail clients, FTP clients and so forth. To see what applications are installed on your computer, follow these directions:

1. Click **Start** on the Taskbar, point to **Settings**, and click **Control Panel**. The Control Panel opens.

2. Double-click the **Add/Remove Programs** icon. The Add/Remove Programs Properties window opens, as shown in Figure 13-1.

3. Click the **Install/Uninstall** tab to see the list of software applications installed on this PC. If you want to uninstall software, select the software and click the **Add/Remove** button.

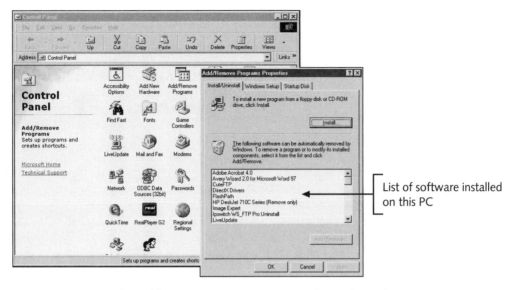

List of software installed
on this PC

Figure 13-1   Use the Add/Remove Programs icon in Control Panel to manage
Windows 98 components and software installed on the PC

Most well-written software applications include an uninstall utility. When Windows 98 unin-
stalls software, it executes the application's uninstall utility. If the utility is not present,
Windows 98 deletes the application from the hard drive, but sometimes some of the application's components are left in the Windows folders, which might cause problems for other
applications.

Because not everyone needs all the components that come with Windows 98, Windows 98
does not install all the components during a normal installation. To know which Windows 98
components are installed, use the Control Panel. Follow these directions:

13

1. On the Control Panel, double-click the **Add/Remove Programs** icon. Select
   the **Windows Setup** tab; see Figure 13-2. This window lists all the categories of
   components that are included with Windows 98. If a category is checked, at least
   some of the components in this category are installed.

2. To see which components are installed, click the name of the category and click
   Details. The details of that category are displayed. For example, in Figure 13-2,
   two of the seven Internet Tools are installed.

3. If you want to install a Windows 98 component, select the component by clicking
   in the check box on the detailed window and click **OK**. You might be asked to
   insert the original Windows 98 CD in the CD-ROM drive so that Windows 98
   can retrieve the component, and then reboot the PC. If you don't want to install
   any new components, click **Cancel** in each open window.

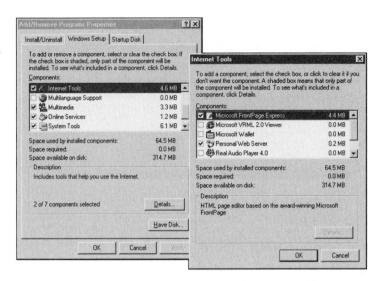

Figure 13-2   Use the Windows Setup tab on the Add/Remove Programs Properties window to install and uninstall Windows components

Finding Out Information from the Microsoft Web Site

When you are having a problem with software or hardware on a PC, one thing you should do is check the Microsoft web site. The Microsoft web site contains a wealth of information about problems with Windows 98 and also points to the FTP site where you can download patches and new releases.

The Microsoft Knowledge Base

The Microsoft web site contains a knowledge base. Remember that a knowledge base is a comprehensive source of information, and some knowledge bases can be accessed via the Web. The Microsoft knowledge base contains information about problems with Windows 98, how to solve these problems, and information about new releases. Follow these directions to use the Microsoft knowledge base on the Microsoft web site:

1. Using a web browser, access the web site *support.microsoft.com*. This is the first page of the Knowledge Base Search page, as shown in Figure 13-3.

2. Specify the Microsoft product and what you want to search for, and then enter a descriptive text. Click **Go**. For example, if you select Windows 98 as the Microsoft product, and perform a keyword search on TCP/IP, the list of articles showing in Figure 13-4 appears. This list contains 170 articles on the subject.

3. Click on an article to read it. For offline viewing, you can print the article or save it to a file on your hard drive.

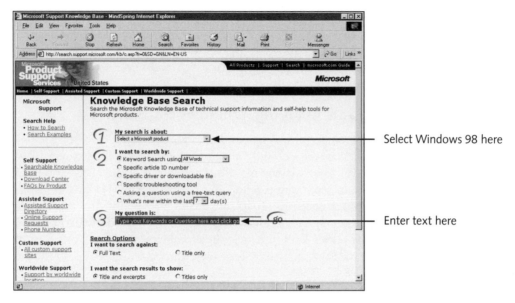

Select Windows 98 here

Enter text here

Figure 13-3   The Microsoft Knowledge Base provides technical support information and self-help tools for Microsoft products

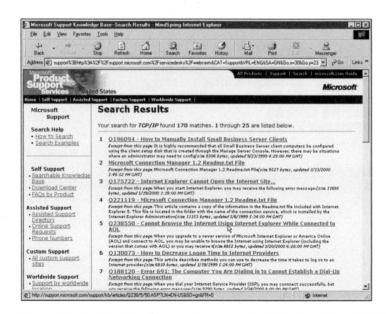

Figure 13-4   Results of a search concerning Windows 98 and TCP/IP included 170 articles

13

If you want to develop your PC troubleshooting skills, it is well worth your time to learn to use this knowledge base and be familiar with the type of information you will find here. For example, the knowledge base provides explanations for many Microsoft error messages. You can enter the specific error message in the text box and retrieve a description of the cause of the error and what to do about it.

Downloading and Applying Windows 98 Patches

If you are having problems with Windows 98 or with installing new software or hardware, you can check the Microsoft web site for updates to Windows 98. If you find one that will fix your problem, you can then download and install the update. It's a good idea to check the site periodically, to see if any patches are available for newly-discovered problems. For example, Microsoft has recently provided updates in response to security problems in Outlook Express. Windows 98 in general has not provided good protection against hackers. Microsoft has issued several fixes to handle these problems. Microsoft calls a patch or fix for a Microsoft product a Service Pack. Follow these directions to download the latest Service Pack for Windows 98:

1. Access the web site, *windowsupdate.microsoft.com*. Click **Product Updates**.

2. The site examines your installation of Windows 98 and compiles a list of updates that apply to your system. Figure 13-5 shows an example of the Windows Update web site.

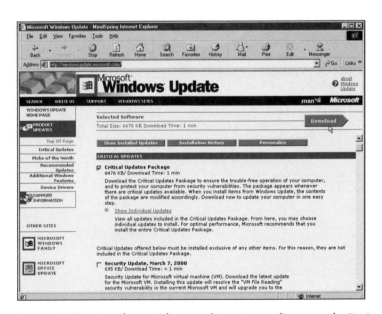

Figure 13-5   Use the *windowsupdate.microsoft.com* web site to get the latest Windows updates

3. Check the updates you want to download. Several updates, including the Critical Updates Package showing in Figure 13-5, must be downloaded and installed individually. Directions on the screen give you instructions about these limitations.

4. Click **Download** to begin the downloading process.

5. After the files are downloaded, you are asked to restart your machine before the changes can take effect.

Tools to Troubleshoot Windows 98

The purpose of this section is to give you a general understanding of how to approach a problem with Windows 98. You will learn about the tools that are included with Windows 98 and a little about how to use them. Generally, Windows 98 problems can be divided into two categories:

- Problems that prevent Windows 98 from loading successfully. The Startup menu is one tool that you can use to troubleshoot loading problems.

- Problems that occur after Windows 98 is loaded. Windows provides a variety of system tools that you can use to discover the source of problems that occur after Windows 98 starts up.

The next sections discuss these two different types of problems and some potential solutions.

The Startup Menu

When you load Windows 98, the first thing you see is the Windows 98 logo screen, followed by the Windows desktop; Windows 98 loads without ever displaying the Startup Menu. The exception to this is when you configure Windows 98 to display the menu every time it loads, but this is not the normal setting. However, there are times when you might want to display the menu so you can use it to troubleshoot a problem loading Windows 98. To see the Startup Menu, hold down the Ctrl key while booting. The Microsoft Windows 98 Startup Menu options are listed below. Option 7 displays only for Windows 98 First Edition.

13

1. Normal

2. Logged (\BOOTLOG.TXT)

3. Safe mode

4. Step-by-step confirmation

5. Command prompt only

6. Safe mode command prompt only

7. Previous version of MS-DOS

Here's a discussion of what each option offers:

- **Normal** starts Windows 98 as it would when you bypass this menu.

- **Logged** starts Windows 98 normally but with loading activities recorded in a file named Bootlog.txt. This file can be a useful tool to diagnose Windows 98 problems.

- **Safe mode** starts Windows 98 with a minimum default configuration to give you an opportunity to correct an error in the configuration. For example, if you installed a modem card that has caused Windows 98 to hang when it loads, this option causes Windows 98 to bypass loading the modem card drivers. You can then uninstall the modem drivers and try the driver installation again. If Windows 98 cannot load normally, but does load successfully in Safe mode, then you can assume that some hardware or software is causing the problem and must be uninstalled. Another way of starting Windows 98 in Safe mode is to press F5 when the message "Starting Windows 98" displays.

- **Step-by-step confirmation** asks you for confirmation before executing each command in the Windows 98 startup files. If the problem occurs while these startup files are being executed, you can most likely identify the command in a startup file that is causing the problem.

- The other options on the Startup Menu all provide a command prompt instead of loading the Windows desktop. Using a command prompt is beyond the scope of this chapter, but it is a tool that a PC technician can sometimes use to diagnose and solve a problem when the desktop refuses to load.

If none of the options on the Startup Menu allow you to load Windows 98 correctly, then the next option is to start up the PC from a floppy disk that contains enough of the operating system to boot the PC. Again, how to boot from a floppy disk and what to do once you have booted are beyond the scope of this chapter. Just know that, if a technician must boot from a floppy disk to get your PC going, then the operating system on the hard drive is corrupted or the hard drive itself is damaged.

Windows 98 System Tools

Once Windows 98 loads successfully, problems can occur with the operating system itself, with the hardware, or with the applications software installed on the system. This section looks at some of the tools available to solve these problems and also explains how Windows 98 relates to software and hardware so that you can have an understanding of what these tools are doing.

The Windows Registry   When a hardware device or applications software is installed on a computer, Windows 98 records information about that installation in a database called the Windows Registry. Later, when the OS loads, it reads that information in the Registry to know how to configure and interact with the device or application. In addition, applications can use the Registry to store their own information that they can later use to "remember" user preferences and other options. Every time you change a Windows setting, install a new Windows background, share a printer over the network, change your Windows default printer, or many other similar tasks, the Registry is changed.

Therefore, the Registry is a repository of various pieces of information used by Windows 98 and other software. Because of its heavy and varied uses, the Registry sometimes gets corrupted. A corrupted Registry can be the source of all kinds of problems such as incorrectly displayed fonts, lost software options, network connections that don't work, and applications that refuse to run.

Windows Registry Checker   Because the Registry is so critical to your PC, Windows 98 has a **Registry Checker** that makes a backup copy of the Registry every day you load Windows 98. The Registry Checker keeps the last five days of backups.

If Windows 98 fails to load and it recognizes that the problem is caused by a corrupted Registry, the Registry Checker automatically restores the Registry from the last successful backup. From the perspective of the user, these events go somewhat like this:

- The system fails. Perhaps there is an error message or the system simply hangs.

- The user reboots, and the system displays a message saying that it is attempting to recover from a failure.

- Windows 98 loads, but the user notices that recent changes are lost. This is because the corrupted Registry was replaced with the last successful backup. Any changes made to the system since this last backup are lost. You might find it necessary to reinstall software, change Control Panel settings or other such things, to get the system current.

Sometimes you can use the Registry Checker to undo a bad software installation. If you have installed software that is not working and you are not able to uninstall the software, you can use the Registry to revert back to a version before the installation. Because Windows 98 keeps all its knowledge about installed software in the Registry, all records of the installation are effectively lost to Windows 98. Everything will appear as it was before the installation with the exception that the folders and files written to the hard drive by the installation will still be there.

To manually restore the Registry to a previous backup, follow these directions:

1. Hold down the **Ctrl** key while booting to display the Windows Startup Menu.

2. Select the option **Command prompt only**.

3. At the command prompt, enter this command: **ScanReg/Restore.** A screen appears that lets you select which backup to use. Select the most recent backup before the installation and continue to follow the directions on the screen.

4. Once Windows 98 is successfully loaded, check to see if the problem is solved.

The Registry Checker is a feature that is new with Windows 98 and is not included with Windows 95. Windows 98 offers several of these types of utilities that make the OS easier to troubleshoot and maintain over Windows 95. These features are one of the reasons people choose to upgrade to Windows 98.

ScanDisk and Defragmenter

Computers need a certain amount of unused hard disk space available for optimum performance. The system uses the hard disk space to hold information temporarily as you install software, connect to the Internet, open and close a browser and perform routine tasks. Without enough free disk space, a system moves very slowly, and it might not be able to connect to the Internet or use Internet resources. One thing to do when you encounter a slow system is to look at the hard drive as the source of the problem and use the following tools to clean it up.

Windows 98, as well as older operating systems, offers tools to keep the hard drive free of unnecessary data, fix problems with the hard drive, and improve hard drive performance. In addition, there are several routine tasks that you can perform to speed up operation. The first thing you should do is delete temporary files that are no longer needed and empty the Recycle Bin. The Recycle Bin is a folder where Windows 98 keeps files that have been deleted. Even though the file is no longer available after you have deleted it, it is still taking up space on the hard drive until you empty the Recycle Bin. Windows 98 offers a handy way to delete temporary files and empty the Recycle Bin in one easy step. Follow these directions to do that:

1. Close all open applications.

2. Click **Start** on the Taskbar, then point to **Programs**, **Accessories**, and **System Tools**. The System Tools menu opens, as shown in Figure 13-6.

3. Select **Disk Cleanup**. If you have more than one logical drive (for example, drive C and drive D) on your system, a window opens asking which drive. Select the drive and click **OK**. The Disk Cleanup window opens, as shown in Figure 13-7.

4. Make sure all options are checked and click **OK** to delete unneeded temporary files and empty the Recycle Bin.

5. Windows 98 asks, "Are you sure you want to delete files?" Click **Yes** and the operation continues.

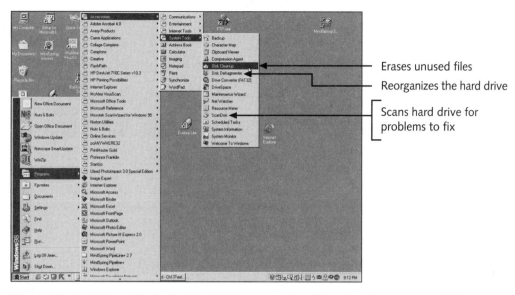

Erases unused files

Reorganizes the hard drive

Scans hard drive for problems to fix

Figure 13-6   System Tools that can help improve hard drive performance include Disk Cleanup, Disk Defragmenter, and ScanDisk

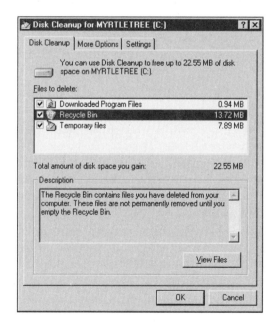

Figure 13-7   Use Disk Cleanup to remove unwanted files from the hard drive

The next thing to do to improve the performance of a hard drive is to scan the drive for errors and fix those errors. Hard drives accumulate errors over time. For example, if an application is open and a user turns off a PC while Windows 98 is still running, the result can be incomplete file fragments left on the hard drive. Sometimes files are not where the operating system thinks they are, two or more files claim to contain the same data on the hard drive, or data on the hard drive does not belong to any file. All these types of errors are called file system errors. **ScanDisk** is the tool to fix these errors. Follow these directions to scan the hard drive and repair errors in the file system:

1. Close all open applications.

2. Click **Start** on the Taskbar, then point to **Programs, Accessories,** and **System Tools.** Then click **ScanDisk.** The ScanDisk window opens, as shown in Figure 13-8.

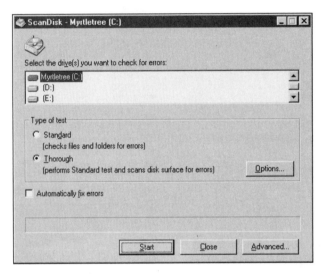

Figure 13-8   Use ScanDisk to scan the hard drive for errors and repair those errors

3. ScanDisk offers two options: Standard and Thorough. The Standard option checks every file and folder on the hard drive looking for inconsistencies and repairing any errors it finds. The Thorough option does this, and in addition, it scans the hard drive surface looking for problems on the surface that might cause data to be lost in the future. If it finds a segment of the surface that does not look good, it marks that segment as bad so that data will not be written there in the future. The Thorough option takes longer, but you should use it in order to get the best benefit from ScanDisk. Select **Thorough** and click **Start.**

4. As ScanDisk finds errors, it asks if you want it to repair those errors. Click **OK** to repair the error.

5. When the process is completed, ScanDisk reports what it found and corrected. Click **Close** in the report window.

Disk Defragmenter, also showing in Figure 13-6, reorganizes the data on the hard drive so that each file is located in only a single place on the hard drive, rather than fragmented over the drive in several locations. When a hard drive is first installed and is still relatively empty, Windows 98 writes each file to the hard drive in a single continuous location. However, as many files are written to the drive and then deleted over time, and new files are written, the space available for new files becomes fragmented—some here, some there. Windows 98 is then forced to write a single file into several small locations on the drive. When it's time to read the file, Windows 98 must move all over the drive to retrieve the one file, causing performance to slow down. **Disk Defragmenter** reorganizes all these files so that, once again, all files are written into a single place on the drive. If you see a decrease in system performance, use Disk Defragmenter. Follow these directions:

1. Close all open applications.

2. Click **Start** on the Taskbar, then point to **Programs**, **Accessories**, and **System Tools**. Then click **Disk Defragmenter**. If you have more than one logical drive (for example, drive C and drive D) on your system, a window opens asking which drive you want to defragment, as shown in Figure 13-9. Select the drive and click **OK**.

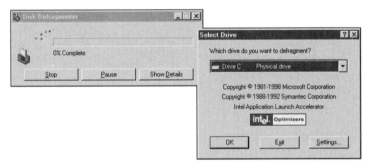

Figure 13-9   To improve performance, use Disk Defragmenter to reorganize files on the hard drive

3. Defragmenter shows a progress bar as it works. The process is slow as many files are read and rewritten to the drive. When done, it asks if you want to exit Defragmenter. Click **Yes**.

All the three tools discussed here should be used on a regular basis to keep a hard drive error-free and performing well.

SECURITY ON A PC

Because the Internet was not designed to offer a great deal of protection from intrusion, most users and organizations put some kind of security in place to protect themselves when using the Internet. Firewalls and proxy servers were discussed in Chapter 10 and installing and troubleshooting them are covered later in this chapter. In addition, you can do some things at your personal computer to improve security. Because viruses are commonly distributed from one PC to another, it is very important to have antivirus software running on a PC. This section explains how to use passwords on your PC to help provide security and manage antivirus software on the PC.

Passwords on a PC

Passwords can be assigned to the computer hardware, the operating system, and individual files and folders. This section addresses how to do all three.

Every computer has a microchip on the main circuit board inside the computer (called the system board) that can hold some basic information about the setup of the system. This information stored on the microchip is called setup or CMOS (pronounced "c-moss") setup after the type of microchip, which is a CMOS chip. When you turn off the PC, no electricity reaches the system board, but the microchip still holds its data because of a small battery installed on the system board near the chip. This data includes the system date and time, what type of hard drive is installed on the system, and where the system must first look to find an operating system when it first boots. Also included in this data is an optional startup password. If the password is present, a user must enter the password when the system first boots in order to use the computer.

To set or change the startup password, you must access the setup information when the PC first starts up. On the initial startup screen you can see a message that says "Press Del to access setup" or "Press F8 to access setup." The message may differ, depending on the system board. Press the specified key and the setup screen appears.

Setup programs vary from one computer manufacturer to another. Look in the manual that came with your computer or system board for specific instructions to set the password. However, caution is in order. If you forget your password, you will not be able to use your computer! In the event you do forget it, there is a way out. Have a qualified PC technician open the computer case and reset the CMOS setup information back to default settings, which will cause the PC to "forget" the password.

You can also enter a password for Windows 98. This operating system password is normally used for Windows networks so that the network can know who is using the PC in order to set user preferences and user privileges. A Windows 98 password is kept in the Windows Registry and can be set or changed by following these directions:

1. Click **Start** on the Taskbar, then point to **Settings**, and click the **Control Panel**. The Control Panel opens.

2. Double-click the **Passwords** icon. The Password Properties window opens, as shown in Figure 13-10.

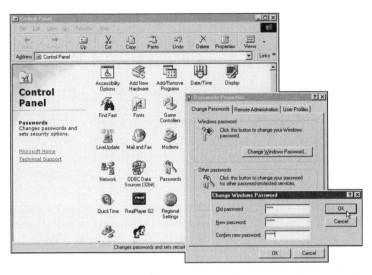

Figure 13-10   Set a Windows password using the Password icon in Control Panel

3. Click the **Change Passwords** tab, then click the **Change Windows Password** button. The Change Windows Password dialog box opens; this is also shown in Figure 13-10.

4. Enter the old password, if there is one. Enter the new password once, and then again, to confirm the password. Click **OK** to close the dialog box and **OK** to close the Passwords Properties box. Next time you load Windows 98, a dialog box opens, asking for the password.

This method sets the password that must be entered to load Windows 98 on a personal stand-alone computer. If you are connected to a network, check with the Network Administrator to find out how to set your password for the network. Your network password must also be entered when you first load Windows 98.

Many applications have features that allow you to set a password that applies to a specific document. You can also set passwords on individual files and folders that are shared on a network. For file and printer sharing to work, the PC must have Client for Microsoft Networks and File and Printer Sharing for Microsoft Networks installed and enabled. A network administrator normally does this when configuring a PC to connect to a LAN. The process is described later in the chapter.

For example, if you are connected to a LAN and want to share a folder on your hard drive with some people but not with everyone on the LAN, you can set a password that must be entered in order to access the folder. Follow these example directions to place password protection on a folder on your drive C named \data:

1. Using Windows Explorer, select the folder C:\data. Right-click the folder name. If the system is configured for file and printer sharing, the drop-down menu lists Sharing. Select **Sharing**. See Figure 13-11. The Data Properties dialog box opens, as shown in Figure 13-12.

13

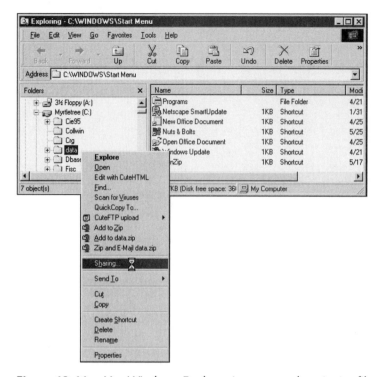

Figure 13-11 Use Windows Explorer to password protect a file or folder shared on the network

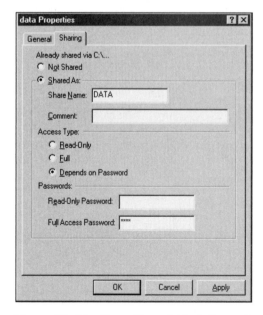

Figure 13-12 Use a file or folder's Properties window to share the resource on the network and assign it a password

2. Click the **Shared As** option button and enter a name for the shared folder. In the figure, the name is DATA. This action makes the folder available to others on the network. They can see the folder when they open Network Neighborhood on their desktop.

3. In the section labeled Access Type, click the **Depends on Password** option button.

4. To allow others the right to make changes to the folder, enter a password under **Full Access Password**. For read-only access, enter a different password. Click **OK** to exit the window.

5. Distribute the two passwords to those people who need to access the folder. You control the access rights by selecting the password you give.

Managing Antivirus Software

Recall from Chapter 12 that a virus is a malicious program that attaches itself to another program or macro within a document file. A virus can replicate itself, and is intended to do harm when executed. Over 55% of viruses are spread by attachments to e-mail messages. A user opens an attachment and the virus executes, infecting the system. To protect your PC against viruses, install and run antivirus software. Use software that loads automatically each time your PC boots. Whenever you boot your system, the antivirus software scans memory and the very beginning of your hard drive where startup information is loaded. It is also a good idea to use antivirus software that scans each e-mail attachment as the attachment is downloaded to look for viruses.

Antivirus software must be updated in order to stay abreast of new viruses. The software can only find viruses that it knows to look for; therefore the antivirus software manufacturer is constantly providing updates to the software as new viruses are discovered. Use software that provides an easy way to download these updates from the manufacturer's web site.

For example, McAfee VirusScan checks to see how long it has been since you have downloaded an update. If it is longer than 30 days, it suggests that you update the software. If you agree, it connects to the Internet, loads a browser, and accesses the McAfee web site. By following the directions on the web site, you can access the web page showing in Figure 13-13 where you can download the updates. McAfee keeps information about viruses in DAT files. Once you purchase the software, you can keep these DAT files current for free. You can also get upgrades to the software for a yearly maintenance fee.

Table 13-1 lists several antivirus software products and the manufacturer's web site. When you suspect a virus has infected your system, check these web sites for information about the virus. Search on the name of the virus in the message that the virus displays when it executes. If the antivirus site can provide you with information about the virus, most likely their software can destroy it.

13

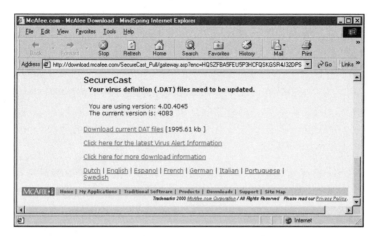

Figure 13-13   Download updates to antivirus software to keep the software current

Table 13-1   Antivirus software

Antivirus Software	Web Site
Norton AntiVirus by Symantec, Inc.	www.symantec.com
Dr. Solomon's Software	www.drsolomon.com
McAfee VirusScan by McAfee Associates, Inc.	www.mcafee.com
ESafe by Aladdin Knowledge Systems, Ltd.	www.esafe.com
F-Prot by FRISK Software International	www.complex.is/f-prot
Command AntiVirus by Command Software	www.commandcom.com
PC-cillin by Trend Micro (for home use)	www.antivirus.com
NeaTSuite by Trend Micro (for networks)	www.antivirus.com

SOLVING BROWSER PROBLEMS

As you know, the two most popular browsers are Internet Explorer and Netscape Navigator. This section looks at problems you might encounter with both these browsers and how to solve them.

Slow Performance

If a browser is showing slow performance, here are some things to try:

Clean Up the Hard Drive

The entire system might be sluggish because of poor hard drive performance. Perform the clean up, scan disk, and defragment processes discussed earlier in the chapter. A hard drive needs a minimum of 100 MB of free space in order to manage temporary files and processes.

If the hard drive doesn't have that much free space, look for software applications that are not being used that you can uninstall.

Check System Resources

A system might not be configured for optimal performance or the system resources might need to be upgraded. In general, a system can be improved by upgrading memory, the hard drive, or the processor in order to improve performance when accessing the Internet. However, you don't want to upgrade one component so that it is significantly faster or better than other components in a system because the overall gain will be lessened by the other slower components. In other words, a system can improve by moderate upgrades of any one component or even all components, but don't make the mistake of investing a lot of money to upgrade one or two components, when what you really need is a new system. Don't expect a huge gain in performance as long as other components in the system are still old and slow.

To verify that the system resources are being used to their best advantage and to see if more resources are needed, first get a report of what resources are on the system and how effectively they are being used:

1. Click **Start** on the Taskbar, point to **Programs**, **Accessories**, and **System Tools.** Then click **System Information.** The Microsoft System Information window opens. See Figure 13-14.

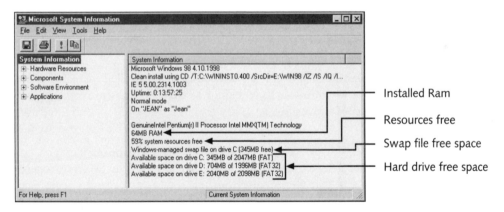

Figure 13-14   Use the Microsoft System Information window to determine the resources available to the system

2. Determine how much memory is installed in the system. In this window, memory is called RAM (Random Access Memory) and RAM is measured in MB. One MB is one megabyte or about 1 million bytes of memory. A byte is the amount of memory required to store a single character or number in a computer. For Windows 98, you should have at least 32 MB of RAM, but 64 or 128 MB is preferred. If you have less than 64 MB, consider adding more RAM. To add more

RAM, consult a qualified PC technician. RAM is relatively inexpensive and the upgrade takes less than 20 minutes. You can see a major improvement in system performance when RAM is adequate. However, if you have a very old PC (older than six years) with a slow processor (for example, an Intel 486), then adding more RAM (more than 64 MB) might not help because the overall system performance will never exceed the performance of this slow processor.

3. Check the free space on the hard drive that is available for the Windows swap file. A swap file is a file on the hard drive that Windows 98 uses if it runs low on memory. Windows 98 stores things in the swap file that it would have stored in memory. Because the swap file is assigned to a logical drive (drive C in Figure 13-14), it can only be as big as the free space on that hard drive. Windows 98 will decrease and increase the size of the swap file as it needs to, according to how much space is available. If the drive has little free space, follow previous directions in the chapter to free up some space. You should allow space for the swap file to be about the same as the amount of memory you have installed. For example, if you have 64 MB of RAM, allow about 64 MB for the swap file.

4. Check the percentage of system resources that are free. In Figure 13-14, 59% of system resources are currently not used. If that percentage is low (less than 40%) when the browser is open, look for applications that you can close. Open applications are listed in the taskbar at the bottom of the Windows 98 desktop. Even though they are reduced to an entry in the taskbar and don't have a window open on the desktop, they are still using system resources. Close any open applications and make it a practice to use the browser with all other applications closed.

5. When you have finished examining system resources, close the window. Click **File**, then click **Exit**.

Windows 98 has another name for the swap file; it's also called virtual memory. For best performance, Windows 98 needs the freedom to manage the size of the swap file (virtual memory). Follow these directions to verify that Windows 98 is configured to manage its own virtual memory:

1. On the Windows desktop, right-click the **My Computer** icon. Select **Properties** on the drop-down menu that appears. The System Properties window opens, as shown in Figure 13-15.

2. Click the **Performance** tab. Click the **Virtual Memory** button. The Virtual Memory window opens. This window is also shown in Figure 13-15.

3. Verify that the option button labeled **Let Windows manage my virtual memory settings** is checked. If it is not selected, select it now. Click **OK** to exit the Virtual Memory window and **OK** to exit the System Properties window.

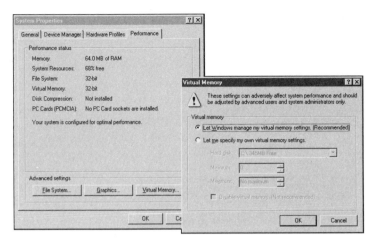

Figure 13-15   For best system performance, verify that Windows 98 is allowed to manage virtual memory settings

Internet Explorer   If Internet Explorer is showing a slowdown in performance even after you have performed the previous tasks, try the following procedures:

1. Right-click the **Internet Explorer** icon on the desktop and select **Properties** on the drop-down menu. The Internet Properties window opens, as shown in Figure 13-16. (If the icon is not on the desktop, double-click on the **Internet** icon in Control Panel.)

2. Click **Delete Files** under the Temporary Internet files heading to clean out the IE cache. The Delete Files dialog box appears asking you to confirm the deletion. Click **OK**. IE must search through the entire cache each time it accesses a web page. If the cache is too big, performance is affected.

3. Click **Clear History** under the History heading to clean out the short cuts cache. The Internet Options dialog box appears asking you to confirm the deletions. Click **OK**. If this cache gets too big, performance can be slowed down. Also, if you reduce the days that Internet Explorer keeps pages in the history folder, performance might improve as there will be less material for Internet Explorer to search. For example, change the days to keep pages in history from the default value of 20 to 7.

4. Click **OK** to close the window.

13

Figure 13-16   Use the Internet Properties window to control the Internet Explorer environment

Netscape Navigator   Use the following procedure to improve performance in Netscape Navigator:

1. Click **Edit** on the menu bar, then click **Preferences**. The Preferences window opens, as shown in Figure 13-17. Click the **+** to the left of Advanced and then click **Cache**.

2. Click the **Clear Disk Cache** button. You might also try selecting the option in the lower part of this window to tell Navigator to stop using the cache. Under the statement, "Document in cache is compared to document on network," select **Never**. Try this for a while to see if performance improves.

3. Click **OK** to exit the window.

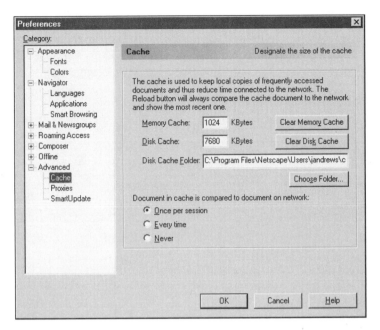

Figure 13-17   Clean out the Netscape Navigator cache to improve browser performance

Browser Updates and Patches

Browser manufacturers are continually improving their products, and generally speaking, you will want to keep the most current version of the browser on your PC in order to take advantage of the latest features and fixes to known problems. However, if you have an older computer or operating system, you might not want to update to a browser that requires a lot of system resources, as your older PC might not be able to support it. In this case, it's better to keep an older version on your PC unless you are having problems with the version.

If you are using Internet Explorer, check the Windows support web site at *support.microsoft.com* for specific problems with Internet Explorer. Search on the product and the error message for articles that describe the problem and possible solutions. Also check the Windows update web site at *windowsupdate.microsoft.com* for updates or patches for known Internet Explorer problems. Download the patch and install it following the same general instructions for Windows 98 patches discussed earlier in the chapter.

If you are not using the latest version of Internet Explorer, try downloading the latest version. If you use your browser for banking on the Internet, be sure to download the version of Internet Explorer for 128-bit encryption in order to get the better security features discussed in Chapter 12. If the new version gives problems on your system, you can revert back to your original version by uninstalling the new version, following the directions given in Chapter 8.

For Netscape Navigator, you can download the latest version of Navigator from the Netscape web site at *www.netscape.com*. (A quick way to get to the right place on the site is

13

to click Help and Software Updates from the browser menu in Navigator.) There is also a link on the site to frequently asked questions about SmartUpdate, the software that takes you through the download and install process. Look at Figure 13-18 to see SmartUpdate. Use these questions and answers to troubleshoot problems installing Navigator.

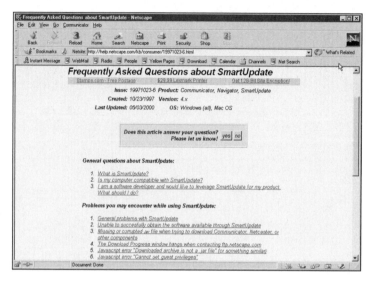

Figure 13-18   Use Netscape's FAQ list to help troubleshoot a problem when installing Netscape Navigator

Also, notice on the web page in Figure 13-18, the link to download the 128-bit encryption version of Navigator. Be sure to use this version if you do banking over the Internet.

TROUBLESHOOTING INTERNET CONNECTIONS

Recall from Chapter 2 that you learned about the TCP/IP suite of protocols. In that chapter, you learned about the OSI layers as they apply to the Internet and how each hardware and software component fits into these layers. In Chapter 8 you learned how to configure the hardware, operating system, and applications software so that they can use the Internet. If this material seems unclear to you, review it again before you continue with this chapter.

The remainder of this chapter addresses how to deal with problems when a PC connects to the Internet. You will learn about the tools that are included with Windows 98 to troubleshoot problems with TCP/IP. You will also get a close look at a comprehensive troubleshooting situation that involves all of the OSI layers, including problems with hardware, operating system configuration, and applications software. You can follow along in a real-life, on-site troubleshooting session in which a small company is attempting to bring up a LAN and connect all its users to the Internet. But first, turn your attention to the TCP/IP tools you will be using to solve these connectivity problems.

TCP/IP Utilities for Problem Solving

When TCP/IP is installed as a Windows 95 or Windows 98 component, a group of utility tools are installed that can be used to troubleshoot problems with TCP/IP. This section looks at each tool and describes when and how to use it. Table 13-2 lists each of the ten utilities and the purpose of each.

Table 13-2   Utilities installed with TCP/IP on Windows

Command	Description
ARP	Manages the IP-to-Ethernet address translation tables that are used to find the MAC address of a host on the network when the IP address is known
Ipconfig	Displays the IP address of the host and other configuration information
FTP	Transfers files over a network. This utility was discussed in earlier chapters.
Nbtstat	Displays current information about TCP/IP and NetBIOS when both are being used on the same network
Netstat	Displays information about current TCP/IP connections
Ping	Verifies there is a connection on a network between two hosts
Route	Allows you to manually control network routing tables
Telnet	Allows you to remotely control another computer on the network. Telnet was discussed in earlier chapters
Tracert	Traces and displays the route taken from the host to a remote destination. Tracert is one example of a trace routing utility
Winipcfg	Displays IP address and other configuration information

Most of these commands are entered from a command prompt. You can access a command prompt using two different methods: the Run dialog box or a command window. To access the Run dialog box, click Start on the Taskbar, and click Run to display the box. Then enter the command and click OK. A disadvantage of using this method is that the results of some commands are difficult to read as they quickly appear and disappear.

To access a command prompt window, click Start on the Taskbar, point to Programs, then click MS-DOS Prompt. Another way to access this command window is to type Command in the Run dialog box. The MS-DOS command prompt window appears; this is sometimes called a DOS box. From this command prompt window, you can enter a Windows or DOS command, including any of those in Table 13-2. You can easily view the results of the command in the window. In a project at the end of this chapter, you will get the opportunity to use the command window to practice these TCP/IP utility commands.

To solve problems that occur when first connecting to the Internet, you will find that the most useful utilities are ping, Ipconfig, and WinIPcfg. WinIPcfg and Ipconfig display the same information, but WinIPcfg has more functionality than does Ipconfig as you'll see in the next section. The advantage Ipconfig has over WinIPcfg is that Ipconfig does not require a GUI Windows interface as WinIPcfg does. If you are working from a command prompt, then use

13

Ipconfig rather than WinIPcfg. In the upcoming troubleshooting situation, you will see how ping and WinIPcfg are used to help in the troubleshooting process.

In addition to the utilities that are automatically installed with TCP/IP, another useful utility is Microsoft SNMP Agent. This utility can be installed after you install TCP/IP, and you can find it on the Windows 98 CD. **SNMP (Simple Network Management Protocol)** provides system management for networks. A system manager can monitor remote connections to computers running Windows 98 with SNMP Agent. For more information about SNMP, see RFC 1156.

Review the Steps for Connecting to the Internet

Let's briefly review the steps to connecting to the Internet as discussed in Chapter 8, and then you'll learn what to do when the connection does not work. Here are the steps to connect to the Internet. This is a summary of the information in Chapter 8:

- **Step 1:** Install and set up the hardware device that will be used to make the connection to the Internet. Use a modem to connect over regular phone lines. Use a network card to connect over cable modem, DSL, or a LAN. If you use a modem, then the modem is configured to use PPP, which is the protocol that is needed so that TCP/IP can be used over phone lines.

- **Step 2:** Bind TCP/IP to the device. Recall that TCP/IP is a Windows component, so if it is not installed, you must first install it before you bind it to the device. Once TCP/IP is bound to the device, then you should see the entry in the Network window. Figure 13-19 shows an example of a system that has both a modem and a network call installed. TCP/IP has been bound to each device so either device can be used to connect to the Internet.

- **Step 3:** Configure the entry in the Network window of the Control Panel. After TCP/IP has been bound to the device, then you must configure the binding correctly, according to the way the PC connects to the network. Recall that one option is static versus dynamic IP addresses and, in some cases, you must specify the gateway to the Internet. (Recall that to configure the entry, you should select it and click the Properties button on the Network window.)

- **Step 4:** Test the connection. After the configuration is finished, the next step is to access the Internet. For a modem dial-up connection, you must dial up your ISP. For cable modem, DSL and a company LAN, the connection is "always up." In either case, you're ready to try your browser to see if you can connect to a web site.

Suppose you get to Step 4 and attempt to use the browser to access a web site on the Internet and the attempt fails. You now need the tools listed at the beginning of this section. First, let's look at two tools, WinIPcfg and ping, examine what each does, and see how to use it. Then you'll go through a step-by-step process for troubleshooting a failed connection.

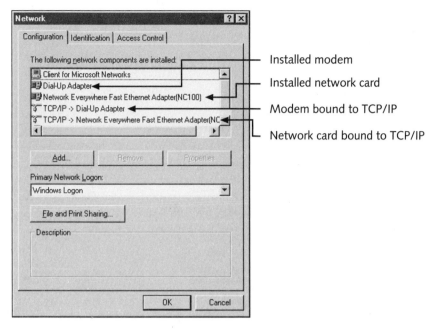

Figure 13-19   The Network window shows hardware installed that can be used to connect to a network and the network protocol assigned to the device

WinIPcfg

WinIPcfg reports the configuration information about the current TCP/IP connection for a device. To use the utility, click Start, click Run, and type winipcfg in the Run dialog box. The IP Configuration window opens, as shown in Figure 13-20. There is a selection box on the window that lists the currently installed devices that are bound to TCP/IP. In this system, there is a network card and a modem card both configured to use TCP/IP. You can choose the particular settings you want to see by choosing the device from the drop down list under the heading Ethernet Adapter Information. The network card is showing in Figure 13-20 and the modem card is showing in Figure 13-21.

13

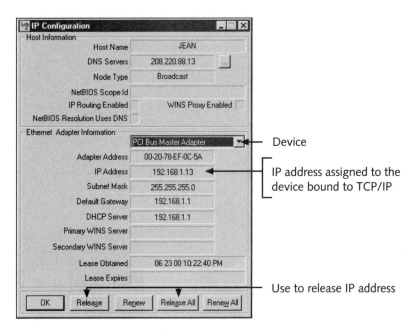

Figure 13-20 Use the WinIPcfg utility to view current information about a TCP/IP connection for a device

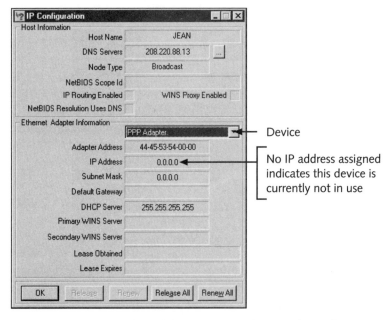

Figure 13-21 The selected device is a modem configured to use TCP/IP over PPP and is currently not in use

Compare the two figures. The network card is a PCI Bus Master Adapter card that is currently assigned an IP address. The modem card is listed as PPP Adapter because it is configured to use TCP/IP over PPP. There is no IP address assigned to the modem card, which means that it is currently not connected to the Internet. Note the Release and Renew buttons at the bottom of the IP Configuration window. Click Release to cause the device to disconnect from the network and click Renew to renew the connection. Sometimes this will cause a failed connection to work.

If the computer is getting dynamically assigned IP addresses from a remote host, such as when connecting to an ISP or a proxy server on a LAN, then a new IP address is assigned when you click Renew. Sometimes this action will heal a failed connection. If you release the connection and then attempt to renew it, but the system fails to get a new IP address, then use ping to test for connectivity with the remote host that is to assign you the IP address.

Ping

Ping is used to find out if one computer can communicate with another over a network that is using TCP/IP. When you issue ping from the command prompt, followed by an IP address or a domain name, ping communicates over a TCP/IP network to another node on the network. An example is shown in Figure 13-22, in which ping is used to test the connection between the host and a web site. Packets are exchanged back and forth and reported on the screen to verify connectivity on the network. If ping works, then you know that the two nodes are communicating at the Transport layer of the OSI model. If communication is happening at this layer, then you also know that all layers underneath the Transport layer are also working. If you cannot use ping successfully, then try these things:

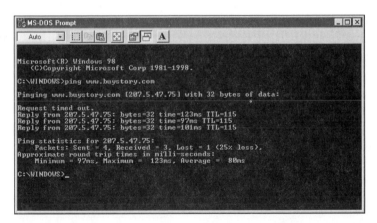

Figure 13-22   Use the ping command to test communication with another host

- Reboot the PC to verify that TCP/IP has been loaded. Verify all the configuration settings in the Network window.

- Use WinIPcfg to verify that the PC has been assigned an IP address

- If you tried to ping using a domain name, use the IP address of the remote host instead. If that works, then the problem is with name resolution.

- Try to ping a different computer. Can you communicate with any other computer on the network? If not, then try removing TCP/IP and reinstalling it. Perhaps the initial installation was corrupted.

- Check the physical connections. Is the network cable plugged in or is there a phone connection? Do you get a dial tone?

If all these fail to produce results, you might need to turn to a network technician or PC technician to solve the problem. The following discussion shows an example of what can go wrong and how professional technicians solved the several problems that occurred when a small company attempted to bring up a LAN and connect to the Internet.

Network Analyzers and Network Monitors

The Windows 98 TCP/IP utilities can be useful in many troubleshooting situations, but sometimes they cannot get to the bottom of a networking problem. Other tools that are more expensive and require more training in order to use them effectively are network analyzers and network monitors. A network analyzer, sometimes called a sniffer, is a portable device that can be hand-carried to a network location and set up to monitor and diagnose problems with a network. A network analyzer can help you troubleshoot difficulties that can occur because of problems with the hardware or software. It can identify problems with cabling, jacks, network cards, hubs and other hardware that work at the lower levels of the OSI model. A network analyzer can also diagnose problems with TCP/IP including TCP/IP packet errors. It can analyze where a packet is coming from or going to, and if the protocols within the packet are used correctly. The packets can be captured and analyzed at any point on the network such as when the cabling is connected to a wall jack. The analyzer can be attached between the cable and the jack and can read and analyze packets as they pass by.

One problem that you might encounter when using a network analyzer is that the analyzer can capture too much data, making it difficult to wade through all the data to search for what applies to the problem at hand. For that reason, a network analyzer allows you to specify filters that weed out data that is not involved in the problem. A network analyzer can be a laptop computer with a proprietary operating system and other software specifically designed to capture and analyze packets on a network. One example of a sniffer is Network Associates' NetXRay.

A **network monitor** is a software program that can be installed on one computer on the network to analyze data on the network. Network monitors are significantly less expensive than network analyzers, but don't always provide all the information needed to solve a problem. This is because they are installed on a computer with an operating system that filters out bad packets, such as Windows 98 or Windows 2000 Server. Thus the network monitoring software doesn't always get to see the packets that give evidence of a problem. Examples of network monitoring software are LANalyzer by Novell for Novell Netware networks using IPX/SPX protocols and Network Monitor by Microsoft for TCP/IP networks.

CONNECTING A SMALL COMPANY LAN TO THE INTERNET

This section looks at how one company set up a network, and connected that network to the Internet. It examines the process from start to finish, and describes in detail the problems that were encountered along the way, and the solutions to those problems.

The company is Golden Locators, LLC, (*www.goldenlocators.com*) a small vehicle-locating company. The network that Golden Locators wanted to install was simple. It has these features:

- The network consists of six PCs in a peer-to-peer arrangement.

- One computer on the network acts as the proxy server to connect the LAN to the Internet using cable modem.

- All computers connect to a 16-port hub that is installed in an electrical closet.

The configuration for the LAN and Internet connection is showing in Figure 13-23. As you look at the process of bringing up this small LAN, it will seem that anything that can go wrong, did go wrong during this installation. The story is true and, as the network was being set up, those people in charge certainly felt that way! Follow along as you are included in the troubleshooting process.

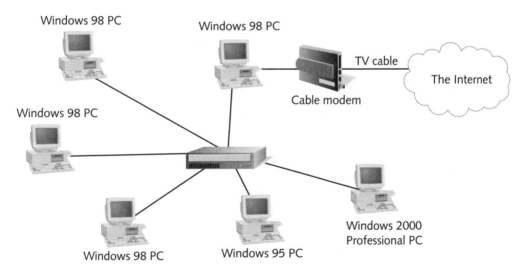

Figure 13-23   Cable modem connected to one PC on a small LAN can provide Internet connectivity for all users on the LAN

Installing the Network Cables in the Office

Golden Locators hired a building contractor to customize the building for the company's needs. Included in that contract was the installation of network cabling and phone lines at each workstation. The contractor used Cat5 cabling (recall from Chapter 2 that Cat5 refers to a grade of Ethernet cable that can accommodate either 10 mbps or 100 mbps Ethernet) and culminated every cable from each workstation in an electrical closet that was strategically located in the center of the building. The contractor left the cable dangling in the closet on one end and hanging from a metal box at the other end.

Next the company hired a communications company to install the in-house phone system and the network cabling connections. The communications company installed wall outlets for each phone line and network connection, as shown in Figure 13-24, and installed the hub in the electrical closet. Figure 13-25 shows a photo of the hub.

The technicians who did the installation were very competent when it came to the phone system, but told the Golden Locators owner, "We don't know much about networks, but I think the hub is installed correctly." This is definitely a clue that something might be wrong!

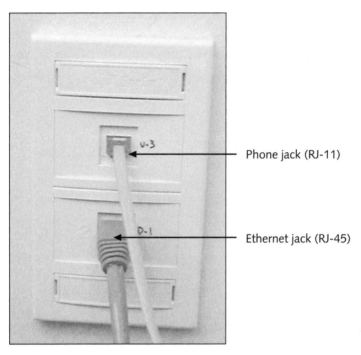

Phone jack (RJ-11)

Ethernet jack (RJ-45)

Figure 13-24   Wall outlet has a regular phone jack called an RJ-11 jack, and an Ethernet LAN jack called an RJ-45 jack

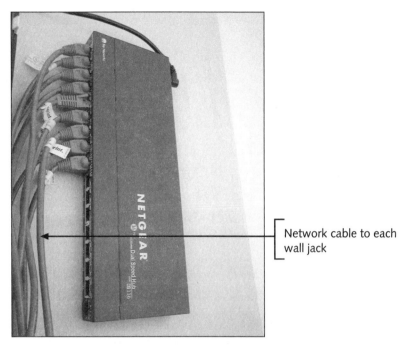

Network cable to each wall jack

Figure 13-25   A hub is mounted on a wall in the electrical closet to connect all nodes on the LAN

Connecting the PCs to the Network

The next step was to connect the PCs to the network and configure each one to access each other and the Internet. The company hired another organization, Omega Computers (*www.omegacomputers.com*), a network service company, to do the job. This company installs PCs, servers, routers, printers and other equipment on networks and installs and configures the software on these devices. It does not handle cabling or hub installation.

When Tim Hayden, the network technician, arrived on site, he first needed to plan the installation. It was decided that one PC that was connected to cable modem should act as the proxy server and DHCP server to all other PCs on the LAN. See Figure 13-26. The proxy server was named INET and all others PCs would be named according to their primary user. Private IP addresses would be used for the LAN.

The proxy server needed two network cards. One card connected to the LAN and needed a private IP address which was designated as 192.168.1.1. The other network card would connect to the cable modem. It would receive a dynamic IP address from the ISP when it connected to the ISP through cable modem. The proxy server and DHCP software on the INET PC was SyGate by Sybergen (*www.sygate.com*), first introduced in Chapter 10. Because this PC is used to connect two networks (the LAN and the ISP network) using the same protocols, it is logically a router. One network card belongs to the LAN and the other network card belongs to the ISP network.

13

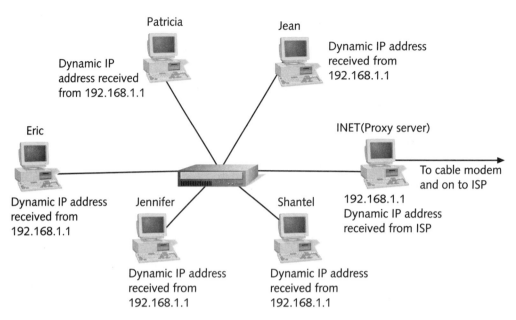

Figure 13-26 One PC acts as the proxy server and DHCP server for all PCs on the LAN

 TIP Windows 98 Second Edition, Windows 2000 and Internet Explorer Version 5 offer a proxy server component called Internet Connection Sharing (ICS). If all PCs on the network had ICS, it could have been used in this network installation instead of SyGate.

After developing his plan, Tim's first job was to install network cards in those PCs that did not already have them, and install the driver software to manage the cards. Next, he connected the network cable to the back of each PC and tested for connectivity. The first two PCs connected successfully to the LAN and communicated with one another with no problem. Here is the procedure that Tim followed in order to install the network cards:

1. Open the PC case and install a network card in an empty expansion slot on the system board. Replace the case cover, plug in the PC and turn it on.

2. When the PC boots up, it recognizes that new hardware is present and begins the Windows 98 automated process of installing a new hardware device. The Add New Hardware Wizard opens, as shown in Figure 13-27. Rather than select the device from the list of devices supported by Windows, click **Have Disk** and insert the floppy disk that was included in the box with the network card. This disk contains the device drivers (software to control a device) provided by the manufacturer. Windows 98 copies the files from the floppy disk and completes the process of installing the network card.

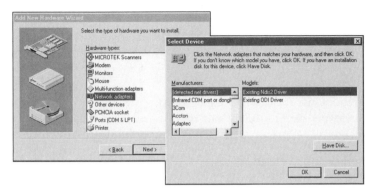

Figure 13-27   When installing a new device, to use the drivers from the device manufacturer, click Have Disk

Installing TCP/IP and Setting up the Network Software

Once the hardware was installed, Tim needed to install and configure the network software, including TCP/IP. Here is the procedure Tim used to set up TCP/IP on each PC on the network:

1. Access the Control Panel and double-click the **Network** icon. The Network window opens.

2. Click **Add** to display the Select Network Component Type window, as shown in Figure 13-28.

13

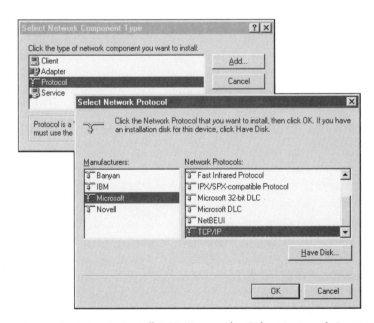

Figure 13-28   To install TCP/IP, use the Select Network Protocol window

3. Click **Protocol** and the Select Network Protocol window opens. Select **Microsoft** on the left and **TCP/IP** on the right. See Figure 13-28. Click **OK**. The system asks for the Microsoft Windows 98 CD and requests that you reboot the system.

The next job was to bind TCP/IP to the network card. Here is how to do it:

1. After the reboot, use the Control Panel to open the Network window again, select the network card in the list of network devices and click **Properties**, as shown in Figure 13-29. The network card Properties dialog box opens.

2. Select the **Bindings** tab and check **TCP/IP**, then click **OK**. You should now be able to see TCP/IP bound to the network card in the Network window.

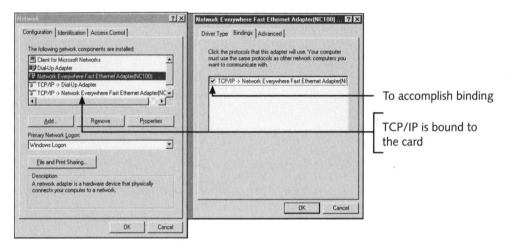

Figure 13-29   Bind TCP/IP to the network card so the card uses TCP/IP as its network protocol

3. Click the entry **TCP/IP -> Network card** in the Network window and click **Properties**. The TCP/IP Properties window opens.

4. Click the **IP Address** tab and select **Obtain an IP address automatically**, as shown in Figure 13-30.

TIP
Compare Figure 13-29 to Figure 13-30. In Figure 13-29 you are looking at the properties of the network card (Data Link and Physical layers of the OSI model) and in Figure 13-30 you are looking at the properties of TCP/IP bound to the network card (Transport and Network layers of the OSI model).

5. Click the **DNS Configuration** tab and select **Disable DNS**. When the PC first connects to the LAN and receives an IP address, it will be told the IP address of the DNS server.

6. Click the **Gateway** tab and add the gateway IP address. See Figure 13-31. The gateway for the LAN is the proxy server in Figure 13-26. Its IP address is 192.168.1.1.

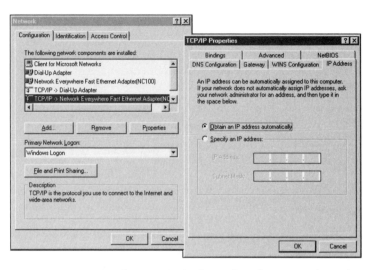

Figure 13-30   Configure TCP/IP bound to the network card

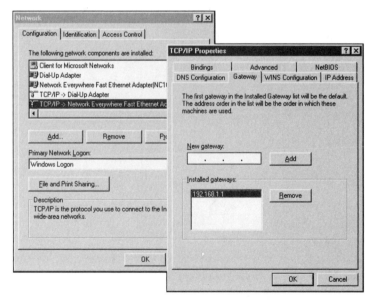

13

Figure 13-31   The gateway IP address is that of the proxy server. This PC will contact this IP address when it needs Internet access

The next thing Tim had to do was to install the necessary client and services software so that users can share files and printers on the network. Each user can share folders on his or her PC and allow others on the network to use a printer that is installed on the PC. One Windows 98 component is used to share folders and printers with others on the network (server side), and another component is needed to use those resources shared by other PCs (client side). Each PC needs both components so it can share its resources and use other shared resources. Also, the computer needs a name so that others on the LAN can address it using Network Neighborhood. To install both components and name the computer, you would use these procedures:

1. Use the Control Panel to access the Network window. In the Network window, click **Add**. The Select Network Component Type dialog box opens.

2. Select **Client** and click **Add**. The Select Network Client window opens. See Figure 13-32.

3. Select **Microsoft** on the left and **Client for Microsoft Networks** on the right. Click **OK** and insert the Windows 98 CD.

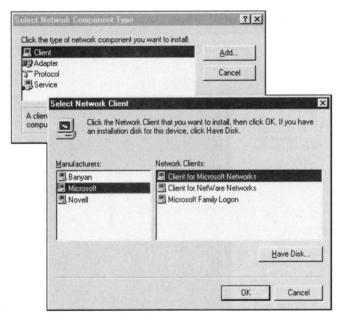

Figure 13-32 Install Client for Microsoft Networks so that users on the LAN can connect to other PCs to share files, folders, and printers

4. Install the service for sharing files and printers with others on the Microsoft network. In the Network window, click **Add.** The Select Network Component Type dialog box opens.

5. Click **Service** and click **Add**. The Select Network Service window opens. See Figure 13-33.

6. Select **File and printer sharing for Microsoft Networks** and click **OK**. Insert the Windows 98 CD.

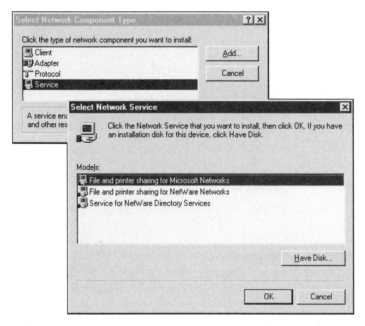

Figure 13-33   Install file and printer sharing for Microsoft Networks to be used to share files and printers on a LAN

13

7. The next step is to turn on file and printer sharing. In the Network window, click **File and Print Sharing**. The File and Print Sharing window opens. See Figure 13-34. Check both options to share both files and printers and click **OK**.

8. Finally, you need to name the computer so that others can recognize it on the LAN. From the Network window, click the **Identification** tab. See Figure 13-35. Give the computer a name and assign it to a workgroup. Put all computers on the LAN that need to share resources in the same workgroup, and name each PC a unique name.

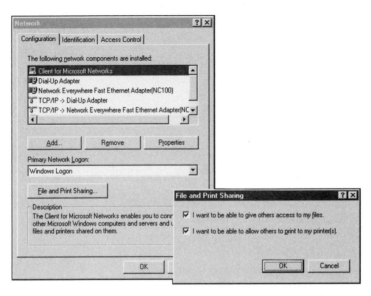

Figure 13-34   Turn on file and printer sharing so others on the LAN can access resources on this PC

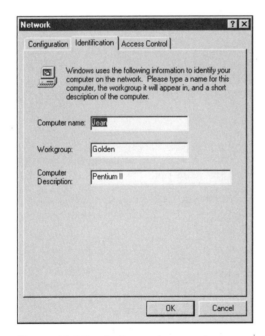

Figure 13-35   Assign each computer a name in a workgroup so that others in the workgroup can see the computer in Network Neighborhood

Recall from earlier in the chapter that to share a resource on a LAN, right-click a folder or file name in Windows Explorer or a printer name in the Printers window and select Sharing on the drop-down menu. In the Sharing window, check Shared As, give the resource a name, and click OK.

The last thing Tim had to do after all these steps was reboot the system so that all changes could take affect. Tim expected to have connectivity on the LAN. He knew that to see others on the LAN, he needed to double-click the Network Neighborhood icon on the desktop, as shown in Figure 13-36.

Figure 13-36   Use Network Neighborhood to view all users on the LAN in the same workgroup

Troubleshooting LAN Connectivity Problems

When Tim attempted to view others on the LAN using Network Neighborhood, he encountered trouble immediately. He discovered that two PCs on the LAN could see one another, but when he attempted to connect the remaining PCs, he could not attain connectivity. To troubleshoot the problem, he began with the network cards and hub.

A network card normally has two lights on the card. One light stays on (is steady) when the card senses connectivity and the other light blinks as communication happens. The hub also has a light for each port that is steady when connectivity is good. Tim checked the lights on the network card and the corresponding light on the hub. He noticed that three of the hub lights that should have been lit were not lit, and that the lights on the three network cards also were not lit. He tinkered with the network wall outlet at one of these PCs and discovered that if he removed the network wall jack and replaced it with a spare jack in his tool kit, he could get the correct lights on the network card. However, he only had one spare jack with him, so was not able to get the others working. He assumed the remaining PCs had a similar problem and turned the problem back to the communications company.

The next day the communications company arrived on site with the proper equipment and experienced technicians to troubleshoot the cabling and hub installation. They used a network analyzer to test each cable connection to determine that the hub was working, each jack was wired correctly, and that all cables were attached correctly at both ends. They discovered that four wall jacks had been wired incorrectly and they replaced these jacks. When they left the site, all hub lights and all network card lights were lit correctly.

Tim returned the next day to continue with the installation. The next three PCs came up just fine, so now five of the six PCs were connected to the LAN, and Network Neighborhood on each PC saw all five. Because the proxy server and DHCP server software was not yet installed, the PCs were not able to get an IP address from the server. When this is the case, the PC will select its own private IP address, but TCP/IP will still work on the LAN and resources can still be shared within a workgroup.

The feature whereby a PC will automatically use its own private IP address when no DHCP server is available is new to Windows 98 (it was not available with Windows 95) and is called **automatic private IP addressing**. If a PC that is configured to get its IP address from a DHCP server does not find a DHCP server when it first connects to the network, it assigns itself an IP address. The IP address has the format of 169.254.x.x. Later, if the PC discovers a DHCP server has become available, it gets its IP address from the server. Use WinIPcfg to tell if a PC has used automatic private IP addressing. See Figure 13-37. The IP address is labeled IP Autoconfiguration Address. If the IP address were assigned by the DHCP server or if it were a static IP address, then the label would be simply IP Address. In addition, if automatic private IP addressing is used, the IP address is in the format 169.254.x.x.

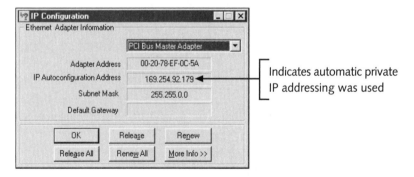

Figure 13-37   Use WinIPcfg to determine if automatic private IP addressing under Windows 98 was used

Setting up the Proxy Server

Next Tim turned his attention to the PC that would act as the proxy server. The physical setup for this PC is shown in Figure 13-38. The PC had two network cards—one for the LAN and one for cable modem, as shown in Figure 13-39. The rear of the cable modem is shown in Figure 13-40.

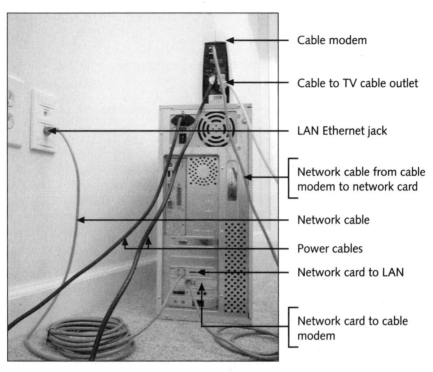

Cable modem

Cable to TV cable outlet

LAN Ethernet jack

Network cable from cable
modem to network card

Network cable

Power cables

Network card to LAN

Network card to cable
modem

Figure 13-38   This PC is connected to two networks; one network is to the ISP using cable
modem and the other network is a LAN

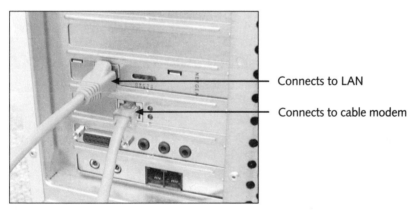

Connects to LAN

Connects to cable modem

Figure 13-39   Two network cards each provide a port—one for cable modem and one to
the LAN

13

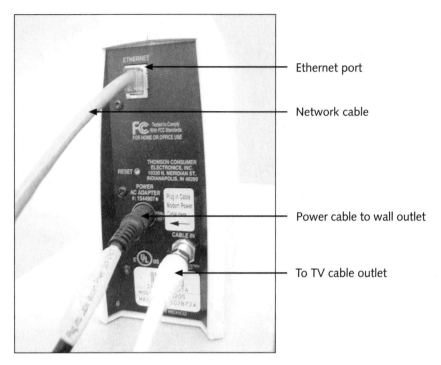

Figure 13-40   Rear of a cable modem

Tim first configured the card to connect to the cable modem ISP. Chapter 8 covered the details of that configuration, so they are not repeated here. After he completed the configuration, Tim had access to the Internet from this one PC. His next job was to install and configure SyGate and configure the PC to connect to the LAN.

Tim accessed the *www.sygate.com* web site and downloaded SyGate. He followed the installation instructions to install the software. Figure 13-41 shows the configuration screen for SyGate. The range of private IP addresses are visible on the configuration screen, as well as the IP addresses of the DNS servers provided by the cable modem ISP.

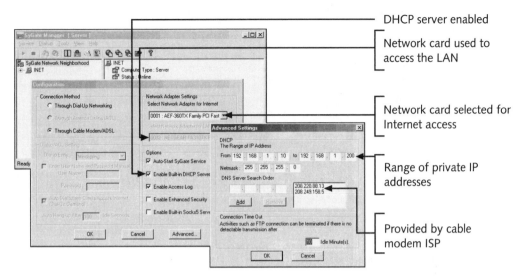

Figure 13-41   The DHCP server is configured to use a range of private IP addresses and to use the DNS server IP addresses supplied by the cable modem ISP

The network card that is connected to the LAN is bound to TCP/IP according to the instructions earlier in the chapter. Unlike the other PCs on the LAN, which had IP addresses that were assigned automatically, this PC needed a static IP address. Tim therefore needed to assign a static IP address to TCP/IP that was bound to the network card. Here is how to do this:

1. Use the Control Panel to access the Network window, then click the entry **TCP/IP -> Network card** and click **Properties**. The TCP/IP Properties window opens.

2. Select the **IP Address** tab. Click the option button **Specify an IP address** to assign a static IP address. See Figure 13-42. The subnet mask is 255.255.255.0 which means that the network is not divided into subnets.

Tim configured file and print sharing, and assigned the workgroup name and the computer name, just as he did for all other PCs on the LAN. Recall that the name of the proxy server PC was INET (refer back to Figure 13-26).

Tim rebooted the PC for all changes to take effect. After the reboot, to verify that the PC was configured correctly, he used WinIPcfg. To use WinIPcfg, click Start on the Taskbar, click Run and type/<lc> winipcfg in the Run dialog box. Figure 13-43 shows an IP Configuration window for each network card installed in the PC. (To see the IP configuration for each network card on the screen at the same time, issue the WinIPcfg command twice.)

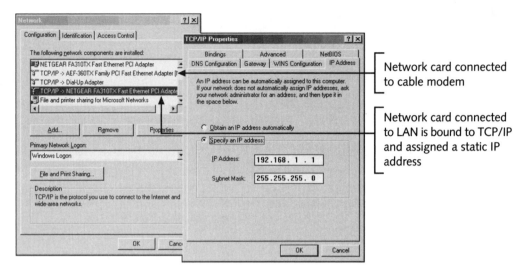

Figure 13-42 One network card is assigned a static IP address and the other network card is assigned a dynamic IP address

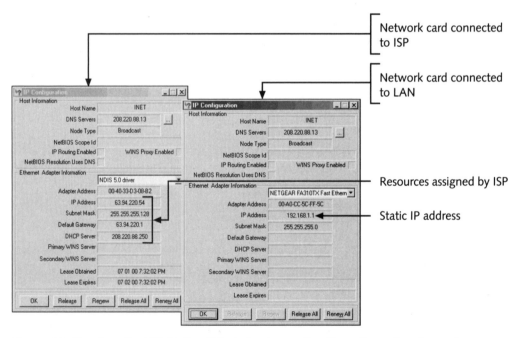

Figure 13-43 Run the WinIPcfg utility twice to see the IP configuration for each network card on the screen at the same time

Troubleshooting Internet Connectivity Problems

All appeared to be working well until Tim discovered that he could not access the Internet from one of the other PCs on the LAN. He also noted that this same PC could not see the INET PC in Network Neighborhood. Here are the things he did to troubleshoot the problem:

1. From the PC named JENNIFER on the network, he used ping to attempt to communicate with INET. The ping command failed.

2. He used the WinIPcfg command to verify that the JENNIFER PC had obtained an IP address from the INET DHCP server and noted that the IP address for JENNIFER was 192.168.1.3, which was within the range of IP addresses that the DHCP server on INET could assign. This was puzzling because the JENNIFER PC would have had to communicate with INET to get the IP address when it first started up, but now Tim could not communicate with INET using ping. He tried using WinIPcfg to release and renew the IP address. He noticed that sometimes the JENNIFER PC could pick up an IP address and sometimes it could not.

3. Tim verified the installation of TCP/IP on the LAN network card on INET. All looked well, but he still could not get the JENNIFER PC to view the Internet. He uninstalled and reinstalled TCP/IP on the INET PC, reconfigured everything and tried again, without success.

4. He called technical support at his company and talked through everything. Technical support asked if any other PC on the LAN could access the Internet. Tim checked and discovered that one PC briefly accessed a web site and then stopped communicating.

5. Technical support at his company suggested he call the help desk of the cable modem ISP and ask for assistance.

6. Tim called the cable modem company help desk. They recycled the connection and talked Tim through the installation once again, verifying the configuration on INET for both the LAN network card and the cable modem network card. Still Tim had no success.

7. Tim went back and forth between other computers and INET using ping to attempt to communicate. As he did so, he noticed that occasionally a ping command would work and then all communication would stop again.

8. Then Tim remembered something. When he had first sat down at the INET PC, he had seen a firewall software running (not SyGate), which was set to automatically start up when Windows 98 loaded. He had closed the firewall software, but had not uninstalled it. He decided to uninstall the software and reboot the INET PC.

When he rebooted, everything worked perfectly! All PCs could connect to the Internet and could view all other PCs in Network Neighborhood. The free shareware software that had been downloaded from the Internet was causing a problem so that the INET PC refused to communicate with other PCs on the LAN. The strange thing was that the software was not

13

running, but it was still causing a problem! Uninstalling the software was the solution. There's a valuable lesson in this experience: Take nothing for granted. Even factors that seem unimportant can contribute to a connectivity problem.

REAL PEOPLE, REAL PROBLEMS, REAL SOLUTIONS
A SLOW SITE?

The site that had been launched for Mears and Company seemed to be doing just what the company expected after six months of being live. Susan Lewis, who had managed the site from its inception, was happy with the results they were receiving. Mears and Company manufactures orthopedic supplies in Miami, Florida. The company was feeling the positive impact of the informative site from both customers and field representatives.

Although Susan was pleased with the site, there was one puzzling problem that started not long after the site began getting traffic. Every once in a while, a visitor would complain that the site took a long time to load into their web browser. At first, she shrugged off the complaints and blamed it on the visitor's connection to the Internet. But as traffic continued to increase to the site, so did the complaints. She knew that something must be wrong with the site, even though she had never encountered the same problem.

A call was made to the web development firm that produced the site. The manager of the firm assured Susan that the site was technically sound, and that all graphics had been optimized for quick loading.

After the conversation with the development firm, Susan asked the customer service representatives to start following up with customers who had mentioned the poor performance of the site. She wanted to find out where the visitors were physically located, and what time of day they encountered the problem.

The results were gathered a month later. Susan was surprised to find that 98% of the visitors that had mentioned the slow response of the site were located in Florida! She didn't know why this was happening because whenever she visited the Mears and Company site, it seemed to work just fine.

Next Susan called the company that hosted the web site. Susan explained the issue, and a test was run on the integrity and performance of the web server. The technician reported that the server was running, as it should, with no problems. She insisted that there must be a problem. The tech then asked her to perform a routing trace routine on the site from her location. Susan had never heard of this so the tech explained that the routing trace routine would produce a report that tell them how a request from a browser to the web site was "routed" through the Internet to reach the site.

The first trace route reported that it took 33 hops, or exchanges of carrier networks, and over 20 seconds to reach the site. A second and third routine were run, with the same result. Now the technician knew what was wrong. After confirming that Susan was located in Florida, he explained that currently that state had the most adverse Internet infrastructure in the entire United States! He went on to give details about how his company had other customers located in Florida with the same problem. The tech then ran a trace route routine to the Mears and Company site from a server located in the New York City area. The report showed only five hops in less than five seconds. It was also clear to Susan why the problem was not noticed from her office— she would never see the difference!

Soon after Susan found out what was wrong, she learned that plans were under way to rebuild and improve the Internet infrastructure in the state of Florida. The company's site continues to grow and attract new business, mainly in the North and West.

CHAPTER SUMMARY

❏ Downloading a patch for Windows 98 from the Microsoft web site can sometimes solve problems with Windows 98 and software installed under Windows 98.

❏ During a typical Windows 98 installation, not all Windows 98 components are installed, but you can install them later.

❏ To view the Windows 98 components installed on a PC and install new ones, use the Add/Remove Programs icon in Control Panel.

❏ Microsoft calls a patch or fix for Windows software a Service Pack. To download the latest Service Pack from Microsoft, use the *windowsupdate.microsoft.com* site.

❏ Windows 98 has a Startup Menu that does not normally display when Windows 98 loads. You can force the menu to display by holding down the Ctrl key while booting.

❏ Options on the Windows Startup Menu include Normal, Logged, Safe Mode, Step-by-step confirmation, Command prompt only, Safe mode command prompt only, and Previous version of MS-DOS.

❏ If none of the options on the Startup menu allows you to load Windows 98, you should boot from a floppy disk and troubleshoot problems with the hard drive.

❏ The Windows Registry is a small database of information about Windows 98 setup options, configuration settings, software installations, and user preferences. In addition, applications software can record information in the Registry.

❏ Because the Registry has heavy and varied uses, it can get corrupted. When this happens, Windows 98 Registry Checker can automatically restore the Registry from a previously backed up copy.

13

❏ You can manually restore the Registry from a previously backed up copy using the ScanReg/Restore command at a command prompt. You might want to do this to recover from a failed software installation.

❏ Registry Checker is new with Windows 98 and is not included with Windows 95.

❏ For optimum performance, regularly clean up and fix any problems with the hard drive.

❏ Under Windows System Tools, use the Disk Cleanup, ScanDisk and Defragmenter to clean and fix the hard drive.

❏ ScanDisk checks all files and folders on the hard drive for errors and corruption and fixes problems when it can. It can also scan the surface of the hard drive for problems that might cause data to later get corrupted.

❏ To secure your PC and files on it, you can use a startup password that is kept in setup information on the system board, a Windows 98 logon password, or individual passwords assigned to specific folders and files on the hard drive.

❏ Use antivirus software to protect against viruses. Set the software to run each time the PC is booted. It is also a good idea to use antivirus software that will automatically scan e-mail attachments for viruses because this is the way most viruses are spread.

❏ Use antivirus software that gives you the opportunity to download upgrades to the software and new information about viruses from the manufacturer's web site. Be sure to keep the software current because new viruses are continually discovered and the software must know about these viruses in order to scan for and delete them successfully.

❏ If a system is performing slowly, it may not be able to connect to the Internet or use Internet applications.

❏ To improve slow performance, clean up the hard drive and check system resources to verify that there are enough resources and that the resources present are being effectively used.

❏ Windows 98 needs at least 32 MB of RAM, but can benefit from 64 MB or even 128 MB to get optimal performance.

❏ A hard drive should have at least 100 MB of free disk space for temporary files.

❏ For optimal performance, verify that Windows 98 has been set to manage its virtual memory, which is preferred to manually controlling virtual memory.

❏ For slow browsers, try cleaning out the disk cache and deleting history files.

❏ Browser manufacturers sometimes offer fixes or patches to their browsers. Download these fixes or the latest version of the browser from the manufacturer's web site.

❏ When TCP/IP is installed as a Windows component, several utilities that can be used in solving problems with TCP/IP are also installed, including ARP, IPconfig, FTP, Nbtstat, Netstat, ping, Route, Telnet, Tracert, and WinIPcfg.

❑ Microsoft SNMP Agent can be installed from the Windows 9x CD, and is used to manage and monitor a TCP/IP network.

❑ Ping is used to verify connectivity between two hosts on a network.

❑ WinIPcfg reports IP configuration information and can release and renew IP addresses on a network. This can help when troubleshooting problems on the network.

❑ When connecting a PC to a network, first install the network card and its drivers and, for a TCP/IP network, bind TCP/IP to the card using the Network window accessed from the Control Panel. The next step is to configure TCP/IP to connect to the network.

❑ When troubleshooting problems with a network connecting to the Internet, first verify that the network card and hub connectivity is working and then turn your attention to how TCP/IP is configured for the network.

KEY TERMS

automatic private IP addressing — The feature whereby a PC automatically uses its own private IP address when no DHCP server is available.

Disk Defragmenter — A Windows and DOS utility that reorganizes files on a hard drive so that files are written to the drive in contiguous segments.

network monitor — Utility software installed on one computer on the network to analyze data on the network.

Registry — A Windows database that stores configuration information about Windows 9x, user preferences and software settings.

Registry Checker — A Windows 98 utility that makes a backup copy of the Windows Registry every day Windows is loaded and keeps the last five days of backups.

ScanDisk — A Windows and DOS utility that fixes file system errors on a hard drive.

SNMP (Simple Network Management Protocol) — A protocol used to provide system management for networks.

SNMP Agent — A TCP/IP utility included with Windows that allows a PC using Windows to be monitored by network administrators responsible for managing a network.

13

REVIEW QUESTIONS

1. What is the purpose of the web site *windowsupdate.microsoft.com*? When might you use this site?

2. List the steps to know what Windows 98 components are installed on a PC.

3. How do you display the Windows 98 Startup menu?

4. What is the purpose of loading Windows 98 in Safe mode?

5. When does the option "Previous version of MS-DOS" appear in the Windows 98 Startup menu?

6. When you change a Windows 98 user preferences setting, where is that change recorded so that Windows 98 can apply the change next time Windows 98 loads?

7. What is the Windows 98 tool that backs up the Windows 98 Registry on a daily basis?

8. What command is used at a Windows 98 command prompt to restore the Registry from a previous backup?

9. What Windows 98 command will reorganize the files on a hard drive so they are each written in contiguous segments?

10. What is the difference between a Standard and Thorough scan of the hard drive using ScanDisk?

11. Where is a startup password stored on a PC?

12. Where is a Windows logon password stored on a PC?

13. List three brands of antivirus software and the web sites of the manufacturers.

14. Another name for a Windows swap file is _____.

15. If you have an older 486 PC that is performing slowly when accessing the Internet, why might it not be wise to upgrade the memory or hard drive in order to improve performance?

16. What TCP/IP utility displays the route taken from the host to a remote destination?

17. What two TCP/IP utilities will display the current IP address assigned to the host?

18. What is one TCP/IP utility that is not automatically installed when TCP/IP is installed?

19. What physical device is installed in a PC to connect to the Internet using DSL?

20. What TCP/IP utility is used to cause the PC to release its IP address and request a new one from the DHCP server?

21. When a PC is connected to two networks, what is the minimum number of network cards that must be installed in that PC?

22. If a PC on a LAN is accessing the Internet through a proxy server, what entry is made under the Gateway tab of the TCP/IP Properties window when configuring TCP/IP on the PC?

23. When PCs on a LAN are sharing files and printers, each PC must have a host name. List the steps to assign that name to a PC, assuming the correct Windows components are installed and enabled.

24. What is the name of the icon on the Windows 98 desktop used to view other host computers connected to a LAN?

25. A network card is working at what two layers of the OSI model? TCP/IP bound to the network card is working at what two layers of the OSI model?

HANDS-ON PROJECTS

Using Net.Medic Diagnostic Software

Net.Medic by VitalSoft is a software program that can diagnose problems with an Internet connection. Download a free demo version of the software from the manufacturer web site (*www.ins.com/software/medic*). Run the software on your PC and print a diagnostic screen.

Using AGNetTools Diagnostic Software

AGNetTools by AG Group, Inc. provides a variety of tools to diagnose connections to the Internet. Download it from the manufacturer web site (*www.aggroup.com*) or the ZDNet site (*www.zdnet.com*). Install and run the software. Use it to perform these three tests: Ping Scan, TraceRoute, and Name Scan. Print the screens showing the results of each command.

Solving Browser Problems

Follow these instructions to solve problems with Netscape Navigator:

1. List the steps to access the Netscape web site and search for information about a problem. Search the site for information about Error 403.6, IP Restriction error. Print any information you find about the error.

2. Print the Netscape web site page that allows you to use SmartUpdate to download the latest fixes for Netscape Navigator. Download the update and apply it to your browser.

3. Perform the procedures discussed in the chapter to clean out the browser cache.

Now do the same three steps above for Microsoft Internet Explorer:

1. List the steps to access the Microsoft web site and search for information about a problem. Search the site for information about Error 403.6, IP Restriction error. Print any information you find about the error.

2. Print the Microsoft web site page that allows you to use the update wizard to download the latest fixes for Internet Explorer. Download the update and apply it to your browser.

3. Perform the procedures discussed in the chapter to clean out the browser cache.

13

Using TCP/IP Utilities

1. Use the WinIPcfg command to display detailed information about the current TCP/IP connection. Print the resulting screen.

2. From a command window, use the IPConfig command to display IP configuration information. Print the resulting screen. An easy way to print the results of a command from a command window is to add the parameter >PRN at the end of the command line (for example, IPConfig >PRN).

3. Access a web site. While the site is downloading data, use the Netstat command to display information about the connection. Print the screen showing the output of Netstat. To do this, first have a command window open. Use your browser to access a web site. Quickly go to the command window and enter the Netstat command.

4. Use the ping command to ping a web site. Print the screen showing the results of the command.

5. Use Route Print command to show the currently active routes available to your host. Print the screen showing the results. (Enter the command: Route Print >prn)

6. Use Tracert to trace the route to the web site zdnet.com. From a command window, enter the command **tracert www.zdnet.com**. Print the results.

Create a Small LAN with Internet Access

To do this project, you will need two computers that have network cards installed, a network cable and a connection to the Internet by way of a regular phone line, cable modem, or DSL. Follow these general directions to create a network and allow both computers to access the Internet. The setup is showing in Figure 13-44. The two PCs in the figure and the directions below are labeled PC1 and PC2.

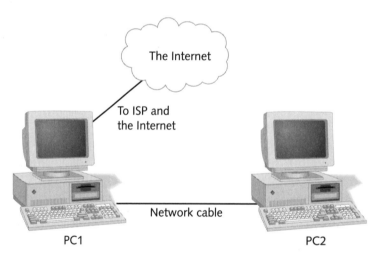

Figure 13-44   A simple network with Internet connectivity

1. Using a network cable, connect one end of the cable to the network port on PC1, and the other end of the cable to the network port on PC2.

2. Bind TCP/IP to each network card and configure the two PCs for static IP addressing. Assign PC1 the IP address 192.168.1.1, and assign PC2 the IP address 192.168.1.2.

3. Configure the two PCs so that Network Neighborhood on each desktop shows both computers.

4. Share a folder on each PC and verify that each PC can access the folder on the other PC. Print screens showing these shared folders.

5. Connect one PC to the Internet using either its modem or a second network card that connects to cable modem or DSL. Follow the directions from your ISP to configure the device making the connection. Verify that the PC has Internet connectivity by accessing several web sites.

6. Configure PC2 to access the Internet through PC1, using PC1 as the proxy server. Download SyGate or similar proxy server software on PC1 and use the software to provide Internet access for PC2. (If both PCs use Windows 98 Second Edition, you can use ICS instead of SyGate or other third-party proxy server software.)

CASE PROJECT

Test Your Web Site from a Fresh Installation

If you have a PC that you can use to create a freshly built Windows 98 environment, do the following to install Windows 98, connect to the Internet, and troubleshoot accessing your personal web site.

This exercise will completely erase everything on your hard drive, so only do it if you have access to a PC that has nothing of value on the hard drive! To do the exercise, you will need a blank floppy disk and the Windows 98 CD (not the Windows 98 Upgrade CD, which requires more information than is given below). In a lab environment, follow specific instructions from your instructor.

13

1. Create a Windows 98 Startup disk: From the Control Panel, double-click the **Add/Remove Programs** icon. Click the **Startup Disk** tab. See Figure 13-45. Insert a floppy disk in the drive and click **Create Disk**. Everything on the disk will be erased and Windows 98 places enough of the operating system on the disk to boot the system.

2. Totally erase everything on the hard drive: Boot from the Startup Disk and enter this command at the command prompt: **FORMAT C:/S**

3. Install Windows 98: Place the Windows 98 CD in the CD-ROM drive. Enter **D:Setup** at the command prompt, substituting the drive letter for the CD-ROM drive in the command line. The Windows 98 Setup menu displays as in Figure 13-46. Perform a typical installation. Windows 98 might ask you to restart the PC several times. Follow instructions on the screen.

4. Install and configure the software necessary to connect to the Internet. This step depends on your type of connection (phone line, LAN, cable modem, DSL, etc). Follow instructions in this chapter and Chapter 8 to connect. For LAN connections, follow the instructions of your lab instructor or network administrator to configure your PC to connect to the LAN.

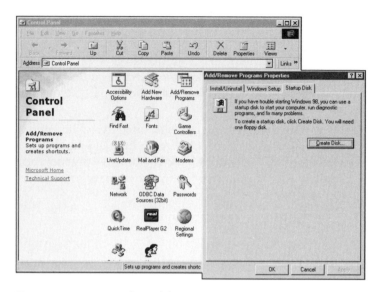

Figure 13-45   Use the Add/Remove Programs icon to create a Windows 98 system disk

5. Download the latest browser from either the Netscape or Microsoft web site.

6. Access your personal web site using the browser. Test every link or option on your web site, downloading plug-ins as necessary.

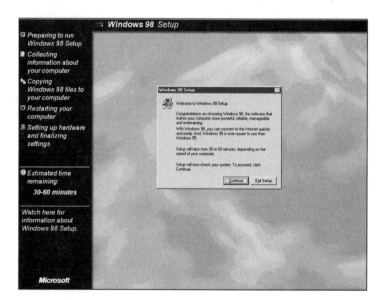

Figure 13-46   Windows 98 Setup screen

14

DOING BUSINESS ON THE WEB

In this chapter, you will learn

- ◆ The different ways that the Web can be used to conduct business, including intranets, extranets, and the Internet
- ◆ How companies attract and retain customers
- ◆ The importance of copyrights and how to get copyrights for your work
- ◆ Different aspects of conducting international business on the Web

Most companies today are keenly aware of the increasing importance of doing business on the Web, and many businesses have web sites that advertise their companies and market their goods and services. It has been said that within the next five years there will be no "Internet companies" because all companies will have an Internet presence. Having a web site will be viewed like having a computer is today—something that is simply assumed. Just as Chapter 13 brought together information from previous chapters about supporting personal computers connected to the Internet, this chapter brings together information from several previous chapters about electronic commerce. You'll learn about the different technologies and software products available to conduct business over the Internet and about legal concerns surrounding these transactions. But first, let's look at one success story that sets the pace for the many possibilities presented in this chapter.

BUSINESSES ON THE WEB

Jeff Bezos decided that the Internet was an ideal place for a business. Customers could shop from their homes any time of the day. Although he knew that he wanted to create an e-business, he was unsure of what type of business he wanted to create, so he made a list of about 20 items that he thought he could sell. Then Bezos analyzed the list to determine which item would work best for an e-business. When he looked at selling books, he realized the great potential. Bookstores cannot carry all the books that are in publication today; rather, they carry only a small percentage of the total books. If he created an e-business, he could offer customers most of the books in-print today, and although some of the books might take longer to get, it would not take any longer for him to special order a book than it would take a bookstore.

Customers typically purchase books after reading the information on the cover. If Bezos could provide the information on the cover, including a synopsis, customers would be willing to purchase the books online. And by adding customer reviews to the book listings, customers could share thoughts and recommend the books to others. This increased the willingness of customers to purchase the books online and helped create the atmosphere of community similar to that attained when people gather in bookstores and discuss books over a cup of coffee.

Another important aspect that Bezos considered was shipping. Books could easily be shipped. They do not require any special handling, and the costs for shipping books is minimal. They are also not as likely as other items to be damaged during shipping, which was another advantage.

After settling on creating an e-business that focused on selling books, Bezos created Amazon.com (*www.amazon.com*), which has become one of the largest e-businesses on the Internet today. Its home page is shown in Figure 14-1.

Why Sell on the Web?

It was estimated that business on the Web in the United States in 1999 exceeded $7 billion and is expected to double in the year 2000. With this volume, businesses are looking at what brings customers to the Web, what they want to buy there, how they want to buy, and what the business must do to meet the demands. Reasons to sell on the Web include:

- The cost of taking orders over the Web is less than most types of order taking, including in-store, over the phone, and on-site.
- Processing and administrative costs are less.
- Orders over the Web have proven to be less prone to errors than orders taken over the phone.
- Customers can easily comparison shop and conveniently make purchases any time of the day or night.

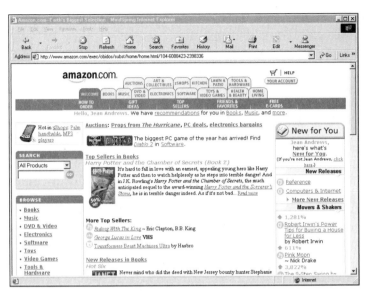

Figure 14-1   Amazon.com began from a logical assessment of what might best sell over the Internet

- Customers sometimes feel more comfortable making buying decisions when salesmen are not present.

- For business-to-business (B2B) sales, having a web presence for order taking implies having command of current technologies.

Even with many compelling reasons to sell on the Web, businesses are reluctant to begin the process. Some of the barriers that prevent businesses from developing a web presence for selling products and services include:

- There is insufficient security on the Internet; customers cannot confirm whom they are doing business with and that financial information will be kept private.

- Customers are concerned about the risk of receiving bad merchandise and about inadequate return policies.

- Systems to receive payments are difficult to implement and businesses don't have enough knowledge of the software and processes involved.

- Electronic commerce for the consumer is not an integrated part of our culture. It is sometimes difficult to use and requires some degree of computer literacy.

- There is inconsistency in taxation laws, legal issues, and international agreements.

- There are no established business models and not enough in-house expertise. It is difficult to justify the cost.

- Businesses are concerned about losing their identity and personal contact with their customers, and losing the ability to negotiate with the customer.

14

Most of the disadvantages listed above are rooted in the fact that doing business on the Web is new. As with other new technologies, it takes time to not only develop the technology, but to develop the business vision, expertise, and culture to use it. As the Internet industry matures, many of the above reasons not to do business on the Web will no longer be of concern. In the future, every business will consider the ability to take orders over the Internet just as essential as the ability to use computers to do bookkeeping or the ability to use telephones to take customer orders.

What to Sell

The Internet is so diverse that you can sell just about anything, but most e-businesses can be classified as selling products, selling services, or a combination of the two. Amazon.com is an example of an e-business that focuses on selling products. Amazon.com began by offering books, but now the company offers musical CDs and tapes, electronics, software, tools, toys, and a myriad of other products, as well as books. And there are countless other web sites that offer products to customers, even some that sell such niche-market products as Wicks' End (*www.wicksend.com*), a site that specializes in selling candles.

Although products are usually the first thing that many people think of when they think of creating an e-business, many popular sites sell services over the Internet. Computerjobs.com (*www.computerjobs.com*) offers personnel placement services for information technology positions. The company's customers are other companies that are looking for IT professionals. Those companies pay a fee to Computerjobs.com so that the job can be posted on the site. Once the job has been posted, anyone looking for a job can reply to the post with his or her resume. Computerjobs.com also lets users create a profile, and the system matches jobs based on the profile.

Other services that are available over the Internet include resume writing services, loan application services, weight loss consultation, and banking services. As the Internet grows, e-businesses are becoming more diverse in what they sell. The next section looks at some of the newer concepts in e-businesses that are emerging today.

Downloadable Files

If you sell an item that can be presented to the customer in a file, it is possible to offer the customer the ability to immediately download the file once the payment has been processed. For example, if you are hosting a site that sells financial management software, you can save money by having the customer download the software and the documentation rather than spending the money to mail the CDs or floppy disks to the customer. Giving the customer the ability to download the files also benefits the customer because it allows instant gratification. The customer receives the product right away, which is an effective selling point because one reason customers cite for not using the Web is that they have to wait for the products to be delivered.

Plans Now (*www.plansnow.com*) is one company that offers customers the option to download files once payment is processed. Plans Now sells woodworking plans. When customers go to the web site, the customer can view pictures of various projects. See Figure 14-2. Clicking on the picture brings up details about the plans, including how many pages the file is, what type of pictures are included, and the cost.

Figure 14-2   Products on this e-commerce site are immediately downloaded to the consumer in a file

14

Most of these sites save their document files in PDF format so that the customer can view the file without any special software. Recall that Adobe (*www.adobe.com*) offers free downloadable browser plug-in software that can be used to display PDF files.

Auctions

eBay (*www.ebay.com*) is well known for its auctions. The company allows customers to post items they wish to sell and allows other customers to bid on the items. For each item posted on the site, the customer must pay a fee for posting the item, and a percentage of the final sale price (between 1 and 5%). These fees are paid to eBay, and no fees are paid when browsing the items or bidding on an item.

When the item is posted, the seller can designate a minimum bid amount, to prevent someone from paying a dollar for an item worth fifty. Also a time frame is assigned to the item. Bidding only takes place within the time frame, and the person who submitted the highest bid at the closing time for the item wins the item. Figure 14-3 shows how auction items are displayed. The seller is responsible for making sure the item is delivered to the buyer, and the buyer is responsible for making sure payment is made. See Figure 14-4.

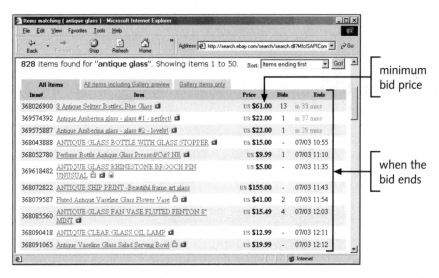

minimum
bid price

when the
bid ends

Figure 14-3   EBay.com shows bidders the minimum bid for an item and when the bidding
will end

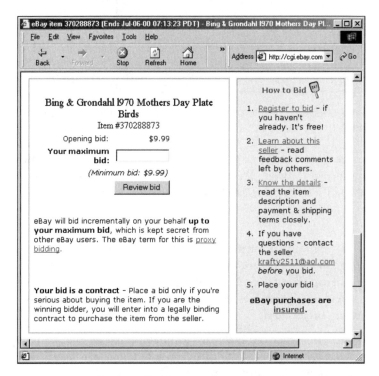

Figure 14-4   Placing a bid in an online auction is considered a legally binding contract if
you win the bid

Auctions provide a unique and profitable e-business if they are done correctly. The company that hosts the auction has no inventory. Instead, the customers provide the inventory. The company is not responsible for shipping; again, that is left to the customers.

Although it may sound like eBay has it easy because all the work appears to be done by the customers, setting up and running an auction site involves a lot of work. The company must make sure that the bidders pay the sellers and the sellers pay eBay and send the merchandise. They also must monitor the items listed to make sure that no illegal items are posted. There have been many news reports of eBay having items like kidneys and "one little brother" for sale, neither of which can legally be sold!

Application Service Providers

Another new trend in e-business is to become an application service provider. An **application service provider (ASP)** stores application software (such as accounting packages) on its web server so that customers can use the software via the Internet. The software packages are more advanced than off-the-shelf software and can offer many features that a small- to medium-size company could not afford if purchasing the software directly.

One company that is emerging as a leading application service provider is Intacct Corp. (*www.intacct.com*). Intacct offers accounting services and software to its customers, and it lets their customers access these services and the software over the Web. The software is stored on the company's web server, and users can access it through the Web with a unique password and user ID. As Figure 14-5 shows, the system lets users create accounts and manage those accounts over the Internet.

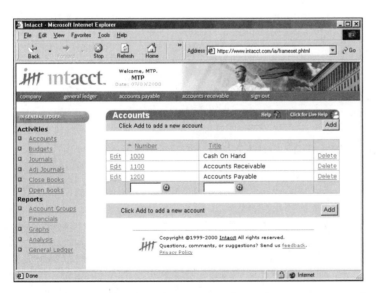

Figure 14-5   Application Service Providers relieve a company from much of the overhead of supporting a software application in-house

The use of application service providers can be appealing to mid-sized companies. Because another company is responsible for hosting the software, the company using the software does not have to worry about maintaining it, providing storage for their data, or providing in-house technical support for the software or data. All they need is a connection to the Internet. The cost of leasing the software is much less than the cost of purchasing and supporting the software. The customer leases the software by paying a monthly fee to use the software over the Internet.

E-tailing

E-tailing refers to the selling of retail goods over the Internet. It is a more specialized category than e-business, which can include selling both goods and services. Because e-tailing has become popular, some companies have begun offering e-tailware. **E-tailware** refers to software that is dedicated to creating on-line catalogs and maintaining e-businesses.

Although many people think that e-tailing simply involves setting up a web page and waiting for the money to roll in, there is a lot more involved with the sales process. An ideal sales transaction follows the steps below:

1. The customer finds and browses your web site.

2. The customer finds a product that he is interested in purchasing, and completes the order form.

3. The item is added to a shopping cart (list of items prior to purchase) and the customer can continue shopping.

4. When the customer "checks out," software designed to handle credit card transactions is used to process payment.

5. The product is shipped to the customer.

But there are things that can prevent this process from flowing as easily as described in the steps above, including billing problems and returned merchandise. As e-commerce grows, the number of companies that are designed to help you with these problems also increases.

Dot.com Companies That Don't Sell Anything

In all the previous examples, the e-commerce site sells a service or a product. Sometimes a commercial web site provides a service that is not billed to the customer when the customer uses the site. Instead, the cost of the service is passed on to the customer indirectly, through some other business cost. For example, Writealoan.com, Inc. (*www.writealoan.com*) provides a service to mortgage companies and banks and their customers by providing a web site where customers can enter the information needed to originate a loan. The service is paid for by the mortgage company or bank and is passed on to the customer as part of the expense of making the loan. Because Writealoan.com has no other source of income than what is generated from the web site, it is called a dot.com company. In contrast, many companies have a web presence on the Internet and also generate their revenue from other sources. The web site is there to advertise their product or services, increase revenue, and as a service to their customers. These companies are sometimes called brick-and-click companies. An example of a brick-and-click company is Barnes and Noble (*www.barnesandnoble.com*). It sells books from retail stores and also from its web site.

But what about those dot.com companies that don't sell a product or service from their site? How do they stay in business? An example of a web site that has no apparent direct revenue is *www.stockmarketcontest.com* by Rcontest.com, Inc. The site is free and offers prizes for winning the contest. These companies depend on advertisements on the site, and the fact that the value today's market places on a dot.com company is not in the revenue it generates, but in the number of unique hits to the site per day, called the hit rate. People invest in these companies based on this hit rate, expecting the value of their stock to go up as the hit rate improves and others invest in the company. The income generated by a dot.com company can consist solely of money from investors who are unconcerned that the company generates no revenue.

These non-revenue generating web sites don't need to be able to receive orders or payments from the site. The remainder of this chapter focuses on web sites that perform revenue-generating business transactions from the site.

HOW BUSINESS IS DONE ON THE WEB

A web site that can take an order for a product or service can be very simple or very complex. This section looks at the basic requirements for doing business on the Web and also looks at some of the companies that have emerged to help other companies meet these requirements.

Just how simple can e-commerce be? A business can have a web site that is used solely to advertise the business, or products and services can be listed on the site in a table or as text on the page. Sites that use this approach list a toll free number for a customer to call to place an order. That's as simple as it can get.

A business can also put a form on the web page. Recall from previous chapters that a form is used in HTML on a web page to receive input from a user. Data entered on a form can be posted to the web server for processing or can be sent to someone's e-mail address. Using this method, the Web is nothing more than an unsecured message center. Once a business receives the e-mail message or reads a text file or database on the server, the business transaction proceeds the same as it would if the customer had mailed in an order or given the order over the phone. In fact, the next step in processing the order might be to manually key the data into the in-house order-processing system.

Many companies begin business on the Web using these simple methods or even simpler ones. However, it's not a good idea to ask a customer to include credit card information in an unsecured e-mail message. And, if traffic is high and there are many different products and

14

services to sell, these methods quickly prove inadequate. More powerful tools are needed which include the following:

- A **catalog server** is software that can list multiple products and give the customer the opportunity to search for these products.

- **Shopping cart software** allows a customer to select several products for a single transaction.

- **Transaction processing (TP) software** receives credit or debit card information, validates the card information, and passes the transaction to the bank. Besides handling the payment processing, the software can also track when the order is shipped or backordered.

- An **Internet merchant account** is a relationship or account between a business taking credit or debit card transactions over the Internet, and the merchant bank or other financial institution that can process the money transaction.

A business can provide all of the above components in-house or can outsource these components to another company. A business might choose to outsource some of these components and keep others in-house. For example, a company might maintain its own catalog software, outsource the shopping cart and transaction processing software to another company and keep the Internet merchant account in-house. If a company outsources the Internet merchant account, then it is in fact passing the sale to another company which becomes the first company's reseller. The next section looks at each of these four components and at some of the options to consider when making purchasing and outsourcing decisions about them.

Online Cataloging

Most e-businesses have some type of catalog for use in their web site. The type of catalog that is used depends greatly on the size of the company and the number of items that are offered. When customers first access the Amazon.com web site, they can search for products, as shown in Figure 14-6.

Notice in the figure that Amazon.com lets the customer search by keyword, so if you were looking for an Italian cookbook, you could enter "Italian Cookbook" and view the results. Notice also that the search may be limited to certain products, such as books, rather than searching all products. This prevents the web site from retrieving items that are of no interest to you. When the customer enters a search, Amazon.com's search engine looks through the database of items and returns those items that meet the criteria entered by the customer, with links to more search results; see Figure 14-7.

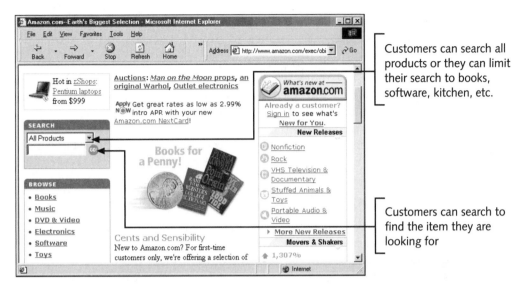

Customers can search all products or they can limit their search to books, software, kitchen, etc.

Customers can search to find the item they are looking for

Figure 14-6   Catalog software includes a search feature

Figure 14-7   The search for Italian cookbooks resulted in three popular cookbooks and a link to more search results

When Amazon.com sells a new product, it first enters the product into the database. As items are entered in the database, descriptive keywords are also entered. Those words are used when

14

the customer initiates a search. The search engine does not limit itself to looking at just keywords; it also searches titles and authors for possible matches. Items often fall into more than one category. You can see in Figure 14-7 that the book *The Complete Italian Vegetarian Cookbook* appeared. That book also appears if you search for vegetarian cookbooks.

As you can see, an e-business web site must do more then just list items that are available. Unless the number of items is very small, a catalog should offer customers the ability to search for items. The catalog should have a database that customers can search, and the catalog should enable a customer to search in several different ways. For example, if you know you need a red shirt, it would be helpful to be able to search by color as well as type of clothing. Another desirable feature of catalogs is the ability to show other items the customer might be interested in purchasing based on his first selection. For example, in Figure 14-8, the shopping bag shows that the customer has selected a T-shirt to purchase. One the right hand side of the screen is a column showing other items that the customer may also be interested in.

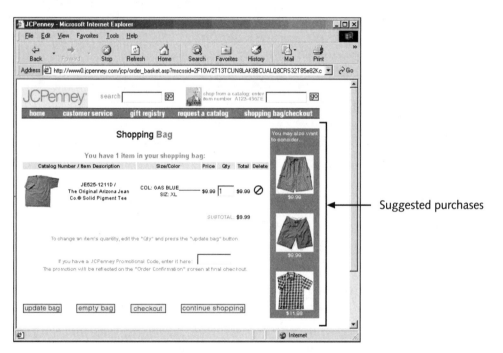

Suggested purchases

Figure 14-8   Catalog software makes suggestions for new purchases based on customer selections

A business can write its own catalog software, purchase the software, or use another company to provide the catalog service for its web site. When purchasing catalog software, look for an easy-to-use interface that allows you to change product lines, prices, and product descriptions and images. Look for a database that can contain online images of each product as well as search utilities that make it easy to provide search features to customers.

Another option is to outsource your online catalog to a catalog service company. There are several different companies that offer catalog services, and a few offer their services for free. Bigstep.com (*www.bigstep.com*) and Freemerchant.com (*www.freemerchant.com*) both offer free services to set up an e-business. Both companies provide services that let you set up a catalog using graphical user interfaces.

Shopping Cart Software

If the web site offers multiple products, shopping cart software is needed to hold the selections in a list until the customer is ready to check out. Just as with catalog software, a business can write its own shopping cart software, purchase the software, or lease the service from another company.

Shopping cart software is sometimes called a shopping bag or commerce cart. Some software allows the customer to "park" a selection in a shopping list. Later, when the customer returns to this web site, he or she can retrieve the shopping list and continue shopping. Figure 14-9 shows an example of shopping cart software.

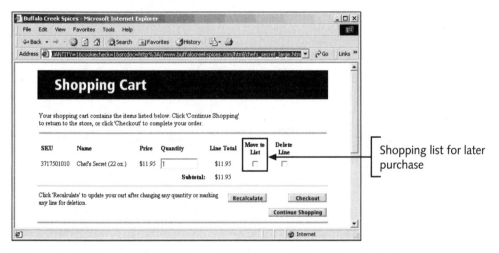

Shopping list for later purchase

Figure 14-9   Shopping cart software lets the customer delete a selection, move it to a future shopping list, check out, or continue shopping

14

Some web hosting services even offer free shopping cart software. Precision Web Hosting and Design (*www.precisionweb.net*) gives customers the ability to set up e-commerce sites that use their free shopping cart software. The software supports most of the standard shopping cart features including sales tax calculations, offline ordering using printed forms, and built-in inventory control.

Taking Orders and Receiving Payments on the Web

Virtually all e-businesses offer some type of electronic payment. But there are several factors that must be considered when taking electronic payments, which is why many companies rely on other companies to provide secure electronic payments. The process of receiving a credit card transaction is diagrammed in Figure 14-10. The process goes something like this:

- The customer enters information about an order including credit card information, which is received by the web server and passed to transaction processing (TP) software.

- The TP software validates the credit card information by way of a gateway to a financial institution.

- The institution authorizes or declines the credit card information, and then the TP software accepts or declines the transaction.

- The seller's software updates a database or flat file with the order information and passes the information to the gateway and on to the financial institution.

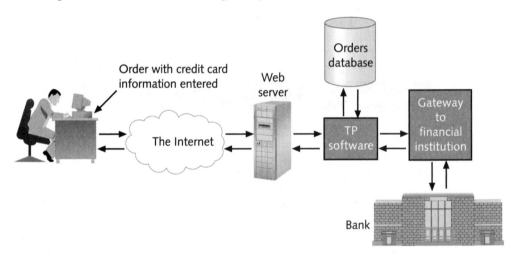

Figure 14-10   Credit card transactions are processed by way of a gateway to financial institutions

Systems that automate the transaction process are not new. Many industries have been using OLTP (online transaction processing) for years. OLTP automates business processes and allows companies to complete these processes with little downtime, minimal errors, and increased security. OLTP is used to book airline seating, handle ATM transactions, and process online business transactions.

Just as with other software used to build an e-commerce site, you can write, purchase, or lease the transaction processing software. If you use a leasing service, the service company has the gateway to the financial institutions in place and gives you several options of banks that you can use for your Internet merchants account. If you are purchasing TP software, look for features that allow you to track orders, including shipping information, returned merchandise, and problems with payment processing. TP software should also have an interface that is easy for you to use to record this information. For example, when the product ships, someone in the shipping department should be able to easily record that fact along with a tracking number if there is one. Customers should also be able to track their shipments and view the tracking number and any information you want them to see about the order in progress.

There are several choices for software to use as the gateway to the financial institutions. CashRegister by CyberCash Corporation is probably the most popular choice. When using CyberCash software, the web site does not need to retain credit card information unless it is kept for future transactions. If the web site doesn't retain the information, the user is assured more security. CyberCash also offers a full line of transaction processing software. For more information, see *www.cybercash.com*.

Using Third-Party Web Sites for Transaction Processing

When a third-party web site is used to manage the transaction processing for a retail web site, the third-party company usually maintains a database of products and orders for the retailer. Figure 14-11 shows how the process works. It goes something like this:

- The retailer displays products to users. When the user clicks a button to select a product for purchase, the retail site points the user's browser to the third-party site to put the item in a shopping cart managed by the TP company.

- Shopping cart software interacts with the product database and displays a web page to the user showing items in the shopping cart. The TP company directs the user's browser back to the retail site.

- When the user clicks a button to complete the purchase, again the retailer points the user's browser to the TP web site where the information about the purchase is collected and the information is recorded in an order database.

- As Figure 14-10 shows, the TP software is also responsible for interfacing with a gateway to a financial institution to charge the customer's credit card with the purchase.

14

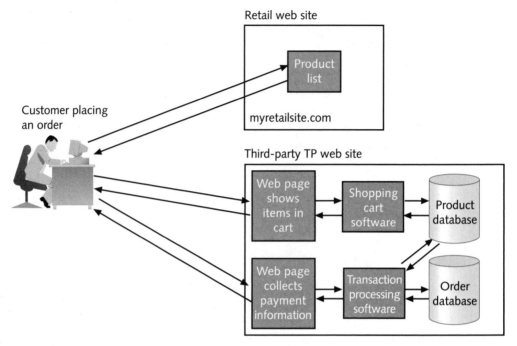

Figure 14-11 A third-party transaction processing web site can do much of the work for a retailer doing business on the Web

This section next looks at a few examples of companies that offer software products and services that collectively are called store front software. These products include catalog, shopping cart and transaction processing software.

One company that provides store front services is Internet Billing Company, or Ibill (*www.ibill.com*). The company handles all aspects of transaction processing. It helps companies set up an Internet merchant account with a bank with which Ibill is associated. Companies that use Ibill software are able to accept all major credit cards, as well as checking account funds. With Ibill's billing software, customers can give authorization to have funds automatically withdrawn from their checking accounts.

 TIP Even though you can use a debit card to buy something from the Web, it is not advised. Instead, use a credit card to decrease your risk.

Another service that Ibill offers is the option for customers to pay their bill by dialing a 900 number. Some customers are leery of sending their credit card information over the Internet, but they have become comfortable with giving the information over the phone. Ibill encourages these customers to purchase items over the Internet by offering the 900-number option when paying their bills.

When an e-commerce site uses a third-party company to do some of the chores, the web developer creates links to the company's site, in this case Ibill. In the example that follows, you will learn to write the HTML so that you can use Ibill to provide the shopping cart and transaction processing for an e-commerce site. The sample web page is shown in Figure 14-12 and the HTML to build the page is listed below with detailed explanations. Regardless of the third-party service company used, the steps to building an e-commerce site are similar.

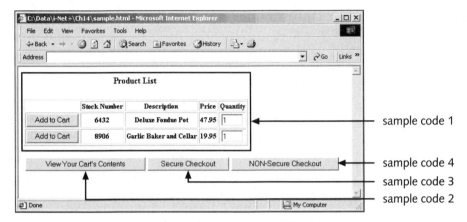

Figure 14-12   When a user clicks one of the buttons on this page, the action is passed to a third-party company to process the request

The following is a step-by-step process that a business uses to set up its e-commerce site using Ibill transaction processing. This code is sample code 1 in Figure 14-12 and creates a table of products for sale.

```
 1. <Table Border="1">
 2.    <Caption> <H3>Product List</H3></Caption>
 3.    <TR>
 4.       <TH></TH>
 5.       <TH>Stock Number </TH>
 6.       <TH>Description</TH>
 7.       <TH>Price</TH>
 8.       <TH>Quantity</TH>
 9.    </TR>

10.    <TR>
11.       <Form method="POST" action="https://
          secure.ibill.com/cgi-win/ccprod/iprod.exe">
12.          <input type="hidden" name="reqtype" value="add
             2cart">
13.          <input type="hidden" name="account"
             value="9000">
14.          <input type="hidden" name="catnum"
             value="6432">
```

14

```
15.        <input type="hidden" name="return"
           value="www.myretailsite.com">
16.        <TH><input type="Submit" border=0 value="Add
           to Cart"></TH>
17.        <TH>6432</TH>
18.        <TH>Deluxe Fondue Pot</TH>
19.        <TH>47.95</TH>
20.        <TH><input type="text" name="qty" size="3"
           maxlength="3" value="1"></TH>
21.     </Form>
22.   </TR>

23. <TR>
24.     <Form method="POST" action="https://
           secure.ibill.com/cgi-win/ccprod/iprod.exe">
25.        <input type="hidden" name="reqtype" value=
           "add2cart">
26.        <input type="hidden" name="account" value=
           "9000">
27.        <input type="hidden" name="catnum" value=
           "8906">
28.        <input type="hidden" name="return" value=
           "www.myretailsite.com">
29.        <TH><input type="Submit" border=0 value=
           "Addto Cart"></TH>
30.        <TH>8906</TH>
31.        <TH>Garlic Baker and Cellar</TH>
32.        <TH>19.95</TH>
33.        <TH><input type="text" name="qty" size="3"
           maxlength="3" value="1"></TH>
34.     </Form>
35.   </TR>

36. </Table>
```

The web page defined above and shown in Figure 14-12, displays two products for sale, a Deluxe Fondue Pot and a Garlic Baker and Cellar. Each item has an "Add to Cart" button in the row that links to the Ibill site so that the item, including the quantity and the SKU (stock-keeping unit), can be added to the shopping cart for this customer. Here is an explanation of each HTML line used to create the table and the actions:

- Lines 1 through 9 build the beginning of the table including the column headings, Stock Number, Description, Price, and Quantity.

- Line 10 begins the first row for a product.

- Line 11 contains the <Form> tag that identifies the URL to the ibill site.

- Line 12 contains a hidden (not displayed by the user's browser) value that is passed to the Ibill site that identifies the action to take (add2cart).

- Line 13 contains the account number of the merchant that identifies the merchant to Ibill (9000).

- Line 14 contains the catalog number or SKU for the item that is to be added to the cart (6432).

- Line 15 gives the URL that Ibill should point the customer's browser to when the action has been completed.

- Line 16 contains the submit button that starts the action.

- Lines 17, 18, and 19 contain information displayed on the user's browser about the item.

- Line 20 contains the input tag that allows the user to specify the quantity ordered.

- Line 21 ends the form and line 22 ends the row in the table.

- Lines 23 through 35 repeat this HTML for the next product item. Everything is the same except the catalog number submitted to Ibill and the information displayed on the user's browser screen.

- Line 36 ends the table.

When the user clicks the Add to Cart button, the item is added to that user's shopping cart. Also shown in Figure 14-12 is the View Your Cart's Contents button. Here is the HTML used to create the button, which is labeled sample code 2 in the figure:

```
1. <form method="post"
         action="http://secure.ibill.com/cgi-win/ccprod/
         iprod.exe">
2. <input type="hidden" name="reqtype" value="viewcart">
3. <input type="hidden" name="account" value="9000">
4. <input type="hidden" name="return" value=
   "www.myretailsite.com">
5. <input type="submit" name="submit" value="View Your Cart'
   Contents">
6. </form>
```

Line 2 in the code shown above passes the action "viewcart" to Ibill. The program running on the ibill site (iprod.exe) receives the request and returns the contents of the user's shopping cart to the browser. Line 3 identifies the merchant to Ibill and line 4 tells Ibill where to point the customer's browser when the customer is finished viewing the contents. While the customer views the contents of the shopping cart, the URL showing in the browser's address box will be Ibill.com and not myretailsite.com. When you are making purchases on retail sites, you can easily tell if the site is using third-party companies by looking for these different URLs while the transaction is in progress. Figure 14-13 shows a sample of what the Ibill web page might look like when the user requests to view the shopping cart contents.

14

Figure 14-13   Sample shopping cart view from Ibill

Next, we look at the button shown in Figure 14-12, labeled "Secure Checkout" and compare that to the button that offers a non-secured checkout. A customer must use the non-secured checkout if his or her browser does not support Secure Socket Layer (SSL) encryption.

Here is the HTML to create the button "Secure Checkout," labeled sample code 3 in Figure 14-12:

```
1. <form method="post"
        action="https://secure.ibill.com/cgi-
        win/ccprod/iprod.exe">
2. <input type="hidden" name="reqtype" value="checkout">
3. <input type="hidden" name="account" value="9000">
4. <input type="hidden" name="return" value=
   "www.myretailsite.com">
5. <input type="submit" name="submit" value=
   "Secure Checkout">
6.</form>
```

Compare the HTML above to that below, which is for a non-secure checkout. Note that the only difference besides the text written on the button is the protocol specified in the <form> tags. Putting https in the URL rather than http tells the web site to use SSL when communicating. All credit card information sent over the Internet is encrypted when using SSL. If others intercepted the information as it is being transmitted, it would not be possible to read it.

Below is the HTML code for a non-secure checkout labeled sample code 4 in Figure 14-12:

```
1. <form method="post"
        action="http://secure.ibill.com/cgi-win/ccprod/
        iprod.exe">
2. <input type="hidden" name="reqtype" value="checkout">
```

```
3. <input type="hidden" name="account" value="9000">
4. <input type="hidden" name="return" value=
   "www.myretailsite.com">
5. <input type="submit" name="submit" value="NON-Secure
   Checkout">
6. </form>
```

After the customer clicks either the secured or non-secured checkout button and the post command is executed from your retail site, the ibill web site takes the transaction and displays a checkout screen to the user. See Figure 14-14 for a sample of the checkout screen, which asks the user to give financial information.

Once the Ibill site has received this information, this happens:

- Ibill charges the customer credit card for the transaction amount.

- Ibill sends a receipt to the customer and gives the customer a URL on the Ibill site that he or she can use to check on the progress of the order.

- Ibill sends an e-mail message to the retailer with the order information and sends the purchase order to the retailer.

- The retailer ships the product to the customer.

- The retailer goes to the Ibill site and updates the Ibill database with information about the shipment (tracking number, date shipped, or the backorder date).

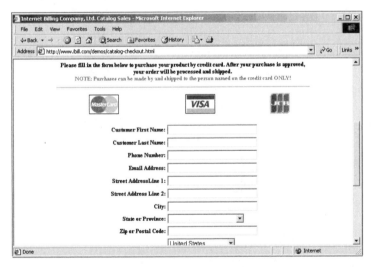

Figure 14-14   Completing the checkout process

- If the customer wants to check on the progress of the order, this information about the shipment can be viewed on the Ibill site.

- Using the Ibill site, at any time you can get a detailed or summary report of your sales for a given date range.

You have just seen what the HTML might look like when a retail site uses a third party company to manage the shopping cart and transaction processing software and the process that is used to manage orders. Before the web site can go live, the retail company must subscribe to an account with Ibill or another company that offers similar services and set up an Internet merchants account with a financial institution. When a company subscribes to Ibill, an account number is assigned (9000 was used in the above example). This account number must be included in all information posted to the Ibill site to identify the retailer to Ibill. In addition, before the retail site can go live, the company must update the catalog database on the Ibill site. Each product SKU, description, price, shipping charges, and the URL on your site where the user can view the product's description must be entered in the ibill database and kept current. Notice in the example above that the price was not passed from the retail site to the Ibill site, just the SKU and quantity. Information about the item kept on the Ibill site was required to complete the transaction.

There are many third-party transaction processing companies offering their services to e-commerce retailers. Services can include shopping cart, transaction processing, catalog services, web hosting services, customer sales tracking, and inventory tracking. In addition, some of these companies sell the software that you can use to keep all of these processes inhouse.

The following table shows a list of companies that provide services or software for e-commerce solutions:

Table 14-1   E-commerce service providers

CashRegistrer	www.cybercash.com
Commerce Cart	www.icat.com
Commerce servers by IBM	www-4.ibm.com/software/webservers/commerce/servers
Commerce servers by Microsoft	www.microsoft.com/siteserver/commerce
Digital Storefronts	www.digitalstorefronts.com
Internet Billing	www.ibill.com
Intershop Communications	www.intershop.com
O'Reilly and Associates	www.oreilly.com
Smith Micro Software	www.smithmicro.com

Returned Merchandise

When you purchase an item from a retail store and decide to return it, you can simply return to the store with your receipt and return the merchandise. Although it is an easy process for the customer, it is not as easy for the retailer. Less than half of all merchandise that is returned can be sold as new; the rest must be sold at reduced prices. When customers return merchandise to a physical store, the associates can examine the merchandise prior to giving a refund. E-businesses have to approach returns a little differently.

In order to help an e-commerce business handle its returns, companies like The Return Exchange (*www.thereturnexchange.com*) offer their assistance. When a customer wants to return merchandise, he or she completes a form, and The Return Exchange issues a Return Merchandise Authorization (RMA), which the customer must have to return any merchandise. The merchandise is then sent to The Return Exchange (instead of the original merchant), where the company checks the quality of the merchandise and determines if it is to be returned to the vendor, returned to merchant's stock, or liquidated. If the product is liquidated, The Return Exchange auctions it off.

ATTRACTING AND RETAINING CUSTOMERS TO YOUR WEB SITE

Having a good product or service to sell is a key part of creating an effective e-business, but the business will not be successful if people do not use your web site. You must also keep the customers returning to your site.

Remember that creating a business on the Internet is very different from creating a business in a physical location that customers must visit. When people visit a store, they often do not want to be inconvenienced by having to go to other stores to price shop. It is not worth their time to drive to another store, see if that store carries the product, and if it is more expensive, return to the first store. However, with the Internet, comparison shopping is simple; the customer does not have to leave his computer. That is why it is so important to make sure that once you get customers to your web site, they keep returning.

Web Page Design and Ease of Use

There are several factors that play into web page design, but it is important to make sure that customers will not leave once they see your site downloading. The site you build must make customers want to see the site and return to the site. Recall that the best sites are those that build a sense of community with users and make it quick and easy to use the site. There are several things that you can do to make your site more attractive to customers. A few are listed below:

14

- Avoid using blinking text. Although the customer will notice it, it is distracting and will often not be read.

- Put the most important information at the top of the web page. If a customer does not find what she is looking for at the top, she will often go to another site.

- Don't overload the site with graphics and sounds. Graphics and sounds make the web page take too long to download, especially if the customer has a slow connection.

- Include complete contact information, with an e-mail address, mailing address, and phone number.

- If a page is too large, put the information on several pages.

- Add the company's mission statement or philosophy to the web site to increase customer comfort with your company.

- Limit your use of colors to two or three.

- Provide a search box so that customers can easily find items they are looking for, and keep the search box at the top of the page instead of hiding it at the bottom.

Frames

As you recall from Chapter 1, frames are often used to organize a web page, because they allow different information to be displayed in different sections of the screen. Remember, too, that each frame displays a different HTML file. Because each frame shows a different file, it is possible to have pages from more than one web site showing on the same screen, each in its own frame. For example, if you have a web site that helps consumers choose a doctor, you might have a link for hospitals with which the doctors are affiliated. Instead of having the hospital's site display in the whole window, you have it display in a frame and have your site's information display in the other frame. To do this, you must use the NAME attribute within <FRAME> to give each frame a name. For example, to set a frame name to "info", use this tag:

```
<FRAME NAME="info">
```

Then you can set the page to go in the frame using the TARGET attribute of the <A HREF> tag, as shown below.

```
<A HREF=http://www.buystory.com TARGET="info">
```

Some designers do not like to have their web pages displayed within frames of another web site. To avoid having your web page shown within a frame of another web site, you can use the following script.

```
If <self!=top> (self location=top.location)
```

When you place links to other web sites on your web site, to avoid having web pages from another site display within frames on your web site, you can add TARGET="_top" when you are entering a URL for another site, as shown below.

```
<A HREF=http://www.buystory.com TARGET="_top">
```

Marketing

E-businesses must use marketing techniques just like any other business. Companies all use advertising, press releases, and word-of-mouth, whether they reside on the Internet or on Main Street. But there are other marketing techniques that have become popular with e-businesses because they work so well with customers who surf the Internet. Two primary techniques that are used today with e-businesses are affiliate networks and syndication.

Affiliate Networks

An **affiliate network** is a group of sites that work together to attract new customers for each other. The affiliated sites contain small advertisements for the other sites in their network, as shown in Figure 14-15. The Internet is full of affiliate networks. Think of all the web sites that you go to that have a link to Amazon.com. Those sites are affiliated with Amazon.com.

affiliate sites

Figure 14-15   Affiliate sites advertise each others sites on their web pages

If you are affiliated with Amazon.com, you have a small advertisement for Amazon on your site. Every time someone uses the link on your site to access Amazon.com, you make money. Affiliates are also set up so that if a customer uses your link to go to a web site and then purchases something, you can make a commission off the sale, as well as the money you make because the customer used your link to get to the site. Note that the affiliation does not have to go both ways. In other words, just because your site is affiliated with Amazon.com and has a link to their site, Amazon.com does not have to (and probably wouldn't) have a link to your site.

Because sites make money if the link is used to generate a sale, the sites try to place the promotions in places that are likely to cause the reader to click the advertisement. For example, if a golf site had an article on Tiger Woods, they would likely place an advertisement for his biography on the page with the article. Because people who are reading the article are more likely to want to purchase the book than someone reading about the history of golf, this placement makes the most sense. Placing the advertisement in the most effective location helps increase your commission and helps increase sales for the owner of the advertisement.

There are several different ways to become part of an affiliate network. If you had the time and contacts, you could set up your own affiliation, but this is not a likely solution for most

14

web site owners. A more popular way to join an affiliate network is to join an organization with the primary goal of maintaining affiliate networks. One such group is Be Free (*www.befree.com*) which maintains a huge group of affiliated sites and allows anyone to join for free. Once you join, you can select the affiliates that you wish to have on your web site, and you will receive money for each person that uses your link to access the affiliated web site.

Syndication

Another option to enhance your marketing efforts is to use syndication. **Syndication** is when you have another person or company write part of your web page for the purpose of attracting and retaining customers. For example, if you are a small company, you may not have the resources or the time to properly keep a web page up-to-date with current events. One example is a small golf company that has a web site that sells golf accessories online. One way to keep customers returning to your web page is to display golf news on the first page. This process is often time consuming, especially if you have a small staff. If you don't have the resources to keep up with the news and write the articles, you can hire another company to write the articles for you. This allows you to continue to work on the e-business you have created, and it keeps customers returning to view the news and hopefully purchase some products.

One company that offers syndicated articles to be used on web pages is Screaming Media (*www.screamingmedia.com*). See an example of their site in Figure 14-16. Screaming Media allows customers to select categories for which they want to receive information, or they can design a custom filter if one of the categories is not quite right for the customer. Then Screaming Media collects information and articles from various sources. The content collected is sent through the filter, and anything that matches what the customer is looking for is sent to the customer. The information can be sent in HTML, XML, flat file, or data that is formatted to be inserted into the customer's database. Screaming Media also offers an editor to make it especially simple to insert the text into a web page.

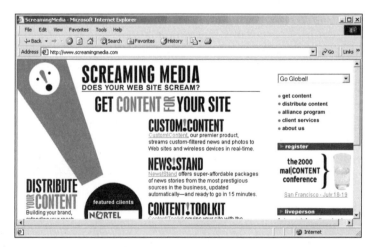

Figure 14-16   Screaming Media provides news, stock quotes and other interesting information for attracting customers to web sites

Search Engines

When you are looking for information on the Web, one of the first things you do is go to a search engine. Some of the more popular search engines include Yahoo! (*www.yahoo.com*), Lycos (*www.lycos.com*), and Alta Vista (*www.altavista.com*). To increase traffic to your web site, you have to make sure that the popular search engines recognize your site. If they don't, many people will never find your site.

Earlier chapters covered search engines and how they work, but here is a quick review. There are three major parts to every search engine: a spider, an index, and the search engine utility itself. The spider, also known as a crawler, robot, or bot, is a program that continuously searches the Internet for new web pages. When it finds a new page, it scans the page to find out what the page is about, and then it creates an entry for the web site in its database. Spiders also make sure that all the web pages in the database are current by periodically rechecking the web page. If the web page no longer exists, it is deleted from the database.

The data about web pages is kept in a database that is sometimes called the **index**. The index contains every web page that the spider finds. Although the spider is constantly searching for web pages that are new or have been deleted, updating the index takes some time, so it is often out-of-date. An out-of-date index can cause the search engine to display links to web pages that do not exist.

The last part of the search engine is the actual search engine itself, which is the program installed on the search engine's web site that searches through the index to return web pages that match the criteria you entered.

The key to having a successful web site is to make sure that search engines have your web site in their database. There are several keys to increasing the number of search engines that find your web site. The four most important things that you can do to increase the number of search engines that find your site are listed below.

1. **Title**. The title is often considered the most important part of a web page because it is the first thing a spider looks for when it is searching for new web pages. The spider searches the title to find out how to classify the web site in its database. Therefore, your title should describe what information is contained in the web site.

2. **First Paragraph**. Many spiders look beyond the title and skim the first paragraph that appears on the web page. This is why you often get the first few sentences of the web page when you perform a search. Because the first paragraph is used to classify the web site, you should make sure that it contains words that are directly related to the site. Don't start with a paragraph that talks about another subject, because it may bring the wrong people to your site, and it will eliminate the customers you want from locating you.

3. **Description**. When using HTML, you can add a <meta> tag to the code, and use it to enter a description of the web site. Many search engines do not recognize the <meta> tag, but for those that do, it is a good way to increase the

14

number of hits your web site receives. An example of the <meta> tag used with description is shown below:

<META NAME="description" CONTENT="The best source of fishing supplies on the Web!">

The first part of the tag (**META NAME="description"**) tells the system that the CONTENT that follows is the description of the web site.

4. **Keywords**. Another way that the <meta> tag can be used is to enter keywords for your site. When you enter keywords, try to enter the same keywords that people searching for your site would use. For example, if your site was about the different ways to cook barbecue, you would want to enter all the different ways barbecue can be spelled. A comma, as shown below, separates each keyword.

<META NAME="keywords" CONTENT="Barbecue, Barbeque, barbecue, barbeque, bar-b-q, bar-b-que, bbq, sauce, ribs, grill, recipes">

Notice some of the words are spelled incorrectly. If you are using a word that can be easily misspelled or mistyped, it is a good idea to type in the incorrect word as well as the correct word, because it is likely that the person searching may spell the word wrong.

In addition to positioning your web site to be cataloged by spiders, you can register your site with the search engines. For example, the company Submit It, will register your web site with over 400 search engines and directories for a fee of $59 per year. See *www.submitit.com*.

Security Features

Consumers who do not make purchases over the Internet often mention security as one of their primary concerns. If customers are concerned about the security of your web site, they are not likely to purchase products from your site. There are certain things that you can do to make your site more secure for your users. Many of the options for creating a secure site were outlined in Chapter 12, but this section covers some additional features of secure web sites.

As you will remember, VeriSign is a certification agency, which means that they distribute digital certificates. Part of their responsibility is to verify the identity of companies or people to whom they have issued a digital certificate. Companies that have been issued a digital certificate will often display the VeriSign symbol on their web sites, and many have a link verifying the identity of the company that owns the web site. Figure 14-17 shows an example of the verification provided by VeriSign.

As the figure shows, VeriSign indicates the name of the web site, provides the status of the certificate, and shows when the certificate is valid. In addition, information about the server is provided. The purpose of a web page like the one in Figure 14-17 is to assure the user that the company is legitimate and is not trying to portray itself as another party. It also confirms that the site has standards in place to prevent any data sent to and from the site from being read or stolen by another party.

Figure 14-17   MediaPlay uses VeriSign to prove to customers that the web page showing on the browser screen truly belongs to MediaPlay

Push and Pull Technologies

There are two technologies that are used when information is transmitted over the Internet: push and pull. The difference between the two is which side (client or server) initiates the transfer of information.

The more dominant of the two technologies is the **pull technology**, which is used when the client "pulls" information from the server. An example of pull technology includes using a search engine to find a site. First you enter keywords to indicate what you are looking for, and then the search engine responds with sites that match your request. Essentially you are "pulling" the information from the server.

On the other hand, **push technology** works by having information automatically delivered to the client. For example, if you receive a newsletter daily via e-mail, the message is being pushed to you. You do not have to submit daily requests for the newsletter, and you do not have to go to the Internet to get the information. Push technology also works with intranets. Employees can receive information about new stock options, health insurance, and benefits packages. With push technology, the company can send the information to all its employees to make sure that they receive the information. They can also indicate that only a certain group or department is to receive the information.

Recall from Chapter 10 the difference between a list server and a newsgroup server. A list server sends messages that have been posted to the list members' e-mail boxes, and the newsgroup servers collect the posted articles and the users have to retrieve the articles manually. A list server uses push technology, while a newsgroup server uses pull technology.

14

Channel Definition Format

Microsoft has developed a file format called Channel Definition Format (CDF), which allows web developers to offer subscriptions to users. The subscriptions consist of information and documents that are updated regularly and then sent to subscribers. When new information is added to the web site, it is automatically sent to the subscriber using push technology. CDF is actually an application of XML, and requires Internet Explorer 4 or higher.

Users can also schedule when information is sent to them—daily, weekly, or monthly—instead of having the information automatically sent when it is updated. The updates are sent to the user, and the user can then view the sites offline at any time desired. The technology is popular for people who have laptops and spend time away from an Internet connection. For example, people who travel can view their favorite sites while they are flying even though they do not have a connection to the Internet.

Systems that automate the transaction process are not new. Many industries have been using OLTP (online transaction processing) for years. OLTP automates business processes and allows companies to complete these processes with little downtime, minimal errors, and increased security. OLTP is used to book airline seating, handle ATM transactions, and process online business transactions.

Customer Support

When you are building an e-business, you want to make sure your customers can get support easily. If a customer has to search through a list of frequently asked questions or send an e-mail to the Technical Support Department and wait for a reply, that customer is likely to find another web site that offers better support. Also, customers do not want to have to call for support because many dial-up home subscribers have only one telephone line. Several solutions are being created to help e-businesses offer technical support to their Internet customers.

VoIP

One solution to this problem is to offer Voice over IP (VoIP). **VoIP** is the use of the Internet Protocol to deliver voice. VoIP is especially useful for home computer users. If a customer has only one telephone line, and it is being used for the Internet connection, the customer can still talk to a customer service representative using VoIP.

Because VoIP is still a new technology, it is uncertain what standards will emerge. There are several protocols that exist for VoIP, and the most popular protocols used today include H.323, session initiation protocol (SIP), and media gateway control (MEGACO). Even though it will take some time for standards and voice quality to be developed, VoIP is an option for customer support because customers can access the technicians while they are still dialed into the Internet.

Lipstream Networks (*www.lipstream.com*) offers VoIP technology. The technology they offer requires that a small amount of code be added to the web site so that a link appears. When customers click on the link, a program is automatically installed on the customer's machine so that they can use VoIP. The customer must have a sound card, speakers and a microphone installed on their machine to use the service.

Text Chat

Another solution is to offer **text chat**, which allows a user to open a text box and exchange messages in real time with the support person. Programs like AOL Instant Messenger and MSN Messenger Service have made text chats popular. The programs allow two or more people to type messages back and forth while they are online. Because the customer is already online and has the necessary equipment (a browser and Internet connection), using a text chat can be a good way to offer support.

When the user goes to a web site that uses text chat boxes, he can click on a special link for chat help. When the link is activated, a text box appears in a separate window, and a support person begins the conversation by asking if he can help. Mindspring (*www.mindspring.com*) is one company that uses text chat for customer support. As shown in Figure 14-18, Mindspring has a link that customers can click on to access live online technical support.

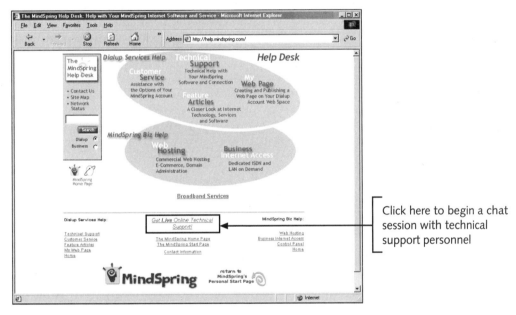

Figure 14-18   MindSpring offers chat sessions to support its customers

When you first click on the link to live technical support, the site asks you to enter your nickname and your e-mail address. Once that information has been entered, a chat box appears that tells you how long the wait is until you can talk to a technical support representative. Once a technician becomes available, the chat begins, and you can ask your question. Figure 14-19 shows the chat box.

One company that sells software packages for text-based chat boxes is LivePerson (*www.liveperson.com*). LivePerson's text boxes allow customer service representatives to "talk" to their customers while the customers are still on the Web. See Figure 14-20. The software also lets the customer service representative open a new browser window on the customer's PC and bring up any web page. This prevents the customer from typing the URL incorrectly.

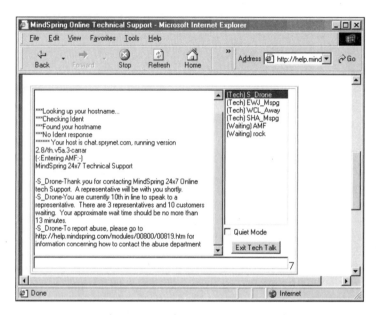

Figure 14-19   Chat sessions let customers get online, live technical support while connected to the Internet

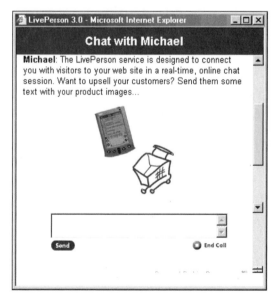

Figure 14-20   Place a chat session link on your web site to attract and keep customers using your site

ELECTRONIC DATA INTERCHANGE (EDI)

Electronic Data Interchange (EDI) is a standard format that two computers can use to transfer information when conducting business transactions between institutions, corporations, and governments. The type of information that is transmitted with EDI can include orders, bills of lading, receipts, invoices, and so forth. EDI allows these documents, which traditionally would have to be completed on paper and mailed to the other party, to be transmitted electronically. Figure 14–21 illustrates how EDI works.

EDI has been an integral part of corporate business for over 30 years. Because of the Internet, the cost of implementing EDI has dropped, which makes it possible for smaller companies to afford the technology.

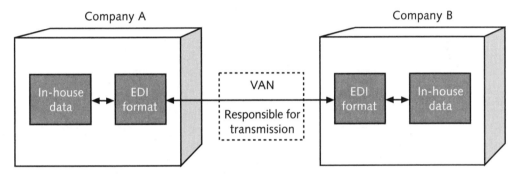

Figure 14-21   Companies convert data to EDI format before it is sent to another company by way of a VAN (value added network)

The two businesses using EDI to exchange information are called **trading partners**. Each trading partner must conform to the EDI standards. There are three categories of standards, which define how data is formatted for transmission between companies: EDI ASC X12 (sometimes called EDI ANSI X.12), UNTDI2, and EDIFACT. **EDI ASC X12** is primarily used in North America. **UNTDI2** was at one time primarily used in Europe but is now used mostly in the United Kingdom. The prevalent standard for international use is **EDIFACT**, which is a standard that developed from the best features of EDI ASCX12 and UNTDI2. The American National Standards Institute (ANSI) (*www.ansi.org*) is the organization that is responsible for the oversight of EDI ASC X12. This committee meets three times a year to create and maintain the EDI standards.

Part of the standards of EDI include defining the rules of forming transaction sets. **Transaction sets** are data formats that have been set up for common transactions, such as shipping instructions, invoices, and acknowledgements. The transaction sets describe what information should appear and in what order. The transaction sets outline exactly how the file should be created. For example, the first ten characters may be the customer number, and the next eight characters may be the date. If a file is created with the date as the first ten characters, the computer that receives the file will read the date as the customer number. As

14

you can see, it is very important to make sure all files are in the specified format. The transaction sets also have information on which data is mandatory, and which information is optional.

EDI is best used to process files containing hundreds of transactions, but can be used for only a single transaction. For example, the steps below explain the EDI process for purchasing an item between trading partners.

1. The buyer enters the information for the order in his computer system, including all details of the order such as what he wishes to purchase and where it should be sent.

2. The computer converts the information to a file that conforms to EDI standards and sends the file to the seller.

3. The seller receives the EDI transaction in his computer system. The computer system converts the file to a readable order.

4. The seller processes the order and determines if the order can be filled. If there are problems with the order, the seller contacts the buyer to resolve any problems.

5. The seller fills and ships the order. Once the order has been shipped, the seller makes note of it on her system, and the computer sends an EDI transaction to the buyer notifying him of what was shipped and when.

6. The buyer receives the merchandise and the order is complete.

The above steps outline the basics steps that take place with EDI, but there are many other transactions that can be incorporated into the EDI process. For example, if the buyer ordered several items and the seller did not have all the merchandise in stock, the seller could send an EDI transaction to notify the customer that some of the items were going to be cut. Acknowledgements, used to notify the sender that you received the file they sent, are also common with EDI.

The benefits of EDI are the cost savings and the convenience. Obviously, because the amount of paperwork is reduced, the cost of the paper is also reduced. Fewer people are needed because the data does not have to be entered twice. Before transactions were completed with EDI, the information had to be entered twice: once for each company. But with EDI, the information is electronically transferred, so it only has to be entered once. And when you cut the number of times the information has to be entered, you also cut the chance of errors.

To implement EDI, a company needs three things: EDI standards, EDI software, and a method of transmitting the EDI data. Software can be purchased that converts in-house data to the EDI standards or the software can be written in-house to do the conversion. Once the data is in EDI format, it can be transmitted to the receiving corporation by one of several means: a floppy disk or magnetic tape in the mail, a leased dedicated circuit, or by way of a third-party company that provides the communication service for other companies. These communication companies are called VANs (Value Added Networks). There are several VANs and an organization might use more than one depending on the corporations with whom it does business. Examples of VANs are AutoLink, DIALnet, and AT&T Easylink. A VAN is responsible for receiving the EDI file and getting it to its destination. Before the Internet, this was most often done by dedicated circuits and the service was expensive. Due to the Internet, the cost is much lower and small businesses can afford it. A VAN can sell a packaged service to a company implementing EDI, that can include the EDI software, training for business and technical employees in an organization, and on-going help desk support.

COPYRIGHT, LICENSES AND TRADEMARKS

The Internet has become a breeding ground for copyright infringement, although most people are unaware of the laws they are breaking. For example, the creators of unofficial fan pages of popular TV shows, bands, and collectibles are known for copying pictures and sounds from other pages when creating their own pages. Some of the companies that own this material are watching and shutting down sites that use copyrighted materials or trademarks without permission. One web site that was targeted was a site for fans of the television show King of the Hill. The site (*www.wfu.edu/~bwilson/koth.html*) was contacted by Twentieth Century Fox and asked to remove all audio clips. Now all the site contains is the letter they received from the lawyers.

Another example is *www.napster.com*, a web site that acts as a host for people who wish to share audio files. When the company was sued by the music industry, a federal court ruled that the free downloading of copyrighted music files must stop. The next morning, Napster posted this message on the web site, "The Judge's ruling is essentially this: that one-to-one non-commercial file sharing violates the law."

Protecting Intellectual Property

Intellectual property that can be legally protected includes the following:

- Literary works, such as books, newspaper articles, computer software, and web pages

- Dramatic works, such as plays and skits (copyright also covers any music in the work)

- Audiovisual works, such as motion pictures

- Musical works, such as songs (copyright covers both the music and the words)

- Sound recordings, including short voice recordings

- Pictorial, graphic, and sculptural works, such as photographs and drawings

- Architectural works, such as drawings of buildings

- Pantomimes and choreographic works, such as dances

Trademarks, copyrights and licenses are all intended to protect intellectual property. Each is described next.

14

What Is a Trademark?

A **trademark** is a name, symbol, or other mark that is used to represent a product or a company. Companies go through a lot of work and money to make sure that the general public recognizes their trademarks. It is because of this great expense and time that companies are particular about their trademarks.

A trademark cannot be used without expressed permission from the owner of the trademark. Although that sounds like a simple rule to follow, often trademark infringement occurs because the person creating an image was not aware he or she was violating the law.

Trademark problems on the Web include trademark infringement and cybersquatting. Trademark infringement happens when a web site uses another company's name or trademark on the site without permission or disparages another company's name or mark. Two laws that can effectively be used to prevent trademark infringement online are the Lanham Act and the Anti-Dilution Act.

Cybersquatting is when someone registers a domain name using another company's mark or name and then tries to sell the domain name to that company. The Anti-Cybersquatting Protection Act gives established trademark owners the right to sue for damages and prevents use of the mark by others. Also, effective December, 1999, ICANN adopted its Uniform Domain Name Dispute Resolution Policies which allow for a quick, inexpensive, and mandatory online proceeding for getting these domain names back from squatters in the top level .com, .net, and .org domains. There have been well over 1,000 proceedings instituted since ICANN's rules became effective.

What Is a Copyright?

A **copyright** is a type of protection that is offered to creators of original works. These works are known as intellectual property. Computer software is covered by the laws of copyright, as are the contents of web pages, and any written work, artwork, music, or photography that is distributed by electronic means. The copyright gives the creator of the works the right to copy, distribute, display, or perform the work. Under the copyright, no one *other* than the author can do these things unless the author gives permission to do so.

What Is a License?

Another way of protecting intellectual property is with a **license**, which gives the owner of the license the right to use the product as outlined by the license agreement. A license is issued by the owner of the copyright and has specific limitations. Licensing is a common method of selling software. What you are buying, when you purchase software at a store or over the Internet, is the license to use the software and not the software itself. To fully purchase the software, you would be purchasing the copyright to the software, and then it would be yours to do anything with that you wanted to.

When a user purchases a license, he or she is authorized to use the software. A person who does not own a license to the software is not necessarily authorized to use it. Although the user has a license, under copyright law, he or she is not authorized to make copies of the software, although the law does allow for one backup copy to be made.

A software license generally gives you the right to install and use the software. It does not generally give you the right to distribute or give copies of the software to third parties. You may not disassemble the software or rent or lease it to others. The specific agreement that is stated in the software license is called an **end-user license agreement** (**EULA**) (pronounced "U-la"). When you install software, the EULA displays as part of the installation process and you are asked to agree to the license agreement. When you click "I agree" or a similar button, you are held legally responsible for complying with the agreement. "I agree" buttons can also be placed on web sites to make users agree to the licensing terms before downloading software from the web site. These agreements are legally binding.

Figure 14-22 shows an example of a licensing agreement for Eudora, an e-mail client that can be downloaded from the Internet for free. When you accept the terms of agreement to get the software for free, you are agreeing to "sponsor mode" which places ads on the software screens. If you pay for the software, then no ads display.

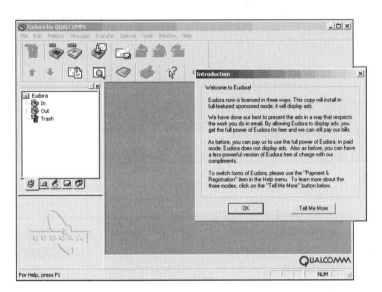

Figure 14-22   Eudora e-mail software can be downloaded for free in "sponsor mode," which displays ads on Eudora windows

How to Copyright Material

It is not necessary to apply for a copyright for material to be protected under the copyright laws, but many people still feel more comfortable when they have registered their works. Registering allows the creator to sue if anyone uses the work without permission. If the work is not registered, the creator cannot sue, even though the work is protected under copyright laws. The owner of the work must register the work before filing a lawsuit.

The other advantage to registering your work is that registration allows you to collect statutory damages. However, to collect statutory damages, the work must be registered within three months from when the work was first published or performed. If the work is not registered within the three-month time frame, you are eligible to collect only actual damages.

The registration process is not difficult. In order to register, you must know which of the categories of intellectual property listed in the above section your work falls into, because each category has a different form. These forms can be downloaded in PDF format from the Copyright web site (*lcweb.loc.gov/copyright/*). Once the form has been completed, you must send a registration fee (usually around $30 for a single copyright) and a copy of the work (or a partial copy, depending on the work) along with the form to the Copyright office.

The Copyright office will not send an acknowledgement that they received your information, but once the application has been processed, you will receive a certificate of registration indicating that the copyright has been accepted, or you will receive a letter outlining why your application for copyright was rejected.

Copyright Laws

The Federal Copyright Act of 1976 protects the exclusive rights of copyright holders. For owners of material that was copyrighted after January 1, 1978, the copyright does not expire until 50 years after the owner's death. For items copyrighted prior to January 1, 1978, the copyright expires 75 years after the first publication date of the item.

The copyright laws allow for the fact that software can get damaged, and The Federal Copyright Act of 1976 gives legal users of software the right to make one backup copy. Other rights are based on what the copyright holder allows. In 1990, the United States Congress passed the Software Rental Amendment Act, which prevents the renting, leasing, lending, or sharing of software without the expressed written permission of the copyright holder.

In 1992, Congress instituted criminal penalties for software copyright infringement, which include imprisonment for up to five years and/or fines of up to $250,000, for the unlawful reproduction or distribution of 10 or more copies of software. In short, it is illegal for a person to give an unauthorized copy of software to another individual, even if they work for the same organization.

INTERNATIONAL BUSINESS ON THE WEB

Because the Internet is not limited by countries and time zones, neither is e-commerce. But, expanding your e-business to include other countries requires you to have an understanding of the traditions and cultures of the other country. Many companies have learned the hard way of the barriers that can exist when cross-selling merchandise. Many people are familiar with the story of General Motors' unsuccessful attempt to sell its Chevy Nova in Latin America. Once they found out that *no va* means "will not go" in Spanish, General Motors realized their mistake.

Multi-Lingual and Multi-Character Concerns

Having a web site that can be accessed by people from all over the globe means that your web site may not be understood by all your customers. And as the General Motors example above shows, a simple misunderstanding can cost a company a considerable amount of business.

HTML was originally created to support English, but as the Web grew, it became apparent that users spoke many languages and web pages had to be designed to accommodate all users. HTML 4 includes a LANG attribute to support an increased number of languages. The attribute is frequently used in documents that are written in multiple languages. The attribute can be combined with other tags, such as the paragraph tag, as shown below.

```
<P LANG="en">This is English.</P>
<P LANG="fr">C'est Francais.</P>
```

For more information on the LANG attribute, refer to RFC 1766.

Although purchasing items over the Internet has become popular in the United States, consumers in Japan are not as interested in using credit cards for purchases. They generally prefer to pay with cash, and they are not comfortable making purchases on-line. Softbank (*www.softbank.com*) helped come up with a solution that would allow the Japanese culture to participate in e-commerce, yet still allow them to pay with cash.

Softbank created a program that allows customers to order items over the Internet and pick up and pay for the items at the local 7-Eleven. This approach is the exact opposite of the approach that is taken in the United States where e-businesses appeal to customers because they don't have to leave their homes to purchase and receive items. But the approach is working in Japan, and Softbank continues to offer international e-business solutions.

Legal and Regulatory Concerns

14

The legal world is still trying to catch up with the fast growth of the Internet and e-commerce. In a traditional shopping situation, when a person purchases an item or a service, both the buyer and seller are in the same location. This makes it easy to determine jurisdiction if there is a dispute. However, with e-business, the buyer could very easily be in another country. In fact, the buyer may not even know in which country the seller is located. This makes it difficult for a government to claim jurisdiction. Usually jurisdiction is determined by a contract that has been agreed to by both countries. But because the whole idea of jurisdiction over Internet transactions is still relatively new, it will be some time before all the questions regarding jurisdiction are answered.

The basis of an e-commerce transaction is a **contract**, or an agreement, between two parties for the transfer of a service or good in return for another service or good (often money). For a contract to be valid, it must be offered by one party and accepted by another party. The offer must be a clear explanation of what is to be exchanged, and how the exchange is to take place. A good offer should be clear and unambiguous. When an offer is accepted, meaning the terms of the offer are agreed to by the other party, the contract is sealed.

Although people often think of contracts as long, drawn out documents, a contract can be made using e-mail. If you send an e-mail to your friend inviting her to lunch on Friday, and she sends a reply agreeing to meet you at your favorite café at noon, you have created a contract. Your friend would be unlikely to sue you if you did not show for lunch, but you still have the terms of a contract outlined in your e-mails.

These contracts are all over the Web. Many sites request that you agree to certain terms before you can log on. One site that uses the contracts is the auction site eBay. The site will not succeed if the people bidding on items do not purchase the items when they win an auction. So, eBay reminds people that when they bid, they are agreeing to a contract that says that the winner of the auction agrees to pay the seller the winning bid price.

REAL PEOPLE, REAL PROBLEMS, REAL SOLUTIONS
TALK TO THE VISITOR

E-Liza.com (*www.e-liza.com*) is different than most electronic commerce web sites on the Internet today. What sets the site apart from most is the attention the owner has given to making sure visitors turn into repeat customers. The company sells unusual and one-of-a-kind gifts from selected artisans via an elaborate e-commerce system. When the owner decided to build the Internet-based company, she knew that there must be solid shopping components—including very good navigation, a gift reminder service, and a detailed profiling system. She also knew that it would take a little more than a good catalog selection to attract and retain customers.

In doing research for the new company, the entrepreneur visited several e-commerce shopping sites. She was able to quickly identify something that was missing from most of them: the ability to ask the store a question on the spot about a product. She thought that if she could have received an answer about a product while she was at the site, she might have made a purchase. She also discovered that very few sites would suggest items if looking for a gift. The lack of interaction with a sales person troubled her. She wanted her site to be much like the experience a shopper receives when walking in to a retail storefront.

In building E-Liza.com, two extra systems were installed. One was to offer live help on the site. Wherever a shopper is within E-Liza.com, he or she can ask a real person a question. Whether the visitor has a question about a specific product or wanted to inquire further about the return policy, an answer is a click away.

The second system was to offer a personal shopping service. The owner's idea was that if a visitor was in need of a unique item, or was having problems finding the right gift, a live person could be reached that was familiar with the product line. The personal shopping service could also give the company the chance to make sure the customers found what they were looking for. This could catch the attention of the visitor and narrowed down the chances that they would head for another site because the product wasn't found.

The owner of E-Liza.com has proven that the two systems have made a difference. The list of customers that return for more purchases continues to grow. By giving the customer a chance to ask questions or get direction about a purchase, the site has a unique quality that makes a difference in attracting customers.

CHAPTER SUMMARY

❑ There are many reasons to sell on the Web including lower costs, fewer errors, and easy access for customers.

❑ Reasons not to sell on the Web include limited security, customer concerns, no established business models, and a lack of personal contact between companies and customers.

❑ Items sold on the Web can usually be classified as services, products, or a combination of the two.

❑ As the Internet's popularity increases, e-business are coming up with unique ways to offer products and services over the Web, such as providing downloadable files, hosting auctions, and becoming application service providers.

❑ The basic steps for a sales transaction include the customer finding and browsing a web site, the customer selecting and ordering a product, and the business shipping the product to the customer. Steps can be added, depending on the situation.

❑ E-businesses can have very simple web sites. For example, a business may just use its web site to list products and a toll-free phone number that customers can call to place orders.

❑ Web sites for e-businesses can also be complex, and can require special hardware and software, such as a catalog server, shopping cart software, transaction processing software, and an Internet merchant account. These components can be either in-house or the company can outsource them to another provider.

❑ Unless a company is very small, it should have some type of catalog on its web site to allow customers to search for items.

❑ When creating a catalog, a company can write its own catalog software, purchase the software, or use another company to provide the catalog service.

❑ E-businesses also need some type of shopping cart software to allow customers to select an item, browse the web site more, and select another item without losing the first item selected.

❑ Many companies use other companies to handle credit card transactions since there are so many different factors that must be addressed with credit card transactions.

❑ When a credit card transaction is processed, transaction processing software must be used. Transaction processing software should allow you to track orders, return merchandise, and handle payment problems.

14

❑ Many sites hire a third party company to handle credit card transactions. When this happens, the customer first goes to the retailer's site to select items to purchase, but once the customer is ready to select items to purchase and begin the payment process, the customer is directed to the third party company (often without the customer's knowledge).

❑ When writing HTML code for a secure credit card transaction, Secure Socket Layer encryption is used. Using the <form> tag in HTML, the user can indicate that the protocol that should be used is Secure Socket Layer encryption.

❑ Many third party companies offer e-businesses various services including shopping carts, transaction processing, catalog services, web hosting services, customer sales tracking, returned merchandise, and inventory tracking.

❑ When creating a web site for an e-business, the site must be designed so that it will attract customers. A good web site puts the important information at the top of the page, does not use too many sounds and graphics, and includes complete contact information.

❑ When marketing a web site, e-businesses often use affiliate networks or syndication.

❑ There are three major parts to a search engine: a spider, an index, and the search engine utility itself.

❑ In order to increase the number of search engines that find your web site, you should make sure you have a descriptive title and first paragraph, and include <meta> tags for the description and keywords to the HTML code.

❑ Having a digital certificate for your company increases security for your web site, and helps customers trust your site.

❑ Information can be transmitted over the Internet using one of two technologies: push or pull.

❑ Customer support for e-businesses can come in the form of Voice over IP or text chat, in addition to the traditional Frequently Asked Questions list that appears on many web pages.

❑ EDI has been an integral part of communication between large corporations for over 30 years.

❑ Trading partners using EDI must conform to transaction sets when sending data to ensure the receiver of the data will understand the information being sent.

❑ A copyright gives the creator of the work the right to copy, distribute, display or perform the work, but it does not give permission for anyone else to copy, distribute, display or perform the work.

❑ Licensing is a common method of selling computer software.

❑ Trademarks cannot be used without the expressed permission from the owner of the trademark.

❑ It is not required to register for a copyright, but if you have not registered the work, you are not entitled to sue if someone illegally uses the work.

❏ The Federal Copyright Act of 1976 protects the exclusive rights of copyright holders, but it also gives the legal users of software the right to make one backup copy.

❏ The Software Rental Amendment Act of 1990 prevents the renting, leasing, lending, or sharing of software without the expressed permission of the copyright holder.

❏ The legal world is still trying to catch up with the growth of the Internet and e-businesses. Regulations over the Internet are still being worked out, and it will probably take some time before all the questions regarding legal concerns and the Internet are answered.

KEY TERMS

affiliate network — A group of companies that work together by promoting each other's web sites.

application service provider (ASP) — A company that stores application software on its web site to allow customers to use the software via the Internet.

catalog server — Software that stores multiple products and allows customer to search for products by keyword or name.

contract — An agreement between two parties for the transfer of a service or good in return for another service or good (such as money).

copyright — Protection offered to the creators of intellectual property which gives the creator, and no one else, the right to copy, distribute, display, or perform the work.

cybersquatting — When someone registers a domain name using another company's name or trademark with the intention of selling the domain name to that company.

EDI ASC X12 — An EDI standard that is primarily used in North America. Also called EDI ANSI X.12.

EDIFACT — An EDI standard which was developed by determining the best features of EDI ASC X12 and UNTDI2.

electronic data interchange (EDI) — A standard format that two computers can use to communicate information relating to business transactions such as orders, invoices, and receipts.

end–user license agreement (EULA) — An agreement that is stated in a software license. When the software is installed, the user must agree to the EULA.

e-tailing — The selling of goods and services over the Internet.

e-tailware — Software that is designed to help users create on-line catalogs and maintain e-businesses.

index — A database used by search engines. The database contains information about web pages so that when a user performs a search, the search engine can access the database to find any matches for the user.

Internet merchant account — An account used by an e-business which takes credit card transactions over the Internet. The account works as a relationship between the e-business and the merchant bank or other financial institution that can process the money transaction.

14

license — A document issued by the owner of the copyright, which gives the owner of the license limited rights to use the product. The rights are outlined in the license.

pull technology — In a client-server environment, when the client requests information from the server, and pulls that information down.

push technology — In a client-server environment, when the server sends information to the client without the client requesting the information first.

shopping cart software — Software that allows customers to select an item, then browse the site for more items, and select another item. All the items are kept in a database so they can be purchased in a single transaction.

syndication — The process of hiring another company or individual to write a specific portion of your web site (such as the latest health news) on a regular basis.

text chat — A technology that allows users to type messages back and forth and which prevents others from reading those messages.

trademark — A name, symbol, or other mark that is used to represent a product or company.

trading partners — Two businesses that exchange information using EDI.

transaction processing (TP) software — Software that is used to handle a credit card transaction over the Internet. The software receives the card information, validates the information received, and passes the transaction to the bank.

transaction sets — Data formats that outline which information should appear in each section of the file and exactly how the file should be created. Transaction sets exist for all common business transactions.

UNTDI2 — An EDI standard that was once common in Europe, but is now primarily used in the United Kingdom.

VoIP (Voice over IP) — A system that uses the Internet Protocol to deliver voice between two parties on the Internet.

REVIEW QUESTIONS

1. List five reasons why companies are interesting in selling their products over the Internet.

2. List five disadvantages to doing business over the Web.

3. What are the responsibilities of a company that hosts an auction site?

4. What size companies do application service providers appeal to and why?

5. List the basic steps of a sales transaction.

6. Outline the procedure used during an Internet credit card transaction.

7. Name different services that e-businesses often outsource to third parties?

8. What is the HTML code used to indicate that Secure Socket Layer encryption should be used?

9. Give six tips to creating an effective web site.

10. Explain how an affiliate network works.

11. If you are affiliated with a site, do they have to be affiliated with your site?

12. When would it be beneficial to use syndication on your web site?

13. What are the three major parts of a web site?

14. List four things you can do to increase the chances of your web site being found by search engines.

15. Why is it beneficial for a company to have a digital certificate?

16. Explain the difference between push and pull technologies and give examples of each.

17. What are the hardware requirements for VoIP?

18. What are the three categories of standards used by EDI?

19. What organization is responsible for overseeing EDI ASC X12?

20. What is required to implement EDI in a company?

21. How is a copyright different from a license?

22. Whom do you contact to register a work to be copyrighted?

23. What did the Federal Copyright Act of 1976 do?

24. What are the criminal penalties for software copyright infringement?

25. What two things must occur for a contract to be considered valid?

HANDS-ON PROJECTS

Investigate Digital Certificates

You are working for a small company that is interested in offering their products to customers over the Internet. Your boss knows of digital certificates, but he is not sure what the advantage is to using a digital certificate. You have been asked to do the research for him. Investigate at least two different companies that supply digital certificates. Determine the costs involved for each company and the advantages and disadvantages.

Research the Copyright Symbol

You are writing documents that are being published on the Web, but you are currently not using the copyright symbol with your work. Someone brought it to your attention that you need to make sure you indicate that the work has been copyrighted, but you are not sure of the laws regarding using the copyright symbol. Do research to find out when you can use the copyright symbol.

14

Research Third Party Companies

Your e-business is just getting started, and you do not have the resources to write your own catalog, shopping cart, and transaction processing software. Research a third-party company (other than those mentioned in this chapter) that will offer these services. Find out the cost, any limitations, what services are offered, and any additional information that will help make an informed decision. Write a brief report on your findings, indicating whether or not you would recommend this company.

Research Internet Merchant Accounts

Your company currently requires customers to call a customer service representative to purchase items, but is interested in automating the process and allowing customers to order merchandise over the Internet. In order to do this, the company will have to be able to take credit cards over the Internet. Check with your local banks to see if they offer Internet merchant accounts. Find out how much the fees are and what transaction software the banks use.

CASE PROJECT

Add Meta Tags to Your Web Site

Add to your web site <meta> tags with a description and a list of keywords. Make sure the description and keywords properly reflect the content of your web site, and add enough keywords so that they are useful.

EXAM OBJECTIVES FOR I-NET+ CERTIFICATION

The following table lists the domains covered on the i–Net+ Certification exam and the weight assigned to each domain. The remainder of this appendix lists each objective covered in the exam and indicates where the objective is covered in this book. For more information about i–Net+ Certification see the CompTIA web site at *www.comptia.org*.

Domain	% of Examination (approximately)
1.0 I-Net Basics	10%
2.0 I-Net Clients	20%
3.0 Development	20%
4.0 Networking	25%
5.0 I-Net Security	15%
6.0 Business Concepts	10%

Domain 1.0 I-NET BASICS

Objective	Chapter: Section
1.1. Describe a URL, its functions and components, different types of URLs, and use of the appropriate type of URL to access a given type of server. Content may include the following: • Protocol • Address • Port	• Chapter 1: Using Web Browsers • Chapter 2: Physical Addresses, IP Addresses, Ports, Domain Names • Chapter 4: FTP using a Web Browser, Newsgroups, Gophers
1.2. Identify the issues that affect Internet site functionality (e.g., performance, security and reliability). Content may include the following: • Bandwidth • Internet connection points • Audience access • Internet Service Provider (ISP) • Connection types • Corrupt files • Files taking too long to load • Inability to open files • Resolution of graphics	• Chapter 1: How an Internet Service Provider Works • Chapter 3: Testing Your Site • Chapter 4: MIME • Chapter 5: Plug-ins, Optimizing Page Download Time • Chapter 6: Pre-launch Testing • Chapter 10: Ability to Monitor Performance • Chapter 11: Bandwidth Technologies
1.3. Describe the concept of caching and its implications. Content may include the following: • Server caching • Client caching • Proxy caching • Cleaning out client-side cache • Server may cache information as well • Web page update settings in browsers	• Chapter 8: Managing the Web Browser Cache • Chapter 10: Cache Server, Proxy Server • Chapter 11: Internet-in-a-Box • Chapter 13: Solving Browser Problems
1.4. Describe different types of search indexes—static index/site map, keyword index, full text index. Examples could include the following: • Searching your site • Searching content • Indexing your site for a search	• Chapter 1: Finding Information on the Web • Chapter 14: Search Engines

DOMAIN 2.0 I-NET CLIENTS

A

Objective	Chapter: Section
2.1. Describe the infrastructure needed to support an Internet client. Content could include the following: • TCP/IP stack • Operating system • Network connection • Web browser • E-mail • Hardware platform (PC, handheld device, WebTV, Internet phone)	• Chapter 2: How Data Travels Across Interconnected Networks • Chapter 4: E-mail • Chapter 8: Installing and Managing Internet Explorer or Netscape Navigator • Chapter 11: Internet Infrastructure • Chapter 9: WebTV and Other Internet Appliances (entire chapter)
2.2. Describe the use of Web browsers and various clients (e.g., FTP clients, Telnet clients, e-mail clients, all-in-one clients/universal clients) within a given context of use. Examples of context could include the following: • When you would use each • The basic commands you would use (e.g., put and get) with each client (e.g., FTP, Telnet)	• Chapter 1: Using Web Browsers • Chapter 4: E-mail, FTP, Telnet and Newsgroups (entire chapter)
2.3. Explain the issues to consider when configuring the desktop. Content could include the following: • TCP/IP configuration (NetBIOS name server such as WINS, DNS, default gateway, subnet mask • Host file configuration • DHCP versus static IP • Configuring browser (proxy configuration, client-side caching)	• Chapter 8: Internet Clients (entire chapter) • Chapter 13: Connecting a Small Company LAN to the Internet
2.4. Describe MIME types and their components. Content could include the following: • Whether a client can understand various e-mail types (MIME, HTML, uuencode) • The need to define MIME file types for special download procedures such as unusual documents or graphic formats	• Chapter 4: MIME

Objective	Chapter: Section
2.5. Identify problems related to legacy clients (e.g., TCP/IP sockets and their implication on the operating system). Content could include the following: • Checking revision date, manufacturer/vendor • Troubleshooting and performance issues • Compatibility issues • Version of the Web browser	• Chapter 13: Solving Windows 98 and Other Software Problems, Solving Browser Problems, Browser Updates and Patches
2.6. Explain the function of patches and updates to client software and associated problems. Content could include the following: • Desktop security • Virus protection • Encryption levels • Web browsers • E-mail clients	• Chapter 13: Solving Windows 98 and Other Software Problems, Solving Browser Problems, Browser Updates and Patches
2.7. Describe the advantages and disadvantages of using a cookie and how to set cookies. Content could include the following: • Setting a cookie without the knowledge of the user • Automatically accepting cookies versus query • Remembering everything the user has done • Security and privacy implications	• Chapter 6: All About Cookies • Chapter 12: Cookies

DOMAIN 3.0 DEVELOPMENT

Objective	Chapter: Section
3.1. Define programming-related terms as they relate to Internet applications development. Content could include the following: • API • CGI • SQL • SAPI • DLL—dynamic linking and static linking • Client and server-side scripting	• Chapter 6: Why Programming?, Server-Side Programming Protocols, Learning to Use Scripts • Chapter 7: Using SQL to Access a Database
3.2. Describe the differences between popular client-side and server-side programming languages. Examples could include the following: • Java • JavaScript • Perl • C • C++ • Visual Basic • VBScript • Jscript • XML • VRML • ASP Content could include the following: • When to use the languages • When they are executed	• Chapter 3: The Future of HTML • Chapter 5: Proprietary Multimedia File Formats • Chapter 6: Survey of Programming Languages Used on the Internet, Learning to Use Scripts
3.3. Describe the differences between a relational database and a non-relational database.	• Chapter 7: Introduction to Relational Databases
3.4. Identify when to integrate a database with a web site and the technologies used to connect the two.	• Chapter 7: Introduction to Relational Databases, Setting up a Database on a Web Site
3.5. Demonstrate the ability to create HTML pages. Content could include the following: • HTML document structure • Coding simple tables, headings, forms • Compatibility between different browsers • Difference between text editors and GUI editors • Importance of creating cross-browser coding in your HTML	• Chapter 3: Build Your Own Web Site (entire chapter) • Chapter 6: Why Programming?, Learning to Use Scripts, Pre-Launch Testing

Objective	Chapter: Section
3.6. Identify popular multimedia extensions or plug-ins. Examples could include the following: • QTVR (quick time) • Flash • Shockwave • RealPlayer • Windows Media Player	• Chapter 5: Sights and Sounds of the Internet, Movies and Videos on the Web, Proprietary Multimedia File Formats, Video Conferencing over the Internet
3.7. Describe the uses and benefits of various multimedia file formats. Examples could include the following: • GIF • GIF89a • JPEG • PNG • PDF • RTF • TIFF • PostScript • EPS • BMP • MOV • MPEG • AVI • BINHex • Streaming media • Non-streaming media	• Chapter 4: Background Information about Attached Files, MIME File Types • Chapter 5: Enhancing Web Sites with Graphics and Sound, Storing Sound in Files, Graphics on Web Pages
3.8. Describe the process of pre-launch site/application functionality testing. Content could including the following: • Checking hot links • Testing different browsers • Testing to ensure it does not corrupt your e-commerce site • Load testing • Access to the site • Testing with various speed connections	• Chapter 3: Learning and Using HTML, Testing Your Site • Chapter 6: Pre-launch Testing

DOMAIN 4.0 NETWORKING AND INFRASTRUCTURE

Objective	Chapter: Section
4.1. Describe the core components of the current Internet infrastructure and how they relate to each other. Content may include the following: • Network access points • Backbone	• Chapter 1: Introduction to the Internet Infrastructure • Chapter 11: What is the Internet Infrastructure?, Understanding LANs and How They Work, Internetworking Devices
4.2. Identify problems with Internet connectivity from source to destination for various types of servers. Examples could include the following: • E-mail • Slow server • Website	• Chapter 4: E-mail Clients and E-mail Servers: How They Interact • Chapter 7: Web Hosting • Chapter 13: Troubleshooting Internet Connections
4.3. Describe Internet domain names and DNS. Content could include the following: • DNS entry types • Hierarchical structure • Role of root domain server • Top level or original domains—edu, com, mil, net, gov, org • Country level domains — .uk	• Chapter 2: Domain Names • Chapter 10: How a Browser Accesses a Web Server, DNS Server (Name Server)
4.4. Describe the nature, purpose, and operational essentials of TCP/IP. Content could include the following: • What addresses are and their classifications (A, B, C, D) • Determining which ones are valid and which ones are not (subnet masks) • Public versus private IP addresses	• Chapter 2: Addressing on the Internet, Routing on the Internet
4.5. Describe the purpose of remote access protocols. Content could include the following: • SLIP • PPP • PPTP • Point-to-point/multipoint	• Chapter 8: Using a Phone Line to Connect to the Internet • Chapter 12: Virtual Private Networks

Objective	Chapter: Section
4.6. Describe how various protocols or services apply to the function of a mail system, web system, and file transfer system. Content could include the following: • POP3 • SMTP • HTTP • FTP • NNTP (news servers) • TCP/IP • LDAP • LPR • Telnet • Gopher	• Chapter 2: The OSI Model Applied to the Internet • Chapter 4: E-mail Protocols and How They Work, How FTP Works, Telnet, Newsgroups, Gophers • Chapter 10: Directory Server, LPD Server
4.7. Describe when to use various diagnostic tools for identifying and resolving Internet problems. Content could include the following: • Ping • WinIPCfg • IPC Config • ARP • Trace Routing Utility • Network Analyzer • Netstat	• Chapter 13: Troubleshooting Internet Connections, Connecting a Small Company LAN to the Internet
4.8. Describe hardware and software connection devices and their uses. Content could include the following: • Network interface card • Various types of modems including analog, ISDN, DSL, and cable • Modem setup and commands • Adapter • Bridge • Internet-in-a-box • Cache-in-a-box • Hub • Router • Switch • Gateway • NOS • Firewall	• Chapter 8: Using a Phone Line to Connect to the Internet, Using Cable Modem, ISDN, or DSL to Connect to the Internet, Connecting a PC on a LAN to the Internet • Chapter 12: Firewalls • Chapter 11: Operating Systems on the Network, Internetworking Devices

A

Objective	Chapter: Section
4.9. Describe various types of Internet band-width technologies (link types). Content could include the following: • T1/E1 • T3/E3 • Frame relay • X.25 • ATM • DSL	• Chapter 1: Introduction to the Internet Infrastructure • Chapter 11: Understanding LANs and How They Work, Bandwidth Technologies
4.10. Describe the purpose of various servers—what they are, their functionality, and features. Content could include the following: • Proxy • Mail • Mirrored • Cache • List • Web (HTTP) • News • Certificate • Directory (LDAP) • E-commerce • Telnet • FTP	• Chapter 4: E-mail, FTP • Chapter 7: Web Hosting • Chapter 10: Servers and What They Do (entire chapter)

DOMAIN 5.0 I-NET SECURITY

Objective	Chapter: Section
5.1. Define the following Internet security concepts: access control, encryption, auditing and authentication, and provide appropriate types of technologies currently available for each. Examples could include the following: • Access control—access control list, firewall, packet filters, proxy • Authentication—certificates, digital signatures, non-repudiation • Encryption—public and private keys, secure socket layers (SSL), S/MIME, digital signatures, global versus country-specific encryption standards • Auditing—intrusion detection utilities, log files, auditing logs • SET (Secure Electronic Transactions)	• Chapter 12: Types of Intrusion, Protection Strategies, Virtual Private Networks

Objective	Chapter: Section
5.2. Describe VPN and what it does. Content could include the following: • VPN is encrypted communications • Connecting two different company sites via an Internet VPN (extranet) • Connecting a remote user to a site	• Chapter 12: Virtual Private Networks
5.3. Describe various types of suspicious activities. Examples could include the following: • Multiple login failures • Denial of service attacks • Mail flooding/spam • Ping floods • SYN floods	• Chapter 12: Types of Intrusions
5.4. Describe access security features for an Internet server (e.g., e-mail server, web server). Examples could include the following: • User name and password • File level • Certificate • File-level access: read, write, no access	• Chapter 8: Configuring a PC to Share Resources with Others on the LAN • Chapter 12: Protection Strategies
5.5. Describe the purpose of antivirus software and when to use it. Content could include the following: • Browser/client • Server	• Chapter 12: Protecting Against Viruses • Chapter 13: Managing AntiVirus Software
5.6. Describe the differences between the following as they relate to security requirements: • Intranet • Extranet • Internet	• Chapter 12: Protection Strategies

DOMAIN 6.0 BUSINESS CONCEPTS

A

Objective	Chapter: Section
6.1. Explain the issues involved in copy-righting, trademarking, and licensing. Content could include the following: • How to license copyright materials • Scope of your copyright • How to copyright your material anywhere • Consequences of not being aware of copyright issues, not following copy-right restrictions	• Chapter 14: Copyright, Licenses, and Trademarks
6.2. Identify the issues related to working in a global environment. Content could include the following: • Working in a multi-vendor environ-ment with different currencies, etc. • International issues—shipping, supply chain • Multi-lingual or multi-character issues (Unicode) • Legal and regulatory issues	• Chapter 14: How Business is Done on the Web, International Business on the Web
6.3. Define the following web-related mechanisms for audience development (i.e., attracting and retaining an audience): • Push technology • Pull technology	• Chapter 14: Attracting and Retaining Customers to Your Web Site
6.4. Describe the differences between the following from a business standpoint: • Intranet • Extranet • Internet	• Chapter 12: Protection Strategies • Chapter 14: Businesses on the Web, How Business is Done on the Web
6.5. Define e-commerce terms and concepts Content could include the following: • EDI • Business to Business • Business to Consumer • Internet commerce • Merchant systems • Online Cataloging • Relationship management • Customer self-service • Internet marketing	• Chapter 14: Businesses on the Web, How Business is Done on the Web, Attracting and Retaining Customers to Your Web Site, Electronic Data Interchange (EDI), Copyright, Licenses, and Trademarks, International Business on the Web

B

ORGANIZATIONS THAT STANDARDIZE THE INTERNET

This appendix describes several organizations that are responsible for developing world-wide standards for the many technical aspects of the Internet.

AMERICAN NATIONAL STANDARDS INSTITUTE (ANSI)

The American National Standards Institute (ANSI) is dedicated to promoting the use of U.S. standards internationally. It was a founding member of the International Organization for Standardization (explained later in this appendix), and is still directly associated with that organization. ANSI does not develop standards—rather, it is responsible for ensuring that qualified groups achieve a consensus.

ANSI members are drawn from a wide variety of organizations from around the world, including corporations, educational institutions, and governments. For details about ANSI and information on membership, go to *www.ansi.org*.

DIRECTORY INTEROPERABILITY FORUM (DIF)

The Directory Interoperability Forum (DIF) was created to accelerate the creation of applications that employ open directories. The forum is primarily concerned with directory structures that are based on LDAP standards. DIF works to make such directories more useable. At the same time, it strives to promote the use of applications based on open directories, which can be run using any directory.

DIF has an open membership policy, and is made up of teams that meet at least four times a year. Currently the teams focus on topics such as ISV (independent software vendor) programs, standards, SDKs (software development kits), and marketing. You can find more information about DIF at *www.directoryforum.org*.

Highway 1

Highway 1 is dedicated to informing the U.S. government about new technologies and the effect that they might have on our society, economy, and public policy. The organization hosts discussions focusing on key issues related to the Internet. Highway 1 works with Cisco Systems, IBM, MCI Worldcom, Microsoft, NCS and other organizations in order to achieve its goals. For more information about Highway 1, go to *www.highway1.org*.

Institute of Electrical and Electronics Engineers, Inc. (IEEE)

The Institute of Electrical and Electronics Engineers, Inc. IEEE is a non-profit organization that focuses on technical topics such as computer engineering, telecommunications, electric power, consumer electronics, and biomedical technology. IEEE publishes almost 30 percent of the world's literature on electrical, electronic, and computer engineering and science.

IEEE offers both professional and student memberships. Members are assigned to local groups. Members gather regularly at local meetings to discuss current issues in the profession and to network with other professionals. You can find membership information at *www.ieee.org*.

International Multimedia Teleconferencing Consortium (IMTC)

The International Multimedia Teleconferencing Consortium (IMTC) works to establish international standards for interoperable multimedia teleconferencing. IMTC is a result of the merger of The Consortium for Audiographics Teleconferencing Standards, Inc. (CATS) and the Multimedia Communications Community of Interest (MCCOI). After IMTC was formed, it merged with the Personal Conferencing Work Group (PCWG). As a result, the organization consists of over 150 companies from around the globe.

IMTC members include Internet application developers and service providers, end users, telecommunications service providers, educational institutions, government agencies, and non-profit organizations. You can find more details about the organization and membership at *www.imtc.org*.

International Organization for Standardization (ISO)

The International Organization for Standardization (ISO) is dedicated to promoting standardization in technologies used in the international exchange of goods and services. ISO is best known for creating the OSI reference model and the OSI protocol suite.

You may notice that ISO is not an acronym for International Organization for Standardization. It was not meant to be. ISO means "equal" in Greek, and the founders felt it was a good representation of their organization.

ISO member organizations are divided into three categories: member body, correspondent member, and subscriber member. Only one member body is allowed from each country, and that member is then charged with representing that country's standards. The member body for the United States is the American National Standards Institute (ANSI). Countries that do not yet have established standards are allowed a correspondent membership in ISO. The subscriber membership is reserved for countries with very small economies. Currently, 130 countries are represented in ISO. For more information about the organization, visit *www.iso.ch*.

INTERNATIONAL TELECOMMUNICATION UNION (ITU)

The International Telecommunication Union (ITU) works to set standards for the telecommunication industry. The organization recognizes that telecommunications were once viewed as public utilities, but are now seen as tools of commerce. ITU makes recommendations for the telecommunications industry including regulatory concerns, growth issues, and new technology advancements.

Various groups within ITU focus on individual issues. These groups include Radio-Communication (ITU-R), Telecom Standardization (ITU-T), and Telecom Development (ITU-D). You can find more information about ITU and its component groups at *www.itu.int*.

INTERNATIONAL WEBCASTING ASSOCIATION (IWA)

The International Webcasting Association (IWA) focuses on the delivery of multimedia services to consumers and businesses. IWA is interested in both audio and visual multimedia, and although most of the members use Internet transmission, some members focus on distributing multimedia through other networks.

IWA membership is open to companies that work with or are interested in multimedia technology. The organization is led by a board of directors, the members of which were instrumental in the creation of IWA. These board members include Apple Computer, Microsoft, Morgan Stanley Dean Witter, Real Networks, and TVontheWeb. For information about IWA, go to *www.webcasters.org*.

INTERNET CORPORATION FOR ASSIGNED NAMES AND NUMBERS (ICANN)

The Internet Corporation for Assigned Names and Numbers (ICANN) works to coordinate the management of the directory system used on the Internet. Among other things, ICANN focuses on the domain name system, the root server system, IP address space allocation, and protocol parameter assignment. The group works to ensure that the Internet continues to be a stable environment for users worldwide.

In order to make ICANN a true representation of Internet users, the organization offers At Large Memberships. At Large Members receive regular updates about the organization, and they are allowed to help choose the Board of Directors through a worldwide online election. You can find information about ICANN at *www.icann.org*.

INTERNET ENGINEERING TASK FORCE (IETF)

The Internet Engineering Task Force (IETF) is an international community of computer associates concerned with the architecture and operation of the Internet. The organization is best known for its publication of Requests for Comments (RFCs). You can find copies of RFCs on IETF's web site at *www.ietf.org*.

The organization is open to anyone interested in joining. Members are divided into work groups that focus on particular topics (such as security, the Internet, and routing), and each group corresponds by mailing lists. Although most correspondence is done through electronic communication, the organization also meets three times a year.

INTERNET MAIL CONSORTIUM (IMC)

The Internet Mail Consortium (IMC) is dedicated to managing and promoting electronic mail and the use of the Internet. The group focuses on expanding the use of electronic mail in commerce, studying the role of new technologies, and making electronic mail easier to use for everyone.

Membership in IMC is generally limited to companies and organizations that deal directly with Internet mail, including software vendors who sell Internet mail packages, hardware vendors who offer mail servers, and companies who have Internet mail gateways. You can find information about the organization and membership requirements at *www.imc.org*.

INTERNET SOCIETY

The Internet Society (ISOC) is an organization of professionals who work with the Internet. Its goal is to help expand the Internet and to ensure that any new technologies are compatible with each other and with the Internet. ISOC offers memberships to both individuals and organizations. Members receive subscriptions to the magazine **OnTheInternet** and to the electronic newsletter **ISOC Forum**. You can obtain membership information from the society's web page at *www.isoc.org*.

IP MULTICAST INITIATIVE (IPMI)

IP Multicast Initiative (IPMI) is a forum that was created to help accelerate the adoption of IP Multicast (an IETF standard). The group is working to become the leading comprehensive source of information regarding IP Multicast. IPMI also works to increase the demand for IP Multicast products and services.

Membership in IPMI is limited to companies that work with or provide products or services that are related to IP Multicast. The IPMI web site (*www.ipmulticast.com*) includes a list of vendors that provide IP Multicast products and services.

NATIONAL COMMITTEE FOR INFORMATION TECHNOLOGY STANDARDS (NCITS)

The National Committee for Information Technology Standards (NCITS) works to provide standards in the computer industry, focusing on multimedia, intercommunication, storage media, databases, security, and programming languages. The organization previously operated under the name Accredited Standards Committee X3, and it participates in the development of international and national standards.

NCITS offers memberships to organizations that directly deal with or are affected by standards-based information technology. The organization divides members into three groups: producers, consumers, and general interest. NCITS works to keep members active by requiring that members attend two of every three meetings. You can find more information about the organization and membership at *www.ncits.org*.

ORGANIZATION FOR THE ADVANCEMENT OF STRUCTURED INFORMATION STANDARDS (OASIS)

The Organization for the Advancement of Structured Information Standards (OASIS) works for the adoption of product-independent formats such as SGML, XML, and HTML. The organization's goal is to provide formats that can be used universally. In addition to product-independent formats, OASIS works to ensure that formats are easy to adopt and use, and are practical for real-life applications.

A range of professionals makes up the organization, including providers, users, and specialists. Memberships are available for both companies and individuals. Members receive special benefits such as access to the OASIS open forum, where various issues and products are discussed. You can find additional information about OASIS at *www.oasis-open.org*.

PORTABLE APPLICATION STANDARDS COMMITTEE (PASC)

The Portable Application Standards Committee (PASC) is a committee within IEEE. PASC works to maintain the POSIX family of standards. POSIX (Portable Operating System Interface for UNIX) is an IEEE standard that outlines a set of operating-system services.

Applications that follow the POSIX standard can be ported between systems. Although POSIX was originally created for UNIX, it can be implemented on other systems as well.

You can join PASC without joining IEEE, although dual membership is encouraged. There are two ways to be a member of PASC. The first is to participate in the quarterly meetings, which are held in the United States and periodically in Europe. In addition, you can partake in work groups by reviewing and commenting on PASC materials that are distributed through mailing lists and the Internet. You can find additional information about PASC at *www.pasc.org*.

US Internet Industry Association (USIIA)

The US Internet Industry Association (USIIA) focuses on the development and growth of Internet commerce, content, and connectivity. The organization works as an advocate for the industry on issues such as copyright, taxation, electronic commerce, open access, and privacy. Previously known as the Association of Online Professionals (AOP), USIIA promotes awareness on current issues facing the electronic world.

The organization is open to both individuals and corporations, and the benefits of joining include legal representation and assistance, a database of legislative information related to the Internet, employment services, and networking opportunities. You can find information about USIIA at *www.usiia.org*.

World Wide Web Consortium (W3C)

The World Wide Web Consortium (W3C) was founded to develop protocols to be used by the World Wide Web and to make sure that the Web continues to be a functional tool. The organization provides a wealth of information about the World Wide Web, including specifications and sample code.

While the W3C does not allow for individual memberships, it does accept applications from companies and other organizations. Some of W3C's members include Apple Computer, IBM Corporation, the Library of Congress, and Toyota Motor Corporation. You can find more information about W3C at *www.w3.org*.

C

HTML Reference

This appendix contains a list of some of the most valuable HTML tags used in designing web pages. Some tags or attributes may not work for certain HTML versions or for certain browsers or programs.

Structural Tags

<HTML>...</HTML>

- **Purpose**: Identifies the beginning and end of an HTML document. All HTML documents should contain these tags. <HTML> should be the first tag in the document, and </HTML> should be the last.

<HEAD>...</HEAD>

- **Purpose**: Identifies the beginning and end of a header. A header contains general information about the document, and the browser does not display the contents of the header. All HTML documents should contain these tags, and the tags should be inserted immediately after the initial HTML tag.

- **Syntax with examples**:

| <HEAD>HTML Lessons</HEAD> | Creates the header "HTML Lessons" |
| <HEAD>Page 2</HEAD> | Creates the header "Page 2" |

<TITLE>...</TITLE>

- **Purpose**: Marks the title for the web page that will be displayed in the title bar of the browser window. Place these tags between the HEAD tags.

■ **Syntax with examples**:

<HEAD><TITLE>Learning HTML</TITLE></HEAD>	Creates the title within the header.

<META NAME="KEYWORDS" CONTENT="...">

■ **Purpose**: Identifies key words related to the web page so that search and index-ing services can locate the page. This tag is optional, but increases the chances of your web page being located and viewed by web users. Place this tag between your HEAD tags and after the TITLE tags.

■ **Syntax with examples**:

<META NAME="KEYWORDS" CONTENT="cow milk farm">	Search engines will list this web page under the keywords cow, milk, or farm.

<META NAME="DESCRIPTION" CONTENT="...">

■ **Purpose**: Creates a description of your web page for display by search engines and indexing services. Again, this tag is optional, but providing a description of your web page up front increases the chances of someone selecting it from a long list. This tag also goes between the HEAD tags.

■ **Syntax with examples**:

<META NAME="DESCRIPTION" CONTENT="This is my personal web site.">	This web page would be described in a search results list as "This is my personal web site."
<META NAME="DESCRIPTION" CONTENT="LEARN HOW TO CREATE YOUR OWN WEB PAGE!!!">	This web page would be described in a search result as "LEARN HOW TO CREATE YOUR OWN WEB PAGE!!!"

<BODY>...</BODY>

■ **Purpose**: Indicates the body of the document, which is displayed by the browser. Codes and tags before and after the BODY tags will not be visible on the web page. All HTML documents should contain these tags.

■ **Syntax with examples**:

<BODY>Welcome! This is my personal web page.</BODY>	Only the text between the tags will appear on the web page.

BGCOLOR="…"

- **Purpose**: Sets the background color, and is used within a TABLE, TR, TH, or TD tag.

- **Attributes**: You may create a color background by including the BGCOLOR= "#rrggbb" or "name" attribute. The "#rrggbb" is a code that identifies colors to a computer. Some common colors are #000000 for black, #00CC00 for green, #0000CC for purple, and #CC0000 for red. You may also use some names for colors, such as "black", "green", "blue", "purple", "red", "silver", "aqua", "fuchsia", "olive", "white", "teal", or "yellow" (using the "name" attribute).

- **Syntax with examples**:

<TABLE BGCOLOR="#CC0000">	Creates a red background in the table.
<TH BGCOLOR="purple">	Creates a purple background in the heading cell.

BACKGROUND="…"

- **Purpose**: Uses an image for the background. It is used within a BODY tag.

- **Attributes**: The image attribute should indicate the path for the source of the image, and the browser will automatically tile an image that does not fill the screen.

- **Syntax with examples**:

<BODY BACKGROUND="cocacola.gif">	Displays the web page on a background of the cocacola image.

BODY TAGS

- **Purpose**: Forces a line break.

- **Syntax with examples**:

My favorite color is blue. 	Creates a line break after the sentence.
 My favorite number is 7.	Creates a line break before the sentence.

C

<P>...</P>

- **Purpose**: Marks the beginning and end of a paragraph.

- **Attributes**: The paragraph can be aligned LEFT, RIGHT, CENTER, or JUSTIFY by using the ALIGN="..." attribute.

- **Syntax with examples**:

<P>What is your favorite pet? I personally like dogs, but cats and birds are okay, too.</P>	Creates a paragraph of the three sentences and wraps the text throughout the paragraph.
<P ALIGN="CENTER">Cows eat grass. I would prefer not to.</P>	Both sentences are part of the same paragraph, which is centered on the page.

<HR>

- **Purpose**: Inserts a horizontal line in the document.

- **Attributes**: The horizontal line's size and width can be determined using the SIZE=n and WIDTH=n attributes, respectively, with n being the size in pixels or the width in pixels or the relative width percentage of the document. The horizontal line can also be aligned to the LEFT, RIGHT, or CENTER using the ALIGN="..." attribute.

- **Syntax with examples**:

Dogs and cats are popular pets. <HR>	Creates a horizontal line underneath the sentence.
Pets: <HR SIZE=15 WIDTH=30% ALIGN="LEFT"> Dog Cat Bird Fish 	Creates a horizontal line 15 pixels thick, 30% the length of the document, and aligned to the left underneath the word "Pets" and over the word "Dog".

BORDER="0"

- **Purpose**: Controls the size of the border surrounding a picture, table, link, heading, photograph, etc.

- **Attributes**: Border="0" removes a border that would be present by default; border="1" creates a thin border while border="10" creates a much thicker border.

- **Syntax with examples**:

`<TABLE BORDER="1"> ... </TABLE>`	Creates a thin border around a table.

`<A HREF="http://www.cocacola.com">`
`<IMG SRC="cocacola.gif"`
`BORDER="0"></A>`
	Removes the border that would have automatically been added to this hyperlink.

FONT TAGS

`<B>...</B>`

- **Purpose**: Marks the beginning and end of bold face text.

- **Syntax with examples**:

`<B>Cows eat grass.</B>`	The sentence looks like: **Cows eat grass**.
`My family lived on <B>dairy farms</B>.`	Only the words **dairy farms** will be bold.

`<I>...</I>`

- **Purpose**: Italicizes text.

- **Syntax with examples**:

`<I>Drink Milk</I>`	The sentence looks like: *Drink Milk*
`I <I>love</I> milk!`	Only the word *love* will be italicized.

`<U>...</U>`

- **Purpose**: Underlines text.

- **Syntax with examples**:

`<U>If the cow kicks over the bucket,` `you just have to start over!</U>`	The sentence looks like: <u>If the cow kicks over the</u> <u>bucket, you just have to start over!</u>
`Our dogs are <U>very</U> well` `behaved.`	Only the word <u>very</u> will be underlined.

<S>...</S> or <STRIKE>...</STRIKE>

- **Purpose**: Overstrikes text.

- **Syntax with examples**:

<STRIKE>Make a left turn.</STRIKE>	The sentence looks like: ~~Make a left turn.~~
Make a <S>right</S>left turn.	Only the word ~~right~~ is struck out.

<FONT>...</FONT>

- **Purpose**: Sets a specific font.

- **Attributes**: The color and size of the selected font can be changed from the text's font by using the COLOR="#rrggbb" or "name" and the SIZE="n" attributes, where "#rrggbb" refers to a color code, "name" refers to a color name, and "n" refers to the font size using a scale of 1 to 7. The default size is 4, and the new size can be set by using relative "+" or "-" settings, or by using absolute numbers 1 through 7.

- **Syntax with examples**:

<FONT SIZE="2" COLOR="33CCFF"> The tiny bird peaked out at the blue sky from the safety of his nest.</FONT>	Changes the text selection to a small size and colors it light blue, even though the rest of the document text could be a different size and color.
<FONT SIZE="+5" COLOR="red">He saw a hawk circling overhead!</FONT>	Changes the text selection by a factor of plus 5 and colors the text red.

<H1>...</H1>
<H2>...</H2>
...
<H6>...</H6>

- **Purpose**: Formats size and boldness of font. Use heading tags to format titles and subtitles.

- **Attributes**: H1 uses a large, bold face font. H2 uses a slightly smaller font, and so forth. H6 uses the smallest heading font. Headings can also be aligned to the LEFT, RIGHT, or CENTER using the ALIGN="..." attribute.

- **Syntax with examples**:

`<H1 ALIGN="CENTER">Book 1</H1>`	Shows "Book 1" as the main heading, which is centered on the page.
`<H2>Chapter 1</H2>`	Shows "Chapter 1" as the sub-heading.
`<H3>Verse 1</H3>`	Shows "Verse 1" as the next sub-heading.

`<SUB>...</SUB>`, `<SUP>...</SUP>`

- **Purpose**: Changes text to subscript or superscript, respectively.

- **Syntax with examples**:

Fill the test tube with H`<SUB>`2`</SUB>`O.	The sentence looks like: Fill the test tube with H_2O.
The formula for a square's area is s`<SUP>`2`</SUP>`.	The sentence looks like: The formula for a square's area is s^2.

`<BIG>...</BIG>`

- **Purpose**: Enlarges text.

- **Syntax with examples**:

`<BIG>You can do it!</BIG>`	Enlarges "You can do it!"
`<BIG><B>I KNOW you can!</B></BIG>`	Enlarges and bolds "I KNOW you can!"

`<BLINK>...</BLINK>`

- **Purpose**: Makes text blink. This tag works only in Netscape Navigator.

- **Syntax with examples**:

`<BLINK>Drink Milk</BLINK>`	"Drink Milk" blinks on the screen.
`<BLINK>Drink<I>Coca-Cola</I></BLINK>`	"Drink" blinks, "Coca-Cola" is italicized and also blinks.

- **Purpose**: Creates a non-breaking space.
- **Syntax with examples**:

Left Right	Creates a space between "Left" and "Right" without breaking the line and appears like this: "Left Right."

TABLE TAGS

<TABLE>...</TABLE>

- **Purpose**: Marks the beginning and end of a table.
- **Attributes**: BORDER=n creates a border around the table, with "n" determining the size of the border in pixels. The border color can be set using the tag BORDERCOLOR="#rrggbb" or "name", with "#rrggbb" being the color code or "name" being the name of the color. This attribute only works in Internet Explorer. The tag CELLSPACING=n determines the amount of space in pixels between the cells of the table.
- **Syntax with examples**:

<TABLE BORDER=3>...</TABLE>	These tags would create a table with a 3-pixel wide border.
<TABLE BORDER=0 CELLSPACING=5>...</TABLE>	This table would not have a border at all and would space the cells 5 pixels apart.

<CAPTION>...</CAPTION>

- **Purpose**: Creates the title of the table that is written above the table. This is an optional table tag.
- **Attributes**: The alignment of the caption can be controlled using the ALIGN="..." tag, with the alignment options being LEFT, RIGHT, TOP or BOTTOM.
- **Syntax with examples**:

<CAPTION ALIGN="RIGHT"> <B>My Pets</B></CAPTION>	Bolds the title for the table called "**My Pets**" and aligns the caption to the right of the page.
<CAPTION ALIGN="TOP"> Local Farmers</CAPTION>	Creates the title "Local Farmers" and aligns it to the top.

<TH>...</TH>

- **Purpose**: Creates a column heading over one column in a table. This is an optional table tag.

- **Attributes**: The column can be aligned using the ALIGN="..." tag with the alignment options being LEFT, RIGHT, CENTER, JUSTIFY, or CHAR; the CHAR alignment means the column will align either with the decimal or with some other character as specified by CHAR="...". The vertical alignment is controlled using VALIGN="..." with the options being TOP, MIDDLE, or BOTTOM. The number of columns used by a particular cell can be specified by COLSPAN=n, and similarly, the number of rows used by a cell can be specified with ROWSPAN=n, with "n" being the number of cells.

- **Syntax with examples**:

<TH ALIGN="LEFT" VALIGN="TOP">Animal</TH>	Creates the column heading "Animal" and aligns the heading within the cell to the left and top of the cell.
<TH COLSPAN=2>Name</TH> <TH ROWSPAN=2>Color</TH>	Creates two column headings, "Name" and "Color", on the same row and will use two columns for the "Name" cell and two rows for the "Color" cell.

<TR>...</TR>

- **Purpose**: Marks the beginning and end of one row of a table.

- **Attributes**: The column can be aligned using the ALIGN="..." tag with the alignment options being LEFT, RIGHT, CENTER, JUSTIFY, or CHAR; the CHAR alignment means the column will align either with the decimal or with some other character as specified by CHAR="...". The vertical alignment is controlled using VALIGN="..." with the options being TOP, MIDDLE, or BOTTOM.

- **Syntax with example**:

<TR ALIGN="CENTER">Pets I Have</TR> <TR ALIGN="LEFT">Pets I Want</TR>	Creates two rows in a table showing the phrase "Pets I Have" and "Pets I Want", respectively. The first row is aligned to the center, and the second row is aligned to the left.

<TD>...</TD>

- **Purpose**: Marks the beginning and end of one cell in one row of a table.

- **Attributes**: The column can be aligned using the ALIGN="..." tag with the alignment options being LEFT, RIGHT, CENTER, JUSTIFY, or CHAR; the CHAR alignment means the column will align either with the decimal or with some other character as specified by CHAR="...". The vertical alignment is controlled using VALIGN="..." with the options being TOP, MIDDLE, or BOTTOM. The number of columns used by a particular cell can be specified by COLSPAN=n, and similarly, the number of rows used by a cell can be specified with ROWSPAN=n, with "n" being the number of cells.

- **Syntax with examples**:

<TR> <TD COLSPAN=2>Frostie</TD> <TD>Gray</TD> </TR>	Creates one row with "Frostie" in one cell, taking up two columns, and "Gray" in the next cell of the same row.

Sample Table:

<CAPTION ALIGN="RIGHT"> My Favorite Animals</CAPTION> <TABLE BORDER=3> <TR VALIGN="MIDDLE"> <TH ALIGN="CENTER">Name</TH> <TH ALIGN="CENTER">Type</TH> </TR> <TR> <TD>Frostie</TD> <TD>Sheltie</TD> </TR> <TR> <TD>Kawika</TD> <TD>Sheltie</TD> </TR> <TR> <TD>Shamu</TD> <TD>Orca</TD> </TR> </TABLE>	Creates a table with the caption reading "My Favorite Animals", a border 3 pixels wide, two columns labeled "Name" and "Type", and three rows below the heading row. The table headings are vertically aligned in the middle of their cells and horizontally aligned to the center of each cell.

ILLUSTRATION TAGS

<IMG>

- **Purpose**: Inserts an image file in the document. Be sure to include the path to the file relative to the location of the web page.

- **Attributes**: The SRC="URL" attribute indicates where the image can be found. When adding an image, you should also indicate what text to display should the image not download properly. Do this using the ALT="..." attribute. The alignment of the image can be controlled using the ALIGN="..." attribute. Also, the thickness of the border around the image, the height and width of the image, and the vertical and horizontal (white) space around the image can be controlled using the following respective attribute codes: BORDER=n, HEIGHT=n, WIDTH=n, VSPACE=n, and HSPACE=n, where "n" equals the number of pixels.

- **Syntax with examples**:

<IMG SRC="cocacola.gif" ALT="Drink Coca-Cola" ALIGN="center" BORDER=2>	Inserts clip art from a file named cocacola.gif, aligns the image in the center of the document with a small border around it, and displays "Drink Coca-Cola" if the image does not download.
<IMG SRC="Images/cow.jpg" ALT="Dairy Cow" WIDTH=200 VSPACE=50>	Inserts the photograph from the file called Images/cow.jpg, makes the photograph 200 pixels wide with 50 pixels space on top and bottom, and displays "Dairy Cow" if the image does not download correctly.

<MARQUEE>

- **Purpose**: Creates a scrolling text marquee. This tag works only in Internet Explorer.

- **Attributes**: The marquee can be aligned with the ALIGN="..." attribute, with the options being TOP, MIDDLE, or BOTTOM. The action of the marquee is determined using BEHAVIOR="...", where the marquee either behaves as a SCROLL, SLIDE, or ALTERNATE. The background color is determined using BGCOLOR="#rrggbb" or "name", where "#rrggbb" is the color code or "name" is the name of the color. The height and width are controlled with HEIGHT="..." and WIDTH="n", respectively, and each is determined either in pixels or as a percentage of the respective screen dimension. The LOOP="..." attribute sets the number of times the marquee loops, and the SCROLLAMOUNT=n determines the number of pixels between each successive loop.

- **Syntax with Examples**:

<MARQUEE BEHAVIOR="SCROLL" LOOP="15" HEIGHT="25">Don't forget to e-mail me!	Creates a marquee that scrolls fifteen times at a height of 25 pixels.
<MARQUEE BEHAVIOR="ALTERNATE" LOOP="INFINITE" SCROLLAMOUNT=10>Come again soon!	Creates a marquee that alternates between scroll and slide, loops infinitely, and inserts 10 pixels of space between each successive loop.

<BGSOUND>

- **Purpose**: Determines background sounds. This tag works only in Internet Explorer.

- **Attributes**: SRC="URL" works like the image SRC above—it indicates where to find the sound file, which can be in WAV, AU, or MID format. The LOOP="…" indicates how many times to repeat the sound file. The <BGSOUND> tag only works with Internet Explorer.

- **Syntax with Example**:

<BGSOUND SRC=moo.wav>	Adds the background sounds from the WAV file moo.wav to the page.

INTERACTIVE TAGS

<A HREF="#section-name">...</A>

- **Purpose**: Uses the anchor tag to create a link. Marks the text or graphic as a link to a section name within the same document or to another web page on this or another site.

- **Syntax with examples**:

<A HREF="#Section1">How Fluid Milk is Processed</A>	This link appears as "How Fluid Milk is Processed" and points to the Section 1 target further down in the document.
<A HREF="http://www.cocacola.com"> <IMG SRC= "cocacola.gif"></A>	This hyperlink appears as the clip art picture from the file cocacola.gif and points to the web site www.cocacola.com.

<A NAME="section-name">...</A>

- **Purpose**: Uses the anchor tag to create a position in the document as the link target, or position that the link points to.

- **Syntax with examples**:

<A NAME="Section1"> Processing Fluid Milk</A>	This link target appears as "Processing Fluid Milk" and is pointed to by the earlier "Section 1" link.
<A NAME="Photos"><IMG SRC= "Images/cow.jpg"></A>	This link target appears as the photograph from the file called Images/cow.jpg and is pointed to by an earlier "Photos" link.

<FORM ACTION="mailto:myaddress@mindspring.com" METHOD="POST">...</FORM>

- **Purpose**: Uses the FORM tag to allow data to be received and sent back to the web server. Certain parts must be included.

- **Attributes**: The ACTION portion tells the browser where to put the data once it is submitted. You should input your e-mail address after the "mailto:" phrase. The METHOD portion tells the browser how to send the data. Another possible value for METHOD is "GET".

- **Syntax with examples**: See example below.

<INPUT>

- **Purpose**: Allows a user to input information.

- **Attributes**: SIZE=n determines the size of the object as the number of pixels unless the TYPE attribute is set to either TEXT or PASSWORD, in which case SIZE indicates the number of characters for the INPUT tag. MAXLENGTH=n determines the maximum number of characters allowed within a field. The TYPE="..." tag allows for a variety of types of fields; options include TEXT, PASSWORD, CHECKBOX, RADIO, SUBMIT, RESET, HIDDEN, FILE, BUTTON, and IMAGE. The "TEXT" TYPE tag allows a user to enter data into a text box. The NAME="..." attribute defines the text box to the browser for when the data is sent to the e-mail address. The "SUBMIT" TYPE tag creates a Submit button. The VALUE="..." attribute of "SUBMIT" is the text that displays on the button.

■ **Syntax with examples**: Combine the FORM and INPUT tags as follows:

1. <FORM ACTION= "mailto:myaddress@mindspring.com" METHOD="POST"> 2. Enter your name: <INPUT TYPE= "TEXT" NAME="Friend" MAXLENGTH=10> 3. <INPUT TYPE="SUBMIT" VALUE= "Send"> 4.</FORM>	Creates a line "Enter your name:" with a text box that allows a maximum of 10 characters and a Submit button for e-mailing information to myaddress@mindspring.com.
1. <FORM ACTION= "mailto:myaddress@mindspring.com" METHOD="POST"> 2. <P>Your name: <INPUT TYPE= "TEXT" NAME="Friend" SIZE=10 MAXLENGTH=10></P> 3. Your favorite pet is a: 4. <INPUT TYPE="RADIO" NAME="Favorite">Dog 5. <INPUT TYPE="RADIO" NAME="Favorite">Cat 6. <INPUT TYPE="SUBMIT" VALUE= "Send"> 7. <INPUT TYPE="RESET" VALUE= "Reset"> 8. </FORM>	Creates one line requesting the user's name and provides a text box for the data. The text box appears 10 characters long and only allows 10 characters. Then starts another line requesting the user's favorite pet with radio buttons in front of each choice. Finally, creates two buttons: a submit button and a reset button. The non-breaking space code " " puts a little space between the Send button and the Reset button.

SPECIAL SYMBOLS

■ **Purpose**: Some symbols cannot simply be typed on the keyboard, so HTML requires special codes for these symbols. Listed below are a few that may be helpful.

Symbol	Code	Symbol	Code
¡	&#161 or &iexcl	µ	&#181 or &micro
¢	&#162 or &cent	¶	&#182 or &para
£	&#163 or &pound	¸	&#184 or &cedil
§	&#167 or &sect	¿	&#191 or &iquest
©	&#169 or &copy	À	&#192 or &Agrave
®	&#174 or &reg	Á	&#193 or &Aacute
°	&#176 or &deg	Æ	&#198 or &AElig

D

COMMON HTTP ERROR MESSAGES

This appendix contains a list of some of the most common HTML error messages and their meanings. HTTP status codes are three-digit numbers that are generated by the server based on HTTP standards described in RFC 2068, 2616, 2816, and 2817. The codes can be grouped by the general meanings. Codes with numbers 200–299 indicate that a successful transaction took place. Codes numbered 300–399 indicate redirection. Numbers 400–499 are reserved for error messages that indicate a problem was created by the client. And the last range of codes, 500–599, is used to indicate the server has a problem or cannot fulfill the client request. The list below contains the most common codes, as found on the Hobson Square web site, *www.hobsonsquare.com*

Sometimes a browser displays messages to the user that might or might not indicate it has received an HTTP status code from the server. This list of error messages displayed by a browser and their meanings was taken from the Pioneer Internet web site, *www.pldi.net.*

Message	Meaning
Bad File Request	An online form or the HTML code for an online form has an error.
Failed DNS Lookup	The web site's URL couldn't be translated into a valid IP address.
Helper Application Not Found	You have attempted to download a file that needs a helper application, and the browser cannot find it.
Not Found	The page that the hyperlink points to no longer exists.
Site Unavailable	One of several things can cause this message: either too many users are trying to access the site, the site is down for maintenance, there is "noise" on the line, or the site no longer exists. Typing the wrong address can also produce this message.

Code	Meaning
200	Request completed successfully.
201	Data sent, request was a POST.
202	Request accepted, but results unknown.
204	Request fulfilled, but no new information sent to client.
301	Data request has been moved. Server should provide client with new URL.
302	Data found at different URL. Server should provide client with correct URL.
303	Available at different URL, should be retrieved using GET.
304	Request contained **if-modified-since field**. Server indicating file not modified since the date specified, server will not resend the requested document.
400	Requested syntax wrong.
401	The request included an **Authorization** field, but the client (browser) did not supply one.
403	Request for a file that is presently set to forbidden, so the file can't be sent. A browser sometimes reports this status as "Connection Refused by Host".
404	Server can't find the requested URL. Frequently indicates user made a typo in entering the URL string.
405	Server didn't understand the METHOD supplied by the client.
406	Resource found, but not sent. Type of resource incompatible based on information passed between server and client.
408	Client did not produce the request before server timed out.
410	Resource no longer available, server has no forwarding URL.
500	Unfortunately, this error can mean almost anything and will frequently halt execution of a CGI script dead in its tracks. Usually the only message you will see is "Server encountered an internal error and can't continue."
501	Server does not support the method being requested. For CGI scripts, a 501 error may mean the server isn't set up to support CGI scripts outside their designation subdirectory. Therefore the method (typically POST) fails since it isn't supported in other directories.
502	Server attempted to retrieve resource from another server or gateway with this secondary server failing to return a valid response on the calling server.
503	Server is too busy and unavailable to process the request. Server may send a special header (called a Retry-After header) to the client that specifies how long the client should wait before trying again.
504	Similar to error #502, but secondary server timed-out before the request could be completed.
505	HTTP version not supported.

Glossary

10Base2 — An Ethernet standard that operates at 10 Mbps and uses small coaxial cable up to 200 meters long. Also called Thinnet.

10Base5 — An Ethernet standard that operates at 10 Mbps and uses thick coaxial cable up to 500 meters long. Also called Thicknet.

100BaseFX — A variation of 100BaseT that supports fiber optic cable.

100BaseT — An Ethernet standard that operates at 100 Mbps and uses STP cabling. Also called Fast Ethernet.

822 messages — Error messages that occur during e-mail transactions. 822 messages are named after RFC 822, which is the RFC that defines them.

access control — A feature of a server that limits which files or directories a user can read or write to based on his user ID.

adapter address — *See* MAC address.

address resolution — The process of discovering an IP address for a domain name.

Address Resolution Protocol (ARP) — A protocol used by TCP/IP that dynamically or automatically translates IP addresses into physical network addresses (MAC addresses).

ADODB (ActiveX Data Object Database) — A Microsoft technology designed to provide a standard set of commands to interface between a program and a database.

ADSL — *See* Asymmetric Digital Subscriber Line.

Advanced Research Projects Agency Network (ARPANet) — The first interconnected network used for free exchange of information between universities, the Department of Defense, and research organizations; a precursor to the Internet.

Advanced Television Enhancement Forum (ATVEF) — An organization that provides direction and standards for the interactive television industry.

affiliate network — A group of companies that work together by promoting each other's web sites.

AIFF file — A sound file that uses the format originally developed for Apple computers.

alert box — A message box that can be displayed on the user's screen by a JavaScript to get the user's attention.

alternate gateway — An alternate router that is used if the default gateway is down. *See* gateway.

amplifier repeater — A repeater that does not distinguish between noise and signal. It amplifies both.

anchor tag — An HTML tag that marks text or a graphic that links to another location in the same document or a different document. Anchor tags create hyperlinks. *See* hyperlink.

anonymous FTP site — An FTP site that does not require a user to log in with a valid ID or password. Anonymous FTP sites are used to download files, but not used to receive uploaded files.

Application layer — The OSI layer responsible for interfacing with the application using the network.

Application Program Interface (API) — A method used by an application program to call another program to perform a utility task.

application service provider (ASP) — A company that stores application software on its web site to allow customers to use the software via the Internet.

argument — In programming, an argument qualifies or modifies the action that is stated in a command.

ASCII files — Text files stored in ASCII format. ASCII stands for the American Standard Code for Information Interchange. ASCII characters are 7-bit characters; each character is assigned a number from 0 to 255. Compare to binary files.

ASP (Active Server Pages) — A Microsoft technology that allows a web page to contain a server-side script. Some objects that are built into ASP scripting are the request, response, scripting and server objects.

Asymmetric Digital Subscriber Line (ADSL) — A type of DSL line that is asymmetric, which means that data travels downstream at one speed and upstream at a different (slower) speed.

ATM (asynchronous transfer mode) — Network technology that uses cells of a fixed length to transmit data.

attribute — A part of an HTML tag that describes how the tag should handle certain tasks.

AU file — A sound file format originally developed for UNIX computers.

authentication — The process of verifying that a person or computer is actually who or what they say they are.

authoritative name server — The primary or secondary name server over a zone, containing the most authoritative information about domain names in that zone.

automatic private IP addressing — The feature whereby a PC automatically uses its own private IP address when no DHCP server is available.

AVI (Audio Video Interleaved) — An older Windows video format that is not as well compressed as more recent file formats such as MPEG or QuickTime.

backbone — A network that connects other networks.

(BDC) backup domain controller — A server on a Windows NT network that contains a read-only copy of the domain database.

bandwidth — The transmission speed of data.

base64 — An encoding method used by MIME to convert a binary file to a 7-bit ASCII text format so that it can be attached to an e-mail message.

Basic Rate Interface (BRI) — An ISDN standard that allows for two B channels and one D channel on a single ISDN line. A B channel is equivalent to a regular phone line and a D channel is a slower channel used for control. *See* PRI.

batch file — A file with a .BAT file extension that contains a list of DOS-like commands to be executed as a group.

BGP (Border Gateway Protocol) — A routing protocol used by routers to manage data packets destined for remote locations of the Internet. It is sometimes called the long-distance protocol.

binary files — Files that use all 8 bits in a byte and are usually not readable by humans. Binary files include graphics files, executable files, sound files; any type of file that is not in ASCII format. Compare to ASCII files.

binding — Associating an OSI layer to a layer above it or below it, for example, when an IP address (Network layer) is associated with a MAC address (Data Link layer).

BinHex — A program used by an Apple Macintosh computer to convert a binary file to a 7-bit ASCII text file format so that it can be attached to an e-mail message. Another BinHex program on the receiving computer must convert the file back to binary.

bit-mapped image — An image format that makes up an image from many dots. Also called raster image.

BLOB (Binary Large Object) — In a database, a data type used to hold large quantities of data such as that required for photographs, video clips, images and audio.

BMP (Bit-mapped) — An older file format that stores an image as many dots of varying colors.

BNC connector — A connector used with coaxial cable. It is often called a T-connector because of the T shape. The long end of the T connects to the NIC and the two short ends can connect to cable or end a bus formation with a terminator.

BRI — *See* Basic Rate Interface.

broadcast — A message sent from a single host to multiple hosts.

browser extension — *See* plug-in.

bus topology — A LAN in which all the devices are daisy-chained together on a single communication line. Bus topology does not have a central connection point.

C — A programming language that provides direct access by the programmer to low-level hardware devices such as memory.

C++ — An updated version of C that is object-oriented.

cable modem — A technology that uses cable TV lines for analog data transmission requiring a modem at each end. From the modem, a network cable connects to a NIC in the user's PC.

cache — Areas of memory or secondary storage where data is kept so that it can be used a second time.

cache-in-a-box — The hardware and software necessary to implement web and FTP caching for a network.

cache server — A server that can reside on a router or computer that caches information retrieved from the Internet in case it is requested again, in order to reduce traffic over the Internet and improve performance on the local network.

cancelbot — An Internet robot used by news servers to cull out articles that have the same body content as other articles in order to avoid unnecessary traffic on the Internet and avoid wasting server resources.

canonical name — As applies to domain names, a name added to the beginning of a domain name that serves as a subcategory of the domain, such as *support.microsoft.com*, where support is the canonical name.

card — As applies to WML, a section of a WML file (a deck) that fits on the screen of a wireless Internet device – *See* deck.

Cascading Style Sheets (CSS) — A specification for style sheets, developed by the World Wide Web Consortium, which defines how a style sheet controls the formatting of an HTML document. *See* style sheets.

catalog server — Software that stores multiple products and allows customer to search for products by keyword or name.

CAU (controlled-access unit) — *See* MSAU.

cells — Used in ATMs, cells are packets of data that are a fixed length of 53 bytes.

certificate server — A server that issues and revokes certificates, which are binary data used to identify a user on the Internet in order to secure electronic business transactions.

certification authority — An agency that is authorized to distribute digital certificates.

CGI (Common Gateway Interface) — Specifications and protocols used by programs on the server to customize a web page before it is downloaded to the browser. For example, CGI determines how a program can read information in a query string included in the URL to the web site.

channel — One chat room on a chat network. A channel can be either a private or public chat room.

Channel Service Device (CSU) — A device that acts as a safe electrical buffer between a LAN and a public network such as that accessed by a T1 line.

checksum — A number that is calculated for a data file using a mathematical formula. A checksum usually uses the number of bits in the data as part of the formula to produce a unique number.

chroot mode — A function of UNIX that restricts the portion of the file system that a service running on the UNIX platform can access.

ciphertext — Encrypted data that is generated by an encryption program.

circuit-switching network — A type of network that creates a physical or virtual dedicated circuit between end points. After the connection is established, data flows continuously from point to point. The public telephone network is an example of a circuit-switching network. Compare to data-packet network.

clickable map — *See* image map.

client — A software program or computer that requests information from another software program on another computer.

client-side script — A script embedded in a web page that is performed by the browser either before the browser displays the page or when the user clicks a button or performs some other action on the page.

client-to-client security — The type of protection strategy that is needed when two individuals communicate over the Internet. It includes protection strategies for e-mail exchanges and FTP.

client-to-gateway security — The type of protection from intrusion needed by a private network or intranet. In client-to-gateway security, one user accesses the network via a secure gateway.

client-server — A computer concept where one computer (the client) requests information from another computer (the server).

client-server database model — A method to optimize performance of a database that is being used by multiple users on a network. Some of the database management software resides on the user's PC and some of it resides on the server that is holding the database. The client/server model replaced the earlier file server model.

client-server model — A network of computers that have one or more computers that control the resources for all computers on the network. Also called domain model.

coaxial cable — Networking cable used with 10-Mbps Ethernet.

CODEC (compressor/decompressor) — Compressing and later decompressing sound, animation, and video files. MPEG is a common example of a file that goes through the CODEC process. Also stands for coder/decoder when referring to digital-to-analog conversion.

collision — When two computers send a signal on the same channel at the same time.

command — In programming, an order to perform an action, such as "open a file."

command-driven interface — A software interface that requires the user to enter a command to achieve a desired result. MS-DOS is an example of software that uses this type of interface. Compare to GUI.

compiling — In programming, the process of changing the source code so that the computer's processor can execute the program.

connection-oriented protocol — In networking, a protocol that confirms that a good connection has been made, before transmitting data to the other end. An example of a connection protocol is TCP.

connectionless protocol — A protocol such as UDP that does not require a connection before sending a packet. A connectionless protocol provides no guarantee that a packet will arrive at its destination. An example of a UDP transmission is a broadcast to all nodes on a network.

contention-based — A network system in which each computer on the system must compete for the opportunity to transmit a signal on the network.

contract — An agreement between two parties for the transfer of a service or good in return for another service or good (such as money).

cookie — Data that is sent from a web server to the client and is stored on the client's hard drive.

copyright — Protection offered to the creators of intellectual property which gives the creator, and no one else, the right to copy, distribute, display, or perform the work.

CSMA/CD (Carrier Sense Multiple Access with Collision Detection) — A protocol that Ethernet networks use to monitor the network to determine if the line is free before sending a transmission.

CSS — *See* Cascading Style Sheets.

CSU — *See* Channel Service Device.

CSU/DSU — A combination of two devices that serves as the entry point to a T1 or other public network channel. *See* CSU and DSU.

cybersquatting — When someone registers a domain name using another company's name or trademark with the intention of selling the domain name to that company.

daemon — In UNIX, a program that runs in the background to support or serve other programs.

data communication equipment (DCE) — A device, such as a modem, that is responsible for the communication between two other devices, such as a PC and a server.

Data Link layer — The OSI layer that disassembles packets and reassembles data into packets, preparing the packets to be passed onto the physical media.

data mart — A portion of the data in a data warehouse that is identified as useful to a certain target group of data miners.

data mining — Studying data in a data warehouse with the intention of discovering information useful to predict future direction for a company.

data path — On a system board, a group of embedded wires on which data can travel. A data path is part of a bus.

data terminal equipment (DTE) — The term used to refer to a computer and a remote computer or terminal to which the computer or terminal is attached.

data throughput — The measurement of data capacity, stated in bits per second (bps), thousands of bits per second (Kbps), or millions of bits per second (Mbps).

data warehouse — A repository of data that has been collected into one or more databases, but is no longer needed for current processing. Data warehouses are used to discover market trends and for forecasting.

database administrator — The person responsible for the overall integrity of the data in a database and the security to the database. The database administrator also monitors the performance of the database software and can adjust parameters to optimize performance.

database engine — The database applications software that provides an interface between the user and the DBMS.

database management system (DBMS) — Software that controls a database, receiving commands from the user or other software and executing those commands on the database. The DBMS is responsible for maintaining the integrity of the database structure. Also called relational database management system (RDBMS).

database server — The computer that contains the database and the DBMS.

database structure — The design of a database including the number of tables in the database, the field names of each column within a table, the primary key of each table and how tables can relate to one another.

DBMS — *See* database management system.

DCE — *See* data communications equipment.

de facto standard — A standard that does not have an official backing, but is considered a standard because of widespread use and acceptance by the industry.

deck — As applies to WML, a file containing text to be displayed on wireless Internet devices. *See* card.

dedicated private network (DPN) — A type of private network where two or more sites communicate over a private, dedicated line such as a T1 line or lease a portion of a shared circuit such as Frame Relay. Compare to virtual private network.

default gateway — The main gateway or unit that sends or receives packets addressed to other networks.

default web page — A web page that is designated as the page to send if no specific page is requested. This page is usually the introductory page of a web site. Also called a home page.

Denial of Service (DoS) — Attacks on servers which are designed to overload the server, therefore preventing it from processing legitimate requests.

device driver — A small program stored on a hard drive that tells the computer how to communicate with an input/output device such as a printer or modem.

DHCP (Dynamic Host Configuration Protocol) server — A service that assigns dynamic IP addresses to computers on a network when they first access the network.

Dial-Up Networking (DUN) — A Windows utility that allows a modem connected to a phone line to look and act like a network card, so other higher-level utilities and software can use a phone line to connect to a network.

dialogue — A series of transmissions between two computers that accomplishes a task such as sending an e-mail message.

digital certificate — An electronic profile that can be used when sending messages to authenticate the sender of the message. A digital certificate includes a key used to decode messages. Also called digital ID.

Digital Service Unit or Data Service Unit (DSU) — A device that connects a data terminal equipment (DTE) to a digital communication line such as a T1 line, that insures that the data is formatted correctly.

Digital Subscriber Line (DSL) — A leased digital phone line that uses direct connection (always up). A DSL line connects to a data converter installed at your site, which connects to your PC by way of a network cable and network card. DSL lines are rated at 5 Mbps, about 50 times faster than regular phone lines.

digitize — The process of converting analog data, such as sound, to digital representation of the data in binary (0s and 1s).

directory — A database that tracks resources on a network.

directory server — A server that accesses and manages a directory.

Disk Defragmenter — A Windows and DOS utility that reorganizes files on a hard drive so that files are written to the drive in contiguous segments.

distributed database — A database that is stored on more than one computer. Portions of the database can be presented to the user in such a way that the user is unaware that the data is coming from more than one computer.

DLL (dynamic linked library) — A utility program that is called by another program to perform a specific task. For example, a Windows print DLL is called by Microsoft Word to print a document, so that Word does not need to manage the print process. On Windows 9x, DLL files are normally stored in the \Windows\System folder.

DNS (Domain Name Service or Domain Name System) — A distributed pool of information (called the name space) that keeps track of assigned domain names and their corresponding IP addresses, and the system that allows a host to locate information in the pool.

DNS record — *See* resource record.

DOCSIS (Data Over Cable Service Interface Specifications) — The communications standards that are used by cable modem.

domain — In Windows NT, a logical group of networked computers, such as those on a college campus, that share a centralized directory database of user account information and security for the entire domain.

domain controller — A server on a Windows NT network that contains a database of user accounts and passwords that controls access to the network.

domain model — *See* client-server model.

domain name — A unique, text-based name that identifies an IP address. Typically, domain names in the United States end in .edu, .gov, .com, .org, or .net. Domain names can also include a country code, such as .uk for the United Kingdom.

DOS — *See* Denial of Service.

DSL — *See* Digital Subscriber Line.

DSU — *See* Digital Service Unit.

DTE — *See* data terminal equipment.

dumb terminal — Used with a mainframe computer, the terminal is little more than a monitor and keyboard that is used to connect to the mainframe as an input/output device. All processing of data is done on the mainframe.

DUN — *See* Dial-up Networking.

DVMRP (Distance Vector Multicast Routing Protocol) — A routing protocol used by routers for connectionless data packet delivery to a group of hosts.

Dynamic Host Configuration Protocol (DHCP) — The protocol of a server that manages dynamically assigned IP addresses. DHCP is supported by Windows 9x, Windows NT, and Windows 2000.

dynamic IP addressing — An assigned IP address that is used for the current session only. When the session is terminated, the IP address is returned to the list of available addresses.

dynamic web page — A web page that can be customized by a script or program.

e-commerce — Buying and selling products and services over the Internet.

e-commerce server — A server designed to handle all aspects of e-commerce, including taking orders, processing payments, sending verifications, and printing packing slips.

e-tailing — The selling of goods and services over the Internet.

e-tailware — Software that is designed to help users create on-line catalogs and maintain e-businesses.

ECMAScript (European Computer Manufacturers Association) — A scripting language that encompasses both JavaScript and Jscript, developed with input from both Netscape and Microsoft, designed to ultimately replace both JavaScript and JScript.

EDI — *See* electronic data interchange.

EDI ASC X12 — An EDI standard that is primarily used in North America. Also called EDI ANSI X.12.

EDIFACT — An EDI standard which was developed by determining the best features of EDI ASC X12 and UNTDI2.

EIA/TIA-232 standard — *See* RS-232 standard.

electronic data interchange (EDI) — A standard format that two computers can use to communicate information relating to business transactions such as orders, invoices, and receipts.

Encapsulated PostScript (EPS) — A file format developed by Adobe that includes directions for printing a document to a PostScript printer, and also includes a print preview of the document.

encryption — The process of coding data to prevent unauthorized parties from viewing or changing the data.

end-user license agreement (EULA) — An agreement that is stated in a software license. When the software is installed, the user must agree to the EULA.

EPS — *See* Encapsulated PostScript.

executable file — A program file that normally has a .EXE file extension. Using Windows 9x, to execute a program file, from Windows Explorer, double click on the file name.

Extensible HyperText Markup Language (XHTML) — Proposed future evolution of

HTML. XHTML is an application of XML. *See* Extensible Markup Language.

Extensible Markup Language (XML) — An evolution of SGML that allows developers to create their own tags within a markup language like XHTML.

external viewer — *See* helper application.

extranet — A network between two or more organizations that is a private physical or virtual network

fat server — A powerful server that is used to support the software, processing and data needs of a thin client.

FDDI (fiber distributed data interface) — A ring-based network that does not require a centralized hub and can transfer data at a rate of 100 Mbps.

field — In a relational database, a single entry in a table that occurs at the intersection of one row and one column and the data contained within that entry.

field name — In a relational database, the column heading on a column within a table.

firewall — Software or hardware that limits traffic between the Internet and a private network or single computer.

firmware — A combination of hardware and software that works together as a unit. Network cards have firmware that controls how the card sends data onto the network cables.

fixed wireless — A technology that uses an antenna or similar receiver/transmitter device for wireless communication, which can be used for Internet access in remote locations.

flame — A rude message sent over the Internet.

Flash — A popular multimedia file format developed by Macromedia. Flash uses vector-based, streaming data to produce animation, graphics, audio and interactivity.

flooding — The indiscriminate sending of messages to every host connected to a computer, which can be a waste of network resources.

form — As it applies to HTML, an object in a document that allows the user to input data, which is e-mailed to a recipient identified at the top of the form or is sent back to a program running on the web server.

fractional T1 line — A T1 line that has more than one company leasing the line. Each company is given a specific number of channels, totaling 24.

frame — As applies to web sites two or more web pages designed to be displayed in a web browser at the same time, either side by side or stacked top to bottom. Each frame can have its own scroll bars.

frame relay — A packet-switching communication protocol that uses digital technology, which can support data transmission speeds of up to 1.544 Mbps.

FTP (File Transfer Protocol) — The protocol used to transfer files over the Internet such that the file does not need to be converted to ASCII format before transferring.

FTP Site — A computer that is running an FTP server application.

full text index — A method of locating items on a web site. A full text index searches the entire contents of a web site for the specific word or phrase the you enter in a full text search box. The word or phrase need not have been designated as a keyword.

function — A segment of a program that is assigned a name and sits dormant until called by a command from somewhere else in the program to perform a given task.

G.Lite — A communication standard sponsored by ITU used by ADSL.

gateway — Any device that connects two networks of differing protocols or a device that provides a network with access to another network.

gateway-to-gateway security — The type of protection from intrusion needed by a virtual private network, to ensure reliable and secure communication among private networks that belong to the same organization, but which are located in different places.

GIF — *See* Graphical Interchange Format.

GIF89 — A version of GIF image that supports animation, transparent background and interlacing.

Gopher — A distribution system for text documents stored on UNIX computers. A Gopher is the service responsible for tracking the documents and presenting them to users who access the system.

Gopher protocol — The protocol used by a Gopher service. *See* Gopher.

Gopher space — The top-down hierarchical structure of all the documents on a UNIX computer that is managed by a Gopher server.

graphical user interfaces (GUI) — A software interface that provides icons, menus, and windows in order for a user to command the software. Windows is an example of software that uses a GUI. Compare to command-driven interface.

Graphics Interchange Format (GIF) — A type of compressed bit-mapped graphics file used to hold clip art. The file can contain up to 256 colors. The clip art can have a transparent background and be animated. GIF files have a .gif file extension.

GUI— *See* graphical user interface.

hardware address — *See* MAC address.

helper application — An application used by e-mail client software to interpret and display an attached file to the user. Also called external viewer.

hierarchical database — A database architecture that uses a top-down design with major categories at the top and less significant categories at the bottom. The Windows 98 Registry is an example of a hierarchical database.

hop — The trip a packet makes between two routers or a router and its final destination.

hop count — The number of routers a packet passes through as it goes from source to destination. If the hop count exceeds the TTL, the packet is discarded.

host name — A name that identifies a computer, printer, or other device on a network.

Hosts — A text file located in the Windows folder that contains NetBIOS names and their associated IP addresses, that is used for name resolution for a NetBIOS over TCP/IP network.

hot link — *See* hyperlink.

HTML — *See* Hypertext Markup Language.

HTTP — *See* Hypertext Transfer Protocol.

hub — A device used to join or connect all the nodes of a LAN in a star formation.

hyperlink — A tag in a hypertext document that links the location of the tag to another point in the same or to a different document. Also called hot link or link.

hypertext — Text in a document that is written with hyperlinks, which are connections between specially marked texts and other locations in the same document or other documents. The hypertext document can be read in a non-linear fashion as the reader moves from one location in the document to other locations by way of the hyperlinks.

Hypertext Markup Language (HTML) — A markup language used for hypertext documents on the World Wide Web. The language uses tags to format the document, create hyperlinks, and mark locations for graphics.

hypertext reference — *See* hyperlink.

Hypertext Transfer Protocol (HTTP) — The protocol used by the World Wide Web.

ICMP — *See* Internet Control Message Protocol.

ICMP flood — *See* ping flood.

IEEE1284 — A standard for parallel communication used by parallel ports and cables.

image map — A graphic on a web page that contains multiple hyperlinks. Also called clickable map.

IMAP (Internet Message Access Protocol) — An e-mail protocol that has more functionality than its predecessor, POP. IMAP can archive messages in folders on the e-mail server and can allow the user to choose to not download attachments to files.

IMAP4 (Internet Message Access Protocol, version 4) — Version 4 of the IMAP protocol. *See* IMAP.

index — A database used by search engines. The database contains information about web pages so that when a user performs a search, the search engine can access the database to find any matches for the user.

initialization file (INI file) — A text file that contains information about application setup and user preferences, which is read by an application when the application first loads.

inoculation — The process of calculating two checksums, one before and one after data is transmitted, and comparing those checksums to ensure that a file has not been altered.

Integrated Services Digital Network (ISDN) — A communications standard that can carry digital data simultaneously over two or more channels on a single pair of wires (BRI standard) at about five times the speed of a regular phone line connection, or up to 23 channels for heavy business use (PRI standard).

interactive television — A technology to combine a web browser such as WebTV with a television show so that a user can interact with a web site that is synchronized with the TV show.

interlacing — The method of staggering the presentation of data so as to give the overall effect of a smooth transition. Graphics that are interlaced are built on a screen one layer at a time.

Internet — A group of computer networks around the world that are connected to each other to create one very large network.

Internet appliance — A device other than a computer that is used to access the Internet as a client with limited applications.

Internet Control Message Protocol (ICMP) — Part of the IP layer that is used to transmit error messages and other control messages to hosts and routers.

Internet Explorer — Made by Microsoft, the most popular web browser.

Internet-in-a-box — A device that acts as web server, e-mail server, and basic network server to provide Internet access.

Internet merchant account — An account used by an e-business which takes credit card transactions over the Internet. The account works as a relationship between the e-business and the merchant bank or other financial institution that can process the money transaction.

Internet Network Information Center (InterNIC) — The central group that assigns and keeps track of all Internet IP addresses on the organizational level.

Internet Protocol address (IP address) — A 32-bit address consisting of four numbers separated by periods, used to uniquely identify a device on a network that uses TCP/IP protocols. The first numbers identify the network; the last numbers identify a host. An example of an IP address is 206.96.103.114.

Internet Protocol Security (IPsec) — A suite of protocols that are used for private communication over the Internet.

Internet Relay Chat (IRC) — The applications software used by chat rooms on the Internet.

Internet Service Provider (ISP) — A business that provides individuals and companies with access to the Internet.

Internet telephony — The technology of using the Internet to make phone calls.

intranet — A private TCP/IP network used by a large company.

intrusion detection software — Software that monitors activity on a network to alert the network administrator of any suspicious activity.

IPsec — *See* Internet Protocol security.

IP address — *See* Internet Protocol address.

IP phone — An Internet appliance used to initiate or receive a phone call made over the Internet. It uses a direct connection to the Internet. For example, it connects to a LAN, cable modem or DSL line.

IP telephony switch — A device that can make the switch between PSTN and IP.

IP Telephony terminal — A device such as a PC that can be used to initiate or receive voice communication over the Internet.

IP version 6 (IPv6) — A proposed new version of the Internet Protocol proposed by the Internet Engineering Task Force in 1995. The current version of IP is version 4.

IPX/SPX (Internetwork Packet Exchange/Sequenced Packet Exchange) — Protocol used by Novell Netware, which corresponds to the TCP/IP protocols.

IRC — *See* Internet Relay Chat.

ISA bus — A bus or group of wires embedded on a system board that provide a group of expansion slots on the system board that can be used to attach expansion cards, such as a modem card, to the board. An ISA bus can have either an 8-bit or 16-bit data path.

ISAPI (Internet Server Application Programming Interface) — A technology developed by Microsoft to be used by the web server Internet Information Server (IIS), so that programs on a web site can be written to interact with the web server as a DLL.

ISDN — *See* Integrated Services Digital Network.

ISP — *See* Internet Service Provider.

ITSP (Internet Telephony Service Provider) — An organization similar to an ISP that provides access to the regular telephone system from the Internet. An ITSP is used when you want to make a phone call on the Internet to a regular telephone.

Java — An object-oriented programming language developed by Sun Microsystems. Programs written in Java are designed to easily port to different platforms and operating systems without having to alter the programming code.

Java applet — A small Java program that can be downloaded to a browser and used to perform tasks that the browser cannot do, such as add multimedia effects to a web page.

Java Server Pages (JSP) — A technology developed by Sun Microsystems that uses Java programs called Java servlets in HTML to be executed by the web server before the web page is downloaded.

Java servlet — A short Java program embedded in an HTML document.

Java Speech API (JSAPI) — An interface used by Java programs developed by Sun to recognize voice and convert text to speech.

JavaBean — A short Java program designed to work as a reusable component or object in many different situations.

JavaScript — A scripting language developed by Netscape to be used with Netscape Navigator, but which can now be used by web servers as well as clients.

JDBC (Java Database Connectivity) — A technology similar to ODBC that provides an interface between a Java program and a database.

Joint Photographic Experts Group (JPEG) file — A type of compressed file commonly used to hold photographs. The file can contain up to 1.6 million colors or be gray scale and does not allow a transparent background.

JScript — Microsoft's version of JavaScript developed to be used with Internet Explorer.

jump link — *See* link target.

kernel — Core portion of an operating system that loads applications and manages files, memory, and other resources.

key — Part of the formula that is used to encode and decode information. A key must be used when data is encoded, then again to decode the data.

keyword — A word that has a special pre-defined meaning to the software interpreting a command or instruction.

keyword index — A method of locating items on a web site based on an internal list of preselected terms, known as keywords. Usually presented in the form of a field where you can enter a term you wish to search for. Compare to full text index.

knowledge base — A collection of articles, frequently-asked-questions (FAQs), definitions and procedures offered by an organization as part of its customer service.

LAN (local area network) — A network that covers a relatively small geographical area.

Layer 2 Forwarding (L2F) — A tunneling protocol which connects two computers through the Internet, providing them with a secure connection.

Layer 2 Tunneling Protocol (L2TP) — A tunneling protocol that combines PPTP and L2F to allow Internet Service Providers to operate virtual private networks.

LDAP (Lightweight Directory Access Protocol) — A protocol used by client and server software to access a directory.

license — A document issued by the owner of the copyright, which gives the owner of the license limited rights to use the product. The rights are outlined in the license.

line protocol — A protocol used to send data packets destined for a network over phone lines. PPP and SLIP are examples of line protocols.

link — *See* hyperlink.

link target — The point in a document that is assigned a section name and is the destination point for a link or hyperlink identified somewhere else in the document. Also called jumplink.

list server — Software to maintain and manage a list of e-mail addresses and messages to multiple addresses on the list.

LMHosts — A text file located in the Windows folder that contains NetBIOS names and their associated IP addresses, that is used for name resolution for a NetBIOS over TCP/IP network.

log file — A text file that is used to record activity and events encountered or done by an application.

lossy compression — A data compression method that drops redundant and near-redundant data, losing some quality in the process, but producing a much smaller data file.

LPD (Line Printer Daemon) — A server that is responsible for receiving and processing print jobs that are sent over the Internet.

LPR (Line Printer Remote) — The protocol that controls how print jobs are sent to printers over the Internet.

MAC (Media Access Control) — An element of the Data Link layer protocol that provides compatibility with the Physical layer. A network card address is often called a MAC address. *See* MAC address.

MAC address — A 6-byte hex hardware address unique to each NIC card and assigned by manufacturers. The address is often printed on the adapter. An example is 00 00 0C 08 2F 35. Also called adapter address or physical address.

macro — A script stored in a Word or Excel document for later execution. *See* script.

mail flooding — A type of denial of service attack in which an SMTP host is sent a large number of huge e-mails, thus overloading the system.

man in the middle — An attack in which e-mail, files, chat dialogs, and other data are intercepted as they are being transmitted across a network.

MAPI — A specification that allows an application to interact with an e-mail client to send and receive e-mail.

MAU (multistation access unit) — *See* MSAU.

meta robot tag — A meta tag that contains a list of keywords left there for web robots to find so that the web page can be located by a search engine.

meta tag — A type of tag in a web page that contains information about the page such as the title of the page and the editor that was used to create the page.

metafile — A file that contains information about other files.

MIDI (Musical Instrument Digital Interface) — A standard for transmitting sound from musical devices, such as electronic keyboards, to computers where it can be digitally stored.

MIME (Multipurpose Internet Mail Extensions) — A protocol that allows non-text files to be attached to e-mail messages or downloaded to a web browser along with a web page. MIME identifies a file as belonging to a category and a subcategory such as Image/gif. Files are encoded using a method that the SMTP protocol can handle when it processes the e-mail message.

mirrored server — A server that is an exact replica of another server that is used to reduce traffic on the main server. This improves performance for the benefit of the user. Mirrored servers also serve as a backup for the main server in case the main server fails.

modem — From MOdulate/DEModulate. A device that modulates digital data from a computer to an analog format that can be sent over telephone lines, then demodulates it back into digital form.

Mosaic — The first web browser sold to the general public that supported graphics.

MP3 — A high-quality audio format that uses MPEG, Version 3 technology.

MSAU (multistation access unit) — A centralized hub used in token ring networks to connect stations. Also called CAU and MAU.

Multi-Purpose Internet Mail Extensions — *See* MIME.

multicasting — A message sent by one host to multiple hosts, such as when a video conference is broadcasted to several hosts on the Internet.

multiple log-in failures — A type of failure caused by a user's repeated attempts to log on to a system with an invalid username and/or password.

multiplexing — The process of dividing a single channel into multiple channels that can carry voice, data, video, or other signals.

multipoint connection — A connection between two devices in which more than one physical connection is used to create the appearance of a single connection. Two computers connected to each other using two phone lines and two modems on each computer is an example of a multipoint connection.

multiprocessor computer — A computer that contains more than one CPU designed for powerful large-scale applications and network traffic.

NADN (nearest active downstream neighbor) — In a token ring environment, the station that receives the token just after the current station.

name server — A server that has part of the name space or information needed to resolve a domain name.

name space — The total information that is distributed over many name servers that relate domain names to IP addresses.

NAP— *See* Network Access Point.

NAT— *See* Network Address Translator.

NAUN (nearest active upstream neighbor) — In a token ring environment, the station that receives the token just prior to the current station.

NetBIOS (Network Basic Input Output System) — A Windows application programming interface (API) that allows one application to communicate with another application on the same LAN. NetBIOS cannot be used to cross from one network to another because it does not support routing.

NetBT (NetBIOS over TCP/IP) — A protocol that is used when NetBIOS program calls are made over a TCP/IP network.

netiquette (network etiquette) — Basic rules of courtesy used when sending electronic messages.

Netscape Navigator — A web browser that is part of the Netscape Communicator suite of software.

Network Access Point (NAP) — One of four original locations in the United States that serve as major connection points for backbone networks in the U.S. The NAPs were created by the National Science Foundation in 1993.

Network Address Translator (NAT) — A process that converts private IP addresses on a LAN to the proxy server's IP address before the data packet is sent over the Internet.

Network layer — The OSI layer responsible for routing packets.

network architecture — The overall design of a network. It includes hardware, software, and protocols.

network mask — The portion of the IP address that identifies the network; sometimes called a subnet mask. Not all networks use network masks.

network monitor — Utility software installed on one computer on the network to analyze data on the network.

newsgroup — An Internet or private network service that provides a forum for group members to post articles and respond to them.

NNTP (Network News Transfer Protocol) — The protocol used by newsgroup server and client software.

node — Each computer, workstation, or device on a network.

non-repudiation — The process of verifying that a transaction occurred, including verifying the people or entities involved with the transaction.

non-repudiation of delivery — Providing proof that a specific message was received by its intended recipient, so that the receiver cannot deny getting the message.

non-repudiation of origin — Providing proof of the origin of a message so that the sender cannot deny sending it.

non-streaming data — Multimedia data that is first downloaded from a web site and then played. Compare to streaming data.

NOS (network operating system) — An operating system that resides on the controlling computer in the network. The NOS controls what software, data, and devices a user can access.

NT1 (Network Termination 1) — A device used in an ISDN setup that is the point of interchange between the phone company and your internal home or business network. (An NT1 is a box outside your house where your ISDN line connects to the phone company service.)

object — In programming, anything that is addressed by the program as an entity with properties, attributes and rules that the program must follow in order to use the object.

object code — In programming, source code that has been compiled into instructions that can be executed by the computer.

object image — See vector image.

octet — An 8-bit number that is part of an IP address. IP addresses are composed of four 8-bit numbers, separated by periods.

ODBC (Open Database Connectivity) — A technology initially developed by the SQL Access Group and later supported by most database and operating system manufacturers that provides a connection between an application and a database on a network.

Oracle — A high-end, highly reliable database and DBMS originally designed for a UNIX system, which is popular on the Internet for database-enabled web sites.

OSPF (Open Shortest Path First) — A routing protocol built to improve on the shortcomings of RIP, used by routers that use multicasting instead of broadcasting to exchange routing information among routers.

overhead — The storage space, computing power and other resources needed by software or hardware that do not directly add to the intrinsic value of the software or hardware.

packet — Segments of network data that also include header, destination addresses, and trailer information that are sent as a unit using electronic communication. Also called datagram.

packet-switching network — A network that works by sending data broken down into individual packets from point-to-point. Each packet is capable of taking a different route to the destination and then the data is reassembled at the destination point. The Internet is an example of a packet-switching network. Compare to circuit-switching network.

page — *See* web page.

Page Description Language (PDL) — A language used to communicate printing instructions to a printer.

password — A group of characters that a user must enter, in addition to the user ID, to gain access to a network.

PCI bus — A bus on a system board that provides four or more expansion slots that can be used to attach expansion cards such as a modem to the board. A PCI bus has a 32-bit data path.

PDC (primary domain controller) — Used in Windows NT, the server that stores and controls a database of user accounts, group accounts, and computer accounts.

PDF (Portable Document Format) — A proprietary file format by Adobe Systems, designed to retain a document's formatting. You can view a PDF file with Adobe Acrobat Reader, a free helper application that can be downloaded from the Adobe web site (*www.adobe.com*).

peer-to-peer model — A network of computers that are all equals, or peers. Each computer has the same amount of authority and each can act as a server to the other computers.

Perl (Practical Extraction and Report Language) — A programming language originally used to write UNIX shell scripts, but now commonly used to write CGI scripts.

physical address — *See* MAC address.

Physical layer — The OSI layer responsible for interfacing with the network media (cabling).

ping — A program that allows one computer to send a packet to another computer and then receive a reply.

ping flood — A type of denial of service attack that happens when a host is flooded with ping requests to the point that the server cannot function; also known as ICMP flooding.

ping of death — A type of denial of service attack that happens when a ping is sent with a packet larger than the standard 64 bytes, causing the system that received the ping request to shut down.

pixel — The smallest unit of space on a monitor that can be addressed by software. Screen resolutions are normally given in pixels, for example, 1024 by 768 pixels.

Platform for Internet Content Selection (PICS) — An independent organization that provides a voluntary rating system for web pages.

Plug and Play — A technology in which the operating system and BIOS are designed to automatically configure new hardware devices to eliminate system resource conflicts (such as IRQ and I/O address conflicts).

plug-in — Software that enhances the ability of a browser to handle certain file types. Also called browser extension.

PNG (Portable Network Graphics) — A graphics format that uses lossless compression, interlacing and transparent background color.

Point of Presence (POP) — A phone number that a user can dial to connect to an Internet Service Provider.

point-to-multipoint — A connection between one device and several other devices where data travels from the original device to multiple destinations. An example of point-to-multipoint communication is cable modem.

point-to-point — A dedicated connection between two devices using a single physical connection.

Point-to-Point Protocol (PPP) — A protocol that governs the methods for communicating via modems and dial-up telephone lines. The Windows Dial-Up Networking utility uses PPP.

Point-to-Point Tunneling Protocol (PPTP) — Tunneling protocol that is based on PPP, which allows two computers to maintain a secure connection over the Internet.

POP (Post Office Protocol) — The protocol used by an e-mail server and client when the client requests to download e-mail messages. POP is being slowly outdated by the IMAP protocol. *See* IMAP.

POP account — The name of an e-mail account on an e-mail server where a user receives messages.

POP3 (Post Office Protocol, version 3) — Version 3 of the POP protocol. *See* POP.

port — A number assigned to a process on a computer so that the process can be found by TCP/IP.

port scanning script — A script or program that a hacker can use to discover an open port on a computer. A hacker can use an open port to penetrate a computer or network and steal data.

Portable Network Graphics (PNG) — A graphics file used for clip art that supports a transparent background, but does not support animated clip art.

PostScript — A page description language developed by Adobe Systems, used to communicate printing directions to a PostScript printer.

PPP (Point-to-Point Protocol) — A line protocol used by Dial-Up Networking and other software to send data packets over phone lines. PPP works at the Data Link layer of the OSI model and can support TCP/IP and NetBIOS packets.

PPP Multilink (MP) — A Windows utility that allows a PC with more than one modem or other communication device to create a multipoint connection.

Presentation layer — The OSI layer that compresses and decompresses data and interfaces with the Application layer and the Session layer.

Pretty Good Privacy encryption (PGP) — A popular encryption protocol that uses three keys: a private key, a public key, and a short key that is generated by the encryption software.

PRI — *See* Primary Rate Interface.

primary key — In a relational database, the field or fields that are defined as the entries that make a single row unique within the table. Therefore, no two rows within a table can have the same primary key.

Primary Rate Interface (PRI) — An ISDN standard designed for heavy business use that allows for up to 23 B channels and 1 D channel on a single ISDN leased line. *See* BRI.

private IP addresses — An IP address that is used on a private TCP/IP network that is isolated from the Internet.

private key encryption — An encryption protocol that uses a single key, the private key, for both encryption and decryption. Also called symmetric encryption.

process — An executing instance of a program, together with the program resources. There can be more than one process running for a program at the same time. One process for a program happens each time the program is loaded into memory or executed.

program — A list of instructions to be executed by the operating system or some other software. A program is normally stored on a computer in a program file with a .EXE, .COM, or .SYS file extension.

programming language — A set of commands, and arguments to those commands that have a predetermined meaning to the software executing the program. Examples of programming languages are C++, Visual Basic, and Java.

programming protocol — A set of rules or standards by which programs interact with other programs or resources.

progressive JPEG — A JPEG format that fades a photograph on the screen one layer at a time.

protected mode — A mode of CPU operation. When a CPU operates in protected mode, it accesses memory and the hard drive indirectly, using a 32-bit data path.

protocol — The rules for communication used by a computer program when communicating with another program.

protocol isolation — A type of network security whereby computers on the network don't use TCP/IP and therefore cannot communicate over the Internet.

proxy server — A server that acts as an intermediary between another computer and the Internet. The proxy server substitutes its own IP address for the IP address of the computer on the network making a request, so that all traffic over the Internet appears to be coming from only this one IP address.

public IP address — An IP address available to the Internet. *See* private IP address.

public key encryption — An encryption protocol that uses two keys, a public key for encryption, and a private key for decryption. Also called asymmetric encryption.

Public Key Infrastructure (PKI) — A group of parties who subscribe to a public key encryption service such as VeriSign in order to communicate over the Internet in privacy.

Public Switched Telephone Network (PSTN) — The traditional public telephone network, which uses a circuit-switching technology.

pull technology — In a client-server environment, when the client requests information from the server, and pulls that information down.

push technology — In a client-server environment, when the server sends information to the client without the client requesting the information first.

PVC (permanent virtual circuit) — A permanent logical connection between two nodes or fixed end points that allows data to follow any number of paths when being transmitted.

query — A request for data from a database that can be used for an on-screen display or in a printed report. Most database queries are done using SQL. *See* SQL.

query string — A text-based expression that is included in a URL to a web server to pass information to the web page or CGI program that is requested.

QuickTime — A popular video file format developed by Apple. QuickTime files have a .MOV file extension.

QuickTime Virtual Reality (QTVR) — A version of a QuickTime file format that supports 3D rendering.

quoted-printable — An encoding method used by MIME to convert a text-based file to a 7-bit format so that it can be attached to an e-mail message.

raster image — *See* bit-mapped image.

read access — As applied to network privileges, read access allows a user the right to view a file, but not make any changes to it.

real mode — A mode of CPU operation. When a CPU operates in real mode, it accesses memory and the hard drive directly, using a 16-bit data path.

record — In a relational database, one row within one table of the database.

recordset — In Microsoft ADODB technology, a group of records in a database currently available to a program to be written to or read from.

Registry — A Windows database that stores configuration information about Windows 9x, user preferences and software settings.

Registry Checker — A Windows 98 utility that makes a backup copy of the Windows Registry every day Windows is loaded and keeps the last five days of backups.

relational database — A database architecture that holds data in a group of tables that can be related to one another by columns they have in common. Most databases today use this structure.

relational database management system (RDBMS) — *See* database management system.

repeater — A device that amplifies signals on a network so they can be transmitted further down the line.

Request For Comment (RFC) — A document that proposes a change in standards or protocols for the Internet. An RFC can be presented by different organizations, but is done under the general guidance of the Internet Architecture Board (IAB).

resolver — A computer searching for the IP address for a domain name.

resource record — A record on a name server that contains information relating domain names to IP addresses.

Reverse Address Resolution Protocol (RARP) — A protocol used to translate the unique hardware NIC addresses into IP addresses (the reverse of ARP).

REC — *See* Request For Comment.

RIP (Router Information Protocol) — An older routing protocol used by routers to build routing tables by broadcasting messages to all routers on the network.

RJ-45 connector — An attachment used with UTP (Unshielded Twisted Pair cable) that connects the cable to the NIC.

RMF (Rich Music Format) — A proprietary audio file format developed by Beatnik. It requires a Beatnik Player plug-in on the client, which is supported by Netscape Navigator.

root server — A server managed by Network Solutions that contains the highest authoritative information about domain names.

router — A device used on networks to send packets across multiple networks, finding the best available route.

RS-232 standard — The standard that determines the design and function of a serial port or serial cable. Also called the EIA/TIA-232 standard.

RSVP (Resource Reservation Setup Protocol) — A protocol that allows you to reserve bandwidth for upcoming streaming data.

RTF (Rich Text Format) — A file format that converts a word processing document to ASCII code so that another word processor can read and edit the file.

RTP (Real Time Transport Protocol) — A protocol used to transmit real-time data, such as audio, video or simulation data over the Internet. RTP is defined by RFC 1889.

RTSP (Real Time Streaming Protocol) — A protocol that establishes and controls time-synchronized streams of continuous media such as audio and video. RTSP uses the RTP protocol and acts as a network remote control for multimedia servers.

SAM (security accounts manager) — Used in Windows NT, the database of user accounts, group accounts, and computer accounts.

sampling — Part of the process of converting sound or video from analog to digital format, whereby a sound wave or image is measured at uniform time intervals and saved as a series of smaller representative blocks.

ScanDisk — A Windows and DOS utility that fixes file system errors on a hard drive.

script — A list of programming commands stored in a text file to be executed by the operating system or other software. An example of a script is a Perl script stored in a file.

search engine — Software that can be used to search a site, group of sites or the World Wide Web for information. Search engines that search the entire Web use software called spiders or robots to locate information which is stored in a database on the search site for later retrieval.

Secure Electronic Transaction (SET) — A protocol that offers a secure medium for credit card transactions using digital signatures.

Secure Multi-Purpose Internet Mail Extensions (S/MIME) — A secure version of MIME that works like public key encryption.

secure sockets layers — A protocol that uses both the sender's and receiver's public and private keys to ensure a secure transaction.

security gateway — A device that provides security for a network. *See* firewall.

security policy server — A server that is responsible for authenticating users who have access to a private network.

segmentation — When a larger network is divided into smaller segments to increase speed and reliability.

Serial Line Internet Protocol (SLIP) — An older, mostly outdated line protocol used to send data packets over phone lines. SLIP does not support encrypted data as does PPP.

serial port — A port on the back of a computer used for transmitting data serially or in single file. Serial ports are used by a mouse, modem, or other device that uses serial communication with a computer. A serial port has either 9 or 25 pins.

server — (1) A software program that interacts with client software in a client-server environment. (2) A computer that runs server software and responds to requests for information from client computers.

server-side script — A script that is performed by the server before a web page is downloaded to the browser. The script can be stored alone in a CGI file or embedded in a web page.

service — A program that runs in the background to support or serve other programs.

Session layer — The OSI layer that makes and manages an extended connection between two hosts on a network.

shell — An operating system component responsible for providing an interface for users to enter OS commands.

shell script — A list of operating system commands to be executed by the OS shell. In Windows 9x, a shell script is called a batch file. An example of a shell script or batch file is AUTOEXEC.BAT.

Shockwave — A popular multimedia file format developed by Macromedia that produces video and audio streaming data.

shopping cart — Software used by a commercial web site to hold information about the selections a user has made before the purchase is completed.

signal-regenerating repeater — A repeater that is able to distinguish between noise and signal. It reads the signal and retransmits the signal without the accompanying noise.

site map — On a web page, a list of all the pages on a site, showing how the pages are organized. You can select the page you want to view from the list.

SLIP — *See* Serial Line Internet Protocol.

smart card — A card that can hold data and can be used for authentication when accessing a computer or network.

SMAU (smart multistation access unit) — *See* MSAU.

SMTP (simple mail transfer protocol) — The protocol used by e-mail clients and servers to send e-mail messages over the Internet. *See* POP and IMAP.

SNMP (Simple Network Management Protocol) — A protocol that is included with Windows but must be installed separately that provides system management for TCP/IP networks.

SNMP Agent — A TCP/IP utility included with Windows that allows a PC using Windows to be monitored by network administrators responsible for managing a network.

socket — A virtual connection from one computer to another, such as that between a client and a server. Higher-level protocols such as HTTP use a socket to pass data between two computers. A socket is assigned a number for the current session, which is used by the high-level protocol. A socket contains the IP address and the port number.

software patch — A segment of computer code that fixes a bug or provides a new feature. Software patches can be downloaded from a software manufacturer's web site and then installed over existing software.

source file — In programming, a list of commands that have been entered by a programmer in a specific programming language. These commands cannot be executed until after they have been changed, or compiled, so that the computer's processor can understand them.

spam — Unsolicited e-mail messages that are usually trying to sell a product and are sent in bulk to large groups.

Speech Application Programming Interface (SAPI) — An application interface developed by Microsoft for voice recognition and converting text to speech.

spider — *See* web crawler.

SQL — *See* Structured Query Language.

SQL Server — A high-end, robust database and database management system made by Microsoft for a Windows system.

SSI (Server Side Includes) — A simple form of server-side scripting that allows you to use variable values which can be included in the HTML code before it is sent to the browser.

Standard Generalized Markup Language (SGML) — A standard for several markup languages, including HTML.

star topology — A LAN in which all the devices are connected to a central hub.

stateful — A device or process that manages data or an activity and is concerned with all aspects of the data or activity.

stateless — A device or process that manages data or some activity without regard to all details of the data or activity.

static index — On a web page, an index in the form of a predetermined list of terms that allows you to select what you want to see. Usually appears in the form of a drop-down list.

static IP addressing — IP addresses permanently assigned to a workstation.

static web page — A web page that never changes unless the developer edits the page contents.

STP (shielded twisted-pair) — A cable that is made of one or more twisted pairs of wires, which is surrounded by a metal shield.

streaming data — Multimedia data that is played as it is being downloaded. Video conferencing and listening to the radio from a web site are two examples of streaming data.

Structured Query Language (SQL) — A set of commands and arguments used to manage a database that is universally accepted as the defacto standard by the industry. Most relational databases accept SQL commands.

style sheet — A text file with a .css file extension that contains rules about how a browser should display a web page. A style sheet can include information such as what font to use when displaying text, what background color to use, or what margins to use. A style sheet is attached to an HTML document, and controls the formatting of that document.

subject directory — A method for locating information on the World Wide Web by which keywords are manually registered into a database for later retrieval.

subnet mask — Defines which portion of the host address within an IP address is being borrowed to define separate subnets within a network.

subnetwork — Divisions of a large network, consisting of smaller separate networks (to prevent congestion). Each subnetwork (also called a subnet) is assigned a logical network IP name.

SVC (switched virtual circuit) — A logical point-to-point connection that depends on switches to decide the best path to send the data. ATM uses SVC.

SYN flooding — A flooding attack that uses the synchronization feature of TCP to cause a server to shut down.

syndication — The process of hiring another company or individual to write a specific portion of your web site (such as the latest health news) on a regular basis.

T-carrier — A system that provides leased digital communications lines through a common carrier such as Bell Atlantic or MCI; typically used for voice and data transmission.

TA (Terminal Adapter) — An internal or external device that converts an ISDN data stream into a signal that is suitable for a regular analog telephone or a computer. Sometimes called an ISDN card or ISDN box.

tag — A code in an HTML document that is used for formatting, inserting graphics, and creating hyperlinks. Most often, a tag has a beginning point and an ending point and each point is enclosed in angle brackets. For example, to bold text, use <B> to begin boldface and </B> to end boldface.

TCP/IP (Transmission Control Protocol/Internet Protocol) — The suite of protocols that supports communication on the Internet. TCP is responsible for error checking, and IP is responsible for routing.

TCP/IP stack — A group of TCP/IP utilities and protocols that make up the total TCP/IP group needed to support traffic over a TCP/IP network such as the Internet. TCP/IP software on a PC is sometimes called the TCP/IP stack.

telephony — Telephone technology.

Telnet — A service or daemon that allows a computer to be controlled from a remote computer. Telnet applications use the Telnet protocol.

text chat — A technology that allows users to type messages back and forth and which prevents others from reading those messages.

thicknet — *See* 10Base5 Ethernet.

thin client — A computer that does little processing of data, contains a limited version of an operating system and applications software, and depends on a fat server for its data and most of the software it needs.

thin client/fat server model — A client-server model in which the client computer performs little if any processing because the majority of the processing is done by the server.

thinnet — *See* 10Base2 Ethernet.

TIFF (Tagged Image File Format) — A bit-mapped file format used to hold photographs, graphics and screen captures. TIFF files can be rather large and so are not commonly used on web sites.

Time To Live (TTL) — The time that data is considered to be good, before it must be verified or discarded.

token — A frame that is used on token ring networks used to send data from one station to the next.

topology — The arrangement used to connect modes on a LAN, either in a star or a bus function.

trademark — A name, symbol, or other mark that is used to represent a product or company.

trading partners — Two businesses that exchange information using EDI.

transaction processing (TP) software — Software that is used to handle a credit card transaction over the Internet. The software receives the card information, validates the information received, and passes the transaction to the bank.

transaction sets — Data formats that outline which information should appear in each section of the file and exactly how the file should be created. Transaction sets exist for all common business transactions.

transparent background — A background that is designed to display as the same color as the background of the web page.

Transport layer — The OSI layer that verifies data and requests a resend when the data is corrupted.

Trivial FTP — A file transfer protocol, similar to FTP, with fewer commands, usually used for multicasting.

Trojan horse — A program that appears to perform legitimate functions, but actually is damaging to the system.

TTL — *See* Time To Live.

tunneling — A process by which a packet is encapsulated in a special secure protocol so that the packet can be sent through the Internet.

UDP — *See* User Datagram Protocol.

Unicode — A 16-bit character set that is expected to ultimately replace ASCII. Unicode includes most of the world's writing systems including the Asian character set.

Uniform Resource Locator (URL) — An address for a resource on the Internet. A URL can contain the protocol used by the resource, the name of the computer, and the path and name of a file on the computer.

UNTDI2 — An EDI standard that was once common in Europe, but is now primarily used in the United Kingdom.

UseNet — A popular and free system of newsgroups on the Internet containing thousands of newsgroups.

User Datagram Protocol (UDP) — A connectionless protocol that does not require a connection to send a packet and does not guarantee that the packet arrives at its destination. UDP works at the Transport layer.

user ID — A code that indicates who the user is. The user ID has certain rights associated with it, including rights to files, functions, and programs.

UTP (unshielded twisted-pair) — A cable that is made of one or more twisted pairs of wires, which is not surrounded by a metal shield. Compare to STP.

Uudecode — The program that converts a uuencoded file back into the original binary file that it was before it was attached to an e-mail message. *See* uuencode.

Uuencode — An encoding program on a UNIX computer that converts a binary file to a format that can be attached to an e-mail message using the SMTP protocol. Uuencode files have a .UU or .UUE file extension. *See* uudecode.

VBI (vertical blanking interval) — In a television analog data stream, the interval that does not carry visual data needed to cover the time it takes for the pointer beam to move from the bottom of one frame to the top of the next frame. The VBI carries hyperlink information for interactive television.

VBScript — A subset of Visual Basic designed to be used as a web page scripting language.

vector image — An image format that composes an image from a series of mathematical equations. Also called object image.

virtual hosting — A server that provides personal web space on a computer by assigning a folder to the web site, but might assign the folder its own IP address or give it the right to run its own processes.

virtual private network (VPN) — A network that uses a public network, usually the Internet, to provide a secure connection between two private networks or a node and a private network.

virtual server — A server that is used by many customers who share the space and processing power for their web sites, FTP sites, and mail sites. Virtual servers provide customers with unique IP addresses, each of which point to the same computer, but to different folders. A virtual server runs its own processes or programs separately from other programs that are running for other virtual servers on the same computer.

virus — A program that can replicate itself by attaching itself to other programs, and which can cause damage to your computer or network, ranging in severity from mild to disastrous.

Visual Basic (VB) — A popular, object-oriented Microsoft programming language that is easy to learn and interacts well with Windows.

VoIP (Voice over IP) — The protocol used to send voice data over the Internet.

VRML (Virtual Reality Modeling Language) — A language used to create interactive animation on web sites. VRML is not as well-used as it once was, because it's easier for developers to use Flash or Shockwave plug-in software rather than developing their own code.

WAP — *See* Wireless Application Protocol.

wave file — A Windows audio file commonly used on web sites for short, low-quality sound.

web browser — A client software program that requests information from another program (the web server) on the World Wide Web.

web crawler — Software that searches the web looking for keywords to record in a search engine database. Also called web robot, spider.

web host — A computer that runs a web server application and stores web site files.

web page — As it pertains to the World Wide Web, a file containing hypertext that is transmitted from a web server to a web browser. The web browser can then display the page to the user. Also called page.

web robot — *See* web crawler.

web server — Computer software that retrieves information in the form of web pages, and delivers those web pages to web browsers upon request. Also, the computer that is running the web server software.

web site — A group of web page files and multimedia files that work together to provide information on the World Wide Web.

WebTV — A system for displaying information from the Internet on a television screen and to support interactive television.

WebTV for Windows — A Windows component that supports television on a PC by way of a TV tuner card.

Windows Internet Naming Service (WINS) — A Microsoft resolution service with a distributed database that tracks relationships between domain names and IP addresses. Compare to DNS.

Windows Sockets (WinSock) — A part of the TCP/IP utility software that manages API calls from applications to other computers on a TCP/IP network.

Wireless Application Protocol (WAP) — A protocol that specifies how information from the Internet is formatted, transmitted and received by wireless Internet appliances.

WML (Wireless Markup Language) — A markup language that is used to build web pages for transmission to wireless devices using the WAP protocol.

World Wide Web (WWW) — One of several applications that use the Internet. This application is a massive accumulation of information stored on computers around the globe in web pages or hypertext documents, graphics, sound, and other multimedia files.

World Wide Web Consortium (W3C) — An organization that controls the standards of HTML and web communications.

worm — A program that spreads copies of itself throughout the network without needing a host program.

write access — As applied to network privileges, a user with write access to a file can view it, change it, and save changes to that file.

W3C — *See* World Wide Web Consortium.

WWW — *See* World Wide Web.

X.25 — A packet-switching communication protocol which uses analog technology and which can support data transmission speeds of up to 56 Kbps.

XHTML — *See* Extensible Hypertext Markup Language.

XML — *See* Extensible Markup Language.

zone — The group of computers on one or more networks that a name server is responsible for, and which contain the most authoritative information about the domain names assigned to these computers.

Index